Teach
Yourself
PERL 5 FOR
WINDOWS NT®

in 21 days

Teach Yourself
PERL 5 FOR
WINDOWS NT®
in 21 days

Tony Zhang
David Till

SAMS
PUBLISHING

201 West 103rd Street
Indianapolis, Indiana 46290

To my first PC—a very slow and expensive IBM clone by today's standards. But I will never forget the joy when I brought it home.

—TZ

Copyright © 1997 by Sams Publishing

International Standard Book Number: 0-672-31047-3

Library of Congress Catalog Card Number: 96-72076

2000   99   98   97   4   3   2   1

Interpretation of the printing code: the rightmost double-digit number is the year of the book's printing; the rightmost single-digit, the number of the book's printing. For example, a printing code of 97-1 shows that the first printing of the book occurred in 1997.

Composed in AGaramond and Courier by Macmillan Computer Publishing

Printed in the United States of America

Trademarks

Publisher and President   Richard K. Swadley
Publishing Manager   Greg Wiegand
Director of Editorial Services   Cindy Morrow
Managing Editor   Kitty Wilson Jarrett
Assistant Marketing Managers   Kristina Perry, Rachel Wolfe

Acquisitions Editor
Sharon Cox

Development Editor
Fran Hatton

Software Development Specialist
Brad Meyers

Production Editor
Mary Ann Abramson

Copy Editor
Kim Hannel

Indexer
Ben Slen

Editorial Coordinator
Katie Wise

Technical Edit Coordinator
Lynette Quinn

Editorial Assistants
Carol Ackerman
Andi Richter
Rhonda Tinch-Mize

Cover Designer
Tim Amrhein

Book Designer
Gary Adair

Copy Writer
Peter Fuller

Production Team Supervisors
Brad Chinn
Charlotte Clapp

Production
Georgiana Briggs
Jeanne Clark
Michael Dietsch
Svetlana Dominguez
Polly Lavrick

Overview

Contents

Acknowledgments

This book could not have been written in such a short time without the help and support from many people inside and outside Sams Publishing.

Among them, Dr. Ed Ferguson, my mentor at Texas Instruments, coached me when I first began working with Perl. Ed, thank you!

It was Sharon Cox, at Sams Publishing, who found me and gave me the chance to write down what I've known and learned about Perl 5 for Win32. As editors for the book, Sharon and Fran Hatton have given me a lot of encouragement and help in every phase of the book's creation. Kenneth Albanowski, the technical reviewer of the book, has provided valuable feedback, which improves the quality of the book in many places.

I also want to thank Mary Ann Abramson, Kim Hannel, and the other members of the editorial team for their hard work. Many of them I have not talked to directly, but I do appreciate all their efforts and contributions to the book.

Ellen, my lovely wife, who is a college professor teaching comparative philosophy, inspires me to look at this wired world from the metaphysical perspective.

Last but not least, I must acknowledge my parents, who gave me not only love and affection, but also the opportunity to get a better education when I was in China.

About the Authors

Tony Zhang

Tony Zhang is a software developer who is currently working at Texas Instruments (TI) in Dallas, Texas. He has broad range of experience on various computers, from mainframes, minis, and workstations to PCs. Besides his application-level programming experience in GUI, client/server, databases, and networking, Tony has gained tremendous knowledge of computer system-level design and programming since he joined the Microprocessor Business Unit at TI. With an advanced degree in physics, he has published dozens of papers on lasers and mathematical modeling as well as computer programming. When he's not programming, he likes photography, painting, reading, writing, and swimming.

You can reach Tony through Sams Publishing or by e-mailing to

`tt-zhang@ti.com.`

David Till

David Till is a technical writer working in Toronto, Ontario, Canada. He holds a master's degree in computer science from the University of Waterloo; programming languages was his major field of study. He has also worked in compiler development and on version-control software. He lists his hobbies as "writing, comedy, walking, duplicate bridge, and fanatical support of the Toronto Blue Jays."

Tell Us What You Think!

As a reader, you are the most important critic and commentator of our books. We value your opinion and want to know what we're doing right, what we could do better, what areas you'd like to see us publish in, and any other words of wisdom you're willing to pass our way. You can help us make strong books that meet your needs and give you the computer guidance you require.

Do you have access to CompuServe or the World Wide Web? Then check out our CompuServe forum by typing GO SAMS at any prompt. If you prefer the World Wide Web, check out our site at http://www.mcp.com.

 NOTE

> If you have a technical question about this book, call the technical support line at 317-581-3833.

As the publishing manager of the group that created this book, I welcome your comments. You can fax, e-mail, or write me directly to let me know what you did or didn't like about this book—as well as what we can do to make our books stronger. Here's the information:

FAX: 317-581-4669

E-mail: programming_mgr@sams.samspublishing.com

Mail: Greg Wiegand
          Sams Publishing
          201 W. 103rd Street
          Indianapolis, IN 46290

Introduction

"Is it not a pleasure to learn and to repeat or practice what has been learned?"

— Confucius

With many clearly described examples and useful exercises, this book is designed to teach you the programming language of Perl 5 for Win32 in just 21 days. You'll find out that Perl is powerful enough to perform many sophisticated programming tasks, yet is easy to learn and use.

Besides the clear explanation of the concepts and terminology of Perl, there are many sample programs and exercises in this book. You can run and modify these Perl programs repeatedly on your computer to help you understand Perl.

Who Should Read This Book?

When we wrote this book, we assumed our audience had no previous programming experience. In particular, no knowledge of the C programming language is required for our audience, like you, to learn about programming with Perl from this book.

Of course, learning Perl will be a snap if you are familiar with other programming languages. The only assumption this book does make is that you are familiar with the basics of using Windows NT, as well as Windows 95.

Special Features of This Book

This book contains some special elements that clarify points and make it easier for you to understand the features and concepts of Perl 5 for Win32 as they are introduced:

- ☐ Syntax boxes
- ☐ DO/DON'T boxes
- ☐ Notes
- ☐ Warnings
- ☐ Tips

Syntax boxes explain some of the more complicated features of Perl 5 for Win32, such as the control structures. Each syntax box consists of a formal definition of the feature followed by an explanation. Here is an example of a syntax box:

The syntax of the for statement is

```
for (expr1; expr2; expr3) {
        statement_block
}
```

expr1 is the loop initializer. It is evaluated only once, before the start of the loop.

expr2 is the conditional expression that terminates the loop. The conditional expression in *expr2* behaves just like the ones in `while` and `if` statements: If its value is `0`, the loop is terminated, and if its value is nonzero, the loop is executed.

statement_block is the collection of statements that is executed if (and when) *expr2* has a nonzero value.

expr3 is executed once per iteration of the loop, and is executed after the last statement in *statement_block* is executed.

(You'll learn more about `if` later in the book.)

DO/DON'T boxes present the do's and don'ts for a particular task or features of Perl. Here is an example of such a box:

Do	Don't

DON'T confuse the | operator (bitwise OR) with the || operator (logical OR).

DO make sure you are using the proper bitwise operator. It's easy to slip and assume you want bitwise OR when you actually want bitwise AND.

(Don't worry about these operators now. They are covered on Day 4 in this book.)

Notes are explanations of interesting properties of a particular Perl program feature. Take a look at the following example of a note:

NOTE

In left-justified output, the value being displayed appears at the left end of the value field. In right-justified output, the value being displayed appears at the right end of the value field.

Warnings warn you of programming pitfalls to avoid. Here is a typical warning:

WARNING

> You cannot use the `last` statement inside the `do` statement. The `do` statement is actually implemented differently, although it behaves like the other control structures.

Tips are hints on how to write your Perl programs better. The following is an example of a tip:

TIP

> It is a good idea to use all uppercase letters for your file-variable names. This makes it easier to distinguish file-variable names from other variable names, as well as from reserved words.

Programming Examples

As mentioned before, this book contains many useful programming examples with explanations. These examples show you how to use Perl features and functions in your own programs.

Each example has a listing of the Perl program, the input required and the output generated by the program, and an analysis of how the program works. Special icons are used to point out each part of the example: Type, Input-Output, and Analysis.

In an Input-Output example, like the one shown in Listing IN.1, there are some special typographic conventions. The input you enter is shown in **bold monospace** type, and the output generated by the system of the program is shown in plain monospace type. The system prompt (`c:\>` in the examples in this book) is also shown so that you know when a command is to be entered on the command line.

TYPE **Listing IN.1. A simple Perl program with comments.**

```
1:  # pIN_1.pl
2:  # this program reads a line of input, and write
3:  # the line back out
4:  $inputline = <STDIN>;  # read in a line
5:  print STDOUT $inputline;
```

```
C:\> perl pIN_1.pl
This is a line of input.
This is a line of input.
C:\>
```

Line 1 saves the name of the Perl program. Lines 2 and 3 are comments, not executable lines of code. Line 4 reads a line of input. Line 5 writes the line of input on your screen.

End-of-Day Q&A and Workshop

Each day ends with a *Q&A* section that contains answers to common questions relating to the lesson of that day. Following the Q&A section is a *Workshop* that consists of quiz questions and programming exercises. The exercises often include BUG BUSTER exercises that help you spot some of the common bugs in Perl programs. The answers to these quiz questions, as well as sample solutions for the exercises, are presented in Appendix B, "Answers."

To help you solidify your understanding of each day's lesson, you are encouraged to try to answer the quiz questions and finish the exercises provided in the workshop before you move to the next day's lesson.

Conventions Used in This Book

Different typefaces are used in this book to help you differentiate between Perl code and regular English, and to identify important concepts:

☐ Actual Perl code is typeset in a special monospace font. You'll see this font used in listings, the Input-Output examples, and code snippets. In the explanations of Perl features, commands, filenames, statements, variables, and any text you see on the screen are also typeset in this font.

☐ Command input and anything that you are supposed to enter appear in a **bold monospace** font. You'll see this mainly in the Input-Output sections of the examples.

☐ Placeholders in syntax descriptions appear in an *italic monospace* font. Replace the placeholder with the actual filename, parameter, or whatever element it represents.

☐ *Italics* highlight technical terms when they first appear in the text and are sometimes used to emphasize important points.

☐ When a line of code is too long to fit on only one line of this book, it is broken at a convenient place and continued to the next line. The continuation of the line is preceded by a code continuation character (➥). You should type a line of code that has this character as one long line without breaking it.

What You'll Learn in 21 Days

In your first week of learning Perl 5 for Win32, you'll learn enough of the basics to write many useful Perl programs. Here is a summary of what you're going to learn in Week 1:

- ☐ **Day 1, "Getting Started—Perl for Windows NT,"** tells you how to get Perl 5 for Win32, how to run Perl programs on Windows NT or Windows 95, and how to read from your keyboard and write to your screen.

- ☐ **Day 2, "Basic Operators and Control Flow,"** teaches you about simple arithmetic, how to assign a value to a scalar variable, and how to control execution using conditional statements.

- ☐ **Day 3, "Understanding Scalar Values,"** teaches you about integers, floating-point numbers, and character strings. Also, it shows you that all three are interchangeable in Perl 5 for Win32.

- ☐ **Day 4, "More Operators,"** tells you all about operators and expressions in Perl 5 for Win32 and talks about operator association and precedence.

- ☐ **Day 5, "Lists and Array Variables,"** introduces you to lists, which are collections of values, and to array variables, which store lists.

- ☐ **Day 6, "Reading from and Writing to Files,"** tells you how to interact with your file system by reading from input files, writing to output files, and testing for particular file attributes.

- ☐ **Day 7, "Pattern Matching,"** describes pattern matching in Perl 5 for Win32 and shows you how to substitute values and translate sets of characters in text strings.

By the end of Week 2, you'll have mastered almost all the features of Perl 5 for Win32; you'll also have learned about many of the Perl library functions. The following is a summary of what you'll learn in the second week:

- ☐ **Day 8, "More Control Structures,"** discusses the control-flow statements not covered in the previous lessons.

- ☐ **Day 9, "Using Subroutines,"** shows you how to break your Perl program into smaller and more manageable chunks.

- ☐ **Day 10, "Associative Arrays,"** introduces one of the most powerful and useful constructs in Perl 5 for Win32—arrays—and shows you how you can use these arrays to simulate other data structures.

- ☐ **Day 11, "Formatting Your Output,"** shows you how to use Perl 5 for Win32 to produce tidy reports.

- ☐ **Day 12, "File-System, String, and Mathematical Functions,"** demonstrates how to interact with your system's directory structure. It also describes the Perl functions that operate on strings or perform trigonometric and other mathematical operations.

☐ **Day 13, "Process, Scalar-Conversion, and List-Manipulation Functions,"** introduces the Perl library functions that interact with processes running on the system, convert values from one form to another, or work with lists and array variables.

☐ **Day 14, "Packages, Modules, and System Functions,"** describes the features of packages and modules in Perl and shows you how to include them in your programs. The Perl system library functions and socket-manipulation functions are also introduced on this day.

You'll know all the features and capabilities of Perl 5 for Win32 by the end of Week 3. More advanced features and applications of Perl, such as references, object-oriented programming, and CGI programming with Perl, are also introduced in Week 3. Take a look at the summary:

☐ **Day 15, "Perl 5 for Win32 Module Extensions,"** introduces the most important Perl module extensions for Windows 32-bit operating systems such as Windows NT. Day 15 reminds you to pay more attention to some of the Win32 module extensions because they contain bugs in the current version (build 110) of Perl 5 for Win32. Also, some tricks to get around the bugs are demonstrated in sample programs on Day 15.

☐ **Day 16, "Command-Line Options,"** describes the options you can supply with Perl 5 for Win32 to control how your program runs.

☐ **Day 17, "System Variables,"** explains the system variables that are included automatically as part of every Perl program.

☐ **Day 18, "References in Perl 5 for Win32,"** introduces the hard and symbolic references in Perl 5 for Win32, as well as multidimensional arrays and hashes.

☐ **Day 19, "Object-Oriented Programming in Perl,"** describes the *object-oriented programming* (OOP) features added to Perl 5. Because Perl 5 for Win32 is the Perl 5 version for Windows 32-bit operating systems, you can take advantage of the OOP features in your programming applications with Perl 5 for Win32.

☐ **Day 20, "CGI Programming with Perl 5 for Win32,"** introduces *Common Gateway Interface* (CGI) programming as one of the most exciting and important applications of Perl. Also, the basics of the Internet and HTML formats are covered. The content of Day 20 helps you start with CGI programming.

☐ **Day 21, "The Perl Debugger,"** shows how to use the built-in Perl debugger to discover errors quickly.

Have fun reading this book!

Tony Zhang

Plano, Texas

January 1997

At a Glance

In your first week of learning Perl 5 for Win32, you'll learn enough of the basics to write many useful Perl programs. Here's an indication of what you're going to learn in Week 1:

Day 1, "Getting Started—Perl for Windows NT"
Day 2, "Basic Operators and Control Flow"
Day 3, "Understanding Scalar Values"
Day 4, "More Operators"
Day 5, "Lists and Array Variables"
Day 6, "Reading from and Writing to Files"
Day 7, "Pattern Matching"

1

2

3

4

5

6

7

Day 1

Getting Started—Perl for Windows NT

Welcome to the world of Perl for Windows NT. *Teach Yourself Perl 5 for Windows NT in 21 Days* has been written to help you to get started right away. Today you will learn about the following:

- ☐ What Perl is and why it is useful
- ☐ Why to use Perl with Windows NT
- ☐ What role Perl can play for IIS and CGI programming on the Internet or on an intranet
- ☐ How to get Perl for Windows NT
- ☐ How to run Perl programs on Windows NT
- ☐ How to write simple Perl programs
- ☐ What the difference is between interpreted and compiled programming languages

What Is Perl?

Designed and maintained by Larry Wall, Perl is an acronym that stands for Practical Extraction and Report Language. It was first developed as a tool for writing programs in the UNIX system. So far, Perl has been ported to many other operating systems, including Windows NT. The reasons that make Perl such a popular and challenging language across almost all platforms are

- ☐ Perl is relatively easy to learn and use because it was designed primarily to be practical. No complex data structures are required when you start writing your Perl programs.

- ☐ Perl has rich, built-in features to easily manipulate text, files, and processes. Perl entails the power and flexibility of a high-level programming language such as C. In fact, many of the features of Perl are directly borrowed from C.

- ☐ Perl is ideal for offering quick solutions to programming problems because it doesn't require a special compiler and linker to convert the program you write into machine-readable code. Instead, all you need to do is to write the program and have the Perl interpreter run it.

- ☐ Perl source code, as well as binary code, is freely available. You can always modify and recompile it to write useful programs to fit your needs. As you will see later in this book, you can add your own extensions to Perl for programming on Windows NT.

You don't need to be a computer guru to play with Perl. But if you already have some working experience with other programming languages, learning Perl is even easier. You'll know enough about Perl to solve many problems by the end of Day 2, "Basic Operators and Control Flow."

Windows NT

Windows NT is a relatively new operating system. Microsoft is committed to making it transcend the 20th century. Currently, Microsoft is engaging in two Windows NT products: Windows NT Workstation and Windows NT Server.

Windows NT Workstation is designed to run high-end engineering or mission-critical client/server applications. On the other hand, Windows NT Server—with additional packages such as a network monitor tool, TCP/IP server services, Internet Information Server (IIS), and more—is targeted at the enterprise network operating-system market.

What you learn from this book can be applied to both Windows NT Workstation and Windows NT Server because the two products are based on the same core technologies; they have more similarities than differences. Therefore, I use Windows NT to refer to both Windows NT Workstation and Windows NT Server in this book.

Windows NT (both the workstation and server) has the following important features:

☐ It can run different applications simultaneously. Windows NT native applications are the 32-bit Win32 applications. Win32 provides Windows NT with power, robustness, and speed.

☐ It is a portable operating system that can be run on computers with various types of CPUs, such as Intel's x86, IBM/Motorola's PowerPC, and DEC's Alpha or MIPS.

☐ It is a secure operating system supporting integrated C2-level security. It also supports computers with multiple CPUs, which enables you to run more tasks simultaneously in a shorter period of time.

☐ Its built-in networking protocols and services are completely 32-bit. They consist of TCP/IP for the Internet, dial-up networking, NetBEUI, peer-to-peer networking, and client services for NetWare.

In short, Windows NT is a multitasking and multiuser operating system that plays a dynamic role in the information age.

Windows NT versus Windows 95

Windows 95 is a successor to 16-bit Windows 3.*x*, targeted at users with 386 (or better) computers equipped with 4MB (or more) of RAM. Those machines make up a large market that Windows NT cannot address because NT's hardware requirements are too demanding.

However, Windows 95 reaches the goal to cover the market at the expense of not fully supporting registry functions, security functions, event-logging functions, and some other features found in Windows NT. In fact, you can still find a significant amount of 16-bit code hidden inside Windows 95.

Microsoft uses Windows 95 as a transitional operating system bridging to the world of 32-bit Windows operating system (that is, Windows NT) and applications. In addition, Windows NT 4.0, the latest NT version, adapts a more popular, functional user interface employed first by Windows 95 (see Figure 1.1). By doing so, Microsoft makes it easier and smoother for the user when it's time to transplant from a Windows 95 platform to Windows NT.

Some extensions found in Perl for Windows NT may not work properly on Windows 95. More details are covered on Day 16, "Command-Line Options."

Figure 1.1.
The desktop user interface of Windows NT 4.0.

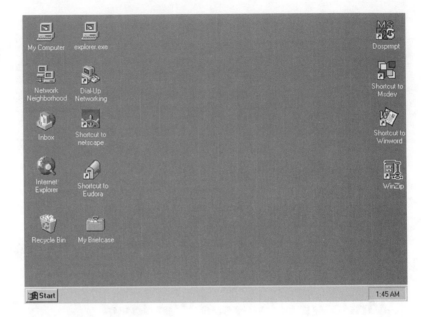

Windows NT versus UNIX

The UNIX operating system was originally developed at AT&T Bell Laboratories in the late 1960s. Today, you can find the UNIX system running on different machines, ranging from PCs and workstations to large mainframe systems.

UNIX and Windows NT have many similarities. Both operating systems are scalable and portable. Both of them have rich, built-in features to support multitasking and networking. In addition, Windows NT can communicate with UNIX systems through the TCP/IP protocol suite and the basic TCP/IP connectivity applications such as FTP, Telnet, and Ping.

UNIX and Windows NT will coexist for a while (if not forever). Although Perl was originally designed and used on the UNIX platform, you'll see more and more applications written in Perl for Windows NT.

There is, however, an obvious difference between UNIX and Windows NT (and Windows 95 and DOS as well). In UNIX, pathnames are specified with the forward slash (/) operator, whereas in Windows NT (and DOS and Windows 95 as well) the backslash (\) is used.

In the UNIX environment, you can run a program with any arbitrary filename as long as the system knows the program contains executable statements. In Windows NT, only files with the specific extension names—for instance, `.exe` or `.bat`—are recognized by the system as the default executable files. That explains why, in the Windows NT version of Perl, there is a utility program called `pl2bat.exe` that has been created to convert a Perl script file to a batch file. On Day 16 you'll learn more about how to run Perl programs in your Windows NT environment.

NOTE

> This book assumes that you have basic knowledge of using the Windows NT 4 operating system.
>
> For those who are new to Windows NT 4, *Peter Norton's Complete Guide to Windows NT 4 Workstation* (published by Sams, 1996) is a good book to start with.

Perl for Win32

The distribution of the Perl language for Windows NT is normally called Perl for Win32, because Win32 is the native and primary subsystem for Windows NT. Perl 5 for Win32, referring to the current version of Perl for Win32, is a straight port from the UNIX version of Perl 5 with extra NT-specific functionality provided via module extensions. I'll elaborate on these extensions on Day 16.

The latest build of Perl 5 for Win32, as this book is being written, is build 110 ported from Perl5.001m. We're going to use this build thoroughly to write our Perl programs. Also, two terms, Perl for Win32 and Perl 5 for Win32, are used interchangeably in this book.

Perl, IIS, and CGI Programming

The Internet Information Server (IIS) is one of the latest products from Microsoft. IIS provides services, such as document publishing, file transmission, and information searching and indexing, for hosting an Internet or intranet information repository on Windows NT.

The Internet has been exploding in popularity over recent years. You can use many services, such as World Wide Web (WWW) publishing and FTP for file transfers, provided by the servers globally connected on the Internet.

The Common Gateway Interface (CGI) is designed and used to run programs for a client (like you) on the server (IIS, for instance). Perl is one of the most popular languages used to create CGI applications. Programming CGI requires knowledge of the Internet.

An introduction on IIS and CGI programming is offered on Day 20, "CGI Programming with Perl 5 for Win32."

NOTE

> Originally sponsored by the U.S. government, the term *Internet* now refers to an independent and vast system that loosely connects millions of people, computers, databases, and other information repositories all over the world.
>
> The term *intranet*, on the other hand, stands for a private network having a specific owner. Information on an intranet is shared internally.

How Do I Find Perl?

Perl is generally available on most machines operated by UNIX, Windows NT, OS/2, or other operating systems.

To find out whether Perl for Win32 already is available on your computer, check the place where you normally keep your executable programs, or check the directory access defined in the Windows NT registry. In a Windows 95 system, you can verify the accessibility of directories defined in AUTOEXEC.BAT.

If you don't find Perl on your computer, it's time to get on the Internet.

Where Can I Get Perl?

You can obtain a copy of Perl with file transfer protocol (FTP) over the Internet. For instance, you can use the command

```
ftp prep.ai.mit.edu
```

to connect you to the main Free Software Foundation source repository at MIT.

You could also use your favorite Internet browser to visit the main Perl home page at http://www.perl.com to get documents, samples, news, and releases of Perl.

Another alternative is to visit the Yahoo! Perl page at

```
http://www.yahoo.com/Computers_and_Internet/Programming_Languages/Perl
```

Where Can I Get Perl for Win32?

Perl for Win32 is ported from the UNIX version and distributed for free by a company called Hip Communications, Inc., with funding from Microsoft. The main Perl for Win32 home page is maintained by Hip Communications, Inc., at http://www.perl.hip.com.

Computers with x86, Alpha, MIPS, or PowerPC chips are currently supported by Perl for Win32.

NOTE As this book is being written, I have been told that "The Perl people from Hip Communications (of Perl for Win32 fame) have started a new venture, ActiveWare." You can visit the new Perl for Win32 home page at ActiveWare's Web page, http://www.ActiveWare.com.

The following is a sample FTP session that transfers a copy of the Perl for Win32 distribution. Let's assume that you want to receive a copy of the compiled binary file, 110-i86.zip, for your x86 machine. The items shown in boldface type are what you would enter during the session. I start it from a directory called download located on my c: drive.

```
C:\download>ftp ftp.perl.hip.com
Connected to ftp.perl.hip.com.
220 gitco Microsoft FTP Service (Version 2.0)
Name (ftp.perl.hip.com(none)): anonymous
331 Anonymous access allowed, send identity (e-mail name) as password.
Password:
230 Anonymous user logged in.
ftp> cd ntperl/perl5.001m/CurrentBuild
250 CWD command successful.
Ftp> ls
200 PORT command successful.
150 Opening ASCII mode data connection for file list.
110-Alp.zip
110-i86.zip
110-Ppc.zip
110-scr.zip
readme.txt
Rel110.txt
Splits
226 Transfer complete.
84 bytes received in 0.00 seconds (84000.00 Kbytes/sec)
ftp> binary
200 Type set to I.
ftp> get 110-i86.zip
200 PORT command successful.
150 Opening BINARY mode data connection for 110-i86.zip(1144634 bytes).
226 Transfer complete.
1144634 bytes received in 46.96 seconds (24.37 Kbytes/sec)
ftp> quit
221
C:\download>
```

The sample FTP session is a copy from my screen. You may have a similar session with minor differences because of the system varieties.

Here's an explanation of what's in the sample session:

☐ The command ftp ftp.perl.hip.com connects you to the FTP site at Hip Communications.

☐ The user ID (Name) anonymous tells FTP that you want to perform an anonymous FTP operation.

☐ When FTP asks for a password, enter your e-mail address. This lets the FTP site administrator know who is using the archives of the site. (For security reasons, the password is not displayed when you type it.)

☐ The command `cd ntperl/perl5.001m/CurrentBuild` sets your current working directory to be the directory containing the Perl for Win32 files.

☐ The command `ls` lists all filenames under the current directory. In this case, you see the compressed binary files `110-Alp.zip`, `110-i86.zip`, `110-Ppc.zip`, and other text files about the release and bug fixes. This command is optional; you may skip it if you like.

☐ The `binary` command tells FTP that the file you'll be receiving contains unreadable (nontext) characters.

☐ The `get` command copies the file `110-i86.zip` from the FTP site to your own site which, for instance, is the directory `download` on your `C:` drive in the sample session. (It's usually best to do this in off-peak hours to make things easier for other Internet users—it takes a while.)

☐ The `quit` command disconnects from the FTP site and returns you to your own system.

 TIP

> If your internal network system prevents you from directly connecting to the FTP site, contact your systems administrator to find out the gateway name that has to be connected first. Then, in most cases, you just type in `anonymous@ftp.perl.hip.com` as the username. After entering your e-mail address as the password, you should be able to download a copy of Perl for Win32 simply by following the rest of the steps shown in the preceding sample FTP session.

You've retrieved the Perl 5 for Win32 distribution. Now, you can install the Perl interpreter in accordance with the following steps:

1. Move the file you just received (`110-i86.zip`, for instance) to a directory that you have created or reserved for the installation.

2. You can decompress the `110-i86.zip` file by using almost any decompression utility software available on your computer, or you can use the widely distributed shareware WinZip to decompress it. The directory containing all Perl 5 for Win32 files is called `Perl5` by default.

3. Next, open a command prompt, such as a DOS prompt, in your Windows NT environment. Change to the `Perl5` directory and run the `install.bat` file by typing `INSTALL` at the command prompt.

4. Follow the instructions issued by the installation file. If you need more information on the installation, read `install.txt`, which you can find in your Perl directory.

If you download only the source code of Perl for Win32, you have to compile it on your target machine that is supported by Windows NT.

The file structure of an installed Perl 5 for Win32 is illustrated in Figure 1.2.

Figure 1.2.

The file structure of Perl 5 for Win32.

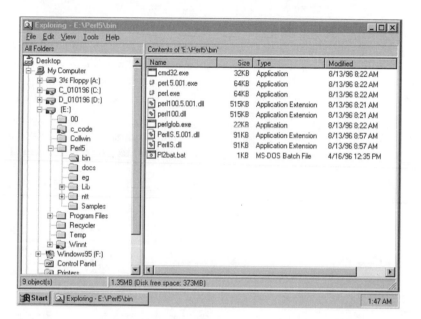

NOTE

WinZip is a file-decompressing utility program that supports long filenames and a variety of file-compression formats. You can learn more about the program from the Web page at `http://www.winzip.com`.

To uninstall Perl for Win32, you have to use the `uninstall.bat` file that comes with the Perl for Win32 package. Then you have to remove the Perl for Win32 files yourself, because `uninstall.bat` just clears out the Windows NT Registry settings.

If you are interested in the latest news on Perl for Win32, you can sign up for the mailing list at the Web page: `http://www.activeware.com/cgi-bin/ntperl/addto-mail-list.pl5`.

You can also send an e-mail to `ListManager@ActiveWare.com`. Type the following in the message body:

```
join Perl-Win32-Users
```

Running a Perl Program on Windows NT

To run a Perl program on Windows NT, do the following:

1. Using your favorite editor (almost any text editor is fine), type the program, and save it in a file. By default, `.pl` is the extension name for a Perl program file.

2. Open a command prompt and type in something like this:

   perl `drive:\path\filename`

   where `perl`, the Perl interpreter, reads the statements saved in the Perl program under the filename and then asks Windows NT to run the statements; `drive:\path\` gives the name of the drive and the directory in which the Perl program resides; and `filename` refers to the name of the Perl program you want to run on your Windows NT system.

   For instance, if your Perl program is called `MyPerl.pl` and is located in a directory called `MyDir` on drive `C:`, you just need to type the following from a command prompt:

   `perl c:\Mydir\MyPerl.pl`

   and press the Enter key to start it.

NOTE

On the UNIX system, you have to put `#!/usr/local/bin/perl`, or something similar, at the first line of a Perl program to indicate to the system where to find the Perl interpreter.

TIP

There is another cool way to run your Perl programs. You can use the Explorer on Windows NT to associate the Perl interpreter, `perl.exe`, with your Perl program files. It's better to follow consistent naming conventions to name your Perl program files. For instance, if you always use the extension `.pl` for your Perl files, you can associate `perl.exe` to any files with extension name `.pl` by choosing Open With from the File menu in the Explorer. If `perl.exe` appears in the list of application programs, highlight it. Otherwise, click the Other button to find `perl.exe` and select it.

After you set up the association, you should be able to run any Perl program file by just double-clicking on the filename from the Explorer.

You can launch a Perl program in a similar manner on Windows 95, too.

If Something Goes Wrong

If your Perl program does not run, one of two things may account for the problem:

- [ ] Your Windows NT system can't find the Perl program you've created and saved.
- [ ] Your Windows NT system can't find `perl.exe`, the Perl interpreter.

If you see this error message on your screen

```
Can't open perl script "C:\MyDir\MyPerl.pl": No such file or directory
```

or something similar, your Windows NT system couldn't find the file `MyPerl.pl`. Check the drive name and directory name; make sure you gave the Windows NT system the right names. Also make sure your Perl program is saved properly under the filename `MyPerl.pl`.

If you see the following message

```
Bad command or file name
```

or something similar, this means that you didn't install the Perl interpreter successfully on your machine. You can run the Registry Editor, `Regedit.exe`, to check whether the installation of Perl has been done correctly. If not, you need to reinstall Perl for Win32 to your computer.

On my computer, I installed Perl 5 for Win32 on drive `E:` in a directory called `Perl5`. Here is what I found from the Registry Editor on my machine:

```
HKEY_LOCAL_MACHINE\Software\Microsoft\ResourceKit\PERL5
BIN        "E:\Perl5\bin"
HTML-DOCS  "E:\Perl5\docs"
PRIVLIB    "E:\Perl5\lib"
```

See Figure 1.3 for an illustration of the registry.

If you have Microsoft Internet Information Server (IIS) installed on your computer, you have one more registry key to check.

You might want to ask your systems administrator for help if you still have trouble running your Perl programs.

Figure 1.3.

The Windows NT Registry of Perl 5 for Win32.

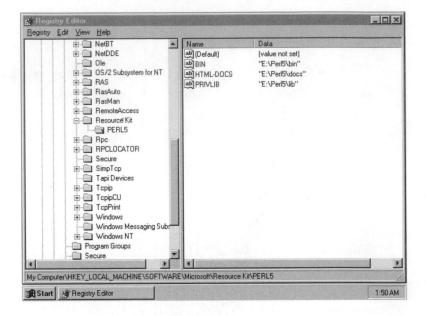

TIP

There is a quick way to check whether you've installed the Perl interpreter properly. Open a command prompt and type `perl -v`.

If the Perl interpreter has been installed successfully, you'll see the following text printed on the screen:

```
This is perl, version 5.001

Unofficial patchlevel 1m.

[ Copyright information – skipped here ]

Perl for Win32 Build 110

Built Aug 13 1996@08:18:50

[ License information – skipped here ]
```

The command `perl -v` asks for the version number of Perl running on your computer. When the Perl interpreter sees the option `-v`, it prints out the information about itself and then exits without doing anything else.

Hello, World!—A Sample Perl Program

Congratulations, if Perl 5 for Win32 is now available on your system. Listing 1.1 is a simple program that illustrates how easy it is to use Perl. This program prints out the string "Hello, World!" on your computer screen.

 Listing 1.1. A simple Perl program that prints a string.

```
1: # This is my first Perl program, called p1_1.pl
2: # It's just a simple perl program.
3: # It was made on Nov. 24, 1996 by Tony Zhang.
4: $mystring = "Hello, World!";
5: print ($mystring);            # print a string to screen
```

```
C\:>perl  p1_1.pl
Hello, World!
C:\>
```

ANALYSIS   Lines 1 to 3 are the comments. Line 4 defines a string, "Hello, World!". Line 5 prints the string to your computer screen.

Comments, Comments, and Again, Comments

From time to time, you need to read or modify your Perl programs that you created several days or several months ago. It's better to write down what the purposes of the programs are and when you wrote them.

Because Perl has a reputation for being unreadable, it's recommended that you use comments whenever you think a line of code is not easy to understand.

As you have just noticed in Listing 1.1, line 1 shows you the name of the Perl program. Line 2 tells you what the program is all about. And line 3 reminds you when you wrote the program.

is the *comment character* to the Perl interpreter. Whenever the Perl interpreter sees #, it ignores the rest of that line. Comments can be lines of their own, or they can be appended to lines containing code:

```
# The following line prints a string to screen
print ($mystring);        # print a string to screen
```

NOTE

> It's convenient for me to assume that the current directory, `c:\` in our case, always contains the Perl programs that we want to run. Although you can put your Perl programs anywhere, you are recommended to save your Perl programs into a dedicated directory, and make sure the programs are accessible to `perl.exe`. For instance, you may save your Perl programs in a directory called `c:\Perlcode`, or something similar.
>
> Certainly, you can name your programs anything you like. For the sake of illustration and discussion, this book has adopted the convention of using a name that corresponds to the listing number. For instance, the program in Listing 1.1 is called `p1_1.pl`. The default extension name, `.pl`, is used.
>
> In this book, the program name is used in the Input-Output examples and in the Analysis section where the listing is discussed in detail. When you follow the Input-Output example, just remember to substitute your program's name for the one shown in the example.

Statements and Tokens

Let's start with line 4 in Listing 1.1:

```
$mystring = "Hello, World!";
```

This is an example of a statement. A *statement* is one task for the Perl interpreter to perform. A Perl program is indeed a collection of statements performed one at a time.

A statement consists of smaller units, called *tokens*. In line 4, there are four tokens: `$mystring`, `=`, `"Hello, World!"`, and `;`.

Usually, tokens can be separated by as many spaces and tabs as you want. For example, the following statements are identical in Perl:

```
$mystring = "Hello, World!";

$mystring='Hello, World!';

$mystring        =        "Hello, World!";
```

A Perl statement can take up several lines of code. For example, the following statement is equivalent to the preceding ones:

```
$mystring
=
"Hello, World!"
;
```

White Space

In Perl, *white space* refers to the collection of spaces, tabs, and new lines separating one token from another.

White space can be used to make your Perl programs more readable. The examples in this book use white space in the following ways:

☐ New statements always start on a new line.

☐ One blank space is used to separate one token from another (except in special cases, some of which you'll see today).

The = and ; Tokens

Now come back to line 4 in Listing 1.1. The first token, $mystring, is an example of a *scalar variable*. In Perl, a scalar variable is used to store one piece of information.

The = token, called the *assignment operator*, tells the Perl interpreter to store the item specified by the expression to the right of the = in the place specified by the expression to the left of the =. In Listing 1.1, the item on the right of the assignment operator is the "Hello, World!" token, and the item to the left of the assignment operator is the $mystring token. Therefore, "Hello, World!" is stored in the scalar variable $mystring.

The last token in the statement, ;, is a special one that separates one statement from others. Scalar variables and assignment operators are discussed on Day 2.

Standard Input and Output

Before we go further, let's modify line 4 in Listing 1.1 and save it as p1_2.pl, which is shown in Listing 1.2. Line 4 of Listing 1.2 is now formatted to take a line of input entered by the user like you.

TYPE **Listing 1.2. A simple Perl program that prints an input line.**

```
1: # This is my second Perl program, called p1_2.pl
2: # It's just a simple perl program.
3: # It was made on Nov. 24, 1996 by Tony Zhang.
4: $mystring = <STDIN>;
5: print ($mystring);                    # print a string to screen
```

```
C:\>perl  p1_2.pl
Hello, World!
Hello, World!
C:\>
```

The behavior of the program in Listing 1.2 is identical to that of Listing 1.1 except that line 4 of Listing 1.2 takes a line of input—that is, "Hello, World!"—instead of the one embedded in the program. Listing 1.2 puts more power into your hands.

As you may already have figured out, the statement

```
$mystring = <STDIN>;
```

consists of four tokens: $mystring, =, <STDIN>, and ;.

The new token, <STDIN>, represents a line of input from the *standard input file*. The standard input file, or *STDIN* for short, typically contains everything you enter when running a program.

For instance, when you start p1_2.pl and enter

```
Hello, World!
```

the line you enter is stored in STDIN, the standard input file.

<STDIN> tells the Perl interpreter to read one line from the standard input file, where a *line* is defined to be a string of characters terminated by a new line. In our example, when the Perl interpreter sees <STDIN>, it reads in

```
Hello, World!
```

Then the assignment operator (=) assigns Hello, World! to the scalar variable $mystring.

Now let's consider the statement in line 5 of Listing 1.2, which is

```
print ($mystring);
```

In this case, the print function's task is to send data to the *standard output file*. The standard output file, pointed to by the file handle *STDOUT*, stores data that is to be written to your computer screen.

The print **Library Function**

print is a built-in *library function*. In Perl for Win32, built-in library functions are provided as part of the Perl interpreter; each library function performs a useful task.

In Listing 1.2, print sends $mystring to the standard output file. We know that line 4 assigns the line of input, Hello, World!, for instance, to $mystring. Therefore, print sends the content of $mystring to the standard output file that displays the content on your screen.

print can take as many arguments as you give to it; it prints each argument, starting with the first one. You can also tell print to write to any other specified file. More details about print are covered on Day 6, "Reading from and Writing to Files."

NOTE
If the Perl interpreter sees another <STDIN> in a different statement, the interpreter reads the line of data from the standard input file. The line of data that the interpreter read earlier is destroyed unless it has been saved somewhere else.

Error Messages

You may misspell or forget to add a token in a statement when writing a Perl program. Normally, the Perl interpreter is able to detect errors and tell you where the errors are located in your program.

Listing 1.3 is identical to Listing 1.2, except that it contains one small error.

 Listing 1.3. A program containing an error.

```
1: # This is my third Perl program, called p1_3.pl
2: # This program contains an error !!!
3: # It's made on Nov. 24, 1996 by Tony Zhang.
4: $mystring = <STDIN>
5: print ($mystring);                    # print a string to screen
```

```
C:\> perl p1_3.pl
Syntax error in file p1_3.pl at line5, near "print"
Execution of p1_3.pl aborted due to compilation errors.
C:\>
```

When you try to run the program shown in Listing 1.3, an error message appears on the screen. This means that the Perl interpreter has found error(s). In this example, the Perl interpreter detects that line 4 of the program is missing its closing ; token.

TIP
You have to fix all errors in your Perl program before you can run it. You may use the syntax check option, -c, built into the Perl interpreter, to detect any syntax problems in your program. The following is an example of using this option:

```
perl -c p1_3.pl
```

Strengths and Weaknesses of Perl

It's easy to run a Perl program. All you need to do is to create the program and run it with the assistance of the Perl interpreter. Languages such as Perl that are processed by an interpreter are known as *interpreted languages.*

If you write a program in a *compiled language*, however, you must translate the program into machine-readable code by calling a special program known as a *compiler*. In addition, library code might need to be added by another special program known as a *linker*. Once the compiler and linker have done their jobs, the result is a program called an *executable file* that can be executed on your machine. If an error is found in your program, you have to fix the error and then compile and link the program all over again.

It should be noted that interpreted programs cannot run unless the interpreter is available. Compiled programs, on the other hand, can be transferred to any machine that understands them.

Sometimes, you may find that it's relatively difficult to read a Perl program. Also, when you distribute your Perl solutions, you have to give away your source code. The reason is—you got it—Perl is an interpreted language.

NOTE   It's true that there are no "formal" supports for either Perl or Perl for Win32. But you're never really stuck, because you can find the solutions from so many Perl books, including this one, on the shelves. Plus, there are many Perl user groups virtually and actively existing on the Internet. You can get a lot of help from people involved in the groups.

Summary

Today you learned that Perl is an easy-to-use interpreted language that has the power and flexibility of a high-level programming language such as C.

You understand now that the distribution of Perl for Windows NT is called Perl for Win32, or more specifically Perl 5 for Win32. Perl 5 for Win32 consists of the code ported directly from the UNIX version of Perl 5 plus NT-specific functionality provided via module extensions.

You have learned that Windows NT is a robust 32-bit operating system that is capable of running mission-critical applications or high-performance Internet servers (IIS, for instance), and that you can use Perl for Win32 in CGI programming on Windows NT to provide services on the Internet or on an intranet.

You have seen two very simple Perl programs. The first one writes an embedded string to the standard output file, whereas the second one reads a line of input from the standard input file and writes the line to the standard output file. The standard input file stores everything you type from your keyboard, and the standard output file stores everything your Perl program sends to your screen.

You have learned that you can add comments to your Perl programs, that a program with proper comments is more readable, and that a comment must be preceded by a #.

You now know that a Perl program consists of statements. The statements are executed one at a time. Each statement has several tokens—smaller units that may be separated by white space. Each statement is separated by the token ;.

You have learned that a Perl program can call library functions to perform certain predefined tasks. print is one of the built-in library functions. Library functions are passed arguments that tell a function what to do.

The Perl interpreter reads and executes the Perl programs you write. If it detects an error in the program, it shows you an error message. You have to fix the error before the interpreter can run your program successfully.

In the last section, "Strengths and Weaknesses of Perl," you learned about the differences between interpreted languages, such as Perl 5 for Win32, and compiled languages.

Q&A

Q Is there any particular editor I need to use with Perl?

A No. You can use any text editor you can find on your computer because Perl programs are ordinary text files.

Q Why do I need to make my Perl programs accessible to the Perl interpreter before running my program?

A Perl programs are ordinary text files. The Windows NT operating system does not know how to run them unless you make them accessible to the Perl interpreter, perl.exe. Perl interpreter is an executable program to Windows NT. The Perl interpreter can read your Perl program, interpret the statements in the program, and tell Windows NT to run them accordingly.

Q Can I use print to print other things besides input lines?

A Yes. You'll learn more about how you can use print on Day 3, "Understanding Scalar Values."

Q Why are Perl and Perl for Win32 available for free?

A This encourages the dissemination of computer knowledge and capabilities.

It works like this: You can get Perl, or Perl for Win32, for free, and you can use it to write interesting and useful programs. If you want, you can give these programs away and let other people write interesting and useful programs based on your programs. In this way, everybody benefits.

You can always modify the source code and repackage it as you want, though you must tell everybody that your version is a modification of the original. Also, you can sell your Perl programs, but make sure you don't borrow anything from somebody else's program unless you get permission.

Workshop

The Workshop provides quiz questions and exercises to help you solidify your understanding of the material covered and gain experience by practicing what you've learned. Try to digest the quiz and exercise answers before continuing to the next day; you can find them in Appendix B, "Answers."

Quiz

1. Where can you get Perl 5 for Win32?

2. What does the Perl interpreter do?

3. Define the following terms:

    a. statement

    b. token

    c. argument

    d. standard input file

    e. standard output file

4. What is a comment, and where can it appear?

5. Where is Perl 5 for Win32 ported from?

6. What is a library function?

7. How do you start to run a Perl program on Windows NT?

Exercises

1. Modify p1_1.pl to print the string twice.

2. Modify p1_2.pl to read and print two different input lines.

3. Modify p1_2.pl to read two input lines and print only the second one.

4. **BUG BUSTER:** What is wrong with the following program?

```
# Exercise 4 -- bug buster
$mystring = <STDIN>
print ($mystring);
```

5. **BUG BUSTER:** Why won't the following program print anything?

```
# Exercise 5 -- bug buster
$mystring - <STDIN>;
# print my string!   Print ($mystring);
```

6. What does the following program do?

```
# Exercise 6:
$inputline = <STDIN>;
$inputline2 = <STDIN>;
print ($inputline2);
print ($inputline);
```

Day **2**

Basic Operators and Control Flow

Today's lesson gives you the information you need to write some simple Perl programs. You'll learn the following:

☐ More about scalar variables and how to assign values to them

☐ The basic arithmetic operators and how they work with scalar variables

☐ What an expression is

☐ How to use the `if` statement and the `==` operator to test for simple conditions

☐ How to specify two-way and multi-way branches using `else` and `elsif`

☐ How to write simple loops using the `while` and `until` statements

Storing in Scalar Variable Assignment

As you've learned from yesterday's lesson, the following statement assigns a line of input from the keyboard to the scalar variable $inputline:

```
$inputline = <STDIN>;
```

This section tells you more about variables such as $inputline and how to assign values to these variables.

The Definition of a Scalar Variable

The variable $inputline is an example of a *scalar variable*. A scalar variable stores exactly one item—a line of input, a piece of text, or a number, for example. Items that can be stored in scalar variables are called *scalar values*.

You'll learn more about scalar values on Day 3, "Understanding Scalar Values." For today, all you need to remember is that a scalar variable stores exactly one value, and that value is termed a scalar value.

Scalar Variable Syntax

The name of a scalar variable consists of the character $ followed by at least one letter, which is followed by any number of letters, digits, or underscore characters (that is, the _ character).

The following are examples of legal scalar variable names:

```
$x
$var
$my_variable
$var2
$a_new_variable
```

These, however, are not legal scalar variable names:

variable	Because the $ character is missing
$	Because there must be at least one letter in the name
$47x	Because second character must be a letter
$_var	Again, because the second character must be a letter
$variable!	Because you can't have a ! in a variable name
$new.var	Because you can't have a . in a variable name

Perl variables are case sensitive. This means that the following variables are different:

```
$VAR
$var
$Var
```

Your variable name can be as long as you like:

```
$this_is_a_really_long_but_legal_name
$this_is_a_really_long_but_legal_name_that_is_different
```

The $ character is necessary because it ensures that the Perl interpreter can distinguish scalar variables from other kinds of Perl variables, which you'll see on later days.

 TIP

> Variable names should be long enough to be self-explanatory but short enough to be easy to read and easy to type.

Assigning a Value to a Scalar Variable

The following statement contains the Perl *assignment operator*, which is the = character:

```
$inputline = <STDIN>;
```

Remember that this statement tells Perl that the line of text read from the standard input file, represented by <STDIN>, is to become the new value of the scalar variable $inputline.

You can use the assignment operator to assign other values to scalar variables as well. For example, in the following statement the number 42 is assigned to the scalar variable $var:

```
$var = 42;
```

A second assignment to a scalar variable supersedes any previous assignments. In these two statements

```
$var = 42;
$var = 113;
```

the old value of $var, 42, is destroyed, and the value of $var becomes 113.

Assignment statements can assign text to scalar variables as well. Consider the following statement:

```
$name = "inputdata";
```

In this statement, the text inputdata is assigned to the scalar variable $name.

Note that the quotation marks (the " characters) on either end of the text are not part of the text assigned to $name. This is because the " characters are just there to enclose the text.

Spaces or tabs contained inside the pair of " characters are treated as part of the text:

```
$name = "John Q Hacker";
```

Here, the spaces on either side of the Q are considered part of the text.

In Perl, enclosed text such as John Q Hacker is known as a *character string*, and the surrounding " characters are an example of *string delimiters*. You learn more about character strings tomorrow; for now, all you need to know is that everything inside the " characters is treated as a single unit.

Performing Arithmetic

As you've seen, the assignment operator = takes the value to the right of the = sign and assigns it to the variable on the left of the =:

```
$var = 42;
```

Here, the value 42 is assigned to the scalar variable $var.

In Perl, the assignment operator is just one of many *operators* that perform tasks, or *operations*. Each operation consists of the following components:

- ☐ The operator, such as the assignment operator (=)
- ☐ One or more *operands*, such as $var and 42

This might sound a little confusing, but it's really quite straightforward. To illustrate, Table 2.1 lists some of the basic arithmetic operators that Perl supports.

Table 2.1. Basic arithmetic operators.

Operator	Operation
+	Addition
–	Subtraction
*	Multiplication
/	Division

You use these operators in the same way you use them when you do arithmetic on paper. For example, the following statement adds 17 and 5 and then assigns the result, 22, to the scalar variable $var:

```
$var = 17 + 5;
```

You can perform more than one arithmetic operation in a single statement like this one, which assigns 19 to $var:

```
$var = 17 + 5 - 3;
```

You can use the value of a variable in an arithmetic operation, as follows:

```
$var1 = 11;
$var2 = $var1 * 6;
```

The second statement takes the value currently stored in $var1, 11, and multiplies it by 6. The result, 66, is assigned to $var2.

Now examine the following statements:

```
$var = 11;
$var = $var * 6;
```

As you can see, $var appears twice in the second statement. What Perl does in this case is straightforward:

1. The first statement assigns the value 11 to $var.

2. In the second statement, the Perl interpreter retrieves the current value of $var, 11, and multiplies it by 6, producing the result 66.

3. This result, 66, is then assigned to $var (destroying the old value, 11).

As you can see, there is no ambiguity. Perl uses the old value of $var in the arithmetic operation, and then it assigns the result of the operation to $var.

NOTE

Perl always performs multiplication and division before addition and subtraction—even if the addition or subtraction operator appears first. It does this to conform to the rules of arithmetic. For example, in the following statement

```
$var = 5 + 6 * 4;
```

$var is assigned 29: 6 is multiplied by 4, and then 5 is added to the result.

An Example: A Miles-to-Kilometers Conversion

To see how arithmetic operators work, take a look at Listing 2.1, which performs a simple miles-to-kilometers and kilometers-to-miles conversion.

TYPE | **Listing 2.1. Miles-to-kilometers converter.**

```
1:  # p2_1.pl
2:
3:  print ("Enter the distance to be converted:\n");
4:  $originaldist = <STDIN>;
5:  chop ($originaldist);
6:  $miles = $originaldist * 0.6214;
7:  $kilometers = $originaldist * 1.609;
8:  print ($originaldist, " kilometers = ", $miles,
9:          " miles\n");
10: print ($originaldist, " miles = ", $kilometers,
11:         " kilometers\n");
```

OUTPUT

```
C:\> perl p2_1.pl
Enter the distance to be converted:
10
10 kilometers = 6.2139999999999995 miles
10 miles = 16.09 kilometers
C:\>
```

ANALYSIS Line 3 of this program asks for a distance to convert. To do this, it prints the following text on your screen:

```
Enter the distance to be converted:
```

Note that the \n at the end of the text is not printed. The \n is a special sequence of characters that represents the newline character; when the print library function sees \n, it starts a new line of output on your screen. (You'll learn more about special sequences of characters such as \n on Day 3.)

At this point, you can enter any number you like in response to the program's request for a distance. Make sure to press Enter after typing in a number. The input/output example shows an entry of 10.

Line 4 retrieves the line of input you entered and then assigns it to the variable named $originaldist.

Line 5 calls the library function chop, which gets rid of the closing newline character that is part of the input line you entered. This library function is described in the following section, "The chop Library Function."

Line 6 determines the number of miles that is equivalent to 10 kilometers and assigns this number to the variable $miles.

Line 7 determines the number of kilometers that is equivalent to 10 miles and assigns this number to the variable $kilometers.

Lines 8–11 print the values of the variables $miles and $kilometers.

NOTE

> Different machines handle floating-point numbers (numbers containing a decimal point) in different ways. Because of this, the numbers displayed in your Listing 2.1 output might not be exactly the same as the numbers shown here. These minor differences will appear whenever a floating-point number is printed.
>
> For more information on difficulties with floating-point numbers, refer to the discussion of round-off errors on Day 3.

2

The chop **Library Function**

The program shown in Listing 2.1 calls a special library function, chop. This function assumes that a line of text is stored in the variable passed to it; chop's job is to delete the character at the right end of the line of text. Consider this example:

```
$line = "This is my line";
chop ($line);
```

After chop is called, the value of $line becomes

```
This is my lin
```

Here's why Listing 2.1 uses chop. The statement

```
$originaldist = <STDIN>;
```

assigns a line of input from the standard input file to the variable $originaldist. When you type

```
10
```

and press Enter, the line of input assigned to $originaldist consists of three characters: the 1, the 0, and a newline character. When chop is called, the newline character is removed, and $originaldist now contains the value 10, which can be used in arithmetic operations.

You'll learn more about using lines of input in arithmetic operations and about conversions from lines of input to numbers on Day 3. For now, just remember to call chop after reading a number from the standard input file.

```
$originaldist = <STDIN>;
chop ($originaldist);
```

Expressions

Now that you know a little more about operators, operands, and how they both work, it's time to learn some more terminology as well as the details about exactly what Perl is doing when it evaluates operators such as the arithmetic operators and the assignment operator.

In Perl, a collection of operators and operands is known as an *expression*. Each expression yields a *result*, which is the value you get when the Perl interpreter *evaluates* the expression (that is, when the Perl interpreter performs the specified operations). For example, in the simple expression

```
4 * 5
```

the result is 20, or 4 times 5.

You can think of an expression as a set of subordinate expressions. Consider this example:

```
4 * 5 + 3 * 6
```

When the Perl interpreter evaluates this expression, it first evaluates the subexpressions `4 * 5` and `3 * 6`, yielding the results `20` and `18`. These results are then (effectively) substituted for the subexpressions, leaving the following:

```
20 + 18
```

The Perl interpreter then performs the addition operation, and the final result of the expression is `38`.

Consider the following statement:

```
$var = 4 * 5 + 3;
```

As you can see, the Perl interpreter multiplies 4 by 5, adds 3, and assigns the result, 23, to `$var`. Here's what the Perl interpreter is doing, more formally, when it evaluates this expression (`$var = 4 * 5 + 3`):

1. The subexpression `4 * 5` is evaluated, yielding the result `20`. The expression being evaluated is now

   ```
   $var = 20 + 3
   ```

   because the multiplication operation has been replaced by its result.

2. The subexpression `20 + 3` is evaluated, yielding `23`. The expression is now

   ```
   $var = 23
   ```

3. Finally, the value `23` is assigned to `$var`.

Here's one more example, this time using the value of a variable in an expression:

```
$var1 = 15;
$var2 = $var1 - 11;
```

When the Perl interpreter evaluates the second expression, it does the following:

1. It retrieves the value currently stored in $var1, which is 15, and replaces the variable with its value. This means the expression is now

   ```
   $var2 = 15 - 11
   ```

   and $var1 is out of the picture.

2. The Perl interpreter performs the subtraction operation, yielding

   ```
   $var2 = 4
   ```

3. $var2 is thus assigned the value 4.

NOTE

> An expression and a statement are two different things. A statement, however, can contain a Perl expression. For example, the statement
>
> ```
> $var2 = 4;
> ```
>
> contains the Perl expression
>
> ```
> $var2 = 4
> ```
>
> and is terminated by a semicolon (;).
>
> The distinction between statements and expressions will become clearer when you encounter other places where Perl statements use expressions. For example, expressions are used in conditional statements, which you'll see later today.

Assignments and Expressions

The assignment operator, like all Perl operators, yields a result. The *result* of an assignment operation is the value assigned. For example, in the expression

```
$var = 42
```

the result of the expression is 42, which is the value assigned to $var.

Because the assignment operator yields a value, you can use more than one assignment operator in a single expression:

```
$var1 = $var2 = 42;
```

In this example, the subexpression

```
$var2 = 42
```

is performed first. (You'll learn why on Day 4, "More Operators," in the lesson about operator precedence.) The result of this subexpression is 42, and the expression is now

```
$var1 = 42
```

At this point, 42 is assigned to $var1.

Other Perl Operators

So far, you have encountered the following Perl operators, which are just a few of the many operators Perl supports:

☐ The assignment operator, =.

☐ The arithmetic operators +, −, *, and /.

You'll learn about additional Perl operators on Day 4.

Introduction to Conditional Statements

So far, the Perl programs you've seen have had their statements executed in sequential order, from top to bottom. For example, consider the kilometers-to-miles conversion program you saw in Listing 2.1:

```
# p2_1.pl

print ("Enter the distance to be converted:\n");
$originaldist = <STDIN>;
chop ($originaldist);
$miles = $originaldist * 0.6214;
$kilometers = $originaldist * 1.609;
print ($originaldist, " kilometers = ", $miles,
       " miles\n");
print ($originaldist, " miles = ", $kilometers,
       " kilometers\n");
```

When the Perl interpreter executes this program, it starts at the top of the program and executes each statement in turn. When the final statement is executed, the program terminates.

All the statements in this program are *unconditional statements*—that is, they always are executed sequentially, regardless of what is happening in the program. In some situations, however, you might want to have statements that are executed only when certain conditions are true. These statements are known as *conditional statements*.

Perl supports a variety of conditional statements. In the following sections, you will learn about these conditional statements:

Statement	Description
if	Executes when a specified condition is true.
if-else	Chooses between two alternatives.
if-elsif-else	Chooses among more than two alternatives.
while and until	Repeats a group of statements a specified number of times.

Perl also has other conditional statements, which you'll learn about on Day 8, "More Control Structures."

The if Statement

The if statement is the simplest conditional statement used in Perl. The easiest way to explain how the if statement works is to show you a simple example:

```
if ($number) {
        print ("The number is not zero.\n");
}
```

The if statement consists of everything from the word if to the closing brace character }. This statement consists of two parts:

☐ The code between the if and the open brace character {.

☐ The code between the { and the close brace character }.

The first part is known as a *conditional expression*; the second part is a set of one or more statements called a *statement block*. Let's look at each part in detail.

The Conditional Expression

The first part of an if statement—the part between the parentheses—is the *conditional expression* associated with the if statement. This conditional expression is just like any other expression you've seen so far; in fact, you can use any legal Perl expression as a conditional expression.

When the Perl interpreter sees a conditional expression, it evaluates the expression. The result of the expression is then placed in one of two classes:

☐ If the result is a nonzero value, the conditional expression is true.

☐ If the result is zero, the conditional expression is false.

The Perl interpreter uses the value of the conditional expression to decide whether to execute the statements between the { and } characters. If the conditional expression is true, the statements are executed. If the conditional expression is false, the statements are not executed.

In the example you have just seen,

```
if ($number) {
        print ("The number is not zero.\n");
}
```

the conditional expression consists of the value of the variable $number. If $number contains something other than zero, the conditional expression is true, and the statement

```
print ("The value is not zero.\n");
```

is executed. If $number currently is set to zero, the conditional expression is false, and the print statement is not executed.

Listing 2.2 is a program that contains this simple if statement.

TYPE Listing 2.2. A program containing a simple example of an if statement.

```
1:  # p2_2.pl
2:
3:  print ("Enter a number:\n");
4:  $number = <STDIN>;
5:  chop ($number);
6:  if ($number) {
7:          print ("The number is not zero.\n");
8:  }
9:  print ("This is the last line of the program.\n");
```

OUTPUT
```
C:\> perl p2_2.pl
Enter a number:
5
The number is not zero.
This is the last line of the program.
C:\>
```

ANALYSIS
Lines 3, 4, and 5 of Listing 2.2 are similar to lines you've seen before. Line 3 tells you to enter a number, line 4 assigns the line you've entered to the variable $number, and line 5 throws away the trailing newline character.

Lines 6–8 constitute the if statement itself. As you have seen, this statement evaluates the conditional expression consisting of the variable $number. If $number is not zero, the expression is true, and the call to print is executed. If $number is zero, the expression is false, and the call to print is skipped; the Perl interpreter thus jumps to line 9.

The Perl interpreter executes line 9 and prints the following regardless of whether the conditional expression in line 6 is true or false:

```
This is the last line of the program.
```

Now that you understand how an `if` statement works, you're ready to see the formal syntax definition for the `if` statement.

SYNTAX

The syntax for the `if` statement is

```
if (expr) {
        statement_block
}
```

Here, `expr` refers to the conditional expression, which evaluates to either true or false. `statement_block` is the group of statements that is executed when `expr` evaluates to true.

WARNING

> If you are familiar with the C programming language, you probably have noticed that the `if` statement in Perl is syntactically similar to the `if` statement in C. There is one important difference, however: In Perl, the braces (`{` and `}`) must be present.

The following statement is illegal in Perl because the `{` and `}` are missing:

```
if ($number)
        print ("The value is not zero.\n");
```

Perl does support a syntax for single-line conditional statements. This is discussed on Day 8.

The Statement Block

The second part of the `if` statement, the part between the `{` and the `}`, is called a *statement block*. A statement block consists of any number of legal Perl statements (including no statements, if you like), separated by semicolons.

In the following example, the statement block consists of one statement:

```
print ("The value is not zero.\n");
```

NOTE

> A statement block can be completely empty. In this statement, for instance
>
> ```
> if ($number == 21) {
> }
> ```
>
> there is nothing between the `{` and `}`, so the statement block is empty. This is perfectly legal Perl code, although it's not necessarily useful.

Testing for Equality Using ==

So far, the only conditional expression you've seen is an expression consisting of a single variable. Although you can use any expression you like and any operators you like, Perl provides special operators that are designed for use in conditional expressions. One such operator is the *equality-comparison operator*, ==.

The == operator, like the other operators you've seen so far, requires two operands or subexpressions. Unlike the other operators, however, it yields one of two possible results: true (not-zero) or false (zero). (The other operators you've seen yield a numeric value as a result.) The == operator works like this:

☐ If the two subexpressions evaluate to the same numeric value, the == operator yields the result *true*.

☐ If the two subexpressions have different values, the == operator yields the result *false*.

Because the == operator returns either true or false, it is ideal for use in conditional expressions, because conditional expressions are expected to evaluate to either true or false. For an example, look at Listing 2.3, which compares two numbers read in from the standard input file.

Listing 2.3. A program that uses the equality-comparison operator to compare two numbers entered at the keyboard.

TYPE

```
1:  # p2_3.pl
2:
3:  print ("Enter a number:\n");
4:  $number1 = <STDIN>;
5:  chop ($number1);
6:  print ("Enter another number:\n");
7:  $number2 = <STDIN>;
8:  chop ($number2);
9:  if ($number1 == $number2) {
10:       print ("The two numbers are equal.\n");
11: }
12: print ("This is the last line of the program.\n");
```

OUTPUT

```
C:\> perl p2_3.pl
Enter a number:
17
Enter another number:
17
The two numbers are equal.
This is the last line of the program.
C:\>
```

2

ANALYSIS Lines 3–5 are again similar to statements you've seen before. They print a message on your screen, read a number into the variable `$number1`, and chop the newline character from the number.

Lines 6–8 repeat the preceding process for a second number, which is stored in `$number2`.

Lines 9–11 contain the `if` statement that compares the two numbers. Line 9 contains the conditional expression

```
$number1 == $number2
```

If the two numbers are equal, the conditional expression is true, and the `print` statement in line 10 is executed. If the two numbers are not equal, the conditional expression is false, so the `print` statement in line 10 is not executed; in this case, the Perl interpreter skips to the first statement after the `if` statement, which is line 12.

Line 12 is executed regardless of whether the conditional expression in line 9 is true. It prints the following message on the screen:

```
This is the last line of the program.
```

WARNING

Make sure that you don't confuse the `=` and `==` operators. Because any expression can be used as a conditional expression, Perl is quite happy to accept statements such as

```
if ($number = 5) {
        print ("The number is five.\n");
}
```

Here, the `if` statement is evaluated as follows:

1. The number 5 is assigned to `$number`, and the following expression yields the result `5`:
   ```
   $number = 5
   ```

2. The value `5` is nonzero, so the conditional expression is true.

3. Because the conditional expression is true, this statement is executed:
   ```
   print ("The number is five.\n");
   ```

Note that the `print` statement is executed regardless of what the value of `$number` was before the `if` statement. This is because the value `5` is assigned to `$number` by the conditional expression.

To repeat: Be careful when you use the `==` operator!

Other Comparison Operators

The `==` operator is just one of many comparison operators that you can use in conditional expressions. For a complete list, refer to Day 4.

Two-Way Branching Using `if` and `else`

When you examine Listing 2.3 (shown previously), you might notice a problem. What happens if the two numbers are not equal? In that case, the statement

```
print ("The two numbers are equal.\n");
```

is not printed. In fact, nothing is printed.

Suppose you want to modify Listing 2.3 to print one message if the two numbers are equal and another message if the two numbers are not equal. One convenient way of doing this is with the `if-else` statement.

Listing 2.4 is a modification of the program in Listing 2.3. It uses the `if-else` statement to print one of two messages, depending on whether the numbers are equal.

TYPE   **Listing 2.4. A program that uses the `if-else` statement.**

```
1:  # p2_4.pl
2:
3:  print ("Enter a number:\n");
4:  $number1 = <STDIN>;
5:  chop ($number1);
6:  print ("Enter another number:\n");
7:  $number2 = <STDIN>;
8:  chop ($number2);
9:  if ($number1 == $number2) {
10:         print ("The two numbers are equal.\n");
11: } else {
12:         print ("The two numbers are not equal.\n");
13: }
14: print ("This is the last line of the program.\n");
```

OUTPUT
```
C:\> perl p2_4.pl
Enter a number:
17
Enter another number:
18
The two numbers are not equal.
This is the last line of the program.
C:\>
```

ANALYSIS Lines 3–8 are identical to those in Listing 2.3. They read in two numbers, assign them to $number1 and $number2, and chop their newline characters.

Line 9 compares the value stored in $number1 to the value stored in $number2. If the two values are equal, line 10 is executed, and the following message is printed:

```
The two numbers are equal.
```

The Perl interpreter then jumps to the first statement after the if-else statement—line 14.

If the two values are not equal, line 12 is executed, and the following message is printed:

```
The two numbers are not equal.
```

The interpreter then continues with the first statement after the if-else—line 14.

In either case, the Perl interpreter executes line 14, which prints the following message:

```
This is the last line of the program.
```

SYNTAX

The syntax for the if-else statement is

```
if (expr) {
        statement_block_1
} else {
        statement_block_2
}
```

As in the if statement, *expr* is any expression (it is usually a conditional expression). *statement_block_1* is the block of statements that the Perl interpreter executes if *expr* is true, and *statement_block_2* is the block of statements that are executed if *expr* is false.

Note that the else part of the if-else statement cannot appear by itself; it must always follow an if.

TIP

In Perl, as you've learned, you can use any amount of white space to separate tokens. This means that you can present conditional statements in a variety of ways.

The examples in this book use what is called the *one true brace* style:

```
if ($number == 0) {
        print ("The number is zero.\n");
} else {
        print ("The number is not zero.\n");
}
```

In this brace style, the opening brace ({) appears on the same line as the if or else, and the closing brace (}) starts a new line.

Other programmers insist on putting the braces on separate lines:

```
if ($number == 0)
{
        print ("The number is zero.\n");
}
  else
{
        print ("The number is not zero.\n");
}
```

Still others prefer to indent their braces:

```
if ($number == 0)
    {
        print ("The number is not zero.\n");
    }
```

I prefer the one true brace style because it is both legible and compact. However, it doesn't really matter what brace style you choose, provided that you follow these rules:

- ☐ The brace style is consistent. Every `if` and `else` that appears in your program should have its braces displayed in the same way.
- ☐ The brace style is easy to follow.
- ☐ The statement blocks inside the braces always should be indented in the same way.

If you do not follow a consistent style, and you write statements such as

```
if ($number == 0) { print ("The number is zero"); }
```

you'll find that your code is difficult to understand, especially when you start writing longer Perl programs.

Multi-Way Branching Using `elsif`

Listing 2.4 (which you've just seen) shows how to write a program that chooses between two alternatives. Perl also provides a conditional statement, the `if-elsif-else` statement, which selects one of more than two alternatives. Listing 2.5 illustrates the use of `elsif`.

2

TYPE **Listing 2.5. A program that uses the** `if-elsif-else` **statement.**

```
1:  # p2_5.pl
2:
3:  print ("Enter a number:\n");
4:  $number1 = <STDIN>;
5:  chop ($number1);
6:  print ("Enter another number:\n");
7:  $number2 = <STDIN>;
8:  chop ($number2);
9:  if ($number1 == $number2) {
10:         print ("The two numbers are equal.\n");
11: } elsif ($number1 == $number2 + 1) {
12:         print ("The first number is greater by one.\n");
13: } elsif ($number1 + 1 == $number2) {
14:         print ("The second number is greater by one.\n");
15: } else {
16:         print ("The two numbers are not equal.\n");
17: }
18: print ("This is the last line of the program.\n");
```

OUTPUT
```
C:\> perl p2_5.pl
Enter a number:
17
Enter another number:
18
The second number is greater by one.
This is the last line of the program.
C:\>
```

ANALYSIS   You already are familiar with lines 3–8. They obtain two numbers from the standard input file and assign them to $number1 and $number2, chopping the terminating newline character in the process.

Line 9 checks whether the two numbers are equal. If the numbers are equal, line 10 is executed, and the following message is printed:

```
The two numbers are equal.
```

The Perl interpreter then jumps to the first statement after the if-elsif-else statement, which is line 18.

If the two numbers are not equal, the Perl interpreter goes to line 11. Line 11 performs another comparison. It adds 1 to the value of $number2 and compares it with the value of $number1. If the two values are equal, the Perl interpreter executes line 12, printing the message

```
The first number is greater by one.
```

The interpreter then jumps to line 18—the statement following the if-elsif-else statement.

If the conditional expression in line 11 is false, the interpreter jumps to line 13. Line 13 adds 1 to the value of `$number1` and compares it with the value of `$number2`. If these two values are equal, the Perl interpreter executes line 14, which prints

```
The second number is greater by one.
```

on the screen. The interpreter then jumps to line 18.

If the conditional expression in line 13 is false, the Perl interpreter jumps to line 15 and executes line 16, which prints

```
The two numbers are not equal.
```

on the screen. The Perl interpreter continues with the next statement, which is line 18.

If you have followed the program logic to this point, you've realized that the Perl interpreter eventually reaches line 18 in every case. Line 18 prints this statement:

```
This is the last line of the program.
```

SYNTAX

The syntax of the `if-elsif-else` statement is as follows:

```
if (expr_1) {
        statement_block_1
} elsif (expr_2) {
        statement_block_2
} elsif (expr_3) {
        statement_block_3
...
} else {
        default_statement_block
}
```

Here, `expr_1`, `expr_2`, and `expr_3` are conditional expressions. `statement_block_1`, `statement_block_2`, `statement_block_3`, and `default_statement_block` are blocks of statements.

The `...` indicates that you can have as many `elsif` statements as you like. Each `elsif` statement has the same form:

```
} elsif (expr) {
        statement_block
}
```

Syntactically, an `if-else` statement is just an `if-elsif-else` statement with no `elsif` parts.

If you like, you can leave out the `else` part of the `if-elsif-else` statement, as follows:

```
if (expr_1) {
        statement_block_1
} elsif (expr_2) {
        statement_block_2
} elsif (expr_3) {
        statement_block_3
```

2

```
    . . .
}
```

Here, if none of the expressions *expr_1*, *expr_2*, *expr_3*, and so on are true, the Perl interpreter just skips to the first statement following the `if-elsif-else` statement.

NOTE

The `elsif` parts of the `if-elsif-else` statement must appear between the `if` part and the `else` part.

Writing Loops Using the `while` **Statement**

The conditional statements you've seen so far enable the Perl interpreter to decide between alternatives. However, each statement in the Perl programs that you have seen is either not executed or is executed only once.

Perl also enables you to write conditional statements that tell the Perl interpreter to repeat a block of statements a specified number of times. A block of statements that can be repeated is known as a *loop*.

The simplest way to write a loop in Perl is with the `while` statement. Here is a simple example of a `while` statement:

```
while ($number == 5) {
        print ("The number is still 5!\n");
}
```

The `while` statement looks similar to the `if` statement, but it works in a different way. Here's how:

1. First, the conditional expression located between the parentheses is tested.

2. If the conditional expression is true, the statement block between the { and } is executed. If the expression is false, the statement block is skipped, and the Perl interpreter jumps to the statement following the `while` statement. (This is called *exiting the loop*.)

3. If the statement block is executed, the Perl interpreter jumps back to the start of the `while` statement and tests the conditional expression over again. (This is the looping part of the `while` statement, because at this point the Perl interpreter is executing a statement it has executed before.)

The statement block in the `while` statement is repeated until the conditional expression becomes false. This means that the statement

```
while ($number == 5) {
        print ("The number is still 5!\n");
}
```

loops forever (which is referred to as going into an *infinite loop*) if the value of $number is 5, because the value of $number never changes and the following conditional expression is always true:

```
$number == 5
```

For a more useful example of a while statement—one that does not go into an infinite loop—take a look at Listing 2.6.

TYPE Listing 2.6. A program that demonstrates the while statement.

```
1:  # p2_6.pl
2:
3:  $done = 0;
4:  $count = 1;
5:  print ("This line is printed before the loop starts.\n");
6:  while ($done == 0) {
7:          print ("The value of count is ", $count, "\n");
8:          if ($count == 3) {
9:                  $done = 1;
10:         }
11:         $count = $count + 1;
12: }
13: print ("End of loop.\n");
```

OUTPUT

```
C:\> perl p2_6.pl
This line is printed before the loop starts.
The value of count is 1
The value of count is 2
The value of count is 3
End of loop.
C:\>
```

ANALYSIS

Lines 3–5 prepare the program for looping. Line 3 assigns the value 0 to the variable $done. (As you'll see, the program uses $done to indicate whether or not to continue looping.) Line 4 assigns the value 1 to the variable $count. Line 5 prints the following line to the screen:

```
This line is printed before the loop starts.
```

The while statement appears in lines 6–12. Line 6 contains a conditional expression to be tested. If the conditional expression is true, the statement block in lines 7–11 is executed. At this point, the conditional expression is true, so the Perl interpreter continues with line 7.

Line 7 prints the current value of the variable $count. At present, $count is set to 1. This means that line 7 prints the following on the screen:

```
The value of count is 1
```

Lines 8–10 test whether $count has reached the value 3. Because $count is 1 at the moment, the conditional expression in line 8 is false, and the Perl interpreter skips to line 11.

Line 11 adds 1 to the current value of $count, setting it to 2.

Line 12 is the bottom of the while statement. The Perl interpreter now jumps back to line 6, and the whole process is repeated. Here's how the Perl interpreter continues from here:

- ☐ Line 6: $done == 0 is true, so continue.
- ☐ Line 7: Print The value of count is 2 on the screen.
- ☐ Line 8: $count is 2; $count == 3 is false, so skip to line 11.
- ☐ Line 11: 1 is added to $count; $count is now 3.
- ☐ Line 12: Jump back to the start of the loop, which is line 6.
- ☐ Line 6: $done == 0 is true, so continue.
- ☐ Line 7: Print The value of count is 3 on the screen.
- ☐ Line 8: $count is 3; $count == 3 is true, and the if statement block is executed.
- ☐ Line 9: $done is set to 1. Execution continues with the first statement after the if, which is line 11.
- ☐ Line 11: $count is set to 4.
- ☐ Line 12: Jump back to line 6.
- ☐ Line 6: $done == 0 is now false, because the value of $done is 1. The Perl interpreter exits the loop and continues with the first statement after while, which is line 13.

Line 13 prints the following message on the screen:

```
End of loop.
```

At this point, program execution terminates because there are no more statements to execute.

The syntax for the while statement is

```
while (expr) {
        statement_block
}
```

As you can see, the while statement is syntactically similar to the if statement. expr is a conditional expression to be evaluated, and statement_block is a block of statements to be executed while expr is true.

Nesting Conditional Statements

The `if` statement in Listing 2.6 (shown previously) is an example of a *nested conditional statement*. It is contained inside another conditional statement (the `while` statement). In Perl, you can nest any conditional statement inside another. For example, you can have a `while` statement inside another `while` statement, as follows:

```
while (expr_1) {
        some_statements
        while (expr_2) {
                inner_statement_block
        }
        some_more_statements
}
```

Similarly, you can have an `if` statement inside another `if` statement, or you can have a `while` statement inside an `if` statement.

You can nest conditional statements inside `elsif` and `else` parts of `if` statements as well:

```
if ($number == 0) {
        # some statements go here
} elsif ($number == 1) {
        while ($number2 == 19) {
                # here is a place for a statement block
        }
} else {
        while ($number2 == 33) {
                # here is a place for another statement block
        }
}
```

The braces (`{` and `}`) around the statement block for each conditional statement ensure that the Perl interpreter never gets confused.

 TIP

> If you plan to nest conditional statements, it's a good idea to indent each statement block to indicate how many levels of nesting you are using. If you write code such as the following, it's easy to get confused:
>
> ```
> while ($done == 0) {
> print ("The value of count is", $count, "\n");
> if ($count == 3) {
> $done = 1;
> }
> $count = $count + 1;
> }
> ```
>
> Although this code is correct, it's not easy to see that the statement
>
> ```
> $done = 1;
> ```

is actually inside an `if` statement that is inside a `while` statement. Larger and more complicated programs rapidly become unreadable if you do not indent properly.

Looping Using the `until` Statement

Another way to loop in Perl is with the `until` statement. It is similar in appearance to the `while` statement, but it works in a different way.

☐ The `while` statement loops *while* its conditional expression is true.

☐ The `until` statement loops *until* its conditional expression is true (that is, it loops as long as its conditional expression is *false*).

Listing 2.7 contains an example of the `until` statement.

TYPE **Listing 2.7. A program that uses the `until` statement.**

```
1:  # p2_7.pl
2:
3:  print ("What is 17 plus 26?\n");
4:  $correct_answer = 43;      # the correct answer
5:  $input_answer = <STDIN>;
6:  chop ($input_answer);
7:  until ($input_answer == $correct_answer) {
8:          print ("Wrong! Keep trying!\n");
9:          $input_answer = <STDIN>;
10:         chop ($input_answer);
11: }
12: print ("You've got it!\n");
```

OUTPUT
```
C:\> perl p2_7.pl
What is 17 plus 26?
39
Wrong! Keep trying!
43
You've got it!
C:\>
```

ANALYSIS Lines 3 and 4 set up the loop. Line 3 prints the following question on the screen:

```
What is 17 plus 26?
```

Line 4 assigns the correct answer, 43, to `$correct_answer`.

Lines 5 and 6 retrieve the first attempt at the answer. Line 5 reads a line of input and stores it in `$input_answer`. Line 6 chops off the newline character.

Line 7 tests whether the answer entered is correct by comparing `$input_answer` with `$correct_answer`. If the two are not equal, the Perl interpreter continues with lines 8–10; if they are equal, the interpreter skips to line 12.

Line 8 prints the following on the screen:

```
Wrong! Keep trying!
```

Line 9 reads another attempt from the standard input file and stores it in `$input_answer`. Line 10 chops off the newline character. At this point, the Perl interpreter jumps back to line 7 and tests the new attempt.

The interpreter reaches line 12 when the answer is correct. At this point, the following message appears on the screen, and the program terminates:

```
You've got it!
```

The syntax for the `until` statement is

```
until (expr) {
        statement_block
}
```

As in the `while` statement, `expr` is a conditional expression, and `statement_block` is a statement block.

Summary

Today, you have learned about scalar variables and how to assign values to them. Scalar variables and values can be used by the arithmetic operators to perform the basic arithmetic operations of addition, subtraction, multiplication, and division. The `chop` built-in library function removes the trailing newline character from a line, enabling you to read scalar values from the standard input file.

A collection of operations and their values is known as an expression. The values operated on by a particular operator are called the operands of the operator. Each operator yields a result, which then can be used in other operations. An expression can be divided into subexpressions, each of which is evaluated in turn.

Today you were introduced to the idea of a conditional statement. A conditional statement consists of two components: a conditional expression, which yields a result of either true or false; and a statement block, which is a group of statements that is executed only when the conditional expression is true.

One operator commonly used in conditional expression is the `==` operator, which returns true if its operands are numerically equal, and returns false if its operands are not.

You learned about the following conditional statements today:

- ☐ The `if` statement, which is executed only if its conditional expression is true
- ☐ The `if-else` statement, which chooses between two alternatives
- ☐ The `if-elsif-else` statement, which chooses among multiple alternatives
- ☐ The `while` statement, which loops while a condition is true
- ☐ The `until` statement, which loops until a condition is true

You also learned about nesting conditional statements, as well as about infinite loops and how to avoid them.

Q&A

Q Which should I use, the `while` statement or the `until` statement?

A It doesn't matter, really; it just depends on which, in your judgment, is easier to read.

Once you learn about the other comparison operators on Day 4, you'll be able to use the `while` statement wherever you can use an `until` statement, and vice versa.

Q In Listing 2.7, you read input from the standard input file in two separate places. Is there any way I can reduce this to one?

A Yes, by using some of the other statements described on Day 8.

Q Do I really need both a `$done` variable and a `$count` variable in Listing 2.6?

A No. On Day 4 you'll learn about comparison operators, which enable you to test whether a variable is less than or greater than a particular value. At that point, you won't need the `$done` variable.

Q How many `elsif` parts can I have in an `if-elsif-else` statement?

A Effectively, as many as you like.

Q How much nesting of conditional statements does Perl allow? Can I put an `if` inside a `while` that is inside an `if` that is inside an `until`?

A Yes. You can nest as many levels deep as you like. Generally, though, you don't want to go too many levels down because your program will become difficult to read.

The logical operators, which you'll learn about on Day 4, make it possible to produce more complicated conditional expressions. They'll eliminate the need for too much nesting.

Workshop

The Workshop provides quiz questions to help you solidify your understanding of the material covered and exercises to give you experience in using what you've learned. Try to understand the quiz and exercise answers before you go on to tomorrow's lesson. You can find the answers in Appendix B, "Answers."

Quiz

1. Define the following terms:
   a. expression
   b. operand
   c. conditional statement
   d. statement block
   e. infinite loop

2. When does a `while` statement stop looping?

3. When does an `until` statement stop looping?

4. What does the `==` operator do?

5. What is the result when the following expression is evaluated?

   ```
   14 + 6 * 3 - 10 / 2
   ```

6. Which of the following are legal scalar variable names?
   a. `$hello`
   b. `$_test`
   c. `$now_is_the_time_to_come_to_the_aid_of_the_party`
   d. `$fries&gravy`
   e. `$96tears`
   f. `$tea_for_2`

Exercises

1. Write a Perl program that reads in a number, multiplies it by 2, and prints the result.

2

2. Write a Perl program that reads in two numbers and does the following:

- ☐ It prints `Error: can't divide by zero` if the second number is `0`.

- ☐ If the first number is `0` or the second number is `1`, it just prints the first number (because no division is necessary).

- ☐ In all other cases, it divides the first number by the second number and prints the result.

3. Write a Perl program that uses the `while` statement to print out the first 10 numbers (1–10) in ascending order.

4. Write a Perl program that uses the `until` statement to print out the first 10 numbers in descending order (10–1).

5. **BUG BUSTER:** What is wrong with the following program? (Hint: There might be more than one bug!)

```
# exercise 2_5

$value = <STDIN>;
if ($value = 17) {
        print ("You typed the number 17.\n");
else {
        print ("You did not type the number 17.\n");
}
```

6. **BUG BUSTER:** What is wrong with the following program?

```
# exercise2_6

# program which prints the next five numbers after the
# number typed in
$input = <STDIN>;
chop ($input);
$input = $input + 1;        # start with the next number;
$input = $terminate + 5;    # we want to loop five times
until ($input == $terminate) {
        print ("The next number is ", $terminate, "\n");
}
```

Day **3**

Understanding Scalar Values

Today's lesson describes everything you need to know about scalar values in Perl. Today, you learn about the following:

- ☐ Scalar values
- ☐ How integers are represented
- ☐ Floating-point values
- ☐ The octal and hexadecimal notations
- ☐ Character strings, and using the double-quote and single-quote characters to enclose them
- ☐ Escape sequences
- ☐ The interchangeability of character strings and numeric values

What Is a Scalar Value?

Basically, a *scalar value* is one unit of data. This unit of data can be either a number or a chunk of text.

There are several types of scalar values that Perl understands. Today's lesson describes each of them in turn and shows you how you can use them.

Integer Scalar Values

The most common scalar values in Perl programs are *integer scalar values*, also known as *integer constants* or *integer literals*.

An integer scalar value consists of one or more digits, optionally preceded by a plus or minus sign and optionally containing underscores.

Here are a few examples:

```
14
10000000000
-27
1_000_000
```

You can use integer scalar values in expressions or assign them to scalar variables, as follows:

```
$x = 12345;
if (1217 + 116 == 1333) {
        # statement block goes here
}
```

Integer Scalar Value Limitations

In Perl, there is a limit on the size of integers included in a program. To see what this limit is and how it works, take a look at Listing 3.1, which prints out integers of various sizes.

TYPE   **Listing 3.1. A program that displays integers and illustrates their size limitations.**

```
1:  # p3_1.pl
2:
3:  $value = 1234567890;
4:  print ("first value is ", $value, "\n");
5:  $value = 1234567890123456;
6:  print ("second value is ", $value, "\n");
7:  $value = 12345678901234567890;
8:  print ("third value is ", $value, "\n");
```

3

OUTPUT

```
C:\> perl p3_1.pl
first value is 1234567890
second value is 1234567890123456
third value is 12345678901234567168
C:\>
```

ANALYSIS

This program assigns integer scalar values to the variable $value and then prints the value of $value.

Lines 3 and 4 store and print the value 1234567890 without any difficulty. Similarly, lines 5 and 6 successfully store and print the value 1234567890123456.

Line 7 attempts to assign the value 12345678901234567890 to $value. Unfortunately, this number is too big for Perl to understand. When line 8 prints out the value assigned to $value, it prints out

```
12345678901234567168
```

As you can see, the last three digits have been replaced with different values.

Here's what has happened: Perl actually stores integers in the floating-point registers on your machine. In other words, integers are treated as if they are floating-point numbers (numbers containing decimal points).

On most machines, floating-point registers can store approximately 16 digits before running out of space. As the output from line 8 shows, the first 17 digits of the number 12345678901234567890 are remembered and stored by the Perl interpreter, and the rest are thrown away. This means that the value printed by line 8 is not the same as the value assigned in line 7.

This somewhat annoying limitation on the number of digits in an integer can be found in almost all programming languages. In fact, many programming languages have an upper integer limit of 4294967295 (which is equal to 2^{32} minus 1).

The number of digits that can be stored varies from machine to machine. For a more detailed explanation, refer to the discussion of precision in the following section, "Floating-Point Scalar Values."

WARNING

An integer constant that starts with a 0 is a special case:

```
$x = 012345;
```

The 0 at the beginning of the constant (also known as a leading zero) tells the Perl interpreter to treat this as an octal integer constant. To find out about octal integer constants, refer to the section called "Using Octal and Hexadecimal Notation" later today.

Floating-Point Scalar Values

In Perl, a floating-point scalar value consists of all the following:

- ☐ An optional minus sign (–)
- ☐ A sequence of digits, optionally containing a decimal point
- ☐ An optional exponent

Here are some simple examples of floating-point scalar values:

```
11.4
-275
-0.3
.3
3.
```

The optional exponent tells the Perl interpreter to multiply or divide the scalar value by a power of 10. An exponent consists of all of the following:

- ☐ The letter e (E is also acceptable)
- ☐ An optional + or –
- ☐ A one-, two-, or three-digit number

The number in the exponent represents the value by which to multiply or divide, represented as a power of 10. For example, the exponent e+01 tells the Perl interpreter to multiply the scalar value by 10 to the power of 1, or 10. This means that the scalar value 8e+01 is equivalent to 8 multiplied by 10, or 80.

Similarly, the exponent e+02 is equivalent to multiplying by 100, e+03 is equivalent to multiplying by 1,000, and so on. The following scalar values are all equal:

```
541e+01
54.1e+02
5.41e+03
```

A negative exponent tells the Perl interpreter to divide by 10. For example, the value 54e-01 is equivalent to 54 divided by 10, or 5.4. Similarly, e-02 tells the Perl interpreter to divide by 100, e-03 tells it to divide by 1,000, and so on.

The exponent e+00 is equivalent to multiplying by 1, which does nothing. Therefore, the following values are equal:

```
5.12e+00
5.12
```

If you like, you can omit the + when you multiply by a power of 10:

```
5.47e+03
5.47e03
```

3

Listing 3.2 shows how Perl works with and prints out floating-point scalar values.

Listing 3.2. A program that displays various floating-point scalar values.

Type

```
1:  # p3_2.pl
2:
3:  $value = 34.0;
4:  print ("first value is ", $value, "\n");
5:  $value = 114.6e-01;
6:  print ("second value is ", $value, "\n");
7:  $value = 178.263e+19;
8:  print ("third value is ", $value, "\n");
9:  $value = 1234567890000000000000000000000;
10: print ("fourth value is ", $value, "\n");
11: $value = 1.23e+999;
12: print ("fifth value is ", $value, "\n");
13: $value = 1.23e-999;
14: print ("sixth value is ", $value, "\n");
```

Output

```
C:\> perl p3_2.pl
first value is 34
second value is 11.460000000000001
third value is 1.7826300000000001e+21
fourth value is 1.2345678899999999e+29
fifth value is Infinity
sixth value is 0
C:\>
```

Analysis As in Listing 3.1, this program stores and prints various scalar values. Line 3 assigns the floating-point value 34.0 to $value. Line 4 then prints this value. Note that because there are no significant digits after the decimal point, the Perl interpreter treats 34.0 as if it is an integer.

Line 5 assigns 114.6e-01 to $value, and line 6 prints this value. Whenever possible, the Perl interpreter removes any exponents, shifting the decimal point appropriately. As a result, line 6 prints out

11.460000000000001

which is 114.6e-01 with the exponent e-01 removed and the decimal point shifted one place to the left (which is equivalent to dividing by 10).

Note that the number printed by line 6 is not exactly equal to the value assigned in line 5. This is a result of *round-off error*. The floating-point register cannot contain the exact value 11.46, so it comes as close as it can. It comes pretty close—in fact, the first 16 digits are correct. This number of correct digits is known as the *precision*, and it is a property of the machine on which you are working; the precision of a floating-point number varies from machine to machine. (The machine on which I ran these test examples supports a floating-point precision of 16 or 17 digits. That's about normal.)

Line 6 shows that a floating-point value has its exponent removed whenever possible. Lines 7 and 8 show what happens when a number is too large to be conveniently displayed without the exponent. In this case, the number is displayed in scientific notation.

In *scientific notation*, one digit appears before the decimal point, and all the other significant digits (the rest of the machine's precision) follow the decimal point. The exponent is adjusted to reflect this. In this example, the number

```
178.263e+19
```

is converted into scientific notation and becomes

```
1.7826300000000001e+21
```

As you can see, the decimal point has been shifted two places to the left, and the exponent has, as a consequence, been adjusted from 19 to 21. As before, the 1 at the end is an example of round-off error.

If an integer is too large to be displayed conveniently, the Perl interpreter converts it to scientific notation. Lines 9 and 10 show this. The number

```
123456789000000000000000000000
```

is converted to

```
1.2345678899999999e+29
```

Here, scientific notation becomes useful. At a glance, you can tell approximately how large the number is. (In conventional notation, you can't do this without counting the zeros.)

Lines 11 and 12 show what happens when the Perl interpreter is given a number that is too large to fit into the machine's floating-point register. In this case, Perl just prints the word Infinity.

The maximum size of a floating-point number varies from machine to machine. Generally, the largest possible exponent that can be stored is about e+308.

Lines 13 and 14 illustrate the case of a number having a negative exponent that is too large (that is, it's too small to store). In such cases, Perl either gets as close as it can or just prints 0.

The largest negative exponent that produces reliable values is about e-309. Below that, accuracy diminishes.

Floating-Point Arithmetic and Round-Off Errors

The arithmetic operations you saw on Day 2, "Basic Operators and Control Flow," also work on floating-point values. On that day, you saw an example of a miles-to-kilometers conversion program that uses floating-point arithmetic.

When you perform floating-point arithmetic, you must remember the problems with precision and round-off errors. Listing 3.3 illustrates what can go wrong and shows you how to attack this problem.

Listing 3.3. A program that illustrates round-off error problems in floating-point arithmetic.

```
1:  # p3_3.pl
2:
3:  $value = 9.01e+21 + 0.01 - 9.01e+21;
4:  print ("first value is ", $value, "\n");
5:  $value = 9.01e+21 - 9.01e+21 + 0.01;
6:  print ("second value is ", $value, "\n");
```

OUTPUT
```
C:\> perl p3_3.pl
first value is 0
second value is 0.01
C:\>
```

ANALYSIS Line 3 and line 5 both subtract 9.01e+21 from itself and add 0.01. However, as you can see when you examine the output produced by line 4 and line 6, the order in which you perform the addition and subtraction has a significant effect.

In line 3, a very small number, 0.01, is added to a very large number, 9.01e+21. If you work it out yourself, you see that the result is 9.0100000000000000000001e+21.

The final 1 in the preceding number can be retained only on machines that support 24 digits of precision in their floating-point numbers. Most machines, as you've seen, handle only 16 or 17 digits. As a result, the final 1, along with some of the zeros, is lost, and the number instead is stored as 9.0100000000000000e+21.

This is the same as 9.01e+21, which means that subtracting 9.01e+21 yields 0. The 0.01 is lost along the way.

Line 5, however, doesn't have this problem. The two large numbers are operated on first, yielding 0, and then 0.01 is added. The result is what you expect: 0.01.

The moral of the story: Floating-point arithmetic is accurate only when you bunch together operations on large numbers. If the arithmetic operations are on values stored in variables, it might not be as easy to spot this problem.

```
$result = $number1 + $number2 - $number3;
```

If $number1 and $number3 contain large numbers and $number2 is small, $result is likely to contain an incorrect value because of the problem demonstrated in Listing 3.3.

Using Octal and Hexadecimal Notation

So far, all the integer scalar values you've seen have been in what normally is called *base 10* or *decimal notation*. Perl also enables you to use two other notations to represent integer scalar values:

- ☐ Base 8 notation, or *octal*
- ☐ Base 16 notation, or *hexadecimal* (sometimes shortened to *hex*)

To use octal notation, put a zero in front of your integer scalar value:

```
$result = 047;
```

This assigns 47 octal, or 39 decimal, to $result.

To use hexadecimal notation, put 0x in front of your integer scalar value, as follows:

```
$result = 0x1f;
```

This assigns 1f hexadecimal, or 31 decimal, to $result.

Perl accepts either uppercase letters or lowercase letters as representations of the digits a through f:

```
$result = 0xe;
$result = 0xE;
```

Both of the preceding statements assign 14 (decimal) to $result.

If you are not familiar with octal and hexadecimal notations and would like to learn more, read the following sections. They explain how to convert numbers to different bases. If you are familiar with this concept, you can skip to the section called "Character Strings."

Decimal Notation

To understand how the octal and hexadecimal notations work, take a closer look at what the standard decimal notation actually represents.

In decimal notation, each digit in a number has one of 10 values: the standard numbers 0 through 9. Each digit in a number in decimal notation corresponds to a power of 10. Mathematically, the value of a digit x in a number is

```
x * 10 to the exponent n,
```

where n is the number of digits you have to skip before reaching x.

This might sound complicated, but it's really straightforward. For example, the number 243 can be expressed as follows:

- ☐ 2 * 10 to the exponent 2 (which is 200), plus
- ☐ 4 * 10 to the exponent 1 (which is 40), plus
- ☐ 3 * 10 to the exponent 0 (which is 3 * 1, which is 3)

Adding the three numbers together yields 243.

Octal Notation

Working through these steps might seem like a waste of time when you are dealing with decimal notation. However, once you understand this method, reading numbers in other notations becomes simple.

For example, in octal notation, each digit x in a number is

```
x * 8 to the exponent n
```

where x is the value of the digit, and n is the number of digits to skip before reaching x. This is the same formula as in decimal notation, but with the 10 replaced by 8.

Using this method, here's how to determine the decimal equivalent of 243 octal:

- ☐ 2 * 8 to the exponent 2, which is 2 * 64, or 128, plus
- ☐ 4 * 8 to the exponent 1, which is 4 * 8, or 32, plus
- ☐ 3 * 8 to the exponent 0, which is 3 * 1, or 3

Adding 128, 32, and 3 yields 163, which is the decimal notation equivalent of 243 octal.

Hexadecimal Notation

Hexadecimal notation works the same way, but with 16 as the base instead of 10 or 8. For example, here's how to convert 243 hexadecimal to decimal notation:

- ☐ 2 * 16 to the exponent 2, which is 2 * 256, or 512, plus
- ☐ 4 * 16 to the exponent 1, which is 4 * 16, or 64, plus
- ☐ 3 * 16 to the exponent 0, which is 3 * 1, or 3

Adding these three numbers together yields 579.

Note that the letters a through f represent the numbers 10 through 15, respectively. For example, here's the hexadecimal number fe in decimal notation:

☐ 15 * 16 to the exponent 1, which is 15 * 16, or 240, plus

☐ 14 * 16 to the exponent 0, which is 14 * 1, or 14

Adding 240 and 14 yields 254, which is the decimal equivalent of fe.

Why Bother?

You might be wondering why Perl bothers supporting octal and hexadecimal notation. Here's the answer: Computers store numbers in memory in binary (base 2) notation, not decimal (base 10) notation. Because 8 and 16 are multiples of 2, it is easier to represent stored computer memory in base 8 or base 16 than in base 10. (You could use base 2, of course; however, base 2 numbers are clumsy because they are very long.)

NOTE   Perl supports base 2 operations on integer scalar values. These operations, called *bit-manipulation operations*, are discussed on Day 4, "More Operators."

Character Strings

Yesterday, you saw that Perl enables you to assign text to scalar variables. In the following statement, for instance

```
$var = "This is some text";
```

the text This is some text is an example of what is called a *character string* (frequently shortened to just *string*). A character string is a sequence of one or more letters, digits, spaces, or special characters.

The following subsections show you

☐ How you can substitute for scalar variables in character strings

☐ How to add escape sequences to your character strings

☐ How to tell the Perl interpreter not to substitute for scalar variables

NOTE   C programmers should be advised that character strings in Perl do not contain a hidden null character at the end of the string. In Perl, null characters can appear anywhere in a string. (See the discussion of escape sequences later today for more details.)

Using Double-Quoted Strings

Perl supports *scalar variable substitution* in character strings enclosed by double quotation-mark characters. For example, consider the following assignments:

```
$number = 11;
$text = "This text contains the number $number.";
```

When the Perl interpreter sees `$number` inside the string in the second statement, it replaces `$number` with its current value. This means that the string assigned to `$text` is actually

```
This text contains the number 11.
```

The most immediate practical application of this is in the `print` statement. So far, many of the `print` statements you have seen contain several arguments, as in the following:

```
print ("The final result is ", $result, "\n");
```

Because Perl supports scalar variable substitution, you can combine the three arguments to `print` into a single argument, as in the following:

```
print ("The final result is $result\n");
```

NOTE

From now on in this book, examples and listings that call `print` use scalar variable substitution because it is easier to read. The substitution is normally called interpolation.

Escape Sequences

Character strings that are enclosed in double quotes accept *escape sequences* for special characters. These escape sequences consist of a backslash (\) followed by one or more characters. The most common escape sequence is \n, which represents the newline character as shown in this example:

```
$text = "This is a string terminated by a newline\n";
```

Table 3.1 lists the escape sequences recognized in double-quoted strings.

Table 3.1. Escape sequences in strings.

Escape Sequence	Description
\a	Bell (beep)
\b	Backspace

continues

Table 3.1. continued

Escape Sequence	Description
\cn	The Ctrl+n character
\e	Escape
\E	Ends the effect of \L, \U, or \Q
\f	Form feed
\l	Forces the next letter into lowercase
\L	All following letters are lowercase
\n	Newline
\r	Carriage return
\Q	Do not look for special pattern characters
\t	Tab
\u	Force next letter into uppercase
\U	All following letters are uppercase
\v	Vertical tab

The \Q escape sequence is useful only when the string is used as a pattern. Patterns are described on Day 7, "Pattern Matching."

The escape sequences \L, \U, and \Q can be turned off by \E, as follows:

```
$a = "T\LHIS IS A \ESTRING"; # same as "This is a STRING"
```

To include a backslash or double quote in a double-quoted string, precede the backslash or quote with another backslash:

```
$result = "A quote \" in a string";
$result = "A backslash \\ in a string";
```

A backslash also enables you to include a $ character in a string. For example, the statements

```
$result = 14;
print("The value of \$result is $result.\n");
```

print the following on your screen:

```
The value of $result is 14.
```

You can specify the ASCII value for a character in base 8 or octal notation using \nnn, where each n is an octal digit. For example:

```
$result = "\377";
```

You can also use hexadecimal notation to specify the ASCII value for a character. To do this, use the sequence \xnn, where each n is a hexadecimal digit.

```
$result = "\xff";        # this is also 255
```

Listing 3.4 is an example of a program that uses escape sequences. This program takes a line of input and converts it to a variety of cases.

TYPE **Listing 3.4. A case-conversion program.**

```
1:  # p3_4.pl
2:
3:  print ("Enter a line of input:\n");
4:  $inputline = <STDIN>;
5:  print ("uppercase: \U$inputline\E\n");
6:  print ("lowercase: \L$inputline\E\n");
7:  print ("as a sentence: \L\u$inputline\E\n");
```

OUTPUT
```
C:\> perl p3_4.pl
Enter a line of input:
tHis Is My INpUT LiNE.
uppercase: THIS IS MY INPUT LINE.
lowercase: this is my input line.
as a sentence: This is my input line.
C:\>
```

ANALYSIS Line 3 of this program reads a line of input and stores it in the scalar variable $inputline.

Line 5 replaces the string $inputline with the current value of the scalar variable $inputline. The escape character \u tells the Perl interpreter to convert everything in the string into uppercase until it sees a \E character; as a result, line 4 writes the contents of $inputline in uppercase.

Similarly, line 6 writes the input line in all lowercase characters by specifying the escape character \L in the string.

Line 7 combines the escape characters \L and \u. The \L specifies that everything in the string is to be in lowercase; however, the \u special character temporarily overrides this and tells the Perl interpreter that the next character is to be in uppercase. When this character—the first character in the line—is printed, the \L escape character remains in force, and the rest of the line is printed in lowercase. The result is as if the input line is a single sentence in English. The first character is capitalized, and the remainder is in lowercase.

Single-Quoted Strings

Perl also enables you to enclose strings using the ' (single quotation mark) character:

```
$text = 'This is a string in single quotes';
```

There are two differences between double-quoted strings and single-quoted strings. The first difference is that scalar variables are replaced by their values in double-quoted strings but not in single-quoted strings. The following is an example:

```
$string = "a string";
$text = "This is $string";  # becomes "This is a string"
$text = 'This is $string';  # remains 'This is $string'
```

The second difference is that the backslash character, \, does not have a special meaning in single-quoted strings. This means that the statement

```
$text = 'This is a string.\n';
```

assigns the following string to $text:

```
This is a string.\n
```

The \ character is special in only two instances for single-quoted strings. The first is when you want to include a single-quote character (') in a string.

```
$text = 'This string contains \', a quote character';
```

The preceding line of code assigns the following string to $text:

```
This string contains ', a quote character
```

The second instance is to escape the backslash itself.

```
$text = 'This string ends with a backslash \\';
```

The preceding code line assigns the following string to $text:

```
This string ends with a backslash \
```

As you can see, the double backslash makes it possible for the backslash character (\) to be the last character in a string.

WARNING

Single-quoted strings can be spread over multiple lines. The statement

```
$text = 'This is two
lines of text
';
```

is equivalent to the statement

```
$text = "This is two\nlines of text\n";
```

If you forget the closing ' for a string, the Perl interpreter is likely to get quite confused because it won't detect an error until after it starts processing the next line.

3

Interchangeability of Strings and Numeric Values

As you've seen, you can use a scalar variable to store a character string, an integer, or a floating-point value. In scalar variables, a value that was assigned as a string can be used as an integer whenever it makes sense to do so, and vice versa. In the following example

```
$string = "43";
$number = 28;
$result = $string + $number;
```

the value of `$string` is converted to an integer and added to the value of `$number`. The result of the addition, 71, is assigned to `$result`.

Another instance in which strings are converted to integers is when you are reading a number from the standard input file. The following is some code similar to code you've seen before:

```
$number = <STDIN>;
chop ($number);
$result = $number + 1;
```

This is what is happening: When `$number` is assigned a line of standard input, it really is being assigned a string. For instance, if you enter 22, `$number` is assigned the string 22\n (the \n represents the newline character). The chop function removes the \n, leaving the string 22, and this string is converted to the number 22 in the arithmetic expression.

WARNING

If a string contains characters that are not digits, the string is converted to 0 when used in an integer context. For example:

```
$result = "hello" * 5;
# this assigns 0 to $result, since "hello" becomes 0
```

This is true even if the string is a valid hexadecimal integer, as in the following:

```
$result = "0xff" + 1;
```

In cases like this, Perl does not tell you that anything has gone wrong, and your results might not be what you expect.

Also, strings containing misprints might not contain what you expect. For example:

```
$result = "12O34";        # the letter O, not the number 0
```

When converting from a string to an integer, Perl starts at the left and continues until it sees a letter that is not a digit. In the preceding instance, 12O34 is converted to the integer 12, not 12034.

Initial Values of Scalar Variables

In Perl, all scalar variables have an initial value of undef, which is usually treated as an empty (null) string, " ". This means that you do not need to define a value for a scalar variable. (Day 14 introduces the details of undef.)

This short program is perfectly legal Perl:

```
$result = $undefined + 2;   # $undefined is not defined
print ("The value of \$result is $result.\n");
```

The output is

```
The value of $result is 2.
```

Because $undefined is not defined, the Perl interpreter assumes that its value is the null string. This null string is then converted to 0, because it is being used in an addition operation. The result of the addition, 2, is assigned to $result.

 TIP

Although you can use uninitialized variables in your Perl programs, you shouldn't. If your Perl program gets to be large (as many complicated programs do), it might be difficult to determine whether a particular variable is supposed to be appearing for the first time or is a spelling mistake that should be fixed. To avoid ambiguity and to make life easier for yourself, initialize every scalar variable before using it.

Summary

Perl supports two kinds of scalar values: integers and character strings.

Integers can be specified using any of three notations: standard (decimal) notation, octal notation, and hexadecimal notation. Octal notation is indicated by a leading 0, and hexadecimal notation is indicated by a leading 0x. Integers are stored as floating-point values and can be as long as the machine's floating-point precision (usually 16 digits or so).

Floating-point numbers can consist of a string of digits that contain a decimal point and an optional exponent. The exponent's range can be anywhere from about e-309 to e+308. (This value might be different on some machines.) When possible, floating-point numbers are displayed without the exponent; failing that, they are displayed in scientific notation (one digit before the decimal point).

When you use floating-point arithmetic, be alert for round-off errors. Performing arithmetic operations in the proper order—operating on large numbers first—might yield better results.

You can enclose character strings in either double quotes (") or single quotes ('). If a scalar variable name appears in a character string enclosed in double quotes, the value of the variable is substituted for its name. Escape characters are recognized in strings enclosed in double quotes; these characters are indicated by a backslash (\).

Character strings in single quotes do not support escape characters, with the exception of \\ and \'. Scalar variable names are not replaced by their values.

Strings and integers are freely interchangeable in Perl whenever it is logically possible to do so.

Q&A

Q **If Perl character strings are not terminated by null characters, how does the Perl interpreter know the length of a string?**

A The Perl interpreter keeps track of the length of a string as well as its contents. In Perl, you do not need to use a null character to indicate "end of string."

Q **Why does Perl use floating-point registers for floating-point arithmetic even though they cause round-off errors?**

A Basically, it's a performance issue. It's possible to write routines that store floating-point numbers as strings and convert parts of these strings to numbers as necessary; however, you often don't need more than 16 or so digits of precision anyway.

Applications that need to do high-speed arithmetic calculations of great precision usually run on special computers designed for that purpose.

Q **What happens if I forget to call** chop **when reading a number from the standard input file?**

A As it happens, nothing. Perl is smart enough to ignore white space at the end of a line that consists only of a number. However, it's a good idea to get into the habit of using chop to get rid of a trailing newline at all times, because the trailing newline becomes significant when you start doing string comparisons. (You'll learn about string comparisons on Day 4.)

Workshop

The Workshop provides quiz questions to help you solidify your understanding of the material covered and exercises to give you experience in using what you've learned. Try to understand the quiz and exercise answers before you go on to tomorrow's lesson. You can find the answers in Appendix B, "Answers."

Quiz

1. Define the following terms:
   a. round-off error
   b. octal notation
   c. precision
   d. scientific notation

2. Convert the following numbers from octal notation to decimal:
   a. 0377
   b. 06
   c. 01131

3. Convert the following numbers from hexadecimal notation to decimal notation:
   a. 0xff
   b. 0x11
   c. 0xbead

4. What does the following line print?

   ```
   print ("I am bored\b\b\b\b\bhappy!\n");
   ```

5. Suppose the value of $num is 21. What string is assigned to $text in each of the following cases?

   a. $text = "This string contains $num.";
   b. $text = "\\$num is my favorite number.";
   c. $text = 'Assign \$num to this string.';

6. Convert the following numbers to scientific notation:
   a. 43.71
   b. 0.000006e-02
   c. 3
   d. -1.04

3

Exercises

1. Write a program that prints every number from 0 to 1 that has a single digit after the decimal place. (That is, 0.1, 0.2, and so on.)

2. Write a program that reads a line of input and prints out the following:

   ☐ 1 if the line consists of a nonzero integer

   ☐ 0 if the line consists of 0 or a string

   (Hint: Remember that character strings are converted to 0 when they are converted to integers.)

3. Write a program that asks for a number and keeps trying until you enter the number 47. At that point, it prints Correct! and rings a bell.

4. **BUG BUSTER:** What is wrong with the following program?

```
# exercise 4:

$inputline = <STDIN>;
print ('here is the value of \$inputline\', ": $inputline");
```

5. **BUG BUSTER:** What is wrong with the following code fragment?

```
$num1 = 6.02e+23;
$num2 = 11.4;
$num3 = 5.171e+22;
$num4 = -2.5;
$result = $num1 + $num2 - $num3 + $num4;
```

6. **BUG BUSTER:** What is wrong with the following statement?

```
$result = "26" + "0xce" + "1";
```

Day **4**

More Operators

On Day 2, "Basic Operators and Control Flow," you learned about the following operators:

- [ ] The arithmetic operators +, --, *, and /
- [ ] The comparison operator, ==
- [ ] The assignment operator, =

Today, you will learn about the rest of the operators that Perl provides, as well as about operator associativity and precedence. The operators are

- [ ] The arithmetic operators **, %, and - (unary negation)
- [ ] The other integer- and string-comparison operators
- [ ] The logical operators
- [ ] The bit-manipulation operators
- [ ] The assignment operators
- [ ] Autoincrement and autodecrement
- [ ] Concatenating and repeating strings
- [ ] The comma and conditional operators

Using the Arithmetic Operators

The arithmetic operators that you have seen so far—the +, --, *, and / operators—work the way you expect them to. That is, they perform the operations of addition, subtraction, multiplication, and division.

Perl also supports three other arithmetic operations:

- ☐ Exponentiation
- ☐ The remainder operation
- ☐ Unary negation

Although these operators aren't as intuitively obvious as the ones you've already seen, they are quite easy to use.

Exponentiation

The *exponentiation operator*, **, provides a convenient way to multiply a number by itself repeatedly. For example, here is a simple Perl statement that uses the exponentiation operator:

```
$x = 2 ** 4;
```

The expression 2 ** 4 means "take four copies of 2 and multiply them." This statement assigns 16 to the scalar variable $x.

Note that the following statements are equivalent, but the first statement is much more concise:

```
$x = 2 ** 7;
$x = 2 * 2 * 2 * 2 * 2 * 2 * 2;
```

When an exponentiation operator is employed, the *base value* (the value to the left of the **) is the number to be repeatedly multiplied. The number to the right, called the *exponent*, is the number of times the multiplication is to be performed. Here are some other simple examples of the exponentiation operator:

```
$x = 9 ** 2;        # 9 squared, or 81
$x = 2 ** 3;        # 2 * 2 * 2, or 8
$x = 43 ** 1;       # this is just 43
```

The ** operator also works on the values stored in variables:

```
$x = $y ** 2;
```

Here, the value stored in $y is multiplied by itself, and the result is stored in $x. $y is not changed by this operation.

```
$x = 2 ** $y;
```

In this case, the value stored in $y becomes the exponent, and $x is assigned 2 multiplied by itself $y times.

You can use the exponent operator with non-integer or negative exponents:

```
2 ** -5              # this is the fraction 1/32
5 ** 2.5             # this is 25 * the square root of 5
```

Listing 4.1 shows an example of a simple program that uses the exponential operator. It prompts for a number, $exponent, and prints out 2 ** $exponent.

TYPE **Listing 4.1. A program that prints out the powers of 2.**

```
1:  # p4_1.pl
2:
3:  # this program asks for a number, n, and prints 2 to the
4:  # exponent n
5:
6:  print ("Enter the exponent to use:\n");
7:  $exponent = <STDIN>;
8:  chop ($exponent);
9:  print ("Two to the power $exponent is ",
10:        2 ** $exponent, "\n");
```

OUTPUT
```
C:\> perl p4_1.pl
Enter the exponent to use:
16
Two to the power 16 is 65536
C:\>
```

ANALYSIS   The program shown in Listing 4.1 is useful if you have to use, or be aware of, numbers such as 4,294,967,295 (the largest number that can be stored in a 32-bit unsigned integer) and 2,147,483,647 (the largest number that can be stored in a 32-bit signed integer). The former is equivalent to 2 ** 32 - 1, and the latter is equivalent to 2 ** 31 - 1.

Do **Don't**

DON'T use the exponent operator with a negative base and a non-integer exponent:

```
(-5) ** 2.5          # error
```

The result of this expression is a complex (non-real) number (just as, for instance, the square root of –2 is a complex number). Perl does not understand complex numbers without further help from external packages.

> **DON'T** produce a result that is larger than the largest floating-point number your machine can understand:
>
> ```
> 10 ** 999999        # error
> ```
>
> In this example, the exponent is too large to be stored on most machines.

The Remainder Operator

The *remainder operator* retrieves the remainder resulting from the division of one integer by another. Consider the following simple example:

```
$x = 25 % 4;
```

In this case, 25 divided by 4 yields 6, with a remainder of 1. The remainder, 1, is assigned to $x.

The % operator does not work on values that are not integers. Non-integers are converted to integers, as follows:

```
$x = 24.77 % 4.21;  # same as 25 % 4
```

Because division by 0 is impossible, you can't put a 0 to the right of a % operator:

```
$x = 25 % 0;        # error: can't divide by 0
$x = 25 % 0.1;      # error: 0.1 is converted to 0
```

Unary Negation

The *unary negation operator* is a – character in front of a single value. (This distinguishes it from the subtraction operator, which appears between two values.) It is equivalent to multiplying the value by –1, as illustrated by this example:

```
- 5;                # identical to the integer -5
- $y;               # equivalent to $y * -1
```

Using Comparison Operators

On Day 2 you learned about the equality comparison operator (==), which compares two values and tests whether they are equal:

```
$x = $a == $b;
```

Recall that the value of $x depends on the values stored in $a and $b:

☐ If $a equals $b, $a == $b is true, and $x is assigned a nonzero value.

☐ If $a is not equal to $b, $a == $b is false, and $x is assigned 0.

The == operator is an example of a *comparison operator*. Comparison operators are most commonly used in control statements such as the if statement, as follows:

```
if ($a == $b) {
        print("$a is equal to $b\n");
}
```

In Perl, the comparison operators are divided into two classes:

☐ Comparison operators that work with numbers

☐ Comparison operators that work with strings

Integer-Comparison Operators

Table 4.1 defines the integer-comparison operators available in Perl.

Table 4.1. Integer-comparison operators.

Operator	Description
<	Less than
>	Greater than
==	Equal to
<=	Less than or equal to
>=	Greater than or equal to
!=	Not equal to
<=>	Comparison returning 1, 0, or -1

Here are simple examples of each of the first six operators in Table 4.1:

```
$x < 10          # true if the value of $x is less than 10
$x > 10          # true if $x is greater than 10
$x == 10         # true if $x is equal to 10
$x <= 10         # true if $x is less than or equal to 10
$x >= 10         # true if $x is greater than or equal to 10
$x != 10         # true if $x is not equal to 10
```

Each of these operators yields one of two values:

☐ True, or a nonzero number

☐ False, or 0

The <=> operator is a special case. Unlike the other integer-comparison operators, <=> returns one of three values:

- [ ] 0, if the two values being compared are equal
- [ ] 1, if the first value is greater
- [ ] -1, if the second value is greater

For example, consider the following statement:

```
$y = $x <=> 10;
```

These are the possible results:

- [ ] If $x is greater than 10, the first value in the comparison is greater, and $y is assigned 1.
- [ ] If $x is less than 10, the second value in the comparison is greater, and $y is assigned -1.
- [ ] If $x is equal to 10, $y is assigned 0.

Integer Comparisons and Readability

In any given statement, it's best to use the comparison that can be most easily read. For example, consider the following:

```
if (3.2 < $x) {
        # conditionally executed stuff goes here
}
```

Although the expression 3.2 < $x is perfectly valid, it isn't easy to read because variables usually appear first in comparisons. Instead, it would be better to use

```
if ($x >= 3.2) {
    ...
```

because it is easier to understand. I'm not sure exactly why this is true; I think it's related to the way the English language is spoken. You will find it easier if you keep the variable on the left.

String-Comparison Operators

For every numeric-comparison operator, Perl defines an equivalent string-comparison operator. Table 4.2 lists each string-comparison operator, the comparison it performs, and the equivalent numeric-comparison operator.

Table 4.2. String- and numeric-comparison operators.

String operator	Comparison operation	Equivalent numeric operator
lt	Less than	<
gt	Greater than	>
eq	Equal to	==
le	Less than or equal to	<=
ge	Greater than or equal to	>=
ne	Not equal to	!=
cmp	Compare, returning 1, 0, or -1	<=>

Perl compares strings by determining their places in alphabetical order. For example, the string aaa is less than the string bbb, because aaa appears before bbb when they are sorted alphabetically.

Here are some examples of string-comparison operators in action:

```
$result = "aaa" lt "bbb";    # result is true
$result = "aaa" gt "bbb";    # result is false
$result = "aaa" eq "bbb";    # result is false
$result = "aaa" le "aaa";    # result is true
$result = "aaa" ge "bbb";    # result is false
$result = "aaa" ne "aaa";    # result is false
$result = "aaa" cmp "bbb";   # result is -1
```

If you are familiar with the C programming language, you might have noticed that the behavior of the cmp operator is identical to that of the C function strcmp().

String Comparison versus Integer Comparison

You might be thinking: If strings and integers are equivalent in Perl, why do we need two kinds of comparison operators?

To answer this, consider the strings 123 and 45. The result when these two strings are compared depends on whether a string or an integer comparison is being performed.

```
$result = "123" < "45";
$result = "123" lt "45";
```

In the first statement, the strings 123 and 45 are converted to integers, and 123 is compared to 45. The result is false, and $result is assigned 0 because 123 is not less than 45.

In the second statement, 123 is alphabetically compared to 45. Because 123 is alphabetically less than 45, the result in this case is true, and $result is assigned a nonzero value.

Because these results are different, you must ensure that you are using the proper comparison operator every time. If you don't, your program can contain errors that are not easy to spot. For instance, consider the following:

```
$var1 = "string 1";
$var2 = "string 2";
$result = $var1 == $var2;    # this statement is bad
```

Because == is a numeric-comparison operator, the values string 1 and string 2 are converted to integers before the comparison is performed. Because both strings are non-numeric, they are both converted to the integer 0, and the following comparison becomes true:

```
$var1 == $var2
```

This is probably not what you want.

Comparison and Floating-Point Numbers

There is one thing to keep in mind when you use comparison operators: Floating-point numbers don't always behave properly in comparisons.

Take a look at Listing 4.2.

TYPE Listing 4.2. A program that contains a floating-point comparison.

```
1:  # p4_2.pl
2:
3:  $value1 = 14.3;
4:  $value2 = 100 + 14.3 - 100;
5:  if ($value1 == $value2) {
6:          print("value 1 equals value 2\n");
7:  } else {
8:          print("value 1 does not equal value 2\n");
9:  }
```

OUTPUT
```
C:\> perl p4_2.pl
value 1 does not equal value 2
C:\>
```

ANALYSIS At first glance, you might think that $value1 and $value2 are identical. However, when you run this program, you get the following:

```
value 1 does not equal value 2
```

What is wrong? To find out, print out the values of $value1 and $value2 before doing the comparison:

```
$value1 = 14.3;
$value2 = 100 + 14.3 - 100;
print("value 1 is $value1, value2 is $value2\n");
if ($value1 == $value2) {
        print("value 1 equals value 2\n");
} else {
        print("value 1 does not equal value 2\n");
}
```

When you run this program, you get the following output:

```
value 1 is 14.300000000000001, value 2 is 14.299999999999997
value 1 does not equal value 2
```

Well, Perl isn't lying; $value1 and $value2 *are* different. What happened?

To understand what's going on, consider what happens when you take an ordinary calculator and tell it to divide 8 by 3. The actual answer is

```
2.6666666...
```

with the number of 6s being infinite. Because your calculator can't display an infinite number of 6s, what it displays is something like the following:

```
2.6666666667
```

This is as close to the actual number as your calculator can get. The difference between the actual number and the number displayed is an example of a *round-off error*.

Round-off errors often occur when Perl (or almost any other programming language) stores a floating-point number or adds a number to a floating-point number. The statement

```
$value1 = 14.3;
```

actually assigns

```
14.300000000000001
```

to $value1, because 14.3 cannot be exactly represented in the machine's floating-point storage. When 100 is added to this number and subtracted again, the result is

```
14.299999999999997
```

Note that both numbers are very close to 14.3 but aren't exactly 14.3 due to round-off errors. What's worse, each number is affected by a different set of round-off errors, so the two numbers are not identical.

Be very careful when you use floating-point numbers in comparisons, because round-off errors might affect your results.

Using Logical Operators

The comparison operators you've seen so far are sufficient if you need to test for only one condition before executing a particular code segment, as in this example:

```
if ($value == 26) {
        # the code to execute if the condition is true
}
```

Suppose, however, that a particular section of code is to be executed only when a variety of conditions are true. You can use a sequence of `if` statements to test for the conditions, as follows:

```
if ($value1 == 26) {
        if ($value2 > 0) {
                if ($string1 eq "ready") {
                        print("all three conditions are true!\n");
                }
        }
}
```

This is tiresome to write, and not particularly easy to read, either.

Fortunately, Perl provides an easier way to deal with multiple conditions: the *logical operators*. The following logical operators are defined:

`$a || $b`	Logical OR: true if either is nonzero
`$a && $b`	Logical AND: true only if both are nonzero
`! $a`	Logical NOT: true if `$a` is zero

Perl 5 also defines these logical operators:

`$a or $b`	Another form of logical OR
`$a and $b`	Another form of logical AND
`not $a`	Another form of logical NOT
`$a xor $b`	Logical XOR: true if either `$a` or `$b` is nonzero, but not both

The `or`, `and`, and `not` operators listed are identical to `||`, `&&`, and `!`, except that their precedence is lower. (*Operator precedence* determines the order in which operators are evaluated; it is discussed later today.)

In each case, the result of the operation performed by a logical operator is nonzero if true and `0` if false:

```
$a = 5;
$b = 0;
$a || $b;                 # true: $a is not zero
```

```
$b || $a;          # also true
$a && $b;          # false: $b is zero
! $a;              # false: $a is nonzero, so ! $a is zero
! $b;              # true: $b is zero, so ! $b is nonzero
```

These logical operators enable you to test for multiple conditions more conveniently. Instead of writing, for example, this code

```
if ($value1 == 26) {
        if ($value2 > 0) {
                if ($string1 eq "ready") {
                        print("all three conditions are true!\n");
                }
        }
}
```

you now can write this code instead:

```
if (($value == 26) && ($value2 > 0) && ($string1 eq "ready")) {
        print("all three conditions are true!\n");
}
```

In each case, the result is the same: the `print` operation is performed only when `$value` is 26, `$value2` is greater than 0, and `$string1` is ready.

Evaluation Within Logical Operators

When Perl sees a logical AND operator or a logical OR operator, the expression on the left side of the operator is always evaluated first. For example, consider the following:

```
$a = 0;
$b = 106;
$result = $a && $b;
```

When Perl is evaluating the expression `$a && $b`, it first checks whether `$a` is 0. If `$a` is 0, `$a && $b` must be false regardless of the value of `$b`, so Perl doesn't bother checking the value of `$b`. (This is called *short-circuit evaluation*.)

Similarly, in the following example, Perl doesn't bother checking `$b`, because `$a` is nonzero and therefore `$a || $b` must be true:

```
$a = 43;
$b = 11;
$result = $a || $b;
```

You can take advantage of the order of evaluation of expressions in `||` or `&&` to safeguard your code:

```
$x == 0 || $y / $x > 5
```

Here is how the preceding statement protects you from division-by-zero errors:

☐ If $x is not 0, $x == 0 is false, so Perl evaluates $y / $x > 5. This cannot produce a division-by-zero error because $x is guaranteed to be some value other than 0.

☐ If $x is 0, $x == 0 is true. This means that

```
$x == 0 || $y / $x > 5
```

is true, so Perl doesn't bother evaluating the expression to the right of the ||. As a result, the expression

```
$y / $x > 5
```

is not evaluated when $x is 0, and the division-by-zero error is avoided.

Logical Operators as Subexpressions

Expressions that contain logical operators can be contained in larger expressions. The following is an example:

```
$myval = $a || $b || $c;
```

Here, Perl evaluates the expression $a || $b || $c and assigns its value to $myval.

To understand the behavior of this statement, recall that the || operator evaluates its subexpressions in the order given and evaluates a subexpression only if the previous subexpression is zero. This means that $b is evaluated only if $a is zero.

When the logical OR operator is used in a larger expression, its value is the last subexpression actually evaluated, which is the first subexpression of the logical OR operator that is nonzero. This means that

```
$myval = $a || $b || $c;
```

is equivalent to

```
if ($a != 0) {
        $myvalue = $a;
} elsif ($b != 0) {
        $myvalue = $b;
} else {
        $myvalue = $c;
}
```

The logical AND operator works in the same way, but isn't as useful. The statement

```
$myval = $a && $b && $c;
```

4

is equivalent to

```
if ($a == 0) {
        $myvalue = $a;
} elsif ($b == 0) {
        $myvalue = $b;
} else {
        $myvalue = $c;
}
```

This means that $myval is set to either 0 or the value of $c.

Using Bit-Manipulation Operators

Perl enables you to manipulate the binary digits (or *bits*) of an integer using its *bit-manipulation operators*. To understand how Perl does this, first look at what a bit is and how computers store integers. Once you understand how bits work, you can easily figure out how the bit-manipulation operators work. (If you are familiar with binary notation and the computer representation of an integer, feel free to skip the following section.)

What Bits Are and How They Are Used

On Day 3, "Understanding Scalar Values," you learned that Perl understands three different notations for integers:

- [ ] Standard notation, or base 10
- [ ] Octal notation, or base 8
- [ ] Hexadecimal notation, or base 16

However, when a computer stores an integer, it uses none of these notations; instead, it uses base 2, or *binary notation*.

In binary notation, every number is represented as a series of 0s and 1s. For instance, the number 124 is represented as

```
01111100
```

To understand how to get from base-10 notation to binary notation, recall what the number 124 represents. When we write "124," what we really mean is the following:

- [ ] 4 multiplied by 1, plus
- [ ] 2 multiplied by 10, plus
- [ ] 1 multiplied by 100

In grade school, your teacher probably said these digits represented the "ones place," the "tens place," and the "hundreds place." Each "place" is 10 times larger than the place to its right. This means that you also can think of 124 as follows:

☐ 4 multiplied by 1 (or 10 to the exponent 0), plus

☐ 2 multiplied by 10 to the exponent 1, plus

☐ 1 multiplied by 10 to the exponent 2

In binary notation, you can use this same method, but replace the 10s with 2s. Here's how to use this method to figure out that the binary number 01111100 is equivalent to 124 in standard notation. Starting from the right, you have:

☐ 0 multiplied by 2 to the exponent 0, which is 0

☐ 0 multiplied by 2 to the exponent 1, which is 0

☐ 1 multiplied by 2 to the exponent 2, which is 4

☐ 1 multiplied by 2 to the exponent 3, which is 8

☐ 1 multiplied by 2 to the exponent 4, which is 16

☐ 1 multiplied by 2 to the exponent 5, which is 32

☐ 1 multiplied by 2 to the exponent 6, which is 64

☐ 0 multiplied by 2 to the exponent 7, which is 0

Adding 2, 8, 16, 32, and 64 gives you 124.

Each of the 0s and 1s in the binary number 01111100 is called a *bit* (which is short for *bi*nary digi*t*). Each bit can have only two possible values: 0 or 1.

In computers, integers are stored as a sequence of bits. This sequence of bits is normally 8, 16, or 32 bits long, depending on the size and configuration of your computer. In the examples in today's lesson, 8-bit integers are assumed; to convert an 8-bit binary number to a 16-bit binary number, just add eight zeros to the left. For example, the following numbers are equivalent:

```
01111100            # 124 as an 8-bit integer
0000000001111100    # 124 as a 16-bit integer
```

The examples in today's lesson use 8-bit integers. The Perl bitwise operators will work on integers of any size.

The Bit-Manipulation Operators

The following bit-manipulation operators are supported in Perl:

☐ The & (bitwise AND) operator

☐ The | (bitwise OR) operator

☐ The ^ (bitwise XOR or "exclusive or") operator

☐ The ~ (bitwise NOT) operator

☐ The << (left shift) and >> (right shift) operators

The Bitwise AND Operator

In Perl, the & operator represents the bitwise AND operation. This operation works as follows:

☐ The value to the left side of the & (also called the *left operand* of the & operation) is converted to an integer, if necessary.

☐ The value to the right side of the & (the *right operand*) also is converted to an integer.

☐ Each bit of the left operand is compared to the corresponding bit of the right operand.

☐ If a pair of corresponding bits both have the value 1, the corresponding bit of the result is set to 1. Otherwise, the corresponding bit of the result is set to 0.

This might sound complicated, but when you take a look at an example, you'll see that it's pretty easy to figure out. For instance, consider the following:

```
$result = 124.3 & 99;
```

First, the left operand, 124.3, is converted to an integer, becoming 124. (The right operand, 99, does not need to be converted.) Next, take a look at the binary representations of 124 and 99:

```
01111100            # this is 124 in binary
01100011            # this is 99 in binary
```

When you examine each pair of bits in turn, you can see that only the second and third pairs (from the left) are both 1. Thus, the & operation yields the following binary result:

```
01100000
```

This is 96 in standard notation. As a consequence, the statement

```
$result = 124.3 & 99;
```

assigns 96 to $result.

Do	Don't

DO use the & operator with strings, provided the strings can be converted to numbers, as follows:

```
$result = "124.3" & "99";
```

Remember: Strings and integers are interchangeable in Perl.

DON'T confuse the `&` operator with the `&&` operator. The `&&` operator performs a logical AND operation, not a bitwise AND operation. For example, the statement

```
$result = 124.3 && 99;
```

assigns a nonzero value to `$result` (because `124.3` and `99` are both nonzero). This nonzero value is not likely to be the result you want.

The Bitwise OR Operator

The bitwise OR operator, `|`, also compares two integers one bit at a time. However, in the bitwise OR operation, a result bit is 1 if either of the corresponding bits in the operands is 1.

To see how this works, look at another example:

```
$result = 124.3 | 99;
```

Here's how this operation is performed:

- [ ] As before, the two operands are converted to integers if necessary. The operands become 124 and 99; in binary representation, these are, as before,

  ```
  01111100
  01100011
  ```

- [ ] Each bit of the left operand is compared with the corresponding bit in the right operand. If either of the corresponding bits is 1, the corresponding result bit is 1.

In this example, every bit becomes 1 except the first one, because at least one of each of the other pairs is a 1. Therefore, the result is

```
01111111
```

which translates to 127. This means that the following statement assigns `127` to `$result`:

```
$result = 124.3 | 99;
```

Do	Don't

DO make sure you are using the proper bitwise operator. It's easy to slip and assume you want bitwise OR when you really want bitwise AND. (Trust me.)

DON'T confuse the `|` operator (bitwise OR) with the `||` operator (logical OR).

The Bitwise XOR Operator

The bitwise XOR ("exclusive or") operator, ^, is similar to the bitwise OR operator, but it's a little more demanding. In the bitwise OR operation, a result bit is 1 if either of the corresponding bits in the operands is 1. In the bitwise XOR operation, a result bit is 1 if *exactly one* of the corresponding bits in the operands is 1.

Here is an example of the bitwise XOR operation:

```
$result = 124.3 ^ 99;
```

This works as follows:

☐ As before, 124.3 is converted to 124, and the binary representations of the two operands are as follows:

```
01111100            # this is 124
01100011            # this is 99
```

☐ Each bit of the left operand is compared with the corresponding bit of the right operand. The corresponding result bit is set to 1 if exactly one of the bits in the operands is 1.

In this case, the result is

```
00011111
```

which is 31. To work through how you get this result, consider the following:

☐ The first bit of the left operand and the first bit of the right operand are both 0. This means the first bit of the result is 0.

☐ The second bit of the left operand and the second bit of the right operand both arc 1. Therefore, the second bit of the result is 0, not 1.

☐ The same applies for the third bits: Both are 1, so the result bit is 0.

☐ The fourth bit of the left operand is 1, and the fourth bit of the right operand is 0. Here, exactly one of the bits is 1, so the result bit becomes 1.

☐ Same for the fifth and sixth pairs: The first bit is 1 and the second is 0, so the result is 1.

☐ The seventh bit of the left operand is 0, and the seventh bit of the right operand is 1. Again, exactly one of the bits is 1, and the result bit is also 1.

☐ Same for the eighth pair: The first bit is 0, the second is 1, so the result is 1.

From this, you can determine that the following statement assigns 31 to $result:

```
$result = 124.3 ^ 99;
```

4

The Bitwise NOT Operator

Unlike the other bitwise operators you've seen so far, the bitwise NOT operator, ~, is a *unary operator*, meaning it works on only one operand.

The way it works is straightforward, as follows:

1. The operand is converted to an integer, if necessary.
2. Each bit of the operand is examined. If a bit is 0, the corresponding result bit is set to 1, and vice versa.

For example, consider the following:

```
$result = ~99;
```

The binary representation of 99 is

```
01100011
```

Applying the bitwise NOT operation to this number produces

```
10011100
```

This number, in standard notation, is 156. Therefore, the following statement assigns 156 to `$result`:

```
$result = ~99;
```

Note that the number of bits used to store an integer affects the results produced by the ~ operator. For example, if integers are stored in 16 bits on your computer, the number 99 is represented as

```
0000000001100011
```

This means that applying ~ to this number yields

```
1111111110011100
```

which is 65436 in standard notation. As a consequence, the statement

```
$result = ~99;
```

assigns `65436`, not `156`, to `$result`. (On a computer with 32-bit integers, the value assigned is `4294967196`.)

The Shift Operators

Perl enables you to shift the bits of an integer using the *shift operators*, << (shift left) and >> (shift right). For example, in the statement

```
$result = $x >> 1;
```

every bit of the value stored in $x is shifted one place to the right, and the result is assigned to $result ($x itself is not changed).

To see how this works, consider the following example:

```
$result = 99 >> 1;
```

As you saw earlier, the binary representation of 99 is

```
01100011
```

Shifting every bit right one place yields

```
00110001
```

Note that a 0 is added at the far left, and the bit at the far right disappears.

Because 00110001 in binary notation is the same as 49 in standard notation, the following statement assigns 49 to $result:

```
$result = 99 >> 1;
```

The <<, or shift-left, operator works in the same way:

```
$result = 99 << 1;
```

The shift-left operator works as follows:

```
01100011           # the binary representation of 99
11000110           # after shifting left 1 bit
```

The result of the shift is 198, which is assigned to $result.

Do	Don't

DO remember that when you use the >> operator, the bits on the right are lost. For example:

```
$result1 = 17 >> 1;
$result2 = 16 >> 1;
```

In this case, $result1 and $result2 are the same value, 8. This is because the rightmost bit is shifted out in both cases.

DON'T shift left too far, or you might not get the result you want. For example, if you are using 16-bit integers, the statement

```
$result = 35000 << 1;
```

does not assign 70000 to $result as you might think it would because the largest value that can be stored in a 16-bit integer is 65536.

Shifting and Powers of 2

In the following statement, the variable $result is assigned the value 49:

```
$result = 99 / 2;
```

Take a look at the binary representations of 99 and 49:

```
01100011          # 99 in binary form
00110001          # 49 in binary form
```

As you can see, dividing by 2 is identical to shifting right one bit—in each case, every bit is moved one place to the right. Similarly, shifting right two bits is equivalent to dividing by 4:

```
$result = 99 / 4;   # $result is assigned 24
01100011            # 99 in binary
00011000            # 24 in binary
```

Multiplying by 4 is similar to shifting left two bits:

```
$result = 17 * 4;   # $result is assigned 68
00010001            # 17 in binary
01000100            # 68 in binary
```

The general rules are as follows:

☐ Shifting left n bits, where n is some number greater than zero, is equivalent to multiplying by `2**n`.

☐ Shifting right n bits, where n is some number greater than zero, is equivalent to dividing by `2**n`.

In the early days of programming, many programmers used shift operators in place of multiplication and division wherever possible, because the shift operations were usually more efficient. (In fact, some compilers would optimize their code by converting multiplication and division to shifts.) Today, it's usually best to use the shift operators when you are manipulating bits, and to use the multiplication and division operators when you're actually doing arithmetic. This will make your programs easier to understand.

Using the Assignment Operators

As you saw on Day 2, the assignment operator = associates, or assigns, a value to a variable. For example, the statement

```
$result = 42;
```

assigns the value 42 to the variable $result.

The = operator can appear more than once in a single statement. For example, in the statement

```
$value1 = $value2 = "a string";
```

the character string `a string` is assigned to both `$value1` and `$value2`.

Perl also supports other assignment operators, each of which combines an assignment with another operation. For example, suppose that you want to add a value to a scalar variable and assign the result to the following variable:

```
$var = $var + 1;
```

Another way to write this is with the `+=` assignment operator:

```
$var += 1;
```

This statement adds the value 1 to the existing value of `$var`.

An assignment operator exists for just about every bitwise operator and arithmetic operator that Perl supports. Table 4.3 lists the assignment operators supported in Perl.

Table 4.3. The assignment operators.

Operator	Operations performed
=	Assignment only
+=	Addition and assignment
--=	Subtraction and assignment
*=	Multiplication and assignment
/=	Division and assignment
%=	Remainder and assignment
**=	Exponentiation and assignment
&=	Bitwise AND and assignment
|=	Bitwise OR and assignment
^=	Bitwise "exclusive or" and assignment

Table 4.4 shows examples of the assignment operators, along with equivalent statements that use operators you've seen earlier.

Table 4.4. Examples of assignment operators.

Statement using assignment operator	Equivalent Perl statement
`$a = 1;`	none (basic assignment)
`$a --= 1;`	`$a = $a -- 1;`
`$a *= 2;`	`$a = $a * 2;`
`$a /= 2;`	`$a = $a / 2;`
`$a %= 2;`	`$a = $a % 2;`
`$a **= 2;`	`$a = $a ** 2;`
`$a &= 2;`	`$a = $a & 2;`
`$a |= 2;`	`$a = $a	2;`
`$a ^= 2;`	`$a = $a ^ 2;`

Assignment Operators as Subexpressions

Any expression that contains an assignment operator can appear on the left side of another assignment operator. The following is an example:

```
($a = $b) += 3;
```

In cases such as this, the assignment enclosed in parentheses is performed first. This assignment is then treated as a separate subexpression whose value is the variable to which it is being assigned. For example, `$a = $b` has the value `$a`.

This means that the statement shown previously is equivalent to the following two statements:

```
a = $b;
$a += 3;
```

TIP

Don't use assignments in this way unless you absolutely have to. At first glance, the statement

```
($a = $b) += 3;
```

appears to add `3` to `$b` as well as to `$a`.

4

Using Autoincrement and Autodecrement

So far, you've seen two ways to add 1 to a scalar variable:

```
$a = $a + 1;
$a += 1;
```

The first method uses the standard assignment operator = and the addition operator +, and the second method uses the addition assignment operator +=.

Perl also supports a third method of adding 1 to a scalar variable: the *autoincrement operator*, or ++. Here are some examples of the ++ operator in action:

```
$a++;
++$a;
$result = $a++;
$result2 = ++$a;
```

In each case, the ++ operator tells Perl to add 1 to the value stored in $a.

In some of the examples, the ++ is in front of the variable it is affecting, whereas in others the ++ follows the variable. If the ++ is first, the operation is a *pre-increment* operation; if the ++ follows, the operation is a *post-increment* operation.

The Autoincrement Operator: Pre-Increment

To understand how the pre-increment operation works, first recall that you can use a single statement to assign a value to more than one variable, as follows:

```
$var1 = 43;
$var2 = $var1 += 1;
```

Here, the original value stored in $var1, 43, has 1 added to it. The result, 44, becomes the new value of $var1. This new value of 44 is then assigned to $var2.

The pre-increment operation works in the same way:

```
$var1 = 43;
$var2 = ++$var1;
```

The following code fragment tells Perl to add 1 to $var1 before doing anything else:

```
++$var1
```

As a result, $var1 becomes 44 before the value of $var1 is assigned to $var2. Therefore, $var2 is assigned 44.

The ++ operator is most frequently used in while statements. Listing 4.3 provides an example of a simple program that uses the ++ operator in a while statement.

4

TYPE
Listing 4.3. A program that uses the pre-increment operation.

```
1:  # p4_3.pl
2:  $value = 0;
3:  while (++$value <= 5) {
4:          print("value is now $value\n");
5:  }
6:  print("all done\n");
```

OUTPUT
```
C:\> perl p4_3.pl
value is now 1
value is now 2
value is now 3
value is now 4
value is now 5
all done
C:\>
```

ANALYSIS
Note that the pre-increment operation enables you to add 1 to $value and test it all at the same time. This means that you no longer have to remember to add the following:

```
$value = $value + 1;
```

at the bottom of the while statement, which means that you are less likely to write a while statement that goes on forever.

Now see what happens when you change

```
while (++$value <= 5) {
```

to this

```
while (++$value <= 0) {
```

and then run the program again. This time, you get the following:

```
all done
```

Because the ++ operator is in front of $value, 1 is added to $value before testing. This means that $value is not less than or equal to 0 when the while statement is executed for the first time; as a result, the code inside the while statement is never executed.

The Autoincrement Operator: Post-Increment

The post-increment operator also adds 1 to the variable with which it is associated. However, its behavior is slightly different:

```
$var1 = 43;
$var2 = $var1++;
```

When the ++ operator appears after the variable, the ++ operator is performed *after* everything else is finished. This means that the original value of $var1, 43, is assigned to $var2. After this assignment is completed, 1 is added to $var1 and the new value of $var1 becomes 44.

To see how this works in while statements, examine Listing 4.4. Although it is similar to Listing 4.3, it performs a post-increment operation instead of a pre-increment operation.

TYPE

Listing 4.4. A program that uses the post-increment operation.

```
1:   # p4_4.pl
2:   $value = 0;
3:   while ($value++ <= 5) {
4:           print("value is now $value\n");
5:   }
6:   print("all done\n");
```

OUTPUT

```
C:\> perl p4_4.pl
value is now 1
value is now 2
value is now 3
value is now 4
value is now 5
value is now 6
all done
C:\>
```

ANALYSIS You are probably wondering why the output of Listing 4.4 contained the following line:

```
value is now 6
```

To figure out what happened, examine the value stored in $value each time the condition in the while statement is tested. Table 4.5 lists the contents of $value when the condition is tested, the result of the test, and the contents of $value immediately after the condition is tested (after the ++ operator is applied).

Table 4.5. Condition evaluation.

$value at time of test	Result	$value after test
0	true (0 <= 5)	1
1	true (1 <= 5)	2
2	true (2 <= 5)	3

continues

Table 4.5. continued

$value at time of test	Result	$value after test
3	true (3 <= 5)	4
4	true (4 <= 5)	5
5	true (5 <= 5)	6
6	false (6 <= 5)	7 (exit while)

As you know, when the condition at the top of a while statement is true, the code inside the statement is executed, which in this case is

```
print("value is now $value\n");
```

This is why the following line appears:

```
value is now 6
```

$value is 5 at the time the condition is tested, so the result is true.

To fix this problem, change the while condition to the following and run the program again:

```
while ($value < 5) {
```

This is the output you get from the changed program:

```
value is now 1
value is now 2
value is now 3
value is now 4
value is now 5
all done
```

Now, when $value is 5, the statement

```
while ($value++ < 5)
```

is false, and the code inside while is not executed.

The Autodecrement Operator

As you've seen, the ++ operator adds 1 to the value of the variable it is associated with and can appear either before or after the variable. The -- operator, or *autodecrement operator*, works in the same way, but it subtracts 1 from the value of the variable it is associated with, as follows:

```
$a--;
--$a;
$result = $a--;
$result2 = --$a;
```

When the -- operator is in front of the variable, the operation is a *pre-decrement* operation, which means that 1 is subtracted from the variable before anything else happens.

```
$var1 = 56;
$var2 = --$var1;
```

This subtracts 1 from $var1 and assigns the result, 55, back to $var1. The value 55 is then assigned to $var2.

When the -- operator follows the variable, the operation is a *post-decrement* operation, which means that 1 is subtracted from the variable after everything else happens.

```
$var1 = 56;
$var2 = $var1--;
```

This assigns 56 to $var2 and then subtracts 1 from $var1, which means that $var1 now has the value 55.

Do   **Don't**

DO be careful when you use the autoincrement and autodecrement operators. As you've seen, it's easy to get confused and tell your program to loop one too many times or one too few.

I tend not to use these operators in while statements except in very simple cases, because they can get confusing. A better solution is to use the for statement, which you'll learn about on Day 8, "More Control Structures."

DON'T use ++ or -- on both sides of a single variable, as in this statement, because it isn't allowed in Perl:

```
++$var1--;
```

DON'T use autoincrement or autodecrement on a variable and then use the variable again in the same statement:

```
$var1 = 10;
$var2 = $var1 + ++$var1;
```

Is $var2 now 20, 21, or 22? It's impossible to tell. Even different versions of Perl can produce different results!

Using Autoincrement with Strings

If a string value contains only alphabetic characters, the ++ operator can be used to "add one" to a string. In other words, the operator replaces the last character of the string with the next letter of the alphabet. The following is an example:

```
$stringvar = "abc";
$stringvar++;
```

Here, $stringvar now contains abd.

Note that this works only with ++, not --:

```
$stringvar = "abc";
$stringvar--;
```

The -- operator treats abc as a number, which means that it is equivalent to 0. The resulting value of $stringvar is, therefore, -1.

Auto-incrementing strings using ++ also works on uppercase letters:

```
$stringvar = "aBC";
$stringvar++;
```

The value stored in $stringvar is now aBD.

If the last letter of the string is z or Z, ++ converts this letter to a or A, and then "adds one" to the second-to-last character of the string:

```
$stringvar = "abz";
$stringvar++;            # $stringvar now contains "aca"
$stringvar = "AGZZZ";
$stringvar++;            # $stringvar now contains "AHAAA"
```

This also works if the string contains one or more trailing digits:

```
$stringvar = "ab4";
$stringvar++;            # $stringvar now contains "ab5"
```

As in numeric operations, incrementing a string that ends in 9 carries over to the next character of the string. This works regardless of whether the next character is a digit or an alphabetic character.

```
$stringvar = "bc999";
$stringvar++;            # $stringvar now contains "bd000"
```

WARNING

Incrementing string values using ++ works only if the variable has not already been converted to a number.

```
$stringvar = "abc";
$stringvar += 5;
$stringvar++;
```

Here, the value of $stringvar is 6 because abc is converted to 0 by the += operator in the second statement.

Also note that this does not work if the string value contains any character other than a letter or digit, or if a digit is located in the middle of the string:

4

```
$stringvar = "ab*c";
$stringvar++;
$stringvar = "ab5c";
$stringvar++;
```

In both of these cases, the value stored in `$stringvar` is converted to its numeric equivalent, zero, before the `++` operation is performed. This means that `$stringvar` is assigned the value of `1`.

The String-Concatenation and -Repetition Operators

So far, the Perl operators you've seen operate only on integers. (To be exact, they can also operate on strings, but they convert the strings to integers first.) Perl also supports the following special operators that manipulate strings:

☐ The `.` operator, which *concatenates* (joins together) two strings

☐ The `x` operator, which repeats a string

☐ The `.=` operator, which combines concatenation and assignment

The String-Concatenation Operator

The string-concatenation operator, `.`, joins two strings together. For example, the following statement assigns the string `potatohead` to `$newstring`:

```
$newstring = "potato" . "head";
```

You can use the `.` operator with variables, as in this example:

```
$string1 = "potato";
$string2 = "head";
$newstring = $string1 . $string2;
```

This also assigns `potatohead` to `$newstring`. Note that the values of `$string1` and `$string2` are not changed by the `.` operator: `$string1` still has the value `potato`, and `$string2` still has the value `head`.

The String-Repetition Operator

The string-repetition operator, `x` (literally the letter *x*), makes multiple copies of a string and joins the copies together, as shown in this example:

```
$newstring = "t" x 5;
```

This statement takes five copies of the string t and joins them together, producing the string ttttt. This string is then assigned to the variable $newstring.

You can use variables as operands for the x operator, if you like, as follows:

```
$copystring = "t";
$repeats = 5;
$newstring = $copystring x $repeats;
```

The only restriction is that the variable on the right of the x must contain an integer or a value that can be converted to an integer.

Do	Don't

DO make sure you leave a space between the x operator and the values or variables on either side:

```
$newstring = $oldstring x 5;       # this is correct
$newstring = $oldstringx 5;        # incorrect
$newstring = $oldstring x5;        # also incorrect
```

Normally, you don't need to put spaces between an operator and its operands:

```
$x = $x + 1;                       # this is OK
$x=$x+1;                           # this is also OK
```

You need spaces around the x because the letter *x* can appear in variable names. (For example, $oldstringx is a perfectly valid variable name.)

Concatenation and Assignment

The .= operator combines the operations of string concatenation and assignment. For example, the following statements

```
$a = "be";
$a .= "witched";              # $a is now "bewitched"
```

are equivalent to these statements:

```
$a = "be";
$a = $a . "witched";
```

You can use the .= operator to write a very simple program that reads multiple lines of input and joins them into a single string. This program is shown in Listing 4.5.

TYPE
Listing 4.5. A program that reads input lines and concatenates them.

```
1:  # p4_5.pl
2:  $resultstring = "";
3:  print("Enter your input -- type an empty line to quit\n");
4:  $input = <STDIN>;
5:  chop ($input);
6:  while ($input ne "") {
7:          $resultstring .= $input;
8:          $input = <STDIN>;
9:          chop ($input);
10: }
11: print ("Here is the final string:\n");
12: print ("$resultstring\n");
```

OUTPUT
```
C:\> perl p4_5.pl
Enter your input -- type an empty line to quit
this
is
a
test

Here is the final string:
thisisatest
C:\>
```

ANALYSIS
As you can see from the output of Listing 4.5, the four input lines are joined and have become a single string.

Note that there is a much simpler way to do this in Perl: using the built-in function join(). You'll learn about join() on Day 5, "Lists and Array Variables."

Other Perl Operators

Perl also supports two other operators that do not fit into any of the preceding categories:

☐ The comma operator

☐ The conditional operator

The Comma Operator

The *comma operator* (,) is an operator borrowed from the C programming language. It guarantees that a particular part of an expression (the part before the ,) is evaluated first.

Here is an example of a simple statement that uses the , operator:

```
$var1 += 1, $var2 = $var1;
```

Because the , operator indicates that the left operand is to be performed first, 1 is added to $var1 before $var1 is assigned to $var2. In effect, the , operator breaks a statement into two separate statements, as follows:

```
$var1 += 1;
$var2 = $var1;
```

In fact, the only real reason to use the , operator is when two operations are so closely tied together that it is easier to understand the program if they appear as part of the same expression.

The comma operator is often used in conjunction with the = operator, as follows:

```
$val = 26;
$result = (++$val, $val + 5);
```

In this statement, the

```
++$val
```

operation is performed first, because it appears before the , operator. This adds 1 to $val, which means that $val now has the value 27. Then this new value of $val has 5 added to it, and the result, 32, is assigned to $result.

Note that the following expression is enclosed in parentheses:

```
++$val, $val + 5
```

This indicates that this set of operations is to be performed first. Had the parentheses not been present, the statement would have been

```
$result = ++$val, $val + 5;
```

In this case, everything before the comma would be performed first:

```
$result = ++$val
```

This means that $result would be assigned 27, not 32.

You'll learn more about parentheses and the order of operations later today, in the section titled "The Order of Operations."

The Conditional Operator

The *conditional operator* also is borrowed from the C programming language. Unlike the other operators you've seen, the conditional operator requires three operands, as follows:

☐ A condition to test

☐ A value that is to be used when the test condition is true (evaluates to a nonzero value)

☐ A value that is to be used when the test condition is false

The first two operands are separated by the character ?, and the second and third operands are separated by the character :.

Here is a simple example of an expression that uses the conditional operator:

```
$result = $var == 0 ? 14 : 7;
```

Here, the test condition is the expression

```
$var == 0
```

If this expression is true, the value 14 is assigned to $result. If it is false, the value 7 is assigned to $result.

As you can see, the conditional operator behaves just like the if and else statements. The expression

```
$result = $var == 0 ? 14 : 7;
```

is identical to the following:

```
if ($var == 0) {
        $result = 14;
} else {
        $result = 7;
}
```

The difference between the conditional operator and the if-else construct is that the conditional operator can appear in the middle of expressions. For example, the conditional operator can be used as another way to prevent division by 0, as follows:

```
$result = 43 + ($divisor == 0 ? 0 : $dividend / $divisor);
```

Here, $result is assigned the value 43 plus the result of $dividend divided by $divisor, unless $divisor is 0. If $divisor is 0, the result of the division is assumed to be 0, and $result is assigned 43.

Listing 4.6 is a simple program that reads from the standard input file and compares the input line with a predetermined password.

TYPE **Listing 4.6. A very simple password checker.**

```
1:  # p4_6.pl
2:  print ("Enter the secret password:\n");
```

continues

Listing 4.6. continued

```
3:  $password = "bluejays";
4:  $inputline = <STDIN>;
5:  chop ($inputline);
6:  $outputline = $inputline eq $password ?
7:          "Yes, that is the correct password!\n" :
8:          "No, that is not the correct password.\n";
9:  print ($outputline);
```

```
C:\> perl p4_6.pl
Enter the secret password:
orioles
No, that is not the correct password.
C:\>
```

ANALYSIS When you run p4_6.pl and type in a random password, you get the results shown in the Input-Output example.

The advantage of using the conditional operator here is that the assignment to $outputline occurs in only one place, and the statement is much more concise. If you use if and else, you need two assignments to $outputline and five lines, as follows:

```
if ($inputline eq $password) {
        $outputline = "Yes, that is the correct password!\n";
} else {
        $outputline = "No, that is not the correct password.\n");
}
```

Of course, the if and else statements are easier to use when things get more complex. Consider the following example:

```
if ($var1 == 47) {
        print("var1 is already 47\n");
        $is_fortyseven = 1;
} else {
        $var1 = 47;
        print("var1 set to 47\n");
        $is_fortyseven = 0;
}
```

You can write this using the conditional operator if you use the comma operator, as follows:

```
$var1 == 47 ? (print("var1 is already 47\n"), $is_fortyseven = 1) :
        ($var1 = 47, print("var1 set to 47\n"), $is_fortyseven = 0);
```

As you can see, this is difficult to understand. The basic rules are as follows:

☐ Use the conditional operator for very simple conditional statements.

☐ Use if and else for everything else.

Conditional Operators on the Left Side of Assignments

In Perl 5, you can use the conditional operator on the left side of an assignment. This enables you to assign a value to either one of two variables, depending on the result of a conditional expression.

```
$condvar == 43 ? $var1 : $var2 = 14;
```

This statement checks whether `$condvar` has the value of `43`. If it does, `$var1` is assigned `14`. If it doesn't, `$var2` is assigned `14`.

Normally, you won't want to use conditional operators in this way because your code will become difficult to follow. Although the following code is a little less efficient, it performs the same task in a way that is easier to understand:

```
$condvar == 43 ? $var1 = 14 : $var2 = 14;
```

The Order of Operations

Perl, like all programming languages, has a clearly defined set of rules that determine which operations are to be performed first in a particular expression. The following three concepts help explain these rules:

- ☐ The concept of *precedence*
- ☐ The concept of *associativity*
- ☐ The capability to override precedence and associativity using *parentheses*

Precedence

In grade school, you learned that certain arithmetic operations always are performed before other ones. For example, multiplication and division always are performed before addition and subtraction. Look at the following line:

```
4 + 5 * 3
```

Here, the multiplication is performed first, even though the addition is encountered first when the statement is read from left to right. Because multiplication always is performed first, it is said to have higher *precedence* than addition.

Table 4.6 defines the precedence of the operators in Perl. The items at the top of the table have the highest precedence, and the items at the bottom have the lowest.

Table 4.6. Operator precedence.

Operator	Operation Performed
++, --	Autoincrement and autodecrement
-, ~, !	Operators with one operand
**	Exponentiation
=~, !~	Pattern-matching operators
*, /, %, x	Multiplication, division, remainder, repetition
+, -, .	Addition, subtraction, concatenation
<<, >>	Shifting operators
-e, -r, and so on	File-status operators
<, <=, >, >=, lt, le, gt, ge	Inequality-comparison operators
==, !=, <=>, eq, ne, cmp	Equality-comparison operators
&	Bitwise AND
|, ^	Bitwise OR and "exclusive or"
&&	Logical AND
||	Logical OR
..	List-range operator
? and :	Conditional operator (together)
=, +=, -=, *=, and so on	Assignment operators
,	Comma operator
not	Low-precedence logical NOT
and	Low-precedence logical AND
or, xor	Low-precedence logical OR and XOR

Using this table, you can determine the order of operations in complicated expressions. For example:

```
$result = 11 * 2 + 6 ** 2 << 2;
```

To determine the order of operations in this expression, start at the top of Table 4.6 and work down. The first operator you see is **, which means that it is performed first, leaving

```
$result = 11 * 2 + 36 << 2;
```

The next operator you find in the table is the * operator. Performing the multiplication leaves the following:

```
$result = 22 + 36 << 2;
```

The + operator is next:

```
$result = 58 << 2;
```

Next up is the << operator:

```
$result = 232;
```

The = operator is last on the list and assigns 232 to $result.

You might have noticed that Table 4.6 contains some operators that you've not yet seen and that you'll learn about later:

- ☐ The list-range operator, defined on Day 5
- ☐ The file-status operators, defined on Day 6, "Reading from and Writing to Files"
- ☐ The pattern-matching operators, =~ and !~, defined on Day 7, "Pattern Matching"

Associativity

The rules of operator precedence enable you to determine which operation to perform first when an expression contains different operators. But what should you do when an expression contains two or more operators that have the same precedence?

In some cases, it doesn't matter what order you perform the operations in. For example:

```
$result = 4 + 5 + 3;
```

Here, $result gets 12 no matter which addition is performed first. However, for some operations the order of evaluation matters:

```
$result = 2 ** 3 ** 2;
```

Here, if you perform the leftmost exponentiation first, $result is assigned 8 ** 2, or 64. If you perform the rightmost exponentiation first, $result is assigned 2 ** 9, or 512.

Because the order of operations is sometimes important, Perl defines the order in which operations of the same precedence are to be performed. Operations that are performed right-to-left (with the rightmost operation performed first) are said to be *right associative*. Operations that are performed left-to-right (with the leftmost operation performed first) are *left associative*.

Table 4.7 lists the associativity for each of the Perl operators. The operators are sorted according to precedence (in the same order as Table 4.6).

Table 4.7. Operator associativity.

Operator	Associativity
++, --	Not applicable
-, ~, !	Right-to-left
**	Right-to-left
=~, !~	Left-to-right
*, /, %, x	Left-to-right
+, --, .	Left-to-right
<<, >>	Left-to-right
-e, -r, and so on	Not applicable
<, <=, >, >=, lt, le, gt, ge	Left-to-right
==, !=, <=>, eq, ne, cmp	Left-to-right
&	Left-to-right
|, ^	Left-to-right
&&	Left-to-right
||	Left-to-right
..	Left-to-right
? and :	Right-to-left
=, +=, --=, *=, and so on	Right-to-left
,	Left-to-right
not	Left-to-right
and	Left-to-right
or, xor	Left-to-right

From Table 4.7, you see that the exponentiation operator is right associative. This means that in

```
$result = 2 ** 3 ** 2;
```

`$result` is assigned 512, because the rightmost ** operation is performed first.

Perl enables you to force the order of evaluation of operations in expressions. To do this, use parentheses as follows:

```
$result = 4 * (5 + 3);
```

4

In this statement, 5 is added to 3, and then that total is multiplied by 4, yielding 32.

You can use as many sets of parentheses as you like:

```
$result = 4 ** (5 % (8 -- 6));
```

Here, the result is 4:

- ☐ 8 - 6 is performed, leaving 4 ** (5 % 2)
- ☐ 5 % 2 is performed, leaving 4 ** 1
- ☐ 4 ** 1 is 4

Do   **Don't**

DO use parentheses whenever you aren't sure whether a particular operation is to be evaluated first. For example, I don't know many programmers who remember that addition operators are evaluated before shifts:

```
$result = 4 << 2 + 3;
```

And virtually no one remembers that && has higher precedence than ||:

```
if ($value == 0 || $value == 2 && $value2 == "hello") {
      print("my condition is true\n");
}
```

You can make life a lot easier for people who read your code if you use parentheses when the order of evaluation is not obvious. For example:

```
$result = 4 << (2 + 3);
if ($value == 0 || ($value == 2 && $value2 == "hello")) {
      print("my condition is true\n");
}
```

DO use multiple lines, extra spaces, and indentations to make complicated expressions easier to read. For example:

```
if ($value == 0 ||
      ($value == 2 && $value2 == "hello")) {
```

Here, it's obvious that there are two main conditions to be tested and that one of them contains a pair of subconditions.

DON'T leave out closing parentheses by mistake.

```
$result = 4 + (2 << ($value / 2);    # error
```

This statement will be flagged as erroneous because you are missing a closing parenthesis.

A handy way of checking whether you have enough parentheses in complicated expressions is to use this simple trick:

1. Start at the left end of your expression.
2. Starting from 0, add 1 for every left parenthesis you see.
3. Subtract 1 for every closing parenthesis you see.

If your final result is 0, you have enough opening and closing parentheses. (This doesn't guarantee that you've put the parentheses in the right places, but at least you now know that you have enough of them.)

Summary

Today you learned about the operators that Perl supports. Each operator requires one or more operands, which are the values on which the operator operates. A collection of operands and operators is known as an expression.

The operators you learned how to use are as follows:

- ☐ The arithmetic operators (+, -, *, /, %, **) and unary negation operator (-)
- ☐ The integer-comparison operators ==, !=, <, >, <=, >=, and <=>
- ☐ The string-comparison operators eq, ne, lt, gt, le, ge, and cmp
- ☐ The logical operators ||, &&, and !
- ☐ The bit-manipulation operators |, &, ^, ~, <<, and >>
- ☐ The assignment operators =, +=, --=, *=, /=, %=, **=, !=, &=, ^=, and .=
- ☐ The autoincrement operator ++
- ☐ The autodecrement operator --
- ☐ The string-concatenation operator .
- ☐ The string-repetition operator x
- ☐ The comma operator ,
- ☐ The conditional operator (? and : together)

You have also learned about operator precedence and associativity, two concepts that tell you which operators in an expression usually are performed first. Operator precedence and associativity can be controlled by putting parentheses around the operations you want to perform first.

Q&A

Q Is there a limit on how large my expressions can be?

A Effectively, no. There is a limit, but it's so large that no one would possibly want to create an expression that long because it would be impossible to read or understand.

It's easier to understand expressions if they are shorter.

Q Is it better to use += or ++ when adding 1 to a variable?

A It's best to use ++ when using a variable as a counter in a `while` statement (or in other loops, which you learn about on Day 8). For other addition operations, you should use +=.

Q Why are some operators left associative and others right associative?

A Most operators are left associative, because we normally read from left to right.

The assignment operator is right associative because it's easier to read that way. For instance:

```
$var1 = $var2 = 5;
```

If the assignment operator happened to be left associative, `$var1` would be assigned the old value of `$var2`, not `5`. This would not be obvious to a casual reader of the program.

Exponentiation is right associative because that's how exponentiation is performed in mathematics.

Other operators that are right associative are easier to read from right to left.

Workshop

The Workshop provides quiz questions to help you solidify your understanding of the material covered and exercises to give you experience in using what you've learned. Try to understand the quiz and exercise answers before you go on to tomorrow's lesson. You can find the answers in Appendix B, "Answers."

Quiz

1. Define the following terms:
    a. operator
    b. operand
    c. expression
    d. precedence
    e. associativity

2. What operation is performed by the following operators?
    a. `&&`
    b. `&`
    c. `^`
    d. `ne`
    e. `.`

3. What operators perform the following operations?
    a. string-equality comparison
    b. remainder
    c. string duplication
    d. bitwise OR
    e. numeric greater-than-or-equal-to

4. What is the binary (base 2) representation of the following numbers?
    a. 171
    b. 1105
    c. 0

5. What is the standard (base 10) representation of the following numbers?
    a. 01100100
    b. 00001111
    c. 01000001

6. What is the value of the following expressions?
    a. `17 * 2 ** 3 / 9 % 2 << 2`
    b. `0 && (171567 * 98275 / 1174.5 ** 4)`
    c. `1171 ^ 904`
    d. `"abc" . "de" x 2`

4

Exercises

1. Write a program that uses the << operator to print out the first 16 powers of 2.

2. Rewrite the following statement using the conditional operator:

```
if ($var1 == 5 || $var2 == 7) {
        $result = $var1 * $var2 + 16.5;
} else {
        print("condition is false\n");
        $result = 0;
}
```

3. Rewrite the following expression using the `if` and `else` statements:

```
$result = $var1 <= 26 ? ++$var2 : 0;
```

4. Write a program that reads two integers from standard input (one at a time), divides the first one by the second one, and prints out the quotient (the result) and the remainder.

5. Why might the following statement not assign the value 5.1 to $result?

```
$result = 5.1 + 100005.2 -- 100005.2;
```

6. Determine the order of operations in the following statement and add parentheses to the statement to indicate this order:

```
$result = $var1 * 2 << 5 + 3 || $var2 ** 3, $var3;
```

7. What value is assigned to $result by the following code?

```
$var1 = 43;
$var2 = 16;
$result = ++$var2 == 17 ? $var1++ * 2 - 5 : ++$var1 * 3 -- 11;
```

8. **BUG BUSTER:** Find and fix the bugs in the following program:

```
# exercise 8:

$num = <STDIN>;
chop ($num);
$x = "";
$x += "hello";
if ($x != "goodbye" | $x == "farewell") {
        $result = $num eq 0 ? 43;
} else {
        $result = ++$num++;
}
print("the result is $result\n");
```

Day 5

Lists and Array Variables

The Perl programs you have seen so far deal with *scalar values*, which are single units of data, and *scalar variables*, which can store one piece of information.

Perl also enables you to define an ordered collection of values, known as a *list*; this collection of values can be stored in variables known as *array variables*.

Today's lesson describes lists and array variables, and it shows you what you can do with them. Today, you will learn about the following:

- ☐ What lists are
- ☐ The relationship between scalar variables and lists
- ☐ Storing lists in array variables
- ☐ Accessing an element of an array variable or list

- [ ] How to use list ranges
- [ ] Assigning to array variables
- [ ] Assigning to scalar variables from array variables
- [ ] Retrieving the length of a list
- [ ] Using array slices
- [ ] Using an array to store input
- [ ] Sorting a list or array variable
- [ ] Reversing a list or array variable
- [ ] Creating a string from a list
- [ ] Creating a list from a string

Introducing Lists

A *list* is a sequence of scalar values enclosed in parentheses. The following is a simple example of a list:

```
(1, 5.3, "hello", 2)
```

This list contains four elements, each of which is a scalar value: the numbers 1 and 5.3, the string hello, and the number 2.

Lists can be as long as needed, and they can contain any scalar value. A list can have no elements at all, as follows:

```
()
```

This list also is called an *empty list*.

NOTE

> A list with one element and a scalar value are different entities. For example, the list
>
> ```
> (43.2)
> ```
>
> and the scalar value
>
> ```
> 43.2
> ```
>
> are not the same thing. This is not a severe limitation, though, because one can be converted to or assigned to the other. See the section titled "Assigning to Scalar Variables from Array Variables" later today.

5

Scalar Variables and Lists

A scalar variable name can always be included as part of a list. In this case, the current value of the scalar variable becomes the list element value. Look at this example:

```
(17, $var, "a string")
```

If `$var` has been assigned the value 26, the second element of the list becomes 26. (It remains 26 even if a different value is assigned to `$var`.)

Similarly, you can use the value of an expression as an element of a list:

```
(17, 26 << 2)
```

This list contains two elements: 17 and 104 (which is 26 left-shifted two places). Expressions in lists, like other expressions, can contain scalar variables:

```
(17, $var1 + $var2)
```

Here, the expression `$var1 + $var2` is evaluated, and its value becomes the second element of the list.

Lists and String Substitution

Because character strings are scalar values, they can be used in lists, as follows:

```
("my string", 24.3, "another string")
```

You can substitute for scalar variable names in character strings in lists, as follows:

```
($value, "The answer is $value")
```

This list contains two elements: the value of the scalar variable `$value` and a string containing the contents of `$value`. If the current value of `$value` is 26, the two elements of the list are 26 and `The answer is 26`.

Storing Lists in Array Variables

Perl enables you to store lists in special variables designed for that purpose. These variables are called *array variables* (or *arrays* for short).

The following is an example of a list being assigned to an array variable:

```
@array = (1, 2, 3);
```

Here, the list `(1, 2, 3)` is assigned to the array variable `@array`.

Note that the name of the array variable starts with the character @. This enables Perl to distinguish array variables from other kinds of variables—for example, scalar variables, which start with the character $. As with scalar variables, the second character of the variable name must be a letter, while subsequent characters of the name can be letters, numbers, or underscores. Array variable names can be as long as you like.

The following are legal array-variable names:

```
@my_array
@list2
@_array
@a_very_long_array_name_with_lots_of_underscores
```

The following are not legal array-variable names:

```
@1array          # can't start with a number
@a.new.array     # . is not a legal variable-name character
```

When an array variable is first created (that is, seen for the first time), it is assumed to contain the empty list () unless it is assigned to a not-empty list.

NOTE

Because Perl uses @ and $ to distinguish array variables from scalar variables, the same name can be used in an array variable and in a scalar variable. Look at this example:

```
$var = 1;
@var = (11, 27.1, "a string");
```

Here, the name var is used in both the scalar variable $var and the array variable @var. These are two completely separate variables.

Normally, you won't want to use the same name in both an array and a scalar variable because it's confusing.

Accessing an Element of an Array Variable

After you have assigned a list to an array variable, you can refer to any element of the array variable as if it were a scalar variable.

For example, to assign the first element of the array variable @array to the scalar variable $scalar, use the following statement:

```
$scalar = $array[0];
```

5

The character sequence [0] is an example of a *subscript*. A subscript indicates a particular element of an array. In this case, 0 refers to the first element of the array. Similarly, the subscript 1 refers to the second element of the array, as follows:

```
$scalar = $array[1];
```

Here, the second element of the array @array is assigned to $scalar. The general rule is this:

An array subscript *n*, where *n* is any non-negative integer, always refers to array element *n*+1.

This notation is employed to ensure compatibility with the C programming language, which also starts its array subscripting with 0.

You can assign a scalar value to an individual array element in the same way:

```
@array = (1, 2, 3, 4);
$array[3] = 5;
```

After the second assignment, the value of @array becomes

```
(1, 2, 3, 5)
```

This is because the fourth element of the array has been replaced.

NOTE

If you try to access an array element that does not exist, undef is returned. Here, undef is equivalent to an empty string. For instance,

```
@array = (1, 2, 3, 4);
$scalar = $array[4];
```

Here, $array[4] refers to the fifth element of @array, which does not exist. In this case, $scalar is assigned undef.

5

You can use the value of a scalar variable as a subscript, as follows:

```
$index = 1;
$scalar = $array[$index];
```

Here, the value of $index, 1, becomes the subscript. This means that the second element of @array is assigned to $scalar.

WARNING

When you use a scalar variable as a subscript, make sure that the value stored in the scalar variable corresponds to an array element that exists. Look at this example:

```
@array = (1, 2, 3, 4);
$index = 4;
$scalar = $array[$index];
```

> Here, the third statement tries to access the fifth element of @array, which does not exist. In this case, $scalar is assigned undef, and the Perl interpreter doesn't tell you that anything went wrong.

More Details on Array Element Names

Note that the first character of an array-element variable name is the $ character, not the @ character. For example, to refer to the first element of the array @potato, use

```
$potato[0]
```

and not

```
@potato[0]
```

The basic rule is as follows: Things that reference one value—such as scalar variables and array elements—must start with a $.

> **NOTE**
>
> Even though references to elements of array variables start with a $, the Perl interpreter still has no trouble distinguishing scalar variables from array-variable elements. For example, if you have defined a scalar variable $potato and an array variable @potato, the Perl interpreter uses the subscript to distinguish between the scalar variable and the array-variable element:
>
> ```
> $result = $potato;        # the scalar variable $potato
> $result = $potato[0];     # the first element of @potato
> ```

Using Lists and Arrays in Perl Programs

Now that you have seen how lists and array variables work, it's time to take a look at a simple program that uses them. Listing 5.1 is a simple program that prints the elements of a list.

TYPE   **Listing 5.1. A program that prints the elements of a list.**

```
1:  # p5_1.pl
2:
3:  @array = (1, "chicken", 1.23, "\"Having fun?\"", 9.33e+23);
4:  $count = 1;
5:  while ($count <= 5) {
```

```
6:              print ("element $count is $array[$count-1]\n");
7:              $count++;
8:  }
```

OUTPUT
```
C:\> perl p5_1.pl
element 1 is 1
element 2 is chicken
element 3 is 1.23
element 4 is "Having fun?"
element 5 is 9.3300000000000005+e23
C:\>
```

ANALYSIS Line 3 assigns a list containing five elements to the array variable @array.

Line 5 tests whether $count is less than or equal to 5. This conditional expression ensures that the while statement loops five times.

Line 6 prints the current value of $count and the corresponding element of @array. Note that the expression used in the subscript is $count-1, not $count, because subscripting starts from 0. For example, when count is 3, the subscript is 2, which means that the third element of @array is printed.

When you examine line 6, you see that Perl lets you substitute for array elements in character strings. When the Perl interpreter sees $array[$count-1] in the character string, it replaces this array element name with its corresponding value.

Listing 5.2 is another example of a program that uses arrays. This one is a little more interesting; it uses the built-in functions rand and int to generate random integers between 1 and 10.

5

TYPE **Listing 5.2. A program that generates random integers between 1 and 10.**

```
1:  # p5_2.pl
2:
3:  # collect the random numbers
4:  $count = 1;
5:  while ($count <= 100) {
6:          $randnum = int( rand(10) ) + 1;
7:          $randtotal[$randnum] += 1;
8:          $count++;
9:  }
10:
11: # print the total of each number
12: $count = 1;
13: print ("Total for each number:\n");
14: while ($count <= 10) {
15:         print ("\tnumber $count: $randtotal[$count]\n");
16:         $count++;
17: }
```

OUTPUT
```
C:\> perl p5_2.pl
Total for each number:
            number 1: 11
            number 2: 8
            number 3: 13
            number 4: 6
            number 5: 10
            number 6: 9
            number 7: 12
            number 8: 11
            number 9: 11
            number 10: 9
C:\>
```

ANALYSIS   This program is divided into two parts: The first part collects the random numbers, and the second part prints them.

Line 5 ensures that the loop *iterates* (is performed) 100 times. You can just as easily have the program generate any other quantity of random numbers just by changing the value in this conditional expression.

Line 6 generates a random number between 1 and 10 and assigns it to the scalar variable `$randnum`. To see how it does this, first note that the code fragment

```
int ( rand (10) )
```

actually is two function calls, one inside another. When the Perl interpreter sees this, it first calls the inner one, which is `rand`. The value returned by `rand` becomes the argument to the built-in function `int`.

Here's how line 6 generates a random number:

1. First, it calls the Perl library function `rand`. This function generates a floating-point random number between 0 and 1 and then multiplies it by the argument it is passed. In this program, `rand` is passed `10`, which means that the random number is multiplied by 10 and is now a floating-point number that is greater than 0 and less than 10.

2. The value returned by `rand` is then passed to the library function `int`, which takes a floating-point number and gets rid of the non-integer part. This operation is known as *truncation*. The integer produced by this truncation operation becomes the return value of the function. For example, the following returns `5`:

   ```
   int (5.7)
   ```

   In this program, `int` truncates the random number returned by `rand` and returns the resulting integer, which is now a random number between 0 and 9.

3. The value `1` is added to the number returned by `int`, resulting in a random number between 1 and 10.

4. This number is assigned to the scalar variable `$randnum`.

Line 7 now adds 1 to the element of the array `@randtotal` corresponding to the number generated. For example, if the random number is 7, the array element `$randtotal[7]` has 1 added to it.

NOTE

> As you can see, line 7 works even though `@randtotal` is not initialized. When the program refers to an array element for the first time, the Perl interpreter assumes that the element has an initial value of the null string (`""`). In other words, the array element starts out with `undef`. This null string is converted to 0, which means that adding 1 for the first time produces the result 1, which is what you want.

The second part of the program, which prints the total of each random number, starts with lines 12 and 13. These lines get things started by resetting the counter variable `$count` to 1 and printing an introductory message.

The conditional expression in line 14 ensures that the loop iterates 10 times—once for each possible random number.

Line 15 prints the total for a particular random number.

Using Brackets and Substituting for Variables

As you have just seen, Perl lets you substitute for array-element variable names in strings, as follows:

```
print ("element $count is $array[ $count-1]\n");
```

This might lead to problems if you want to include the characters [and] in character strings. For example, suppose that you have defined the scalar variable `$var` and the array variable `@var`. The character string

```
"$var[0]"
```

substitutes the value of the first element of `@var` in the string. To substitute the value of `$var` and keep the `[0]` as it is, you must use one of the following:

```
"${var}[0]"
"$var\[0]"
"$var" . "[0]"
```

The character string

```
"${var}[0]"
```

uses the brace characters { and } to keep var and [separate; this tells the Perl interpreter to substitute for the variable $var, not $var[0]. After the substitution, the brace characters are not included in the string.

To include a brace character after a $, use a backslash, as follows:

```
"$\{var}"
```

This character string contains the text ${var}.

The character string

```
"$var\[0]"
```

uses \ to indicate that the [character is to be given a different meaning than normal; in this case, this means that [is to be treated as a printable character and not as part of the variable name to be substituted.

The expression

```
"$var" . "[0]"
```

consists of two character strings joined together by the . operator. Here, the Perl interpreter replaces the first character string with the current value of $var.

Using List Ranges

Suppose that you want to define a list consisting of the numbers 1 through 10, inclusive. You can do this by typing each of the numbers in turn:

```
(1, 2, 3, 4, 5, 6, 7, 8, 9, 10)
```

However, there is a simpler way to do it: Use the *list range operator*, which is .. (two consecutive period characters). The following is an example of a list created using the list-range operator:

```
(1..10)
```

This tells Perl to define a list that has a first value of 1, a second value of 2, and so on up to 10.

The list-range operator can be used to define part of a list.

```
(2, 5..7, 11)
```

This list consists of five elements: the numbers 2, 5, 6, 7, and 11.

List-range operators can be used with floating-point values. Look at this example:

```
(2.1..5.3)
```

This list consists of four elements: 2.1, 3.1, 4.1, and 5.1. Each element of the list is one greater than the previous element, and the last element of the list is the largest possible number less than or equal to the number to the right of the .. operator. Here, 5.1 is less than 5.3, so it is included in the list; however, 6.1 is greater than 5.3, so it is not included.

NOTE

If the value to the left of the .. operator is greater than the value to the right, an empty list is created.

```
(4.5..1.6)
```

Because 4.5 is greater than 1.6, this list is empty.

If the two values are equal, a one-element list is created.

```
(3..3)
```

This is equivalent to the list (3).

List-range operators can specify ranges of strings. For example, the list ("aaa", "aab", "aac", "aad") can be expressed as ("aaa".."aad"). Similarly, the list ("BCY", "BCZ", "BDA", "BDB") is equivalent to ("BCY".."BDB"), and the statement @alphabet = ("a".."z"); creates a list consisting of the twenty-six lowercase letters of the alphabet and assigns this list to the array variable @alphabet.

List ranges also enable you to use strings to specify numbers that contain leading zeros:

```
@day_of_month = ("01".."31");
```

This statement creates a list consisting of the strings 01, 02, 03, and so on, up to 31, and then assigns this list to @day_of_month. Because each string contains two characters, this array is suitable for use when you are printing a date in a format such as 08-June-1960.

Expressions and List Ranges

The values that define the range of a list-range operator can be expressions, and these expressions can contain scalar variables. For example:

```
($var1..$var2+5)
```

This list consists of all values between the current value of $var1 and the current value of the expression $var2+5.

Listing 5.3 is an example of a program that uses list ranges. This program asks for a start number and an end number, and it prints all the numbers between them.

Listing 5.3. A program that uses list ranges to print a list of numbers.

TYPE

```
 1:  # p5_3.pl
 2:
 3:  print ("Enter the start number:\n");
 4:  $start = <STDIN>;
 5:  chop ($start);
 6:  print ("Enter the end number:\n");
 7:  $end = <STDIN>;
 8:  chop ($end);
 9:  @list = ($start..$end);
10:  $count = 0;
11:  print ("Here is the list:\n");
12:  while ($list[$count] != 0 || $list[$count-1] == -1 ||
13:          $list[$count+1] == 1) {
14:          print ("$list[$count]\n");
15:          $count++;
16:  }
```

OUTPUT

```
C:\> perl p5_3.pl
Enter the start number:
-2
Enter the end number:
2
Here is the list:
-2
-1
0
1
2
C:\>
```

ANALYSIS   Lines 3 through 5 retrieve the start of the range to be printed. Line 3 retrieves the number from the standard input file. Line 4 assigns the resulting number to the scalar variable $start. Line 5 chops the trailing newline character.

Lines 6 through 8 repeat the same process for the end of the range, assigning the end of the range to the scalar variable $end.

Line 9 creates a list that consists of the numbers between $start and $end, and stores the list in the array variable @list.

Line 10 initializes the counter variable $count to 0.

Line 11 is a print statement that indicates that the list is about to be printed.

Lines 12 and 13 are the start of the loop that prints the range. The conditional expression to be evaluated consists of three subexpressions that are operands for the logical OR operator, ||. If any one of these subexpressions is true, the loop continues.

5

The first subexpression tests for the end of the range. To do this, it takes advantage of the fact that an unidentified list element is equal to the null string and that the null string is equivalent to 0. When the list element `$list[$count]` is undefined, the following subexpression is false:

```
$list[$count] != 0
```

The second and third subexpressions cover the cases in which 0 is actually a part of the list. If the list to be printed contains 0, one or both of the following conditions must be true:

- [ ] The number 1 must be the next element in the list.
- [ ] The number –1 must be the previous element in the list.

The second and third subexpressions test for these conditions. If either or both of these conditions are true, at least one of the following subexpressions also must be true:

```
$list[$count-1] == -1
$list[$count+1] == 1
```

This ensures that the loop continues. Of course, this doesn't cover the case in which the list consists of just 0; however, that's not a meaningful case. (If you want to be finicky, you can add a special chunk of code that prints 0 if `$start` and `$end` are both 0, but that's not really worth bothering with.)

After this, the rest of the program is straightforward. Line 14 prints a number in the range, line 15 adds 1 to the counter variable `$count`, and line 16 ends the `while` statement.

TIP

One of the problems with Perl is that it is sometimes difficult to distinguish the following scalar variable or array-element values:

- [ ] The null string `""`, which is converted to 0 in numeric expressions
- [ ] An undefined variable or element, which defaults to the null string, which in turn is converted to 0 in numeric expressions
- [ ] The string 0, which is converted to the number 0 in numeric expressions
- [ ] A non-numeric string such as `string`, which is converted to 0 in numeric expressions

There are several ways of dealing with this confusion:

- [ ] Retrieve the length of the list stored in an array variable before processing it. This ensures that you don't go past the end of the list. See the section titled "Retrieving the Length of a List" later in today's lesson for more details on how to do this.

5

☐ Compare the value with the string `0` rather than the number 0, as follows:

```
if ($value eq "0") ...
```

This handles the strings that convert to `0` in numeric expressions that are not 0 itself. (It doesn't handle strings such as `0000` or `0.0`, which you might want your program to consider equivalent to 0; to deal with these, see the discussion of the `split` function later in today's lesson.)

☐ Initialize the scalar variable or array element to a value other than `0` that you know is not going to appear naturally in your program, such as `-99999`.

Which particular method is best depends on the program you want to write, the input it expects, and how bulletproof the program needs to be.

More on Assignment and Array Variables

So far, you've seen that you can assign lists to array variables:

```
@array = (1, 2, 3, 4, 5);
```

You've also seen that you can assign an element of an array to a scalar variable:

```
$scalar = $array[3];
```

The following sections describe the other ways you can use assignment with lists and array variables.

Copying from One Array Variable to Another

You also can assign one array variable to another:

```
@result = @original;
```

Here, the list currently stored in the array variable `@original` is copied to the array variable `@result`. Each element of the new array `@result` is the same as the corresponding element of the array `@original`. Listing 5.4 shows that this is true.

Listing 5.4. A program that copies an array and compares the elements of the two arrays.

TYPE

```
1:  # p5_4.pl
2:
3:  @array1 = (14, "cheeseburger", 1.23, -7, "toad");
4:  @array2 = @array1;
5:  $count = 1;
6:  while ($count <= 5) {
7:          print("element $count: $array1[$count-1] ");
8:          print("$array2[$count-1]\n");
9:          $count++;
10: }
```

OUTPUT

```
C:\> perl p5_4.pl
element 1: 14 14
element 2: cheeseburger cheeseburger
element 3: 1.23 1.23
element 4: -7 -7
element 5: toad toad
C:\>
```

ANALYSIS Line 3 assigns the list

```
(14, "cheeseburger", 1.23, -7, "toad")
```

to the array variable @array1. Line 4 then copies this array into a second array variable, @array2.

The rest of the program prints the elements of each array, as follows:

☐ Line 5 initializes the counter variable $count to 1.

☐ The conditional expression in line 6 ensures that the loop is performed five times.

☐ Lines 7 and 8 print the matching element of each array. (Note that the subscript is $count-1, not $count, because the subscript 0 is the first element of the array.)

☐ Line 9 adds 1 to the counter variable $count.

NOTE

> You can assign a list to multiple arrays in one statement. For example:
>
> ```
> @array1 = @array2 = (1, 2, 3);
> ```
>
> This assigns a copy of the list (1, 2, 3) to both @array1 and @array2.

5

Using Array Variables in Lists

As you've already seen, lists can contain scalar variables:

```
@list = (1, $scalar, 3);
```

Here, the value of the scalar variable $scalar becomes the second element of the list assigned to @list.

You also can specify that the value of an array variable is to appear in a list, as follows:

```
@list1 = (2, 3, 4);
@list2 = (1, @list1, 5);
```

Here, the value of the array variable @list1—the list (2, 3, 4)—is substituted for the name @list1, and the resulting list (1, 2, 3, 4, 5) is assigned to @list2.

Listing 5.5 shows an example of a list being contained in another list.

TYPE

Listing 5.5. A program that assigns a list as part of another list.

```
1:  # p5_5.pl
2:
3:  @innerlist = " never ";
4:  @outerlist = ("I", @innerlist, "fail!\n");
5:  print @outerlist;
```

OUTPUT

```
C:\> perl p5_5.pl
I never fail!
C:\>
```

ANALYSIS
Although this program is quite simple, it contains a couple of new tricks. The first of these is in line 3. Here, a scalar value, " never " (note the surrounding spaces), is assigned to the array variable @innerlist. This works because the Perl interpreter automatically converts the scalar value into a one-element list before assigning it to the array variable.

Line 4 assigns a list to the array variable @outerlist. This list is assembled by taking the following list

```
("I", @innerlist, "fail!\n")
```

and substituting in the current value of the array variable @innerlist. As a result, the list assigned to @outerlist is

```
("I", " never ", "fail!\n")
```

Line 5 prints the list. To do this, it calls the library function `print` and passes it the array variable `@outerlist`. When `print` is given an array variable or a list to print, it prints each element in turn. This means that the following is written to the standard output file:

```
I never fail!
```

Note that `print` doesn't leave any spaces between the elements of the list when it prints them. The only reason the output is readable is because the character string contains spaces around `never`. This means that `print` isn't usually used to print a list of numbers in this way:

```
@list = (1, 2, 3);
print @list;
```

This prints the following, which isn't quite what you want:

```
123
```

TIP

In Listing 5.5, the argument passed to the `print` function is not enclosed in parentheses. This is perfectly acceptable. In Perl for Win32, the parentheses enclosing arguments to functions are optional. For example, when you call the library function `chop`, instead of writing

```
chop ($number);
```

you can write

```
chop $number;
```

Although this saves a few extra keystrokes, it makes things a little less readable.

Besides, eliminating the parentheses can lead to problems. Consider the following example:

```
$fred = "Fred";
print (("Hello, " . $fred . "!\n") x 2);
```

This code prints

```
Hello, Fred!
Hello, Fred!
```

In this case, the parentheses enclosing the arguments to `print` are absolutely necessary. Without them, you have

```
print ("Hello, " . $fred . "!\n") x 2;
```

When the Perl interpreter sees this statement, it assumes that `print` is being called with the following argument, which is not what you want:

```
"Hello, " . $fred . "!\n"
```

As always in programming, the basic rule to follow is this: Do whatever makes your program easier to work with, and use your best judgment.

5

Substituting for Array Variables in Strings

As you have seen, Perl does not leave spaces if you pass an array variable to `print`:

```
@array = (1, 2, 3);
print (@array, "\n");
```

This prints the following on your screen:

```
123
```

To get around this problem, put the array you want to print into a string:

```
print ("@array\n");
```

When the Perl interpreter sees the array variable inside the string, it substitutes the values of the list assigned to the array variables and leaves a space between each pair of elements. For example:

```
@array = (1, 2, 3);
print ("@array\n");
```

This prints the following on your screen:

```
1 2 3
```

Assigning to Scalar Variables from Array Variables

Consider the following assignment, which you've already seen:

```
@array = ($var1, $var2);
```

Here, the values of the scalar variables `$var1` and `$var2` are used to form a two-element list that is assigned to the array variable `@array`.

Perl also enables you to take the current value of an array variable and assign its components to a group of scalar variables. For example:

```
@array = (5, 7);
($var1, $var2) = @array;
```

Here, the first element of the list currently stored in `@array`, 5, is assigned to `$var1`. The second element, 7, is assigned to `$var2`.

Additional elements in an array, if they exist, are ignored. For example:

```
@array = (5, 7, 11);
($var1, $var2) = @array;
```

Here, 5 is assigned to `$var1`, 7 is assigned to `$var2`, and 11 is not assigned to anything.

If there are more scalar variables than elements in an array variable, the excess scalar variables are assigned the null string, as follows:

```
@array = (5, 7);
($var1, $var2, $var3) = @array;
```

This assigns 5 to $var1 and 7 to $var2. Because there are not enough elements in @array to assign anything to $var3, $var3 is assigned the null string, "".

NOTE

You also can assign to several scalar variables using a list. For example:

```
($var1, $var2, $var3) = ("one", "two", "three");
```

This assigns one to $var1, two to $var2, and three to $var3.

As with array variables, extra values in the list are ignored and extra scalar variables are assigned the null string, as follows:

```
($var1, $var2) = (1, 2, 3);       # 3 is ignored
($var1, $var2, $var3) = (1, 2);  # $var3 is now ""
```

Retrieving the Length of a List

As you've seen, lists and array variables can be any length you want. As a consequence, Perl provides a way of determining the length of the list assigned to an array variable.

Here's how it works: If an array variable (or list) appears anywhere that a scalar value is expected, the Perl interpreter obtains a scalar value by calculating the length of the list assigned to the array variable.

For example, consider the following example:

```
@array = (1, 2, 3);
$scalar = @array;
```

In the assignment to $scalar, the Perl interpreter replaces @array with the length of the list currently assigned to @array, which is 3. $scalar, therefore, is assigned the value 3.

WARNING

Note that the following two statements are not equivalent:

```
$scalar = @array;
($scalar) = @array;
```

In the first statement, the length of the list in @array is assigned to $scalar. In the second statement, the first element of @array is assigned to $scalar.

It is important to remember that $scalar and ($scalar) are not the same thing. $scalar is a scalar variable, and ($scalar) is a one-element list containing $scalar.

5

Being able to access the length of an array is useful if you want to write a loop that performs an operation on every element of an array. Listing 5.6 is an example of a program that does just that.

TYPE

Listing 5.6. A program that prints every element of an array.

```
1:  # p5_6.pl
2:
3:  @array = (14, "cheeseburger", 1.23, -7, "toad");
4:  $count = 1;
5:  while ($count <= @array) {
6:          print("element $count: $array[$count-1]\n");
7:          $count++;
8:  }
```

OUTPUT

```
C:\> perl p5_6.pl
element 1: 14
element 2: cheeseburger
element 3: 1.23
element 4: -7
element 5: toad
C:\>
```

ANALYSIS The only new feature of this program is line 5, which compares the counter variable $count to the length of the array @array. Because the list assigned to @array contains five elements, the conditional expression

```
$count <= @array
```

ensures that the loop iterates five times.

Once again, note that the subscript in line 6 is $count-1, not $count. This caution bears repeating: It is very easy to forget to subtract 1 when you use a value as a subscript.

If you like, you can write your loop in a different way and use $count as a subscript. For example:

```
$count = 0;
while ($count < @array) {
        print ("element $count+1: $array[ $count]\n");
}
```

As you can see, this isn't any easier to follow because you now have to remember these two things:

☐ The conditional expression now must use the < operator, not the <= operator. If you use <= here, the loop iterates six times, not five.

☐ The value of `$count` is now not the same as the element you are referring to. For instance, if you are printing the third element of the array, `$count` has the value 2. This means that references to `$count`, such as

```
element $count+1:
```

must add 1 to the value of `$count` to get the result you want.

As you can see, there is no intuitive or obvious way of writing programs that loop through arrays. Generally, it's best to pick the way that is easiest for you to remember.

WARNING

You cannot retrieve the length of a list without first assigning the list to an array variable. For example:

```
@array = (10, 20, 30);
$scalar = @array;
```

This assigns 3 to `$scalar`. Compare this with the following statement:

```
$scalar = (10, 20, 30);
```

This statement actually assigns 30 to `$scalar`, not 3. In this statement, the subexpression

```
(10, 20, 30)
```

is treated as three scalar values separated by comma operators.

For more details on the comma operator, refer to the section titled "The Comma Operator" on Day 4, "More Operators."

Using Array Slices

As you've seen, array subscripting enables you to change or access one element of an array. For example:

```
$var = $array[2];
$array[2] = $var;
```

Perl enables you to access more than one element of an array at a time in much the same way. Following is a simple example:

```
@subarray = @array[0,1];
```

Here, the code fragment

```
@array[0,1]
```

refers to the first two elements of the list stored in the array variable. This portion of the array is known as an *array slice*. An array slice is treated just like any other list. In the statement

```
@subarray = @array[0,1];
```

the list consisting of the first two elements of @array is assigned to the array variable @subarray.

Here is another example:

```
@slice = @array[1,2,3];
```

This statement assigns the array slice consisting of the second, third, and fourth elements of @array to the array variable @slice.

WARNING

Although single elements of an array are referenced using the $ character, array slices are referenced using @:

```
$var = $array[0];
@subarray = @array[0,1];
```

The basic rules are as follows:

☐ References to single items, such as scalar variables or single array elements, start with a $.

☐ References to array variables or array slices, which refer to lists, start with a @.

Listing 5.7 shows a simple example of an array slice.

Listing 5.7. A program that demonstrates the use of an
TYPE   array slice.

```
1:  # p5_7.pl
2:
3:  @array = (1, 2, 3, 4);
4:  @subarray = @array[1,2];
5:  print ("The first element of subarray is $subarray[0]\n");
6:  print ("The second element of subarray is $subarray[1]\n");
```

OUTPUT
```
C:\> perl p5_7.pl
The first element of subarray is 2
The second element of subarray is 3
C:\>
```

ANALYSIS Line 3 of this program assigns the following list to the array variable `@array`:

```
(1, 2, 3, 4)
```

Line 4 assigns a slice of the array variable `@array` to the array variable `@subarray`. The array slice

```
@array[1,2]
```

specifies that the second and third elements of the array are to be treated as a list and assigned to `@subarray`.

> **NOTE**
>
> In array slices, as in references to single elements of an array, subscripts start from `0`. For example, the array slice
>
> ```
> @array[1,2]
> ```
>
> refers to the second and third elements of an array.

The final two lines of the program print the two elements of the array variable `@subarray`. As you can see, these elements are identical to the second and third elements of `@array`.

Using List Ranges in Array-Slice Subscripts

Perl provides a convenient way to refer to large array slices. Instead of writing

```
@array[0,1,2,3,4]
```

to refer to the first five elements of array `@array`, you can use the list range operator, as follows:

```
@array[0..4]
```

This enables you to assign large array slices easily:

```
@subarray = @array[0..19];
```

This assigns the first 20 elements of `@array` to `@subarray`.

Using Variables in Array-Slice Subscripts

You can use the value of a scalar variable in a list range in an array slice subscript. The following is an example:

```
$endrange = 19;
@subarray = @array[0..$endrange];
```

5

Here, the scalar variable $endrange contains the upper limit of the array slice, which in this case is 19. This means that the array slice to assign is

@array[0..19]

which assigns the first 20 elements of @array to @subarray.

You can also use the list stored in an array variable to define an array slice. Listing 5.8 shows how this works.

TYPE

Listing 5.8. A program that uses an array variable as an array-slice subscript.

```
1:  # p5_8.pl
2:
3:  @array = ("one", "two", "three", "four", "five");
4:  @range = (1, 2, 3);
5:  @subarray = @array[@range];
6:  print ("The array slice is: @subarray\n");
```

OUTPUT

```
C:\> perl 5_8.pl
The array slice is: two three four
C:\>
```

ANALYSIS   Line 3 of this program assigns the following list to the array variable @array:

("one", "two", "three", "four", "five")

Line 4 assigns the list (1, 2, 3) to the array variable @range, which is to serve as the list range.

Line 5 uses the value of @range as the array subscript for an array slice. Because @range contains (1, 2, 3) the slice of @array that is selected consists of the second, third, and fourth elements. These elements are then assigned to the array variable @subarray.

Line 6 prints the selected array slice. When the Perl interpreter sees the variable name @subarray in the character string to be printed, it substitutes the value of @subarray for its name. Because @subarray is inside a character string, the Perl interpreter leaves a space between each pair of elements when printing.

Compare line 6 with the following:

print (@subarray, "\n");

Here, print leaves no spaces between the elements of @subarray, which means that it prints

twothreefour

Which outcome you want depends, of course, on what you want your program to do.

5

Assigning to Array Slices

You can assign to array slices using the notation you have just seen. The following is an example:

```
@array[0,1] = ("string", 46);
```

Here, the first two elements of `@array` become `string` and `46`, respectively.

You can use list-range operators and variables when you assign to array slices as well. The following is an example:

```
@array[0..3] = (1, 2, 3, 4);
@array[0..$endrange] = (1, 2, 3, 4);
```

If there are more items in the array slice than in the list, the extra items in the array slice are assigned the null string, as follows:

```
@array[0..2] = ("string1", "string2");
```

The third element of `@array` now holds the null string.

If there are fewer items in the array slice than in the list, the extra items in the list are ignored, as in the following:

```
@array[0..2] = (1, 2, 3, 4);
```

In this assignment, the fourth element in the list, `4`, is not assigned to anything.

When an array slice is assigned to, the remainder of the array is not changed. Listing 5.9 shows how this works.

TYPE **Listing 5.9. A program that assigns to an array slice.**

```
1:  # p5_9.pl
2:
3:  @array = ("old1", "old2", "old3", "old4");
4:  @array[1,2] = ("new2", "new3");
5:  print ("@array\n");
```

OUTPUT
```
C:\> perl p5_9.pl
old1 new2 new3 old4
C:\>
```

ANALYSIS In the preceding program, the only statement that did not appear in previous programs is line 4, which assigns the list (`"new2"`, `"new3"`) to the array slice of `@array` consisting of the second and third elements. This assignment changes the value of `@array` from

```
("old1", "old2", "old3", "old4")
```

to

```
("old1", "new2", "new3", "old4")
```

Line 5 then prints the changed array.

Overlapping Array Slices

As you've seen, Perl enables you to use array slices on either side of an assignment statement. The following is an example:

```
@newarray = @array[2,3,4];
@array[2,3,4] = @newarray;
```

This means that you can assign from one array slice to another, even if the two slices overlap, as in the following:

```
@array[1,2,3] = @array[2,3,4];
```

The Perl interpreter has no problem with this statement because it copies the list stored in @array[2,3,4] into a temporary location (invisible to you) before assigning it to @array[1,2,3].

Listing 5.10 provides an example of overlapping array slices in use.

 Listing 5.10. A program containing overlapping array slices.

```
1:  # p5_10.pl
2:
3:  @array = ("one", "two", "three", "four", "five");
4:  @array[1,2,3] = @array[2,3,4];
5:  print ("@array\n");
```

```
C:\> perl p5_10.pl
one three four five five
C:\>
```

 Line 4 is an example of an assignment with overlapping array slices. At the time of assignment, the array slice @array[2,3,4] contains the list

```
("three", "four", "five")
```

This list consists of the last three elements of @array. Assigning this list to @array[1,2,3] means that the list stored in @array changes from

```
("one", "two", "three", "four", "five")
```

to

```
("one", "three", "four", "five", "five")
```

NOTE

Overlapping array slices of varying lengths are dealt with in the same way as other array-slice assignments of non-matching lengths. For example:

```
@array = (1, 2, 3, 4, 5);
@array[0..2] = @array[3,4];
```

This assignment assigns the array slice `@array[3,4]`, which is the list `(4, 5)`, to the array slice `@array[0..2]`. After this assignment, the value of `@array` is the list

```
(4, 5, "", 4, 5)
```

The third element of `@array` is now the null string because there are only two elements in the array slice being assigned.

Using the Array-Slice Notation as a Shorthand

So far, I've been using the following array-slice notation to refer to consecutive elements of an array:

```
@array[0,1]
```

In Perl for Win32, however, there is no real difference between an array slice and a list containing consecutive elements of the same array. For example, the following statements are equivalent:

```
@subarray = @array[0,1];
@subarray = ($array[0], $array[1]);
```

Because of this, you can use the array-slice notation to refer to any elements of an array, regardless of whether they are in order. For example, the following two statements are equivalent:

```
@subarray = ($array[4], $array[1], $array[3]);
@subarray = @array[4,1,3];
```

In both cases, the array variable `@subarray` is assigned a list consisting of three elements: the fifth, second, and fourth elements of `@array`.

You can use this array-slice notation in a variety of ways. For example, you can assign one element of an array multiple times:

```
@subarray = @array[0,0,0];
```

This creates a list consisting of three copies of the first element of @array and then assigns this list to @subarray.

The array-slice notation provides an easy way to swap elements in a list. The following is an example:

```
@array[1,2] = @array[2,1];
```

This statement swaps the second and third elements of @array. As with the overlapping array slices you saw earlier, the Perl interpreter copies @array[2,1] into a temporary location before assigning it, which ensures that the assignment takes place properly.

For an example of a program that swaps array elements, look at Listing 5.11, which sorts the elements in an array using a simple sort algorithm.

TYPE **Listing 5.11. A program that sorts an array.**

```
 1:  # p5_11.pl
 2:
 3:  # read the array from standard input one item at a time
 4:  print ("Enter the array to sort, one item at a time.\n");
 5:  print ("Enter an empty line to quit.\n");
 6:  $count = 1;
 7:  $inputline = <STDIN>;
 8:  chop ($inputline);
 9:  while ($inputline ne "") {
10:          $array[$count-1] = $inputline;
11:          $count++;
12:          $inputline = <STDIN>;
13:          chop ($inputline);
14:  }
15:
16:  # now sort the array
17:  $count = 1;
18:  while ($count < @array) {
19:          $x = 1;
20:          while ($x < @array) {
21:                  if ($array[$x - 1] gt $array[$x]) {
22:                          @array[$x-1,$x] = @array[$x,$x-1];
23:                  }
24:                  $x++;
25:          }
26:          $count++;
27:  }
28:
29:  # finally, print the sorted array
30:  print ("@array\n");
```

OUTPUT
```
C:\> perl p5_11.pl
Enter the array to sort, one item at a time.
Enter an empty line to quit.
foo
baz
dip
bar

bar baz dip foo
C:\>
```

ANALYSIS This program is divided into three parts:

☐ Reading the array

☐ Sorting the array

☐ Printing the array

Lines 3–14 read the array into the variable @array. The conditional expression in line 9, $inputline ne "", is true as long as the line is not empty. (Recall that an empty line consists of just the newline character, which the library function chop removes.) In this example, the list foo baz dip bar is read into the array variable @array.

Lines 17–27 perform the sort. The sort consists of two loops, one inside the other. The inner loop works like this:

1. Line 21 compares the first item in the list with the item next to it. If the first item is greater, line 22 swaps the two items. Otherwise, the two items are left where they are. In this example, foo is greater than baz, so foo becomes the second element in the list. At this point, the list is

   baz foo dip bar

2. The program then loops back to line 21, which now compares the second pair in the list (the second and third elements). The new second element, foo, is compared to dip. foo is greater, so foo becomes the new third element, and dip becomes the second element:

   baz dip foo bar

3. Line 20 terminates the loop when the last pair is compared. (Note that the conditional expression compares the inner counting variable $x with the length of the array variable @array. When $x becomes equal to @array, every pair of elements in the list has been compared.)

At this point, the largest element in the list is at the far end of the list:

baz dip bar foo

The largest value in the list, foo, has been moved to the far right end of the list, where it belongs. The other elements have been displaced to make room.

Lines 17–19 and 26–27 contain the outer loop. This outer loop just makes sure that the inner loop is repeated $n-1$ times, where n is the number of elements in the list. When the inner loop is repeated a second time, the second-largest element moves up to the second position from the right:

```
baz bar dip foo
```

The final pass through the inner loop sorts the final two elements:

```
bar baz dip foo
```

Line 30 then prints the sorted list.

> **NOTE**
>
> You'll never need to write a program that sorts values in a list because Perl has a library function, `sort`, that does it for you. See the section "Array Library Functions" later today for more details.

Reading an Array from the Standard Input File

In the programs you have seen so far, single lines of input are read from the standard input file and stored in scalar variables:

```
$var = <STDIN>;
```

In this case, every appearance of `<STDIN>` means that another line of input is obtained from the standard input file.

Perl also provides a quicker approach: If you assign `<STDIN>` to an array variable instead of to a scalar variable, the Perl interpreter reads in all of the data from the standard input file at once and assigns it. For example, the statement

```
@array = <STDIN>;
```

reads everything typed in and assigns it all to the array variable `@array`. The variable `@array` now contains a list; each element of the list is a line of input.

Listing 5.12 is an example of a simple program that reads its input data into an array.

TYPE
Listing 5.12. A program that reads data into an array and writes the array.

```
1:  # p5_12.pl
2:
3:  @array = <STDIN>;
4:  print (@array);
```

OUTPUT

```
C:\> perl p5_12.pl
Here is my first line of data.
Here is another line.
Here is the last line.
^Z
Here is my first line of data.
Here is another line.
Here is the last line.
C:\>
```

ANALYSIS As you can see, this program is very short. Line 3 reads the input from the standard input file. In this example, the input that is entered consists of the three lines

```
Here is my first line of data.
Here is another line.
Here is the last line.
```

followed by the Ctrl+Z key combination. Ctrl+Z produces a special character that indicates end of file; when the Perl interpreter sees this, it knows there is no more input.

After line 3 is executed, the array variable @array contains a list comprising three elements: the three lines of input you just entered. The last character of each input line is the newline character (because you didn't call chop to get rid of it).

Line 4 prints the lines of input you just read. Note that you do not need to separate the lines with spaces or newline characters because each line in @array is terminated by a newline character.

5

WARNING

When you use the following statement

```
@array = <STDIN>;
```

every line of input you enter is stored in @array all at once. If you enter a lot of input, @array can get very large.

Use this statement only when you really need to work with the entire input file at once.

Array Library Functions

Perl provides a number of built-in library functions that work on lists and array variables. You can use them to do the following:

☐ Sort array elements in alphabetical order

☐ Reverse the elements of an array

☐ Remove the last character from all elements of an array

☐ Merge the elements of an array into a single string

☐ Split a string into array elements

The following sections describe these array library functions.

Sorting a List or Array Variable

The library function `sort` sorts the elements of an array in alphabetical order and returns the sorted list.

The syntax for the `sort` library function is

```
retlist = sort (array);
```

In this syntax, `array` is the list to sort, and `retlist` is the sorted list.

Here are some examples:

```
@array = ("this", "is", "a", "test");
@array2 = sort (@array);
```

After `sort` is called, the value of `@array2` is the list

```
("a", "is", "test", "this")
```

Note that `sort` does not modify the original list. The statement

```
@array2 = sort (@array);
```

does not change the value of `@array`. To replace the contents of an array variable with the sorted list, put the array variable on both sides of the assignment, as follows:

```
@array = sort (@array);
```

▲ Here, the sorted list is put back in `@array`.

5

WARNING

> The sorted list must be assigned to an array variable in order to be used. The statement
>
> ```
> sort (@array);
> ```
>
> doesn't do anything useful because the sorted list is not assigned to anything.

Note that `sort` treats its items as strings, not integers; items are sorted in alphabetical, not numeric, order. Here's an example:

```
@array = (70, 100, 8);
@array = sort (@array);
```

In this case, `sort` produces

```
(100, 70, 8)
```

not

```
(8, 70, 100)
```

Because `sort` is treating the elements of the list as strings, the strings to be sorted are 70, 100, and 8. When sorting characters that are not alphabetic, `sort` looks at the internal representation of the characters to be sorted. If you are not familiar with ASCII (which will be described shortly), this might sound complicated, but it's not too difficult to understand.

Here's how it works: When Perl (or any other programming language) stores a character such as r or 1, what it actually does is store a unique eight-bit number that corresponds to this character. For example, the letter r is represented by the number 114, and 1 is represented by the number 49. Every possible character has its own unique number.

The `sort` function uses these unique numbers to determine how to sort character strings. When sorting 70, 100, and 8, `sort` looks at the unique numbers corresponding to 7, 1, and 8, which are the first characters in each of the strings. As it happens, the unique number for 1 is less than that for 7, which is less than that for 8 (which makes sense when you think of it). This means that 100 is "less than" 70, and 70 is "less than" 8.

Of course, if two strings have identical first characters, `sort` then compares the second characters. For example, when `sort` sorts 72 and 7$, the first characters are identical; `sort` then compares the unique number representing 2 with the number representing $. As it happens, the number for $ is smaller, so 7$ is "less than" 72.

5

NOTE

The set of unique numbers that correspond to the characters understood by the computer is known as the *ASCII character set*. See Appendix C in this book.

Most computers today use the ASCII character set, with a couple of exceptions as follows:

☐ Some IBM computers use an IBM-developed character set called *EBCDIC*. EBCDIC works the same way as ASCII. In both cases, a character such as r or 1 is translated into a number that represents it. The only difference between EBCDIC and ASCII is that the translated numbers are different.

☐ Computers that print a variety of spoken languages, or that deal with languages such as Japanese or Chinese, use a more complicated 16-bit code to represent the wide variety of characters they understand.

You don't really need to worry about what character set your machine uses, except to take note of the sorting order.

Using Other Sort Keys

Normally, sort sorts in alphabetical order. You can tell the Perl interpreter to sort using any criterion you like. To learn more about sort keys, refer to Day 9, "Using Subroutines."

Reversing a List or Array Variable

The library function reverse reverses the order of the elements in a list or array variable and returns the reversed list.

 SYNTAX

The syntax for the reverse library function is

```
retlist = reverse (array);
```

array is the list to reverse, and *retlist* is the reversed list.

Here is an example:

```
@array = ("backwards", "is", "array", "this");
@array2 = reverse(@array);
```

The value assigned to @array2 is the list

```
("this", "array", "is", "backwards")
```

 As with sort, reverse does not change the original array.

If you like, you can sort and reverse the same list by passing the list returned by sort to reverse. Listing 5.13 shows an example of this. It reads lines of data from the standard input file and sorts them in reverse order.

Listing 5.13. A program that sorts input lines in reverse order.

TYPE

```
1:  # p5_13.pl
2:
3:  @input = <STDIN>;
4:  @input = reverse (sort (@input));
5:  print (@input);
```

OUTPUT

```
C:\> perl p5_13.pl
foo
bar
dip
baz
^z
foo
dip
baz
bar
C:\>
```

ANALYSIS   Line 3 reads all the input lines from the standard input file into the array variable @input. Each element of input consists of a single line of input terminated with a newline character.

Line 4 sorts and reverses the input line. First, sort is called to sort the input lines in alphabetical order. (Recall that when one library function appears inside another, the innermost one is called first.) The list returned by sort is then passed to reverse, which reverses the order of the elements of the list. The result is a list sorted in reverse order, which is then assigned to @input.

Line 5 prints the sorted lines. Because each line is terminated by a newline character, no extra spaces or newline characters need to be added to make the output readable.

TIP

If you like, you can omit the parentheses to the call to reverse. This gives you the following statement:

```
@input = reverse sort (@input);
```

Here is a case where eliminating a set of parentheses actually makes the code more readable; it is obvious that the statement sorts @input in reverse order.

5

Using chop on Array Variables

As you've seen, the chop library function removes the last character from a character string. The following is an example:

```
$var = "bathe";
chop ($var);      # $var now contains "bath"
```

The chop function also can work on lists in array variables. If you pass an array variable to chop, it removes the last character from every element in the list stored in the array variable. For example:

```
@list = ("rabbit", "12345", "quartz");
chop (@list);
```

After chop is called, the list stored in @list is

```
("rabbi", "1234", "quart")
```

The chop function often is used on arrays read from the standard input file, as shown in the following:

```
@array = <STDIN>;
chop (@array);
```

This call to chop removes the newline character from each input line. In the following section, you will see programs in which this is helpful.

Creating a Single String from a List

The library function join creates a single string from a list of strings, which then can be assigned to a scalar variable.

The syntax for the join library function is

```
string = join (array);
```

array is the list to join together, and *string* is the resulting character string.

The following is an example using join:

```
$string = join(" ", "this", "is", "a", "string");
```

The first element of the list supplied to join contains the characters that are to be used to join together the parts of the created string. In this example, $string becomes this is a string.

join can specify other join strings besides " ". For example, the following statement uses a pair of colons to join the strings:

```
$string = join("::", "words", "and", "colons");
```

In this statement, $string becomes words::and::colons.

You can use any list or array variable as part or all of the argument to join. For example:

```
@list = ("here", "is", "a");
$string = join(" ", @list, "string");
```

This assigns here is a string to $string.

Listing 5.14 is a simple program that uses join. It joins together all the input lines from the standard input file.

TYPE

Listing 5.14. A program that takes its input and joins it into a single string.

```
1:  # p5_14.pl
2:
3:  @input = <STDIN>;
4:  chop (@input);
5:  $string = join(" ", @input);
6:  print ("$string\n");
```

OUTPUT

```
C:\> perl p5_14.pl
This
is
my
input
^z
This is my input
C:\>
```

ANALYSIS Line 3 reads all of the input lines into the array variable @input. Each element of @input is a single line of input terminated by a newline character.

Line 4 passes the array variable @input to the library function chop, which removes the last character from each element of the list stored in @input. This removes all the trailing newline characters.

Line 5 calls join, which joins all the input lines into a single string. The first argument passed to join is " ", which tells join to put one space between each pair of lines. This turns the list

```
("This", "is", "my", "input")
```

into the string

```
This is my input
```

Line 6 prints the string produced by join. Note that the call to print has to specify a newline character because all the newline characters in the input lines have been removed by the call to chop.

5

NOTE

> You may not be able to get the right results displayed on the screen by running Perl programs such as p5_12.pl or p5_14.pl in the Windows 95 environment. This is an example illustrating that Perl 5 for Win32 does not fully support Windows 95.

Splitting a String into a List

As you've seen, the library function `join` creates a character string from a list. To undo the effects of `join`—to split a character string into separate items—call the function `split`.

SYNTAX

The syntax for the library function `split` is

```
array = split (string);
```

string is the character string to split, and *array* is the resulting array.

The following is a simple example of the use of `split`:

```
$string = "words::separated::by::colons";
@array = split(/::/, $string);
```

The first argument passed to `split` tells it where to break the string into separate parts. In this example, the first argument is `::` (two colons); because there are three pairs of colons in the string, `split` breaks the string into four separate parts. The result is the list

```
("words", "separated", "by", "colons")
```

which is assigned to the array variable `@array`.

NOTE

> The `/` characters surrounding the `::` in the call to `split` indicate that the `::` is a *pattern* to be matched. Perl supports a wide variety of special pattern-matching sequences, which you will learn about on Day 7, "Pattern Matching."

The `split` function is used in a variety of applications. Listing 5.15 uses `split` to count the number of words in the standard input file.

TYPE   **Listing 5.15. A simple word-count program.**

```
1:  # p5_15.pl
2:
3:  $wordcount = 0;
```

5

```
4:  $line = <STDIN>;
5:  while ($line ne "") {
6:          chop ($line);
7:          @array = split(/ /, $line);
8:          $wordcount += @array;
9:          $line = <STDIN>;
10: }
11: print ("Total number of words: $wordcount\n");
```

```
C:\> pero p5_15.pl
Here is some input.
Here are some more words.
Here is my last line.
^z
Total number of words: 14
C:\>
```

ANALYSIS When you enter a Ctrl+Z (end-of-file) character and read it using <STDIN>, the resulting line is the null string. Line 5 of this program tests for this null string.

Note that line 5 has no problem distinguishing the end of file from a blank input line because a blank input line contains the newline character, and chop has not yet been called. Once the Perl interpreter knows that the program is not at the end of file, line 6 can be called; it chops the newline character off the end of the input line.

Line 7 splits the input line into words. The first argument to split, / /, indicates that the line is to be broken whenever the Perl interpreter sees a space. The resulting list is stored in @array.

Because each element of the list in @array is one word in the input line, the total number of words in the line is equivalent to the number of elements in the array. Line 8 takes advantage of this to count the number of words in the input line. Here's how line 8 works:

☐ When an array variable appears in a place where the Perl interpreter normally expects a scalar value, the number of elements in the list stored in the array variable is substituted for the variable name. In this program, when the Perl interpreter sees @array, it replaces it with the number of elements in @array.

☐ Because the number of elements in the array is the same as the number of words in the input line, the statement

```
$wordcount += @array;
```

actually adds the number of words in the line to $wordcount.

NOTE

Listing 5.15 does not work properly if an input line contains more than one space between words. The following is an example:

```
This  is a line
```

Because there are two spaces between This and is, the split function breaks

This is

into three words: This, an empty word " ", and is. Because of this, the line

This is a line

appears to contain five words when it really contains only four.

To get around this problem, what you need is a pattern that matches one or more spaces. To learn about special patterns such as this, see Day 7.

Listing 5.16 is an example of a program that uses split, join, and reverse to reverse the word order of the input read from the standard input file.

Listing 5.16. A program that reverses the word order of the input file.

TYPE

```
1:  # p5_16.pl
2:
3:  @input = <STDIN>;
4:  chop (@input);
5:
6:  # first, reverse the order of the words in each line
7:  $currline = 1;
8:  while ($currline <= @input) {
9:          @words = split(/ /, $input[$currline-1]);
10:         @words = reverse(@words);
11:         $input[$currline-1] = join(" ", @words, "\n");
12:         $currline++;
13: }
14:
15: # now, reverse the order of the input lines and print them
16: @input = reverse(@input);
17: print (@input);
```

OUTPUT

```
C:\> perl p5_16.pl
This sentence
is in
reverse order.
^z
order. reverse
in is
sentence This
C:\>
```

ANALYSIS Line 3 reads all of the standard input file into the array @input. Line 4 then removes the trailing newline characters from the input lines.

Lines 7–13 reverse each individual line. Line 7 compares the current line number, stored in $currline, with the number of lines of input. (Recall that the number of elements in the list is used whenever an array variable appears where a scalar value is expected.)

Line 9 splits a line of input into words. The first argument to split, / /, indicates that a split is to occur every time a space is seen. The list of words is stored in the array variable @words.

Line 10 reverses the order of the list of words stored in @words. After the list has been reversed, line 11 joins the input line back together again. Note that line 11 appends a newline character to the input line.

Now that the words in each individual line have been reversed, all that the program needs to do is reverse the order of the lines themselves. Line 16 accomplishes this.

Line 17 prints the reversed input file. Note that the period character (.) appears at the end of the first word; this is because the reversing program isn't smart enough to detect and get rid of it. (You can use split to get rid of this, too, if you like.)

Other List-Manipulation Functions

Perl provides several other list-manipulation functions also. To learn about these, refer to Day 13, "Process, Scalar-Conversion, and List-Manipulation Functions."

Summary

In today's lesson, you learned about lists and array variables. A list is an ordered collection of scalar values. A list can consist of any number of scalar values.

Lists can be stored in array variables, which are variables whose names begin with the character @.

Individual elements of array variables can be accessed using subscripts. The subscript 0 refers to the first element of the list stored in the array variable, the subscript 1 refers to the second element, and so on. If an array element is not defined, it is assumed to hold the null string (""). If a previously undefined array element is assigned to, the array grows appropriately.

The list-range operator provides a convenient way to create a list containing consecutive numbers.

You can copy lists from one array variable to another. In addition, you can include an array variable in a list, which means that the list stored in the array variable is copied into the list containing the array-variable name.

Array-variable names can appear in character strings; in this case, the elements of the list are included in place of the variable name, with a space separating each pair of elements.

You can assign values to scalar variables from array variables, and vice versa.

If an array variable appears in a place where a scalar variable is expected, the length of the list stored in the array variable is used.

You can access any part of a list stored in an array variable by using the array-slice notation. You can assign values to array slices, and they can be used anywhere a list is expected.

The entire contents of the standard input file can be stored in a single array variable.

The library functions `sort` and `reverse` sort and reverse lists, respectively. The function `chop` removes the last character from each element of a list. The function `split` breaks a single string into a collection of list elements. The function `join` takes a collection of list elements and joins them into a single string.

Q&A

Q How can I tell whether a reference to an array variable such as `@array` refers to the stored list or to the length of the list?

A It's usually pretty easy to tell. In a lot of places, using a list makes no sense:

```
$result = $number + @array;
```

For example, it makes no sense here to add a list to `$number`, so the length of the list stored in `@array` is used.

Q Why do array elements use `$` for the first character of the element name, and not `@`? Wouldn't it make more sense to refer to an array element as

```
@array[2]
```

because we all know that the `@` indicates an array variable?

A This relates to the first question. The Perl interpreter needs to know as soon as possible whether a variable reference is a scalar value or a list. The `$` indicates right away that the upcoming item is a scalar value.

Eventually, you'll get used to this notation.

Q Is there a difference between an undefined array variable and an array variable containing the empty list?

A No. By default, all array variables contain the empty list. Note, however, that the empty list is not the same as a list containing the null string:

```
@array = ("");
```

This list contains one element, which happens to be a null string.

Q How large an input file can I read in using the following statement?

```
@array = <STDIN>;
```

A Perl imposes no limit on the size of arrays. Your computer, however, has a finite amount of memory, which limits how large your arrays can be.

Q Why does Perl add spaces when you substitute for an array variable in a string?

A The most common use of string substitution is in the `print` statement. Normally, when you print a list you don't want to have the elements of the list running together, because you want to see where one element stops and the next one starts.

To print the elements of a string without spaces between them, pass the list to `print` without enclosing it in a string, as follows:

```
print ("Here is my list", @list, "\n");
```

Q Why does $ appear before 1 in the ASCII character set?

A The short answer is: Just because. (This reasoning occurs more often in computing than you might think.)

Here's a more detailed explanation: On early machines that used the ASCII character set, performance was more efficient if there was a relationship between, for instance, the location of the uppercase alphabetic characters and the lowercase alphabetic characters. (In fact, if you add `0x20`, or 20 hexadecimal, to the ASCII representation of an uppercase letter, you get the corresponding lowercase letter.)

Establishing relationships such as these meant that gaps existed between, for example, the representation of z (which is 90) and the representation of a (which is 97). These gaps are filled by printable non-alphanumeric characters; for example, the representation of [is 91.

As for why $ appears before 1, as opposed to ?, which appears after 1, the explanation is: Just because.

Workshop

The Workshop provides quiz questions to help you solidify your understanding of the material covered and exercises to give you experience in using what you've learned. Try to understand the quiz and exercise answers before you go on to tomorrow's lesson. You can find the answers in Appendix B, "Answers."

Quiz

1. Define the following terms:

    a. list

    b. empty list

    c. array variable

    d. subscript

    e. array slice

2. Assume the following assignments have been performed:

   ```
   @list = (1, 2, 3);
   $scalar1 = "hello";
   $scalar2 = "there";
   ```

   What is assigned to the array variable `@newlist` in each of the following cases?

    a. `@newlist = @list;`

    b. `@newlist = reverse(@list[1,2]);`

    c. `@newlist = ($scalar1, @list[1,1]);`

    d. `@newlist[2,1,3] = @list[1,2,1];`

    e. `@newlist = <STDIN>;`

3. Assume that the following assignments have been performed:

   ```
   @list1 = (1, 2, 3, 4);
   @list2 = ("one", "two", "three");
   ```

   What is the value of `$result` in each of the following cases?

    a. `($dummy, $result) = @list1;`

    b. `$result = @list1;`

    c. `($result) = @list2;`

    d. `($result) = @list1[1..2];`

    e. `$result = $list2[$list1[$list1[0]]];`

    f. `$result = $list2[3];`

4. What is the difference between a list and an array variable?

5. How does the Perl interpreter distinguish between an array element and a scalar variable?

6. How can you ensure that the `@`, `$`, and `[` characters are not substituted for in strings?

7. How can you obtain the length of a list stored in an array variable?

5

8. What happens when you refer to an array element that has not yet been defined?

9. What happens when you assign to an array element that is larger than the current length of the array?

Exercises

1. Write a program that counts all occurrences of the word `the` in the standard input file.

2. Write a program that reads lines of input containing numbers, each of which is separated by exactly one space, and prints out the following:

   a. The total for each line

   b. The grand total

3. Write a program that reads all input from the standard input file and sorts all the words in reverse order, printing out one word per line with duplicates omitted.

4. **BUG BUSTER:** What is wrong with the following statement?

   ```
   $result = @array[4];
   ```

5. **BUG BUSTER:** What is wrong with the following program? (See if you can figure out what's wrong without checking the listings in today's lesson.)

   ```
   @input = <STDIN>;
   $currline = 1;
   while ($currline < @input) {
           @words = split(/ /, $input[$currline]);
           @words = sort(@words);
           $input[$currline] = join(" ", @words);
           $currline++;
   }
   print (@input);
   ```

5

Day 6

Reading from and Writing to Files

So far, you've learned to read input from the standard input file, which stores data that is entered from the keyboard. You've also learned how to write to the standard output file, which sends data to your screen. In today's lesson, you'll learn the following:

☐ How to open a file

☐ How to read from and write to an opened file

☐ How to redirect standard input and standard output and how to use the standard error file

☐ How to close a file

☐ About file-test operators, which determine the status of a file

☐ How to read from multiple files

☐ How to use command-line arguments

Opening a File

Before you can read from or write to a file, you must first open the file. This operation tells the operating system that you are currently accessing the file and that no one else can change it while you are working with it. To open a file, call the built-in library function open.

SYNTAX

The syntax for the open library function is

```
open (filevar, filename);
```

When you call open, you must supply two arguments:

- [ ] filevar represents the name you want to use in your Perl program to refer to the file.

- [ ] filename represents the location of the file on your machine.

The File Variable

The first argument passed to open is the name that the Perl interpreter uses to refer to the file. This name is also known as the *file handle* (or the *file variable*).

A file-handle name can be any sequence of letters, digits, and underscores, as long as the first character is a letter.

The following are legal file-handle names:

```
filename
MY_NAME
NAME2
A_REALLY_LONG_FILE_VARIABLE_NAME
```

The following are *not* legal file-handle names:

```
1NAME
A.FILE.NAME

if
```

if is not a valid file-handle name because it has another meaning; as you've seen, it indicates the start of an if statement. Words such as if that have special meanings in Perl are known as reserved words and cannot be used as names.

 TIP

> It's a good idea to use all uppercase letters for your file-handle names. This makes it easier to distinguish file-handle names from other variable names and from reserved words.

The Filename

The second item passed to open is the name of the file you want to open. For example, if your current working directory contains a file named file1 that you would like to open, you can open it as follows:

```
open(FILE1, "file1");
```

This statement tells Perl that you want to open the file file1 and associate it with the file handle FILE1.

If you want to open a file in a different directory, you can specify the complete pathname, as follows:

```
open(FILE1, "c:/MyDir/MyFile");
```

This opens the file C:/MyDir/MyFile and associates it with the file handle MyFile.

NOTE
> You can skip the drive name if your directory is on the current drive. In our case, you can replace C:/MyDir/MyFile with /MyDir/MyFile, if you're sure the directory MyDir is on the current drive C.
>
> Perl 5 for Win32 allows both forward- and backslashes in pathnames:
>
> C:\MyDir\Myfile

The File Mode

When you open a file, you must decide how you want to access the file. There are three different *file-access modes* (or, simply, *file modes*) available in Perl for Win32:

read mode	Enables the program to read the existing contents of the file, but does not enable it to write into the file
write mode	Destroys the current contents of the file and overwrites them with the output supplied by the program
append mode	Appends output supplied by the program to the existing contents of the file

By default, open assumes that a file is to be opened in read mode. To specify write mode, put a > character in front of the filename that you pass to open, as follows:

```
open (OUTFILE, ">C:\MyDir\MyFile\outfile.txt");
```

This opens the file `C:\MyDir\MyFile\outfile.txt` for writing and associates it with the file handle `OUTFILE`.

To specify append mode, put two `>` characters in front of the filename, as follows:

```
open (APPENDFILE, ">>C:\MyDir\MyFile\appendfile.txt");
```

This opens the file `C:\MyDir\MyFile\appendfile.txt` in append mode and associates it with the file handle `APPENDFILE`.

NOTE

> Here are two things to remember when opening files:
> - [ ] When you open a file for writing, any existing contents are destroyed.
> - [ ] When you open a file in append mode, the existing contents are not destroyed, but you cannot read the file while writing to it.

Checking Whether the open Succeeded

Before you can use a file opened by the open function, you should first check whether the open function is actually giving you access to the file. The open function enables you to do this by returning a value indicating whether the file-opening operation succeeded:

- [ ] If open returns a nonzero value, the file has been opened successfully.
- [ ] If open returns 0, an error has occurred.

As you can see, the values returned by open correspond to the values for true and false in conditional expressions. This means that you can use open in `if` and `unless` statements. The following is an example:

```
if (open(MYFILE, "C:\MyDir\MyFile\myfile")) {
        # here's what to do if the file opened
}
```

The code inside the `if` statement is executed only if the file has been successfully opened. This ensures that your programs only read from or write to files that you can access.

NOTE

> If open returns false, you can find out what went wrong by using the file-test operators, which you'll learn about later today.

Reading from a File

Once you have opened a file and have determined that the file is available for use, you can read information from it.

To read from a file, enclose the file handle associated with the file in angle brackets (< and >), as follows:

```
$line = <MYFILE>;
```

This statement reads a line of input from the file specified by the file handle MYFILE and stores the line of input in the scalar variable $line.

Listing 6.1 is a simple program that reads input from a file and writes it to the standard output file.

Listing 6.1. A program that reads lines from a file and prints them.

```
1:  # p6_1.pl
2:
3:  if (open(MYFILE, "file1")) {
4:          $line = <MYFILE>;
5:          while ($line ne "") {
6:                  print ($line);
7:                  $line = <MYFILE>;
8:          }
9:  }
```

OUTPUT

```
C:\> perl p6_1.pl
Here is a line of input.
Here is another line of input.
Here is the last line of input.
C:\>
```

ANALYSIS Line 3 opens the file file1 in read mode, which means that the file is to be made available for reading. file1 is assumed to be in the current working directory. The file handle MYFILE is associated with the file file1.

If the call to open returns a nonzero value, the conditional expression

```
open(MYFILE, "file1")
```

is assumed to be true, and the code inside the if statement is executed.

Lines 4–8 print the contents of file1. The sample output shown here assumes that file1 contains the following three lines:

6

```
Here is a line of input.
Here is another line of input.
Here is the last line of input.
```

Line 4 reads the first line of input from the file specified by the file handle MYFILE, which is file1. This line of input is stored in the scalar variable $line.

Line 5 tests whether the end of the file specified by MYFILE has been reached. If there are no more lines left in MYFILE, $line is assigned the empty string.

Line 6 prints the text stored in $line, which is the line of input read from MYFILE.

Line 7 reads the next line of MYFILE, preparing for the loop to start again.

File Variables and the Standard Input File

Now that you have seen how Perl programs read input from files in read mode, take another look at a statement that reads a line of input from the standard input file.

```
$line = <STDIN>;
```

Here's what is actually happening: The Perl program is referencing the file handle STDIN, which represents the standard input file. The < and > on either side of STDIN tell the Perl interpreter to read a line of input from the standard input file, just as the < and > on either side of MYFILE in

```
$line = <MYFILE>;
```

tell the Perl interpreter to read a line of input from MYFILE.

STDIN is a file handle that behaves like any other file handle representing a file in read mode. The only difference is that STDIN does not need to be opened by the open function because the Perl interpreter does that for you.

Terminating a Program Using die

In Listing 6.1, you saw that the return value from open can be tested to see whether the program actually has access to the file. The code that operates on the opened file is contained in an if statement.

If you are writing a large program, you might not want to put all of the code that affects a file inside an if statement, because the distance between the beginning of the if statement and the closing brace (}) could get very large. For example:

```
if (open(MYFILE, "file1")) {
        # this could be many pages of statements!
}
```

Besides, after a while, you'll probably get tired of typing the spaces or tabs you use to indent the code inside the `if` statement. Perl provides a way around this using the library function `die`.

SYNTAX

The syntax for the `die` library function is

```
die (message);
```

When the Perl interpreter executes the `die` function, the program terminates immediately and prints the message passed to `die`.

For example, the statement

```
die ("Stop this now!\n");
```

prints the following on your screen and terminates the program:

```
Stop this now!
```

Listing 6.2 shows how you can use `die` to smoothly test whether a file has been opened correctly.

Listing 6.2. A program that uses `die` when testing for a successful file-open operation.

TYPE

```
1:  # p6_2.pl
2:
3:  unless (open(MYFILE, "file1")) {
4:          die ("cannot open input file file1\n");
5:  }
6:
7:  # if the program gets this far, the file was
8:  # opened successfully
9:  $line = <MYFILE>;
10: while ($line ne "") {
11:         print ($line);
12:         $line = <MYFILE>;
13: }
```

OUTPUT

```
C:\> perl p6_2.pl
Here is a line of input.
Here is another line of input.
Here is the last line of input.
C:\>
```

ANALYSIS This program behaves the same way as the one in Listing 6.1, except that it prints out an error message when it can't open the file.

6

Line 3 opens the file and tests whether the file opened successfully. Because this is an `unless` statement, the code inside the braces (`{` and `}`) is executed unless the file opened successfully.

Line 4 is the call to `die` that is executed if the file does not open successfully. This statement prints the following message on the screen and exits:

```
cannot open input file file1
```

Because line 4 terminates program execution when the file is not open, the program can make it past line 5 only if the file has been opened successfully.

The loop in lines 9–13 is identical to the loop you saw in Listing 6.1. The only difference is that this loop is no longer inside an `if` statement.

NOTE

> Here is another way to write lines 3–5:
>
> ```
> open (MYFILE, "file1") || die ("Could not open file");
> ```
>
> Recall that the logical OR operator only evaluates the expression on its right if the expression on its left is false. This means that `die` is called only if `open` returns false (if the open operation fails).

Printing Error Information Using `die`

If you like, you can have `die` print the name of the Perl program and the line number of the statement containing the call to `die`. To do this, leave off the trailing newline character in the character string, as follows:

```
die ("Missing input file");
```

If the Perl program containing this statement is called `myprog`, and this statement is line 14 of `myprog`, this call to `die` prints the following and exits:

```
Missing input file at myprog line 14.
```

Compare this with

```
die ("Missing input file\n");
```

which simply prints the following before exiting:

```
Missing input file
```

Specifying the program name and line number is useful in two cases:

□ If the program contains many similar error messages, you can use `die` to specify the line number of the message that actually appeared.

□ If the program is called from within another program, you can use `die` to indicate that this program generated the error.

Reading into Array Variables

Perl enables you to read an entire file into a single array variable. To do this, assign the file handle to the array variable, as follows:

```
@array = <MYFILE>;
```

This reads the entire file represented by MYFILE into the array variable @array. Each line of the file becomes an element of the list that is stored in @array.

Listing 6.3 is a simple program that reads an entire file into an array.

TYPE
Listing 6.3. A program that reads an entire input file into an array.

```
1:  # p6_3.pl
2:
3:  unless (open(MYFILE, "file1")) {
4:          die ("cannot open input file file1\n");
5:  }
6:  @input = <MYFILE>;
7:  print (@input);
```

OUTPUT
```
C:\> perl p6_3.pl
Here is a line of input.
Here is another line of input.
Here is the last line of input.
C:\>
```

ANALYSIS
Lines 3–5 open the file, test whether the file has been opened successfully, and terminate the program if the file cannot be opened.

Line 6 reads the entire contents of the file represented by MYFILE into the array variable @input. @input now contains a list consisting of the following three elements:

```
("Here is a line of input.\n",
 "Here is another line of input.\n",
 "Here is the last line of input.\n")
```

Note that a newline character is included as the last character of each line.

Line 7 uses the `print` function to print the entire file.

6

Writing to a File

After you have opened a file in write or append mode, you can write to the file by specifying the file handle with the `print` function. For example, if you have opened a file for writing using the statement

```
open(OUTFILE, ">outfile");
```

the following statement

```
print OUTFILE ("Here is an output line.\n");
```

writes the following line to the file specified by OUTFILE, which is the file called outfile:

```
Here is an output line.
```

Listing 6.4 is a simple program that reads from one file and writes to another.

Listing 6.4. A program that opens two files and copies one into another.

```
1:  # p6_4.pl
2:
3:  unless (open(INFILE, "file1")) {
4:          die ("cannot open input file file1\n");
5:  }
6:  unless (open(OUTFILE, ">outfile")) {
7:          die ("cannot open output file outfile\n");
8:  }
9:  $line = <INFILE>;
10: while ($line ne "") {
11:         print OUTFILE ($line);
12:         $line = <INFILE>;
13: }
```

OUTPUT This program writes nothing to the screen because all output is directed to the file called outfile.

ANALYSIS Lines 3–5 open file1 for reading. If the file cannot be opened, line 4 is executed, which prints the following message on the screen and terminates the program:

```
cannot open input file file1
```

Lines 6–8 open outfile for writing; the > in >outfile indicates that the file is to be opened in write mode. If outfile cannot be opened, line 7 prints the message

```
cannot open output file outfile
```

on the screen and terminates the program.

The only other line in the program that you have not seen in other listings in this lesson is line 11, which writes the contents of the scalar variable $line on the file specified by OUTFILE.

When this program has completed, the contents of file1 are copied into outfile:

```
Here is a line of input.
Here is another line of input.
Here is the last line of input.
```

WARNING

Make sure that files you open in write mode contain nothing valuable. When the open function opens a file in write mode, any existing contents are destroyed.

The Standard Output File Variable

If you like, your program can reference the standard output file by referring to the file handle associated with the output file. This file handle is named STDOUT.

By default, the print statement sends output to the standard output file, which means that it sends the output to the file associated with STDOUT. As a consequence, the following statements are equivalent:

```
print ("Here is a line of output.\n");
print STDOUT ("Here is a line of output.\n");
```

NOTE

You do not need to open STDOUT because Perl automatically opens it for you.

Merging Two Files into One

In Perl, you can open as many files as you like, provided you define a different file handle for each one. (Actually, there is an upper limit on the number of files you can open, but it's fairly large and also system dependent.) For an example of a program that has multiple files open at one time, take a look at Listing 6.5. This program merges two files by creating an output file consisting of one line from the first file, one line from the second file, another line from the first file, and so on. For example, if an input file named merge1 contains the lines

```
a1
a2
a3
```

6

and another file, merge2, contains the lines

```
b1
b2
b3
```

then the resulting output file consists of

```
a1
b1
a2
b2
a3
b3
```

TYPE **Listing 6.5. A program that merges two files.**

```
1:  # p6_5.pl
2:
3:  open (INFILE1, "merge1") ||
4:          die ("Cannot open input file merge1\n");
5:  open (INFILE2, "merge2") ||
6:          die ("Cannot open input file merge2\n");
7:  $line1 = <INFILE1>;
8:  $line2 = <INFILE2>;
9:  while ($line1 ne "" || $line2 ne "") {
10:         if ($line1 ne "") {
11:                 print ($line1);
12:                 $line1 = <INFILE1>;
13:         }
14:         if ($line2 ne "") {
15:                 print ($line2);
16:                 $line2 = <INFILE2>;
17:         }
18: }
```

OUTPUT
```
C:\> perl p6_5.pl
a1
b1
a2
b2
a3
b3
C:\>
```

ANALYSIS Lines 3 and 4 show another way to write a statement that either opens a file or calls die if the open fails. Recall that the || operator first evaluates its left operand; if the left operand evaluates to true (a nonzero value), the right operand is not evaluated because the result of the expression is true.

Because of this, the right operand, the call to die, is evaluated only when the left operand is false—which happens only when the call to open fails and the file merge1 cannot be opened.

Lines 5 and 6 repeat the preceding process for the file merge2. Again, either the file is opened successfully or the program aborts by calling die.

The program then loops repeatedly, reading a line of input from each file each time. The loop terminates only when both files have been exhausted. If one file is empty but the other is not, the program just copies the line from the non-empty file to the standard output file.

Note that the output from this program is printed on the screen. If you decide that you want to send this output to a file, you can do one of two things:

☐ You can modify the program to write its output to a different file. To do this, open the file in write mode and associate it with a file variable. Then change the print statements to refer to this file variable.

☐ You can redirect the standard output file on the command line.

For a discussion of the second method, see the following section.

Redirecting Standard Input and Standard Output

When you run programs on Windows NT, you can redirect input and output using < and >, respectively, as follows:

```
myprog <input >output
```

Here, when you run the program called myprog, the input for the program is taken from the file specified by input instead of from the keyboard, and the output for the program is sent to the file specified by output instead of to the screen.

When you run a Perl program and redirect input using <, the standard input file handle STDIN now represents the file specified with <. For example, consider the following simple program:

```
$line = <STDIN>;
print ($line);
```

Suppose this program is named myperlprog.pl and is called with the command

```
perl myperlprog.pl <file1
```

In this case, the statement

```
$line = <STDIN>;
```

reads a line of input from file1 because the file handle STDIN represents file1.

6

Similarly, specifying > on the command file redirects the standard output file from the screen to the specified file. For example, consider this command:

```
perl myperlprog.pl <file1 >outfile
```

It redirects output from the standard output file to the file called `outfile`. Now, the following statement writes a line of data to `outfile`:

```
print ($line);
```

The Standard Error File

Besides the standard input file and the standard output file, Perl also defines a third built-in file variable, STDERR, which represents the standard error file. By default, text sent to this file is written to the screen. This enables the program to send messages to the screen even when the standard output file has been redirected to write to a file. As with STDIN and STDOUT, you do not need to open STDERR because it is opened automatically for you.

Listing 6.6 provides a simple example of the use of STDERR. The output shown in the Input-Output example assumes that the standard input file and standard output file have been redirected to files using < and >, as in

```
perl myprog.pl <infile >outfile
```

Therefore, the only output you see is what is written to STDERR.

TYPE **Listing 6.6. A program that writes to the standard error file.**

```
1:  # p6_6.pl
2:
3:  open(MYFILE, "file1") ||
4:          die ("Unable to open input file file1\n");
5:  print STDERR ("File file1 opened successfully.\n");
6:  $line = <MYFILE>;
7:  while ($line ne "") {
8:          chop ($line);
9:          print ("\U$line\E\n");
10:         $line = <MYFILE>;
11: }
```

OUTPUT
```
C:\> perl p6_6.pl
File file1 opened successfully.
C:\>
```

ANALYSIS This program converts the contents of a file into uppercase and sends the converted contents to the standard output file.

Line 3 tries to open `file1`. If the file cannot be opened, line 4 is executed. This calls `die`, which prints the following message and terminates:

```
Unable to open input file file1
```

NOTE

> The function `die` sends its messages to the standard error file, not the standard output file. This means that when a program terminates, the message printed by `die` always appears on your screen, even when you have redirected output to a file.

If the file is opened successfully, line 5 writes a message to the standard error file, which indicates that the file has been opened. As you can see, the standard error file is not reserved solely for errors. You can write anything you want to STDERR at any time.

Lines 6–11 read one line of `file1` at a time and write it out in uppercase (using the escape characters `\U` and `\E`, which you learned about on Day 3, "Understanding Scalar Values").

Closing a File

When you are finished reading from or writing to a file, you can tell the Perl interpreter that you are finished by calling the library function `close`.

The syntax for the `close` library function is

```
close (filevar);
```

`close` requires one argument: the file handle representing the file you want to close. After you have closed the file, you cannot read from it or write to it without invoking `open` again.

Note that you do not have to call `close` when you are finished with a file; Perl automatically closes the file when the program terminates or when you open another file using a previously defined file variable. For example, consider the following statements:

```
open (MYFILE, ">file1");
print MYFILE ("Here is a line of output.\n");
open (MYFILE, ">file2");
print MYFILE ("Here is another line of output.\n");
```

Here, when `file2` is opened for writing, `file1` is closed automatically. The file handle `MYFILE` is now associated with `file2`. This means that the second `print` statement sends the following to `file2`:

```
Here is another line of output.
```

DO use the <> operator, which is an easy way to read input from several files in succession. See the section titled "Reading from a Sequence of Files," later in this lesson, for more information on the <> operator.

DON'T use the same file handle to represent multiple files unless it is absolutely necessary. It is too easy to lose track of which file handle belongs to which file, especially if your program is large or has many nested conditional statements.

Determining the Status of a File

Many of the sample programs in today's lesson call open and test the returned result to see whether the file has been opened successfully. If open fails, it might be useful to find out exactly why the file could not be opened. To do this, use one of the *file-test operators*.

Listing 6.7 provides an example of the use of a file-test operator. This program is a slight modification of Listing 6.6, which is an uppercase-conversion program.

TYPE

Listing 6.7. A program that checks whether an unopened file actually exists.

```
1:  # p6_7.pl
2:
3:  unless (open(MYFILE, "file1")) {
4:          if (-e "file1") {
5:                  die ("File file1 exists, but cannot be opened.\n");
6:          } else {
7:                  die ("File file1 does not exist.\n");
8:          }
9:  }
10: $line = <MYFILE>;
11: while ($line ne "") {
12:         chop ($line);
13:         print ("\U$line\E\n");
14:         $line = <MYFILE>;
15: }
```

OUTPUT

```
C:\> perl p6_7.pl
File file1 does not exist.
C:\>
```

ANALYSIS Line 3 attempts to open the file file1 for reading. If file1 cannot be opened, the program executes the if statement starting on line 4.

Line 4 is an example of a file-test operator. This file-test operator, -e, tests whether its operand, a file, actually exists. If the file file1 exists, the expression -e "file1" returns true, the message File file1 exists, but cannot be opened. is displayed, and the program exits. If file1 does not exist, -e "file1" is false, and the library function die prints the following message before exiting:

```
File file1 does not exist.
```

File-Test Operator Syntax

All file-test operators have the same syntax as the -e operator used in Listing 6.7.

SYNTAX

The syntax for the file-test operators is

-x expr

Here, *x* is an alphabetic character and *expr* is any expression. The value of *expr* is assumed to be a string that contains the name of the file to be tested.

Because the operand for a file-test operator can be any expression, you can use scalar variables and string operators in the expression if you like. For example:

```
$var = "file1";
if (-e $var) {
        print STDERR ("File file1 exists.\n");
}
if (-e $var . "a") {
        print STDERR ("File file1a exists.\n");
}
```

In the first use of -e, the contents of $var, file1, are assumed to be the name of a file, and this file is tested for existence. In the second case, a is appended to the contents of file1, producing the string file1a. The -e operator then tests whether a file named file1a exists.

NOTE

The Perl interpreter does not get confused by the expression

-e $var . "a"

because the . operator has higher precedence than the -e operator. This means that the string concatenation is performed first.

The file-test operators have higher precedence than the comparison operators but lower precedence than the shift operators. To see a complete list of the Perl operators and their precedence, refer to Day 4, "More Operators."

6

The string can be a complete pathname, if you like. The following is an example:

```
if (-e "C:\MyDir\MyFile\file1") {
        print ("The file exists.\n");
}
```

This `if` statement tests for the existence of the file `C:\MyDir\MyFile\file1`.

Available File-Test Operators

Besides `-e`, there are several other most common file-test operators, such as `-r`, `-w`, and `-x`, which test whether a file is readable, writable, or executable, respectively. Also, `-z` tests whether a file is empty; `-s` returns the size of a file. The UNIX version of Perl has a long list of file-test operators; you can find them in the online documents. Be careful when you use those operators on Windows NT, however, because some of them may not work properly in the Windows NT system.

The following sections describe the most common file-test operators and show you how they can be useful. (You'll learn about more of these operators on Day 12, "File-System, String, and Mathematical Functions".)

More on the -e Operator

When a Perl program opens a file for writing, it destroys anything that already exists in the file. This might not be what you want. Therefore, you might want to make sure that your program opens a file only if the file does not already exist.

You can use the `-e` file-test operator to test whether or not to open a file for writing. Listing 6.8 is an example of a program that does this.

TYPE

Listing 6.8. A program that tests whether a file exists before opening it for writing.

```
1:  # p6_8.pl
2:
3:  unless (open(INFILE, "infile")) {
4:          die ("Input file infile cannot be opened.\n");
5:  }
6:  if (-e "outfile") {
7:          die ("Output file outfile already exists.\n");
8:  }
9:  unless (open(OUTFILE, ">outfile")) {
10:         die ("Output file outfile cannot be opened.\n");
11: }
12: $line = <INFILE>;
13: while ($line ne "") {
```

6

```
14:          chop ($line);
15:          print OUTFILE ("\U$line\E\n");
16:          $line = <INFILE>;
17: }
```

```
C:\> perl p6_8.pl
Output file outfile already exists.
C:\>
```

This program is the uppercase-conversion program again; most of it should be familiar to you.

The only difference is in lines 6–8, which use the -e file-test operator to check whether the output file outfile exists. If outfile exists, the program aborts, which ensures that the existing contents of outfile are not lost.

If outfile does not exist, the following expression fails:

```
-e "outfile"
```

and the program knows that it is safe to open outfile because it does not already exist.

Using File-Test Operators in Expressions

If you don't need to know exactly why your program is failing, you can combine all the tests in Listing 6.8 into a single statement, as follows:

```
open(INFILE, "infile") && !(-e "outfile") &&
    open(OUTFILE, ">outfile") || die("Cannot open files\n");
```

Can you see how this works? Here's what is happening: The && operator, logical AND, is true only if both of its operands are true. In this case, the two && operators indicate that the subexpression up to, but not including, the || is true only if all three of the following are true:

```
open(INFILE, "infile")
!(-e "outfile")
open(OUTFILE, ">outfile")
```

All three are true only when the following conditions are met:

- ☐ The input file infile can be opened.
- ☐ The output file outfile does not already exist.
- ☐ The output file outfile can be opened.

If any of these subexpressions is false, the entire expression up to the || is false. This means that the subexpression after the || (the call to die) is executed, and the program aborts.

Note that each of the three subexpressions associated with the `&&` operator is evaluated in turn. This means that the subexpression

```
!(-e "outfile")
```

is evaluated only if

```
open(INFILE, "infile")
```

is true, and that the subexpression

```
open(OUTFILE, ">outfile")
```

is evaluated only if

```
!(-e "outfile")
```

is true. This is exactly the same logic that is used in Listing 6.8.

If any of the subexpressions is false, the Perl interpreter doesn't evaluate the rest of them because it knows that the final result of

```
open(INFILE, "infile") && !(-e "outfile") &&
    open(OUTFILE, ">outfile")
```

is going to be false. Instead, it goes on to evaluate the subexpression to the right of the `||`, which is the call to `die`.

This program logic is somewhat complicated, and you shouldn't use it unless you feel really comfortable with it. The `if` statements in Listing 6.8 do the same thing and are easier to understand; however, it's useful to know how complicated statements such as the following one works because many Perl programmers like to write code that works in this way:

```
open(INFILE, "infile") && !(-e "outfile") &&
    open(OUTFILE, ">outfile") || die("Cannot open files\n");
```

In the next few days, you'll see several more examples of code that exploit how expressions work in Perl for Win32. *Perl hackers*—experienced Perl programmers—often enjoy compressing multiple statements into shorter ones, and they delight in complexity. Be warned.

Testing for Read Permission—the `-r` Operator

Before you can open a file for reading, you must have permission to read the file. The `-r` file-test operator tests whether you have permission to read a file.

Listing 6.9 checks whether the person running the program has permission to access a particular file.

Listing 6.9. A program that tests for read permission on a file.

TYPE

```
 1: # p6_9.pl
 2:
 3: unless (open(MYFILE, "file1")) {
 4:         if (!(-e "file1")) {
 5:                 die ("File file1 does not exist.\n");
 6:         } elsif (!(-r "file1")) {
 7:.                 die ("You are not allowed to read file1.\n");
 8:         } else {
 9:                 die ("File1 cannot be opened\n");
10:         }
11: }
```

OUTPUT

```
C:\> perl p6_9.pl
You are not allowed to read file1.
C:\>
```

ANALYSIS Line 3 of this program tries to open `file1`. If the call to `open` fails, the program tries to find out why.

First, line 4 tests whether the file actually exists. If the file exists, the Perl interpreter executes line 6, which tests whether the file has the proper read permission. If it does not, `die` is called; it then prints the following message and exits:

```
You are not allowed to read file1.
```

NOTE

> You do not need to use the `-e` file-test operator before using the `-r` file-test operator. If the file does not exist, `-r` returns false because you can't read a file that isn't there.
>
> The only reason to use both `-e` and `-r` is to enable your program to determine exactly what is wrong.

6

Checking for Other Permissions

You can use file-test operators to test for other permissions as well. To check whether you have write permission on a file, use the `-w` file-test operator.

```
if (-w "file1") {
        print STDERR ("I can write to file1.\n");
} else {
        print STDERR ("I can't write to file1.\n");
}
```

The -x file-test operator checks whether the file is executable. On Windows NT, files with extension names such as .exe, .bat, or .com are considered to be executable by default. The following is an example:

```
if (-x $filename) {
        print STDERR ("$filename is executable.\n");
} else {
        print STDERR ("$filename is not executable.\n");
}
```

NOTE

> If you are the systems administrator (for example, you are running as user ID root) and have permission to access any file, the -r and -w file-test operators always return true if the file exists. Also, the -x test operator always returns true if the file is an executable program.

Checking for Empty Files

The -z file-test operator tests whether a file is empty. This provides a more refined test for whether to open a file for writing: If the file exists but is empty, no information is lost if you overwrite the existing file.

Listing 6.10 shows how to use -z.

TYPE

Listing 6.10. A program that tests whether the file is empty before opening it for writing.

```
 1:  # p6_10.pl
 2:
 3:  if (-e "outfile") {
 4:          if (!(-w "outfile")) {
 5:                  die ("Missing write permission for outfile.\n");
 6:          }
 7:          if (!(-z "outfile")) {
 8:                  die ("File outfile is non-empty.\n");
 9:          }
10: }
11: # at this point, the file is either empty or doesn't exist,
12: # and we have permission to write to it if it exists
```

OUTPUT

```
C:\> perl p6_10.pl
File outfile is non-empty.
C:\>
```

ANALYSIS Line 3 checks whether the file `outfile` exists using `-e`. If it exists, it can be opened only if the program has permission to write to the file; line 4 checks for this using `-w`.

Line 7 uses `-z` to test whether the file is empty. If it is not, line 7 calls `die` to terminate program execution.

The opposite of `-z` is the `-s` file-test operator, which returns the size of the file if the file is not empty, otherwise zero:

```
$size = -s "outfile";
if ($size == 0) {
        print ("The file is empty.\n");
} else {
        print ("The file is $size bytes long.\n");
}
```

The `-s` file-test operator returns the size of the file in bytes. It can still be used in conditional expressions, though, because any nonzero value (indicating that the file is not empty) is treated as true.

Listing 6.11 uses `-s` to return the size of a file that has its name supplied via the standard input file.

TYPE ## Listing 6.11. A program that prints the size of a file in bytes.

```
1:  # p6.11.pl
2:
3:  print ("Enter the name of the file:\n");
4:  $filename = <STDIN>;
5:  chop ($filename);
6:  if (!(-e $filename)) {
7:          print ("File $filename does not exist.\n");
8:  } else {
9:          $size = -s $filename;
10:         print ("File $filename contains $size bytes.\n");
11: }
```

OUTPUT
```
C:\> perl p6_11.pl
Enter the name of the file:
file1
File file1 contains 128 bytes.
C:\>
```

ANALYSIS Lines 3–5 obtain the name of the file and remove the trailing newline character.

Line 6 tests whether the file exists. If the file doesn't exist, the program indicates this.

6

Line 9 stores the size of the file in the scalar variable $size. The size is measured in bytes (one byte is equivalent to one character in a character string).

Line 10 prints out the number of bytes in the file.

Using File-Test Operators with File Variables

You can use file-test operators on file variables as well as on character strings. In the following example, the file-test operator -w tests the file represented by the file handle MYFILE:

```
if (-w MYFILE) {
        print ("This file is empty!\n");
}
```

As before, this file-test operator returns true if the file is writable and false if it is not.

WARNING

> Remember that file variables can be used only after you open the file. If you need to test a particular condition before opening the file (such as whether the file is nonzero), test it using the name of the file.

Reading from a Sequence of Files

In Perl for Win32, it's easy to write programs that process an arbitrary number of files because there is a special operator, the <> operator, that does all of the file-handling work for you.

To understand how the <> operator works, recall what happens when you put < and > around a file variable:

```
$list = <MYFILE>;
```

This statement reads a line of input from the file represented by the file handle MYFILE and stores it in the scalar variable $list. Similarly, the statement

```
$list = <>;
```

reads a line of input and stores it in the scalar variable $list; however, the file it reads from is contained on the command line. Suppose, for example, a program containing a statement using the <> operator, such as the statement

```
$list = <>;
```

is called myprog and is called using the command

```
$ myprog file1 file2 file3
```

In this case, the first occurrence of the <> operator reads the first line of input from *file1*. Successive occurrences of <> read more lines from *file1*. When *file1* is exhausted, <> reads the first line from *file2*, and so on. When the last file, *file3*, is exhausted, <> returns an empty string, which indicates that all the input has been read.

NOTE

> If a program containing a <> operator is called with no command-line arguments, the <> operator reads input from the standard input file. In this case, the <> operator is equivalent to <STDIN>.
>
> If a file named in a command-line argument does not exist, the Perl interpreter writes the following message to the standard error file:
>
> ```
> Can't open name: No such file or directory
> ```
>
> Here, *name* is a placeholder for the name of the file that the Perl interpreter cannot find. In this case, the Perl interpreter ignores *name* and continues on with the next file in the command line.

To see how the <> operator works, look at Listing 6.12, which displays the contents of the files specified on the command line. (If you are familiar with UNIX, you will recognize this as the behavior of the UNIX utility cat.) The output from Listing 6.12 assumes that files *file1* and *file2* are specified on the command line and that each file contains one line.

Listing 6.12. A program that displays the contents of one or more files.

```
1:  # p6.12.pl
2:
3:  while ($inputline = <>) {
4:         print ($inputline);
5:  }
```

```
C:\> perl p6_12.pl file1 file2
This is a line from file1.
This is a line from file2.
C:\>
```

ANALYSIS Once again, you can see how powerful and useful Perl is. This entire program consists of only five lines, including the header comment and a blank line.

Line 3 both reads a line from a file and tests to see whether the line is the empty string. Because the assignment operator = returns the value assigned, the expression

```
$inputline = <>
```

has the value " " (the null string) if and only if <> returns the null string, which happens only when there are no more lines to read from any of the input files. This is exactly the point at which the program wants to stop looping. (Recall that a "blank line" in a file is not the same as the null string because the blank line contains the newline character.) Because the null string is equivalent to false in a conditional expression, there is no need to use a conditional operator such as ne.

When line 3 is executed for the first time, the first line in the first input file, *file1*, is read and stored in the scalar variable $inputline. Because *file1* contains only one line, the second pass through the loop (and the second execution of line 3) reads the first line of the second input file, *file2*.

After this, there are no more lines in either *file1* or *file2*, so line 3 assigns the null string to $inputline, which terminates the loop.

WARNING

When it reaches the end of the last file on the command line, the <> operator returns the empty string. However, if you use the <> operator after it has returned the empty string, the Perl interpreter assumes that you want to start reading input from the standard input file. (Recall that <> reads from the standard input file if there are no files on the command line.)

This means that you have to be a little more careful when you use <> than when you are reading using <MYFILE> (where MYFILE is a file variable). If MYFILE has been exhausted, repeated attempts to read using <MYFILE> continue to return the null string because there isn't anything left to read.

Reading into an Array Variable

As you have seen, if you read from a file using <STDIN> or <MYFILE> in an assignment to an array variable, the Perl interpreter reads the entire contents of the file into the array, as follows:

```
@array = <MYFILE>;
```

This works also with <>. For example, the statement

```
@array = <>;
```

reads all the contents of all the files on the command line into the array variable @array.

As always, be careful when you use this, because you might end up with a very large array.

Using Command-Line Arguments as Values

As you've seen, the <> operator assumes that its command-line arguments are files. For example, if you start up the program shown in Listing 6.12 with the command

```
C;:\> perl p6_12.pl myfile1 myfile2
```

the Perl interpreter assumes that the command-line arguments myfile1 and myfile2 are files and displays their contents.

Perl enables you to use the command-line arguments any way you want by defining a special array variable called @ARGV. When a Perl program starts up, this variable contains a list consisting of the command-line arguments. For example, the command

```
C:\> perl p6_12.pl myfile1 myfile2
```

sets @ARGV to the list

```
("myfile1", "myfile2")
```

As with all other array variables, you can access individual elements of @ARGV. For example, the statement

```
$var = $ARGV[0];
```

assigns the first element of @ARGV to the scalar variable $var.

You even can assign to some or all of @ARGV if you like. For example:

```
$ARGV[0] = 43;
```

If you assign to any or all of @ARGV, you overwrite what was already there, which means that any command-line arguments that get overwritten are lost.

To determine the number of command-line arguments, assign the array variable to a scalar variable, as follows:

```
$numargs = @ARGV;
```

As with all array variables, using an array variable in a place where the Perl interpreter expects a scalar variable means that the length of the array is used. In this case, $numargs is assigned the number of command-line arguments.

WARNING

C programmers should take note that the first element of @ARGV, unlike argv[0] in C, does not contain the name of the program. In Perl for

6

Win32, the first element of @ARGV is the first command-line argument.

To get the name of the program, use the system variable $0, which is discussed on Day 17, "System Variables."

To see how you can use @ARGV in a program, examine Listing 6.13. This program assumes that its first argument is a word to look for. The remaining arguments are assumed to be files in which to look for the word. The program prints out the searched-for word, the number of occurrences in each file, and the total number of occurrences.

This example assumes that the files *file1* and *file2* are defined and that each file contains the single line

```
This file contains a single line of input.
```

This example is then run with the command

```
C:\> programname single file1 file2
```

where *programname* is a placeholder for the name of the program. (If you are running the program yourself, you can name the program anything you like.)

TYPE   **Listing 6.13. A word-search and counting program.**

```
 1:  # p6_3.pl
 2:
 3:  print ("Word to search for: $ARGV[0]\n");
 4:  $filecount = 1;
 5:  $totalwordcount = 0;
 6:  while ($filecount <= @ARGV-1) {
 7:          unless (open (INFILE, $ARGV[$filecount])) {
 8:                  die ("Can't open input file $ARGV[$filecount]\n");
 9:          }
10:          $wordcount = 0;
11:          while ($line = <INFILE>) {
12:                  chop ($line);
13:                  @words = split(/ /, $line);
14:                  $w = 1;
15:                  while ($w <= @words) {
16:                          if ($words[$w-1] eq $ARGV[0]) {
17:                                  $wordcount++;
18:                          }
19:                          $w++;
20:                  }
21:          }
22:          print ("occurrences in file $ARGV[$filecount]: ");
23:          print ("$wordcount\n");
```

6

```
24:          $filecount++;
25:          $totalwordcount += $wordcount;
26: }
27: print ("total number of occurrences: $totalwordcount\n");
```

OUTPUT

```
C:\> perl p6_13.pl single file1 file2
Word to search for: single
occurrences in file file1: 1
occurrences in file file2: 1
total number of occurrences: 2
C:\>
```

ANALYSIS   Line 3 prints the word to search for. The program assumes that this word is the first argument in the command line and, therefore, is the first element of the array @ARGV.

Lines 7–9 open a file named on the command line. The first time line 7 is executed, the variable $filecount has the value 1, and the file whose name is in $ARGV[1] is opened. The next time through, $filecount is 2 and the file named in $ARGV[2] is opened, and so on. If a file cannot be opened, the program terminates.

Line 11 reads a line from a file. As before, the conditional expression

```
$line = <INFILE>
```

reads a line from the file represented by the file INFILE and assigns it to $line. If the file is empty, $line is assigned the null string, the conditional expression is false, and the loop in lines 11–21 is terminated.

Line 13 splits the line into words, and lines 15–20 compare each word with the search word. If the word matches, the word count for this file is incremented. This word count is reset when a new file is opened.

ARGV **and the** <> **Operator**

In Perl for Win32, the <> operator actually contains a hidden reference to the array @ARGV. Here's how it works:

1. When the Perl interpreter sees the <> for the first time, it opens the file whose name is stored in $ARGV[0].

2. After opening the file, the Perl interpreter executes the following library function:

   ```
   shift(@ARGV);
   ```

   This library function gets rid of the first element of @ARGV and moves every other element over one space. This means that the element x of @ARGV becomes element x-1.

6

3. The <> operator then reads all of the lines of the file opened in step 1.

4. When the <> operator exhausts an input file, the Perl interpreter goes back to step 1 and repeats the cycle again.

If you like, you can modify your program to retrieve a value from the command line and then fix @ARGV so that the <> operator can work properly. If you modify Listing 6.13 to do this, the result is Listing 6.14.

Listing 6.14. A word-search and counting program that **TYPE** uses <>.

```
1:  # p6_14.pl
2:
3:  $searchword = $ARGV[0];
4:  print ("Word to search for: $searchword\n");
5:  shift (@ARGV);
6:  $totalwordcount = $wordcount = 0;
7:  $filename = $ARGV[0];
8:  while ($line = <>) {
9:          chop ($line);
10:         @words = split(/ /, $line);
11:         $w = 1;
12:         while ($w <= @words) {
13:                 if ($words[$w-1] eq $searchword) {
14:                         $wordcount++;
15:                 }
16:                 $w++;
17:         }
18:         if (eof) {
19:                 print ("occurrences in file $filename: ");
20:                 print ("$wordcount\n");
21:                 $totalwordcount += $wordcount;
22:                 $wordcount = 0;
23:                 $filename = $ARGV[0];
24:         }
25: }
26: print ("total number of occurrences: $totalwordcount\n");
```

OUTPUT
```
C:\> perl p6_14.pl single file1 file2
Word to search for: single
occurrences in file file1: 1
occurrences in file file2: 1
total number of occurrences: 2
C:\>
```

ANALYSIS Line 3 assigns the first command-line argument, the search word, to the scalar variable $searchword. This is necessary because the call to shift in line 5 destroys the initial value of $ARGV[0].

6

Line 5 adjusts the array @ARGV so that the <> operator can use it. To do this, it calls the library function `shift`. This function shifts the elements of the list stored in @ARGV. The element in $ARGV[1] is moved to $ARGV[0], the element in $ARGV[2] is moved to $ARGV[1], and so on. After `shift` is called, @ARGV contains the files to be searched, which is exactly what the <> operator is looking for.

Line 7 assigns the current value of $ARGV[0] to the scalar variable $filename. Because the <> operator in line 8 calls `shift`, the value of $ARGV[0] is lost unless the program does this.

Line 8 uses the <> operator to open the file named in $ARGV[0] and to read a line from the file. The array variable @ARGV is shifted at this point.

Lines 9–16 behave as in Listing 6.13. The only difference is that the search word is now in $searchword, not in $ARGV[0].

Line 18 introduces the library function `eof`. This function indicates whether the program has reached the end of the file being read by <>. If `eof` returns true, the next use of <> opens a new file and shifts @ARGV again.

Lines 19–23 prepare for the opening of a new file. The number of occurrences of the search word is printed, the current word count is added to the total word count, and the word count is reset to 0. Because the new filename to be opened is in $ARGV[0], line 23 preserves this filename by assigning it to $filename.

NOTE

> You can use the <> operator to open and read any file you like by setting the value of @ARGV yourself. Look at this example:
>
> ```
> @ARGV = ("myfile1", "myfile2");
> while ($line = <>) {
>         ...
> }
> ```
>
> Here, when the statement containing the <> is executed for the first time, the file myfile1 is opened and its first line is read. Subsequent executions of <> each read another line of input from myfile1. When myfile1 is exhausted, myfile2 is opened and read one line at a time.

6

Summary

Perl accesses files by means of file variables. File variables are associated with files by the `open` statement.

Files can be opened in any of three modes: read, write, and append. A file opened in read mode cannot be written to; a file opened in either of the other modes cannot be read. Opening a file in write mode destroys the existing contents of the file.

To read from an opened file, reference it using <name>, where name is a placeholder for the name of the file handle associated with the file. To write to a file, specify its file handle when calling print.

Perl defines three built-in file variables:

☐ STDIN, which represents the standard input file

☐ STDOUT, which represents the standard output file

☐ STDERR, which represents the standard error file

You can redirect STDIN and STDOUT by specifying < and >, respectively, on the command line. Messages sent to STDERR appear on the screen even if STDOUT is redirected to a file.

The close function closes the file associated with a particular file variable. close never needs to be called unless you want to control exactly when a file is to be made inaccessible.

The file-test operators provide a way of retrieving information on a particular file. The most common file-test operators are

☐ -e, which tests whether a file exists.

☐ -r, -w, and -x, which test whether a file has read, write, and execute permission, respectively.

☐ -z, which tests whether a file is empty.

☐ -s, which returns the size of a file.

You can use -w and -z to ensure that you do not overwrite a non-empty file.

The <> operator enables you to read data from files specified on the command line. This operator uses the built-in array variable @ARGV, whose elements consist of the items specified on the command line.

Q&A

Q How many files can I have open at one time?

A Basically, as many as you like. The actual limit depends on the limitations of your operating system.

Q Why does adding a closing newline character to the text string affect how `die` behaves?

A Perl enables you to choose whether you want the filename and line number of the error message to appear. If you add a closing newline character to the string, the Perl interpreter assumes that you want to control how your error message is to appear.

Q Which is better to use: `<>`, or `@ARGV` and `shift` when appropriate?

A As is often the case, the answer is "It depends." If your program treats almost all the command-line arguments as files, it is better to use `<>` because the mechanics of opening and closing files are taken care of for you. If you are doing a lot of unusual things with `@ARGV`, it is better not to manipulate it to use `<>`, because things can get complicated and confusing.

Q Can I redirect `STDERR`?

A Yes, but there is (normally) no reason why you should. `STDERR`'s job is to report extraordinary conditions, and you usually want to see these, not have them buried in a file somewhere.

Q How many command-line arguments can I specify?

A Basically, as many as your command-line shell can handle.

Q Can I write to a file and then read from it later?

A Yes. To read from a file you have written to, close the file by calling `close` and then open the file in read mode.

Workshop

The Workshop provides quiz questions to help you solidify your understanding of the material covered and exercises to give you experience in using what you've learned. Try to understand the quiz and exercise answers before you go on to tomorrow's lesson. You can find the answers in Appendix B, "Answers."

Quiz

1. Define the following terms:
   a. file handle
   b. reserved word
   c. file mode
   d. append mode

2. From where does the <> operator read its data?

3. What do the following file-test operators do?

    a. -e

    b. -r

    c. -w

4. What are the contents of the array @ARGV when the following Perl program is executed?

```
C:\> perl myprog.pl file1 file2 file3
```

5. How do you indicate that a file is to be opened

    a. in write mode?

    b. in append mode?

    c. in read mode?

6. What is the relationship between @ARGV and the <> operator?

Exercises

1. Write a program that takes the values on the command line, adds them together, and prints the result.

2. Write a program that takes a list of files from the command line and examines their size. If a file is bigger than 10,000 bytes, print

```
File name is a big file!
```

where *name* is a placeholder for the name of the big file.

3. Write a program that copies a file named file1 to file2, and then appends another copy of file1 to file2.

4. Write a program that takes a list of files and indicates, for each file, whether the user has read or write permission.

5. **BUG BUSTER:** What is wrong with the following program?

```
open (OUTFILE, "outfile");
print OUTFILE ("This is my message\n");
```

6

Day 7

Pattern Matching

This lesson describes the pattern-matching features of Perl for Win32. Today, you learn about the following:

- [ ] How pattern matching works
- [ ] The pattern-matching operators
- [ ] Special characters supported in pattern matching
- [ ] Pattern-matching options
- [ ] Pattern substitution
- [ ] Translation
- [ ] Extended pattern-matching features

Introduction to Patterns

A *pattern* is a sequence of characters to be searched for in a character string. In Perl for Win32, patterns are normally enclosed in slash characters:

`/def/`

This represents the pattern `def`.

If the pattern is found, a match occurs. For example, if you search the string `redefine` for the pattern `/def/`, the pattern matches the third, fourth, and fifth characters:

re*def*ine

You already have seen a simple example of pattern matching in the library function `split`:

`@array = split(/ /, $line);`

Here the pattern `/ /` matches a single space, which splits a line into words.

The Match Operators

Perl defines special operators that test whether a particular pattern appears in a character string.

The `=~` operator binds the pattern to the string for testing whether a pattern is matched, as shown in the following:

`$result = $var =~ /abc/;`

The result of the `=~` operation is one of the following:

- ☐ A nonzero value, or true, if the pattern is found in the string
- ☐ `""`, or false, if the pattern is not matched

In this example, the value stored in the scalar variable `$var` is searched for the pattern `abc`. If `abc` is found, `$result` is assigned a nonzero value; otherwise, `$result` is set to `""`.

The `!~` operator is similar to `=~`, except that it checks whether a pattern is not matched:

`$result = $var !~ /abc/;`

Here, `$result` is set to `0` if `abc` appears in the string assigned to `$var`, and to a nonzero value if `abc` is not found.

Because `=~` and `!~` produce either true or false as their result, these operators are ideally suited for use in conditional expressions. Listing 7.1 is a simple program that uses the `=~` operator to test whether a particular sequence of characters exists in a character string.

TYPE **Listing 7.1. A program that illustrates the use of the matching operator.**

```
1:  # p7_1.pl
2:
3:  print ("Ask me a question politely:\n");
4:  $question = <STDIN>;
5:  if ($question =~ /please/) {
6:          print ("Thank you for being polite!\n");
7:  } else {
8:          print ("That was not very polite!\n");
9:  }
```

OUTPUT

```
C:\> perl p7_1.pl
Ask me a question politely:
May I have a glass of water, please?
Thank you for being polite!
C:\>
```

ANALYSIS Line 5 is an example of the use of the operator =~ in a conditional expression. The following expression is true if the value stored in $question contains the word please, and it is false if it does not:

```
$question =~ /please/
```

Match-Operator Precedence

Like all operators, the match operators have a defined precedence. By definition, the =~ and !~ operators have higher precedence than multiplication and division, and lower precedence than the operator **.

For a complete list of Perl operators amé201 their precedence, see Day 4, "More Operators."

Special Characters in Patterns

Perl supports a variety of special characters inside patterns, which enables you to match any of a number of character strings. These special characters are what make patterns useful.

The + Character

The special character + means "one or more of the preceding characters." For example, the pattern /de+f/ matches any of the following:

```
def
deef
deeef
deeeeeeef
```

7

> **NOTE**
>
> Patterns containing + always try to match as many characters as possible. For example, if the pattern
>
> `/ab+/`
>
> is searching in the string
>
> `abbc`
>
> it matches `abb`, not `ab`.

The + special character makes it possible to define a better way to split lines into words. So far, the sample programs you have seen have used

```
@words = split (/ /, $line);
```

to break an input line into words. This works well if there is exactly one space between words. However, if an input line contains more than one space between words, as in

```
Here's multiple   spaces.
```

the call to `split` produces the following list:

```
("Here's", "", "multiple", "", "spaces.")
```

The pattern / / tells `split` to start a new word whenever it sees a space. Because there are two spaces between each word, `split` starts a word when it sees the first space, and then starts another word when it sees the second space. This means that there are now "empty words" in the line.

The + special character gets around this problem. Suppose the call to `split` is changed to this:

```
@array = split (/ +/, $line);
```

Because the pattern / +/ tries to match as many blank characters as possible, the line

```
Here's  multiple   spaces.
```

produces the following list:

```
("Here's", "multiple", "spaces")
```

Listing 7.2 shows how you can use the / +/ pattern to produce a count of the number of words in a file.

Listing 7.2. A word-count program that handles multiple spaces between words.

TYPE

```
1:  # p7_2.pl
2:
3:  $wordcount = 0;
4:  $line = <STDIN>;
5:  while ($line ne "") {
6:          chop ($line);
7:          @words = split(/ +/, $line);
8:          $wordcount += @words;
9:          $line = <STDIN>;
10: }
11: print ("Total number of words: $wordcount\n");
```

OUTPUT

```
C:\> perl p7_2.pl
Here    is    some input.
Here are    some    more words.
Here        is my   last   line.
^z
Total number of words: 14
C:\>
```

ANALYSIS This is the same word-count program you saw in Listing 5.15, with only one change: The pattern / +/ is being used to break the line into words. As you can see, this handles spaces between words properly.

You might have noticed the following problems with this word-count program:

☐ Spaces at the beginning of a line are counted as a word, because split always starts a new word when it sees a space.

☐ Tab characters are counted as a word.

For an example of the first problem, take a look at the following input line:

```
 This line contains leading spaces.
```

The call to split in line 7 breaks the preceding into the following list:

```
("", "This", "line", "contains", "leading", "spaces")
```

This yields a word count of 6, not the expected 5.

There can be, at most, one empty word produced from a line, no matter how many leading spaces there are, because the pattern / +/ matches as many spaces as possible. Note also that the program can distinguish between lines containing words and lines that are blank or contain just spaces. If a line is blank or contains only spaces, the line

```
@words = split(/ +/, $line);
```

7

assigns the empty list to @words. Because of this, you can fix the problem of leading spaces in lines by modifying line 8 as follows:

```
$wordcount += (@words > 0 && $words[0] eq "" ?
               @words-1 : @words);
```

This checks for lines containing leading spaces; if a line contains leading spaces, the first "word" (which is the empty string) is not added to the word count.

To find out how to modify the program to deal with tab characters as well as spaces, see the following section.

The [] Special Characters

The [] special characters enable you to define patterns that match one of a group of alternatives. For example, the following pattern matches def or dEf:

```
/d[eE]f/
```

You can specify as many alternatives as you like:

```
/a[0123456789]c/
```

This matches a, followed by any digit, followed by c.

You can combine [] with + to match a sequence of characters of any length:

```
/d[eE]+f/
```

This matches all of the following:

```
def
dEf
deef
dEef
dEEEeeeEef
```

Any combination of E and e, in any order, is matched by [eE]+.

You can use [] and + together to modify the word-count program you've just seen to accept either tab characters or spaces. Listing 7.3 shows how you can do this.

TYPE

Listing 7.3. A word-count program that handles multiple spaces and tabs between words.

```
1:  # p7_3.pl
2:
3:  $wordcount = 0;
4:  $line = <STDIN>;
```

```
5:  while ($line ne "") {
6:          chop ($line);
7:          @words = split(/[\t ]+/, $line);
8:          $wordcount += @words;
9:          $line = <STDIN>;
10: }
11: print ("Total number of words: $wordcount\n");
```

OUTPUT
```
C:\> perl p7_3.pl
Here is some input.
Here are some more words.
Here is my last line.
^z
Total number of words: 14
C:\>
```

ANALYSIS This program is identical to Listing 7.2, except that the pattern is now /[\t]+/.

The \t special-character sequence represents the tab character, and this pattern matches any combination or quantity of spaces and tabs.

NOTE

> Any escape sequence that is supported in double-quoted strings is supported in patterns. See Day 3, "Understanding Scalar Values," for a list of the escape sequences that are available.

The * and ? Special Characters

As you have seen, the + character matches one or more occurrences of a character. Perl also defines two other special characters that match a varying number of characters: * and ?.

The * special character matches zero or more occurrences of the preceding character. For example, the pattern

```
/de*f/
```

matches df, def, deef, and so on.

This character can also be used with the [] special character.

```
/[eE]*/
```

This matches the empty string as well as any combination of E or e in any order.

7

WARNING

Be sure not to confuse the * special character with the + special character. If you use the wrong special character, you might not get the results that you want.

For example, suppose that you modify Listing 7.3 to call split as follows:

```
@words = split (/[\t ]*/, $list);
```

This matches zero or more occurrences of the space or tab character. When you run this with the input

```
a line
```

here's the list that is assigned to @words:

```
("a", "l", "i", "n", "e")
```

Because the pattern /[\t]*/ matches on zero occurrences of the space or tab character, it matches after every character. This means that split starts a word after every character that is not a space or tab. (It skips spaces and tabs because /[\t]*/ matches them.)

The best way to avoid problems such as this one is to use the * special character only when there is another character appearing in the pattern. Patterns such as

```
/b*[c]/
```

never match the null string, because the matched sequence has to contain at least the character c.

The ? character matches zero or one occurrence of the preceding character. For example, the pattern

```
/de?f/
```

matches either df or def. Note that it does not match deef, because the ? character does not match two occurrences of a character.

Escape Sequences for Special Characters

If you want your pattern to include a character that is normally treated as a special character, precede the character with a backslash \. For example, to check for one or more occurrences of * in a string, use the following pattern:

```
/\*+/
```

The backslash preceding the * tells the Perl interpreter to treat the * as an ordinary character, not as the special character meaning "zero or more occurrences."

To include a backslash in a pattern, specify two backslashes:

```
/\\+/
```

This pattern tests for one or more occurrences of \ in a string.

If you are running Perl 5 for Win32, another way to tell Perl that a special character is to be treated as a normal character is to precede it with the \Q escape sequence. When the Perl interpreter sees \Q, every character following the \Q is treated as a normal character until \E is seen. This means that the pattern

```
/\Q^ab*/
```

matches any occurrence of the string ^ab*, and the pattern

```
/\Q^ab\E*/
```

matches ^a followed by zero or more occurrences of b.

For a complete list of special characters in patterns that require \ to be given their natural meaning, see the section titled "Special-Character Precedence," in today's lesson, which contains a table that lists them.

TIP

In Perl for Win32, any character that is not a letter or a digit can be preceded by a backslash. If the character isn't a special character in Perl, the backslash is ignored.

If you are not sure whether a particular character is a special character, preceding it with a backslash will ensure that your pattern behaves the way you want it to.

Matching Any Letter or Number

As you have seen, the pattern

```
/a[0123456789]c/
```

matches a, followed by any digit, followed by c. Another way of writing this is as follows:

```
/a[0-9]c/
```

7

Here, the range [0-9] represents any digit between 0 and 9. This pattern matches a0c, a1c, a2c, and so on up to a9c.

Similarly, the range [a-z] matches any lowercase letter, and the range [A-Z] matches any uppercase letter. For example, the pattern

```
/[A-Z][A-Z]/
```

matches any two uppercase letters.

To match any uppercase letter, lowercase letter, or digit, use the following range:

```
/[0-9a-zA-Z]/
```

Listing 7.4 provides an example of the use of ranges with the [] special characters. This program checks whether a given input line contains a legal Perl scalar-, array-, or file-variable name. (Note that this program only handles simple input lines. Later examples will solve this problem in a better way.)

TYPE   **Listing 7.4. A simple variable-name validation program.**

```
1:  # p7_4.pl
2:
3:  print ("Enter a variable name:\n");
4:  $varname = <STDIN>;
5:  chop ($varname);
6:  if ($varname =~ /\$[A-Za-z][_0-9a-zA-Z]*/) {
7:          print ("$varname is a legal scalar variable\n");
8:  } elsif ($varname =~ /@[A-Za-z][_0-9a-zA-Z]*/) {
9:          print ("$varname is a legal array variable\n");
10: } elsif ($varname =~ /[A-Za-z][_0-9a-zA-Z]*/) {
11:         print ("$varname is a legal file variable\n");
12: } else {
13:         print ("I don't understand what $varname is.\n");
14: }
```

OUTPUT
```
C:\> perl p7_4.pl
Enter a variable name:
$result
$result is a legal scalar variable
C:\>
```

ANALYSIS   Line 6 checks whether the input line contains the name of a legal scalar variable. Recall that a legal scalar variable consists of the following:

- ☐ A $ character
- ☐ An uppercase or lowercase letter
- ☐ Zero or more letters, digits, or underscore characters

Each part of the pattern tested in line 6 corresponds to one of the aforementioned conditions given. The first part of the pattern, \$, ensures that the pattern matches only if it begins with a $.

NOTE

> The $ is preceded by a backslash, because $ is a special character in patterns. See the following section, "Anchoring Patterns," for more information on the $ special character.

The second part of the pattern,

`[a-zA-Z]`

matches exactly one uppercase or lowercase letter. The final part of the pattern,

`[_0-9a-zA-Z]*`

matches zero or more underscores, digits, or letters in any order.

The patterns in line 8 and line 10 are very similar to the one in line 6. The only difference in line 8 is that the pattern there matches a string whose first character is @, not $. In line 10, this first character is omitted completely.

The pattern in line 8 corresponds to the definition of a legal array-variable name, and the pattern in line 10 corresponds to the definition of a legal file-variable name.

Anchoring Patterns

Although Listing 7.4 can determine whether a line of input contains a legal Perl variable name, it cannot determine whether there is extraneous input on the line. For example, it can't tell the difference between the following three lines of input:

```
$result
junk$result
$result#junk
```

In all three cases, the pattern

`/\$[a-zA-Z][_0-9a-zA-Z]*/`

finds the string $result and matches successfully; however, only the first line is a legal Perl variable name.

To fix this problem, you can use *pattern anchors*. Table 7.1 lists the pattern anchors defined in Perl for Win32.

7

Table 7.1. Pattern anchors in Perl for Win32.

Anchor	Description
^ or \A	Match at beginning of string only
$ or \z	Match at end of string only
\b	Match on word boundary
\B	Match inside word

These pattern anchors are described in the following sections.

The ^ and $ Pattern Anchors

The pattern anchors ^ and $ ensure that the pattern is matched only at the beginning or the end of a string. For example, the pattern

```
/^def/
```

matches def only if these are the first three characters in the string. Similarly, the pattern

```
/def$/
```

matches def only if these are the last three characters in the string.

You can combine ^ and $ to force matching of the entire string, as follows:

```
/^def$/
```

This matches only if the string is def.

In most cases, the escape sequences \A and \z are equivalent to ^ and $, respectively:

```
/\Adef\Z/
```

This also matches only if the string is def.

NOTE

\A and \z behave differently from ^ and $ when the multiple-line pattern-matching option is specified. Pattern-matching options are described later today.

Listing 7.5 shows how you can use pattern anchors to ensure that a line of input is, in fact, a legal Perl scalar-, array-, or file-variable name.

TYPE **Listing 7.5. A better variable-name validation program.**

```
1:  # p7_5.pl
2:
3:  print ("Enter a variable name:\n");
4:  $varname = <STDIN>;
5:  chop ($varname);
6:  if ($varname =~ /^\$[A-Za-z][_0-9a-zA-Z]*$/) {
7:          print ("$varname is a legal scalar variable\n");
8:  } elsif ($varname =~ /^@[A-Za-z][_0-9a-zA-Z]*$/) {
9:          print ("$varname is a legal array variable\n");
10: } elsif ($varname =~ /^[A-Za-z][_0-9a-zA-Z]*$/) {
11:         print ("$varname is a legal file variable\n");
12: } else {
13:         print ("I don't understand what $varname is.\n");
14: }
```

OUTPUT
```
C:\> perl p7_5.pl
Enter a variable name:
x$result
I don't understand what x$result is.
C:\>
```

ANALYSIS The only difference between this program and the one in Listing 7.4 is that this program uses the pattern anchors ^ and $ in the patterns in lines 6, 8, and 10. These anchors ensure that a valid pattern consists of only those characters that make up a legal Perl scalar, array, or file variable.

In the sample output given here, the input

```
x$result
```

is rejected, because the pattern in line 6 is only matched when the $ character appears at the beginning of the line.

Word-Boundary Pattern Anchors

The word-boundary pattern anchors, \b and \B, specify whether a matched pattern must be on a word boundary or inside a word boundary. (A *word boundary* is the beginning or end of a word.)

The \b pattern anchor specifies that the pattern must be on a word boundary. For example, the pattern

```
/\bdef/
```

matches only if def is the beginning of a word. This means that def and defghi match but abcdef does not.

7

You can also use \b to indicate the end of a word. For example,

```
/def\b/
```

matches def and abcdef, but not defghi. Finally, the pattern

```
/\bdef\b/
```

matches only the word def, not abcdef or defghi.

The \B pattern anchor is the opposite of \b. \B matches only if the pattern is contained in a word. For example, the pattern

```
/\Bdef/
```

matches abcdef, but not def. Similarly, the pattern

```
/def\B/
```

matches defghi, and

```
/\Bdef\B/
```

matches cdefg or abcdefghi, but not def, defghi, or abcdef.

The \b and \B pattern anchors enable you to search for words in an input line without having to break up the line using split. For example, Listing 7.6 uses \b to count the number of lines of an input file that contain the word *the*.

Listing 7.6. A program that counts the number of input lines containing the word *the*.

TYPE

```
1:  # p7_6.pl
2:
3:  $thecount = 0;
4:  print ("Enter the input here:\n");
5:  $line = <STDIN>;
```

```
6:  while ($line ne "") {
7:          if ($line =~ /\bthe\b/) {
8:                  $thecount++;
9:          }
10:         $line = <STDIN>;
11: }
12: print ("Number of lines containing 'the': $thecount\n");
```

OUTPUT

```
C:\> perl p7_6.pl
Enter the input here:
Now is the time
for all good men
to come to the aid
of the party.
^z
Number of lines containing 'the': 3
C:\>
```

ANALYSIS This program checks each line in turn to see if it contains the word `the`, and then prints the total number of lines that contain the word.

Line 7 performs the actual checking by trying to match the pattern

```
/\bthe\b/
```

If this pattern matches, the line contains the word `the`, because the pattern checks for word boundaries at either end.

Note that this program doesn't check whether the word `the` appears on a line more than once. It is not difficult to modify the program to do this; in fact, you can do it in several different ways.

The most obvious but most laborious way is to break up lines that you know contain `the` into words, and then check each word, as follows:

```
if ($line =~ /\bthe\b/) {
        @words = split(/[\t ]+/, $line);
        $count = 1;
        while ($count <= @words) {
                if ($words[$count-1] eq "the") {
                        $thecount += 1;
                }
                $count++;
        }
}
```

A cute way to accomplish the same thing is to use the pattern itself to break the line into words:

```
if ($line =~ /\bthe\b/) {
        @words = split(/\bthe\b/, $line);
        $thecount += @words - 1;
}
```

7

In fact, you don't even need the `if` statement. You can do it like this:

```
@words = split(/\bthe\b/, $line);
$thecount += @words - 1;
```

Here's why this works: Every time `split` sees the word `the`, it starts a new word. Therefore, the number of occurrences of `the` is equal to one less than the number of elements in `@words`. If there are no occurrences of `the`, `@words` has the length 1, and `$thecount` is not changed.

WARNING

This trick works only if you know that there is at least one word on the line.

Consider the following code, which tries to use the aforementioned trick on a line that has had its newline character removed using `chop`:

```
$line = <STDIN>;
chop ($line);
@words = split(/\bthe\b/, $line);
$thecount += @words - 1;
```

This code actually subtracts 1 from `$thecount` if the line is blank or consists only of the word `the`, because in these cases `@words` is the empty list and the length of `@words` is 0.

Leaving off the call to `chop` protects against this problem, because there will always be at least one "word" in every line (consisting of the newline character).

Variable Substitution in Patterns

If you like, you can use the value of a scalar variable in a pattern. For example, the following code splits the line `$line` into words:

```
$pattern = "[\\t ]+";
@words = split(/$pattern/, $line);
```

Because you can use a scalar variable in a pattern, there is nothing to stop you from reading the pattern from the standard input file. Listing 7.7 accepts a search pattern from a file and then searches for the pattern in the input files listed on the command line. If it finds the pattern, it prints the filename and line number of the match; at the end, it prints the total number of matches.

This example assumes that two files exist: `file1` and `file2`. Each file contains the following:

```
This is a line of input.
This is another line of input.
```

If you run this program with command-line arguments `file1` and `file2` and search for the pattern `another`, you get the output shown.

TYPE **Listing 7.7. A simple pattern-search program.**

```
1:  # p7_7.pl
2:
3:  print ("Enter the search pattern:\n");
4:  $pattern = <STDIN>;
5:  chop ($pattern);
6:  $filename = $ARGV[0];
7:  $linenum = $matchcount = 0;
8:  print ("Matches found:\n");
9:  while ($line = <>) {
10:         $linenum += 1;
11:         if ($line =~ /$pattern/) {
12:                 print ("$filename, line $linenum\n");
13:                 @words = split(/$pattern/, $line);
14:                 $matchcount += @words - 1;
15:         }
16:         if (eof) {
17:                 $linenum = 0;
18:                 $filename = $ARGV[0];
19:         }
20:  }
21:  if ($matchcount == 0) {
22:          print ("No matches found.\n");
23:  } else {
24:          print ("Total number of matches: $matchcount\n");
25:  }
```

OUTPUT
```
C:\> perl p7_7.pl file1 file2
Enter the search pattern:
another
Matches found:
file1, line 2
file2, line 2
Total number of matches: 2
C:\>
```

ANALYSIS This program uses the following scalar variables to keep track of information:

☐ `$pattern` contains the search pattern read in from the standard input file.

☐ `$filename` contains the file currently being searched.

☐ `$linenum` contains the line number of the line currently being searched.

☐ `$matchcount` contains the total number of matches found to this point.

7

Line 6 sets the current filename, which corresponds to the first element in the built-in array variable @ARGV. This array variable lists the arguments supplied on the command line. (To refresh your memory on how @ARGV works, refer to Day 6, "Reading from and Writing to Files.") This current filename needs to be stored in a scalar variable, because the <> operator in line 9 shifts @ARGV and destroys this name.

Line 9 reads from each of the files on the command line in turn, one line at a time. The current input line is stored in the scalar variable $line. Once the line is read, line 10 adds 1 to the current line number.

Lines 11–15 handle the matching process. Line 11 checks whether the pattern stored in $pattern is contained in the input line stored in $line. If a match is found, line 12 prints out the current filename and line number. Line 13 then splits the line into "words," using the trick described in the earlier section, "Word-Boundary Pattern Anchors." Because the number of elements of the list stored in @words is one larger than the number of times the pattern is matched, the expression @words - 1 is equivalent to the number of matches; its value is added to $matchcount.

Line 16 checks whether the <> operator has reached the end of the current input file. If it has, line 17 resets the current line number to 0. This ensures that the next pass through the loop will set the current line number to 1 (to indicate that the program is on the first line of the next file). Line 18 sets the filename to the next file mentioned on the command line, which is currently stored in $ARGV[0].

Lines 21–25 either print the total number of matches or indicate that no matches were found.

WARNING

Make sure that you remember to include the enclosing / characters when you use a scalar-variable name in a pattern. The Perl interpreter does not complain when it sees the following, for example, but the result might not be what you want:

```
@words = split($pattern, $line);
```

Excluding Alternatives

As you have seen, when the special characters [] appear in a pattern, they specify a set of alternatives to choose from. For example, the pattern

```
/d[eE]f/
```

matches def or dEf.

When the ^ character appears as the first character after the [, it indicates that the pattern is to match any character *except* the ones displayed between the [and]. For example, the pattern

```
/d[^eE]f/
```

matches any pattern that satisfies the following criteria:

- ☐ The first character is d
- ☐ The second character is anything other than e or E
- ☐ The last character is f

NOTE

To include a ^ character in a set of alternatives, precede it with a backslash, as follows:

```
/d[\^eE]f/
```

This pattern matches d^f, def, or dEf.

Character-Range Escape Sequences

In the section titled "Matching Any Letter or Number" earlier in this chapter, you learned that you can represent consecutive letters or numbers inside the [] special characters by specifying ranges. For example, in the pattern

```
/a[1-3]c/
```

the [1-3] matches any of 1, 2, or 3.

Some ranges occur frequently enough that Perl defines special escape sequences for them. For example, instead of writing

```
/[0-9]/
```

to indicate that any digit is to be matched, you can write

```
/\d/
```

The \d escape sequence means "any digit."

Table 7.2 lists the character-range escape sequences, what they match, and their equivalent character ranges.

7

Table 7.2. Character-range escape sequences.

Escape sequence	Description	Range
\d	Any digit	[0-9]
\D	Anything other than a digit	[^0-9]
\w	Any word character	[_0-9a-zA-Z]
\W	Anything not a word character	[^_0-9a-zA-Z]
\s	White space	[\r\t\n\f]
\S	Anything other than white space	[^ \r\t\n\f]

These escape sequences can be used anywhere ordinary characters are used. For example, the following pattern matches any digit or lowercase letter:

```
/[\da-z]/
```

NOTE

The definition of word boundary as used by the \b and \B special characters corresponds to the definition of word character used by \w and \W.

If the pattern /\w\W/ matches a particular pair of characters, the first character is part of a word and the second is not; this means that the first character is the end of a word, and that a word boundary exists between the first and second characters matched by the pattern.

Similarly, if /\W\w/ matches a pair of characters, the first character is not part of a word and the second character is. This means that the second character is the beginning of a word. Again, a word boundary exists between the first and second characters matched by the pattern.

Matching Any Character

Another special character supported in patterns is the period (.) character, which matches any character except the newline character. For example, the following pattern matches d, followed by any non-newline character, followed by f:

```
/d.f/
```

The . character is often used in conjunction with the * character. For example, the following pattern matches any string that contains the character d preceding the character f:

```
/d.*f/
```

Normally, the .* special-character combination tries to match as much as possible. For example, if the string banana is searched using the following pattern, the pattern matches banana, not ba or bana:

/b.*a/

NOTE

There is one exception to the preceding rule: The .* character only matches the longest possible string that enables the pattern match as a whole to succeed.

For example, suppose the string Mississippi is searched using the pattern

/M.*i.*pi/

Here, the first .* in /M.*i.*pi/ matches

Mississippi

If it tried to go further and match

Mississippi

or even

Mississippi

there would be nothing left for the rest of the pattern to match.

When the first .* match is limited to

Mississippi

the rest of the pattern, i.*pi, matches ippi, and the pattern as a whole succeeds.

Matching a Specified Number of Occurrences

Several special characters in patterns you have seen enable you to match a specified number of occurrences of a character. For example, + matches one or more occurrences of a character, and ? matches zero or one occurrences.

Perl enables you to define how many occurrences of a character constitute a match. To do this, use the special characters { and }.

For example, the pattern

/de{1,3}f/

7

matches d, followed by one, two, or three occurrences of e, followed by f. This means that def, deef, and deeef match, but df and deeeef do not.

To specify an exact number of occurrences, include only one value between the { and the }.

```
/de{3}f/
```

This specifies exactly three occurrences of e, which means this pattern only matches deeef.

To specify a minimum number of occurrences, leave off the upper bound:

```
/de{3,}f/
```

This matches d, followed by at least three es, followed by f.

Finally, to specify a maximum number of occurrences, use 0 as the lower bound.

```
/de{0,3}f/
```

This matches d, followed by no more than three es, followed by f.

 NOTE

> You can use { and } with character ranges or any other special character, as follows:
>
> ```
> /[a-z]{1,3}/
> ```
>
> This matches one, two, or three lowercase letters.
> The following matches any three characters:
>
> ```
> /.{3}/
> ```

Specifying Choices

The special character | enables you to specify two or more alternatives to choose from when matching a pattern. For example, the pattern

```
/def|ghi/
```

matches either def or ghi. The pattern

```
/[a-z]+|[0-9]+/
```

matches one or more lowercase letters or one or more digits.

Listing 7.8 is a simple example of a program that uses the | special character. It reads a number and checks whether it is a legitimate Perl integer.

TYPE **Listing 7.8. A simple integer-validation program.**

```
1:  # p7_8.pl
2:
3:  print ("Enter a number:\n");
4:  $number = <STDIN>;
5:  chop ($number);
6:  if ($number =~ /^-?\d+$|^-?0[xX][\da-fA-F]+$/) {
7:          print ("$number is a legal integer.\n");
8:  } else {
9:          print ("$number is not a legal integer.\n");
10: }
```

OUTPUT
```
C:\> perl p7_8.pl
Enter a number:
0x3ff1
0x3ff1 is a legal integer.
C:\>
```

ANALYSIS Recall that Perl integers can be in any of three forms:

☐ Standard base-10 notation, as in 123

☐ Base-8 (octal) notation, indicated by a leading 0, as in 0123

☐ Base-16 (hexadecimal) notation, indicated by a leading 0x or 0X, as in 0X1ff

Line 6 checks whether a number is a legal Perl integer. The first alternative in the pattern,

`^-?\d+$`

matches a string consisting of one or more digits, optionally preceded by a -. (The ^ and $ characters ensure that this is the only string that matches.) This takes care of integers in standard base-10 notation and integers in octal notation.

The second alternative in the pattern,

`^0[xX][\da-fA-F]+$`

matches integers in hexadecimal notation. Take a look at this pattern one piece at a time:

☐ The ^ matches the beginning of the line. This ensures that lines containing leading spaces or extraneous characters are not treated as valid hexadecimal integers.

☐ The -? matches a - if it is present. This ensures that negative numbers are matched.

☐ The 0 matches the leading 0.

☐ The [xX] matches the x or X that follows the leading 0.

☐ The [\da-fA-F] matches any digit, any letter between a and f, or any letter between A and F. Recall that these are precisely the characters that are allowed to appear in hexadecimal digits.

7

☐ The + indicates that the pattern is to match one or more hexadecimal digits.

☐ The closing $ indicates that the pattern is to match only if there are no extraneous characters following the hexadecimal integer.

WARNING

> Beware that the following pattern matches either x *or* one or more of y, not one or more of x or y:
>
> ```
> /x|y+/
> ```
>
> See the section called "Special-Character Precedence" later today for details on how to specify special-character precedence in patterns.

Reusing Portions of Patterns

Suppose that you want to write a pattern that matches the following:

☐ One or more digits or lowercase letters

☐ Followed by a colon or semicolon

☐ Followed by another group of one or more digits or lowercase letters

☐ Another colon or semicolon

☐ Yet another group of one or more digits or lowercase letters

One way to indicate this pattern is as follows:

```
/[\da-z]+[:;][\da-z]+[:;][\da-z]+/
```

This pattern is somewhat complicated and is quite repetitive.

Perl provides an easier way to specify patterns that contain multiple repetitions of a particular sequence. When you enclose a portion of a pattern in parentheses, as in

```
([\da-z]+)
```

Perl stores the matched sequence in memory. To retrieve a sequence from memory, use the special character \n, where *n* is an integer representing the *n*th pattern stored in memory.

For example, the aforementioned pattern can be written as

```
/([\da-z]+)[:;]\1[:;]\1/
```

Here, the pattern matched by [\da-z]+ is stored in memory. When the Perl interpreter sees the escape sequence \1, it matches the matched pattern.

You also can store the sequence `[:;]` in memory, and write this pattern as follows:

`/([\da-z]+)([:;])\1\2\1/`

Pattern sequences are stored in memory from left to right, so `\1` represents the subpattern matched by `[\da-z]+`, and `\2` represents the subpattern matched by `[:;]`.

Pattern-sequence memory is often used when you want to match the same character in more than one place but don't care which character you match. For example, if you are looking for a date in *dd-mm-yy* format, you might want to match

`/\d{2}([\W])\d{2}\1\d{2}/`

This matches two digits, a nonword character, two more digits, the same nonword character, and two more digits. This means that the following strings all match:

```
12-05-92
26.11.87
07 04 92
```

However, the following string does not match:

```
21-05.91
```

This is because the pattern is looking for a – between the `05` and the `91`, not a period.

WARNING

> Beware that the pattern
>
> `/\d{2}([\W])\d{2}\1\d{2}/`
>
> is not the same as the pattern
>
> `/(\d{2})([\W])\1\2\1/`
>
> In the first pattern, any digit can appear anywhere. The second pattern matches any two digits as the first two characters, but then only matches the same two digits again. This means that
>
> ```
> 17-17-17
> ```
>
> matches, but the following does not:
>
> ```
> 17-05-91
> ```

7

Pattern-Sequence Scalar Variables

Note that pattern-sequence memory is only preserved for the length of the pattern. This means that if you define the following pattern (which, incidentally, matches any floating-point number that does not contain an exponent)

```
/-?(\d+)\.?(\d+)/
```

you cannot then define another pattern, such as the following:

```
/\1/
```

and expect the Perl interpreter to remember that \1 refers to the first \d+ (the digits before the decimal point).

To get around this problem, Perl defines special built-in variables that remember the value of patterns matched in parentheses. These special variables are named $n, where n is the nth set of parentheses in the pattern.

For example, consider the following:

```
$string = "This string contains the number 25.11.";
$string =~ /-?(\d+)\.?(\d+)/;
$integerpart = $1;
$decimalpart = $2;
```

In this case, the pattern

```
/-?(\d+)\.?(\d+)/
```

matches 25.11, and the subpattern in the first set of parentheses matches 25. This means that 25 is stored in $1 and is later assigned to $integerpart. Similarly, the second set of parentheses matches 11, which is stored in $2 and later assigned to $decimalpart.

WARNING

The values stored in $1, $2, and so on are destroyed when another pattern match is performed. If you need these values, be sure to assign them to other scalar variables.

There is also one other built-in scalar variable, $&, which contains the entire matched pattern, as follows:

```
$string = "This string contains the number 25.11.";
$string =~ /-?(\d+)\.?(\d+)/;
$number = $&;
```

Here, the pattern matched is 25.11, which is stored in $& and then assigned to $number.

Special-Character Precedence

Perl defines rules of precedence to determine the order in which special characters in patterns are interpreted. For example, the pattern

```
/x|y+/
```

matches either x or one or more occurrences of y, because + has higher precedence than | and is therefore interpreted first.

Table 7.3 lists the special characters that can appear in patterns in order of precedence (highest to lowest). Special characters with higher precedence are always interpreted before those of lower precedence.

Table 7.3. The precedence of pattern-matching special characters.

Special Character	Description
()	Pattern memory
+ * ? {}	Number of occurrences
^ $ \b \B	Pattern anchors
|	Alternatives

Because the pattern-memory special characters () have the highest precedence, you can use them to force other special characters to be evaluated first. For example, the pattern

```
(ab|cd)+
```

matches one or more occurrences of either ab or cd. This matches, for example, abcdab.

WARNING

> Remember that when you use parentheses to force the order of precedence, you also are storing into pattern memory. For example, in the sequence
>
> ```
> /(ab|cd)+(.)(ef|gh)+\1/
> ```
>
> the \1 refers to what ab|cd matched, not to what the . special character matched.

Now that you know all the special-pattern characters and their precedence, look at a program that does more complex pattern matching. Listing 7.9 uses the various special-pattern characters, including the parentheses, to check whether a given input string is a valid twentieth-century date.

TYPE **Listing 7.9. A date-validation program.**

```
1:  # p7_9.pl
2:
3:  print ("Enter a date in the format YYYY-MM-DD:\n");
```

continues

Listing 7.9. continued

```
 4:  $date = <STDIN>;
 5:  chop ($date);
 6:
 7:  # Because this pattern is complicated, we split it
 8:  # into parts, assign the parts to scalar variables,
 9:  # then substitute them in later.
10:
11:  # handle 31-day months
12:  $md1 = "(0[13578]|1[02])\\2(0[1-9]|[12]\\d|3[01])";
13:  # handle 30-day months
14:  $md2 = "(0[469]|11)\\2(0[1-9]|[12]\\d|30)";
15:  # handle February, without worrying about whether it's
16:  # supposed to be a leap year or not
17:  $md3 = "02\\2(0[1-9]|[12]\\d)";
18:
19:  # check for a twentieth-century date
20:  $match = $date =~ /^(19)?\d\d(.)($md1|$md2|$md3)$/;
21:  # check for a valid but non-20th century date
22:  $olddate = $date =~ /^(\d{1,4})(.)($md1|$md2|$md3)$/;
23:  if ($match) {
24:          print ("$date is a valid date\n");
25:  } elsif ($olddate) {
26:          print ("$date is not in the 20th century\n");
27:  } else {
28:          print ("$date is not a valid date\n");
29:  }
```

OUTPUT

```
C:\> perl p7_9.pl
Enter a date in the format YYYY-MM-DD:
1991-04-31
1991-04-31 is not a valid date
C:\>
```

ANALYSIS Don't worry: this program is a lot less complicated than it looks! Basically, this program does the following:

1. It checks whether the date is in the format YYYY-MM-DD. (It allows YY-MM-DD, and also enables you to use a character other than a hyphen to separate the year, month, and date.)

2. It checks whether the year is in the twentieth century.

3. It checks whether the month is between 01 and 12.

4. Finally, it checks whether the date field is a legal date for that month. Legal date fields are between 01 and either 29, 30, or 31, depending on the number of days in that month.

If the date is legal, the program tells you so. If the date is not a twentieth-century date but is legal, the program informs you of this also.

Because the pattern to be matched is too long to fit on one line, this program breaks it into pieces and assigns the pieces to scalar variables. This is possible because scalar-variable substitution is supported in patterns.

Line 12 is the pattern to match for months with 31 days. Note that the escape sequences (such as `\d`) are preceded by another backslash (producing `\\d`). This is because the program actually wants to store a backslash in the scalar variable. (Recall that backslashes in double-quoted strings are treated as escape sequences.) The pattern

```
(0[13578]|1[02])\2(0[1-9]|[12]\d|3[01])
```

which is assigned to `$md1`, consists of the following components:

- ☐ The sequence `(0[13578]|1[02])`, which matches the month values `01`, `03`, `05`, `07`, `08`, `10`, and `12` (the 31-day months)
- ☐ `\2`, which matches the character that separates the day, month, and year
- ☐ The sequence `(0[1-9]|[12]\d|3[01])`, which matches any two-digit number between `01` and `31`.

Note that `\2` matches the separator character because the separator character will eventually be the second pattern sequence stored in memory (when the pattern is finally assembled).

Line 14 is similar to line 12 and handles 30-day months. The only differences between this subpattern and the one in line 12 are as follows:

- ☐ The month values accepted are `04`, `06`, `09`, and `11`.
- ☐ The valid date fields are `01` through `30`, not `01` through `31`.

Line 17 is another similar pattern that checks whether the month is `02` (February) and the date field is between `01` and `29`.

Line 20 does the actual pattern match that checks whether the date is a valid twentieth-century date. This pattern is divided into three parts:

- ☐ `^(19)?\d\d`, which matches any two-digit number at the beginning of a line, or any four-digit number starting with `19`
- ☐ The separator character, which is the second item in parentheses—the second item stored in memory—and thus can be retrieved using `\2`
- ☐ `($md1|$md2|$md3)$`, which matches any of the valid month-day combinations defined in lines 12, 14, and 17, provided it appears at the end of the line

The result of the pattern match, either true or false, is stored in the scalar variable `$match`.

Line 22 checks whether the date is a valid date in any century. The only difference between this pattern and the one in line 20 is that the year can be any one-to-four-digit number. The result of the pattern match is stored in `$olddate`.

7

Lines 23–29 check whether either `$match` or `$olddate` is true and print the appropriate message.

As you can see, the pattern-matching facility in Perl is quite powerful. This program is less than 30 lines long, including comments; the equivalent program in almost any other programming language would be substantially longer and much more difficult to write.

Specifying a Different Pattern Delimiter

So far, all the patterns you have seen have been enclosed by `/` characters.

```
/de*f/
```

These `/` characters are known as *pattern delimiters*.

Because `/` is the pattern-delimiter character, you must use `\/` to include a `/` character in a pattern. This can become awkward if you are searching for a directory such as, for example, `C:/MyDir/MyFile/prog1`:

```
/\C:\/MyDir\/MyFile\/prog1/
```

To make it easier to write patterns that include `/` characters, Perl enables you to use any pattern-delimiter character you like. Therefore, to search for a directory, you can write

```
m!/C:/MyDir/MyFile/prog1!
```

Here, the `m` indicates the pattern-matching operation. If you are using a pattern delimiter other than `/`, you must include the `m`.

WARNING

There are two things you should watch out for when you use other pattern delimiters.

First, if you use the `'` character as a pattern delimiter, the Perl interpreter does not substitute for scalar-variable names. The following matches the string `$var`, not the current value of the scalar variable `$var`:

```
m'$var'
```

Second, if you use a pattern delimiter that is normally a special-pattern character, you will not be able to use that special character in your pattern. For example, if you want to match the pattern `ab?c` (which matches `a`, optionally followed by `b`, followed by `c`) you cannot use the `?` character as a pattern delimiter. The pattern

```
m?ab?c?
```

produces a syntax error, because the Perl interpreter assumes that the `?` after the `b` is a pattern delimiter. You can still use

```
m?ab\?c?
```

but this pattern won't match what you want. Because the `?` inside the pattern is escaped, the Perl interpreter assumes that you want to match the actual `?` character, and the pattern matches the sequence `ab?c`.

Pattern-Matching Options

When you specify a pattern, you also can supply options that control how the pattern is to be matched. Table 7.4 lists these pattern-matching options.

Table 7.4. Pattern-matching options.

Option	Description
g	Match all possible patterns
i	Ignore case
m	Treat string as multiple lines
o	Only evaluate once
s	Treat string as single line
x	Ignore white space in pattern

All pattern options are included immediately after the pattern. For example, the following pattern uses the `i` option to ignore case:

```
/ab*c/i
```

You can specify as many of the options as you like, and the options can be in any order.

Matching All Possible Patterns

The `g` operator tells the Perl interpreter to match all the possible patterns in a string. For example, if you search the string `balata` using the pattern

```
/.a/g
```

which matches any character followed by `a`, the pattern matches `ba`, `la`, and `ta`.

7

If a pattern with the g option specified appears as an assignment to an array variable, the array variable is assigned a list consisting of all the patterns matched. For example,

```
@matches = "balata" =~ /.a/g;
```

assigns the following list to @matches:

```
("ba", "la", "ta")
```

Now, consider the following statement:

```
$match = "balata" =~ /.a/g;
```

The first time this statement is executed, $match is assigned the first pattern matched, which in this case is ba. If this assignment is performed again, $match is assigned the second pattern matched in the string, which is la, and so on until the pattern runs out of matches.

This means that you can use patterns with the g option in loops. Listing 7.10 shows how this works.

TYPE | **Listing 7.10. A program that loops using a pattern.**

```
1:  # p7_10.pl
2:
3:  while ("balata" =~ /.a/g) {
4:          $match = $&;
5:          print ("$match\n");
6:  }
```

OUTPUT
```
C:\> perl p7_10.pl
ba
la
ta
C:\>
```

ANALYSIS The first time through the loop, $match has the value of the first pattern matched, which is ba. (The system variable $& always contains the last pattern matched; this pattern is assigned to $match in line 4.) When the loop is executed for a second time, $match has the value la. The third time through, $match has the value ta. After this, the loop terminates; because the pattern doesn't match anything else, the conditional expression is now false.

Determining the Match Location

If you need to know how much of a string has been searched by the pattern matcher when the g operator is specified, use the pos function:

```
$offset = pos($string);
```

7

This returns the position at which the next pattern match will be started.

You can reposition the pattern matcher by putting `pos()` on the left side of an assignment:

```
pos($string) = $newoffset;
```

This tells the Perl interpreter to start the next pattern match at the position specified by `$newoffset`.

> If you change the string being searched, the match position is reset to the beginning of the string.

Ignoring Case

The `i` option enables you to specify that a matched letter can either be uppercase or lowercase. For example, the following pattern matches `de`, `dE`, `De`, or `DE`:

```
/de/i
```

Patterns that match either uppercase or lowercase letters are said to be case insensitive.

Treating the String as Multiple Lines

The `m` option tells the Perl interpreter that the string to be matched contains multiple lines of text. When the `m` option is specified, the `^` special character matches either the start of the string or the start of any new line. For example, the pattern

```
/^The/m
```

matches the word `The` in

```
This pattern matches\nThe first word on the second line
```

The `m` option also specifies that the `$` special character is to match the end of any line. This means that the pattern

```
/line.$/m
```

is matched in the following string:

```
This is the end of the first line.\nHere's another line.
```

7

Evaluating a Pattern Only Once

The o option enables you to tell the Perl interpreter that a pattern is to be evaluated only once. For example, consider the following:

```
$var = 1;
$line = <STDIN>;
while ($var < 10) {
        $result = $line =~ /$var/o;
        $line = <STDIN>;
        $var++;
}
```

The first time the Perl interpreter sees the pattern /$var/, it replaces the name $var with the current value of $var, which is 1; this means that the pattern to be matched is /1/.

Because the o option is specified, the pattern to be matched remains /1/ even when the value of $var changes. If the o option had not been specified, the pattern would have been /2/ the next time through the loop.

If the pattern never changes, it's very efficient to use the o option.

Treating the String as a Single Line

The s option specifies that the string to be matched is to be treated as a single line of text. In this case, the . special character matches every character in a string, including the newline character. For example, the pattern /a.*bc/s is matched successfully in the following string:

axxxxx \nxxxxbc

If the s option is not specified, this pattern does not match because the . character does not match the newline.

Using White Space in Patterns

One problem with patterns in Perl is that they can become difficult to follow. For example, consider this pattern, which you saw earlier:

/\d{2}([\W])\d{2}\1\d{2}/

Patterns such as this are difficult to follow because there are a lot of backslashes, braces, and brackets to sort out.

Perl 5 for Win32 makes life a little easier by supplying the x option. This tells the Perl interpreter to ignore white space in a pattern unless it is preceded by a backslash. This means that the preceding pattern can be rewritten as the following, which is much easier to follow:

/\d{2} ([\W]) \d{2} \1 \d{2}/x

Here is an example of a pattern containing an actual blank space:

```
/[A-Z] [a-z]+ \ [A-Z] [a-z]+ /x
```

This matches a name in the standard first-name/last-name format (such as `John Smith`). Normally, you won't want to use the `x` option if you're actually trying to match white space, because you wind up with the backslash problem all over again.

The Substitution Operator

Perl enables you to replace part of a string using the substitution operator, which has the following syntax:

```
s/pattern/replacement/
```

The Perl interpreter searches for the pattern specified by the placeholder `pattern`. If it finds `pattern`, it replaces it with the string represented by the placeholder `replacement`. For example:

```
$string = "abc123def";
$string =~ s/123/456/;
```

Here, `123` is replaced by `456`, which means that the value stored in `$string` is now `abc456def`.

You can use any of the pattern special characters in the substitution operator. For example,

```
s/[abc]+/0/
```

searches for a sequence consisting of one or more occurrences of the letters `a`, `b`, and `c` (in any order) and replaces the sequence with `0`.

If you just want to delete a sequence of characters rather than replace it, leave out the replacement string as in the following example, which deletes the first occurrence of the pattern `abc`:

```
s/abc//
```

Using Pattern-Sequence Variables in Substitutions

You can use pattern-sequence variables to include a matched pattern in the replacement string. The following is an example:

```
s/(\d+)/[$1]/
```

This matches a sequence of one or more digits. Because this sequence is enclosed in parentheses, it is stored in the scalar variable `$1`. In the replacement string, `[$1]`, the scalar variable name `$1` is replaced by its value, which is the matched pattern.

7

NOTE

> Because the replacement string in the substitution operator is a string, not a pattern, the pattern special characters, such as [], *, and +, do not have a special meaning. For example, in the substitution
>
> `s/abc/[def]/`
>
> the replacement string is [def] (including the square brackets).

Options for the Substitution Operator

The substitution operator supports several options, which are listed in Table 7.5.

Table 7.5. Options for the substitution operator.

Option	Description
g	Change all occurrences of the pattern
i	Ignore case in pattern
e	Evaluate replacement string as expression
m	Treat string to be matched as multiple lines
o	Evaluate only once
s	Treat string to be matched as single line
x	Ignore white space in pattern

As with pattern matching, options are appended to the end of the operator. For example, to change all occurrences of abc to def, use the following:

```
s/abc/def/g
```

Global Substitution

The g option changes all occurrences of a pattern in a particular string. For example, the following substitution puts parentheses around any number in the string:

```
s/(\d+)/($1)/g
```

Listing 7.11 is an example of a program that uses global substitution. It examines each line of its input, removes all extraneous leading spaces and tabs, and replaces multiple spaces and tabs between words with a single space.

7

TYPE **Listing 7.11. A simple white-space cleanup program.**

```
1:  # p7_11.pl
2:
3:  @input = <STDIN>;
4:  $count = 0;
5:  while ($input[$count] ne "") {
6:          $input[$count] =~ s/^[ \t]+//;
7:          $input[$count] =~ s/[ \t]+\n$/\n/;
8:          $input[$count] =~ s/[ \t]+/ /g;
9:          $count++;
10: }
11: print ("Formatted text:\n");
12: print (@input);
```

OUTPUT
```
C:\> perl p7_11.pl
This is    a   line    of     input.
   Here    is another line.
This       is my  last line of     input.
^Z
Formatted text:
This is a line of input.
Here is another line.
This is my last line of input.
C:\>
```

ANALYSIS This program performs three substitutions on each line of its input. The first substitution, in line 6, checks whether there are any spaces or tabs at the beginning of the line. If any exist, they are removed.

Similarly, line 7 checks whether there are any spaces or tabs at the end of the line (before the trailing newline character). If any exist, they are removed. To do this, line 7 replaces the following pattern (one or more spaces and tabs, followed by a newline character, followed by the end of the line), with a newline character:

`/[ \t]+\n$/`

Line 8 uses a global substitution to remove extra spaces and tabs between words. The following pattern matches one or more spaces or tabs, in any order; these spaces and tabs are replaced by a single space:

`/[ \t]+/`

Ignoring Case

The i option ignores case when substituting. For example, the following substitution replaces all occurrences of the words no, No, NO, and nO with NO (recall that the \b escape character specifies a word boundary):

`s/\bno\b/NO/gi`

Replacement Using an Expression

The e option treats the replacement string as an expression, which it evaluates before replacing. For example, consider the following:

```
$string = "0abc1";
$string =~ s/[a-zA-Z]+/$& x 2/e
```

The substitution shown here is a quick way to duplicate part of a string. Here's how it works:

1. The pattern /[a-zA-Z]+/ matches abc, which is stored in the built-in variable $&.

2. The e option indicates that the replacement string, $& x 2, is to be treated as an expression. This expression is evaluated, producing the result abcabc.

3. abcabc is substituted for abc in the string stored in $string. This means that the new value of $string is 0abcabc1.

Listing 7.12 is another example that uses the e option in a substitution. This program takes every integer in a list of input files and multiplies them by 2, leaving the rest of the contents unchanged. (For the sake of simplicity, the program assumes that there are no floating-point numbers in the file.)

TYPE
Listing 7.12. A program that multiplies every integer in a file by 2.

```
1:  # p7_12.pl
2:
3:  $count = 0;
4:  while ($ARGV[$count] ne "") {
5:          open (FILE, "$ARGV[$count]");
6:          @file = <FILE>;
7:          $linenum = 0;
8:          while ($file[$linenum] ne "") {
9:                  $file[$linenum] =~ s/\d+/$& * 2/eg;
10:                 $linenum++;
11:         }
12:         close (FILE);
13:         open (FILE, ">$ARGV[$count]");
14:         print FILE (@file);
15:         close (FILE);
16:         $count++;
17: }
```

If a file named foo contains the text

```
This contains the number 1.
This contains the number 26.
```

and the name `foo` is passed as a command-line argument to this program, the file `foo` becomes

```
This contains the number 2.
This contains the number 52.
```

 This program uses the built-in variable `@ARGV` to retrieve filenames from the command line. Note that the program cannot use `<>`, because the following statement reads the entire contents of all the files into a single array:

```
@file = <>;
```

Lines 8–11 read and substitute one line of a file at a time. Line 9 performs the actual substitution as follows:

1. The pattern `\d+` matches a sequence of one or more digits, which is automatically assigned to `$&`.

2. The value of `$&` is substituted into the replacement string.

3. The `e` option indicates that this replacement string is to be treated as an expression. This expression multiplies the matched integer by 2.

4. The result of the multiplication is then substituted into the file in place of the original integer.

5. The `g` option indicates that every integer on the line is to be substituted for.

After all the lines in the file have been read, the file is closed and reopened for writing. The call to `print` in line 14 takes the list stored in `@file`—the contents of the current file—and writes them back out to the file, overwriting the original contents.

Doing Evaluation Only Once

As with the match operator, the `o` option to the substitution operator tells the Perl interpreter to replace a scalar-variable name with its value only once. For example, the following statement substitutes the current value of `$var` for its name, producing a replacement string:

```
$string =~ /abc/$var/o;
```

This replacement string then never changes, even if the value of `$var` changes. For example:

```
$var = 17;
while ($var > 0) {
        $string = <STDIN>;
        $string =~ /abc/$var/o;
        print ($string);
        $var--;  # the replacement string is still "17"
}
```

7

Treating the String as Single or Multiple Lines

As in the pattern-matching operator, the s and m options specify that the string to be matched is to be treated as a single line or as multiple lines, respectively.

The s option ensures that the newline character \n is matched by the . special character:

```
$string = "This is a\ntwo-line string.";
$string =~ s/a.*o/one/s;
# $string now contains "This is a one-line string."
```

If the m option is specified, ^ and $ match the beginning and end of any line:

```
$string = "The The first line\nThe The second line";
$string =~ s/^The//gm;
# $string now contains "The first line\nThe second line"
$string =~ s/e$/k/gm;
# $string now contains "The first link\nThe second link"
```

> **TIP**
>
> The \A and \z escape sequences always match only the beginning and end of the string, respectively. (This is the only case where \A and \z behave differently from ^ and $.)

Using White Space in Patterns

The x option tells the Perl interpreter to ignore all white space unless preceded by a backslash. As with the pattern-matching operator, ignoring white space makes complicated string patterns easier to read. The following converts a day-month-year string to the dd-mm-yy format:

```
$string =~ s/\d{2} ([\W]) \d{2} \1 \d{2}/$1-$2-$3/x
```

> **NOTE**
>
> Even if the x option is specified, spaces in the replacement string are not ignored. For example, the following replaces 14/04/95 with 14 - 04 - 95, not 14-04-95:
>
> ```
> $string =~ s/\d{2} ([\W]) \d{2} \1 \d{2}/$1 - $2 - $3/x
> ```

Specifying a Different Delimiter

You can specify a different delimiter to separate the pattern and replacement string in the substitution operator. For example, the following substitution operator replaces /u/bin with /usr/local/bin:

```
s#/u/bin#/usr/local/bin#
```

The search and replacement strings can be enclosed in parentheses or angle brackets:

```
s(/u/bin)(/usr/local/bin)
s</u/bin>/\/usr\/local\/bin/
```

WARNING

> As with the match operator, you cannot use a special character both as a delimiter and in a pattern.
>
> The following substitution will be flagged as containing an error because the . character is being used as the delimiter:
>
> ```
> s.a.c.def.
> ```
>
> The substitution
>
> ```
> s.a\.c.def.
> ```
>
> does work, but it substitutes def for a.c, where . is an actual period and not the pattern special character.

The Translation Operator

Perl also provides another way to substitute one group of characters for another: the tr translation operator. This operator uses the following syntax:

```
tr/string1/string2/
```

Here, *string1* contains a list of characters to be replaced, and *string2* contains the characters that replace them. The first character in *string1* is replaced by the first character in *string2*, the second character in *string1* is replaced by the second character in *string2*, and so on.

Here is a simple example:

```
$string = "abcdefghicba";
$string =~ tr/abc/def/;
```

Here, the characters a, b, and c are to be replaced as follows:

- [ ] All occurrences of the character a are to be replaced by the character d.
- [ ] All occurrences of the character b are to be replaced by the character e.
- [ ] All occurrences of the character c are to be replaced by the character f.

After the translation, the scalar variable $string contains the value defdefghifed.

7

NOTE

> If the string listing the characters to be replaced is longer than the string containing the replacement characters, the last character of the replacement string is repeated. Look at this example:
>
> ```
> $string = "abcdefgh";
> $string =~ tr/efgh/abc/;
> ```
>
> Here, there is no character corresponding to d in the replacement list, so c, the last character in the replacement list, replaces h. This translation sets the value of $string to abcdabcc.
>
> Also note that if the same character appears more than once in the list of characters to be replaced, the first replacement is used:
>
> ```
> $string =~ tr/AAA/XYZ/; replaces A with X
> ```

The most common use of the translation operator is to convert alphabetic characters from uppercase to lowercase, or vice versa. Listing 7.13 provides an example of a program that converts a file to all-lowercase characters.

 TYPE **Listing 7.13. An uppercase-to-lowercase conversion program.**

```
1:  # p7_13.pl
2:
3:  while ($line = <STDIN>) {
4:          $line =~ tr/A-Z/a-z/;
5:          print ($line);
6:  }
```

OUTPUT
```
C:\> perl p7_13.pl
THIS LINE IS IN UPPER CASE.
this line is in upper case.
ThiS LiNE Is iN mIxED cASe.
this line is in mixed case.
^Z
C:\>
```

ANALYSIS This program reads a line at a time from the standard input file, terminating when it sees a line containing the Ctrl+Z (end-of-file) character.

Line 4 performs the translation operation. As in the other pattern-matching operations, the range character (–) indicates a range of characters to be included. Here, the range a-z refers to all the lowercase characters, and the range A-Z refers to all the uppercase characters.

NOTE

There are two things you should note about the translation operator:

- ☐ The pattern special characters are not supported by the translation operator.
- ☐ You can use y in place of tr if you like:

```
$string =~ y/a-z/A-Z/;
```

Options for the Translation Operator

The translation operator supports three options, which are listed in Table 7.6.

The c option (c is for *complement*) translates all characters that are not specified. For example, the statement

```
$string =~ tr/\d/ /c;
```

replaces everything that is not a digit with a space.

Table 7.6. Options for the translation operator.

Option	Description
c	Translate all characters not specified
d	Delete all specified characters
s	Replace multiple identical output characters with a single character

The d option deletes every specified character:

```
$string =~ tr/\t //d;
```

This deletes all the tabs and spaces from $string.

The s option (for *squeeze*) checks the output from the translation. If two or more consecutive characters translate to the same output character, only one output character is actually used. For example, the following replaces everything that is not a digit and outputs only one space between digits:

```
$string =~ tr/0-9/ /cs;
```

Listing 7.14 is a simple example of a program that uses some of these translation options. It reads a number from the standard input file and gets rid of every input character that is not actually a digit.

7

Listing 7.14. A program that ensures that a string consists of nothing but digits.

```
1:   # p7_14.pl
2:
3:   $string = <STDIN>;
4:   $string =~ tr/0-9//cd;
5:   print ("$string\n");
```

OUTPUT

```
C:\> perl p7_14.pl
The number 45 appears in this string.
45
C:\>
```

ANALYSIS   Line 4 of this program performs the translation. The d option indicates that the translated characters are to be deleted, and the c option indicates that every character not in the list is to be deleted. Therefore, this translation deletes every character in the string that is not a digit. Note that the trailing newline character is not a digit, so it is one of the characters deleted.

Extended Pattern-Matching

Perl 5, as well as Perl 5 for Win32, provides some additional pattern-matching capabilities not found in Perl 4.

SYNTAX

Extended pattern-matching capabilities employ the following syntax:

(?<c>pattern)

<c> is a single character representing the extended pattern-matching capability being used, and pattern is the pattern or subpattern to be affected.

The following extended pattern-matching capabilities are supported by Perl 5 for Win32:

☐ Parenthesizing subpatterns without saving them in memory

☐ Embedding options in patterns

☐ Positive and negative look-ahead conditions

☐ Comments

Parenthesizing Without Saving in Memory

In Perl for Win32, when a subpattern is enclosed in parentheses, the subpattern is also stored in memory. If you want to enclose a subpattern in parentheses without storing it in memory, use the ?: extended pattern-matching feature. For example, consider this pattern:

```
/(?:a|b|c)(d|e)f\1/
```

This matches the following:

☐ One of a, b, or c

☐ One of d or e

☐ f

☐ Whichever of d or e was matched earlier

Here, \1 matches either d or e, because the subpattern a|b|c was not stored in memory. Compare this with the following:

```
/(a|b|c)(d|e)f\1/
```

Here, the subpattern a|b|c is stored in memory, and one of a, b, or c is matched by \1.

Embedding Pattern Options

Perl 5 for Win32 provides a way of specifying a pattern-matching option within the pattern itself. For example, the following patterns are equivalent:

```
/[a-z]+/i
/(?i)[a-z]+/
```

In both cases, the pattern matches one or more alphabetic characters; the i option indicates that case is to be ignored when matching.

SYNTAX

The syntax for embedded pattern options is

```
(?option)
```

where option is one of the options shown in Table 7.7.

Table 7.7. Options for embedded patterns.

Option	Description
i	Ignore case in pattern
m	Treat pattern as multiple lines
s	Treat pattern as single line
x	Ignore white space in pattern

The g and o options are not supported as embedded pattern options.

Embedded pattern options give you more flexibility when you are matching patterns. For example:

7

```
$pattern1 = "[a-z0-9]+";
$pattern2 = "(?i)[a-z]+";
if ($string =~ /$pattern1|$pattern2/) {
        ...
}
```

Here, the i option is specified for some, but not all, of a pattern. (This pattern matches either any collection of lowercase letters mixed with digits, or any collection of letters.)

Positive and Negative Look-Ahead

Perl 5 for Win32 enables you to use the ?= feature to define a boundary condition that must be matched in order for the pattern to match. For example, the following pattern matches abc only if it is followed by def:

```
/abc(?=def)/
```

This is known as a positive look-ahead, zero width, condition.

 NOTE

> The positive look-ahead condition is not part of the pattern matched. For example, consider these statements:
>
> ```
> $string = "25abc8";
> $string =~ /abc(?=[0-9])/;
> $matched = $&;
> ```
>
> Here, as always, $& contains the matched pattern, which in this case is abc, **not** abc8.

Similarly, the ?! feature defines a *negative look-ahead condition*, which is a boundary condition that must not be present if the pattern is to match. For example, the pattern /abc(?!def)/ matches any occurrence of abc unless it is followed by def.

Pattern Comments

Perl 5 for Win32 enables you to add comments to a pattern using the ?# feature. For example:

```
if ($string =~ /(?i)[a-z]{2,3}(?# match two or three alphabetic characters)/ {
        ...
}
```

Adding comments makes it easier to follow complicated patterns.

Summary

Perl enables you to search for sequences of characters using patterns. If a pattern is found in a string, the pattern is said to be matched.

Patterns often are used in conjunction with the operators `=~` and `!~` that bind strings for testing pattern match.

Special-pattern characters enable you to search for a string that meets one of a variety of conditions:

☐ The `+` character matches one or more occurrences of a character.

☐ The `*` character matches zero or more occurrences of a character.

☐ The `[]` characters enclose a set of characters, any one of which matches.

☐ The `?` character matches zero or one occurrence of a character.

☐ The `^` and `$` characters match the beginning and end of a line, respectively. The `\b` and `\B` characters match a word boundary or somewhere other than a word boundary, respectively.

☐ The `{}` characters specify the number of occurrences of a character.

☐ The `|` character specifies alternatives, either of which match.

To give a special character its natural meaning in a pattern, precede it with a backslash (`\`).

Enclosing a part of a pattern in parentheses stores the matched subpattern in memory; this stored subpattern can be recalled using the character sequence `\n`, and stored in a scalar variable using the built-in scalar variable `$n`. The built-in scalar variable `$&` stores the entire matched pattern.

You can substitute for scalar-variable names in patterns, specify different pattern delimiters, or supply options that match every possible pattern, ignore case, or perform scalar-variable substitution only once.

The substitution operator, `s`, enables you to replace a matched pattern with a specified string. Options to the substitution operator enable you to replace every matched pattern, ignore case, treat the replacing string as an expression, or perform scalar-variable substitution only once.

The translation operator, `tr`, enables you to translate one set of characters into another set. Options exist that enable you to perform translation on everything not in the list, to delete characters in the list, or to ignore multiple identical output characters.

7

Perl 5 for Win32 provides extended pattern-matching capabilities not provided in Perl 4. To use one of these extended pattern features on a subpattern, put (? at the beginning of the subpattern and) at the end of the subpattern.

Q&A

Q **How many subpatterns can be stored in memory using \1, \2, and so on?**

A Basically, as many as you like. After you store more than nine patterns, you can retrieve the later patterns using two-digit numbers preceded by a backslash, such as \10.

Q **Why does pattern-memory variable numbering start with 1, whereas subscript numbering starts with 0?**

A Subscript numbering starts with 0 to remain compatible with the C programming language. There is no such thing as pattern memory in C, so there is no need to be compatible with it.

Q **What happens when the replacement string in the translate command is left out, as in tr/abc//?**

A If the replacement string is omitted, a copy of the first string is used. This means that

```
tr/abc//
```

does not do anything, because it is the same as

```
tr/abc/abc/
```

If the replacement string is omitted in the substitute command, as in

```
s/abc//
```

the pattern matched—in this case, abc—is deleted.

Q **Why does Perl use both \1 and $1 to store pattern memory?**

A To enable you to distinguish between a subpattern matched in the current pattern (which is stored in \1) and a subpattern matched in the previous statement (which is stored in $1).

Workshop

The Workshop provides quiz questions to help you solidify your understanding of the material covered and exercises to give you experience in using what you've learned. Try to understand the quiz and exercise answers before you go on to tomorrow's lesson. You can find the answers in Appendix B, "Answers."

Quiz

1. What do the following patterns match?

   a. `/a|bc*/`

   b. `/[\d]{1,3}/`

   c. `/\bc[aou]t\b/`

   d. `/(xy+z)\.\1/`

   e. `/^$/`

2. Write patterns that match the following:

   a. Five or more lowercase letters (a–z).

   b. Either the number 1 or the string one.

   c. A string of digits optionally containing a decimal point.

   d. Any letter, followed by any vowel, followed by the same letter again.

   e. One or more + characters.

3. Suppose the variable $var has the value abc123. Indicate whether the following conditional expressions return true or false:

   a. `$var =~ /./`

   b. `$var =~ /[A-Z]*/`

   c. `$var =~ /\w{4-6}/`

   d. `$var =~ /(\d)2(\1)/`

   e. `$var =~ /abc$/`

   f. `$var =~ /1234?/`

4. Suppose the variable $var has the value abc123abc. What is the value of $var after the following substitutions?

   a. `$var =~ s/abc/def/;`

   b. `$var =~ s/[a-z]+/X/g;`

   c. `$var =~ s/B/W/i;`

   d. `$var =~ s/(.)\d.*\1/d/;`

   e. `$var =~ s/(\d+)/$1*2/e;`

5. Suppose the variable $var has the value abc123abc. What is the value of $var after the following translations?

   a. `$var =~ tr/a-z/A-Z/;`

   b. `$var =~ tr/123/456/;`

7

c. `$var =~ tr/231/564/;`

d. `$var =~ tr/123/ /s;`

e. `$var =~ tr/123//cd;`

Exercises

1. Write a program that reads all the input from the standard input file, converts all the common vowels (`aeiou`) to uppercase, and prints the result on the standard output file.

2. Write a program that counts the number of times each digit appears in the standard input file. Print the total for each digit and the sum of all the totals.

3. Write a program that reverses the order of the first three words of each input line (from the standard input file) using the substitution operator. Leave the spacing unchanged, and print each resulting line.

4. Write a program that adds 1 to every number in the standard input file. Print the results.

5. **BUG BUSTER:** What is wrong with the following program?

```
# Exercise 5 - bug buster:

while ($line = <STDIN>) {
        # put quotes around each line of input
        $line =~ /^.*$/"\1"/;
        print ($line);
}
```

6. **BUG BUSTER:** What is wrong with the following program?

```
# Exercise 6 - bug buster:

while ($line = <STDIN>) {
        if ($line =~ /[\d]*/) {
                print ("This line contains the digits '$&'\n");
        }

}
```

In Review

By now, you know enough about programming in Perl 5 for Win32 to write programs that perform many useful tasks. The program in Listing R1.1, which takes a number and prints out its English equivalent, illustrates some of the concepts you've learned during your first week.

1

2

3

4

5

6

7

TYPE **Listing R1.1. Printing the English equivalent of numeric input.**

```perl
 1: # pwk01_1.pl
 2:
 3: # define the string used in printing
 4: @digitword = ("", "one", "two", "three", "four", "five",
 5:     "six", "seven", "eight", "nine");
 6: @digit10word = ("", "ten", "twenty", "thirty", "forty",
 7:     "fifty", "sixty", "seventy", "eighty", "ninety" );
 8: @teenword = ("ten", "eleven", "twelve", "thirteen", "fourteen",
 9:     "fifteen", "sixteen", "seventeen", "eighteen", "nineteen");
10: @groupword = ("", "thousand", "million", "billion", "trillion",
11:     "quadrillion", "quintillion", "sextillion", "septillion",
12:     "octillion", "novillion", "decillion" );
13:
14: # read a line of input and remove all blanks, commas, and tabs;
15: # complain about anything else
16: $inputline = <STDIN>;
17: chop ($inputline);
18: $inputline =~ s/[, \t]+//g;
19: if ($inputline =~ /[^\d]/ ) {
20:     die ("Input must be a number.\n");
21: }
22:
23: #remove leading zeroes
24: $inputline =~ s/^0+//;
25: $inputline =~ s/^$/0/;   #put one back if they're all zero
26:
27: #split into digits: $grouping contains the number of groups
28: # of digits, and $oddlot contains the number of digits in the
29: # first group, which may be only 1 or 2 (e.g., the 1 in 1,000)
30: @digits = split (//, $inputline);
31: if (@digits > 36) {
32:     die ("Number too large for program to handle.\n");
33: }
34: $oddlot = @digits % 3;
35: $grouping = (@digits - 1) /3;
36:
37: # this loop iterates once for each grouping
38: $count = 0;
39: while ($grouping >= 0) {
40:     if ($oddlot == 2) {
41:         $digit1 = 0;
42:         $digit2 = $digits[0];
43:         $digit3 = $digits[1];
44:         $count += 2;
45:     } elsif ($oddlot == 1) {
46:         $digit1 = 0;
47:         $digit2 = 0;
48:         $digit3 = $digits[0];
49:         $count += 1;
50:     } else {            # regular group of three digits
51:         $digit1 = $digits[$count];
52:         $digit2 = $digits[$count+1];
53:         $digit3 = $digits[$count+2];
54:         $count += 3;
```

```
55:        }
56:        $oddlot = 0;
57:        if ($digit1 != 0) {
58:            print ("$digitword[$digit1] hundred ");
59:        }
60:        if (($digit1 != 0 || ($grouping == 0 && $count > 3)) &&
61:            ($digit2 != 0 || $digit3 != 0)) {
62:            print ("and ");
63:        }
64:        if ($digit2 == 1) {
65:            print ("$teenword[$digit3] ");
66:        } elsif ($digit2 != 0 && $digit3 != 0) {
67:            print ("$digit10word[$digit2]-$digitword[$digit3] ");
68:        } elsif ($digit2 != 0 || $digit3 != 0) {
69:            print ("$digit10word[$digit2]$digitword[$digit3] ");
70:        }
71:        if ($digit1 != 0 || $digit2 != 0 || $digit3 != 0) {
72:            print ("$groupword[$grouping]\n");
73:        } elsif ($count <= 3 && $grouping == 0) {
74:            print ("zero\n");
75:        }
76:        $grouping --;
77: }
```

OUTPUT

```
C:\> perl pwk01_1.pl
11,683
eleven thousand
six hundred and eighty-three
C:\>
```

ANALYSIS
This program reads in a number up to 36 digits long and points out its English equivalent, using one line for each group of three digits.

Lines 4–12 define array variables whose lists are the possible words that can be in a number. The variable @digitword lists the digits; @digits10word lists the words that indicate multiples of 10; @teenword lists the words that represent the values from 11 to 19; and @groupword lists the names of each group of digits. Note that some of these lists have an empty first element; this ensures that the array subscripts refer to the correct value. (For example, without the empty word at the beginning of @digitword, $digitword[5] would refer to four, not five.)

Lines 14–21 read the input and check whether it is valid. Valid numbers consist of digits optionally separated by spaces, tabs, or commas. The substitution operator in line 18 removes these valid separations; the conditional expression in line 19 checks whether any invalid separators exist.

If the program reaches line 24, the input number is valid. Line 24 gets rid of any leading zeros (to ensure that, for example, 000071 is converted to 71). If a number consists entirely of zeros, line 24 converts $inputline to the empty string; line 25 tests for this empty string and adds a zero if necessary.

Lines 30–35 split the number into individual digits and create a list of these digits. This list is assigned to the array variable `@digits`. Line 34 determines whether the first group of digits contains fewer than three digits; an example of this is the number 45,771, whose first group of digits consists of only two digits. The scalar variable `$oddlot` is assigned 0 if the first group of digits contains all three digits.

Line 35 calculates the number of groups of digits (including the initial odd lot). This determines the number of times that the upcoming printing loop is to be iterated.

Lines 38–39 actually print the English value for this number. Each group of three digits is printed on its own line. The scalar variable `$count` contains the number of digits printed so far and is used as a subscript for the array variable `@digits`.

To actually print the English value corresponding to a group of three digits, this loop first executes lines 40–57, which assign the values of the digits in the group to three scalar variables: `$digit1`, `$digit2`, and `$digit3`. If the group being handled is the first group, lines 40 and 46 check whether the group is an odd lot. For example, if the first group contains only two digits, the condition in line 40 becomes true, and the variable `$digit1`, which represents the first digit of the group, is assigned 0. Using `$digit1`, `$digit2`, and `$digit3` reduces the complexity of the program because no code following line 57 has to check for the value of `$oddlot`.

The number of digits actually handled is added to the scalar variable `$count` at this point.

Line 58 assigns 0 to `$oddlot`. Subsequent groups of digits always contain three digits.

Lines 59–77 print the English value associated with this particular group of digits as follows:

1. Lines 59–61 print the value of the hundreds place in this group (the first of the three digits).

2. Lines 62–64 check whether the word and needs to appear here. The word and is required in the following cases:

   ☐ `$digit1` is nonzero and one of the other digits is nonzero (as in three hundred and four)

   ☐ `$digit1` is zero, one of the other digits is nonzero, and this is the last group to be handled (as in the and four part of the number 11,004)

3. If the second digit is a 1 (as in 317), one of the "teen words" (such as eleven, twelve, and thirteen) must be used. Line 66 checks for this condition, and line 67 prints the appropriate word.

4. If both of the last digits are defined, they both must be printed, and a dash must separate them (as in forty-two). Line 69 prints this pair of words and the dash.

5. If only one of the last digits is defined, it is printed using line 71. (Note that line 71 actually specifies that both digits are printed; however, because only one is actually nonzero, it is the only one that appears. The digit that is zero appears in the output as the empty string because zero is equivalent to the empty string in Perl for Win32.)

6. Lines 73–74 print the word associated with this group of digits. For example, if this group is the second-to-the-last group of digits, the word `thousand` is printed.

7. Line 75 handles the special case of the number 0. In this case, the word `zero` is printed.

Once the English value for a particular group of digits is printed, the scalar variable `$grouping` has its value decreased by one, and the program continues with the next group of digits. If there are no more digits to print, the program terminates.

WEEK 2

At a Glance

By the end of Week 2, you'll have mastered many features of Perl 5 for Win32; you'll also have learned about many of the Perl built-in library functions. The following is a summary of what you'll learn in Week 2:

Day 8, "More Control Structures"
Day 9, "Using Subroutines"
Day 10, "Associative Arrays"
Day 11, "Formatting Your Output"
Day 12, "File-System, String, and Mathematical Functions"
Day 13, "Process, Scalar-Conversion, and List-Manipulation Functions"
Day 14, "Packages, Modules, and System Functions"

Day 8

More Control Structures

On Day 2, "Basic Operators and Control Flow," you learned about some of the simpler conditional statements in Perl 5 for Win32, including the following:

- [ ] The if statement, which defines statements that are executed only when a certain condition is true
- [ ] The if-else statement, which chooses between two alternatives
- [ ] The if-elsif-else statement, which chooses among multiple alternatives
- [ ] The unless statement, which defines statements that are executed unless a specified condition is true
- [ ] The while statement, which executes a group of statements while a specified condition is true
- [ ] The until statement, which executes a group of statements until a specified condition is true

Today's lesson talks about the other control structures in Perl 5 for Win32. These control structures give you a great deal of flexibility when you are determining the order of execution of your program statement.

Today you learn the following control structures:

- ☐ Single-line conditional statements
- ☐ The `for` statement
- ☐ The `foreach` statement
- ☐ The `do` statement
- ☐ The `last` statement
- ☐ The `next` statement
- ☐ The `redo` statement
- ☐ The `continue` statement
- ☐ Labeled blocks
- ☐ The `goto` statement

Using Single-Line Conditional Statements

On Day 2 you saw the `if` statement, which works as follows:

```
if ($var == 0) {
      print ("This is zero.\n");
}
```

If the statement block inside the `if` statement consists of only one statement, Perl enables you to write this in a more convenient way using a *single-line conditional statement*. This is a conditional statement whose statement block contains only one line of code.

The following single-line conditional statement is identical to the `if` statement defined previously:

```
print ("This is zero.\n") if ($var == 0);
```

Single-line conditional statements also work with `unless`, `while`, and `until`:

```
print ("This is zero.\n") unless ($var != 0);
print ("Not zero yet.\n") while ($var- > 0);
print ("Not zero yet.\n") until ($var- == 0);
```

In all four cases, the syntax of the single-line conditional statement is the same.

The syntax for the single-line conditional statement is

```
statement keyword condexpr
```

Here, *statement* is any Perl statement. *keyword* is if, unless, while, or until. *condexpr* is the conditional expression that is evaluated.

statement is executed in the following cases:

- ☐ If *keyword* is if, statement is executed if *condexpr* is true.
- ☐ If *keyword* is unless, statement is executed unless *condexpr* is true.
- ☐ If *keyword* is while, statement is executed while *condexpr* is true.
- ☐ If *keyword* is until, statement is executed until *condexpr* is true.

To see how single-line conditional expressions can be useful, look at the following examples, starting with Listing 8.1. This is a simple program that copies one file to another. Single-line conditional statements are used to check whether the files opened successfully, and another single-line conditional statement actually copies the file.

Listing 8.1. A program that uses single-line conditional statements to copy one file to another.

```
1:  # p8_1.pl
2:
3:  die ("Can't open input\n") unless (open(INFILE, "infile"));
4:  die ("Can't open output\n") unless (open(OUTFILE, ">outfile"));
5:  print OUTFILE ($line) while ($line = <INFILE>);
6:  close (INFILE);
7:  close (OUTFILE);
```

There is no output; this program writes to a file.

As you can see, this program is clear and concise. Instead of using three lines to open a file and check it, as in

```
unless (open (INFILE, "infile")) {
        die ("Can't open input\n");
    }
```

you can now use just one:

```
die ("Can't open input\n") unless (open(INFILE, "infile"));
```

Line 3 opens the input file. If the open is not successful, the program terminates by calling die.

Line 4 is similar to line 3. It opens the output file and checks whether the file is really open; if the file is not open, the program terminates.

Line 5 actually copies the file. The conditional expression

```
$line = <INFILE>
```

reads a line from the file represented by the file variable INFILE and assigns it to $line. If the line is empty, the conditional expression is false, and the while statement stops executing. If the line is not empty, it is written to OUTFILE.

> **NOTE**
>
> The conditional expression in a single-line conditional statement is always executed first, even though it appears at the end of the statement. For example:
>
> ```
> print OUTFILE ($line) while ($line = <INFILE>);
> ```
>
> Here, the conditional expression that reads a line of input and assigns it to $line is always executed first. This means that print is not called until $line contains something to print. This also means that the call to print is never executed if INFILE is an empty file (which is what you want).
>
> Because single-line conditional expressions are "backward," be careful when you use them with anything more complicated than what you see here.

You can use the single-line conditional statement in conjunction with the autoincrement operator ++ to write a loop in a single line. For example, examine Listing 8.2, which prints the numbers from 1 to 5 using a single-line conditional statement.

Listing 8.2. A program that loops using a single-line conditional statement.

TYPE

```
1:  # p8_2.pl
2:
3:  $count = 0;
4:  print ("$count\n") while ($count++ < 5);
```

OUTPUT

```
C:\> perl p8_2.pl
1
2
3
4
5
C:\>
```

ANALYSIS When the Perl interpreter executes line 3, it first evaluates the conditional expression

```
$count++ < 5
```

8

Because the `++` appears after `$count`, 1 is added to the value of `$count` after the conditional expression is evaluated. This means that `$count` has the value 0, not 1, the first time the expression is evaluated. Similarly, `$count` has the value 1 the second time, 2 the third time, 3 the fourth time, and 4 the fifth time. In each of these five cases, the conditional expression evaluates to true, which means that the loop iterates five times.

After the conditional expression has been evaluated, the `++` operator adds 1 to the value of `$count`. This new value of `$count` is then printed. This means that when the loop is first executed, the call to `print` prints 1, even though the value of `$count` was 0 when the conditional expression was evaluated.

Problems with Single-Line Conditional Statements

Although single-line conditional statements that contain loops are useful, there are problems. Consider Listing 8.2, which you've just seen. It is easy to forget that `$count` has to be initialized to one less than the first value you want to use in the loop, and that the conditional expression has to use the `<` operator, not the `<=` operator.

For example, take a look at the following:

```
$count = 1;
print ("$count\n") while ($count++ < 5);
```

Here, you have to look closely to see that the first value printed is 2, not 1.

Here is another loop containing a mistake:

```
$count = 0;
print ("$count\n") while ($count++ <= 5);
```

This loop iterates six times, not five; the sixth time through the loop, `$count` has the value 5 when the conditional expression is evaluated. The expression evaluates to true, `$count` is incremented to 6, and `print` therefore prints the value 6.

Here is a related but slightly more subtle problem:

```
$count = 0;
print ("$count\n") while ($count++ < 5);
print ("The total number of iterations is $count.\n");
```

This loop iterates five times, which is what you want. However, after the conditional expression is evaluated for the final time, the value of `$count` becomes 6, as follows:

☐ Before the conditional expression is evaluated, `$count` has the value 5.

☐ Because the value of `$count` is not less than 5, the conditional expression evaluates to false, which terminates the loop.

☐ After the conditional expression is evaluated, the `++` operator adds one to `$count`, giving it the value 6.

This means that the final `print` statement prints the following, which is probably not what you want:

```
The total number of iterations is 6.
```

Do	**Don't**

> **DO** use the `for` statement as a convenient way to write a concise, compact loop. It is discussed in the next section.
>
> **DON'T** use the `++` operator to produce a loop in a single-line conditional statement unless it's absolutely necessary. It's just too easy to go wrong with it.

Looping Using the `for` Statement

Many of the programs that you've seen so far use the `while` statement to create a program loop. Here is a simple example:

```
$count = 1;
while ($count <= 5) {
        # statements inside the loop go here
        $count++;
}
```

This loop contains three items that control it:

- ☐ A statement that sets the initial value of the loop. In this loop, the scalar variable `$count` is used to control the number of iterations of the loop, and the statement

  ```
  $count = 1;
  ```

  sets the initial value of `$count` to 1. Statements such as this are called *loop initializers*.

- ☐ A conditional expression that checks to see whether to continue iterating the loop. In this case, the conditional expression

  ```
  $count <= 5
  ```

  is evaluated; if it is false, the loop is terminated.

- ☐ A statement that changes the value of the variable that is tested in the conditional expression. In this loop, the statement

  ```
  count++;
  ```

  adds 1 to the value of `$count`, which is the scalar variable being tested in the conditional expression. Statements such as this are called *loop iterators*.

Perl enables you to put the three components that control a loop together on a single line using a `for` statement. For example, the following statement is equivalent to the loop you've been looking at:

```
for ($count=1; $count <= 5; $count++) {
        # statements inside the loop go here
}
```

Here, the three controlling components—the loop initializer, the conditional expression, and the loop iterator—appear together and are separated by semicolons.

The syntax of the `for` statement is

```
for (expr1; expr2; expr3) {
        statement_block
}
```

expr1 is the loop initializer. It is evaluated only once, before the start of the loop.

expr2 is the conditional expression that terminates the loop. The conditional expression in *expr2* behaves just like the ones in `while` and `if` statements. If its value is 0 (false), the loop is terminated, and if its value is nonzero, the loop is executed.

statement_block is the collection of statements that is executed if (and when) *expr2* has a nonzero value.

expr3 is executed once per iteration of the loop and is executed after the last statement in *statement_block* is executed.

Note	If you know the C programming language, the `for` statement will be familiar to you. The `for` statement in Perl is syntactically identical to the `for` statement in C.

Listing 8.3 is a program based on the example `for` statement you've just seen.

Listing 8.3. A program that prints the numbers from 1 to 5 using the `for` statement.

```
1:  # p8_3.pl
2:
3:  for ($count=1; $count <= 5; $count++) {
4:          print ("$count\n");
5:  }
```

OUTPUT

```
C:\> perl p8_3.pl
1
2
3
4
5
C:\>
```

ANALYSIS

Line 3 of the program is the start of the `for` statement. The first expression defined in the `for` statement, `$count = 1`, is the loop initializer; it is executed before the loop is iterated.

The second expression defined in the `for` statement, `$count <= 5`, tests whether to continue iterating the loop.

The third expression defined in the `for` statement, `$count++`, is evaluated after the last statement in the loop, line 4, is executed.

As you can see from the output, the loop is iterated five times.

TIP

Use the `for` statement instead of `while` or `until` whenever possible; when you use the `for` statement, it is easier to avoid infinite loops.

For example, when you use a `while` statement, it's easy to forget to iterate the loop. The following is an example:

```
$count = 1;

while ($count <= 5) {
print ("$count\n");
}
```

The equivalent statement using `for` is

```
for ($count = 1; $count <= 5; ) {
print ("$count\n");
}
```

When you use the `for` statement, it is easier to notice that the loop iterator is missing.

Using the Comma Operator in a `for` Statement

Some loops need to perform more than one action before iterating. For example, consider the following loop, which reads four lines of input from the standard input file and prints three of them:

```
$line = <STDIN>;
$count = 1;
```

```
while ($count <= 3) {
        print ($line);
        $line = <STDIN>;
        $count++;
}
```

This loop needs two loop initializers and two loop iterators: one of each for the variable $count, and one of each to read another line of input from STDIN.

At first glance, you might think that you can't write this loop using the for statement. However, you can use the comma operator to combine the two loop initializers and the two loop iterators into single expressions. Listing 8.4 does this.

TYPE **Listing 8.4. A program that uses the for statement to read four input lines and write three of them.**

```
1: # p8_4.pl
2:
3: for ($line = <STDIN>, $count = 1; $count <= 3;
4:         $line = <STDIN>, $count++) {
5:         print ($line);
6: }
```

OUTPUT
```
C:\> perl p8_4.pl
This is my first line.
This is my first line.
This is my second line.
This is my second line.
This is my last line.
This is my last line.
This input line is not written out.
C:\>
```

ANALYSIS The loop initializer in this for statement is the expression

```
$line = <STDIN>, $count = 1
```

The comma operator in this expression tells the Perl interpreter to evaluate the first half of the expression—the part to the left of the comma—and then evaluate the second half. The first half of this expression reads a line from the standard input file and assigns it to $line; the second half of the expression assigns 1 to $count.

The loop iterator also consists of two parts:

```
$line = <STDIN>, $count++
```

This expression reads a line from the standard input file and adds 1 to the variable keeping track of when to terminate the loop, which is $count.

Don't use the for statement if you have a large number of loop initializers or loop iterators, because statements that contain a large number of comma operators are difficult to read.

Looping Through a List: The `foreach` Statement

One common use of loops is to perform an operation on every element of a list stored in an array variable. For example, the following loop checks whether any element of the list stored in the array variable @words is the word the:

```
$count = 1;
while ($count <= @words) {
        if ($words[$count-1] eq "the") {
                print ("found the word 'the'\n");
        }
        $count++;
}
```

As you've seen, you can use the for statement to simplify this loop, as follows:

```
for ($count = 1; $count <= @words; $count++) {
        if ($words[$count-1] eq "the") {
                print ("found the word 'the'\n");
        }
}
```

Perl for Win32 provides an even simpler way to do the same thing, using the foreach statement. The following loop, which uses foreach, is identical to the preceding one:

```
foreach $word (@words) {
        if ($word eq "the") {
                print ("found the word 'the'\n");
        }
}
```

SYNTAX

The syntax for the foreach statement is

```
foreach localvar (listexpr) {
        statement_block;
}
```

Here, *listexpr* is any list or array variable, and *statement_block* is a collection of statements that is executed every time the loop iterates.

localvar is a scalar variable that is defined only for the duration of the foreach statement. The first time the loop is executed, *localvar* is assigned the value of the first element of the list in *listexpr*. Each subsequent time the loop is executed, *localvar* is assigned the value of the next element of *listexpr*.

8

Listing 8.5 shows how this works.

TYPE   **Listing 8.5. A demonstration of the `foreach` statement.**

```
1:   # p8_5.pl
2:
3:   @words = ("Here", "is", "a", "list.");
4:   foreach $word (@words) {
5:           print ("$word\n");
6:   }
```

OUTPUT
```
C:\> perl p8_5.pl
Here
is
a
list.
C:\>
```

ANALYSIS   The `foreach` statement in line 4 assigns a word from `@list` to the local variable `$word`. The first time the loop is executed, the value stored in `$word` is the string `Here`. The second time the loop is executed, the value stored in `$word` is `is`. Subsequent iterations assign `a` and `list.` to `$word`.

The loop defined by the `foreach` statement terminates after all of the words in the list have been assigned to `$word`.

NOTE   In Perl for Win32, the `for` statement and the `foreach` statement are actually synonymous. You can use `for` wherever `foreach` is expected, and vice versa.

The `foreach` Local Variable

Note that the scalar variable defined in the `foreach` statement is only defined for the duration of the loop. If a value is assigned to the scalar variable prior to the execution of the `foreach` statement, this value is restored after the `foreach` is executed. Listing 8.6 shows how this works.

TYPE

Listing 8.6. A program that uses the same name inside and outside a `foreach` statement.

```
1:  # p8_6.pl
2:
3:  $temp = 1;
4:  @list = ("This", "is", "a", "list", "of", "words");
5:  print ("Here are the words in the list: \n");
6:  foreach $temp (@list) {
7:          print ("$temp ");
8:  }
9:  print("\n");
10: print("The value of temp is now $temp\n");
```

OUTPUT

```
C:\> perl p8_6.pl
Here are the words in the list:
This is a list of words
The value of temp is now 1
C:\>
```

ANALYSIS   Line 3 assigns 1 to the scalar variable $temp.

The `foreach` statement that prints the words in the list is defined in lines 6–8. This statement assigns the elements of `@list` to `$temp`, one per iteration of the loop.

After the loop is terminated, the original value of `$temp` is restored, which is 1. This value is printed by line 10.

Variables (such as `$temp` in lines 6–8) that are only defined for part of a program are known as *local variables*; variables that are defined throughout a program are known as *global variables*. You'll see more examples of local variables on Day 9, "Using Subroutines."

TIP

It is not a good idea to use `$temp` the way it is used in Listing 8.6—namely, as both a local and a global variable. You might forget that the value of the global variable—in the case of `$temp`, the value 1—is overwritten by the value assigned in the `foreach` statement.

Conversely, you might forget that the value assigned to `$temp` in the `foreach` statement is lost when the `foreach` is finished.

It is better to define a new scalar-variable name for the local variable to avoid confusion.

8

Changing the Value of the Local Variable

Note that changing the value of the local variable inside a `foreach` statement also changes the value of the corresponding element of the list. For example:

```
@list = (1, 2, 3, 4, 5);
foreach $temp (@list) {
        if ($temp == 2) {
                $temp = 20;
        }
}
```

In this loop, when `$temp` is equal to 2, `$temp` is reset to 20. Therefore, the list stored in the array variable `@list` becomes (1, 20, 3, 4, 5).

Use this feature with caution, because it is not obvious that the value of `@list` has changed.

Using Returned Lists in the `foreach` Statement

So far, all of the examples of the `foreach` statement that you've seen have iterated using the contents of an array variable. For example, consider the following:

```
@list = ("This", "is", "a", "list");
foreach $temp (@list) {
        print ("$temp ");
}
```

This loop assigns `This` to `$temp` the first time through the loop, and then assigns `is`, `a`, and `list` to `$temp` on subsequent iterations.

You also can use list constants or the return values from functions in `foreach` statements. For example, the preceding statements can be written as follows:

```
foreach $temp ("This", "is", "a", "list") {
        print("$temp ");
}
```

As before, `$temp` is assigned `This`, `is`, `a`, and `list` in successive iterations of the `foreach` loop.

Listing 8.7 shows how you can use the return value from a function as a loop iterator.

TYPE **Listing 8.7. A program that prints out the words in a line in reverse-sorted order.**

```
1:  # p8_7.pl
2:
3:  $line = <STDIN>;
4:  $line =~ s/^\s+//;
5:  $line =~ s/\s+$//;
6:  foreach $word (reverse sort split(/[\t ]+/, $line)) {
7:          print ("$word ");
8:  }
9:  print ("\n");
```

OUTPUT
```
C:\> perl p8_7.pl
here is my test line
test my line is here
C:\>
```

ANALYSIS Before splitting the input line into words using `split`, this program first removes the leading and trailing white space. (If leading and trailing space is not removed, `split` creates an empty word.) Line 4 removes leading spaces and tabs from the input line. Line 5 removes any trailing spaces and tabs as well as the closing newline character.

Lines 6–8 contain the `foreach` loop. The list used in this loop is created as follows:

1. First, `split` breaks the input line into words. The list returned by `split` is (`"here"`, `"is"`, `"my"`, `"test"`, `"line"`).

2. The list returned by `split` is passed to the built-in function `sort`, which sorts the list. The list returned by `sort` is (`"here"`, `"is"`, `"line"`, `"my"`, `"test"`).

3. The list returned by `sort` is passed to another built-in function, `reverse`. This reverses the sorted list, producing the list (`"test"`, `"my"`, `"line"`, `"is"`, `"here"`).

4. Each element of the list returned by `reverse` is assigned, in turn, to the local scalar variable `$word`, starting with `"test"` and proceeding from there.

Line 7 prints the current value stored in `$word`. Each time the `foreach` loop iterates, a different value in the list is printed.

NOTE

The code fragment

```
foreach $word (reverse sort split(/[\t ]+/, $line))
```

shows why omitting parentheses when calling built-in functions can sometimes be useful. If all the parentheses are included, this becomes

```
foreach $word (reverse(sort(split(/[\t ]+/, $line))))
```

which is not as readable.

The do **Statement**

So far, all of the loops you've seen test the conditional expression before executing the loop. Perl for Win32 enables you to write loops that always execute at least once using the `do` statement.

8

SYNTAX

The syntax for the do statement is

```
do {
        statement_block
} while_or_until (condexpr);
```

As in other conditional statements, such as the if statement and the while statement, *statement_block* is a block of statements to be executed, and *condexpr* is a conditional expression.

while_or_until is either the while keyword or the until keyword. If you use while, *statement_block* loops while *condexpr* is true. For example:

```
do {
        $line = <STDIN>;
} while ($line ne "");
```

This loops while $line is non-empty (in other words, while the program has not reached the end of file).

If you use until, *statement_block* loops until *condexpr* is true. For example:

```
do {
        $line = <STDIN>;
} until ($line eq "");
```

This reads from the standard input file until $line is empty (again, until the end of file is reached).

Listing 8.8 is a simple example of a program that uses a do statement.

TYPE **Listing 8.8. A simple example of a do statement.**

```
1:  # p8_8.pl
2:
3:  $count = 1;
4:  do {
5:          print ("$count\n");
6:          $count++;
7:  } until ($count > 5);
```

OUTPUT
```
C:\> perl p8_8.pl
1
2
3
4
5
C:\>
```

ANALYSIS Lines 4–7 contain the do statement, which loops five times. Line 7 tests whether the counting variable $count is greater than 5.

NOTE

> The do statement can also be used to call subroutines. See Day 9 for more information.

Exiting a Loop Using the `last` Statement

Normally, you exit a loop by testing the conditional expression that is part of the loop. For example, if a loop is defined by the `while` statement, as in

```
while ($count <= 10) {
        # statements go here
}
```

the program exits the loop when the conditional expression at the top of the loop, `$count <= 10`, is false.

In the preceding case, the program can exit the loop only after executing all of the statements in it. Perl for Win32 enables you to define an exit point anywhere in the loop using a special `last` statement.

The syntax for the `last` statement is simple:

```
last;
```

To see how the `last` statement works, take a look at Listing 8.9, which adds a list of numbers supplied by means of the standard input file.

TYPE   **Listing 8.9. A program that exits using the `last` statement.**

```
 1: # p8_9.pl
 2:
 3: $total = 0;
 4: while (1) {
 5:         $line = <STDIN>;
 6:         if ($line eq "") {
 7:                 last;
 8:         }
 9:         chop ($line);
10:         @numbers = split (/[\t ]+/, $line);
11:         foreach $number (@numbers) {
12:                 if ($number =~ /[^0-9]/) {
13:                     print STDERR ("$number is not a number\n");
14:                 }
15:                 $total += $number;
16:         }
17: }
18: print ("The total is $total.\n");
```

OUTPUT

```
C:\> perl p8_9.pl
4 5 7
2 11 6
^Z
The total is 35.
C:\>
```

ANALYSIS
The loop that reads and adds numbers starts on line 4. The conditional expression at the top of this loop is the number 1. Because this is a nonzero number, this conditional expression always evaluates to true. Normally, this means that the `while` statement loops forever; however, because this program contains a `last` statement, the loop eventually terminates.

Line 6 checks whether or not the program has reached the end of the standard input file. To do this, it checks whether the line read from the standard input file, now stored in `$line`, is empty. (Recall that the Ctrl+D character, written here as `^D`, marks the standard input file as empty.)

If the line is empty, line 7, the `last` statement, is executed. This statement tells the Perl interpreter to terminate executing the loop and to continue with the first statement after the loop, which is line 18.

Lines 10–16 add the numbers on the input line to the total stored in the scalar variable `$total`. Line 10 breaks the line into individual numbers, and lines 11–16 add each number, in turn, to `$total`.

Line 12 checks whether each number actually consists of the digits 0–9. The pattern `[^0-9]` matches anything that is not a digit; if the program finds such a character, it flags the number as erroneous. (The program can produce empty words if leading or trailing spaces or tabs exist in the line; this is not a problem, because `[^0-9]` doesn't match an empty word.)

NOTE

You can use the `last` statement with a single-line conditional statement. For example,

```
last if ($count == 5);
```

terminates the loop if the value of `$count` is 5.

WARNING

You cannot use the `last` statement inside the `do` statement. Although the `do` statement behaves like the other control structures, it is actually implemented differently.

Using next to Start the Next Iteration of a Loop

In Perl for Win32, the `last` statement terminates the execution of a loop. To terminate a particular iteration of a loop, use the `next` statement.

Like `last`, the syntax for the `next` statement is simple:

```
next;
```

Listing 8.10 is an example that uses the `next` statement. It sums up the numbers from 1 to a user-specified upper limit and also produces a separate sum of the numbers divisible by 2.

Listing 8.10. A program that sums the numbers from 1 to a specified number and also sums the even numbers.

```
1:  # p8_10.pl
2:
3:  print ("Enter the last number in the sum:\n");
4:  $limit = <STDIN>;
5:  chop ($limit);
6:  $count = 1;
7:  $total = $eventotal = 0;
8:  for ($count = 1; $count <= $limit; $count++) {
9:          $total += $count;
10:         if ($count % 2 == 1) {
11:                 # start the next iteration if the number is odd
12:                 next;
13:         }
14:         $eventotal += $count;
15: }
16: print("The sum of the numbers 1 to $limit is $total\n");
17: print("The sum of the even numbers is $eventotal\n");
```

OUTPUT

```
C:\> perl p8_10.pl
Enter the last number in the sum:
7
The sum of the numbers 1 to 7 is 28
The sum of the even numbers is 12
C:\>
```

ANALYSIS   The loop in lines 8–15 adds the numbers together. The start of the `for` statement, in line 8, loops five times; the counter variable, `$count`, is assigned the values 1, 2, 3, 4, and 5 in successive iterations.

Line 9 adds to the total of all the numbers. This statement is always executed.

Line 10 tests whether the current number—the current value of `$count`—is even or odd. If `$count` is even, the conditional expression

```
$count % 2 == 1
```

is false, and program execution continues with line 14. If the current value of `$count` is odd, the Perl interpreter executes line 12, the `next` statement. This statement tells the Perl interpreter to start the next iteration of the loop.

Note that the loop iterator in the `for` statement, `$count++`, is still executed, even though the `next` statement skips over part of the loop. This ensures that the program does not go into an infinite loop.

Because the `next` statement is executed when the value of `$count` is odd, line 14 is skipped in this case. This means that the value of `$count` is added only when it is even.

WARNING

Be careful when you use `next` in a `while` or `until` loop. The following example goes into an infinite loop:

```
$count = 0;
while ($count <= 10) {
        if ($count == 5) {
                next;
        }
        $count++;
}
```

When `$count` is 5, the program tells Perl to start the next iteration of the loop. However, the value of `$count` is not changed, which means that the expression `$count == 5` is still true.

To get rid of this problem, you need to increment `$count` before using `next`, as in the following:

```
$count = 0;
while ($count <= 10) {
        if ($count == 5) {
                $count++;
                next;
        }
        $count++;
}
```

This, by the way, is why many programming purists dislike statements such as `next` and `last` because it's too easy to lose track of where you are and what needs to be updated.

The next statement enables you to check for and ignore unusual conditions when reading input. For example, Listing 8.11 counts the number of words in the input read from the standard input file. It uses the next statement to skip blank lines.

Listing 8.11. A word-counting program that uses the next statement.

TYPE

```
1:  # p8_11.pl
2:
3:  $total = 0;
4:  while ($line = <STDIN>) {
5:          $line =~ s/^[\t ]*//;
6:          $line =~ s/[\t ]*\n$//;
7:          next if ($line eq "");
8:          @words = split(/[\t ]+/, $line);
9:          $total += @words;
10: }
11: print ("The total number of words is $total\n");
```

OUTPUT

```
C:\> perl p8_11.pl
 Here is my test input.

It contains some words.
^z
The total number of words is 9
C:\>
```

ANALYSIS   After line 4 has read a line of input and checked that it is not empty (which means that the end of file has not been reached), the program then gets rid of leading spaces and tabs (line 5) and trailing spaces, tabs, and the trailing newline (line 6). If a line is blank, lines 5 and 6 turn it into the empty string, for which line 7 tests.

Line 7 contains the next statement as part of a single-line conditional statement. If the line is now empty, the next statement tells the program to go to the beginning of the loop and read in the next line of input.

WARNING

> You cannot use the next statement inside the do statement. Although the do statement behaves like the other control structures, it is actually implemented differently.

8

The redo **Statement**

Perl for Win32 enables you to tell the Perl interpreter to restart an iteration of a loop using the redo statement.

SYNTAX

Like last and next, the syntax for the redo statement is simple:

```
redo;
```

For an example, look at Listing 8.12, which counts the number of words in three non-blank input lines.

TYPE

Listing 8.12. A word-counting program that uses the redo statement.

```
1:  # p8_12.pl
2:
3:  $total = 0;
4:  for ($count = 1; $count <= 3; $count++) {
5:          $line = <STDIN>;
6:          last if ($line eq "");
7:          $line =~ s/^[\t ]*//;
8:          $line =~ s/[\t ]*\n$//;
9:          redo if ($line eq "");
10:         @words = split(/[\t ]/, $line);
11:         $total += @words;
12: }
13: print ("The total number of words is $total\n");
```

OUTPUT

```
C:\> perl p8_12.pl
 Here is my test input.

It contains some words.
^z
The total number of words is 9
C:\>
```

ANALYSIS Line 5 reads a line of input from the standard input file. If this line is empty, the conditional expression in line 6 is true, and the last statement exits the loop. (This ensures that the program behaves properly when there are less than three lines of input.)

Line 7 removes the leading blanks and tabs from this line of input, and line 8 removes the trailing white space. If the resulting line is now empty, the line must originally have been blank. Because this program does not want to include a blank line as one of the three lines in which to count words, line 9 invokes the redo statement, which tells the program to start this loop over. The program returns to line 4, the for statement, but does not increment the value of $count.

WARNING

> You cannot use the redo statement inside the do statement. Although the do statement behaves like the other control structures, it is actually implemented differently.

Note that the redo statement is not recommended because it is too easy to lose track of how many times a program goes through a loop. For example, in Listing 8.12, a quick glance at the for statement in line 4 seems to indicate that the program only loops three times; however, the redo statement might change that.

Listing 8.13 shows an alternate way to solve this problem.

TYPE

Listing 8.13. A program that counts the words in three non-blank lines of input without using the redo statement.

```
1:  # p8_13.pl
2:
3:  $nonblanklines = 0;
4:  while (1) {
5:          $line = <STDIN>;
6:          last if ($line eq "");
7:          $line =~ s/^[\t ]*//;
8:          $line =~ s/[\t ]*\n$//;
9:          if ($line ne "") {
10:                 $nonblanklines += 1;
11:                 @words = split(/[\t ]+/, $line);
12:                 $total += @words;
13:         }
14:         last if ($nonblanklines == 3);
15: };
16: print ("The total number of words is $total\n");
```

OUTPUT

```
C:\> perl p8_13.pl
 Here is my test input.

It contains some words.
^z
The total number of words is 9.
C:\>
```

ANALYSIS This program is identical to the previous one, but it is much easier to understand. It uses a more meaningful variable name—$nonblanklines—which implies that blank lines are a special case.

As in Listing 8.12, if the line is a blank line, lines 7 and 8 turn it into an empty line by removing all white space. When this happens, the condition in line 10 fails, and $nonblanklines is not incremented.

Using Labeled Blocks for Multilevel Jumps

As you've seen, the last, next, and redo statements enable you to exit a loop from anywhere inside its statement block, as follows:

```
while (1) {
        $line = <STDIN>;
        last if ($line eq "");
}
```

If the loop is inside another loop, the last, next, and redo statements quit the inner loop only. Look at this example:

```
while ($line1 = <FILE1>) {
        while ($line2 - <FILE2>) {
                last if ($line2 eq "") {
        }
}
```

Here, the last statement only quits the inner while loop. The outer while loop, which reads from the file represented by FILE1, continues executing.

To quit from more than one loop at once, do the following:

1. Assign a label to the outer loop (the one from which you want to quit).
2. When you use last, next, or redo, specify the label you just assigned.

Listing 8.14 shows an example of a last statement that specifies a label.

TYPE **Listing 8.14. A program that uses a label.**

```
1:  # p8_14.pl
2:
3:  $total = 0;
4:  $firstcounter = 0;
5:  DONE: while ($firstcounter < 10) {
6:          $secondcounter = 1;
7:          while ($secondcounter <= 10) {
```

continues

Listing 8.14. continued

```
8:                    $total++;
9:                    if ($firstcounter == 4 && $secondcounter == 7) {
10:                           last DONE;
11:                    }
12:                    $secondcounter++;
13:            }
14:         $firstcounter++;
15: }
16: print ("$total\n");
```

OUTPUT
```
C:\> perl p8_14.pl
47
C:\>
```

ANALYSIS
The outer while loop starting in line 5 has the label DONE assigned to it. This label consists of an alphabetic character followed by one or more alphanumeric characters or underscores. The colon (:) character following the label indicates that the label is assigned to the following statement (in this case, the while statement).

When the conditional expression in line 9 is true, line 10 is executed. This statement tells the Perl interpreter to jump out of the loop labeled DONE and continue execution with the first statement after this loop. (By the way, this code fragment is just a rather complicated way of assigning 47 to $total.)

WARNING

Make sure that you do not use a label that has another meaning in Perl for Win32. For example, the statement

```
if: while ($x == 0) {      # this is an error in Perl
}
```

is flagged as erroneous, because the Perl interpreter doesn't realize that the if is not the start of an if statement.

You can avoid this problem by using uppercase letters for label names (such as DONE).

```
FILE1: while ($line = <FILE1>) {
...
}
```

The Perl interpreter has no problem distinguishing the label FILE1 from the file variable FILE1, because it is always possible to determine which is which from the context.

8

Using next **and** redo **with Labels**

You can use next and redo with labels as well, as shown in the following example:

```
next LABEL;
redo LABEL;
```

The next statement indicates that the next iteration of the loop labeled LABEL is to be executed. The redo statement indicates that the current iteration of the loop labeled LABEL is to be restarted.

The continue **Block**

In a for statement, the expression following the second semicolon is executed each time the end of the loop is reached or whenever a next statement is executed. For example:

```
for ($i = 1; $i <= 10; $i++) {
        print ("$i\n");
}
```

In this example, the expression $i++, which adds 1 to $i, is executed after the print function is called.

Similarly, you can define statements that are to be executed whenever the end of a while loop or an until loop is reached. To carry out this task, specify a continue statement after the loop:

```
$i = 1;
while ($i <= 10) {
        print ("$i\n");
}
continue {
        $i++;
}
```

A continue statement must be followed by a statement block, which is a collection of zero or more statements enclosed in brace characters. This statement block contains the statements to be executed at the bottom of each loop. In this example, the statement

```
$i++;
```

is executed after each call to print. This while loop therefore behaves like the for loop you've just seen.

The continue statement is executed even if a pass through the loop is prematurely ended by a next statement. It is not executed, however, if the loop is terminated by a last statement.

TIP
> Usually, it is better to use a `for` statement than to use `continue` with a `while` or an `until` statement, because the `for` statement is easier to follow.

The `goto` **Statement**

For the sake of completeness, Perl for Win32 provides a `goto` statement.

The syntax of the `goto` statement is

```
goto label;
```

label is a label associated with a statement, as defined in the earlier section, "Using Labeled Blocks for Multilevel Jumps." The statement to which *label* is assigned cannot be in the middle of a `do` statement or inside a subroutine. (You'll learn about subroutines on Day 9.)

Listing 8.15 is an example of a simple program that uses `goto`.

TYPE **Listing 8.15. A program that uses the `goto` statement.**

```
1:  # p8_15.pl
2:
3:  NEXTLINE: $line = <STDIN>;
4:  if ($line ne "") {
5:          print ($line);
6:          goto NEXTLINE;
7:  }
```

OUTPUT
```
C:\> perl p8_15.pl
Here is a line of input.
Here is a line of input.
^z
C:\>
```

ANALYSIS This program just reads and writes lines of input until the standard input file is exhausted. If the line read into `$line` is not empty, line 6 tells the Perl interpreter to jump back to the line to which the `NEXTLINE` label is assigned, which is line 3.

Note that lines 3–7 are equivalent to the following statement:

```
print ($line) while ($line = <STDIN>);
```

TIP

There is almost never any need to use the `goto` statement. In fact, using `goto` often makes it more difficult to follow the logic of the program. For this reason, using `goto` is not recommended.

Summary

Today you learned about the more complex control structures supported in Perl for Win32.

Single-line conditional statements enable you to put a conditional expression on the same line as the statement to be executed if the condition is satisfied. This enables you to write more concise programs.

The `for` statement enables you to put the loop initializer, the loop iterator, and the conditional expression together on the same line. This makes it more difficult to write code that goes into an infinite loop.

The `foreach` statement enables a program to loop based on the contents of a list. When the loop is first executed, the first element in the list is assigned to a local scalar variable that is only defined for the duration of the loop. Subsequent iterations of the loop assign subsequent elements of the list to this local scalar variable.

The `do` statement enables you to write a loop that executes at least once. Its terminating conditional expression appears at the bottom of the loop, not the top.

The `last` statement tells the Perl interpreter to exit the loop and continue execution with the first statement after the loop. The `next` statement tells the Perl interpreter to skip the rest of this iteration of a loop and start with the next one. The `redo` statement tells the Perl interpreter to restart this iteration of a loop. `last`, `next`, and `redo` cannot be used with the `do` statement.

You can assign a label to a statement, which enables you to use `last`, `next`, and `redo` to exit or restart an outer loop from inside an inner loop.

The `continue` statement enables you to define code to be executed each time a loop iterates.

The `goto` statement enables you to jump to any labeled statement in your program.

Q&A

Q Which control structure is the best one to use as a loop?

A It depends on what you want to do. Consider these:

☐ The `foreach` structure is the best way to perform operations on every element of a list.

□ The `for` statement is the best way to perform an operation a set number of times.

□ The `while` statement is the best way to perform a loop until a particular condition occurs.

□ The `do` statement is useful if you want to perform a loop at least once. (However, it is not as useful as the others, because you cannot use `last`, `next`, or `redo` with it.)

Q **Why does Perl 5 for Win32 bother with the `next`, `last`, and `redo` statements, when the `if-elsif-else` structure can do the job just as well?**

A The `last` and `next` statements are ideal for loops that check for exceptional conditions. For example:

```
for ($count = 1; $count <= 3; $count++) {
        $line = <STDIN>;
        last if ($line eq "");
        $line =~ s/^[\t ]+//;
        $line =~ s/[\t ]+\n$//;
        @words = split(/[\t ]+/, $line);
        $total += @words;
}
```

If the `last` statement did not exist, the only way to implement this would be with another level of nesting and another condition in the `for` statement, as follows:

```
for ($count = 1; $count <= 3 && $line ne ""; $count++) {
        $line = <STDIN>;
        if ($line ne "") {
                $line =~ s/^[\t ]+//;
                $line =~ s/[\t ]+\n$//;
                @words = split(/[\t ]+/, $line);
                $total += @words;
        }
}
```

If your program has to check for several exceptional conditions, you might need several levels of `if` statements to handle them unless you use `next` or `last`.

On the other hand, the `redo` statement should be avoided whenever possible, because it is difficult to follow program logic when it is used.

Q **Is the `goto` statement ever the best way to solve a problem?**

A Almost never. Avoid using the `goto` statement if at all possible.

Q **Why is the conditional expression last in single-line conditional statements?**

A This is to avoid a problem found in the C programming language. In C, you don't need to put braces around the statement block in a conditional statement if the block consists of only one line. For example, the following is legal:

```
if (x == 0)
        printf ("x is zero\n");
```

With this syntax, it is easy to accidentally forget to add the braces when you add another statement to the statement block, as follows:

```
if (x == 0)
        printf ("x is zero\n");
        printf ("this statement is always printed\n");
```

If you glance at this code quickly, you might think that the second call to `printf` is executed only if `x` is `0`. However, this code is really

```
if (x == 0)
        printf ("x is zero\n");
printf ("this statement is always printed\n");
```

In Perl for Win32, this problem does not exist because the only way to write the first statement is

```
print ("x is zero\n") if (x == 0);
```

Q Is a `continue` block executed if a `redo` statement restarts the loop?

A No. The `continue` block is executed only when an iteration of a loop is successfully completed (by reaching the bottom of a loop or a `next` statement).

Workshop

The Workshop provides quiz questions to help you solidify your understanding of the material covered and exercises to give you experience in using what you've learned. Try to understand the quiz and exercise answers before you go on to tomorrow's lesson. The answers can be found in Appendix B, "Answers."

Quiz

1. How many times does the following loop iterate?

```
for ($count = 0; $count < 7; $count++) {
        print ("$count\n");
}
```

2. How many times does the following loop iterate?

```
$count = 1;
do {
        print ("$count\n");
} until ($count++ > 10);
```

3. How many times does the following loop iterate?

```
for ($count = 1; $count <= 10; $count++) {
        last if ($count == 5);
}
```

4. How many times does the following loop iterate?

```
$restart = 0;
for ($count = 1; $count <= 5; $count++) {
        redo if ($restart++ == 1);
}
```

5. Write a single-line conditional statement that quits a loop if $x equals done.

6. Write a single-line conditional statement that restarts a loop if the first element of the list @list is 26.

7. Write a single-line conditional statement that goes to the next iteration of the loop labeled LABEL if $scalar equals #.

8. Write a single-line conditional statement that prints the digits from 1 to 10. (Use a scalar variable, and assume that it has not been previously defined.)

9. What does the continue statement do?

Exercises

1. Write a program that uses the do statement to print the numbers from 1 to 10.

2. Write a program that uses the for statement to print the numbers from 1 to 10.

3. Write a program that uses a loop to read and write five lines of input. Use the last statement to exit the loop if there are less than five lines to read.

4. Write a program that loops through the numbers 1 to 20, printing the even-numbered values. Use the next statement to skip over the odd-numbered values.

5. Write a program that uses the foreach statement to check each word in the standard input file. Print the line numbers of all occurrences of the word the (in uppercase, lowercase, or mixed case).

6. Write a program that uses a while loop and a continue statement to print the integers from 10 down to 1.

7. **BUG BUSTER:** What is wrong with the following code?

```
$count = 1;
do {
        print ("$count\n");
        last if ($count == 10);
        $count++;
} while (1);
```

Day 9

Using Subroutines

Today's lesson shows you how to use subroutines to divide your program into smaller, more manageable modules. Today, you learn about the following:

- [ ] What a subroutine is
- [ ] How to define subroutines
- [ ] How to invoke subroutines
- [ ] How to return a value from a subroutine
- [ ] How to use the return statement
- [ ] How to use local variables in subroutines
- [ ] How to pass arguments to subroutines
- [ ] How to call subroutines from other subroutines
- [ ] The meaning of recursive subroutines
- [ ] How to pass arrays by name in subroutines using aliasing
- [ ] How to use the do statement with subroutines
- [ ] How to use subroutines to change the sort order used by sort
- [ ] How to provide startup and termination code using BEGIN and END
- [ ] How to use AUTOLOAD

What Is a Subroutine?

In Perl for Win32 (or Perl as well), a *subroutine* is a separate body of code designed to perform a particular task. A Perl program executes this body of code by calling or invoking the subroutine; the act of invoking a subroutine is called a *subroutine invocation*.

Subroutines serve two useful purposes:

☐ They break down your program into smaller parts, making it easier to read and understand.

☐ They enable you to use one piece of code to perform the same task multiple times, eliminating needless duplication.

Defining and Invoking a Subroutine

Listing 9.1 shows how a subroutine works. This program calls a subroutine that reads a line from the standard input file and breaks it into numbers. The program then adds the numbers together.

TYPE **Listing 9.1. A program that uses a subroutine.**

```
1:  # p9_1.pl
2:
3:  $total = 0;
4:  &getnumbers;
5:  foreach $number (@numbers) {
6:          $total += $number;
7:  }
8:  print ("the total is $total\n");
9:
10: sub getnumbers {
11:         $line = <STDIN>;
12:         $line =~ s/^\s+|\s*\n$//g;
13:         @numbers = split(/\s+/, $line);
14: }
```

OUTPUT
```
C:\> perl p9_1.pl
11 8 16 4
the total is 39
C:\>
```

ANALYSIS Lines 10–14 are an example of a subroutine. The keyword `sub` tells the Perl interpreter that this is a subroutine definition. The `getnumbers` immediately following `sub` is the name of the subroutine; the Perl program uses this name when invoking the subroutine.

The program starts execution in the normal way, beginning with line 3. Line 4 invokes the subroutine `getnumbers`; the `&` character tells the Perl interpreter that the following name is the name of a subroutine. (This ensures that the Perl interpreter does not confuse subroutine names with the names of scalar or array variables.)

The Perl interpreter executes line 4 by jumping to the first executable statement inside the subroutine, which is line 11. The interpreter then executes lines 11–13.

Lines 11–13 create the array `@numbers` as follows:

- ☐ Line 11 reads a line of input from the standard input file.
- ☐ Line 12 removes the leading and trailing white space (including the trailing newline) from the input line.
- ☐ Line 13 then breaks the input line into numbers and assigns the resulting list of numbers to `@numbers`.

When line 13 is finished, the Perl interpreter jumps back to the main program and executes the line immediately following the subroutine call, which is line 5.

Lines 5–7 add the numbers together by using the `foreach` statement to loop through the list stored in `@numbers`. (Note that this program does not check whether a particular element of `@numbers` actually consists of digits. Because character strings that are not digits are converted to `0` in expressions, this isn't a significant problem.)

The syntax for a subroutine definition is

```
sub subname {
        statement_block
}
```

subname is a placeholder for the name of the subroutine. Like all Perl names, *subname* consists of an alphabetic character followed by one or more letters, digits, or underscores.

statement_block is the body of the subroutine and consists of one or more Perl statements. Any statement that can appear in the main part of a Perl program can appear in a subroutine.

NOTE

The Perl interpreter never confuses a subroutine name with a scalar variable name or any other name, because it can always tell from context which name you are referring to. This means that you can have a subroutine and a scalar variable with the same name. Look at this example:

```
$word = 0;
&word;
```

Here, when the Perl interpreter sees the & character in the second statement, it realizes that the second statement is calling the subroutine named word.

WARNING

When you are defining names for your subroutines, it's best not to use a name belonging to a built-in Perl function that you plan to use.

For example, you could, if you like, define a subroutine named split. The Perl interpreter can always distinguish an invocation of the subroutine split from an invocation of the library function split, because the name of the subroutine is preceded by a & when it is invoked, as follows:

```
@words = &split(1, 2);        # subroutine
@words = split(/\s+/, $line); # library function
```

However, it's easy to leave off the & by mistake (especially if you are used to programming in C, where subroutine calls do not start with an &). To avoid such problems, use subroutine names that don't correspond to the names of library functions.

Perl subroutines can appear anywhere in a program, even in the middle of a conditional statement. For example, Listing 9.2 is a perfectly legal Perl program.

TYPE **Listing 9.2. A program containing a subroutine in the middle of the main program.**

```
1:  # p9_2.pl
2:
3:  while (1) {
4:          &readaline;
5:          last if ($line eq "");
6:          sub readaline {
7:                  $line = <STDIN>;
8:          }
9:          print ($line);
10: }
11: print ("done\n");
```

OUTPUT

```
C:\> perl p9_2.pl
Here is a line of input.
Here is a line of input.
^z
done
C:\>
```

ANALYSIS This program just reads lines of input from the standard input file and writes them straight back out to the standard output file.

Line 4 calls the subroutine readaline. When you examine this subroutine, which is contained in lines 6–8, you can see that it reads a line of input and assigns it to the scalar variable $line.

When readaline is finished, program execution continues with line 5. After line 5 is executed, the program skips over the subroutine definition and continues with line 9. The code inside the subroutine is never directly executed, even if it appears in the middle of a program; lines 6–8 can be executed only by a subroutine invocation, such as is found in line 4.

TIP

Although subroutines can appear anywhere in a program, it usually is best to put all your subroutines at either the beginning of the program or the end. Following this practice makes your programs easier to read.

Forward References to Subroutines

As you have seen, the Perl interpreter uses the & character to indicate that a subroutine is being specified in a statement. In Perl 5 for Win32, as well as in Perl 5, you do not need to supply an & character when calling a subroutine if you have already defined the subroutine. Here's an example:

```
sub readaline {
        $line = <STDIN>;
}
...
readaline;
```

Because the Perl interpreter already knows that readaline is a subroutine, you don't need to specify the & when calling it.

If you prefer to list all your subroutines at the end of your program, you can still omit the & character provided you supply a forward reference for your subroutine, as shown in the following:

```
sub readaline;   # forward reference
...
readaline;
...
```

```
sub readaline {
        $line = <STDIN>;
}
```

The forward reference tells the Perl interpreter that readaline is the name of a subroutine. This means that you no longer need to supply the & when you call readaline.

Occasionally, calling a subroutine without specifying the & character might not behave the way you expect. If your program is behaving strangely, or you are not sure whether to use the & character, supply the & character with your call.

Returning a Value from a Subroutine

Take another look at the getnumbers subroutine from Listing 9.1:

```
sub getnumbers {
        $line = <STDIN>;
        $line =~ s/^\s+|\s*\n$//g;
        @numbers = split(/\s+/, $temp);
}
```

Although this subroutine is useful, it suffers from one serious limitation: It overwrites any existing list stored in the array variable @numbers (as well as any value stored in $line or $temp). This overwriting can lead to problems. For example, consider the following:

```
@numbers = ("the", "a", "an");
&getnumbers;
print ("The value of \@numbers is: @numbers\n");
```

When the subroutine getnumbers is invoked, the value of @numbers is overwritten. If you just examine this portion of the program, it is not obvious that this is what is happening.

To get around this problem, you can use a useful property of subroutines in Perl for Win32: The value of the last expression evaluated by the subroutine is automatically considered to be the subroutine's *return value*.

For example, in the subroutine getnumbers from Listing 9.1, the last expression evaluated is

```
@numbers = split(/\s+/, $temp);
```

The value of this expression is the list of numbers obtained by splitting the line of input. This means that this list of numbers is the return value for the subroutine.

To see how to use a subroutine return value, look at Listing 9.3, which modifies the word-counting program to use the return value from the subroutine getnumbers.

TYPE **Listing 9.3. A program that uses a subroutine return value.**

```
1:  # p9_3.pl
2:
3:  $total = 0;
4:  @numbers = &getnumbers;
5:  foreach $number (@numbers) {
6:          $total += $number;
7:  }
8:  print ("the total is $total\n");
9:
10: sub getnumbers {
11:         $line = <STDIN>;
12:         $line =~ s/^\s+|\s*\n$//g;
13:         split(/\s+/, $line);      # this is the return value
14: }
```

OUTPUT
```
C:\> perl p9_3.pl
11 8 16 4
the total is 39
C:\>
```

ANALYSIS Line 4, once again, calls the subroutine getnumbers. As before, the array variable @numbers is assigned the list of numbers read from the standard input file; however, in this program, the assignment is in the main body of the program, not in the subroutine. This makes the program easier to read.

The only other difference between this program and Listing 9.1 is that the call to split in line 13 no longer assigns anything to @numbers. In fact, it doesn't assign the list returned by split to any variable at all, because it doesn't need to. Line 13 is the last expression evaluated in getnumbers, so it automatically becomes the return value from getnumbers. Therefore, when line 4 calls getnumbers, the list returned by split is assigned to the array variable @numbers.

NOTE

If the idea of evaluating an expression without assigning it confuses you, there's nothing wrong with creating a variable inside the subroutine just for the purpose of containing the return value. For example:

```
sub getnumbers {
        $line = <STDIN>;
        $line =~ s/^\s+|\s*\n$//g;
        @retval = split(/\s+/, $temp); # the return value
}
```

Here, it is obvious that the return value is the contents of @retval.

The only drawback to doing this is that assigning the list returned by split to @retval is slightly less efficient. In larger programs, such

> efficiency costs are worth it, because subroutines become much more comprehensible.
>
> Using a special return variable also eliminates an entire class of errors, which you will see in "Return Values and Conditional Expressions," later today.

You can use a return value of a subroutine any place an expression is expected. For example:

```
foreach $number (&getnumbers) {
       print ("$number\n");
}
```

This `foreach` statement iterates on the list of numbers returned by `getnumbers`. Each element of the list is assigned to `$number` in turn, which means that this loop prints all the numbers in the list, each on its own line.

Listing 9.4 shows another example that uses the return value of a subroutine in an expression. This time, the return value is used as an array subscript.

TYPE Listing 9.4. A program that uses a return value as an array subscript.

```
1:  # p9_4.pl
2:
3:  srand();
4:  print ("Random number tester.\n");
5:  for ($count = 1; $count <= 100; $count++) {
6:          $randnum[&intrand] += 1;
7:  }
8:  print ("Totals for the digits 0 through 9:\n");
9:  print ("@randnum\n");
10:
11: sub intrand {
12:          $num = int(rand(10));
13: }
```

OUTPUT
```
C:\> perl p9_4.pl
Random number tester.
Totals for the digits 0 through 9:
10 9 11 10 8 8 12 11 9 12
C:\>
```

ANALYSIS This program uses the following three built-in functions:

srand   Initializes the built-in random-number generator

rand   Generates a random (non-integral) number greater than zero and less than the value passed to it

int   Gets rid of the non-integer portion of a number

The subroutine `intrand` first calls `rand` to get a random number greater than 0 and less than 10. The return value from `rand` is passed to `int` to remove the fractional portion of the number; this means, for example, that 4.77135 becomes 4. This number becomes the return value returned by `intrand`.

Line 6 calls `intrand`. The return value from `intrand`, an integer between 0 and 9, serves as the subscript into the array variable `randnum`. If the return value from `intrand` is 7, `$randnum[7]` has its value increased by one.

As a consequence, at any given time, the *n*th value of `@randnum` contains the number of occurrences of `n` as a random number.

Line 9 prints out the number of occurrences of each of the 10 numbers. Each number should occur approximately the same number of times (although not necessarily exactly the same number of times).

Return Values and Conditional Expressions

Because the return value of a subroutine is always the last expression evaluated, the return value might not always be what you expect.

Consider the simple program in Listing 9.5. This program, like the one in Listing 9.3, reads an input line, breaks it into numbers, and adds the numbers. This program, however, attempts to do all the work inside the subroutine `get_total`.

Listing 9.5. A program illustrating a potential problem with return values from subroutines.

TYPE

```
 1:  # p9_5.pl
 2:
 3:  $total = &get_total;
 4:  print("The total is $total\n");
 5:
 6:  sub get_total {
 7:          $value = 0;
 8:          $inputline = <STDIN>;
 9:          $inputline =~ s/^\s+|\s*\n$//g;
10:          @subwords = split(/\s+/, $inputline);
11:          $index = 0;
12:          while ($subwords[$index] ne "") {
13:                  $value += $subwords[$index++];
14:          }
15:  }
```

OUTPUT

```
C:\> perl p9_5.pl
11 8 16 4
the total is
C:\>
```

ANALYSIS

Clearly, this program is supposed to assign the contents of the scalar variable $value to the scalar variable $total. However, when line 4 tries to print the total, you see that the value of $total is actually the empty string. What has happened?

The problem is in the subroutine get_total. In get_total, as in all other subroutines, the return value is the value of the last expression evaluated. However, in get_total, the last expression evaluated is not the last expression in the program.

The last expression to be evaluated in get_total is the conditional expression in line 12, which is

```
$subwords[$index] ne ""
```

The loop in lines 12–14 iterates until the value of this expression is 0. When the value of this expression is 0, the loop terminates and the subroutine terminates. This means that the value of the last expression evaluated in the subroutine is 0 and that the return value of the subroutine is 0. Because 0 is treated as the null string by print (0 and the null string are equivalent in Perl for Win32), line 4 prints the following, which isn't what the program is supposed to do:

```
the total is
```

Listing 9.6 shows how you can get around this problem.

TYPE

Listing 9.6. A program that corrects the problem that occurs in Listing 9.5.

```
1:  # p9_6.pl
2:
3:  $total = &get_total;
4:  print("The total is $total.\n");
5:  sub get_total {
6:          $value = 0;
7:          $inputline = <STDIN>;
8:          $inputline =~ s/^\s+|\s*\n$//g;
9:          @subwords = split(/\s+/, $inputline);
10:         $index = 0;
11:         while ($subwords[$index] ne "") {
12:                 $value += $subwords[$index++];
13:         }
14:         $retval = $value;
15: }
```

9

OUTPUT

```
C:\> perl p9_6.pl
11 8 16 4
the total is 39.
C:\>
```

ANALYSIS This program is identical to Listing 9.5 except for one difference: line 15 has been added. This line assigns the total stored in $value to the scalar variable $retval.

Line 15 ensures that the value of the last expression evaluated in the subroutine get_total is, in fact, the total that is supposed to become the return value. This means that line 3 now assigns the correct total to $total, which in turn means that line 4 now prints the correct result.

Note that you don't really need to assign to $retval. The subroutine get_total can just as easily be the following:

```
sub get_total {
        $value = 0;
        $inputline = <STDIN>;
        $inputline =~ s/^\s+|\s*\n$//g;
        @subwords = split(/\s+/, $inputline);
        $index = 0;
        while ($subwords[$index] ne "") {
                $value += $subwords[$index++];
        }
        $value;
}
```

Here, the final expression evaluated by the subroutine is simply $value. The value of this expression is the current value stored in $value, which is the sum of the numbers in the line.

The return **Statement**

Another way to ensure that the return value from a subroutine is the value you want is to use the return statement.

SYNTAX

The syntax for the return statement is

```
return (retval);
```

retval is the value you want your subroutine to return. It can be either a scalar value (including the result of an expression) or a list.

Listing 9.7 provides an example of the use of the return statement.

TYPE **Listing 9.7. A program that uses the `return` statement.**

```
1:  # p9_7.pl
2:
3:  $total = &get_total;
4:  if ($total eq "error") {
5:          print ("No input supplied.\n");
6:  } else {
7:          print("The total is $total.\n");
8:  }
9:
10: sub get_total {
11:         $value = 0;
12:         $inputline = <STDIN>;
13:         $inputline =~ s/^\s+|\s*\n$//g;
14:         if ($inputline eq "") {
15:                 return ("error");
16:         }
17:         @subwords = split(/\s+/, $inputline);
18:         $index = 0;
19:         while ($subwords[$index] ne "") {
20:                 $value += $subwords[$index++];
21:         }
22:         $retval = $value;
23: }
```

OUTPUT
```
C:\> perl p9_7.pl
^z
No input supplied.
C:\>
```

ANALYSIS This program is similar to the one in Listing 9.6. The only difference is that this program checks whether an input line exists.

If the input line does not exist, the conditional expression in line 14 becomes true, and line 15 is executed. Line 15 exits the subroutine with the return value `error`; this means that `error` is assigned to `$total` in line 3.

This program shows why allowing scalar variables to store either numbers or character strings is useful. When the subroutine `get_total` detects the error, it can assign a value that is not an integer to `$total`, which makes it easier to determine that something has gone wrong. Other programming languages, which only enable you to assign either a number or a character string to a particular variable, do not offer this flexibility.

Using Local Variables in Subroutines

The subroutine `get_total` in Listing 9.7 defines several variables that are used only inside the subroutine: the array variable `@subwords` and the four scalar variables `$inputline`, `$value`, `$index`, and `$retval`.

If you know for certain that these variables are going to be used only inside the subroutine, you can tell Perl to define these variables as *local variables* so that the variables do not interfere with variables of a similar name used elsewhere in the program.

In Perl 5 for Win32, as well as in Perl 5, there are two statements used to define local variables:

☐ The my statement, which defines variables that exist only inside a subroutine.

☐ The local statement, which defines variables that do not exist inside the main program, but exist inside the subroutine and any subroutines called by the subroutine. (Calling subroutines from other subroutines is discussed later today.)

Listing 9.8 shows how you can use my to define a variable that exists only inside a subroutine.

NOTE

In Perl for Win32, my and local behave identically and use the same syntax. The only difference between them is that variables created using my are not known outside the subroutine.

TYPE **Listing 9.8. A program that uses local variables.**

```
 1: # p9_8.pl
 2:
 3: $total = 0;
 4: while (1) {
 5:         $linetotal = &get_total;
 6:         last if ($linetotal eq "done");
 7:         print ("Total for this line: $linetotal\n");
 8:         $total += $linetotal;
 9: }
10: print ("Total for all lines: $total\n");
11:
12: sub get_total {
13:         my ($total, $inputline, @subwords);
14:         my ($index, $retval);
15:         $total = 0;
16:         $inputline = <STDIN>;
17:         if ($inputline eq "") {
18:                 return ("done");
19:         }
20:         $inputline =~ s/^\s+|\s*\n$//g;
21:         @subwords = split(/\s+/, $inputline);
22:         $index = 0;
23:         while ($subwords[$index] ne "") {
24:                 $total += $subwords[$index++];
25:         }
26:         $retval = $total;
27: }
```

```
C:\> perl p9_8.pl
11 8 16 4
Total for this line: 39
7 20 6 1
Total for this line: 34
^Z
Total for all lines: 73
C:\>
```

This program uses two scalar variables, both named $total. One copy of $total is defined in the main program and keeps a running total of all of the numbers in all of the lines.

The scalar variable $total is also defined in the subroutine get_total; in this subroutine, $total refers to the total for a particular line, and line 13 defines it as a local variable. Because this copy of $total is only defined inside the subroutine, the copy of $total defined in the main program is not affected by line 15 (which assigns 0 to $total).

> **WARNING**
>
> Because a local variable is not known outside the subroutine, the local variable is destroyed when the subroutine is completed. If the subroutine is called again, a new copy of the local variable is defined.
>
> This means that the following code does not work:
>
> ```
> sub subroutine_count {
>         my($number_of_calls);
>         $number_of_calls += 1;
> }
> ```
>
> This subroutine does not return the number of times subroutine_count has been called. Because a new copy of $number_of_calls is defined every time the subroutine is called, $number_of_calls is always assigned the value 1.

Local variables can appear anywhere in a program, provided they are defined before they are used. It is good programming practice to put all your local definitions at the beginning of your subroutine.

Initializing Local Variables

If you like, you can assign a value to a local variable when you declare it. For example:

```
sub my_sub {
        my($scalar) = 43;
        my(@array) = ("here's", "a", "list");
        # code goes here
}
```

Here, the local scalar variable $scalar is given an initial value of 43, and the local array variable @array is initialized to contain the list ("here's", "a", "list").

Passing Values to a Subroutine

You can make your subroutines more flexible by allowing them to accept values passed from the main program; these values passed from the main program are known as *arguments*.

Listing 9.9 provides a very simple example of a subroutine that accepts three arguments.

TYPE

Listing 9.9. A program that uses a subroutine to print three numbers and their total.

```
1:  # p9_9.pl
2:
3:  print ("Enter three numbers, one at a time:\n");
4:  $number1 = <STDIN>;
5:  chop ($number1);
6:  $number2 = <STDIN>;
7:  chop ($number2);
8:  $number3 = <STDIN>;
9:  chop ($number3);
10: &printnum ($number1, $number2, $number3);
11:
12: sub printnum {
13:         my($number1, $number2, $number3) = @_;
14:         my($total);
15:         print ("The numbers you entered: ");
16:         print ("$number1 $number2 $number3\n");
17:         $total = $number1 + $number2 + $number3;
18:         print ("The total: $total\n");
19: }
```

OUTPUT

```
C:\> perl p9_9.pl
Enter three numbers, one at a time:
5
11
4
The numbers you entered: 5 11 4
The total: 20
C:\>
```

ANALYSIS Line 10 calls the subroutine printnum. Three arguments are passed to printnum: the value stored in $number1, the value stored in $number2, and the value stored in $number3. Note that arguments are passed to subroutines in the same way they are passed to built-in library functions.

9

Line 13 defines local copies of the scalar variables $number1, $number2, and $number3. It then assigns the contents of the system variable @_ to these scalar variables. @_ is created whenever a subroutine is called with arguments; it contains a list consisting of the arguments in the order in which they are passed. In this case, printnum is called with arguments 5, 11, and 4, which means that @_ contains the list (5, 11, 4).

The assignment in line 13 assigns the list to the local scalar variables that have just been defined. This assignment works just like any other assignment of a list to a set of scalar variables. The first element of the list, 5, is assigned to the first variable, $number1; the second element of the list, 11, is assigned to $number2; and the final element, 4, is assigned to $number3.

NOTE

After the array variable @_ has been created, it can be used anywhere any other array variable can be used. This means that you do not need to assign its contents to local variables.

The following subroutine is equivalent to the subroutine in lines 12–19 of Listing 9.9:

```
sub printnum {
        my($total);
        print ("The numbers you entered: ");
        print ("$_[0] $_[1] $_[2]\n");
        $total = $_[0] + $_[1] + $_[2];
        print ("The total: $total\n");
}
```

Here, $_[0] refers to the first element of the array variable @_, $_[1] refers to the second element, and $_[2] refers to the third element.

This subroutine is a little more efficient, but it is harder to read.

TIP

It usually is better to define local variables and assign @_ to them because then your subroutines will be easier to understand.

Listing 9.10 is another example of a program that passes arguments to a subroutine. This program uses the same subroutine to count the number of words and the number of characters in a file.

Listing 9.10. Another example of a subroutine with arguments passed to it.

TYPE

```
1:  # p9_10.pl
2:
3:  $wordcount = $charcount = 0;
4:  $charpattern = "";
5:  $wordpattern = "\\s+";
6:  while ($line = <STDIN>) {
7:          $charcount += &count($line, $charpattern);
8:          $line =~ s/^\s+|\s+$//g;
9:          $wordcount += &count($line, $wordpattern);
10: }
11: print ("Totals: $wordcount words, $charcount characters\n");
12:
13: sub count {
14:         my ($line, $pattern) = @_;
15:         my ($count);
16:         if ($pattern eq "") {
17:                 @items = split (//, $line);
18:         } else {
19:                 @items = split (/$pattern/, $line);
20:         }
21:         $count = @items;
22: }
```

OUTPUT

```
C:\> perl p9_10.pl
This is a line of input.
Here is another line.
^Z
Totals: 10 words, 47 characters
C:\>
```

ANALYSIS This program reads lines from the standard input file until the file is exhausted. Each line has its characters counted and its words counted.

Line 7 determines the number of characters in a line by calling the subroutine count. This subroutine is passed the line of input and the string stored in $charpattern, which is the empty string. Inside the subroutine count, the local variable $pattern receives the pattern passed to it by the call in line 7. This means that the value stored in $pattern is also the empty string.

Lines 16–20 split the input line. The pattern specified in the call to split has the value stored in $pattern substituted into it. Because $pattern currently contains the empty string, the pattern used to split the line is //, which splits the input line into individual characters. As a result, each element of the resulting list stored in @items is a character in the input line.

The total number of elements in the list—in other words, the total number of characters in the input line—is assigned to $count by line 17. Because this is the last expression evaluated in the subroutine, the resulting total number of characters is returned by the subroutine. Line 8 adds this total to the scalar variable $charcount.

Line 8 then removes the leading and trailing white space; this white space is included in the total number of characters—because spaces, tabs, and the trailing newline character count as characters—but is not included when the line is broken into words.

Line 9 calls the subroutine count again, this time with the pattern stored in $wordpattern, which is \s+. (Recall that you need to use two backslashes in a string to represent a single backslash, because the \ character is the escape character in strings.) This value, representing one or more white-space characters, is assigned to $pattern inside the subroutine, and the pattern passed to split therefore becomes /\s+/.

When split is called with this pattern, @items is assigned a list of words. The total number of words in the list is assigned to $count and is returned; line 11 adds this returned value to the total number of words.

Passing a List to a Subroutine

If you like, you can pass a list to a subroutine. For example, the following subroutine adds the element of a list together and prints the result:

```
sub addlist {
        my (@list) = @_;
        $total = 0;
        foreach $item (@list) {
                $total += $item;
        }
        print ("The total is $total\n");
}
```

To invoke this subroutine, pass it an array variable, a list, or any combination of lists and scalar values. For instance,

```
&addlist (@mylist);
&addlist ("14", "6", "11");
&addlist ($value1, @sublist, $value2);
```

In each case, the values and lists supplied in the call to addlist are merged into a single list and then passed to the subroutine.

Because values are merged into a single list when a list is passed to a subroutine, you can only define one list as an argument for a subroutine. The subroutine

```
sub twolists {
        my (@list1, @list2) = @_;
}
```

isn't useful because it always assigns the empty list to @list2, and because @list1 absorbs all of the contents of @_.

This means that if you want to have both scalar variables and a list as arguments to a subroutine, the list must appear last, as follows:

```
sub twoargs {
        my ($scalar, @list) = @_;
}
```

If you call this subroutine using

```
&twoargs(47, @mylist);
```

the value 47 is assigned to $scalar, and @mylist is assigned to @list.

If you like, you can call twoargs with a single list, as follows:

```
&twoargs(@mylist);
```

Here, the first element of @mylist is assigned to $scalar, and the rest of @mylist is assigned to @list.

NOTE

If you find this confusing, it might help to realize that passing arguments to a subroutine follows the same rules as assignment does. For example, you can have

```
($scalar, @list1) = @list2;
```

because $scalar is assigned the first element of @list2. However, you can't have this:

```
(@list1, $scalar) = @list2;
```

because all of @list1 would be assigned to @list2, and $scalar would be assigned the null string.

Calling Subroutines from Other Subroutines

In Perl , you can call subroutines from other subroutines. To call a subroutine from another subroutine, use the same subroutine-invocation syntax you've been using all along. Subroutines that are called by other subroutines are known as *nested subroutine calls* (because one call is "nested" inside the other).

Listing 9.11 is an example of a program that contains a nested subroutine call. It is a fairly simple modification of Listing 9.10 and counts the number of words and characters in three lines of standard input. It also demonstrates how to return multiple values from a subroutine.

TYPE | **Listing 9.11. An example of a nested subroutine.**

```
1:  # p9_11.pl
2:
3:  ($wordcount, $charcount) = &getcounts(3);
4:  print ("Totals for three lines: ");
5:  print ("$wordcount words, $charcount characters\n");
6:
7:  sub getcounts {
8:          my ($numlines) = @_;
9:          my ($charpattern, $wordpattern);
10:         my ($charcount, $wordcount);
11:         my ($line, $linecount);
12:         my (@retval);
13:         $charpattern = "";
14:         $wordpattern = "\\s+";
15:         $linecount = $charcount = $wordcount = 0;
16:         while (1) {
17:                 $line = <STDIN>;
18:                 last if ($line eq "");
19:                 $linecount++;
20:                 $charcount += &count($line, $charpattern);
21:                 $line =~ s/^\s+|\s+$//g;
22:                 $wordcount += &count($line, $wordpattern);
23:                 last if ($linecount == $numlines);
24:         };
25:         @retval = ($wordcount, $charcount);
26: }
27:
28: sub count {
29:         my ($line, $pattern) = @_;
30:         my ($count);
31:         if ($pattern eq "") {
32:                 @items = split (//, $line);
33:         } else {
34:                 @items = split (/$pattern/, $line);
35:         }
36:         $count = @items;
37: }
```

OUTPUT

```
C:\> perl p9_11.pl
This is a line of input.
Here is another line.
Here is the last line.
Totals for three lines: 15 words, 70 characters
C:\>
```

ANALYSIS The main body of this program now consists of only five lines of code, including the special header comment and a blank line. This is because most of the actual work is being done inside the subroutines. (This is common in large programs. Most of these programs call a few main subroutines, which in turn call other subroutines. This approach makes programs easier to read, because each subroutine is compact and concise.)

Line 3 calls the subroutine getcounts, which retrieves the line and character count for the three lines from the standard input file. Because a list containing two elements is returned by getcounts, a standard list-to-scalar-variable assignment can be used to assign the returned list directly to $wordcount and $charcount.

The subroutine getcounts is similar to the main body of the program in Listing 9.10. The only difference is that the while loop has been modified to loop only the number of times specified by the argument passed to getcounts, which is stored in the local variable $numlines.

The subroutine getcounts actually does the word and character counting by calling another subroutine, count. This subroutine is identical to the subroutine of the same name in Listing 9.10.

NOTE

> The @_ variable is a local variable that is defined inside the subroutine. When a subroutine calls a nested subroutine, a new copy of @_ is created for the nested subroutine.
>
> For example, in Listing 9.11, when getcounts calls count, a new copy of @_ is created for count, and the @_ variable in getcounts is not changed.

Recursive Subroutines

In Perl , not only can subroutines call other subroutines, but subroutines actually can call themselves. A subroutine that calls itself is known as a *recursive subroutine*.

You can use a subroutine as a recursive subroutine if the following two conditions are true:

☐ All variables the subroutine uses are local (except those that are not changed by the subroutine).

☐ The subroutine contains code that, one way or another, determines when it should stop calling itself.

When all the variables that a subroutine uses are local, the subroutine creates a new copy of the variables each time it calls itself. This ensures that there is no confusion or overlap.

Listing 9.12 is an example of a program that contains a recursive subroutine. This program accepts a list of numbers and operands that is to be evaluated from right to left, as if the list were a stack whose top is the left end of the list. For example, if the input is

```
-  955  *  26  +  11   8
```

this program adds 11 and 8, multiplies the result by 26, and subtracts that result from 955. This is equivalent to the following Perl expression:

```
955 - 26 * (11 + 8)
```

Listing 9.12. A program that uses a recursive subroutine to perform arithmetic.

TYPE

```
 1:  # p9_12.pl
 2:
 3:  $inputline = <STDIN>;
 4:  $inputline =~ s/^\s+|\s+$//g;
 5:  @list = split (/\s+/, $inputline);
 6:  $result = &rightcalc (0);
 7:  print ("The result is $result.\n");
 8:
 9:  sub rightcalc {
10:          my ($index) = @_;
11:          my ($result, $operand1, $operand2);
12:
13:          if ($index+3 == @list) {
14:                  $operand2 = $list[$index+2];
15:          } else {
16:                  $operand2 = &rightcalc ($index+2);
17:          }
18:          $operand1 = $list[$index+1];
19:          if ($list[$index] eq "+") {
20:                  $result = $operand1 + $operand2;
21:          } elsif ($list[$index] eq "*") {
22:                  $result = $operand1 * $operand2;
23:          } elsif ($list[$index] eq "-") {
24:                  $result = $operand1 - $operand2;
25:          } else {
26:                  $result = $operand1 / $operand2;
27:          }
28: }
```

OUTPUT

```
C:\> perl p9_12.pl
 -    98 *   4 +   12   11
The result is 6.
C:\>
```

ANALYSIS This program starts off by reading a line of input from the standard input file and breaking it into its components, which are stored as a list in the array variable @list.

When given the input

```
 -    98 *   4 +   12   11
```

lines 3–5 produce the following list, which is assigned to @list:

```
("-", "98", "*", "4", "+", "12", "11")
```

Line 6 calls the subroutine `rightcalc` for the first time. `rightcalc` requires one argument, an index value that tells the subroutine what part of the list to work on. Because the first argument here is 0, `rightcalc` starts with the first element in the list.

Line 10 assigns the argument passed to `rightcalc` to the local variable $index. When `rightcalc` is called for the first time, $index is 0.

Lines 13–17 are the heart of this subroutine, because they control whether to call `rightcalc` recursively. The basic logic is that a list such as

```
("-", "98", "*", "4", "+", "12", "11")
```

can be broken into three parts: the first operator, -; the first operand, 98; and a sublist (the rest of the list). Note that the sublist

```
("*", "4", "+", "12", "11")
```

is itself a complete set of operators and operands; because this program is required to perform its arithmetic starting from the right, this sublist must be calculated first.

Line 13 checks whether there is a sublist that needs to be evaluated first. To do this, it checks whether there are more than three elements in the list. If there are only three elements in the list, the list consists of only one operator and two operands, and the arithmetic can be performed right away. If there are more than three elements in the list, a sublist exists.

To evaluate the sublist when it exists, line 16 calls `rightcalc` recursively. The index value passed to this second copy of `rightcalc` is 2; this ensures that the first element of the list examined by the second copy of `rightcalc` is the element with subscript 2, which is *.

At this point, the following is the chain of subroutine invocations, their arguments, and the part of the list on which they are working:

Level 1   Main program
Level 2   `rightcalc(0)—list ("-", "98", "*", "4", "+", "12", "11")`
Level 3   `rightcalc(2)—list ("*", "4", "+", "12", "11")`

When this copy of `rightcalc` reaches line 13, it checks whether the sublist being worked on has just three elements. Because this sublist has five elements, line 16 calls yet another copy of `rightcalc`, this time setting the value of $index to 4. The following is the chain of subroutine invocations after this third call:

Level 1   Main program
Level 2   `rightcalc(0)—list ("-", "98", "*", "4", "+", "12", "11")`
Level 3   `rightcalc(2)—list ("*", "4", "+", "12", "11")`
Level 4   `rightcalc(4)—list ("+", "12", "11")`

When the third copy of this subroutine reaches line 13, it checks whether this portion of the list contains only three elements. Because it does, the conditional expression in line 13 is true. At this point, line 14 is executed for the first time (by any copy of `rightcalc`); it takes the value stored in `$index`—in this case, 4, adds 2 to it, and uses the result as the subscript into `@list`. This assigns 11, the seventh element of `@list`, to `$operand2`.

Lines 18–27 perform an arithmetic operation. Line 18 adds 1 to the value in `$index` to retrieve the location of the first operand; this operand is assigned to `$operand1`. In this copy of `rightcalc`, the subscript is 5 (4+1), and the sixth element of `@list`, 12, is assigned to `$operand1`.

Line 19 uses `$index` as the subscript into the list to access the arithmetic operator for this operation. In this case, the fifth element of `$index` (subscript 4) is +, and the expression in line 19 is true. Line 20 then adds `$operand1` to `$operand2`, yielding `$result`, which is 23. This value is returned by this copy of `rightcalc`.

When the third copy of `rightcalc` returns, execution continues with the second copy of `rightcalc` because the second copy called the third copy. Line 16 of the second copy assigns the return value of the third copy, 23, to `$operand2`. The following is the state of the program after line 16 has finished executing:

Level 1   Main program

Level 2   `rightcalc(0)—list ("-", "98", "*", "4", "+", "12", "11")`

Level 3   `rightcalc(2)—list ("*", "4", "+", "12", "11"), $operand2 is 23`

The Perl interpreter now executes lines 18–27. Because `$index` is 2 in this copy of `rightcalc`, line 18 assigns the fourth element of `@list`, 4, to `$operand1`. Line 21 is true in this case because the operator is *; this means that line 22 multiplies `$operand1` (4) by `$operand2` (23), yielding 92, which is assigned to `$result`.

At this point, the second copy of `rightcalc` is finished, and program execution returns to line 16. This assigns the return value from the second copy, 92, to `$operand2`.

The following is the state of the program after the second copy of `rightcalc` is finished:

Level 1   Main program

Level 2   `rightcalc(0)—list ("-", "98", "*", "4", "+", "12", "11"), $operand2 is 92`

Now you're almost finished; the program is executing only one copy of `rightcalc`. Because `$index` is 0 in this copy of `rightcalc`, line 18 assigns 98 to `$operand1`. Line 23 is true in this case because the operator here is -; line 24 then takes 98 and subtracts 92 from it, yielding a final result of 6.

This final result of 6 is passed to the main program and is assigned to `$result`. (Note that there is no conflict between `$result` in the main program and the various copies of `$result` in `rightcalc` because `$result` is defined as a local variable in `rightcalc`.) Line 7 finally prints this result.

NOTE

> Recursive subroutines are useful when handling complicated data structures such as trees. You will see examples of such complicated data structures on Day 10, "Associative Arrays."

9

Passing Arrays by Name Using Aliases

As you have seen, Perl enables you to pass an array as an argument to a subroutine:

```
&my_sub(@array);
```

When the subroutine `my_sub` is called, the list stored in the array variable `@array` is copied to the variable `@_` defined in the subroutine:

```
sub my_sub {
        my (@subarray) = @_;
        $arraylength = @subarray;
}
```

If the array being passed is large, it might take some time (and considerable space) to create a copy of the array. If your application is operating under time or space limitations, or you just want to make it more efficient, you can specify that the array is to be passed by name.

The following is an example of a similar subroutine that refers to an array by name:

```
sub my_sub {
        local (*subarray) = @_;
        $arraylength = @subarray;
}
```

The `*subarray` definition tells the Perl interpreter to operate on the actual list passed to `my_sub` instead of making a copy.

To call this subroutine, specify `*` instead of `@` with the array variable name, as in the following:

```
@myarray = (1, 2, 3, 4, 5);
&my_sub(*myarray);
```

Specifying `*myarray` instead of `@myarray` indicates that the actual contents of `@myarray` are to be used (and modified, if desired) in `my_sub`. In fact, while the subroutine is being executed, the name `@subarray` becomes identical to the name `@myarray`. This process of creating another name to refer to the same variable is known as *aliasing*. `@subarray` is now an alias of `@myarray`.

When my_sub terminates, @subarray stops being an alias of @myarray. When my_sub is called again with a different argument, as in

```
&my_sub(*anotherarray);
```

the variable @subarray in my_sub becomes an alias for @anotherarray, which means that you can use the array variable @subarray to access the storage in @anotherarray.

Aliasing arrays in this manner has one distinct advantage and one distinct drawback. The advantage is that your program becomes more efficient. You don't need to copy the entire list from your main program to the subroutine. The disadvantage is that your program becomes more difficult to follow. You have to remember, for example, that changing the contents of @subarray in the subroutine my_sub also changes the contents of @myarray and @anotherarray. It is easy to lose track of which name refers to which variable.

There is also another problem with aliasing: It affects all variables with the same name, not just array variables.

For example, consider Listing 9.13, which defines a scalar variable named $foo and an array named @foo, and then aliases @foo. As you'll see, the program aliases $foo as well.

TYPE   **Listing 9.13. A program that demonstrates aliasing.**

```
1:  # p9_13.pl
2:
3:  $foo = 26;
4:  @foo = ("here's", "a", "list");
5:  &testsub (*foo);
6:  print ("The value of \$foo is now $foo\n");
7:
8:  sub testsub {
9:          local (*printarray) = @_;
10:         foreach $element (@printarray) {
11:                 print ("$element\n");
12:         }
13:         $printarray = 61;
14: }
```

OUTPUT
```
C:\> perl p9_13.pl
here's
a
list
The value of $foo is now 61
C:\>
```

ANALYSIS   Line 5 calls the subroutine testsub. The argument, *foo, indicates that the array @foo is to be passed to testsub and aliased.

The local variable definition in line 9 indicates that the array variable @printarray is to become an alias of the array variable @foo. This means that the name printarray is defined to be equivalent to the name foo.

As a consequence, the scalar variable $printarray becomes an alias of the scalar variable $foo. As a consequence, line 13, which seems to assign 61 to $printarray, actually assigns 61 to $foo. This modified value is printed by line 6 of the main program.

NOTE

Aliasing enables you to pass more than one list to a subroutine. Look at this example:

```
@array1 = (1, 2, 3);
@array2 = (4, 5, 6);
&two_array_sub (*array1, *array2);
sub two_array_sub {
        my (*subarray1, *subarray2) = @_;
}
```

In this case, the names array1 and array2 are passed to two_array_sub. subarray1 becomes an alias for array1, and subarray2 becomes an alias for array2.

Using the do **Statement with Subroutines**

Perl enables you to use the do statement to invoke a subroutine. For example, the following statements are identical:

```
&my_sub(1, 2, 3);
do my_sub(1, 2, 3);
```

There is no real reason to use the do statement in this context.

Specifying the Sort Order

By default, the built-in function sort sorts in alphabetical order. The following is an example:

```
@list = ("words", "to", "sort");
@list2 = sort (@list);
```

Here, @list2 is assigned ("sort", "to", "words").

If you like, you can write a subroutine that defines how sorting is to be accomplished. To understand how to do this, first you need to know a little about how sorting works.

When `sort` is given a list to sort, it determines the sort order of the elements of the list by repeatedly comparing pairs of elements. To compare a pair of elements, `sort` calls a special internal subroutine and passes it a pair of arguments. Although the subroutine is not accessible from a Perl program, it basically behaves as follows:

```
sub sort_criteria {
        if ($a gt $b) {
                $retval = -1;
        } elsif ($a eq $b) {
                $retval = 0;
        } else
                $retval = 1;
        }
        $retval;
}
```

This subroutine compares two values, which are stored in `$a` and `$b`. It returns −1 if the first value is greater, 0 if the values are equal, and 1 if the second value is greater. (This, by the way, is how the `cmp` operator works; in fact, the preceding subroutine could compare the two values using a single `cmp` operator.)

To define your own sorting rules, you must write a subroutine whose behavior is identical to the preceding subroutine. This subroutine must use two global variables named `$a` and `$b` to represent the two items in the list currently being compared, and the subroutine must return one of the following values:

-1   If `$a` is to appear before `$b` in the resulting sorted list

0   If `$a` is to be treated as equal to `$b`

1   If `$a` is to appear after `$b` in the resulting sorted list

NOTE

> Even though `$a` and `$b` are global variables that are used by the sorting subroutine, you still can define global variables of your own named `$a` and `$b` without risking their being overwritten.
>
> The built-in function `sort` saves any existing values of `$a` and `$b` before sorting, and then it restores them when sorting is completed.

Once you have written the subroutine, you must specify the subroutine name when calling the function `sort`. For example, if you define a function named `foo` that provides a set of sorting rules, the following statement sorts a list using the rules defined in `foo`:

```
@list2 = sort foo (@list1);
```

Listing 9.14 shows how you can define your own sort criteria. This program sorts a list in the normal order, except that it puts strings starting with a digit last. (By default, strings starting with a number appear before strings starting with a letter, and before some—but not all—special characters.) Strings that begin with a digit are assumed to be numbers and are sorted in numerical order.

TYPE **Listing 9.14. A program that defines sort criteria.**

```
1:  # p9_14.pl
2:
3:  @list1 = ("test", "14", "26", "test2");
4:  @list2 = sort num_last (@list1);
5:  print ("@list2\n");
6:
7:  sub num_last {
8:          my ($num_a, $num_b);
9:
10:         $num_a = $a =~ /^[0-9]/;
11:         $num_b = $b =~ /^[0-9]/;
12:         if ($num_a && $num_b) {
13:                 $retval = $a <=> $b;
14:         } elsif ($num_a) {
15:                 $retval = 1;
16:         } elsif ($num_b) {
17:                 $retval = -1;
18:         } else {
19:                 $retval = $a cmp $b;
20:         }
21:         $retval;
22: }
```

OUTPUT
```
C:\> perl p9_14.pl
test test2 14 26
C:\>
```

ANALYSIS Line 4 sorts the program according to the sort criteria defined in the subroutine num_last. This subroutine is defined in lines 7–22.

This subroutine first determines whether the items are strings that begin with a digit. Line 10 sets the local variable $num_a to a nonzero value if the value stored in $a starts with a digit; similarly, line 11 sets $num_b to a nonzero value if the value of $b starts with a digit.

Lines 12 and 13 handle the case in which both $num_a and $num_b are true. In this case, the two strings are assumed to be digits, and the numeric comparison operator <=> compares their values. The result of the <=> operation is –1 if the first number is larger, 0 if they are equal, and 1 if the second number is larger.

If $num_a is true but $num_b is false, line 15 sets the return value for this subroutine to 1, indicating that the string that does not start with a digit, $b, is to be treated as greater. Similarly, line 17 sets the return value to –1 if $b starts with a digit and $a does not.

If neither string starts with a digit, line 19 uses the normal sort criterion—alphabetical order—to determine which value is larger. Here, the cmp operator is useful. It returns –1 if the first string is alphabetically greater, 0 if the strings are equal, and 1 if the second string is alphabetically greater.

Predefined Subroutines

Perl 5 for Win32 defines three special subroutines that are executed at specific times:

- [ ] The BEGIN subroutine, which is called when your program starts running
- [ ] The END subroutine, which is called when your program terminates
- [ ] The AUTOLOAD subroutine, which is called when your program can't find a subroutine it is supposed to execute.

NOTE

These subroutines are not supported in Perl 4.

Creating Startup Code Using BEGIN

Perl 5 for Win32, as well as Perl 5, enables you to create code that is executed when your program is started. To do this, create a special subroutine named BEGIN. Here's an example:

```
BEGIN {
        print("Hi! Welcome to Perl!\n");
}
```

When your program begins execution, the following line appears on your screen:

```
Hi! Welcome to Perl!
```

The BEGIN subroutine behaves just like any other Perl subroutine. For example, you can define local variables for it or call other subroutines from it.

NOTE

If you like, you can define multiple BEGIN subroutines. These subroutines are called in the order in which they appear in the program.

Creating Termination Code Using END

Perl 5 for Win32, as well as Perl 5, enables you to create code to be executed when your program terminates execution. To do this, define an END subroutine, as in the following example:

```
END {
        print("Thank you for using Perl!\n");
}
```

The code contained in the END subroutine is always executed by your program, even if the program is terminated using die. For example, the code

```
die("Prepare to die!\n");
END {
        print("Ha! You can't kill me!\n");
}
```

displays the following on your screen:

```
Prepare to die!
Ha! You can't kill me!
```

NOTE

You can define multiple END subroutines in your program. In this case, the subroutines are executed in reverse order of appearance, with the last one executed first.

Handling Nonexistent Subroutines Using AUTOLOAD

Perl 5 for Win32 enables you to define a special subroutine named AUTOLOAD that is called whenever the Perl interpreter is told to call a subroutine that does not exist. Listing 9.15 illustrates the use of AUTOLOAD.

TYPE Listing 9.15. A program that uses AUTOLOAD.

```
1: # p9_15.pl
2:
3: &nothere("hi", 46);
4:
5: AUTOLOAD {
6:         print("subroutine $AUTOLOAD not found\n");
7:         print("arguments passed: @_\n");
8: }
```

C:\> **perl p9_15.pl**
subroutine main::nothere not found
arguments passed: hi 46
C:\>

 This program tries to call the nonexistent subroutine `nothere`. When the Perl interpreter discovers that `nothere` does not exist, it calls the AUTOLOAD subroutine.

Line 6 uses a special scalar variable, $AUTOLOAD, that contains the name of the subroutine you tried to call. (The `main::` text that appears before the subroutine name, `nothere`, is the name of the package in which the subroutine is found. By default, all your code is placed in one package, called `main`, so you normally won't need to worry about packages. For more information on creating other packages, see Day 19, "Object-Oriented Programming in Perl.")

When AUTOLOAD is called, the arguments that were to be passed to the nonexistent subroutine are passed to AUTOLOAD instead. This means that the @ array variable contains the list (`"hi"`, `46`), because these are the arguments that were to be passed to `nothere`.

 TIP

> AUTOLOAD is useful if you plan to organize your Perl program into modules, because you can use it to ensure that crucial subroutines from other files actually exist when you need them. For more information about organizing Perl programs into modules, see Day 19.

Summary

Today, you learned about subroutines, which are separated chunks of code intended to perform specific tasks. A subroutine can appear anywhere in your program.

To invoke a subroutine, specify its name preceded by the & character. In Perl 5 for Win32, as well as in Perl 5, the & character is not required if the subroutine exists or if a forward reference is defined.

A subroutine can return a value (either a scalar value or a list). This return value is the value of the last expression evaluated inside the subroutine.

You can define local variables for use inside subroutines. These local variables exist only while the subroutine is being executed. When a subroutine finishes, its local variables are destroyed; if it is invoked again, new copies of the local variables are defined.

You can pass values to subroutines; these values are called arguments. You can pass as many arguments as you like, but only one of these arguments can be a list. If a list is passed to a subroutine, it must be the last argument passed.

The arguments passed to a subroutine are converted into a list and assigned to a special system variable, @_. One copy of @_ exists for each list of arguments passed to a subroutine (that is, @_ is a local variable).

Subroutines can call other subroutines (nested subroutine calls) and even can call themselves (recursive subroutine calls).

You can pass an array variable to a subroutine by name by defining an alias for the variable name. This alias affects all variables of that name. However, using references to pass an array variable to a subroutine is more efficient. References are covered on Day 18.

You can use the do statement to invoke a subroutine, although there is no real reason to do so.

You can define a subroutine that specifies the order in which the elements of a list are to be sorted. To use the sort criteria defined by a subroutine, include its name or body with the call to sort.

The BEGIN subroutine is always executed before your program begins execution. The END subroutine is always executed when your program terminates, even if it was killed off using die. The AUTOLOAD subroutine is executed if your program tries to call a subroutine that does not exist.

Q&A

Q How many levels of nested subroutines can a program have?

A This depends on the amount of memory in your machine. Normally, the limit is large enough for it to be an issue only when you are using recursive subroutines.

Q Which is better: passing entire lists or passing array variables by name?

A As with so many issues in programming, this depends on the situation. If your program needs to be space-efficient or to run as quickly as possible, passing array variables by name might be the best choice.

Another option is to use the global array variable both inside and outside the subroutine. This works well if the array variable is the central repository for program data.

Q When are global variables a good idea? When is it better to pass the contents of a variable to a subroutine?

A If your subroutine is a general-purpose subroutine that performs a task such as breaking a scalar value into words, it's a good idea to pass the value as an argument.

For example:

```
sub breakline {
        local ($line) = @_;
        @words = split(/\s+/, $line);
}
```

If you do not pass the line as an argument, `breakline` will be able to work only with the line stored in a particular scalar variable, which makes it less useful.

On the other hand, if your program stores information in a central array, there's no reason to pass the array or the array name to a subroutine that processes the array. For example, if you are using the array `@occurs` to count all the occurrences of the digits 0 through 9 in a file, there's no reason to pass `@occurs` to a subroutine. For example:

```
sub printcount {
        for ($count = 0; $count <= 9; $count++) {
                print ("$occurs[$count]\n");
        }
}
```

Because `printcount` is not likely to be used with any array except `@occurs`, there's no need to pass it as an argument.

Workshop

The Workshop provides quiz questions to help you solidify your understanding of the material covered and exercises to give you experience in using what you've learned. Try to understand the quiz and exercise answers before you go on to tomorrow's lesson. You can find the answers in Appendix B, "Answers."

Quiz

1. Define the following terms:

    a. subroutine

    b. invocation

    c. argument

2. Consider the following program:

```
$total = 0;
@list = (1, 2, 3);
@list2 = &my_sub;
```

```
sub my_sub {
        local ($total);
        $total = 1;
        @list = (4, 5, 6);
}
```

What are the values stored in the following variables at the end of this program?

   a. `$total`

   b. `@list`

   c. `@list2`

3. What does the following subroutine return?

```
sub sub1 {
        $count = $sum = 0;
        while ($count <= 10) {
                $sum += $count;
                $count++;
        }
}
```

4. What is the value of `@list` at the end of the following program?

```
@list = (1, 2, 3);
&testsub(*list);
sub testsub {
        local (*sublist) = @_;
        $sublist[1] = 5;
}
```

Exercises

1. Write a subroutine that takes two arguments, adds them together, and returns the result.

2. Write a subroutine that counts the number of occurrences of the letter `t` in a string (which is passed to the subroutine). The subroutine must return the number of occurrences.

3. Write a subroutine that takes two filenames as its arguments and returns a nonzero value if the two files have identical contents. Return `0` if the files differ.

4. Write a subroutine that simulates the roll of a die (that is, it generates a random number between 1 and 6) and returns the number.

5. Write a subroutine that uses recursion to print a list in reverse order. The subroutine must recursively call itself to print the entire list; each invocation must print one word of the list. (Assume that the first call to your subroutine passes the value `0` and the list to be printed.)

6. **BUG BUSTER:** What is wrong with the following program?

```
# Exercise 6 - bug buster:

for ($count = 1; $count <= 10; $count++) {
        &print_ten ($count);
}

sub print_ten {
        my ($multiplier) = @_;
        for ($count = 1; $count <= 10; $count++) {
                $printval = $multiplier * 10 + $count;
                print ("$printval\n");
        }
}
```

7. **BUG BUSTER:** What is wrong with the following program?

```
# Exercise 7 - bug buster:

$line = <STDIN>;
@words = split(/\s+/, $line);
$searchword = <STDIN>;
&search_for_word (@words, $searchword);

sub search_for_word {
        local (@searchlist, $searchword) = @_;
        foreach $word (@searchlist) {
                return (1) if ($word eq $searchword);
        }
        $retval = 0;
}
```

8. **BUG BUSTER:** What is wrong with the following program?

```
# Exercise 8 - bug buster:

$line = <STDIN>;
@words = &split_line($line);
print ("@words\n");

sub split_line {
        local ($line) = @_;
        local (@words);
        @words = split(/\s+/, $line);
        if (@words == 0) {
                @words = ("empty list");
        }
}
```

9

Day 10

Associative Arrays

Today's lesson teaches you how to use associative arrays. You'll learn the following:

- ☐ What an associative array is
- ☐ How to access and create an associative array
- ☐ How to copy to and from an associative array
- ☐ How to add and delete associative array elements
- ☐ How to list array indexes and values
- ☐ How to loop using an associative array
- ☐ How to build data structures using associative arrays

To start, take a look at some of the problems that using array variables creates. Once you have seen some of the difficulties created by array variables in certain contexts, you'll see how associative arrays can eliminate these difficulties.

Limitations of Array Variables

In the array variables you've seen so far, you can access an element of a stored list by specifying a subscript. For example, the following statement accesses the third element of the list stored in the array variable @array:

```
$scalar = $array[2];
```

The subscript 2 indicates that the third element of the array is to be referenced.

Although array variables are useful, they have one significant drawback: It's often difficult to remember which element of an array stores what. For example, suppose you want to write a program that counts the number of occurrences of each capitalized word in an input file. You can do this using array variables, but it's very difficult. Listing 10.1 shows you what you have to go through to do this.

Listing 10.1. A program that uses array variables to keep
TYPE | track of capitalized words in an input file.

```
1:  # p10_1.pl
2:
3:  while ($inputline = <STDIN>) {
4:          while ($inputline =~ /\b[A-Z]\S+/g) {
5:                  $word = $&;
6:                  $word =~ s/[;.,:-]$//;  # remove punctuation
7:                  for ($count = 1; $count <= @wordlist;
8:                                  $count++) {
9:                          $found = 0;
10:                         if ($wordlist[$count-1] eq $word) {
11:                                 $found = 1;
12:                                 $wordcount[$count-1] += 1;
13:                                 last;
14:                         }
15:                 }
16:                 if ($found == 0) {
17:                         $oldlength = @wordlist;
18:                         $wordlist[$oldlength] = $word;
19:                         $wordcount[$oldlength] = 1;
20:                 }
21:         }
22: }
23: print ("Capitalized words and number of occurrences:\n");
24: for ($count = 1; $count <= @wordlist; $count++) {
25:         print ("$wordlist[$count-1]: $wordcount[$count-1]\n");
26: }
```

10

OUTPUT

```
C:\> perl p10_1.pl
Here is a line of Input.
This Input contains some Capitalized words.
^Z
Capitalized words and number of occurrences:
Here: 1
Input: 2
This: 1
Capitalized: 1
C:\>
```

ANALYSIS This program reads one line of input at a time from the standard input file. The loop starting on line 4 matches each capitalized word in the line; the loop iterates once for each match, and it assigns the match being examined in this particular iteration to the scalar variable $word.

Once any closing punctuation has been removed by line 6, the program must then check whether this word has been seen before. Lines 7–15 do this by examining each element of the list @wordlist in turn. If an element of @wordlist is identical to the word stored in $word, the corresponding element of @wordcount is incremented.

If no element of @wordlist matches $word, lines 16–20 add a new element to @wordlist and @wordcount.

Definition of Associative Array

As you can see, using array variables creates several problems. First, it's not obvious which element of @wordlist in Listing 10.1 corresponds to which capitalized word. In the example shown, $wordlist[0] contains Here because this is the first capitalized word in the input file, but this is not obvious to the reader.

Worse still, the program has no way of knowing which element of @wordlist contains which word. This means that every time the program reads a new word, it has to check the entire list to see if the word has already been found. This becomes time-consuming as the list grows larger.

All of these problems with array variables exist because elements of array variables are accessed by numeric subscripts. To get around these problems, Perl defines another kind of array, which enables you to access array variables using any scalar value you like. These arrays are called *associative arrays*. (Associative arrays are also called *hashes*.)

To distinguish an associative array variable from an ordinary array variable, Perl uses the % character as the first character of an associative array–variable name, instead of the @ character. As with other variable names, the first character following the % must be a letter, and subsequent characters can be letters, digits, or underscores.

10

The following are examples of associative array–variable names:

```
%assocarray
%a1
%my_really_long_but_legal_array_variable_name
```

NOTE

You can use the same name for an associative array variable and an ordinary array variable. For example, you can define an array variable named `@arrayname` and an associative array variable named `%arrayname`.

The `@` and `%` characters ensure that the Perl interpreter can tell one variable name from another.

Referring to Associative Array Elements

The main difference between associative arrays and ordinary arrays is that associative array subscripts can be any scalar value. For example, the following statement refers to an element of the associative array `%fruit`:

```
$fruit{"bananas"} = 1;
```

The subscript for this array element is `bananas`. Any scalar value can be a subscript. For example:

```
$fruit{"black_currant"}
$number{3.14159}
$integer{-7}
```

A scalar variable can be used as a subscript, as follows:

```
$fruit{$my_fruit}
```

Here, the contents of `$my_fruit` become the subscript into the associative array `%fruit`.

When an array element is referenced, as in the previous example, the name of the array element is preceded by a `$` character, not the `%` character. As with array variables, this tells the Perl interpreter that this is a single scalar item and is to be treated as such.

NOTE

Subscripts for associative array elements are always enclosed in brace brackets (`{}`), not square brackets (`[]`). This ensures that the Perl interpreter is always able to distinguish associative array elements from other array elements.

10

Adding Elements to an Associative Array

The easiest way to create an associative array item is just to assign to it. For example, the statement

```
$fruit{"bananas"} = 1;
```

assigns 1 to the element bananas of the associative array %fruit. If this element does not exist, it is created. If the array %fruit has not been referred to before, it also is created.

This feature makes it easy to use associative arrays to count occurrences of items. For example, Listing 10.2 shows how you can use associative arrays to count the number of capitalized words in an input file. Note how much simpler this program is than the one in Listing 10.1, which accomplishes the same task.

10

TYPE

Listing 10.2. A program that uses an associative array to count the number of capitalized words in a file.

```
1:  # p10_2.pl
2:
3:  while ($inputline = <STDIN>) {
4:          while ($inputline =~ /\b[A-Z]\S+/g) {
5:                  $word = $&;
6:                  $word =~ s/[;.,:-]$//;  # remove punctuation
7:                  $wordlist{$word} += 1;
8:          }
9:  }
10: print ("Capitalized words and number of occurrences:\n");
11: foreach $capword (keys(%wordlist)) {
12:         print ("$capword: $wordlist{$capword}\n");
13: }
```

OUTPUT

```
C:\> perl p10_2.pl
Here is a line of Input.
This Input contains some Capitalized words.
^z
Capitalized words and number of occurrences:
This: 1
Input: 2
Here: 1
Capitalized: 1
C:\>
```

ANALYSIS
As you can see, this program is much simpler than the one in Listing 10.1. The previous program required 20 lines of code to read input and store the counts for each word; this program requires only seven.

As before, this program reads one line of input at a time from the standard input file. The loop starting in line 4 iterates once for each capitalized word found in the input line; each match is assigned, in turn, to the scalar variable $word.

Line 7 uses the associative array %wordlist to keep track of the capitalized words. Because associative arrays can use any value as a subscript for an element, this line uses the word itself as a subscript. Then, the element of the array corresponding to the word has 1 added to its value.

For example, when the word Here is read in, the associative array element $wordlist{"Here"} has 1 added to its value.

Lines 11–13 print the elements of the associative array. Line 11 contains a call to a special built-in function, keys. This function returns a list consisting of the subscripts of the associative array; the foreach statement then loops through this list, iterating once for each element of the associative array. Each subscript of the associative array is assigned, in turn, to the local variable $capword; in this example, this means that $capword is assigned Here, Input, Capitalized, and This—one per each iteration of the foreach loop.

WARNING

An important fact to remember is that associative arrays *always* are stored in "random" order. (Actually, it's the order that ensures fastest access, but, effectively, it is random.) This means that if you use keys to access all the elements of an associative array, there is no guarantee that the elements will appear in any given order. In particular, the elements do not always appear in the order in which they are created.

To control the order in which the associative array elements appear, use sort to sort the elements returned by keys:

```
foreach $capword (sort keys(%wordlist)) {
        print ("$capword: $wordlist{$capword}\n");
}
```

When line 10 of Listing 10.2 is modified to include a call to sort, the associative array elements appear in sorted order.

Creating Associative Arrays

You can create an associative array with a single assignment. To do this, alternate the array subscripts and their values. For example:

```
%fruit = ("apples", 17, "bananas", 9, "oranges", "none");
```

This assignment creates an associative array of three elements:

☐ An element with subscript `apples`, whose value is `17`

☐ An element with subscript `bananas`, whose value is `9`

☐ An element with subscript `oranges`, whose value is `none`

WARNING

> Again, it is important to remember that the elements of associative arrays are not guaranteed to be in any particular order, even if you create the entire array at once.

NOTE

> Perl 5 for Win32, as well as Perl 5, enables you to use either `=>` or `,` to separate array subscripts and values when you assign a list to an associative array. For example:
>
> `%fruit = ("apples" => 17, "bananas" => 9, "oranges" => "none");`
>
> This statement is identical to the previous one, but is easier to understand; the use of `=>` makes it easier to see which subscript is associated with which value.

As with any associative array, you always can add more elements to the array later on. Look at the following example:

```
$fruit{"cherries"} = 5;
```

This adds a fourth element, `cherries`, to the associative array `%fruit` and gives it the value `5`.

Copying Associative Arrays from Array Variables

The list of subscripts and values assigned to `%fruit` in the previous example is an ordinary list like any other. This means that you can create an associative array from the contents of an array variable. For example:

```
@fruit = ("apples", 6, "cherries", 8, "oranges", 11);
%fruit = @fruit;
```

The second statement creates an associative array of three elements—apples, cherries, and oranges—and assigns it to %fruit.

WARNING

> If you are assigning a list or the contents of an array variable to an associative array, make sure that the list contains an even number of elements, because each pair of elements corresponds to the subscript and the value of an associative array element.

Similarly, you can copy one associative array into another. For example:

```
%fruit1 = ("apples", 6, "cherries", 8, "oranges", 11);
%fruit2 = %fruit1;
```

You can assign an associative array to an ordinary array variable in the same way. For example:

```
%fruit = ("grapes", 11, "lemons", 27);
@fruit = %fruit;
```

However, this might not be as useful, because the order of the array elements is not defined. Here, the array variable @fruit is assigned either the four-element list

```
("grapes", 11, "lemons", 27)
```

or the list

```
("lemons", 27, "grapes", 11)
```

depending on how the associative array is sorted.

You can also assign to several scalar variables and an associative array at the same time:

```
($var1, $var2, %myarray) = @list;
```

Here, the first element of @list is assigned to $var1, the second to $var2, and the rest to %myarray.

Finally, an associative array can be created from the return value of a built-in function or user-defined subroutine that returns a list. Listing 10.3 is an example of a simple program that does just that. It takes the return value from split, which is a list, and assigns it to an associative array variable.

TYPE   **Listing 10.3. A program that uses the return value from a built-in function to create an associative array.**

```
1:  # p10_3.pl
2:
3:  $inputline = <STDIN>;
4:  $inputline =~ s/^\s+|\s+\n$//g;
```

```
5:   %fruit = split(/\s+/, $inputline);
6:   print ("Number of bananas: $fruit{\"bananas\"}\n");
```

OUTPUT

```
C:\> perl p10_3.pl
oranges 5 apples 7 bananas 11 cherries 6
Number of bananas: 11
C:\>
```

ANALYSIS This program reads a line of input from the standard input file and eliminates the leading and trailing white space. Line 5 then calls `split`, which breaks the line into words. In this example, `split` returns the following list:

```
("oranges", 5, "apples", 7, "bananas", 11, "cherries", 6)
```

This list is then assigned to the associative array `%fruit`. This assignment creates an associative array with four elements:

Element	Value
oranges	5
apples	7
bananas	11
cherries	6

Line 6 then prints the value of the element `bananas`, which is 11.

Adding and Deleting Array Elements

As you've seen, you can add an element to an associative array by assigning to an element not previously seen, as follows:

```
$fruit{"lime"} = 1;
```

This statement creates a new element of `%fruit` with index `lime` and gives it the value 1.

To delete an element, use the built-in function `delete`. For example, the following statement deletes the element `orange` from the array `%fruit`:

```
delete($fruit{"orange"});
```

Do	Don't

DO use the `delete` function to delete an element of an associative array; it's the only way to delete elements.

DON'T use the built-in functions `push`, `pop`, `shift`, or `splice` with associative arrays because the position of any particular element in the array is not guaranteed.

Listing Array Indexes and Values

As you saw in Listing 10.2, the `keys` function retrieves a list of the subscripts used in an associative array. The following is an example:

```
%fruit = ("apples", 9,
          "bananas", 23,
          "cherries", 11);
@fruitsubs = keys(%fruits);
```

Here, `@fruitsubs` is assigned the list consisting of the elements `apples`, `bananas`, and `cherries`. Note once again that this list is in no particular order. To retrieve the list in alphabetical order, use `sort` on the list:

```
@fruitindexes = sort keys(%fruits));
```

This produces the list `("apples", "bananas", "cherries")`.

To retrieve a list of the values stored in an associative array, use the built-in function `values`. The following is an example:

```
%fruit = ("apples", 9,
          "bananas", 23,
          "cherries", 11);
@fruitvalues = values(%fruits);
```

Here, `@fruitvalues` contains the list `(9, 23, 11)`, not necessarily in this order.

Looping Using an Associative Array

As you've seen, you can use the built-in function `keys` with the `foreach` statement to loop through an associative array. The following is an example:

```
%records = ("Maris", 61, "Aaron", 755, "Young", 511);
foreach $holder (keys(%records)) {
        # stuff goes here
}
```

The variable `$holder` is assigned `Aaron`, `Maris`, and `Young` on successive iterations of the loop (although not necessarily in that order).

This method of looping is useful, but it is inefficient. To retrieve the value associated with a subscript, the program must look it up in the array again, as follows:

```
foreach $holder (keys(%records)) {
        $record = $records{$holder};
}
```

Perl provides a more efficient way to work with associative array subscripts and their values, using the built-in function each, as follows:

```
%records = ("Maris", 61, "Aaron", 755, "Young", 511);
while (($holder, $record) = each(%records)) {
        # stuff goes here
}
```

Every time the each function is called, it returns a two-element list. The first element of the list is the subscript for a particular element of the associative array. The second element is the value associated with that particular subscript.

For example, the first time each is called in the preceding code fragment, the pair of scalar variables (that is, ($holder, $record)) is assigned one of the lists—("Maris", 61), ("Aaron", 755), or ("Young", 511). (Because associative arrays are not stored in any particular order, any of these lists could be assigned first.) If ("Maris", 61) is returned by the first call to each, Maris is assigned to $holder and 61 is assigned to $record.

When each is called again, it assigns a different list to the pair of scalar variables specified. Subsequent calls to each assign further lists, and so on until the associative array is exhausted. When there are no more elements left in the associative array, each returns the empty list.

WARNING

Don't add a new element to an associative array or delete an element from it if you are using the each statement on it. For example, suppose you are looping through the associative array %records using the following loop:

```
while (($holder, $record) = each(%records)) {
        # code goes here
}
```

Adding a new record to %records, such as

```
$records{"Rose"} = 4256;
```

or deleting a record, as in

```
delete $records{"Cobb"};
```

makes the behavior of each unpredictable. This should be avoided.

In Perl 5, as well as in Perl 5 for Windows NT, deleting elements during the each iteration is allowed, though adding elements is not.

Creating Data Structures Using Associative Arrays

You can use associative arrays to simulate a wide variety of data structures found in high-level programming languages. This section describes how you can implement the following data structures in Perl using associative arrays:

- ☐ Linked lists
- ☐ Structures
- ☐ Trees
- ☐ Databases

 NOTE The remainder of today's lesson describes applications of associative arrays but does not introduce any new features of Perl . If you are not interested in applications of associative arrays, you can skip to the next chapter without suffering any loss of general instruction.

Linked Lists

A *linked list* is a simple data structure that enables you to store items in a particular order. Each element of the linked list contains two fields:

- ☐ The value associated with this element
- ☐ A reference, or *pointer*, to the next element in the list

Also, a special *header variable* points to the first element in the list.

Pictorially, a linked list can be represented as in Figure 10.1. As you can see, each element of the list points to the next.

Figure 10.1.
A linked list.

In Perl, a linked list can easily be implemented using an associative array because the value of one associative array element can be the subscript for the next. For example, the following associative array is actually a linked list of words in alphabetical order:

```
%words = ("abel", "baker",
          "baker", "charlie",
          "charlie", "delta",
          "delta", "");
$header = "abel";
```

In this example, the scalar variable $header contains the first word in the list. This word, abel, is also the subscript of the first element of the associative array. The value of the first element of this array, baker, is the subscript for the second element, and so on, as illustrated in Figure 10.2.

Figure 10.2.
A linked list of words
in alphabetical order.

The value of the last element of the subscript, delta, is the null string. This indicates the end of the list.

Linked lists are most useful in applications where the amount of data to be processed is not known, or grows as the program is executed. Listing 10.4 is an example of one such application. It uses a linked list to print the words of a file in alphabetical order.

TYPE | **Listing 10.4. A program that uses an associative array to build a linked list.**

```
1:  # p10_4.pl
2:
3:  # initialize list to empty
4:  $header = "";
5:  while ($line = <STDIN>) {
6:          # remove leading and trailing spaces
7:          $line =~ s/^\s+|\s+$//g;
8:          @words = split(/\s+/, $line);
9:          foreach $word (@words) {
10:                 # remove closing punctuation, if any
11:                 $word =~ s/[.,;:-]$//;
12:                 # convert all words to lower case
13:                 $word =~ tr/A-Z/a-z/;
14:                 &add_word_to_list($word);
15:         }
16: }
17: &print_list;
18:
19: sub add_word_to_list {
20:         local($word) = @_;
21:         local($pointer);
22:
```

continues

Listing 10.4. continued

```
23:              # if list is empty, add first item
24:              if ($header eq "") {
25:                      $header = $word;
26:                      $wordlist{$word} = "";
27:                      return;
28:              }
29:              # if word identical to first element in list,
30:              # do nothing
31:              return if ($header eq $word);
32:              # see whether word should be the new
33:              # first word in the list
34:              if ($header gt $word) {
35:                      $wordlist{$word} = $header;
36:                      $header = $word;
37:                      return;
38:              }
39:              # find place where word belongs
40:              $pointer = $header;
41:              while ($wordlist{$pointer} ne "" &&
42:                      $wordlist{$pointer} lt $word) {
43:                      $pointer = $wordlist{$pointer};
44:              }
45:              # if word already seen, do nothing
46:              return if ($word eq $wordlist{$pointer});
47:              $wordlist{$word} = $wordlist{$pointer};
48:              $wordlist{$pointer} = $word;
49: }
50:
51: sub print_list {
52:         local ($pointer);
53:         print ("Words in this file:\n");
54:         $pointer = $header;
55:         while ($pointer ne "") {
56:                 print ("$pointer\n");
57:                 $pointer = $wordlist{$pointer};
58:         }
59: }
```

OUTPUT

```
C:\> perl p10_4.pl
Here are some words.
Here are more words.
Here are still more words.
^z
Words in this file:
are
here
more
some
still
words
C:\>
```

10

ANALYSIS The logic of this program is a little complicated, but don't despair. Once you understand how this works, you will have all the information you need to build any data structure you like, no matter how complicated.

This program is divided into three parts, as follows:

☐ The main program, which reads input and transforms it into the desired format

☐ The subroutine add_word_to_list, which builds the linked list of sorted words

☐ The subroutine print_list, which prints the list of words

Lines 3–17 contain the main program. Line 4 initializes the list of words by setting the header variable $header to the null string. The loop beginning in line 5 reads one line of input at a time. Line 7 removes leading and trailing spaces from the line, and line 8 splits the line into words.

The inner foreach loop in lines 9–15 processes one word of the input line at a time. If the final character of a word is a punctuation character, line 11 removes it; this ensures that, for example, word. (word with a period) is considered identical to word (without a period). Line 13 converts the word to all-lowercase characters, and line 14 passes the word to the subroutine add_word_to_list.

This subroutine first executes line 24, which checks whether the linked list of words is empty. If it is, line 25 assigns this word to $header, and line 26 creates the first element of the list, which is stored in the associative array %wordlist. In this example, the first word read is here (Here converted to lowercase), and the list looks like Figure 10.3.

Figure 10.3.
*The linked list with
one element in it.*

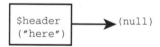

At this point, the header variable $header contains the value here, which is also the subscript for the element of %wordlist that has just been created. This means that the program can reference %wordlist by using $header as a subscript, as follows:

$wordlist{$header}

Variables such as $header that contain a reference to another data item are called *pointers*. Here, $header points to the first element of %wordlist.

If the list is not empty, line 31 checks whether the first item of the list is identical to the word currently being checked. To do this, it compares the current word to the contents of $header, which is the first item in the list. If the two are identical, there is no need to add the new word to the list, because it is already there; therefore, the subroutine returns without doing anything.

The next step is to check whether the new word should be the first word in the list, which is the case if the new word is alphabetically ahead of the existing first word. Line 34 checks this.

If the new word is to go first, the list is adjusted as follows:

1. A new list element is created. The subscript of this element is the new word, and its value is the existing first word.

2. The new word is assigned to the header variable.

To see how this adjustment works, consider the sample input provided. In this example, the second word to be processed is `are`. Because `are` belongs before `here`, the array element `$wordlist{"are"}` is created and is given the value `here`. The header variable `$header` is assigned the value `are`. This means the list now looks like Figure 10.4.

Figure 10.4.
The linked list with two elements in it.

The header variable `$header` now points to the list element with the subscript `are`, which is `$wordlist{"are"}`. The value of `$wordlist{"are"}` is `here`, which means that the program can access `$wordlist{"here"}` from `$wordlist{"are"}`. For example:

```
$reference = $wordlist{"are"};
print ("$wordlist{$reference}\n");
```

The value `here` is assigned to `$reference`, and the `print` statement prints `$wordlist{$reference}`, which is `$wordlist{"here"}`.

Because you can access `$wordlist{"here"}` from `$wordlist{"are"}`, `$wordlist{"are"}` is a pointer to `$wordlist{"here"}`.

If the word does not belong at the front of the list, lines 40–44 search for the place in the list where the word does belong, using a local variable, `$pointer`. Lines 41–44 loop until the value stored in `$wordlist{$pointer}` is greater than or equal to `$word`. For example, Figure 10.5 illustrates where line 42 is true when the subroutine processes `more`.

Figure 10.5.
The linked list when `more` *is processed.*

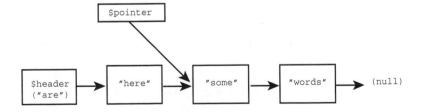

Note that because the list is in alphabetical order, the value stored in `$pointer` is always less than the value stored in `$word`.

If the word being added is greater than any word in the list, the conditional expression in line 41 eventually becomes true. This occurs, for example, when the subroutine processes `some`, as in Figure 10.6.

Figure 10.6.

The linked list when some *is processed.*

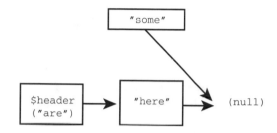

Once the location of the new word has been determined, line 46 checks whether the word already is in the list. If it is, there is no need to do anything.

If the word does not exist, lines 47 and 48 add the word to the list. First, line 47 creates a new element of `%wordlist`, which is `$wordlist{$word}`; its value is the value of `$wordlist{$pointer}`. This means that `$wordlist{$word}` and `$wordlist{$pointer}` now point to the same word, as in Figure 10.7.

Figure 10.7.

The linked list as a new word is being added.

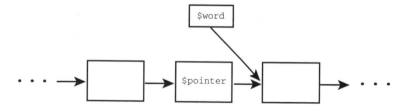

Next, line 48 sets the value of `$wordlist{$pointer}` to the value stored in `$word`. This means that `$wordlist{$pointer}` now points to the new element, `$wordlist{$word}`, that was just created, as in Figure 10.8.

Figure 10.8.

The linked list after the new word is added.

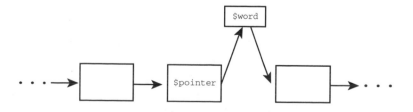

Once the input file has been completely processed, the subroutine `print_list` prints the list, one element at a time. The local variable `$pointer` contains the current value being printed, and `$wordlist{$pointer}` contains the next value to be printed.

NOTE

Normally, you won't want to use a linked list in a program. It's easier just to use `sort` and `keys` to loop through an associative array in alphabetical order, as follows:

```
foreach $word (sort keys(%wordlist)) {
# print the sorted list, or whatever
}
```

However, the basic idea of a pointer, which is introduced here, is useful in other data structures, such as trees, which are described later in today's lesson.

Structures

Many programming languages enable you to define collections of data called *structures*. Like lists, structures are collections of values; each element of a structure, however, has its own name and can be accessed by that name.

Perl does not provide a way of defining structures directly. However, you can simulate a structure using an associative array. For example, suppose you want to simulate the following variable definition written in the C programming language:

```
struct {
        int field1;
        int field2;
        int field3;
} mystructvar;
```

This C statement defines a variable named `mystructvar`, which contains three elements, named `field1`, `field2`, and `field3`.

To simulate this using an associative array, all you need to do is define an associative array with three elements and set the subscripts for these elements to `field1`, `field2`, and `field3`. The following is an example:

```
%mystructvar = ("field1", "",
                "field2", "",
                "field3", "");
```

Like the preceding C definition, this associative array, named `%mystructvar`, has three elements. The subscripts for these elements are `field1`, `field2`, and `field3`. The definition sets the initial values for these elements to the null string.

As with any associative array, you can reference or assign the value of an element by specifying its subscript, as follows:

```
$mystructvar{"field1"} = 17;
```

To define other variables that use the same "structure," all you need to do is create other arrays that use the same subscript names.

Trees

Another data structure that is often used in programs is a *tree*. A tree is similar to a linked list, except that each element of a tree points to more than one other element.

The simplest example of a tree is a *binary tree*. Each element of a binary tree, called a *node*, points to two other elements, called the *left child* and the *right child*. Each of these children points to two children of its own, and so on, as illustrated in Figure 10.9.

Figure 10.9.

A binary tree.

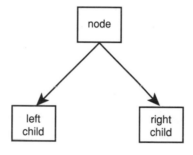

Note that the tree, like a linked list, is a one-way structure. Nodes point to children, but children don't point to their parents.

The following terminology is used when describing trees:

☐ Because each child of a node is a tree of its own, the left child and the right child are often called the *left subtree* and the *right subtree* of the node. (The terms *left branch* and *right branch* are also used.)

☐ The "first" node of the tree (the node that is not a child of another node), is called the *root* of the tree.

☐ Nodes that have no children are called *leaf nodes*.

There are several ways of implementing a tree structure using associative arrays. To illustrate one way of doing so, suppose that you want to create a tree whose root has the value `alpha` and whose children have the values `beta` and `gamma`, as in Figure 10.10.

Figure 10.10.

A binary tree with three nodes.

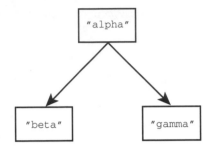

Here, the left child of `alpha` is `beta`, and the right child of `alpha` is `gamma`.

The problem to be solved is this: How can a program associate both `beta` and `gamma` with `alpha`? If the associative array that is to represent the tree is named `%tree`, do you assign the value of `$tree{"alpha"}` to be `beta`, `gamma`, or both? How do you show that an element points to two other elements?

There are several solutions to this problem, but one of the most elegant is as follows: Append the character strings `left` and `right`, respectively, to the name of a node in order to retrieve its children. For example, define `alphaleft` to point to `beta` and `alpharight` to point to `gamma`. In this scheme, if `beta` has children, `betaleft` and `betaright` point to their locations; similarly, `gammaleft` and `gammaright` point to the locations of the children of `gamma`, and so on.

Listing 10.5 is an example of a program that creates a binary tree using this method and then *traverses* it (accesses every node in the tree).

Listing 10.5. A program that uses an associative array to represent a binary tree.

```
1:  # p10_5.pl
2:
3:  $rootname = "parent";
4:  %tree = ("parentleft", "child1",
5:           "parentright", "child2",
6:           "child1left", "grandchild1",
7:           "child1right", "grandchild2",
8:           "child2left", "grandchild3",
9:           "child2right", "grandchild4");
10: # traverse tree, printing its elements
11: &print_tree($rootname);
12:
13: sub print_tree {
14:         local ($nodename) = @_;
15:         local ($leftchildname, $rightchildname);
16:
17:         $leftchildname = $nodename . "left";
```

```
18:             $rightchildname = $nodename . "right";
19:             if ($tree{$leftchildname} ne "") {
20:                     &print_tree($tree{$leftchildname});
21:             }
22:             print ("$nodename\n");
23:             if ($tree{$rightchildname} ne "") {
24:                     &print_tree($tree{$rightchildname});
25:             }
26: }
```

OUTPUT

```
C:\> perl p10_5.pl
grandchild1
child1
grandchild2
parent
grandchild3
child2
grandchild4
C:\>
```

ANALYSIS This program creates the tree depicted in Figure 10.11.

Figure 10.11.

The tree created by Listing 10.5.

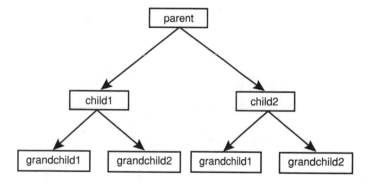

The associative array %tree stores the tree, and the scalar variable $rootname holds the name of the root of the tree. (Note that the grandchild nodes, such as grandchild1, are leaf nodes. There is no need to explicitly create grandchild1left, grandchild1right, and so on because the value of any undefined associative array element is, by default, the null string.)

Once the tree has been created, the program calls the subroutine print_tree to traverse it and print its values. print_tree does this as follows:

1. Line 17 appends left to the name of the node being examined to produce the name of the left child, which is stored in $leftchildname. For example, if the root node, parent, is being examined, the value stored in $leftchildname is parentleft.

2. Similarly, line 18 appends right to the node name and stores the result in $rightchildname.

3. Line 19 checks whether the current node has a left child, which is true if `$tree{$leftchildname}` is defined. (For example, `parent` has a left child, because `$tree{"parentleft"}` is defined.) If the current node has a left child, line 20 recursively calls `print_tree` to print the left subtree (the left child and its children).

4. Line 22 prints the name of the current node.

5. Line 23 checks whether the current node has a right child. If it does, line 24 recursively calls `print_tree` to print the right subtree.

Note that `print_tree` prints the names of the nodes of the tree in the following order: left subtree, node, right subtree. This order of traversal is called *infix mode* or *infix traversal*. If you move line 22 to precede line 19, the node is printed first, followed by the left subtree and the right subtree; this order of traversal is called *prefix mode*. If you move line 22 to follow line 25, the node is printed after the subtrees are printed; this is called *postfix mode*.

Databases

As you have seen, you can build a tree using an associative array. To do this, you build the associative array subscripts by joining character strings together (such as joining the node name and "left"). You can use this technique of joining strings together to use associative arrays to build other data structures.

For example, suppose you want to create a database that contains the lifetime records of baseball players. Each record is to consist of the following:

☐ For non-pitchers, a record consists of games played (GP), home runs (HR), runs batted in (RBI), and batting average (AVG). For example, the record on Lou Gehrig would read as follows:

```
Gehrig: 2164 GP, 493 HR, 1991 RBI, .340 BA
```

☐ For pitchers, a record consists of games pitched (GP), wins (W), and earned run average (ERA). For example, the record on Lefty Grove would read as follows:

```
Grove: 616 GP, 300 W, 3.05 ERA
```

To create a database containing player and pitcher records, you need the following fields:

☐ A name field, for the player's name

☐ A key indicating whether the player was a pitcher

☐ The fields defined in the previous paragraph

You can use an associative array to simulate this in Perl. To do this, build the subscripts for the associative array by concatenating the name of the player with the name of the field being stored by this element of the array. For example, if the associative array is named `%playerbase`, `$playerbase{"GehrigRBI"}`, it contains the career RBI total for Lou Gehrig.

Listing 10.6 shows how to build a player database and how to sequentially print fields from each of the player records.

TYPE **Listing 10.6. A program that builds and prints a database.**

```
1:  # p10_6.pl
2:
3:  @pitcherfields = ("NAME", "KEY", "GP", "W", "ERA");
4:  @playerfields = ("NAME", "KEY", "GP", "HR", "RBI", "BA");
5:
6:  # Build the player database by reading from standard input.
7:  # %playerbase contains the database, @playerlist the list of
8:  # players (for later sequential access).
9:  $playercount = 0;
10: while ($input = <STDIN>) {
11:         $input =~ s/^\s+|\s+$//g;
12:         @words = split (/\s+/, $input);
13:         $playerlist[$playercount++] = $words[0];
14:         if ($words[1] eq "player") {
15:                 @fields = @playerfields;
16:         } else {
17:                 @fields = @pitcherfields;
18:         }
19:         for ($count = 1; $count <= @words; $count++) {
20:                 $playerbase{$words[0].$fields[$count-1]} =
21:                         $words[$count-1];
22:         }
23: }
24:
25: # now, print out pitcher win totals and player home run totals
26: foreach $player (@playerlist) {
27:         print ("$player: ");
28:         if ($playerbase{$player."KEY"} eq "player") {
29:                 $value = $playerbase{$player."HR"};
30:                 print ("$value home runs\n");
31:         } else {
32:                 $value = $playerbase{$player."W"};
33:                 print ("$value wins\n");
34:         }
35: }
```

OUTPUT

```
C:\> perl p10_6.pl
Gehrig      player      2164    493    1991    .340
Ruth        player      2503    714    2217    .342
Grove       pitcher     616     300    3.05
Williams    player      2292    521    1839    .344
Koufax      pitcher     397     165    2.76
^z
Gehrig: 493 home runs
Ruth: 714 home runs
Grove: 300 wins
Williams: 521 home runs
Koufax: 165 wins
C:\>
```

10

ANALYSIS This program has been designed so that it is easy to add new fields to the database. With this in mind, lines 3 and 4 define the fields that are to be used when building the player and pitcher records.

Lines 9–23 build the database. First, line 9 initializes $playercount to 0; this global variable keeps track of the number of players in the database.

Lines 10–12 read a line from the standard input file, check whether the file is empty, remove leading and trailing white space from the line, and split the line into words.

Line 13 adds the player name (the first word in the input line) to the list of player names stored in @playerlist. The counter $playercount then has 1 added to it; this reflects the new total number of players stored in the database.

Lines 14–18 determine whether the new player is a pitcher. If the player is a pitcher, the names of the fields to be stored in this player's record are to be taken from @pitcherfields; otherwise, the names are to be taken from @playerfields. To simplify processing later on, another array variable, @fields, is used to store the list of fields actually being used for this player.

Lines 19–22 copy the fields into the associative array, one at a time. Each array subscript is made up of two parts: the name of the player and the name of the field being stored. For example, Sandy Koufax's pitching wins are stored in the array element KoufaxW. Note that neither the player name nor the field names appear in this loop; this means that you can add new fields to the list of fields without having to change this code.

Lines 26–35 now search the database for all the win and home run totals just read in. Each iteration of the foreach loop assigns a different player name to the local variable $player. Line 28 examines the contents of the array element named $player."KEY" to determine whether the player is a pitcher.

If the player is not a pitcher, lines 29–30 print out the player's home run total by accessing the array element $player."HR". If the player is a pitcher, the pitcher's win total is printed out by lines 32–33; these lines access the array element $player."W".

Note that the database can be accessed randomly as well as sequentially. To retrieve, for example, Babe Ruth's lifetime batting average, you would access the array element $playerbase{"RuthAVG"}. If the record for a particular player is not stored in the database, attempting to access it will return the null string. For example, the following assigns the null string to $cobbavg because Ty Cobb is not in the player database:

```
$cobbavg = $playerbase{"CobbAVG"};
```

As you can see, associative arrays enable you to define databases with variable record lengths, accessible either sequentially or randomly. This gives you all the flexibility you need to use Perl as a database language.

Example: A Calculator Program

Listing 10.7 provides an example of what you can do with associative arrays and recursive subroutines. This program reads in an arithmetic expression, possibly spread over several lines, and builds a tree from it. The program then evaluates the tree and prints the result. The operators supported are +, −, *, /, and () (to force precedence).

This program is longer and more complicated than the programs you have seen so far, but stick with it. Once you understand this program, you will know enough to be able to write an entire compiler in Perl!

TYPE **Listing 10.7. A calculator program that uses trees.**

```
1:  # p10_7.pl
2:  # statements which initialize the program
3:  $nextnodenum = 1;   # initialize node name generator
4:  &get_next_item;     # read first value from file
5:  $treeroot = &build_expr;
6:  $result = &get_result ($treeroot);
7:  print ("the result is $result\n");
8:  # Build an expression.
9:  sub build_expr {
10:         local ($currnode, $leftchild, $rightchild);
11:         local ($operator);
12:         $leftchild = &build_add_operand;
13:         if (&is_next_item("+") || &is_next_item("-")) {
14:                 $operator = &get_next_item;
15:                 $rightchild = &build_expr;
16:                 $currnode = &get_new_node ($operator,
17:                         $leftchild, $rightchild);
18:         } else {
19:                 $currnode = $leftchild;
20:         }
21:  }
22:  # Build an operand for a + or - operator.
23:  sub build_add_operand {
24:         local ($currnode, $leftchild, $rightchild);
25:         local ($operator);
26:         $leftchild = &build_mult_operand;
27:         if (&is_next_item("*") || &is_next_item("/")) {
28:                 $operator = &get_next_item;
29:                 $rightchild = &build_add_operand;
30:                 $currnode = &get_new_node ($operator,
31:                         $leftchild, $rightchild);
32:         } else {
33:                 $currnode = $leftchild;
34:         }
35:  }
```

continues

10

Listing 10.7. continued

```
36: # Build an operand for the * or / operator.
37: sub build_mult_operand {
38:         local ($currnode);
39:         if (&is_next_item("(")) {
40:                 # handle parentheses
41:                 &get_next_item;  # get rid of "("
42:                 $currnode = &build_expr;
43:                 if (! &is_next_item(")")) {
44:                         die ("Invalid expression");
45:                 }
46:                 &get_next_item;  # get rid of ")"
47:         } else {
48:                 $currnode = &get_new_node(&get_next_item,
49:                         "", "");
50:         }
51:         $currnode;  # ensure correct return value
52: }
53: # Check whether the last item read matches
54: # a particular operator.
55: sub is_next_item {
56:         local ($expected) = @_;
57:         $curritem eq $expected;
58: }
59: # Return the last item read; read another item.
60: sub get_next_item {
61:         local ($retitem);
62:         $retitem = $curritem;
63:         $curritem = &read_item;
64:         $retitem;
65: }
66: # This routine actually handles reading from the standard
67: # input file.
68: sub read_item {
69:         local ($line);
70:         if ($curritem eq "EOF") {
71:                 # we are already at end of file; do nothing
72:                 return;
73:         }
74:         while ($wordsread == @words) {
75:                 $line = <STDIN>;
76:                 if ($line eq "") {
77:                         $curritem = "EOF";
78:                         return;
79:                 }
80:                 $line =~ s/\(/ ( /g;
81:                 $line =~ s/\)/ ) /g;
82:                 $line =~ s/^\s+|\s+$//g;
83:                 @words = split(/\s+/, $line);
84:                 $wordsread = 0;
85:         }
86:         $curritem = $words[$wordsread++];
```

10

```
                reate a tree node.
            b get_new_node {
                local ($value, $leftchild, $rightchild) = @_;
                local ($nodenum);
     :          $nodenum = $nextnodenum++;
93:             $tree{$nodenum} = $value;
94:             $tree{$nodenum . "left"} = $leftchild;
95:             $tree{$nodenum . "right"} = $rightchild;
96:             $nodenum;    # return value
97: }
98: # Calculate the result.
99: sub get_result {
100:            local ($node) = @_;
101:            local ($nodevalue, $result);
102:        $nodevalue = $tree{$node};
103:        if ($nodevalue eq "") {
104:                die ("Bad tree");
105:        } elsif ($nodevalue eq "+") {
106:                $result = &get_result($tree{$node . "left"}) +
107:                          &get_result($tree{$node . "right"});
108:        } elsif ($nodevalue eq "-") {
109:                $result = &get_result($tree{$node . "left"}) -
110:                          &get_result($tree{$node . "right"});
111:        } elsif ($nodevalue eq "*") {
112:                $result = &get_result($tree{$node . "left"}) *
113:                          &get_result($tree{$node . "right"});
114:        } elsif ($nodevalue eq "/") {
115:                $result = &get_result($tree{$node . "left"}) /
116:                          &get_result($tree{$node . "right"});
117:        } elsif ($nodevalue =~ /^[0-9]+$/) {
118:                $result = $nodevalue;
119:        } else {
120:                die ("Bad tree");
121:        }
122:}
```

OUTPUT

```
C:\> perl p10_7.pl
11 + 5 *
(4 - 3)
^z
the result is 16
C:\>
```

ANALYSIS   This program is divided into two main parts: a part that reads the input and produces a tree, and a part that calculates the result by traversing the tree.

The subroutines `build_expr`, `build_add_operand`, and `build_mult_operand` build the tree. To see how they do this, first look at Figure 10.12 to see what the tree for the example `11 + 5 * (4 - 3)` should look like.

Figure 10.12.
The tree for the example in Listing 10.7.

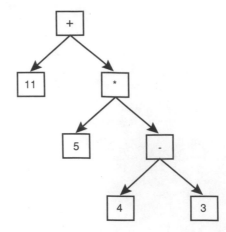

When this tree is evaluated, the nodes are searched in postfix order. First, the left subtree of the root is evaluated, then the right subtree, and finally the operation at the root.

The rules followed by the three subroutines are spelled out in the following description:

1. An *expression* consists of one of the following:

    a. An *add_operand*

    b. An *add_operand*, a + or – operator, and an *expression*

2. An *add_operand* consists of one of the following:

    a. A *mult_operand*

    b. A *mult_operand*, a * or / operator, and an *add_operand*

3. A *mult_operand* consists of one of the following:

    a. A *number* (a group of digits)

    b. An *expression* enclosed in parentheses

The subroutine `build_expr` handles all occurrences of condition 1; it is called (possibly recursively) whenever an *expression* is processed. Condition 1a covers the case in which the expression contains no + or – operators (unless they are enclosed in parentheses). Condition 1b handles expressions that contain one or more + or – operators.

The subroutine `build_add_operand` handles condition 2; it is called whenever an *add_operand* is processed. Condition 2a covers the case in which the add operand contains no * or / operators (except possibly in parentheses). Condition 2b handles add operands that contain one or more * or / operators.

The subroutine `build_mult_operand` handles condition 3 and is called whenever a *mult_operand* is processed. Condition 3a handles multiplication operands that consist of a number. Condition 3b handles multiplication operators that consist of an expression in parentheses; to obtain the subtree for this expression, `build_mult_operand` calls `build_expr` recursively and then treats the returned subtree as a child of the node currently being built.

Note that the tree built by `build_expr`, `build_mult_operand`, and `build_add_operand` is slightly different from the tree you saw in Listing 10.5. In that tree, the value of the node could also be used as the subscript into the associative array. In this tree, the value of the node might not be unique. To get around this problem, a separate counter creates numbers for each node, which are used when building the subscripts. For each node numbered n (where n is an integer), the following are true:

- ☐ `$tree{n}` contains the value of the node, which is the number or operator associated with the node.

- ☐ `$tree{n."left"}` contains the number of the left child of the node.

- ☐ `$tree{n."right"}` contains the number of the right child of the node.

The subroutines `is_next_item`, `get_next_item`, and `read_item` read the input from the standard input file and break it into numbers and operators. The subroutine `get_next_item` "pre-reads" the next item and stores it in the global variable `$curritem`; this lets `is_next_item` check whether the next item to be read matches a particular operator. To read an item, `get_next_item` calls `read_item`, which reads lines of input, breaks them into words, and returns the next word to be read.

The subroutine `get_new_node` creates a tree node. To do this, it uses the contents of the global variable `$nextnodenum` to build the associative array subscripts associated with the node. `$nextnodenum` always contains a positive integer n, which means that the value associated with this node (which is a number or operator) is stored in `$tree{n}`. The locations of the left and right children, if any, are stored in `$tree{n."left"}` and `$tree {n."right"}`.

The subroutine `get_result` traverses the tree built by `build_expr` in postfix order (subtrees first), performing the arithmetic operations as it does so. `get_result` returns the final result, which is then printed.

Note that the main part of this program is only eight lines long! This often happens in more complex programs. The main part of the program just calls subroutines, and the subroutines do the actual work.

NOTE

This program is just the tip of the iceberg: you can use associative arrays to simulate any data structure in any programming language.

Summary

In today's lesson, you learned about associative arrays, which are arrays whose subscripts can be any scalar value.

You can copy a list to an associative array, provided there is an even number of elements in the list. Each pair of elements in the list is treated as an associated array subscript and its value. You also can copy an associative array to an ordinary array variable.

To add an element to an associative array, just assign a value to an element whose subscript has not been previously seen. To delete an element, call the built-in function `delete`. To replace an element, assign a new value to its subscript.

The following three built-in functions enable you to use associative arrays with `foreach` loops:

- ☐ The built-in function `keys` retrieves each associative array subscript in turn.
- ☐ The built-in function `values` retrieves each associative array value in turn.
- ☐ The built-in function `each` retrieves each subscript-value pair in turn (as a two-element list).

Associative arrays are not guaranteed to be stored in any particular order. To guarantee a particular order, use `sort` with `keys`, `values`, or `each`.

Associative arrays can be used to simulate a wide variety of data structures, including linked lists, structures, trees, and databases.

Q&A

Q Are pointers implemented in Perl?

A Yes, if you are using Perl 5 or Perl 5 for Win32; they are discussed on Day 18, "References in Perl 5 for Win32."

Q How can I implement more complicated data structures using associative arrays?

A All you need to do is design the structure you want to implement, name each of the fields in the structure, and use the name-concatenation trick to build your associative array subscript names.

Q What do I do if I want to build a tree that has multiple values at each node?

A There are many ways to do this. One way is to append `value1`, `value2`, and so on, to the name of each node; for example, if the node is named `n7`, `n7value1` could be the associative array subscript for the first value associated with the node, `n7value2` could be the subscript for the second, and so on.

Q What do I do if I want to build a tree that has more than two children per node?

A Again, there are many ways to do this. A possible solution is to use `child1`, `child2`, `child3`, and so on, instead of `left` and `right`.

Q How do I destroy a tree that I have created?

A To destroy a tree, write a subroutine that traverses the tree in postfix order (subtrees first). Destroy each subtree (by recursively calling your subroutine), and then destroy the node you are looking at by calling `delete`.

Note that you shouldn't use `keys` or `each` to access each element of the loop before deleting it. Deleting an element affects how the associative array is stored, which means that `keys` and `each` might not behave the way you want them to.

If you want to destroy the entire associative array in which the tree is stored, you can use the `undef` function, which is described on Day 13, "Process, Scalar-Conversion, and List-Manipulation Functions."

Workshop

The Workshop provides quiz questions to help you solidify your understanding of the material covered and exercises to give you experience in using what you've learned. Try to understand the quiz and exercise answers before you go on to tomorrow's lesson. You can find the answers in Appendix B, "Answers."

Quiz

1. Define the following terms:
    a. associative array
    b. pointer
    c. linked list
    d. binary tree
    e. node
    f. child

2. What are the elements of the associative array created by the following assignment?

    ```
    %list = ("17.2", "hello", "there", "46", "e+6", "88");
    ```

3. What happens when you assign an associative array to an ordinary array variable?

4. How can you create a linked list using an associative array?

5. How many times does the following loop iterate?

```
%list = ("first", "1", "second", "2", "third", "3");
foreach $word (keys(%list)) {
        last if ($word == "second");
}
```

Exercises

1. Write a program that reads lines of input consisting of two words per li⌐

   ```
   bananas 16
   ```

   and creates an associative array from these lines. (The first word is to be
   subscript, and the second word the value.)

2. Write a program that reads a file and searches for lines of the form

   ```
   index word
   ```

   where *word* is a word to be indexed. Each indexed word is to be stored i⌐
   associative array, along with the line number on which it first occurs. (S⌐
   occurrences can be ignored.) Print the resulting index.

3. Modify the program created in Exercise 2 to store every occurrence of ⌐
   line. (Hint: Try building the associative array subscripts using the inde⌐
   non-printable character, and a number.) Print the resulting index.

4. Write a program that reads input lines consisting of a student name an⌐
   numbers representing the student's grades in English, history, mathem⌐
   science, and geography, as follows:

   ```
   Jones 61 67 75 80 72
   ```

   Use an associative array to store these numbers in a database, and then
   the names of all students with failing grades (less than 50) along with ⌐
   they failed.

5. **BUG BUSTER:** What is wrong with the following code?

```
%list = ("Fred", 61, "John", 72,
        "Jack", 59, "Mary", 80);
$surname = "Smith";
foreach $firstname (keys (%list)) {
        %list{$firstname." ".$surname} = %list{$firstname};
}
```

Day 11

Formatting Your Output

The Perl programs you've seen so far produce output using the `print` function, which writes raw, unformatted text to a file.

Perl also enables you to produce formatted output, using print formats and the built-in function `write`. Today's lesson describes how to produce formatted output. You'll learn the following:

☐ How to define a print format (also sometimes known as a *picture format*)

☐ How to use the `write` function

☐ How to add formatted values to a print format

☐ Which value-field formats are available

☐ How to write to other output files

☐ How to specify page headers and the page length

☐ How to format long character strings

☐ How to use the built-in function `printf`

Defining a Print Format

The following is an example of a simple print format:

```
format MYFORMAT =
==================================
Here is the text I want to display.
==================================
.
```

This defines the print format MYFORMAT.

The syntax for print formats is

SYNTAX

```
format formatname =
lines_of_output
.
```

The special keyword format tells the Perl interpreter that the following lines are a print-format definition. The *formatname* is a placeholder for the name of the print format being defined (for example, MYFORMAT). This name must start with an alphabetic character and can consist of any sequence of letters, digits, or underscores.

The *lines_of_output* consists of one or more lines of text that are to be printed when the print format is utilized; these lines are sometimes called *picture lines*. In the MYFORMAT example, there are three lines of text printed: two lines containing = characters, and the line

```
Here is the text I want to display.
```

A print-format definition is terminated with a line containing a period character. This line can contain nothing else; there can be no white space, and the period must be the first character on the line.

Like subroutines, print-format definitions can appear anywhere in program code. However, it usually is best to cluster them either at the beginning or the end of the program.

Displaying a Print Format

To display output using a print format, you need to do two things:

- ☐ Set the system variable $~ to the format you want to use
- ☐ Call the built-in function write

Listing 11.1 is an example of a simple program that displays output using a print format.

Listing 11.1. A program that uses a print format.

```
1:  # p11_1.pl
2:
3:  $~ = "MYFORMAT";
4:  write;
5:
6:  format MYFORMAT =
7:  ===================================
8:  Here is the text I want to display.
9:  ===================================
10: .
```

OUTPUT

```
C:\> perl p11_1.pl
===================================
Here is the text I want to display.
===================================
C:\>
```

 Line 3 of this program assigns the character string MYFORMAT to the system variable $~. This tells the Perl interpreter that MYFORMAT is the print format to use when calling write.

Line 4 calls write, which sends the text defined in MYFORMAT to the standard output file.

Lines 6–10 contain the definition of the print format MYFORMAT.

NOTE

If you don't specify a print format by assigning to $~, the Perl interpreter assumes that the print format to use has the same name as the file variable being written to. In this sample program, if line 3 had not specified MYFORMAT as the print format to use, the Perl interpreter would have tried to use a print format named STDOUT when executing the call to write in line 4, because the call to write is writing to the standard output file.

Displaying Values in a Print Format

Of course, the main reason to use print formats is to format values stored in scalar variables or array variables to produce readable output. Perl enables you to do this by specifying *value fields* as part of a format definition.

11

Each value field specifies a value: the name of a scalar variable, for example, or an expression. When the `write` statement is invoked, the value is displayed in the format specified by the value field.

Listing 11.2 shows how value fields work. This program keeps track of the number of occurrences of the letters a, e, i, o, and u in a text file.

TYPE Listing 11.2. A program that uses value fields to print output.

```
1:  # p11_2.pl
2:
3:  while ($line = <STDIN>) {
4:          $line =~ s/[^aeiou]//g;
5:          @vowels = split(//, $line);
6:          foreach $vowel (@vowels) {
7:                  $vowelcount{$vowel} += 1;
8:          }
9:  }
10: $~ = "VOWELFORMAT";
11: write;
12:
13: format VOWELFORMAT =
14: ============================================================
15: Number of vowels found in text file:
16:         a: @<<<<<   e: @<<<<<
17:         $vowelcount{"a"}, $vowelcount{"e"}
18:         i: @<<<<<   o: @<<<<<
19:         $vowelcount{"i"}, $vowelcount{"o"}
20:         u: @<<<<<
21:         $vowelcount{"u"}
22: ============================================================
23: .
```

OUTPUT

```
C:\> perl p11_2.pl
This is a test file.
This test file contains some vowels.
The quick brown fox jumped over the lazy dog.
^z
============================================================
Number of vowels found in text file:
        a: 3       e: 10
        i: 7       o: 7
        u: 2
============================================================
C:\>
```

ANALYSIS

This program reads one line of input at a time. Line 4 removes everything that is not a, e, i, o, or u from the input line, and line 5 splits the remaining characters into the array @vowels. Each element of @vowels is one character of the input line.

Lines 6–8 count the vowels in the input line by examining the elements of @vowels and adding to the associative array %vowelcount.

Line 10 sets the current print format to VOWELFORMAT; line 11 prints using VOWELFORMAT.

The print format VOWELFORMAT is defined in lines 13–23. Line 16 is an example of a print-format line that contains value fields; in this case, two value fields are defined. Each value field has the format @<<<<<, which indicates six left-justified characters. (For a complete description of the possible value fields, see the section called "Choosing a Value-Field Format" later today.)

When one or more value fields appear in a print-format line, the next line must define the value or values to be printed in this value field. Because line 16 defines two value fields, line 17 defines the two values to be printed. These values are $vowelcount{"a"} and $vowelcount{"e"}, which are the number of occurrences of a and e, respectively.

Similarly, line 18 defines two more value fields to be printed, and line 19 indicates that the values to be printed in these fields are $vowelcount{"i"} and $vowelcount{"o"}. Finally, line 20 defines a fifth value field, and line 21 specifies that $vowelcount{"u"} is to be printed in this field.

> **NOTE**
>
> Here are three things to note about the values specified for value-field formats:
>
> ☐ The lines containing values to be printed are not printed. For example, in Listing 11.2, lines 16, 18, and 20 are printed, but lines 17, 19, and 21 are not.
>
> ☐ The Perl interpreter ignores spacing when it looks for values corresponding to value fields. Many people prefer to line up their values with the corresponding value fields on the previous line, but there is no need to do so.
>
> ☐ The number of values specified must match the number of value fields defined on the previous line.

Creating a General-Purpose Print Format

One disadvantage of print formats as defined in Perl is that scalar-variable names are included as part of the definition. For example, in the following definition, the scalar variable $winnum is built into the print-format definition MYFORMAT:

```
format MYFORMAT =
=========================================================
The winning number is @<<<<<<!
$winnum
=========================================================
.
```

When `write` is called with this print format, as in the following, you have to remember that `$winnum` is being used by MYFORMAT:

```
$~ = "MYFORMAT";
write;
```

If, later on, you accidentally delete all references to `$winnum` in the program, the call to `write` will stop working properly.

One way to get around this problem is to call `write` from within a subroutine, and to use variables local to the subroutine in the print format that `write` uses. Listing 11.3 is a program that does this. It reads a file from the standard input file and prints out the number of occurrences of the five most frequently occurring letters.

Listing 11.3. A program that calls `write` from within a subroutine.

```
1:  # p11_3.pl
2:
3:  while ($line = <STDIN>) {
4:          $line =~ tr/A-Z/a-z/;
5:          $line =~ s/[^a-z]//g;
6:          @letters = split(//, $line);
7:          foreach $letter (@letters) {
8:                  $lettercount{$letter} += 1;
9:          }
10: }
11:
12: $~ = "WRITEHEADER";
13: write;
14: $count = 0;
15: foreach $letter (reverse sort occurrences
16:                 (keys(%lettercount))) {
17:         &write_letter($letter, $lettercount{$letter});
18:         last if (++$count == 5);
19: }
20:
21: sub occurrences {
22:         $lettercount{$a} <=> $lettercount{$b};
23: }
24: sub write_letter {
25:         local($letter, $value) = @_;
26:
27:         $~ = "WRITELETTER";
28:         write;
```

11

```
29: }
30: format WRITEHEADER =
31: The five most frequently occurring letters are:
32: .
33: format WRITELETTER =
34:        @:   @<<<<<<
35:        $letter, $value
36: .
```

```
C:\> perl p11_3.pl
This is a test file.
This test file contains some input.
The quick brown fox jumped over the lazy dog.
^z
The five most frequently occurring letters are:
        t: 10
        e: 9
        i: 8
        s: 7
        o: 6
C:\>
```

ANALYSIS Like the vowel-counting program in Listing 11.2, this program processes one line of input at a time. Line 4 translates all uppercase alphabetic characters into lowercase so that they can be included in the letter count. Line 5 gets rid of all characters that are not letters, including any white space.

Line 6 splits the line into its individual letters; lines 7–9 examine each letter and increment the appropriate letter counters, which are stored in the associative array %lettercount.

Lines 12 and 13 print the following line by setting the current print format to WRITEHEADER and calling write:

```
The five most frequently occurring letters are:
```

Lines 15–19 sort the array %lettercount in order of occurrence. The first letter to appear in the foreach loop is the letter that appears most often in the file. To sort the array in order of occurrence, lines 15 and 16 specify that sorting is to be performed according to the rules defined in the subroutine occurrences. This subroutine tells the Perl interpreter to use the values of the associative array elements as the sort criterion.

Line 17 passes the letter and its occurrence count to the subroutine write_letter. This subroutine sets the current print format to WRITELETTER; this print format refers to the local scalar variables $letter and $value, which contain the values passed to write_letter by line 17. This means that each call to write_letter prints the letter and value currently being examined by the foreach loop.

Note that the first value field in the print format WRITELETTER contains only a single character, @. This indicates that the write field is only one character long (which makes sense, because this is a single letter).

Line 18 ensures that the `foreach` loop quits after the five most frequently used letters have been examined and printed.

TIP

Some programs, such as the one in Listing 11.3, use more than one print-format definition. To make it easier to see which print format is being used by a particular call to `write`, always keep the print-format specification statement and the `write` call together. For example:

```
$~ = "WRITEFORMAT";
write;
```

Here, it is obvious that the call to `write` is using the print format `WRITEFORMAT`.

Formats and Local Variables

In Listing 11.3, you might have noticed that the subroutine `write_letter` calls a subroutine to write out a letter and its value:

```
sub write_letter {
        local($letter, $value) = @_;

        $~ = "WRITELETTER";
        write;
}
```

This subroutine works properly even though the `WRITELETTER` print format is defined outside the subroutine.

Note, however, that local variables defined using `my` cannot be written out using a print format unless the format is defined inside the subroutine. To see this for yourself, change line 25 of Listing 11.3 to the following and run the program again:

```
my($letter,$value) = @_;
```

You will notice that the letter counts do not appear. This limitation is a result of the way local variables defined using `my` are stored by the Perl interpreter. To avoid this difficulty, use `local` instead of `my` when you define local variables that are to be written out using `write`. (For a discussion of `local` and `my`, see Day 9, "Using Subroutines.")

Choosing a Value-Field Format

Now that you know how print formats and `write` work, it's time to look at the value-field formats that are available. Table 11.1 lists these formats.

Table 11.1. Valid value-field formats.

Field	Value-field format
@<<<	Left-justified output
@>>>	Right-justified output
@|||	Centered output
@##.##	Fixed-precision numeric
@*	Multiline text

NOTE

In *left-justified* output, the value being displayed appears at the left end of the value field. In *right-justified* output, the value being displayed appears at the right end of the value field.

In each of the field formats, the first character is a *line-fill character*. It indicates whether text formatting is required. If the @ character is specified as the line-fill character, text formatting is not performed. (For a discussion of text formatting, see the section titled "Formatting Long Character Strings" later today.)

In all cases, except for the multiline value field @*, the width of the field is equal to the number of characters specified. The @ character is included when counting the number of characters in the value field. For example, the following field is five characters wide—one @ character and four > characters:

@>>>>

Similarly, the following field is seven characters wide—four before the decimal point, two after the decimal point, and the decimal point itself:

@###.##

Listing 11.4 illustrates how you can use the value-field formats to produce a neatly printed report. The report is redirected to a file for later printing.

Listing 11.4. A program that uses the various value-field formats.

TYPE

```
1:  # p11_4.pl
2:
3:  $company = <STDIN>;
4:  $~ = "COMPANY";
```

continues

Listing 11.4. continued

```
5:   write;
6:
7:   $grandtotal = 0;
8:   $custline = <STDIN>;
9:   while ($custline ne "") {
10:          $total = 0;
11:          ($customer, $date) = split(/#/, $custline);
12:          $~ = "CUSTOMER";
13:          write;
14:          while (1) {
15:                  $orderline = <STDIN>;
16:                  if ($orderline eq "" || $orderline =~ /#/) {
17:                          $custline = $orderline;
18:                          last;
19:                  }
20:                  ($item, $cost) = split(/:/, $orderline);
21:                  $~ = "ORDERLINE";
22:                  write;
23:                  $total += $cost;
24:          }
25:          &write_total ("Total:", $total);
26:          $grandtotal += $total;
27: }
28: &write_total ("Grand total:", $grandtotal);
29:
30: sub write_total {
31:          local ($totalstring, $total) = @_;
32:          $~ = "TOTAL";
33:          write;
34: }
35:
36: format COMPANY =
37: ************* @|||||||||||||||||||||||||||||||||| *************
38: $company
39: .
40: format CUSTOMER =
41: @<<<<<<<<<<<<<<<<<<<<<<<<<<<<<                   @>>>>>>>>>>>>
42: $customer, $date
43: .
44: format ORDERLINE =
45:            @<<<<<<<<<<<<<<<<<<<<<<<<<<<<<            @####.##
46: $item, $cost
47: .
48: format TOTAL =
49: @<<<<<<<<<<<<<<<                                 @#####.##
50: $totalstring, $total
51:
52: .
```

```
C:\> perl p11_4.pl >report
OUTPUT   Consolidated Widgets, Inc.
         John Doe#Feb 11, 1994
         1 flying widget:171.42
         1 crawling widget:89.99
         Mary Smith#May 4, 1994
         2 swimming widgets:203.43
         ^z
         C:\>
```

The following report is written to the report file:

```
*************    Consolidated Widgets, Inc.    *************
John Doe                                      Feb 11, 1994
            1 flying widget                        171.42
            1 crawling widget                       89.99
Total:                                             261.41

Mary Smith                                     May 4, 1994
            2 swimming widgets                     203.43
Total:                                             203.43

Grand total:                                       464.84
```

ANALYSIS This program starts off by reading the company name from the standard input file and then writing it out. Line 5 writes the company name using the print format COMPANY, which uses a centered output field to display the company name in the center of the line.

After the company name has been printed, the program starts processing data for one customer at a time. Each customer record is assumed to consist of a customer name and date followed by lines of orders. The customer name record uses a # character as the field separator, and the order records use : characters as the separator; this enables the program to distinguish one type of record from the other.

Line 13 prints the customer information using the CUSTOMER print format. This format contains two fields: a left-justified output field for the customer name, and a right-justified output field for the date of the transaction.

Line 22 prints an order line using the ORDERLINE print format. This print format also contains two fields: a left-justified output field indicating the item ordered, and a numeric field to display the cost of the item.

The value-field format @####.## indicates that the cost is to be displayed as a floating-point number. This number is defined as containing, at most, five digits before the decimal point and two digits after.

Finally, the print format TOTAL prints the customer total and the grand total. Because this print format is used inside a subroutine, the same print format can be used to print both totals.

11

Printing Value-Field Characters

As you have seen, certain characters such as @, <, and > are treated as value fields when they are encountered in print formats. Listing 11.5 shows how to actually print one of these special characters using `write`.

TYPE **Listing 11.5. A program that prints a value-field character.**

```
1:  # p11_5.pl
2:
3:  format SPECIAL =
4:  This line contains the special character @.
5:  "@"
6:  .
7:
8:  $~ = "SPECIAL";
9:  write;
```

OUTPUT
```
C:\> perl p11_5.pl
This line contains the special character @.
C:\>
```

ANALYSIS The print-format line in line 4 contains the special character @, which is a one-character value field. Line 5 specifies that the string @ is to be displayed in this value field when the line is printed.

Using the Multiline Field Format

Listing 11.6 uses the multiline field format @* to write a character string over several lines.

TYPE **Listing 11.6. A program that writes a string using the multiline field format.**

```
1:  # p11_6.pl
2:
3:  @input = <STDIN>;
4:  $string = join("", @input);
5:  $~ = "MULTILINE";
6:  write;
7:
8:  format MULTILINE =
9:  ****** contents of the input file: ******
10: @*
11: $string
12: *****************************************
13: .
```

OUTPUT

```
C:\> perl p11_6.pl
Here is a line of input.
Here is another line.
Here is the last line.
^Z
****** contents of the input file: ******
Here is a line of input.
Here is another line.
Here is the last line.
******************************************
C:\>
```

ANALYSIS Line 3 reads the entire input file into the array variable @input. Each element of the list stored in @input is one line of the input file.

Line 4 joins the input lines into a single character string, stored in $string. This character string still contains the newline characters that end each line.

Line 6 calls write using the print format MULTILINE. The @* value field in this print-format definition indicates that the value stored in $string is to be written out using as many lines as necessary. This ensures that the entire string stored in $string is written out.

WARNING

> If a character string contains a newline character, the only way to display the entire string using write is to use the @* multiline value field. If you use any other value field, only the part of the string preceding the first newline character is displayed.

11

Writing to Other Output Files

So far, all of the examples that have used the function write have written to the standard output file. However, you can also use write to send output to other files.

The simplest way to do this is to pass the file to write to as an argument to write. For example, to write to the file represented by the file variable MYFILE using the print format MYFILE, you can use the following statement:

```
write (MYFILE);
```

Here, write writes to the file named MYFILE using the default print format, which is also MYFILE. This is tidy and efficient, but somewhat restricting because, in this case, you can't use $~ to choose the print format to use.

The $~ system variable only works with the *default file variable*, which is the file variable to which write sends output. To change the default file variable, and therefore change the file that $~ affects, call the built-in function select, as follows:

```
select (MYFILE);
```

select sets the default file variable to use when writing. For example, to write to the file represented by the file variable MYFILE using the print format MYFORMAT, you can use the following statements:

```
select(MYFILE);
$~ = "MYFORMAT";
write;
```

Here, the built-in function select indicates that the file to be written to is the file represented by the file variable MYFILE. The statement

```
$~ = "MYFORMAT";
```

selects the print format to be associated with this particular file handle; in this case, the print format MYFORMAT is now associated with the file variable MYFILE.

NOTE

This is worth repeating: Each file variable has its own current print format. An assignment to $~ changes only the print format for the current file variable (the last one passed to select).

Because select has changed the file to be written to, the call to write no longer writes to the standard output file. Instead, it writes to MYFILE. Calls to write continue to write to MYFILE until the following statement is seen:

```
select(STDOUT);
```

This statement resets the write file to be the standard output file.

WARNING

Changing the write file using select not only affects write; it also affects print. For example, consider the following:

```
select (MYFILE);
print ("Here is a line of text.\n");
```

This call to print writes to MYFILE, not to the standard output file. As with write, calls to print continue to write to MYFILE until another call to select is seen.

11

The `select` function is useful if you want to be able to use the same subroutine to write to more than one file at a time. Listing 11.7 is an example of a simple program that does this.

TYPE **Listing 11.7. A program that uses the `select` function.**

```
1:  # p11_7.pl
2:
3:  open (FILE1, ">file1");
4:  $string = "junk";
5:  select (FILE1);
6:  &writeline;
7:  select (STDOUT);
8:  &writeline;
9:  close (FILE1);
10:
11: sub writeline {
12:         $~ = "WRITELINE";
13:         write;
14: }
15:
16: format WRITELINE =
17:         I am writing @<<<<< to my output files.
18:                     $string
19: .
```

OUTPUT

```
C:\> perl p11_7.pl
        I am writing junk    to my output files.
C:\>
```

ANALYSIS Line 5 of this program calls `select`, which sets the default file variable to FILE1. Now, all calls to `write` or `print` write to FILE1, not to the standard output file.

Line 6 calls `writeline` to write a line. This subroutine sets the current print format for the default file variable to WRITELINE. This means that FILE1 now is using the print format WRITELINE, and, therefore, the subroutine writes the following line to FILE1 (which is `file1`):

```
        I am writing junk    to my output files.
```

Line 7 sets the default file variable back to the standard output file variable, STDOUT. This means that `write` and `print` now send output to the standard output file. Note that the current print format for the standard output file is STDOUT (the default), not WRITELINE; the assignment to `$~` in the subroutine WRITELINE affects only FILE1, not STDOUT.

Line 8 calls `writeline` again; this time, the subroutine writes a line to the standard output file. The assignment

```
$~ = "WRITELINE";
```

11

in line 12 associates the print format WRITELINE with the standard output file. This means that WRITELINE is now associated with both STDOUT and FILE1.

At this point, the call to write in line 13 writes the line of output that you see on the standard output file.

Do   **Don't**

DO, whenever possible, call select and assign to $~ immediately before calling write, as follows:

```
select (MYFILE);
$~ = "MYFORMAT";
write;
```

Keeping these statements together makes it clear which file is being written to and which print format is being used.

DON'T use select and $~ indiscriminately, because you might lose track of which print format goes with which file variable, and you might forget which file variable is the default for printing.

Saving the Default File Variable

When select changes the default file variable, it returns an internal representation of the file variable that was last selected. For example:

```
$oldfile = select(NEWFILE);
```

This call to select is setting the current file variable to NEWFILE. The old file variable is now stored in $oldfile. To restore the previous default file variable, you can call select as follows:

```
select ($oldfile);
```

At this point, the default file variable reverts back to its original value (what it was before NEWFILE was selected).

WARNING

> The internal representation of the file variable returned by select is not necessarily the name of the file variable.

You can use the return value from `select` to create subroutines that write to a file, using the print format you want to use, without affecting the rest of the program. For example:

```
sub write_to_stdout {
        my ($savefile, $saveformat);
        $savefile = select(STDOUT);
        $saveformat = $~;
        $~ = "MYFORMAT";
        write;
        $~ = $saveformat;
        select($savefile);
}
```

This subroutine calls `select` to set the default output file to STDOUT, the standard output file. The return value from `select`, the previous default file, is saved in `$savefile`.

Now that the default output file is STDOUT, the next step is to save the current print format being used to write to STDOUT. The subroutine does this by saving the present value of `$~` in another local variable, `$saveformat`. After this is saved, the subroutine can set the current print format to MYFORMAT. The call to `write` now writes to the standard output file using MYFORMAT.

After the call to `write` is complete, the subroutine puts things back the way they were. The first step is to reset `$~` to the value stored in `$saveformat`. The final step is to set the default output file back to the file variable whose representation is saved in `$savefile`.

Note that the call to `select` must appear after the assignment to `$~`. If the call to `select` had been first, the assignment to `$~` would change the print format associated with the original default file variable, not STDOUT.

As you can see, this subroutine doesn't need to know what the default values outside the subroutine are. Also, it does not affect the default values outside the subroutine.

Specifying a Page Header

If you are sending your output to a printer, you can make your output look smarter by supplying text to appear at the top of every page in your output. This special text is called a *page header*.

If a page header is defined for a particular output file, `write` automatically paginates the output to that file. When the number of lines printed is greater than the length of a page, `write` starts a new page.

To define a page header for a file, create a print-format definition with the name of `filename_TOP`, where `filename` is a placeholder for the name of the file variable corresponding to the file to which you are writing. For example, to define a header for writing to standard output, define a print format named STDOUT_TOP, as follows:

```
format STDOUT_TOP =
Consolidated Widgets Inc. 1994 Annual Report
.
```

In this case, when the Perl interpreter starts a new page of standard output, the contents of the print format STDOUT_TOP are printed automatically.

Print formats that generate headers can contain value fields that are replaced by scalar values, just like any other print format. One particular value that is often used in page headers is the current page number, which is stored in the system variable $%. For example:

```
format STDOUT_TOP =
Page @<<.
$%
.
```

In this case, when the first page is printed, the program prints the following header at the top of the page:

```
Page 1.
```

NOTE
By default, $% is initially set to 0 and is incremented every time a new page begins.
To change the pagination, change the value of $% before (or during) printing.

Changing the Header Print Format

To change the name of the print format that prints a page header for a particular file, change the value stored in the special system variable $^.

As with $~, only the value for the current default file can be changed. For example, to use the print format MYHEADER as the header file for the file MYFILE, add the following statements:

```
$oldfile = select(MYFILE);
$^ = "MYHEADER";
select($oldfile);
.
```

These statements set MYFILE to be the current default file, change the header for MYFILE to be the print format MYHEADER, and then reset the current default file to its original value.

11

Setting the Page Length

By default, the page length is 60 lines. To specify a different page length, change the value stored in the system variable $=:

```
$= = 66;      # set the page length to 66 lines
```

This assignment must appear before the first write statement.

WARNING

> If the page length is changed in the middle of the program, the new page length will not be used until a new page is started.

Listing 11.8 shows how you can set the page length and define a page-header print format for your output file.

TYPE

Listing 11.8. A program that sets the length and print format for a page.

```
1:  # p11_8.pl
2:
3:  open (OUTFILE, ">file1");
4:  select (OUTFILE);
5:  $~ = "WRITELINE";
6:  $^ = "TOP_OF_PAGE";
7:  $= = 60;
8:  while ($line = <STDIN>) {
9:          write;
10: }
11: close (OUTFILE);
12:
13: format TOP_OF_PAGE =
14:                                      -- page @<
15:                                            $%
16: .
17: format WRITELINE =
18: @>>>>>>>>>>>>>>>>>>>>>>>>>>>>>>>
19: $line
20: .
```

OUTPUT

```
C:\> perl p11_8.pl
Here is a line of input.
Here is another line.
Here is the last line.
^Z
C:\>
```

The following output is written to the file `file1`:

```
                -- page 1
Here is a line of input.
Here is another line.
Here is the last line.
```

 Line 3 opens the file `file1` for output and associates it with the file variable `OUTFILE`.

Line 4 sets the current default file to `OUTFILE`. Now, when `write` or `print` is called with no file variable supplied, the output is sent to `OUTFILE`.

Line 5 indicates that `WRITELINE` is the print format to be used when writing to the file `OUTFILE`. To do this, it assigns `WRITELINE` to the system variable `$~`. This assignment does not affect the page header.

Line 6 indicates that `TOP_OF_PAGE` is the print format to be used when printing the page headers for the file `OUTFILE`. This assignment does not affect the print format used to write to the body of the page.

Line 7 sets the page length to 60 lines. This page length takes effect immediately, because no output has been written to `OUTFILE`.

Using `print` with Pagination

Normally, you won't want to use `print` if you are using pagination, because the Perl interpreter keeps track of the current line number on the page by monitoring the calls to `write`. If you must use a call to `print` in your program and you want to ensure that the page counter includes the call in its line count, adjust the system variable `$-`. This system variable indicates the number of lines between the current line and the bottom of the page. When `$-` reaches `0`, a top-of-form character is generated, which starts a new page.

The following is a code fragment that calls `print` and then adjusts the `$-` variable:

```
print ("Here is a line of output\n");
$- -= 1;
```

When `$-` has 1 subtracted from its value, the page counter becomes correct.

Formatting Long Character Strings

As you've seen, the `@*` value field prints multiple lines of text. However, this field prints the output exactly as it is stored in the character string. For example, consider Listing 11.9, which uses `@*` to write a multiline character string.

Listing 11.9. A program that illustrates the limitations of the @* value field.

```
1:  # p11_9.pl
2:
3:  $string = "Here\nis an unbalanced line of\ntext.\n";
4:  $~ = "OUTLINE";
5:  write;
6:
7:  format OUTLINE =
8:  @*
9:  $string
10: .
```

OUTPUT

```
C:\> perl p11_9.pl
Here
is an unbalanced line of
text.
C:\>
```

ANALYSIS This call to write displays the character string stored in $string exactly as is. Perl enables you to define value fields in print-format definitions that format text. To do this, replace the initial @ character in the value field with a ^ character. When text formatting is specified, the Perl interpreter tries to fit as many words as possible into the output line.

Listing 11.10 is an example of a simple program that does this.

Listing 11.10. A program that uses a value field that does formatting.

```
1:  # p11_10.pl
2:
3:  $string = "Here\nis an unbalanced line of\ntext.\n";
4:  $~ = "OUTLINE";
5:  write;
6:
7:  format OUTLINE =
8:  ^<<<<<<<<<<<<<<<<<<<<<<<<<<
9:  $string
10: .
```

OUTPUT

```
C:\> perl p11_10.pl
Here is an unbalanced line
C:\>
```

ANALYSIS Line 5 calls write using the print format OUTLINE. This print format contains a value field that specifies that formatting is to take place; this means that the Perl interpreter tries to fit as many words as possible into the line of output. In this case, the first line Here and the four-word string is an unbalanced line fit into the output line.

Note that there are two characters left over in the output line after the four words have been filled in. These characters are not filled, because the next word is not short enough to fit into the space remaining. Only entire words are filled.

One other feature of the line-filling operation is that the substring printed out is actually deleted from the scalar variable $string. This means that the value of $string is now of\ntext.\n. This happens because subsequent lines of output in the same print-format definition can be used to print the rest of the string.

NOTE

> Because the line-filling write operation updates the value used, the value must be contained in a scalar variable and cannot be the result of an expression.

To see how multiple lines of formatted output work, look at Listing 11.11. This program reads a quotation from the standard input file and writes it out on three formatted lines of output.

TYPE
Listing 11.11. A program that writes out multiple formatted lines of output.

```
 1:  # p11_11.pl
 2:
 3:  @quotation = <STDIN>;
 4:  $quotation = join("", @quotation);
 5:  $~ = "QUOTATION";
 6:  write;
 7:
 8:  format QUOTATION =
 9:  Quotation for the day:
10:  --------------------------------------------------------
11:     ^<<<<<<<<<<<<<<<<<<<<<<<<<<<<<<<<<<<<<<<<<<<<<<<<<
12:     $quotation
13:     ^<<<<<<<<<<<<<<<<<<<<<<<<<<<<<<<<<<<<<<<<<<<<<<<<<
14:     $quotation
15:     ^<<<<<<<<<<<<<<<<<<<<<<<<<<<<<<<<<<<<<<<<<<<<<<<<<
16:     $quotation
17:  --------------------------------------------------------
18:  .
```

OUTPUT

```
C:\> perl p11_11.pl
Any sufficiently advanced programming
language is indistinguishable from magic.
^Z
Quotation for the day:
- - - - - - - - - - - - - - - - - - - - - - - - - - - - - - - - - - - - - - - - -
    Any sufficiently advanced programming language is
    indistinguishable from magic.


- - - - - - - - - - - - - - - - - - - - - - - - - - - - - - - - - - - - - - - - -
C:\>
```

ANALYSIS The print format QUOTATION defines three value fields on which formatting is to be employed. Each of the three value fields uses the value of the scalar variable $quotation.

Before write is called, $quotation contains the entire quotation, with newline characters appearing at the end of each input line. When write is called, the first value field in the print format uses as much of the quotation as possible. This means that the following substring is written to the standard output file:

```
Any sufficiently advanced programming language is
```

After the substring is written, it is removed from $quotation, which now contains the following:

```
indistinguishable from magic.
```

Because the written substring has been removed from $quotation, the remainder of the string can be used in subsequent output lines. Because the next value field in the print format also wants to use $quotation, the remainder of the string appears on the second output line and is deleted. Now $quotation is the empty string.

This means that the third value field, which also refers to $quotation, is replaced by the empty string, and a blank line is written out.

WARNING

> The scalar variable containing the output to be printed is changed by a write operation. If you need to preserve the information, copy it to another scalar variable before calling write.

Eliminating Blank Lines when Formatting

You can eliminate blank lines such as the one generated by Listing 11.11. To do this, put a ~ character at the beginning of any output line that is to be printed only when needed.

Listing 11.12 modifies the quotation-printing program to print lines only when they are not blank.

TYPE   **Listing 11.12. A program that writes out multiple formatted lines of output and suppresses blank lines.**

```
 1:  # p11_12.pl
 2:
 3:  @quotation = <STDIN>;
 4:  $quotation = join("", @quotation);
 5:  $~ = "QUOTATION";
 6:  write;
 7:
 8:  format QUOTATION =
 9:  Quotation for the day:
10:  -----------------------------------------------------------
11:  ~    ^<<<<<<<<<<<<<<<<<<<<<<<<<<<<<<<<<<<<<<<<<<<<<<<<<<<<<<
12:       $quotation
13:  ~    ^<<<<<<<<<<<<<<<<<<<<<<<<<<<<<<<<<<<<<<<<<<<<<<<<<<<<<<
14:       $quotation
15:  ~    ^<<<<<<<<<<<<<<<<<<<<<<<<<<<<<<<<<<<<<<<<<<<<<<<<<<<<<<
16:       $quotation
17:  -----------------------------------------------------------
18:  .
```

OUTPUT
```
C:\> perl p11_12.pl
Any sufficiently advanced programming
language is indistinguishable from magic.
^z
Quotation for the day:
-----------------------------------------------------------
    Any sufficiently advanced programming language is
    indistinguishable from magic.
-----------------------------------------------------------
C:\>
```

ANALYSIS   If the quotation is too short to require all the lines, remaining lines are left blank. In this case, the quotation requires only two lines of output, so the third isn't printed.

The program is identical to the one in Listing 11.11 in all other respects. In particular, the value of $quotation after the call to write is still the empty string.

Supplying an Indefinite Number of Lines

While Listing 11.12 suppresses blank lines, it imposes an upper limit of three lines. Quotations longer than three lines are not printed in their entirety. To indicate that the formatted output is to use as many lines as necessary, specify two ~ characters at the beginning of the output line containing the value field. Listing 11.13 modifies the quotation program to allow quotations of any length.

TYPE **Listing 11.13. A program that writes out as many formatted lines of output as necessary.**

```
 1:  # p11_13.pl
 2:
 3:  @quotation = <STDIN>;
 4:  $quotation = join("", @quotation);
 5:  $~ = "QUOTATION";
 6:  write;
 7:
 8:  format QUOTATION =
 9:  Quotation for the day:
10:  -------------------------------------------------------
11:  ~~ ^<<<<<<<<<<<<<<<<<<<<<<<<<<<<<<<<<<<<<<<<<<<<<<<<<
12:      $quotation
13:  -------------------------------------------------------
14:  .
```

OUTPUT
```
C:\> perl p11_13.pl
Any sufficiently advanced programming
language is indistinguishable from magic.
^z
Quotation for the day:
-------------------------------------------------------
   Any sufficiently advanced programming language is
   indistinguishable from magic.
-------------------------------------------------------
C:\>
```

ANALYSIS The ~~ characters at the beginning of the output field indicate that multiple copies of the output line are to be supplied. The output line is to be printed until there is nothing more to print.

In Listing 11.13, two copies of the line are needed.

Formatting Output Using `printf`

If you want to write output that looks reasonable without going to all the trouble of using `write` and `print` formats, Perl provides a built-in function, `printf`, that prints formatted output.

> **NOTE**
>
> If you are familiar with the C programming language, the behavior of `printf` in Perl will be familiar; the Perl `printf` and the C `printf` are basically the same.

The arguments passed to the `printf` function are as follows:

- ☐ The string to be printed, which can contain one or more *field specifiers*
- ☐ One value for each field specifier appearing in the string to be printed

When `printf` sees a field specifier, it substitutes the corresponding value in the `printf` argument list. The representation of the substituted value in the string depends on the field specifier that is supplied.

Field specifiers consist of the `%` character followed by a single character that represents the format to use when printing. Table 11.2 lists the field-specifier formats and the field-specifier character that represents each.

Table 11.2. Field specifiers for `printf`.

Specifier	Description
`%c`	Single character
`%d`	Integer in decimal (base-10) format
`%e`	Floating-point number in scientific notation
`%f`	Floating-point number in "normal" (fixed-point) notation
`%g`	Floating-point number in compact format
`%o`	Integer in octal (base-8) format
`%s`	Character string
`%u`	Unsigned integer
`%x`	Integer in hexadecimal (base-16) format

Here is a simple example of a call to `printf`:

```
printf("The number I want to print is %d.\n", $number);
```

The string to be printed contains one field specifier, `%d`, which represents an integer. The value stored in `$number` is substituted for the field specifier and printed.

Field specifiers also support a variety of options, as follows:

☐ If you are printing an integer using the `d`, `o`, `u`, or `x` format, you can put an `l` character in front of the field-specifier character (as in, for example, `%ld`). This character specifies that the number is a decimal integer in the machine's long integer format (corresponding to the C type `long`). This is useful if your integer is or might be large.

☐ A positive integer following the `%` character indicates the minimum width of the field. For example, `%20s` prints a character string in a field of 20 characters. If the string is not large enough to fill the entire field, it is right-justified (placed at the right end of the field) and padded with blanks. (If the integer starts with a leading `0`, as in `%08d`, the field is padded with zeros, not blanks.)

☐ A negative integer following the `%` character indicates the width of the field and requests left-justification. For example, `%-15s` prints a character string in a field of 15 characters, and it fills the right end of the field with blanks if the string is not large enough.

☐ If you are using a field specifier that prints a floating-point number (`%e`, `%f`, or `%g`), you can specify the number of digits that are to appear after the decimal point. To do this, specify a floating-point number after the `%` character. For example:

`%8.3f`

Here, the number preceding the decimal point is the field width (as before), and the number after the decimal point is the number of decimal places to print.

WARNING

If a floating-point number contains more digits than the field specifier wants, the number is rounded to the number of decimal places needed. For example, if `43.499` is being printed using the field `%5.2f`, the number actually printed is `43.50`.

As with the write value field `@##.##`, `printf` might not always round up when it is handling numbers for which the last decimal place is `5`. This happens because some floating-point numbers cannot be stored exactly, and the nearest equivalent number that can be stored is a slightly smaller number (which rounds down, not up). For example, `43.495` when printed by `%5.2f` might print `43.49`, depending on how `43.495` is stored.

☐ If you are using a field specifier that prints an integer, character, or string, supplying a floating-point number after the `%` character specifies the maximum length of the value to be printed. In the following example, a character string is printed in a 15-character field, but the string itself can be, at most, 10 characters long:

```
%15.10s
```

This guarantees that at least five spaces will appear in the printed line.

You can use `printf` to print to other files. To do this, specify the file variable corresponding to the file to which you want to print, just as you would with `print` or `write`:

```
printf MYFILE ("I am printing %d.\n", $value);
```

This means that changing the current default file using `select` affects `printf`.

Summary

Perl enables you to format your output using print-format definitions and the built-in function `write`. In print-format definitions, you can specify value fields that are to be replaced by either the contents of scalar variables or the values of expressions.

Value fields indicate how to print the contents of a scalar variable or the value of an expression. With a value field, you can specify that the value is to be left-justified (blanks added on the right), right-justified (blanks added on the left), centered, or displayed as a floating-point number.

You also can define value fields that format a multiline character string. Blank lines can be suppressed, and the field can be defined to use as many output lines as necessary.

The built-in function `select` enables you to change the default file to which `write`, `print`, and `printf` send output.

You can break your output into pages by defining a special header print format that prints header information at the top of each page.

The following system variables enable you to control how `write` sends output to a file:

☐ The system variable `$~` contains the name of the print format being used by the current default file.

☐ The system variable `$^` contains the name of the print format being used as a page header by the current default file.

☐ The system variable `$=` contains the number of lines per printed page.

☐ The system variable `$-` contains the number of lines left on the current page.

The built-in function `printf` enables you to format an individual line of text using format specifiers.

Q&A

Q Which is better, `write` or `printf`?

A It depends on what you want to do. If you want to print reports or control pagination, you'll need to use `write`. If you just want individual lines of output to look neat, `printf` might be what you need.

Q How do I generate a page break?

A To do this, set `$-` to `0`. This generates a top-of-form character.

Q Why do value fields that format text modify the contents of the scalar variable containing the text?

A When formatted text is printed, the printed text is removed from the scalar variable, and the part of the string that is not printed is retained. This enables you to use other calls to `write` to print the remainder of the text. In fact, you can print the rest of the text in the scalar variable using a completely different print format.

Q How many print formats can I define?

A Basically, as many as you like, provided the resulting Perl program can still fit in your machine.

Workshop

The Workshop provides quiz questions to help you solidify your understanding of the material covered and exercises to give you experience in using what you've learned. Try to understand the quiz and exercise answers before you go on to tomorrow's lesson. You can find the answers in Appendix B, "Answers."

Quiz

1. Define value fields that print the following:
   a. Ten left-justified characters
   b. Five right-justified characters
   c. Two centered characters
   d. A floating-point number with five digits before the decimal point and three after it
   e. A field that prints as many formatted lines of 30 left-justified characters as necessary

2. What do these fields print?

    a. `@<<<<`

    b. `@||||||`

    c. `@`

    d. `@*`

    e. `~  ^>>>>>>>>>`

3. What do these `printf` field specifiers print?

    a. `%5d`

    b. `%11.4f`

    c. `%010d`

    d. `%-12s`

    e. `%x`

4. Why do certain floating-point numbers have round-off problems?

5. How do you create a page header for an output file?

Exercises

1. Write a program that prints the powers of 2 from `2**1` to `2**10`. Use `write` and a print format to print them three per line. Align the lines so that the right end of each number is lined up with the right end of the corresponding number on the previous line.

2. Repeat Exercise 1 using `printf`.

3. Write a program that reads text and formats it into 40-character lines, left-justified. Put lines of asterisks above and below the text.

4. Write a program that reads a set of dollar values such as `71.43` (one per line). Write out two values per line (the first and second on the first line, and so on). Total each of the resulting columns, and produce a grand total.

5. **BUG BUSTER:** What is wrong with the following program?

```
# Exercise 5 - bug buster:

format STDOUT =
@*
.
while ($line = <STDIN>) {
        chop ($line);
        if ($line eq "") {
                print ("<blank line>\n");
                next;
        }
        write;
}
```

Day 12

File-System, String, and Mathematical Functions

Today, you'll learn how to manage your machine's file system, manipulate character strings, and perform mathematical operations by using some of the built-in library functions in Perl. These functions are divided into four groups:

☐ The file input and output functions

☐ The directory-manipulation functions

☐ The functions that manipulate character strings

☐ The functions that perform mathematical operations

File Input and Output Functions

The following sections describe the built-in library functions that read information from files and write information to files. These library functions perform the following tasks:

- [ ] Basic input and output
- [ ] Skipping or rereading data from a file
- [ ] Reading individual characters from a file
- [ ] Indicating that a file is a binary file

Basic Input and Output Functions

Some of the input and output functions supplied by Perl are discussed in earlier chapters. They are

- [ ] `open`, which lets a program access a file
- [ ] `close`, which terminates file access
- [ ] `print`, which writes a string to a file
- [ ] `write`, which writes information to a file, using a print format
- [ ] `printf`, which formats a string and sends it to a file

The following sections briefly describe these functions again, along with some features of these functions that have not been discussed previously.

The `open` Function

The `open` function enables a Perl program to access a file. It associates a special file handle with each accessed file. The following is an example:

```
open (MYVAR, " C:\data\file");
```

Here, `open` requests access to the file `C:\data\file`, and it associates the file `MYVAR` with this file after it is open. `open` returns a nonzero value if the open succeeds, and `0` if the open fails.

By default, `open` opens a file for reading only. To open a file for writing, put a `>` character in front of the filename, as follows:

```
open (MYVAR, "> C:\data\file");
```

To append information to an existing file, put two `>` characters in front of the filename, as follows:

```
open (MYVAR, ">> C:\data\file");
```

12

Piping Input Using open

The open function enables you to open files in several other ways not previously discussed. For example, to treat the open file as a command that is piping data to this program, put a | character after the filename, like this:

```
open (MYFILE, "dir file*|");
```

This call to open executes the command dir file*. This command creates a temporary file consisting of a list of all files whose names start with file. This file is treated as an input file that is accessible using the file handle MYFILE:

```
$input = <MYFILE>;
```

Listing 12.1 is another example of a program that uses piped input. This program uses the output from the time command to display the current time of the machine.

Listing 12.1. A program that receives input from a piped command.

```
1:  # p12_1.pl
2:
3:  open (MYOUT, "time/T|");
4:  $time = <MYOUT>;
5:  close (MYOUT);
6:  print ("Current time:  $time");
```

OUTPUT

```
C:\> perl p12_1.pl
Current time: 4:25p
C:\>
```

ANALYSIS The time/T command lists the current time according to the Windows NT system.

Line 3 starts the time/T command. The call to open specifies that the output from time/T is to be treated as input to this program, and that the file handle MYOUT is to be used to access this input.

Line 4 reads the first line of the input piped from MYOUT. This is the line read:

```
4:25p
```

Line 5 closes the file handle MYOUT. Line 6 prints the current time, as stored in $time. Note that print does not need to specify a trailing newline character because $time contains one.

Redirecting One File to Another

Listing 12.2 shows how you can do this in Perl.

Listing 12.2. A program that redirects the standard output and standard error files.

TYPE

```
1:  # p12_2.pl
2:
3:  open (STDOUT, ">file1") || die ("open STDOUT failed");
4:  open (STDERR, ">&STDOUT") || die ("open STDERR failed");
5:  print STDOUT ("line 1\n");
6:  print STDERR ("line 2\n");
7:  close (STDOUT);
8:  close (STDERR);
```

OUTPUT This program produces no visible output.

ANALYSIS The following are the contents of the output file `file1`:

```
line 1
line 2
```

Line 3 redirects the standard output file. To do this, it opens the output file `file1` and associates it with the file handle STDOUT; this closes the standard output file.

Line 4 redirects the standard error file. The argument `>&STDOUT` tells the Perl interpreter to use the file already opened and associated with STDOUT. This means that the file handle STDERR refers to the same file as STDOUT.

Lines 5 and 6 write to STDOUT and STDERR, respectively. Because these file handles refer to the same file, both lines are written to `file1`.

Listing 12.3 shows how you can use $| to ensure that your output lines appear in the correct order.

Checking the value of the system variable $| tells whether a particular file is to be buffered (in other words, whether it should use a buffer). If $| is assigned a nonzero value, no buffer is used. As with $~ and $^, assigning to $| affects the current default file, which is the file last specified in a call to `select` (or STDOUT, if `select` has not been called).

Listing 12.3. A program that redirects standard input and output and turns off buffering.

TYPE

```
1:  # p12_3.pl
2:
3:  open (STDOUT, ">file1") || die ("open STDOUT failed");
4:  open (STDERR, ">&STDOUT") || die ("open STDERR failed");
5:  $| = 1;
6:  select (STDERR);
7:  $| = 1;
8:  print STDOUT ("line 1\n");
```

12

```
9:  print STDERR ("line 2\n");
10: close (STDOUT);
11: close (STDERR);
```

 This program produces no visible output.

 The contents of the output file `file1` are now the following:

```
line 1
line 2
```

Line 5 sets $|$ to 1, which tells the Perl interpreter that the current default file does not need to be buffered. Because `select` has not yet been called, the current default file is STDOUT, which means that line 5 turns off buffering for the standard output file (which has been redirected to `file1`).

Line 6 sets the current default file to STDERR, and line 7 once again sets $|$ to 1. This turns off buffering for the standard error file (which has also been redirected to `file1`).

Because buffering has been turned off for both STDERR and STDOUT, lines 8 and 9 write to `file1` right away. This means that the output lines appear in `file1` in the order in which they are printed.

Specifying Read and Write Access

To open a file for both read and write access, specify `+>` before the filename, as follows:

```
open (READWRITE, "+>file1");
```

This opens the file named `file1` for both reading and writing. This enables you to overwrite portions of a file.

Opening a file for reading and writing works best in conjunction with the library functions `seek` and `tell`, which enable you to skip to the middle of a file. (For more information on `seek` and `tell`, refer to the section "Skipping and Rereading Data," later in today's lesson.)

12

 NOTE

You also can use `+<` as the prefix to specify both reading and writing, as follows:

```
open (READWRITE, "+<file1");
```

The prefix `<`, by itself, specifies that the file is to be opened for reading. This means that the following two statements are identical:

```
open (READONLY, "<read");
open (READONLY, "read");
```

The `close` Function

The library function `close` was discussed on Day 6, "Reading from and Writing to Files." It closes a file opened by `open`, as follows:

```
close (MYFILE);
```

Here, `MYFILE` is the file handle (passed to `open`) that is associated with the open file.

NOTE

> If you use `close` to close a pipe, the program will wait for the piped program to terminate. For example:
>
> ```
> open (MYPIPE, "dir file*|");
> close (MYPIPE);
> ```
>
> When `close` is called, the program suspends execution until the command `dir file*` is terminated.

The `print`, `printf`, and `write` Functions

The `print`, `printf`, and `write` functions are also covered in previous chapters, but I'll briefly recap them here.

The `print` function is the simplest function. It writes to the file specified, or to the current default file if no file is specified. For example:

```
print ("Hello, there!\n");
print OUTFILE ("Hello, there!\n");
```

The first statement writes to the current default file (which is STDOUT unless `select` has been called). The second statement writes to the file specified by OUTFILE.

The `printf` function formats a string and sends it to either the file specified or the current default file. For example, the statement

```
printf OUTFILE ("You owe me %8.2f", $owing);
```

takes the value stored in `$owing` and substitutes it for `%8.2f` in the specified string. `%8.2f` is an example of a *field specifier* and indicates that the value stored in `$owing` is to be treated as a floating-point number.

The `write` function uses a print format to send formatted output to the file that is specified or to the current default file. For example:

```
select (OUTFILE);
$~ = "MYFORMAT";
write;
```

This call to write uses the print format MYFORMAT to send output to the file OUTFILE.

For more information on printf or write, refer to Day 11, "Formatting Your Output."

The select Function

The select function is passed a file handle, which becomes the new current default file. Here is an example:

```
select (MYFILE);
```

In this case, MYFILE is now the current default file, which means that calls to print, write, and printf write to MYFILE unless a file handle is explicitly specified.

There is another version of select that takes more than one argument and currently is not implemented in Perl 5 for Win32.

The eof Function

The library function eof checks whether the last input file read has been exhausted. If all the input has been read, eof returns a nonzero value. If there is input remaining, eof returns zero.

The eof function was first introduced on Day 6. You might have noticed on that day that the examples that use eof use it without parentheses. This is because the behavior of eof is a little tricky if you are using it in conjunction with the <> operator; in that case, eof and eof() behave differently.

Listing 12.4 shows how eof interacts with <>. It prints the contents of one or more input files whose names are supplied on the command line. A line of dashes is printed after each input file is completed.

To run this program yourself, create two files named file1 and file2. Put the following in file1:

```
This is a line from the first file.
Here is the last line of the first file.
```

Then, put the following in file2:

```
This is a line from the second and last file.
Here is the last line of the last file.
```

Finally, specify file1 and file2 on the command line when you run this program. For example, if you have called this program program 12_4, run it as follows:

```
C:\> perl p12_4.pl file1 file2
```

This will give you the output shown in the Input-Output example.

12

TYPE   **Listing 12.4. A program that uses** eof **and** <> **together.**

```
1:  # p12_4.pl
2:
3:  while ($line = <>) {
4:        print ($line);
5:        if (eof) {
6:              print ("— end of current file —\n");
7:        }
8:  }
```

OUTPUT
```
C:\> perl p12_4.pl file1 file2
This is a line from the first file.
Here is the last line of the first file.
— end of current file —
This is a line from the second and last file.
Here is the last line of the last file.
— end of current file —
C:\>
```

ANALYSIS   The <> operator in line 3 tells the program to read the next line of input from the input files supplied on the command line. Line 4 then prints the line.

Line 5 calls eof without parentheses. This is the form of eof that you are familiar with. It returns true if the current input file has been completely read.

| When you test for end-of-file, use either eof or eof(), but not both. |

WARNING

Compare the program in Listing 12.4 with Listing 12.5, which uses eof() instead of eof.

TYPE   **Listing 12.5. A program that uses** eof() **and** <> **together.**

```
1:  # p12_5.pl
2:
3:  while ($line = <>) {
4:        print ($line);
5:        if (eof()) {
6:              print ("— end of output —\n");
7:        }
8:  }
```

OUTPUT

```
C:\> perl p12_5.pl file1 file2
This is a line from the first file.
Here is the last line of the first file.
This is a line from the second and last file.
Here is the last line of the last file.
— end of output —
C:\>
```

ANALYSIS

Line 5 of this program calls eof with parentheses. Calls to eof with parentheses return true only when all of the files have been read. If the program is at the end of the first input file, eof() returns false because there is still input to be read.

NOTE

If you like, you can use eof with a particular file. For example:

```
if (eof(MYFILE)) {
        # do end-of-file stuff
}
```

Here, the conditional expression returns true if all of MYFILE has been read.

Also, note that the distinction between eof and eof() is only meaningful when you are using the <> operator. If you are just reading from a single file, it doesn't matter whether you supply parentheses. For example:

```
while ($line = <STDIN>) {
        # stuff goes here
        if (eof) {     # you can also use eof() here
                # more stuff here
        }
}
```

12

Indirect File Handles

When you call any of the functions described so far in today's lesson, you can indicate which file to use by specifying a file handle. However, these functions also enable you to supply a scalar variable in place of a file handle; when you do, the Perl interpreter treats the value stored in the scalar variable as the name of the file handle. For example, consider the following:

```
$filename = "MYFILENAME";
open ($filename, ">file1");
```

This call to open takes the value stored in $filename—MYFILENAME—and uses it as the file-variable name. This means that the file handle MYFILENAME is now associated with the output file file1.

Listing 12.6 is an example of a program that stores a file-variable name in a scalar variable and passes the library variable to Perl input and output functions.

TYPE | **Listing 12.6. A program that uses a scalar variable to store a file handle name.**

```
1:  # p12_6.pl
2:
3:  &open_file("INFILE", "", "file1");
4:  &open_file("OUTFILE", ">", "file2");
5:  while ($line = &read_from_file("INFILE")) {
6:          &print_to_file("OUTFILE", $line);
7:  }
8:
9:  sub open_file {
10:         local ($filevar, $filemode, $filename) = @_;
11:
12:         open ($filevar, $filemode . $filename) ||
13:                 die ("Can't open $filename");
14: }
15: sub read_from_file {
16:         local ($filevar) = @_;
17:
18:         <$filevar>;
19: }
20: sub print_to_file {
21:         local ($filevar, $line) = @_;
22:
23:         print $filevar ($line);
24: }
```

OUTPUT This program produces no output.

ANALYSIS This program is just a fancy way of copying the contents of file1 to file2. Line 3 opens the input file, file1, for reading by calling the subroutine open_file. This subroutine is passed the name of the file handle to use, which is INFILE.

Line 4 uses the same subroutine, open_file, to open the output file, file2, for writing. The file handle OUTFILE is used in this open operation.

Line 5 calls read_from_file to read a line of input and passes it the file-variable name INFILE. Line 18 substitutes the value of $filevar, INFILE, into <$filevar>, yielding the result <INFILE>; then, it reads a line from this input file. Because this line-reading operation is the last expression evaluated in the subroutine, the line read is returned by the subroutine and assigned to $line.

Line 6 then passes OUTFILE and the input line just read to the subroutine print_to_file.

NOTE

All the functions you've seen so far in this chapter—open, close, print, printf, write, select, and eof—enable you to use a scalar variable in place of a file handle.

The functions open, close, write, select, and eof also enable you to use an expression in place of a file handle. The value of the expression must be a character string that can be used as a file handle.

Skipping and Rereading Data

In the programs you've seen so far, input files have always been read in order, starting with the first line of input and continuing on to the end. Perl provides two special functions, seek and tell, that enable you to skip forward or backward in a file so that you can skip or reread data.

The seek Function

The seek function moves backward or forward in a file.

The syntax for the seek function is

```
seek (filevar, distance, relative_to);
```

As you can see, seek requires three arguments:

☐ *filevar*, which is the file handle representing the file in which to skip

☐ *distance*, which is an integer representing the number of bytes (characters) to skip

☐ *relative_to*, which is either 0, 1, or 2

If *relative_to* is 0, the number of bytes to skip is relative to the beginning of the file. If *relative_to* is 1, the skip is relative to the current position in the file (the current position is the location of the next line to be read). If *relative_to* is 2, the skip is relative to the end of the file.

For example, to skip back to the beginning of the file MYFILE, use the following:

```
seek(MYFILE, 0, 0);
```

The following statement skips forward 80 bytes:

```
seek(MYFILE, 80, 1);
```

The following statement skips backward 80 bytes:

```
seek(MYFILE, -80, 1);
```

12

And the following statement skips to the end of the file (which is useful when the file has been opened for reading and writing):

```
seek(MYFILE, 0, 2);
```

The seek function returns true (nonzero) if the skip was successful, and 0 if it failed. It is often used in conjunction with the tell function, described in the next section.

The tell Function

The tell function returns the distance, in bytes, between the beginning of the file and the current position of the file (the location of the next line to be read).

The syntax for the tell function is

```
tell (filevar);
```

filevar, which is required, represents the file whose current position is needed.

For example, the following statement retrieves the current position of the file MYFILE:

```
$offset = tell (MYFILE);
```

> **NOTE**
>
> tell and seek accept an expression in place of a file handle, provided the value of the expression is the name of a file handle.

You can use tell and seek to skip to a particular position in a file. For example, Listing 12.7 uses these functions to print pairs of lines twice each. (This is, of course, not the fastest way to do this.)

TYPE   **Listing 12.7. A program that demonstrates seek and tell.**

```
 1:  # p12_7.pl
 2:
 3:  @array = ("This", "is", "a", "test");
 4:  open (TEMPFILE, ">file1");
 5:  foreach $element (@array) {
 6:          print TEMPFILE ("$element\n");
 7:  }
 8:  close (TEMPFILE);
 9:  open (TEMPFILE, "file1");
10:  while (1) {
11:          $skipback = tell(TEMPFILE);
12:          $line = <TEMPFILE>;
13:          last if ($line eq "");
14:          print ($line);
```

```
15:            $line = <TEMPFILE>;   # assume the second line exists
16:            print ($line);
17:            seek (TEMPFILE, $skipback, 0);
18:            $line = <TEMPFILE>;
19:            print ($line);
20:            $line = <TEMPFILE>;
21:            print ($line);
22: }
```

OUTPUT

```
C:\> perl p12_7.pl
This
is
This
is
a
test
a
test
C:\>
```

ANALYSIS Lines 3–8 of this program create a temporary file named file1 consisting of four lines: This, is, a, and test. Line 9 opens this temporary file for reading.

Lines 10–22 loop through the test file. Line 11 calls tell to obtain the current position of the file before reading the pair of lines. Lines 12–16 read the lines and print them (first testing whether the end of the file has been reached).

Line 17 then calls seek, which positions the file at the point returned by tell in line 11. This means that lines 18 and 20 read the pair of lines that have been read by lines 12 and 15. Therefore, lines 19 and 21 print a second copy of the input lines.

WARNING

You cannot use seek and tell if the file handle actually refers to a pipe. For example, if you open a pipe, using the statement

```
open (MYPIPE, "dir file*|");
```

the following statement makes no sense:

```
$illegal = tell (MYPIPE);
```

System Read and Write Functions

In Perl, the easiest way to read input from a file is to use the `<filevar>` operator, where `filevar` is the file handle representing the file to read. Perl 5 provides two other functions that read from an input file:

☐ read, which is equivalent to the UNIX `fread` function and is ported to Perl 5 for Win32

☐ sysread, which is not supported currently in Perl 5 for Win32

(Also, `syswrite` is not supported in the current version of Perl 5 for Win32.)

The read Function

The `read` function enables you to read an arbitrary number of characters (bytes) into a scalar variable.

The syntax for the `read` function is

```
read (filevar, result, length, skipval);
```

Here, `filevar` is the file handle representing the file to read, `result` is the scalar variable (or array variable element) into which the bytes are to be stored, and `length` is the number of bytes to read.

`skipval` is an optional argument that specifies the number of bytes to skip before reading.

For example:

```
read (MYFILE, $scalar, 80);
```

This call to `read` tries to read 80 bytes from the file represented by the file handle MYFILE, storing the resulting character string in `$scalar`. It returns the number of bytes actually read; if MYFILE is at end of file, it returns 0 (`read` returns the null string if an error occurs).

You can use `read` to append to an existing scalar variable by specifying a fourth argument, which indicates the number of bytes to skip in the scalar variable.

```
read (MYFILE, $scalar, 40, 80);
```

This call to `read` reads another 40 bytes from MYFILE. When copying these bytes into `$scalar`, `read` first skips the first 80 bytes already stored there.

Reading Characters Using getc

Perl provides one other built-in function, `getc`, which reads a single character of input from a file.

The syntax for calls to the `getc` function is

```
char = getc (infile);
```

`infile` is the file handle to a file from which to read, and `char` is the character returned.

For example:

```
$singlechar = getc(INFILE);
```

This statement reads a character from the file represented by INFILE and stores it (as a character string) in the scalar variable $singlechar.

The getc is useful for *hot-key* applications. These applications accept and process input one character at a time rather than one line at a time. Listing 12.8 is an example of such a program. It reads one character at a time and checks whether the character is alphanumeric. If it is, it writes out the next higher letter or number. For example, when you enter a, the program prints out b, and so on. In this example, the alphabetic letters a through z and the digits 0 through 9 are typed in.

TYPE **Listing 12.8. A program that demonstrates the use of** getc.

```
1:  # p12_8.pl
2:
3:  while (1) {
4:          $char = getc(STDIN);
5:          last if ($char eq "\\");
6:          $char =~ tr/a-zA-Z0-9/b-zaB-ZA1-90/;
7:          print ($char);
8:  }
9: print ("\n");
```

OUTPUT
```
C:\> perl p12_8.pl
abcdefghijklmnopqrstuvwxyz0123456789
bcdefghijklmnopqrstuvwxyza1234567890
\
C:\>
```

ANALYSIS The loop in lines 3–8 reads and writes one character per loop iteration when the Enter key is pressed at the end of the line of input text. Line 4 starts off by reading characters from the standard input file using getc.

Line 5 tests whether the character read is a backslash. If it is, the loop terminates. If the character is not a backslash, the program continues with line 6. This line translates all alphanumeric characters to the next-highest letter or number; for example, it translates g to h, E to F, and 7 to 8. The characters z, Z, and 9 are translated to a, A, and 0, respectively.

Line 7 prints out the translated characters.

12

Reading a Binary File Using `binmode`

If your machine distinguishes between text files and binary files (files that contain unprintable characters), your Perl program can tell the system that a particular file is a binary file. To do this, call the built-in function `binmode`.

The syntax for calling the `binmode` function is

```
binmode (filevar);
```

`filevar` is a file handle.

`binmode` expects a file handle (or an expression whose value is the name of a file handle). It must be called after the file is opened, but before the file is read.

The following is an example of a call to `binmode`:

```
binmode (MYFILE);
```

Directory-Manipulation Functions

The input and output functions that you have seen earlier read and write data to files. Perl also provides a group of functions that enable you to manipulate Windows NT directories. Functions exist that enable you to create, read, open, close, delete, and skip around in directories. The following sections describe these functions.

The `mkdir` Function

To create a new directory, call the function `mkdir`.

The syntax for the `mkdir` function is

```
mkdir (dirname, permissions);
```

`mkdir` requires two arguments:

- [ ] `dirname`, which is the name of the directory to be created (which can be a character string or an expression whose value is a directory name)

- [ ] `permissions`, which is an octal (base-8) number specifying the access permissions for the new directory

NOTE

On the Windows NT system, the permissions value does not affect the access permissions of the created directory.

12

`mkdir` returns true (nonzero) if the directory is successfully created. It returns false (0) if the directory is not.

The `chdir` Function

To set a directory to be the current working directory, use the function `chdir`.

The syntax for the `chdir` function is

```
chdir (dirname);
```

`dirname` is the name of the new current working directory.

`chdir` returns true if the current directory is set properly, and false if an error occurs.

For example, to set the current working directory to `C:\user\newdir`, use the following statement:

```
chdir ("C:\user\newdir");
```

NOTE

As with `mkdir`, the directory name passed to `chdir` can be either a character string or an expression whose value is a directory name. For example, the following sets the current directory to be `C:\user\newdir`:

```
$dir = "C:\user\";
chdir ($dir . "newdir");
```

The `opendir` Function

You can have your program examine a list of the files contained in a directory. To do this, the first step is to call the built-in function `opendir`.

The syntax for the `opendir` function is

```
opendir (dirvar, dirname);
```

`dirvar` is the name the program is to use to represent the directory, also known as a *directory handle*, and `dirname` is the name of the directory to open (which can be a character string or the value of an expression).

`opendir` returns true if the open operation is successful, and returns false otherwise.

12

For example, to open the directory named C:\user\mydir, you can use the following
statement:

```
opendir (DIR, "C:\user\mydir");
```

This associates the directory variable DIR with the opened directory.

NOTE

> If you like, you can use the same name as both a directory variable (or
> directory handle) and a file variable (or file handle):
> ```
> opendir (MYNAME, "C:\user\dir");
> open (MYNAME, "C:\data\file");
> ```
> The Perl interpreter always can tell from context whether a name is
> being used as a directory variable or as a file handle. (However, there is
> no real reason to do so. Your programs will be easier to read if you use
> different names to represent files and directories.)

The closedir Function

To close an opened directory, call the closedir function.

The syntax for the closedir function is

```
closedir (mydir);
```

closedir expects one argument: the directory variable associated with the directory to be
closed.

The readdir Function

After opendir has opened a directory, you can access the name of each file or subdirectory
stored in the directory by calling the function readdir.

The syntax for the readdir function is

```
readdir (mydir);
```

Like closedir, readdir is passed the directory variable that is associated with the open
directory.

If the value returned from readdir is assigned to a scalar variable, readdir returns the name
of the first file or subdirectory stored in the directory. For example,

```
$filename = readdir(MYDIR);
```

The first name is returned also if the return value from readdir is assigned to an element of an array variable. Look at this example:

```
$filearray[3] = readdir(MYDIR);
$filearray{"foo"} = readdir(MYDIR);
```

If readdir is called again, it returns the next name in the directory; subsequent calls return other names, continuing until the directory is exhausted. Listing 12.9 uses readdir to list the files and subdirectories in the Per15 directory on my machine.

TYPE

Listing 12.9. A program that lists the files and subdirectories in a directory.

```
1:  # p12_9.pl
2:
3:  opendir(HOMEDIR, "c:/perl5") ||
4:          die ("Unable to open directory");
5:  while (defined($filename = readdir(HOMEDIR))) {
6:          print ("$filename\n");
7:  }
8:  closedir(HOMEDIR);
```

OUTPUT

```
C:\> perl p12_9.pl
.
..
docs
eg
INSTALL.BAT
INSTALL.TXT
Lib
LICENSE.TXT
MANIFEST.TXT
ntt
PL2BAT.BAT
README.TXT
release.txt
Samples
STATUS.TXT
UNINSTALL.BAT
WIN95.TXT
INSTALL.PIF
perl.exe
Perl100.dll
install.log
bin
C:\>
```

ANALYSIS Line 3 opens the directory c:/perl5, which is on my computer. The opendir function associates the directory variable HOMEDIR with c:/perl5.

Lines 5–7 read the name of each file in the directory in turn. Line 6 prints each filename as it is read in.

As you can see, `readdir` reads the names in the order in which they appear in the directory.

The `telldir` and `seekdir` Functions

As you've seen, the library functions `tell` and `seek` enable you to skip backward and forward in a file. Similarly, the library functions `telldir` and `seekdir` enable you to skip backward and forward in a list of directories.

To use `telldir`, pass it the directory variable defined by `opendir`. `telldir` returns the current directory location (where you are in the list of files).

The syntax for the `telldir` function is

```
location = telldir (mydir);
```

Here, `mydir` is the directory variable corresponding to the directory whose file list you are examining, and `location` is assigned the current directory location.

To skip to the directory location returned by `telldir`, call `seekdir`.

The syntax for the `seekdir` function is

```
seekdir(mydir, location);
```

This call to `seekdir` sets the current directory location to the location specified by `location`.

> `seekdir` works only with directory locations returned by `telldir`.
> `seekdir` cannot select an arbitrary position.

WARNING

The `rewinddir` Function

Although being able to skip anywhere you like in a directory list is useful, the most common skipping operation in directory lists is *rewinding* the directory list, or starting over again. Because of this, Perl provides a special function, `rewinddir`, that handles the rewind operation.

The syntax for the `rewinddir` function is

```
rewinddir (mydir);
```

`rewinddir` sets the current directory location to the beginning of the list of files, which lets you read the entire list of files again. As with the other directory functions, `mydir` is the directory variable defined by `opendir`.

The `rmdir` Function

The final directory function supplied by Perl is `rmdir`, which deletes an empty directory.

The syntax for calling the `rmdir` function is

```
rmdir (dirname);
```

`rmdir` returns `true` (nonzero) if the directory `dirname` is deleted successfully, and `false` (zero) if the directory is not empty or cannot be deleted.

File-Attribute Functions

Perl provides several library functions that modify the attributes or behavior of files. These functions can be divided into the following groups:

- ☐ Functions that relocate (rename or delete) files
- ☐ Other file-attribute functions

These groups of functions are described in the following sections.

File-Relocation Functions

Perl provides the following file-relocation functions:

- ☐ `rename`, which moves or renames a file
- ☐ `unlink`, which deletes a file

The `rename` Function

The built-in function `rename` changes the name of a file.

The syntax for the `rename` function is

```
rename (oldname, newname);
```

`oldname` is the old filename, and `newname` is the new filename.

The `rename` function returns true if the rename succeeds, and false if an error occurs.

For example, to change a file named `name1` to `name2`, use the following:

```
rename ("name1", "name2");
```

You can use the value stored in a scalar variable as an argument to `rename`, or any variable or expression whose value is a character string, as follows:

```
rename ($oldname, &get_new_name);
```

12

You can also use `rename` to move a file from one directory to another (provided both directories are in the same file system). For example:

```
rename ("C:\user\name1", "C:\data\name2");
```

WARNING

When `rename` moves a file, as in

```
rename ("name1", "name2");
```

it does not check whether a file named `name2` already exists. Any existing `name2` is destroyed by the `rename` operation.

To get around this problem, use the `-e` file-test operator, which checks whether a named file exists, as follows:

```
-e "name2" || rename (name1, name2);
```

Here, the `||` operator ensures that `rename` is called only when no file named `name2` already exists.

You can use `or` to replace `||` in Perl 5 or Perl 5 for Win32.

The `unlink` Function

To delete a file, use the `unlink` function.

The syntax for the `unlink` function is

SYNTAX

```
num = unlink (filelist);
```

This function takes a list as its argument and deletes all the files named in that list.

`unlink` returns the number of files actually deleted.

The following is an example of a call to `unlink`:

```
@deletelist = ("file1", "file2");
unlink (@deletelist);
```

The function is called `unlink`, instead of `delete`, because that is what UNIX calls it.

Miscellaneous Attribute Functions

The following sections describe other functions supported in Perl 5 for Win32 to retrieve file information.

The `stat` **Function**

The `stat` function retrieves information about a particular file when given a file handle or an expression naming a file.

SYNTAX

The syntax for the `stat` function is

```
stat (file);
```

Here, `file` is either a file handle or an expression naming a file.

`stat` returns a list containing the following elements, in this order:

- ☐ The device on which the file resides
- ☐ The internal reference number (`inode` number) for this file
- ☐ The permissions for the file
- ☐ The number of hard links to the file
- ☐ The numerical user ID of the file owner
- ☐ The numerical group ID of the file owner
- ☐ The device type, if this "file" is actually a device
- ☐ The size of the file (in bytes)
- ☐ When the file was last accessed
- ☐ When the file was last modified
- ☐ When the file status last changed

Some of the items returned by `stat` can be obtained using file-test operators. (See Day 6 for more information on how to use file-test operators.)

The `time` **Function**

The access and modification times returned by `stat` and by the `-A` and `-M` file-test operators are integers representing the number of elapsed seconds from January 1, 1970, to the time the file was accessed or modified.

To obtain the number of elapsed seconds from January 1, 1970, to the present time, call the built-in function `time`.

SYNTAX

The syntax for calls to the `time` function is

```
currtime = time();
```

`currtime` is the returned elapsed-seconds value.

The `gmtime` **and** `localtime` **Functions**

The value returned by `time` can be converted to either Greenwich Mean Time or your computer's local time.

To convert to Greenwich Mean Time, call the `gmtime` function. To convert to local time, call the `localtime` function.

The syntax for the `gmtime` and `localtime` functions is identical:

```
timelist = gmtime (timeval);

timelist = localtime (timeval);
```

Both functions accept the time value returned by `time`, `stat`, or the `-A` and `-M` file-test operators.

Both functions return a list consisting of the following nine elements:

- ☐ Seconds
- ☐ Minutes
- ☐ The hour of the day, which is a value between `0` and `23`
- ☐ The day of the month
- ☐ The month, which is a value between `0` (January) and `11` (December)
- ☐ The year minus 1900. For instance, the year 97 is obtained by 1997–1900
- ☐ The day of the week, which is a value between `0` (Sunday) and `6` (Saturday)
- ☐ The day of the year, which is a value between `0` and `364`
- ☐ A flag indicating whether daylight savings time is in effect

String-Manipulation Functions

This section describes the built-in functions of Perl that manipulate character strings. These functions enable you to do the following:

- ☐ Search for a substring in a character string
- ☐ Create a string
- ☐ Replace a substring within a string

The `index` **Function**

The `index` function provides a way of indicating the location of a substring in a string.

SYNTAX

The syntax for the `index` function is

```
position = index (string, substring);
```

string is the character string to search in, and *substring* is the character string being searched for. *position* returns the number of characters skipped before *substring* is located; if *substring* is not found, position is set to –1.

Listing 12.10 is a program that uses `index` to locate a substring in a string.

TYPE **Listing 12.10. A program that uses the `index` function.**

```
1:  # p12_10.pl
2:
3:  $input = <STDIN>;
4:  $position = index($input, "the");
5:  if ($position >= 0) {
6:          print ("pattern found at position $position\n");
7:  } else {
8:          print ("pattern not found\n");
9:  }
```

OUTPUT

```
C:\> perl p12 10.pl
Here is the input line I have typed.
pattern found at position 8
C:\>
```

ANALYSIS This program searches for the first occurrence of the word `the`. If it is found, the program prints the location of the pattern; if it is not found, the program prints `pattern not found`.

You can use the `index` function to find more than one copy of a substring in a string. To do this, pass a third argument to `index`, which tells it how many characters to skip before starting to search. For example:

```
$position = index($line, "foo", 5);
```

This call to `index` skips five characters before starting to search for `foo` in the string stored in `$line`. As before, if `index` finds the substring, it returns the total number of characters skipped (including the number specified by the third argument to `index`). If `index` does not find the substring in the portion of the string that it searches, it returns –1.

This feature of `index` enables you to find all occurrences of a substring in a string. Listing 12.11 is a modified version of Listing 12.11 that searches for all occurrences of `the` in an input line.

12

Listing 12.11. A program that uses `index` to search a line repeatedly.

`TYPE`

```
 1:  # p12_11.pl
 2:
 3:  $input = <STDIN>;
 4:  $position = $found = 0;
 5:  while (1) {
 6:          $position = index($input, "the", $position);
 7:          last if ($position == -1);
 8:          if ($found == 0) {
 9:                  $found = 1;
10:                  print ("pattern found — characters skipped:");
11:          }
12:          print (" $position");
13:          $position++;
14:  }
15:  if ($found == 0) {
16:          print ("pattern not found\n");
17:  } else {
18:          print ("\n");
19:  }
```

`OUTPUT`

```
C:\> perl p12 11.pl
Here is the test line containing the words.
pattern found — characters skipped: 8 33
C:\>
```

`ANALYSIS`   Line 6 of this program calls `index`. Because the initial value of `$position` is 0, the first call to `index` starts searching from the beginning of the string. Eight characters are skipped before the first occurrence of `the` is found; this means that `$position` is assigned 8.

Line 7 tests whether a match has been found by comparing `$position` with –1, which is the value `index` returns when it does not find the string for which it is looking. Because a match has been found, the loop continues to execute.

When the loop iterates again, line 6 calls `index` again. This time, `index` skips nine characters before beginning the search again, which ensures that the previously found occurrence of `the` is skipped. A total of 33 bytes are skipped before `the` is found again. Once again, the loop continues, because the conditional expression in line 7 is false.

On the final iteration of the loop, line 6 calls `index` and skips 34 characters before starting the search. This time, `the` is not found, `index` returns –1, and the conditional expression in line 7 is true. At this point, the loop terminates.

`NOTE`

> To extract a substring found by `index`, use the `substr` function, which is described later in today's lesson.

12

The `rindex` **Function**

The `rindex` function is similar to the `index` function. The only difference is that `rindex` starts searching from the right end of the string, not the left.

The syntax for the `rindex` function is

```
position = rindex (string, substring);
```

This syntax is identical to the syntax for `index`. *string* is the character string to search in, and *substring* is the character string being searched for. *position* returns the number of characters skipped before *substring* is located; if *substring* is not found, *position* is set to −1.

The following is an example:

```
$string = "Here is the test line containing the words.";
$position = rindex($string, "the");
```

In this example, `rindex` finds the second occurrence of the. As with `index`, `rindex` returns the number of characters between the left end of the string and the location of the found substring. In this case, 33 characters are skipped, and `$position` is assigned 33.

You can specify a third argument to `rindex`, indicating the maximum number of characters that can be skipped. For example, if you want `rindex` to find the first occurrence of the in the preceding example, you can call it as follows:

```
$string = "Here is the test line containing the words.";
$position = rindex($string, "the", 32);
```

Here, the second occurrence of the cannot be matched, because it is to the right of the specified limit of 32 skipped characters. `rindex`, therefore, finds the first occurrence of the. Because there are eight characters between the beginning of the string and the occurrence, `$position` is assigned 8.

Like `index`, `rindex` returns −1 if it cannot find the string it is looking for.

The `length` **Function**

The `length` function returns the number of characters contained in a character string.

The syntax for the `length` function is

```
num = length (string);
```

string is the character string for which you want to determine the length, and *num* is the returned length.

Here is an example using `length`:

```
$string = "Here is a string";
$strlen = length($string);
```

In this example, length determines that the string in $string is 16 characters long, and it assigns 16 to $strlen.

Listing 12.12 is a program that calculates the average word length used in an input file. (This is sometimes used to determine the complexity of the text.) Numbers are skipped.

Listing 12.12. A program that demonstrates the use of

TYPE   length.

```
1:  # p12_12.pl
2:
3:  $wordcount = $charcount = 0;
4:  while ($line = <STDIN>) {
5:          @words = split(/\s+/, $line);
6:          foreach $word (@words) {
7:                  next if ($word =~ /^\d+\.?\d+$/);
8:                  $word =~ s/[,.;:]$//;
9:                  $wordcount += 1;
10:                 $charcount += length($word);
11:         }
12: }
13: print ("Average word length: ", $charcount / $wordcount, "\n");
```

OUTPUT
```
C:\> perl p12_12.pl
Here is the test input.
Here is the last line.
^Z
Average word length: 3.5
C:\>
```

ANALYSIS   This program reads a line of input at a time from the standard input file, breaking the input line into words. Line 7 tests whether the word is a number, and skips it if it is. Line 8 strips any trailing punctuation character from the word, which ensures that the punctuation is not counted as part of the word length.

Line 10 calls length to retrieve the number of characters in the word. This number is added to $charcount, which contains the total number of characters in all of the words that have been read so far. To determine the average word length of the file, line 13 takes this value and divides it by the number of words in the file, which is stored in $wordcount.

Retrieving String Length Using tr

The tr function provides another way of determining the length of a character string, in conjunction with the built-in system variable $_.

SYNTAX

The syntax for the `tr` function is

```
tr/sourcelist/replacelist/
```

sourcelist is the list of characters to replace, and *replacelist* is the list of characters to replace it with. (For details, see the following listing and the explanation provided with it.)

Listing 12.13 shows how `tr` works.

Listing 12.13. A program that uses `tr` to retrieve the length of a string.

```
1:  # p12_13.pl
2:
3:  $string = "here is a string";
4:  $_ = $string;
5:  $length = tr/a-zA-Z /a-zA-Z /;
6:  print ("the string is $length characters long\n");
```

OUTPUT

```
C:\> perl p12 13.pl
the string is 16 characters long
C:\>
```

ANALYSIS

Line 3 of this program creates a string of `here is a string` and assigns it to the scalar variable `$string`. Line 4 copies this string into a built-in scalar variable, `$_`.

Line 5 exploits two features of the `tr` operator that have not yet been discussed:

☐ If the value to be translated is not explicitly specified by means of the `=~` operator, `tr` assumes that the value is stored in `$_`.

☐ `tr` returns the number of characters translated.

In line 5, both the search pattern (the set of characters to look for) and the replacement pattern (the characters to replace them with) are the same. This pattern, `/a-zA-Z /`, tells `tr` to search for all lowercase letters, uppercase letters, and blank spaces and then replace them with themselves. This pattern matches every character in the string, which means that every character is being translated.

Because every character is being translated, the number of characters translated is equivalent to the length of the string. This string length is assigned to the scalar variable `$length`.

`tr` can be used also to count the number of occurrences of a specific character, as shown in Listing 12.14.

TYPE

Listing 12.14. A program that uses `tr` to count the occurrences of specific characters.

```
1:  # p12_14.pl
2:
3:  $punctuation = $blanks = $total = 0;
4:  while ($input = <STDIN>) {
5:          chop ($input);
6:          $total += length($input);
7:          $_ = $input;
8:          $punctuation += tr/,:;.-/,:;.-/;
9:          $blanks += tr/ / /;
10: }
11: print ("In this file, there are:\n");
12: print ("\t$punctuation punctuation characters,\n");
13: print ("\t$blanks blank characters,\n");
14: print ("\t", $total - $punctuation - $blanks);
15: print (" other characters.\n");
```

OUTPUT

```
C:\> perl p12 14.pl
Here is a line of input.
This line, another line, contains punctuation.
^z
In this file, there are:
        4 punctuation characters,
        10 blank characters,
        56 other characters.
C:\>
```

ANALYSIS
This program uses the scalar variable `$total` and the built-in function `length` to count the total number of characters in the input file (excluding the trailing newline characters, which are removed by the call to `chop` in line 5).

Lines 8 and 9 use `tr` to count the number of occurrences of particular characters. Line 8 replaces all punctuation characters with themselves; the number of replacements performed, and hence the number of punctuation characters found, is added to the total stored in `$punctuation`. Similarly, line 9 replaces all blanks with themselves and adds the number of blanks found to the total stored in `$blanks`. In both cases, `tr` operates on the contents of the scalar variable `$_`, because the `=~` operator has not been used to specify another value to translate.

Line 14 uses `$total`, `$punctuation`, and `$blanks` to calculate the total number of characters that are not blank and not punctuation.

NOTE

Many other functions and operators accept `$_` as the default variable on which to work. For example, lines 4–7 of this program also can be written as follows:

```
while (<STDIN>) {
        chop();
        $total += length();
```

For more information on $_, refer to Day 17, "System Variables."

The pos **Function**

The pos function, defined in Perl 5 for Win32, returns the location of the last pattern match in a string. It is ideal for use when repeated pattern matches are specified using the g (global) pattern-matching operator.

SYNTAX

The syntax for the pos function is

```
offset = pos(string);
```

string is the string whose pattern is being matched. *offset* is the number of characters already matched or skipped.

Listing 12.15 illustrates the use of pos.

TYPE
Listing 12.15. A program that uses pos to display pattern-match positions.

```
1: # p12_15.pl
2:
3: $string = "Mississippi";
4: while ($string =~ /i/g) {
5:         $position = pos($string);
6:         print("matched at position $position\n");
7: }
```

OUTPUT
```
C:\> perl p12 15.pl
matched at position 2
matched at position 5
matched at position 8
matched at position 11
C:\>
```

ANALYSIS This program loops every time an i in Mississippi is matched. The number displayed by line 6 is the number of characters to skip to reach the point at which pattern-matching resumes. For example, the first i is the second character in the string, so the second pattern search starts at position 2.

12

> You can also use pos to change the position at which pattern matching
> is to resume. To do this, put the call to pos on the left side of an
> assignment:
>
> ```
> pos($string) = 5;
> ```
>
> This tells the Perl interpreter to start the next pattern search with the
> sixth character in the string. (To restart searching from the beginning,
> use 0.)

The substr **Function**

The substr function lets you assign part of a character string to a scalar variable (or to a
component of an array variable).

The syntax for calls to the substr function is

```
substr (expr, skipchars, length)
```

expr is the character string from which a substring is to be copied; this character string can
be the value stored in a variable or the value resulting from the evaluation of an expression.
skipchars is the number of characters to skip before starting the copying. length is the
number of characters to copy; length can be omitted, in which case the rest of the string is
copied.

Listing 12.16 provides a simple example of substr.

Listing 12.16. A program that demonstrates the use of
TYPE   substr.

```
1:  # p12_16.pl
2:
3:  $string = "This is a sample character string";
4:  $sub1 = substr ($string, 10, 6);
5:  $sub2 = substr ($string, 17);
6:  print ("\$sub1 is \"$sub1\"\n\$sub2 is \"$sub2\"\n");
```

```
C:\> perl p12 16.pl
$sub1 is "sample"
$sub2 is "character string"
C:\>
```

Line 4 calls substr, which copies a portion of the string stored in $string. This call
specifies that 10 characters are to be skipped before copying starts, and that a total

of 6 characters are to be copied. This means that the substring `sample` is copied and stored in `$sub1`.

Line 5 is another call to `substr`. Here, 17 characters are skipped. Because the length field is omitted, `substr` copies the remaining characters in the string. This means that the substring `character string` is copied and stored in `$sub2`.

Note that lines 4 and 5 do not change the contents of `$string`.

String Insertion Using `substr`

In Listing 12.16, which you've just seen, calls to `substr` appear to the right of the assignment operator `=`. This means that the return value from `substr`—the extracted substring—is assigned to the variable appearing to the left of the `=`.

Calls to `substr` can appear on the left of the assignment operator `=` as well. In this case, the portion of the string specified by `substr` is *replaced* by the value appearing to the right of the assignment operator.

SYNTAX

The syntax for these calls to `substr` is basically the same as before:

```
substr (expr, skipchars, length) = newval;
```

Here, `expr` must be something that can be assigned to—for example, a scalar variable or an element of an array variable. `skipchars` represents the number of characters to skip before beginning the overwriting operation, which cannot be greater than the length of the string. `length` is the number of characters to be replaced by the overwriting operation. If `length` is not specified, the remainder of the string is replaced.

`newval` is the string that replaces the substring specified by `skipchars` and `length`. If `newval` is larger than `length`, the character string automatically grows to hold it, and the rest of the string is pushed aside (but *not* overwritten). If `newval` is smaller than `length`, the character string automatically shrinks. Basically, everything appears where it is supposed to without you having to worry about it.

NOTE

By the way, things that can be assigned to are sometimes known as *lvalues*, because they appear to the left of assignment statements (the *l* in *lvalue* stands for "left"). Things that appear to the right of assignment statements are, similarly, called *rvalues*.

This book does not use the terms *lvalue* and *rvalue*, but you might find that knowing them will prove useful when you read other books on programming languages.

12

Listing 12.17 is an example of a program that uses substr to replace portions of a string.

Listing 12.17. A program that replaces parts of a string using substr.

```
1:  # p12_17.pl
2:
3:  $string = "Here is a sample character string";
4:  substr($string, 0, 4) = "This";
5:  substr($string, 8, 1) = "the";
6:  substr($string, 19) = "string";
7:  substr($string, -1, 1) = "g.";
8:  substr($string, 0, 0) = "Behold! ";
9:  print ("$string\n");
```

```
C:\> perl p12 17.pl
Behold! This is the sample string.
C:\>
```

This program illustrates the many ways you can use substr to replace portions of a string.

The call to substr in line 4 specifies that no characters are to be skipped before overwriting, and that four characters in the original string are to be overwritten. This means that the substring Here is replaced by This, and that the following is the new value of the string stored in $string:

```
This is a sample character string
```

Similarly, the call to substr in line 5 specifies that 8 characters are to be skipped and one character is to be replaced. This means that the word a is replaced by the. Now, $string contains the following:

```
This is the sample character string
```

Note that the character string is now larger than the original because the new substring, the, is larger than the substring it replaced.

Line 6 is an example of a call to substr that shrinks the string. Here, 19 characters are skipped, and the rest of the string is replaced by the substring string (because no *length* field has been specified). Now, the following is the value stored in $string:

```
This is the sample string
```

In line 7, the call to substr is passed –1 in the *skipchars* field and is passed 1 in the *length* field. This tells substr to replace the last character of the string with the substring g. (g followed by a period). $string now contains

```
This is the sample string.
```

> If `substr` is passed a *skipchars* value of *–n*, where *n* is a positive integer, `substr` skips to *n* characters from the right end of the string. For example, the following call replaces the last two characters in `$string` with the string `hello`:
>
> ```
> substr($string, -2, 2) = "hello";
> ```

Finally, line 8 specifies that no characters are to be skipped and no characters are to be replaced. This means that the substring `"Behold! "` (including a trailing space) is added to the front of the existing string and that `$string` now contains the following:

```
Behold! This is the sample string.
```

Line 9 prints this final value of `$string`.

TIP

> If you are a C programmer and are used to manipulating strings using pointers, note that `substr` with a length field of 1 can be used to simulate pointer-like behavior in Perl.
>
> For example, you can simulate the C statement
>
> ```
> char = *str++;
> ```
>
> as follows in Perl:
>
> ```
> $char = substr($str, $offset++, 1);
> ```
>
> You'll need to define a counter variable (such as `$offset`) to keep track of where you are in the string. However, this is no more of a chore than remembering to initialize your C pointer variable.
>
> You can simulate the following C statement
>
> ```
> *str++ = char;
> ```
>
> by assigning values using `substr` in the same way:
>
> ```
> substr($str, $offset++, 1) = $char;
> ```
>
> You shouldn't use `substr` in this way unless you really have to. Perl supplies more powerful and useful tools, such as pattern matching and substitution, to get the job done more efficiently.

12

The `study` Function

The `study` function is a special function that tells the Perl interpreter that the specified scalar variable is about to be searched many times.

SYNTAX

The syntax for the `study` function is

```
study (scalar);
```

`scalar` is the scalar variable to be "studied." The Perl interpreter takes the value stored in the specified scalar variable and represents it in an internal format that allows faster access.

Look at this example:

```
study ($myvar);
```

Here, the value stored in the scalar variable `$myvar` is about to be repeatedly searched.

You can call `study` for only one scalar variable at a time. Previous calls to `study` are superseded if `study` is called again.

Case-Conversion Functions

Perl 5 for Win32 provides functions that perform case conversion on strings. These are

- [ ] The `lc` function, which converts a string to lowercase
- [ ] The `uc` function, which converts a string to uppercase
- [ ] The `lcfirst` function, which converts the first character of a string to lowercase
- [ ] The `ucfirst` function, which converts the first character of a string to uppercase

The `lc` and `uc` Functions

SYNTAX

The syntax for the `lc` and `uc` functions is

```
retval = lc(string);
retval = uc(string);
```

`string` is the string to be converted. `retval` is a copy of the string, converted to either lowercase or uppercase:

```
$lower = lc("aBcDe");   # $lower is assigned "abcde"
$upper = uc("aBcDe");   # $upper is assigned "ABCDE"
```

The `lcfirst` and `ucfirst` Functions

The syntax for the `lcfirst` and `ucfirst` functions is

```
retval = lcfirst(string);
retval = ucfirst(string);
```

`string` is the string whose first character is to be converted. `retval` is a copy of the string, with the first character converted to either lowercase or uppercase:

```
$lower = lcfirst("HELLO");  # $lower is assigned "hELLO"
$upper = ucfirst("hello");  # $upper is assigned "Hello"
```

The `quotemeta` Function

The `quotemeta` function, defined in Perl 5 for Win32, places a backslash character in front of any non-word character in a string. The following statements are equivalent:

```
$string = quotemeta($string);
$string =~ s/(\W)/\\$1/g;
```

The syntax for `quotemeta` is

```
newstring = quotemeta(oldstring);
```

`oldstring` is the string to be converted. `newstring` is the string with backslashes added.

`quotemeta` is useful when a string is to be used inside a subsequent pattern-matching operation. It ensures that there are no characters in the string that are to be treated as special pattern-matching characters.

The `join` Function

The `join` function has been used many times in this book. It takes the elements of a list and converts them into a single character string.

The syntax for the `join` function is

```
join (joinstr, list);
```

`joinstr` is the character string that is to be used to glue the elements of `list` together.

Look at this example:

```
@list = ("Here", "is", "a", "list");
$newstr = join ("::", @list);
```

After `join` is called, the value stored in `$newstr` becomes the following string:

```
Here::is::a::list
```

12

The join string, :: in this case, appears between each pair of joined elements. The most common join string is a single blank space; however, you can use any value as the join string, including the value resulting from an expression.

The sprintf Function

The sprintf function behaves like the printf function defined on Day 11, except that the formatted string is returned by the function instead of being written to a file. This enables you to assign the string to another variable.

The syntax for the sprintf function is

```
sprintf (string, fields);
```

string is the character string to print, and *fields* is a list of values to substitute into the string.

Listing 12.18 is an example that uses sprintf to build a string.

Listing 12.18. A program that uses sprintf.

```
1:  # p12_18.pl
2:
3:  $num = 26;
4:  $outstr = sprintf("%d = %x hexadecimal or %o octal\n",
5:           $num, $num, $num);
6:  print ($outstr);
```

```
C:\> perl p12_18.pl
26 = 1a hexadecimal or 32 octal
C:\>
```

ANALYSIS Lines 4 and 5 take three copies of the value stored in $num and include them as part of a string. The field specifiers %d, %x, and %o indicate how the values are to be formatted.

%d   Indicates an integer displayed in the usual decimal (base-10) format

%x   Indicates an integer displayed in hexadecimal (base-16) format

%o   Indicates an integer displayed in octal (base-8) format

The created string is returned by sprintf. Once it has been created, it behaves just like any other Perl character string; in particular, it can be assigned to a scalar variable, as in this example. Here, the string containing the three copies of $num is assigned to the scalar variable $outstr. Line 6 then prints this string.

NOTE

For more information on field specifiers or on how `printf` works, refer to Day 11, which lists the field specifiers defined and provides a description of the syntax of `printf`.

Mathematical Functions

Perl provides functions that perform the standard trigonometric operations, plus some other useful mathematical operations. The following sections describe these functions: `sin`, `cos`, `atan2`, `sqrt`, `exp`, `log`, `rand`, and `srand`.

The `sin` and `cos` Functions

The `sin` and `cos` functions are passed a scalar value and return the sine and cosine, respectively, expressed in radians.

The syntax of the `sin` and `cos` functions is

```
retval = sin (value);
retval = cos (value);
```

value is a placeholder here. It can be the value stored in a scalar variable or the result of an expression; it is assumed to be in radians. See the following section, "The `atan2` Function," to find out how to convert from radians to degrees.

The `atan2` Function

The `atan2` function calculates and returns the arctangent of one value divided by another, in the range –Π to Π.

The syntax of the `atan2` function is

```
retval = atan2 (value1, value2);
```

If *value1* and *value2* are equal, *retval* is the value of Π divided by 4.

Listing 12.19 shows how you can use this to convert from degrees to radians.

12

Listing 12.19. A program that contains a subroutine that converts from degrees to radians.

```
1:  # p12_19.pl
2:
3:  $rad90 = &degrees_to_radians(90);
4:  $sin90 = sin($rad90);
5:  $cos90 = cos($rad90);
6:  print ("90 degrees:\nsine is $sin90\ncosine is $cos90\n");
7:
8:  sub degrees_to_radians {
9:          local ($degrees) = @_;
10:         local ($radians);
11:
12:         $radians = atan2(1,1) * $degrees / 45;
13: }
```

OUTPUT

```
C:\> perl p12_19.pl
90 degrees:
sine is 1
cosine is 6.12303176911118962911e-17
C:\>
```

ANALYSIS The subroutine `degrees_to_radians` converts from degrees to radians by multiplying by Π divided by 180. Because `atan2(1,1)` returns Π divided by 4, all the subroutine needs to do after that is divide by 45 to obtain the number of radians.

In the main body of the program, line 3 converts 90 degrees to the equivalent value in radians (Π divided by 2). Line 4 then passes this value to `sin`, and line 5 passes it to `cos`.

NOTE

The trigonometric operations provided here are sufficient to enable you to perform the other important trigonometric operations. For example, to obtain the tangent of a value, obtain the sine and cosine of the value by calling `sin` and `cos`, and then divide the sine by the cosine.

The `sqrt` Function

The `sqrt` function returns the square root of the value it is passed.

SYNTAX

The syntax for the `sqrt` function is

retval = sqrt (*value*);

value can be any positive number.

12

The `exp` Function

The `exp` function returns the number e `**` `value`, where e is the standard mathematical constant (the base for the natural logarithm) and `value` is the argument passed to `exp`.

The syntax for the `exp` function is

```
retval = exp (value);
```

To retrieve e itself, pass `exp` the value 1.

The `log` Function

The `log` function takes a value and returns the natural (base e) logarithm of the value.

The syntax for the `log` function is

```
retval = log (value);
```

The `log` function undoes `exp`; the expression

```
$var = log (exp ($var));
```

always leaves `$var` with the value it started with (if you factor in round-off error).

The `abs` Function

The `abs` function returns the absolute value of a number. This is defined as follows: If a value is less than zero, `abs` negates it and returns the result.

```
$result = $abs(-3.5);    # returns 3.5
```

Otherwise, the result is identical to the value:

```
$result = $abs(3.5);    # returns 3.5
$result = $abs(0);      # returns 0
```

The syntax for the `abs` function is

```
retval = abs (value);
```

`value` can be any number.

NOTE

`abs` is not defined in Perl 4.

12

The `rand` and `srand` **Functions**

The `rand` and `srand` functions enable Perl programs to generate random numbers.

The `rand` function is passed an integer value and generates a random floating-point number between 0 and the value.

SYNTAX

The syntax for the `rand` function is

```
retval = rand (num);
```

num is the integer value passed to `rand`, and *retval* is a random floating-point number between 0 and the *num*, including 0, but not including *num*. If *num* is omitted, 1 is used.

For example, the following statement generates a number between 0 and 10 and returns it in `$retval`:

```
$retval = rand (10);
```

`srand` initializes the random-number generator used by `rand`. This ensures that the random numbers generated are, in fact, random. (If you do not use `srand`, you'll get the same set of random numbers each time.)

SYNTAX

The syntax for the `srand` function is

```
srand (value);
```

`srand` accepts an integer value as an argument; if no argument is supplied, `srand` calls the `time` function and uses its return value as the random-number seed.

For an example that uses `rand` and `srand`, see the section titled "Returning a Value from a Subroutine" on Day 9, "Using Subroutines."

TIP

> The following values and functions return numbers that can make useful random-number seeds:
>
> ☐ The system variable `$$` contains the process ID of the current program. (See Day 17 for more information on `$$`.)
>
> ☐ `time` returns the current time value.

For best results, combine two or more of these using the `^` (bitwise XOR) operator.

12

Summary

Today, you have learned how to open a file for both reading and writing, and how to associate multiple file handles with a single file. You have also learned how to test for the end of a particular input file or for the end of the last input file.

You have also learned how to skip backward and forward in files and how to read single characters from a file using getc.

Perl provides several functions for manipulating directories. They enable you to create, open, read, close, delete, and skip around in directories. Other Perl functions enable you to move a file from one directory to another, create hard and symbolic links from one location to another, and delete a hard link (or a file).

Functions that search character strings include index, which searches for a substring starting from the left of a string, and rindex, which searches for a substring starting from the right of a string. You can retrieve the length of a character string using length. By using the translate operator tr in conjunction with the system variable $_, you can count the number of occurrences of a particular character or set of characters in a string. The pos function enables you to determine or set the current pattern-matching location in a string.

The function substr enables you to extract a substring from a string and use it in an expression or assignment statement. substr also can be used to replace a portion of a string or append to the front or back end of the string.

The lc and uc functions convert strings to lowercase or uppercase. To convert the first letter of a string to lowercase or uppercase, use lcfirst or ucfirst, respectively.

quotemeta places a backslash in front of every non-word character in a string.

You can create new character strings using join and sprintf. join creates a string by joining elements of a list, and sprintf builds a string using field specifiers that specify the string format.

With the functions that perform mathematical operations, you can obtain the sine, cosine, and arctangent of a value. You also can calculate the natural logarithm and square root of a value, or use the value as an exponent of base e.

You also can generate random numbers and define the seed to use when generating the numbers.

12

Q&A

Q Why does a list of files in a directory appear in unsorted order?

A The list appears in the order in which the files are stored in the directory. This varies, depending on the machine; usually, however, newer files appear at the end of the list.

Q Why are `eof` and `eof()` different?

A The short answer is: just because. The long answer is that an empty list as an argument (as in `eof()`) refers to the list of files on the command line, as does the `<>` in

```
while ($line = <>) ...
```

`eof`, on the other hand, refers only to the file currently being read.

Q How does Perl generate random numbers?

A Basically, by performing arithmetic operations using very large numbers. If the numbers for these arithmetic operations are carefully chosen, a sequence of "pseudo-random" numbers can be generated by repeating the set of arithmetic operations and returning their results.

The random-number seed provided by `srand` supplies the initial value for one of the numbers used in the set of arithmetic operations. This ensures that the sequence of pseudo-random numbers starts with a different result each time.

But these numbers are never truly random, in a mathematical or philosophical sense.

Q What's the difference between the `%c` and `%s` format specifiers in `sprintf`?

A `%c` undoes the effect of the `ord` function. It converts a scalar value into the equivalent ASCII character. (Its behavior is similar to that of the `chr` function in Pascal.)

`%s` treats a scalar value as a character string and inserts it into the string at the place specified.

Workshop

The Workshop provides quiz questions to help you solidify your understanding of the material covered and exercises to give you experience in using what you've learned. Try to understand the quiz and exercise answers before you go on to tomorrow's lesson. You can find the answers in Appendix B, "Answers."

12

Quiz

1. How are the following files being opened?

   a. `open (MYFILE, "<file1");`

   b. `open (MYFILE, "file2|");`

   c. `open (MYFILE, "+>file3");`

   d. `open (MYFILE, ">&STDOUT");`

2. What `sprintf` specifiers produce the following?

   a. A hexadecimal number

   b. An octal number

   c. A floating-point number in exponential format

   d. A floating-point number in standard (fixed) format

3. If the scalar variable `$string` contains `abcdefgh`, what do the following calls return?

   a. `substr ($string, 0, 3);`

   b. `substr ($string, 4);`

   c. `substr ($string, -2, 2);`

   d. `substr ($string, 2, 0);`

4. Assume `$string` contains the value `abcdabcd\n` (the last character being a trailing newline character). What is returned in `$retval` by the following?

   a. `$_ = $string; $retval = tr/ab/ab/;`

   b. `$retval = length ($string);`

Exercises

1. Write a program that reads a directory—for example, the `Per15` directory—on your computer. After the entire list is stored, sort the list into alphabetical order and print the list on the screen.

2. Write a program that prints the natural logarithm of the integers between 1 and 100.

3. Write a program that computes the sum of the numbers from 1 to `10 ** n` for values of *n* from 1 to 6. For each computed value, use `times` to calculate the amount of time each computation takes. Print these calculation times.

4. Write a program that reads an integer value and prints the sine, cosine, and tangent of the value. Assume that the input value is in degrees.

5. Write a program that uses `tr` to count all the occurrences of `a`, `e`, `i`, `o`, and `u` in an input line.

12

6. **BUG BUSTER:** What is wrong with the following program?

```
# Bug buster:
while ($line = <>) {
        print ($line);
        if (eof()) {
                print ("— end of current file —\n");
        }
}
```

Day 13

Process, Scalar-Conversion, and List-Manipulation Functions

Today's lesson describes several groups of functions of Perl:

☐ The functions that handle processes and programs

☐ The functions that convert scalar values from one form to another

You also learn about the built-in Perl functions that manipulate lists and array variables. These functions are divided into two groups:

☐ The functions that manipulate standard array variables and their lists

☐ The functions that manipulate associative arrays

Process- and Program-Manipulation Functions

Perl provides a wide range of functions that manipulate both the program currently being executed and other programs (also called *processes*) running on your machine. These functions are divided into four groups:

- ☐ Functions that start additional processes
- ☐ Functions that stop the current program or another process
- ☐ Functions that control the execution of a program or process
- ☐ Functions that manipulate processes or programs but don't fit into any of the preceding categories

The following sections describe some of process- and program-manipulation functions that are ported to Perl 5 for Win32. Refer to Appendix A, "Unsupported Functions in Perl 5 for Win32," for information.

Starting a Process

Several built-in functions provide different ways of creating processes: `eval`, `system`, and `exec`. These functions are described in the following subsections.

The `eval` Function

The `eval` function treats a character string as an executable Perl program.

SYNTAX

The syntax for the `eval` function is

```
eval (string);
```

Here, `string` is the character string that is to become a Perl program.

For example, these two lines of code

```
$print = "print (\"hello, world\\n\");";
eval ($print);
```

print the following message on your screen:

```
hello, world
```

The character string passed to `eval` can be a character-string constant or any expression that has a value that is a character string. In this example, the following string is assigned to `$print`, which is then passed to `eval`:

```
print ("hello, world\n");
```

The `eval` function uses the special system variable $@ to indicate whether the Perl program contained in the character string has executed properly. If no error has occurred, $@ contains the null string. If an error has been detected, $@ contains the text of the message.

The subprogram executed by `eval` affects the program that called it; for example, any variables that are changed by the subprogram remain changed in the main program. Listing 13.1 provides a simple example of this.

 Listing 13.1. A program that illustrates the behavior of `eval`.

```
1:  # p13_1.pl
2:
3:  $myvar = 1;
4:  eval ("print (\"hi!\\n\"); \$myvar = 2;");
5:  print ("the value of \$myvar is $myvar\n");
```

```
C:\> perl p13_1.pl
hi!
the value of $myvar is 2
C:\>
```

 The call to `eval` in line 4 first executes the statement

```
print ("hi!\n");
```

Then it executes the following assignment, which assigns 2 to $myvar:

```
$myvar = 2;
```

The value of $myvar remains 2 in the main program, which means that line 5 prints the value 2. (The backslash preceding the $ in $myvar ensures that the Perl interpreter does not substitute the value of $myvar for the name before passing it to `eval`.)

NOTE

> If you like, you can leave off the final semicolon in the character string passed to `eval`, as follows:
>
> ```
> eval ("print (\"hi!\\n\"); \$myvar = 2");
> ```
>
> As before, this prints `hi!` and assigns 2 to $myvar.

The `eval` function has one very useful property: If the subprogram executed by `eval` encounters a fatal error, the main program does not halt. Instead, the subprogram terminates, copies the error message into the system variable $@, and returns to the main program.

This feature is very useful if you are moving a Perl program from one machine to another and you are not sure whether the new machine contains a built-in function you need. For example, Listing 13.2 tests whether the `tell` function is implemented.

Listing 13.2. A program that uses `eval` to test whether a function is implemented.

TYPE

```
1:  # p13_2.pl
2:
3:  open (MYFILE, "file1") || die ("Can't open file1");
4:  eval ("\$start = tell(MYFILE);");
5:  if ($@ eq "") {
6:          print ("The tell function is defined.\n");
7:  } else {
8:          print ("The tell function is not defined!\n");
9:  }
```

OUTPUT

```
C:\> perl p13_2.pl
The tell function is defined.
C:\>
```

ANALYSIS   The call to `eval` in line 4 creates a subprogram that calls the function `tell`. If `tell` is defined, the subprogram assigns the location of the next line (which, in this case, is the first line) to read to the scalar variable `$start`. If `tell` is not defined, the subprogram places the error message in `$@`.

Line 5 checks whether `$@` is the null string. If `$@` is empty, the subprogram in line 4 executed without generating an error, which means that the `tell` function is implemented. (Because assignments performed in the subprogram remain in effect in the main program, the main program can call `seek` using the value in `$start`, if desired.) If `$@` is not empty, the program assumes that `tell` is not defined, and it prints a message proclaiming that fact. (This program is assuming that the only reason the subprogram could fail is because `tell` is not defined. This is a reasonable assumption, because you know the file referenced by MYFILE has been successfully opened.)

The `system` Function

You have seen examples of the `system` function in earlier lessons.

SYNTAX

The syntax for the `system` function is

```
system (list);
```

This function is passed a list as follows: The first element of the list contains the name of a program to execute, and the other elements are arguments to be passed to the program.

When `system` is called, it starts a process that runs the program and waits until the process terminates. When the process terminates, the error code is shifted left eight bits, and the resulting value becomes `system`'s return value. Listing 13.3 is a simple example of a program that calls `system`.

 Listing 13.3. A program that calls `system`.

```
1:  # p13_3.pl
2:
3:  @proglist = ("echo", "hello, world!");
4:  system(@proglist);
```

OUTPUT
```
C:\> perl p13_3.pl
hello, world!
C:\>
```

ANALYSIS
In this program, the call to `system` executes the UNIX program `echo`, which displays its arguments. The argument passed to echo is `hello, world!`.

WARNING

When you start another program using `system`, output data might be mixed, out of sequence, or duplicated.

To get around this problem, set the system variable `$|`, defined for each file, to `1`. The following is an example:

```
select (STDOUT);
$| = 1;
select (STDERR);
$| = 1;
```

When `$|` is set to `1`, no buffer is defined for that file, and output is written out right away. This ensures that the output behaves properly when `system` is called.

See "Redirecting One File to Another" on Day 12, "File-System, String, and Mathematical Functions," for more information on `select` and `$|`.

The `exec` Function

The `exec` function is similar to the `system` function, except that it terminates the current program before starting the new one.

SYNTAX

The syntax for the `exec` function is

```
exec (list);
```

This function is passed a list as follows: The first element of the list contains the name of a program to execute, and the other elements are arguments to be passed to the program.

For example, the following statement terminates the Perl program and starts the command `notepad file1`:

```
exec ("notepad file1");
```

Like `system`, `exec` accepts additional arguments that are assumed to be passed to the command being invoked. For example, the following statement executes the command `edit file1`:

```
exec ("edit", "file1");
```

You can specify the name that the system is to use as the program name, as follows:

```
exec "openfile1" ("notepad file1");
```

Here, the command `notepad file1` is invoked, but the program name is set to `openfile1`. (This affects the value of the system variable `$0`, which contains the name of the running program. It also affects the value of `argv[0]` if the program to be invoked was originally written in C.)

WARNING

> `exec` has the same output-buffering problems as `system`. See the description of `system`, earlier in today's lesson, for a description of these problems and how to deal with them.

Terminating a Program or Process

The following sections describe the functions `die`, `warn`, and `exit`, which are all used to terminate a program or process.

The `die` and `warn` Functions

The `die` and `warn` functions provide a way for programs to pass urgent messages back to the user who is running them.

The `die` function terminates the program and prints an error message on the standard error file.

13

The syntax for the `die` function is

```
die (message);
```

`message` is the error message to be displayed.

For example, the call

```
die ("Cannot open input file\n");
```

prints the following message and then exits:

```
Cannot open input file
```

`die` can accept a list as its argument, in which case all elements of the list are printed.

```
@diemsg = ("I'm about ", "to die\n");
die (@diemsg);
```

This prints out the following message and then exits:

```
I'm about to die
```

If the last argument passed to `die` ends with a newline character, the error message is printed as is. If the last argument to `die` does not end with a newline character, the program filename and line number are printed, along with the line number of the input file (if applicable). For example, if line 6 of the file `myprog` is

```
die ("Cannot open input file");
```

the message it prints is

```
Cannot open input file at myprog line 6.
```

The `warn` function, like `die`, prints a message on the standard error file.

The syntax for the `warn` function is

```
warn (message);
```

As with `die`, `message` is the message to be displayed.

`warn`, unlike `die`, does not terminate. For example, the statement

```
warn ("Input file is empty");
```

sends the following message to the standard error file and then continues executing:

```
Input file is empty at myprog line 76.
```

If the string passed to `warn` is terminated by a newline character, the warning message is printed as is. For example, the statement

```
warn("Danger! Danger!\n");
```

sends

```
Danger! Danger!
```

to the standard error file.

Note

> If `eval` is used to invoke a program that calls `die`, the error message printed by `die` is not printed; instead, the error message is assigned to the system variable `$@`.

The `exit` Function

The `exit` function terminates a program.

If you like, you can specify a return code to be passed to the system by passing `exit` an argument using the following syntax:

```
exit (retcode);
```

retcode is the return code you want to pass.

For example, the following statement terminates the program with a return code of `2`:

```
exit(2);
```

Execution-Control Function

The `sleep` function delays the execution of a particular program or process. The `sleep` function is an execution-control function.

The `sleep` Function

The `sleep` function suspends the program for a specified number of seconds.

The syntax for the `sleep` function is

```
sleep (time);
```

time is the number of seconds to suspend program execution.

The function returns the number of seconds that the program was actually stopped.

For example, the following statement puts the program to sleep for 5 seconds:

```
sleep (5);
```

The chop **Function**

The chop function was first discussed on Day 3, "Understanding Scalar Values." It removes the last character from a scalar value.

The syntax for the chop function is

```
chop (var);
```

var can be either a scalar value or a list, as described in the following paragraphs.

Here's an example:

```
$mystring = "This is a string";
chop ($mystring);
# $mystring now contains "This is a strin";
```

chop is used most frequently to remove the trailing newline character from an input line, as follows:

```
$input = <STDIN>;
chop ($input);
```

The argument passed to chop can also be a list. In this case, chop removes the last character from every element of the list. For example, to read an entire input file into an array variable and remove all the trailing newline characters, use the following statements:

```
@input = <STDIN>;
chop (@input);
```

chop returns the character chopped. For example:

```
$input = "12345";
$lastchar = chop ($input);
```

This call to chop assigns 5 to the scalar variable $lastchar.

If chop is passed a list, the last character from the last element of the list is returned:

```
@array = ("ab", "cd", "ef");
$lastchar = chop(@array);
```

This assigns f, the last character of the last element of @array, to $lastchar.

The chomp **Function**

The chomp function, defined in Perl 5 for Win32, checks whether the last characters of a string or list of strings match the input line separator defined by the $/ system variable. If they do, chomp removes them.

The syntax for the chomp function is

```
result = chomp(var)
```

As in the chop function, *var* can be either a scalar variable or a list. If *var* is a list, each element of the list is checked for the input end-of-line string. *result* is the total number of characters removed by chomp.

Listing 13.4 shows how chomp works.

TYPE   **Listing 13.4. A program that uses the chomp function.**

```
1:  # p13_4.pl
2:
3:  $/ = "::";   # set input line separator
4:  $scalar = "testing::";
5:  $num = chomp($scalar);
6:  print ("$scalar $num\n");
7:  @list = ("test1::", "test2", "test3::");
8:  $num = chomp(@list);
9:  print ("@list $num\n");
```

```
C:\> perl p13_4.pl
testing 2
test1 test2 test3 4
C:\>
```

ANALYSIS   This program uses chomp to remove the input line separator from both a scalar variable and an array variable. The call to chomp in line 5 converts the value of $scalar from testing:: to testing. The number of characters removed, 2, is returned by chomp and assigned to $num.

The call to chomp in line 8 checks each element of @list. The first element is converted from test1:: to test1, and the last element is converted from test3:: to test3. (The second element is ignored, because it is not terminated by the end-of-line specifier.) The total number of characters removed, 4 (two from the first element and two from the last), is returned by chomp and assigned to $num.

NOTE

For more information on the $/ system variable, refer to Day 17, "System Variables."

The `hex` **Function**

The `hex` function assumes that a character string is a number written in hexadecimal format, and it converts it into a decimal number (a number in standard base-10 format).

The syntax for the `hex` function is

```
decnum = hex (hexnum);
```

hexnum is the hexadecimal character string, and *decnum* is the resulting decimal number.

The following is an example:

```
$myhexstring = "1ff";
$num = hex ($myhexstring);
```

This call to `hex` assigns the decimal equivalent of `1ff` to `$num`, which means that the value of `$num` is now `511`. The value stored in `$myhexstring` is not changed.

The value passed to the string can contain either uppercase or lowercase letters (provided the letters are between `a` and `f`, inclusive). This value can be the result of an expression, as follows:

```
$num = hex ("f" x 2);
```

Here, the expression `"f" x 2` is equivalent to `ff`, which is converted to `255` by `hex`.

NOTE

To convert a string from a decimal value to a hexadecimal value, use `sprintf` and specify either `%x` (hexadecimal integer) or `%lx` (long hexadecimal integer).

WARNING

`hex` does not handle hexadecimal strings that start with the characters `0x` or `0X`. To handle these strings, either get rid of these characters, using a statement such as

```
$myhexstring =~ s/^0[xX]//;
```

or call the `oct` function, which is described later in today's lesson.

13

The `int` Function

The `int` function turns a floating-point number into an integer by getting rid of everything after the decimal point.

The syntax for the `int` function is

```
intnum = int (floatnum);
```

`floatnum` is the floating-point number, and `intnum` is the resulting integer.

The following is an example:

```
$floatnum = 45.6;
$intnum = int ($floatnum);
```

This call to `int` converts `45.6` to `45` and assigns it to `$intnum`. The value stored in `$floatnum` is not changed.

`int` can be used in expressions as well; for example:

```
$intval = int (68.3 / $divisor) + 1;
```

WARNING

`int` does not round up when you convert from a floating-point number to integer. To round up when you use `int`, add `0.5` first, as follows:

```
$intval = int ($mynum + 0.5);
```

Even then, you still might need to watch out for round-off errors. For example, if `4.5` is actually stored in the machine as, say, `4.499999999`, adding `0.5` might still result in a number less than `5`, which means that `int` will truncate it to `4`.

The `oct` Function

The `oct` function assumes that a character string is a number written in octal format, and it converts it into a decimal number (a number in standard base-10 format).

The syntax for the `oct` function is

```
decnum = oct (octnum);
```

`octnum` is the octal character string, and `decnum` is the resulting decimal number.

The following is an example:

```
$myoctstring = "177";
$num = oct ($myoctstring);
```

This call to oct assigns the decimal equivalent of 177 to $num, which means that the value of $num is now 127. The value stored in $myoctstring is not changed.

The value passed to oct can be the result of an expression, as shown in the following example:

```
$num = oct ("07" x 2);
```

Here, the expression "07" x 2 is equivalent to 0707, which is converted to 455 by oct.

NOTE

> To convert a string from a decimal value to an octal value, use sprintf and specify either %o (octal integer) or %lo (long octal integer).

The oct **Function and Hexadecimal Integers**

The oct function also handles hexadecimal integers whose first two characters start with 0x or 0X:

```
$num = oct ("0xff");
```

This call treats 0xff as the hexadecimal number ff and converts it to 255. This feature of oct can be used to convert any non-standard Perl integer constant.

Listing 13.5 is a program that reads a line of input and checks whether it is a valid Perl integer constant. If it is, it converts it into a standard (base-10) integer.

TYPE **Listing 13.5. A program that reads any kind of integer.**

```
1:  # p13_5.pl
2:
3:  $integer = <STDIN>;
4:  chop ($integer);
5:  if ($integer !~ /^[0-9]+$|^0[xX][0-9a-fA-F]+$/) {
6:          die ("$integer is not a legal integer\n");
7:  }
8:  if ($integer =~ /^0/) {
9:          $integer = oct ($integer);
10: }
11: print ("$integer\n");
```

13

```
C:\> perl p13_5.pl
077
63
C:\>
```

The pattern in line 5 matches one of the following:

☐ One or more digits

☐ A string consisting of 0x or 0X followed by one or more digits or by uppercase or lowercase letters between a and f, inclusive

The first case matches any standard base-10 integer or octal integer (because octal integers start with 0 and consist of the numbers 0 to 7). The second case matches any legal hexadecimal integer. In both cases, the pattern matches only if there are no extraneous characters (blank spaces, or other words or numbers) on the line. Of course, it is easy to use the substitution operator to get rid of these first, if you like.

Line 8 tests whether the integer is either an octal or hexadecimal integer by searching for the pattern /^0/. If this pattern is found, oct converts the integer to decimal, placing the converted integer back in $integer. Note that line 8 does not need to determine which type of integer is contained in $integer, because oct processes both octal and hexadecimal integers.

The ord and chr Functions

The ord and chr functions are similar to the Pascal function of the same name. ord converts a single character to its numeric ASCII equivalent, and chr converts a number to its ASCII character equivalent.

The syntax for the ord function is

```
asciival = ord (char);
```

char is the string whose first character is to be converted, and asciival is the resulting ASCII value.

For example, the following statements assigns the ASCII value for the / character, 47, to $ASCIIval:

```
$ASCIIval = ord("/");
```

If the value passed to ord is a character string that is longer than one character in length, ord converts the first character in the string:

```
$mystring = "/ignore the rest of this string";
$charval = ord ($mystring);
```

Here, the first character stored in $mystring, /, is converted and assigned to $charval.

13

The syntax for the `chr` function is

```
charval = chr (asciival);
```

asciival is the value to be converted, and *charval* is the one-character string representing the character equivalent of *asciival* in the ASCII character set.

For example, the following statement assigns / to `$slash`, because 47 is the numeric equivalent of / in the ASCII character set:

```
$slash = chr(47);
```

NOTE

The ASCII character set contains 256 characters (with the extended character set). As a consequence, if the value passed to `chr` is greater than 256, only the bottom eight bits of the value are used.

This means, for example, that the following statements are equivalent:

```
$slash = chr(47);
$slash = chr(303);
$slash = chr(559);
```

In each case, the value of `$slash` is /.

WARNING

The `chr` function is defined only in Perl 5 and Perl 5 for Win32. If you are using Perl 4, you will need to call `sprintf` to convert a number to a character:

```
$slash = sprintf("%c", 47);
```

This assigns / to `$slash`.

13

The `scalar` **Function**

In Perl, some functions or expressions behave differently when their results are assigned to arrays than they do when assigned to scalar variables. For example, the assignment

```
@var = @array;
```

copies the list stored in `@array` to the array variable `@var`, and the assignment

```
$var = @array;
```

determines the number of elements in the list stored in `@array` and assigns that number to the scalar variable `$var`.

As you can see, @array has two different meanings: an "array meaning" and a "scalar meaning." The Perl interpreter determines which meaning to use by examining the rest of the statement in which @array occurs. In the first case, the array meaning is intended, because the statement is assigning to an array variable. Statements in which the array meaning is intended are called *array contexts*.

In the second case, the scalar meaning of @array is intended, because the statement is assigning to a scalar variable. Statements in which the scalar meaning is intended are called *scalar contexts*.

The scalar function enables you to specify the scalar meaning in an array context.

The syntax for the scalar function is

```
value = scalar (list);
```

list is the list to be used in a scalar context, and *value* is the scalar meaning of the list.

For example, to create a list consisting of the length of an array, you can use the following statement:

```
@array = ("a", "b", "c");
@lengtharray = scalar (@array);
```

Here, the number of elements in @array, 3, is converted into a one-element list and assigned to @lengtharray.

Another useful place to use scalar is in conjunction with the <> operator. Recall that the statement

```
$myline = <MYFILE>;
```

reads one line from the input file MYFILE, and

```
@mylines = <MYFILE>;
```

reads all of MYFILE into the array variable @mylines. To read one line into the array variable @mylines (as a one-element list), use the following:

```
@mylines = scalar (<MYFILE>);
```

Specifying scalar with <MYFILE> ensures that only one line is read from MYFILE.

The pack Function

The pack function enables you to take a list or the contents of an array variable and convert (pack) it into a scalar value in a format that can be stored in actual machine memory or used in programming languages such as C.

13

SYNTAX

The syntax for the `pack` function is

```
formatstr = pack(packformat, list);
```

Here, `list` is a list of values; this list of values can, as always, be the contents of an array variable. `formatstr` is the resulting string, which is in the format specified by `packformat`.

`packformat` consists of one or more *pack-format characters*; these characters determine how the list is to be packed. These pack formats are listed in Table 13.1.

Table 13.1. Format characters for the `pack` function.

Character	Description
a	An ASCII character string padded with null characters
A	An ASCII character string padded with spaces
b	A string of bits, lowest first
B	A string of bits, highest first
c	A signed character (range usually –128 to 127)
C	An unsigned character (usually 8 bits)
d	A double-precision floating-point number
f	A single-precision floating-point number
h	A hexadecimal string, lowest digit first
H	A hexadecimal string, highest digit first
i	A signed integer
I	An unsigned integer
l	A signed long integer
L	An unsigned long integer
n	A short integer in network order
N	A long integer in network order
p	A pointer to a string
s	A signed short integer
S	An unsigned short integer
u	Convert to `uuencode` format
v	A short integer in VAX (little-endian) order
V	A long integer in VAX order
x	A null byte
X	Indicates "go back one byte"
@	Fill with nulls (ASCII 0)

13

One pack-format character must be supplied for each element in the list. If you like, you can use spaces or tabs to separate pack-format characters, because `pack` ignores white space.

The following is a simple example that uses `pack`:

```
$integer = pack("i", 171);
```

This statement takes the number 171, converts it into the format used to store integers on your machine, and returns the converted integer in `$integer`. This converted integer can now be written out to a file or passed to a program, using the `system` or `exec` function.

To repeat a pack-format character multiple times, specify a positive integer after the character. The following is an example:

```
$twoints = pack("i2", 103, 241);
```

Here, the pack format `i2` is equivalent to `ii`.

To use the same pack-format character for all of the remaining elements in the list, use `*` in place of an integer, as follows:

```
$manyints = pack("i*", 14, 26, 11, 83);
```

Specifying integers or `*` to repeat pack-format characters works for all formats except `a`, `A`, and `@`. With the `a` and `A` formats, the integer is assumed to be the length of the string to create.

```
$mystring = pack("a6", "test");
```

This creates a string of six characters (the four that are supplied, plus two null characters).

WARNING

The `a` and `A` formats always use exactly one element of the list, regardless of whether a positive integer is included following the character. For example:

```
$mystring = pack("a6", "test1", "test2");
```

Here, `test1` is packed into a six-character string and assigned to `$mystring`. `test2` is ignored.

To get around this problem, use the `x` operator to create multiple copies of the `a` pack-format character, as follows:

```
$strings = pack ("a6" x 2, "test1", "test2");
```

This packs `test1` and `test2` into two six-character strings (joined together).

The @ format is a special case. It is used only when a following integer is specified. This integer indicates the number of bytes the string must contain at this point; if the string is smaller, null characters are added. For example:

```
$output = pack("a @6 a", "test", "test2");
```

Here, the string `test` is converted to ASCII format. Because this string is only four characters long, and the pack format @6 specifies that the packed scalar value must be six characters long at this point, two null characters are added to the string before `test2` is packed.

The `pack` Function and C Data Types

The most frequent use of `pack` is to create data that can be used by C programs. For example, to create a string terminated by a null character, use the following call to `pack`:

```
$Cstring = pack ("ax", $mystring);
```

Here, the `a` pack-format character converts `$mystring` into an ASCII string, and the `x` character appends a null character to the end of the string. This format—a string followed by null—is how C stores strings.

Table 13.2 shows the pack-format characters that have equivalent data types in C.

Table 13.2. Pack-format characters and their C equivalents.

Character	C Equivalent
c	char
d	double
f	float
i	int
I	unsigned int (or unsigned)
l	long
L	unsigned long
s	short
S	unsigned short

In each case, `pack` stores the value in your local machine's internal format.

13

TIP

> You usually won't need to use `pack` unless you are preparing data for use in other programs.

The `unpack` Function

The `unpack` function reverses the operation performed by `pack`. It takes a value stored in machine format and converts it to a list of values understood by Perl.

SYNTAX

The syntax for the `unpack` function is

```
list = unpack (packformat, formatstr);
```

Here, `formatstr` is the value in machine format, and `list` is the created list of values.

As in `pack`, `packformat` is a set of one or more pack format characters. These characters are basically the same as those understood by `pack`. Table 13.3 lists these characters.

Table 13.3. The pack-format characters, as used by `unpack`.

Character	Description
a	An ASCII character string, unstripped
A	An ASCII character string with trailing nulls and spaces stripped
b	A string of bits, lowest first
B	A string of bits, highest first
c	A signed character (range usually –128 to 127)
C	An unsigned character (usually 8 bits)
d	A double-precision floating-point number
f	A single-precision floating-point number
h	A hexadecimal string, lowest digit first
H	A hexadecimal string, highest digit first
i	A signed integer
I	An unsigned integer
l	A signed long integer
L	An unsigned long integer
n	A short integer in network order
N	A long integer in network order

13

Character	Description
p	A pointer to a string
s	A signed short integer
S	An unsigned short integer
u	Convert (uudecode) a uuencoded string
v	A short integer in VAX (little-endian) order
V	A long integer in VAX order
x	Skip forward a byte
X	Indicates "go back one byte"
@	Go to specified position

In almost all cases, a call to unpack undoes the effects of an equivalent call to pack. For example, consider Listing 13.6, which packs and unpacks a list of integers.

Listing 13.6. A program that demonstrates the relationship between pack and unpack.

```
1:  # p13_6.pl
2:
3:  @list_of_integers = (11, 26, 43);
4:  $mystring = pack("i*", @list_of_integers);
5:  @list_of_integers = unpack("i*", $mystring);
6:  print ("@list_of_integers\n");
```

```
C:\> perl p13_6.pl
11 26 43
C:\>
```

ANALYSIS Line 4 calls pack, which takes all of the elements stored in @list_of_integers, converts them to the machine's integer format, and stores them in $mystring.

Line 5 calls unpack, which assumes that the string stored in $mystring is a list of values stored in the machine's integer format; it takes this string, converts each integer in the string to a Perl value, and stores the resulting list of values in @list_of_integers.

Unpacking Strings

The only unpack operations that do not exactly mirror pack operations are those specified by the a and A formats. The a format converts a machine-format string into a Perl value as is, whereas the A format converts a machine-format string into a Perl value and strips any trailing blanks or null characters.

13

The A format is useful if you want to convert a C string into the string format understood by Perl. The following is an example:

```
$perlstring = unpack("A", $Cstring);
```

Here, $Cstring is assumed to contain a character string stored in the format used by the C programming language (a sequence of bytes terminated by a null character). unpack strips the trailing null character from the string stored in $Cstring and stores the resulting string in $perlstring.

Skipping Characters when Unpacking

The @ pack-format character tells unpack to skip to the position specified with the @. For example, the following statement skips four bytes in $packstring and then unpacks a signed integer and stores it in $skipnum.

```
$skipnum = unpack("@4i", $packstring);
```

NOTE

> If unpack is unpacking a single item, it can be stored in either an array variable or a scalar variable. If an array variable is used to store the result of the unpack operation, the resulting list consists of a single element.

If an * character appears after the @ pack-format character, unpack skips to the end of the value being unpacked. This can be used in conjunction with the x pack-format character to unpack the right end of the packed value. For example, the following statement treats the last four bytes of a packed value as a long unsigned integer and unpacks them:

```
$longrightint = unpack("@* X4 L", $packstring);
```

In this example, the @* pack-format specifier skips to the end of the value stored in $packstring. Then the x4 specifier backs up four bytes. Finally, the L specifier treats the last four bytes as a long unsigned integer, which is unpacked and stored in $longrightint.

WARNING

> The number of bytes unpacked by the s, S, i, I, l, and L formats depends on your machine. Win32 machines store short integers in two bytes of memory, and integer and long integer values in four bytes. However, other machines might behave differently. In general, you cannot assume that programs that use pack and unpack will behave in the same way on different machines.

Using the unpack **Function**

The unpack function enables you to decode files that have been encoded by, for instance, the uuencode encoding program. To do this, use the u pack-format specifier.

NOTE

uuencode is a coding mechanism that converts all characters (including unprintable characters) into printable ASCII characters. This ensures that you can safely transmit files across remote networks.

Listing 13.7 is an example of a program that uses unpack to decode a uuencoded file.

TYPE **Listing 13.7. A program that decodes a uuencoded file.**

```
1:  # p13_7.pl
2:
3:  open (CODEDFILE, "/u/janedoe/codefile") ||
4:          die ("Can't open input file");
5:  open (OUTFILE, ">outfile") ||
6:          die ("Can't open output file");
7:  while ($line = <CODEDFILE>) {
8:          $decoded = unpack("u", $line);
9:          print OUTFILE ($decoded);
10: }
11: close (OUTFILE);
12: close (CODEDFILE);
```

ANALYSIS The file variable CODEDFILE represents the file that was previously encoded by uuencode. Lines 3 and 4 open the file (or die trying). Lines 5 and 6 open the output file, which is represented by the file variable OUTFILE.

Lines 7–10 read and write one line at a time. Line 7 starts off by reading a line of encoded input into the scalar variable $line. As with any other input file, the null string is returned if CODEDFILE is exhausted.

Line 8 calls unpack to decode the line. If the line is a special line created by uuencode (for example, the first line, which lists the filename and the size, or the last line, which marks the end of the line), unpack detects it and converts it into the null string. This means that the program does not need to contain special code to handle these lines.

Line 9 writes the decoded line to the output file represented by OUTFILE.

13

NOTE

You can use `pack` to `uuencode` lists of elements, as in the following:

```
@encoded = pack ("u", @decoded);
```

Here, the elements in `@decoded` are encoded and stored in the array variable `@encoded`. The list in `@encoded` can then be decoded using `unpack`, as follows:

```
@decoded = unpack ("u", @encoded);
```

Although `pack` uses the same `uuencode` algorithm as the UNIX `uuencode` utility, you cannot use the UNIX `uudecode` program on data encoded using `pack`, because `pack` does not supply the header and footer (beginning and ending) lines expected by `uudecode`.

If you really need to use `uudecode` with a file created by writing out the output from `pack`, you'll need to write out the header and footer files as well. (See the UNIX manual page for `uuencode` for more details.)

The vec Function

The `vec` function enables you to treat a scalar value as a collection of chunks, with each chunk consisting of a specified number of bits; this collection is known as a *vector*. Each call to `vec` accesses a particular chunk of bits in the vector (known as a *bit vector*).

SYNTAX

The syntax for the `vec` function is

```
retval = vec (vector, index, bits);
```

vector is the scalar value that is to be treated as a vector. It can be any scalar value, including the value of an expression.

index behaves like an array subscript. It indicates which chunk of bits to retrieve. An index of 0 retrieves the first chunk, 1 retrieves the second, and so on. Note that retrieval is from right to left. The first chunk of bits retrieved when the index 0 is specified is the chunk of bits at the right end of the vector.

bits specifies the number of bits in each chunk; it can be 1, 2, 4, 8, 16, or 32.

retval is the value of the chunk of bits. This value is an ordinary Perl scalar value, and it can be used anywhere scalar values can be used.

Listing 13.8 shows how you can use `vec` to retrieve the value of a particular chunk of bits.

TYPE   **Listing 13.8. A program that illustrates the use of** vec.

```
 1:  # p13_8.pl
 2:
 3:  $vector = pack ("B*", "11010011");
 4:  $val1 = vec ($vector, 0, 4);
 5:  $val2 = vec ($vector, 1, 4);
 6:  print ("high-to-low order values: $val1 and $val2\n");
 7:  $vector = pack ("b*", "11010011");
 8:  $val1 = vec ($vector, 0, 4);
 9:  $val2 = vec ($vector, 1, 4);
10: print ("low-to-high order values: $val1 and $val2\n");
```

OUTPUT
```
C:\> perl p13_8.pl
high-to-low order values: 3 and 13
low-to-high order values: 11 and 12
C:\>
```

ANALYSIS   The call to pack in line 3 assumes that each character in the string 11010011 is a bit to be packed. The bits are packed in high-to-low order (with the highest bit first), which means that the vector stored in $vector consists of the bits 11010011 (from left to right). Grouping these bits into chunks of four produces 1101 and 0011, which are the binary representations of 13 and 3, respectively.

Line 4 retrieves the first chunk of four bits from $vector and assigns it to $val1. This is the chunk 0011, because vec is retrieving the chunk of bits at the right end of the bit vector. Similarly, line 5 retrieves 1101, because the index 1 specifies the second chunk of bits from the right; this chunk is assigned to $val2. (One way to think of the index is as "the number of chunks to skip." The index 1 indicates that one chunk of bits is to be skipped.)

Line 7 is similar to line 3, but the bits are now stored in low-to-high order, not high-to-low. This means that the string 11010011 is stored as the following (which is 11010011 reversed):

11001011

When this bit vector is grouped into chunks of 4 bits, you get the following, which are the binary representations of 12 and 11, respectively:

1100 1011

Lines 8 and 9, like lines 4 and 5, retrieve the first and second chunks of bits from $vector. This means that $val1 is assigned 11 (the first chunk), and $val2 is assigned 12 (the second chunk).

NOTE
You can use vec to assign to a chunk of bits by placing the call to vec to the left of an assignment operator. For example:

vec ($vector, 0, 4) = 11;

13

> This statement assigns 11 to the first chunk of bits in $vector. Because the binary representation of 11 is 1011, the last four bits of $vector become 1011.

The defined Function

By default, all scalar variables and elements of array variables that have not been assigned to are assumed to contain the undefined value.

In some cases, a program might need to know whether a particular scalar variable or array element has been assigned to. The built-in function defined enables you to check for this.

The syntax for the defined function is

```
retval = defined (expr);
```

Here, *expr* is anything that can appear on the left of an assignment statement, such as a scalar variable, array element, or an entire array. (An array is assumed to be defined if at least one of its elements is defined.) *retval* is true (a nonzero value) if *expr* is defined, and false (0) if it is not.

Listing 13.9 is a simple example of a program that uses defined.

Listing 13.9. A program that illustrates the use of defined.

```
1:  # p13_9.pl
2:
3:  $array[2] = 14;
4:  $array[4] = "hello";
5:  for ($i = 0; $i <= 5; $i++) {
6:          if (defined ($array[$i])) {
7:                  print ("element ", $i+1, " is defined\n");
8:          }
9:  }
```

OUTPUT

```
C:\> perl p13_9.pl
element 3 is defined
element 5 is defined
C:\>
```

ANALYSIS

This program assigns values to two elements of the array variable @array: the element with subscript 2 (the third element) and the element with subscript 4 (the fifth element).

The loop in lines 5–9 checks each element of @array to see whether it is defined. Because the third and fifth elements—$array[2] and $array[4], respectively—are defined, defined returns true when $i is 2 and when $i is 4.

NOTE

Many functions that return the null string actually return a special "undefined" value that is treated as if it is the null string. If this undefined value is passed to defined, defined returns false.

Many functions discussed today and on Day 15, "Perl 5 for Win32 Module Extensions," also return the special undefined value when an error occurs.

The general rule is: A function that returns the null string when an error or exceptional condition occurs is usually really returning the undefined value.

The undef **Function**

The undef function undefines a scalar variable, an array element, or an entire array.

The syntax of the undef function is

```
retval = undef (expr);
```

As in calls to defined, expr can be anything that can appear to the left of a Perl assignment statement. retval is always the special undefined value discussed in the previous section, "The defined Function"; this undefined value is equivalent to the null string.

The following are some examples of undef:

```
undef ($myvar);
undef ($array[3]);
undef (@array);
```

In the first case, the scalar variable $myvar becomes undefined. The Perl interpreter now treats $myvar as if it has never been assigned to. Needless to say, any value previously stored in $myvar is now lost.

In the second example, the fourth element of @array is marked as undefined. Its value, if any, is lost. Other elements of @array are unaffected.

In the third example, all the elements of @array are marked as undefined. This lets the Perl interpreter free up any memory used to store the values of @array, which might be useful if your program is working with large arrays. For example, if you have used an array to read in an entire file, as in the following:

```
@bigarray = <STDIN>;
```

you can use the following statement to tell the Perl interpreter that you don't need the contents of the input file and that the interpreter can throw them away:

```
undef (@bigarray);
```

Calls to undef can omit *expr*. In this case, undef does nothing and just returns the undefined value. Listing 13.10 shows how this can be useful.

TYPE **Listing 13.10. A program that illustrates the use of undef to represent an unusual condition.**

```
1:  # p13_10.pl
2:
3:  print ("Enter the number to divide:\n");
4:  $value1 = <STDIN>;
5:  chop ($value1);
6:  print ("Enter the number to divide by:\n");
7:  $value2 = <STDIN>;
8:  chop ($value2);
9:  $result = &safe_division($value1, $value2);
10: if (defined($result)) {
11:         print ("The result is $result.\n");
12: } else {
13:         print ("Can't divide by zero.\n");
14: }
15:
16: sub safe_division {
17:         local ($dividend, $divisor) = @_;
18:         local ($result);
19:
20:         $result = ($divisor == 0) ? undef :
21:                 $dividend / $divisor;
22: }
```

OUTPUT
```
C:\> perl p13_10.pl
Enter the number to divide:
26
Enter the number to divide by:
0
Can't divide by zero.
C:\>
```

ANALYSIS Lines 20 and 21 illustrate how you can use undef. If $divisor is 0, the program is attempting to divide by 0. In this case, the subroutine safe_division calls undef, which returns the special undefined value. This value is assigned to $result and passed back to the main part of the program.

Line 10 tests whether `safe_division` has returned the undefined value by calling the `defined` function. If `defined` returns false, `$result` contains the undefined value, and an attempted division by 0 has been detected.

NOTE

You can use `undef` to undefine an entire subroutine, if you like. The following example

```
undef (&mysub);
```

frees the memory used to store `mysub`; after this, `mysub` can no longer be called.

You are not likely to need to use this feature of `undef`, but it might prove useful in programs that consume a lot of memory.

Array and List Functions

The following functions manipulate standard array variables and the lists that they store:

- ☐ grep
- ☐ splice
- ☐ shift
- ☐ unshift
- ☐ push
- ☐ pop
- ☐ split
- ☐ sort
- ☐ reverse
- ☐ map
- ☐ wantarray

13

The grep Function

The grep function provides a convenient way of extracting the elements of a list that match a specified pattern. (It is named after the UNIX search utility of the same name.)

The syntax for the `grep` function is

```
foundlist = grep (pattern, searchlist);
```

pattern is the pattern to search for. *searchlist* is the list of elements to search in. *foundlist* is the list of elements matched.

Here is an example:

```
@list = ("This", "is", "a", "test");
@foundlist = grep(/^[tT]/, @list);
```

Here, `grep` examines all the elements of the list stored in `@list`. If a list element contains the letter `t` (in either uppercase or lowercase), the element is included as part of `@foundlist`. As a result, `@foundlist` consists of two elements: `This` and `test`.

Listing 13.11 is an example of a program that uses `grep`. It searches for all integers on an input line and adds them together.

TYPE **Listing 13.11. A program that demonstrates the use of `grep`.**

```
1:  # p13_11.pl
2:
3:  $total = 0;
4:  $line = <STDIN>;
5:  @words = split(/\s+/, $line);
6:  @numbers = grep(/^\d+[.,;:]?$/, @words);
7:  foreach $number (@numbers) {
8:          $total += $number;
9:  }
10: print ("The total is $total.\n");
```

OUTPUT

```
C:\> perl p13 11.pl
This line of input contains 8, 11 and 26.
The total is 45.
C:\>
```

ANALYSIS Line 5 splits the input line into words, using the standard pattern `/\s+/`, which matches one or more tabs or blanks. Some of these words are actually numbers, and some are not.

Line 6 uses `grep` to match the words that are actually numbers. The pattern `/^\d+[.,;:]?$/` matches if a word consists of one or more digits followed by an optional punctuation character. The words that match this pattern are returned by `grep` and stored in `@numbers`. After line 6 has been executed, `@numbers` contains the following list:

```
("8,", "11", "26.")
```

Lines 7–9 use a `foreach` loop to total the numbers. Note that the totaling operation works properly even if a number being added contains a closing punctuation character: When the

13

Perl interpreter converts a string to an integer, it reads from left to right until it sees a character that is not a digit. This means that the final word, 26., is converted to 26, which is the expected number.

Because split and grep each return a list and foreach expects a list, you can combine lines 5–9 into a single loop if you want to get fancy:

```
foreach $number (grep (/^\d+[.,;:]?$/, split(/\s+/, $line))) {
        $total += $number;
}
```

As always, there is a trade-off of speed versus readability: This code is more concise, but the code in Listing 13.11 is more readable.

Using grep **with the File-Test Operators**

A useful feature of grep is that it can be used to search for any expression, not just patterns. For example, grep can be used in conjunction with readdir and the file-test operators to search a directory.

Listing 13.12 is an example of a program that searches all the readable files of the current directory for a particular word (which is supplied on the command line). Files whose names begin with a period are ignored.

TYPE

Listing 13.12. A program that uses grep with the file-test operators.

```
1:  # p13_12.pl
2:
3:  opendir(CURRDIR, ".") ||
4:          die("Can't open current directory");
5:  @filelist = grep (!/^\./, grep(-r, readdir(CURRDIR)));
6:  closedir(CURRDIR);
7:  foreach $file (@filelist) {
8:          open (CURRFILE, $file) ||
9:                  die ("Can't open input file $file");
10:         while ($line = <CURRFILE>) {
11:                 if ($line =~ /$ARGV[0]/) {
12:                         print ("$file:$line");
13:                 }
14:         }
15:         close (CURRFILE);
16: }
```

OUTPUT

```
C:\> perl p13 12.pl pattern
file1:This line of this file contains the word "pattern".
myfile:This file also contains abcpatterndef.
C:\>
```

13

ANALYSIS Line 3 of this program opens the current directory. If it cannot be opened, line 4 calls `die`, which terminates the program.

Line 5 is actually three function calls in one, as follows:

1. `readdir` retrieves a list of all of the files in the directory.
2. This list of files is passed to `grep`, which uses the `-r` file test operator to search for all files that the user has permission to read.
3. This list of readable files is passed to another call to `grep`, which uses the expression `!/^\./` to match all the files whose names do not begin with a period.

The resulting list—all the files in the current directory that are readable and whose names do not start with a period—is assigned to `@filelist`.

The rest of the program contains nothing new. Line 6 closes the open directory, and lines 7–16 read each file in turn, searching for the word specified on the command line. (Recall that the built-in array `@ARGV` lists all the arguments supplied on the command line and that the first word specified on the command line is stored in `$ARGV[0]`.) Line 11 prints any lines containing the word to search for, using the format employed by the UNIX `grep` command (the filename, followed by `:`, followed by the line itself).

The `splice` **Function**

The `splice` function enables you to modify the list stored in an array variable. By passing the appropriate arguments to `splice`, you can add elements to the middle of a list, delete a portion of a list, or replace a portion of a list.

SYNTAX

The syntax for the `splice` function is

```
retval = splice (array, skipelements, length, newlist)
```

`array` is the array variable containing the list to be spliced. `skipelements` is the number of elements to skip before splicing. `length` is the number of elements to be replaced. `newlist` is the list to be spliced in; this list can be stored in an array variable or specified explicitly.

If `length` is greater than 0, `retval` is the list of elements replaced by `splice`.

The following sections provide examples of what you can do with `splice`.

Replacing List Elements

You can use `splice` to replace a sublist (a set of elements in a list) with another sublist. The following is an example:

13

```
@array = ("1", "2", "3", "4");
splice (@array, 1, 2, ("two", "three"));
```

This call to `splice` takes the list stored in `@array`, skips over the first element, and replaces the next two elements with the list (`"two"`, `"three"`). The new value of `@array` is the list

```
("1", "two", "three", "4")
```

If the replacement list is longer than the original list, the elements to the right of the replaced list are pushed to the right. For example:

```
@array = ("1", "2", "3", "4");
splice (@array, 1, 2, ("two", "2.5", "three"));
```

After this call, the new value of `@array` is the following:

```
("1", "two", "2.5", "three", "4")
```

Similarly, if the replacement list is shorter than the original list, the elements to the right of the original list are moved left to fill the resulting gap. For example:

```
@array = ("1", "2", "3", "4");
splice (@array, 1, 2, "twothree");
```

After this call to `splice`, `@array` contains the following list:

```
("1", "twothree", "4")
```

NOTE

> You do not need to put parentheses around the list you pass to `splice`. For example, the following two statements are equivalent:
> ```
> splice (@array, 1, 2, ("two", "three"));
> splice (@array, 1, 2, "two", "three");
> ```
> When the Perl interpreter sees the second form of `splice`, it assumes that the fourth and subsequent arguments are the replacement list.

Listing 13.13 is an example of a program that uses `splice` to replace list elements. It reads a file containing a form letter and replaces the string `<name>` with a name read from the standard input file. It then writes out the new letter.

The output shown assumes that the file `form` contains the following:

```
Hello <name>!
This is your lucky day, <name>!
```

13

Listing 13.13. A program that uses `splice` to replace list elements.

```perl
1:  # p13_13.pl
2:
3:  open (FORM, "form") || die ("Can't open form letter");
4:  @form = <FORM>;
5:  close (FORM);
6:  $name = <STDIN>;
7:  @nameparts = split(/\s+/, $name);
8:  foreach $line (@form) {
9:          @words = split(/\s+/, $line);
10:         $i = 0;
11:         while (1) {
12:                 last if (!defined($words[$i]));
13:                 if ($words[$i] eq "<name>") {
14:                         splice (@words, $i, 1, @nameparts);
15:                         $i += @nameparts;
16:                 } elsif ($words[$i] =~ /^<name>/) {
17:                         $punc = $words[$i];
18:                         $punc =~ s/<name>//;
19:                         @temp = @nameparts;
20:                         $temp[@temp-1] .= $punc;
21:                         splice (@words, $i, 1, @temp);
22:                         $i += @temp;
23:                 } else {
24:                         $i++;
25:                 }
26:         }
27:         $line = join (" ", @words);
28: }
29: $i = 0;
30: while (1) {
31:         if (!defined ($form[$i])) {
32:                 $~ = "FLUSH";
33:                 write;
34:                 last;
35:         }
36:         if ($form[$i] =~ /^\s*$/) {
37:                 $~ = "FLUSH";
38:                 write;
39:                 $~ = "BLANK";
40:                 write;
41:                 $i++;
42:                 next;
43:         }
44:         if ($writeline ne "" &&
45:                 $writeline !~ / $/) {
46:                 $writeline .= " ";
47:         }
48:         $writeline .= $form[$i];
49:         if (length ($writeline) < 60) {
50:                 $i++;
51:                 next;
52:         }
53:         $~ = "WRITELINE";
```

13

```
54:          write;
55:          $i++;
56: }
57: format WRITELINE =
58: ^<<<<<<<<<<<<<<<<<<<<<<<<<<<<<<<<<<<<<<<<<<<<<<<<<<<<<<<<<<~
59: $writeline
60: .
61: format FLUSH =
62: ^<<<<<<<<<<<<<<<<<<<<<<<<<<<<<<<<<<<<<<<<<<<<<<<<<<<<<<<<<~~
63: $writeline
64: .
65: format BLANK =
66:
67: .
```

OUTPUT

```
C:\> perl p13 13.pl
Fred
Hello Fred! This is your lucky day, Fred!
C:\>
```

ANALYSIS This program starts off by reading the entire form letter from the file named `form` into the array variable `@form`. This makes it possible to format the form letter output later.

Lines 6 and 7 read the name from the standard input file and break it into individual words. This list of words is stored in the array variable `@nameparts`.

The loop in lines 8–28 reads each line in the form letter and looks for occurrences of the string `<name>`. First, line 9 breaks the line into individual words. This list of words is stored in the array variable `@words`.

The `while` loop starting in line 11 then examines each word of `@words` in turn. Line 12 checks whether the loop has reached the end of the list by calling `defined`; if the loop is past the end of the list, `defined` will return false, indicating that the array element is not defined.

Lines 13–15 check whether a word consists entirely of the string `<name>`. If it does, line 14 calls `splice`; this call replaces the word `<name>` with the words in the name list `@nameparts`.

If a word is not equal to the string `<name>`, it might still contain `<name>` followed by a punctuation character. To test for this, line 16 tries to match the pattern `/^<name>/`. If it matches, lines 17 and 18 isolate the punctuation in a single word. This punctuation is stored in the scalar variable `$punc`.

Lines 19 and 20 create a copy of the name array `@nameparts` and append the punctuation to the last element of the array. This ensures that the punctuation will appear in the form letter where it is supposed to—right after the last character of the substituted name. Line 21 then calls `splice` as in line 14.

After the words in `@words` have been searched and the name substituted for `<name>`, line 27 joins the words back into a single line. As an additional benefit, the multiple spaces and tabs in the original line have now been replaced by a single space, which will make the eventual formatted output look nicer.

13

Lines 30–56 write out the output. The string to be written is stored in the scalar variable $writeline. The program ensures that the form-letter output is formatted by doing the following:

1. First, the print format WRITELINE is defined to use the ^<<<< value-field format. This format fits as much of the contents of $writeline into the line as possible and then deletes the part of $writeline that has been written out.

2. Lines 36–43 enable you to add paragraphs to your form letter. Line 36 tests whether an input line is blank. If it is, the FLUSH print format is used to write out any output from previous lines that has not yet been printed. (Because the output line specified by FLUSH starts with ~~, the line is printed only if it is not blank—in other words, if $writeline actually contains some leftover text.) Then, the BLANK print format writes a blank line.

3. Lines 44–47 check whether a space needs to be placed between the end of one input line and the beginning of the next when formatting.

4. Lines 49–52 ensure that $writeline is always long enough to fill the value field specified by WRITELINE. This guarantees that there will be no unnecessary space in any of the output lines.

5. When @form has been completely read, lines 32–34 ensure that all the output from previous lines has been written by using the FLUSH print format.

(For more information on the print formats used in this example, refer to Day 11, "Formatting Your Output.")

NOTE

You can use splice to splice the contents of a scalar variable into an array. For example:

```
splice (@array, 8, 1, $name);
```

This creates a one-element list consisting of the contents of $name and adds it to the list stored in @array (as the eighth element).

Appending List Elements

You can use splice to add a sublist anywhere in a list. To do this, specify a length field of 0. For example:

```
splice (@array, 5, 0, "Hello", "there");
```

This call to splice adds the list ("Hello", "there") to the list stored in @array. Hello becomes the new sixth element of $list, and there becomes the new seventh element; the existing sixth and seventh elements, if they exist, become the new eighth and ninth elements, and every other element is also pushed to the right.

To add a new element to the end of an existing array, specify a `skipelements` value of −1, as shown in the following:

```
splice (@array, -1, 0, "Hello");
```

This adds `Hello` as the last element of the list stored in `@array`.

Listing 13.14 is an example of a program that uses `splice` to insert an element into a list. This program inserts a word count after every tenth word in a file.

TYPE

Listing 13.14. A program that uses `splice` to insert array elements.

```
 1:  # p13_14.pl
 2:
 3:  $count = 0;
 4:  while ($line = <STDIN>) {
 5:          chop ($line);
 6:          @words = split(/\s+/, $line);
 7:          $added = 0;
 8:          for ($i = 0; $i+$added < @words; $i++) {
 9:                  if ($count > 0 && ($count + $i) % 10 == 0) {
10:                          splice (@words, $i+$added, 0,
11:                                  $count + $i);
12:                          $added += 1;
13:                  }
14:          }
15:          $count += @words - $added;
16:          $line = join (" ", @words);
17:          print ("$line\n");
18:  }
```

OUTPUT

```
C:\> perl p13 14.pl
Here is a line with some words on it.
Here is a line with some words on it.
Here are some more test words to count.
Here 10 are some more test words to count.
A B C D E F G H I J K L M N O P
A B C 20 D E F G H I J K L M 30 N O P
^z
C:\>
```

ANALYSIS This program, like many of the others you have seen, reads one line at a time and breaks the line into words; the array variable `@words` contains the list of words for a particular line.

The scalar variable `$count` contains the number of words in the lines previously read. Lines 8 through 14 read each word in the current input line in turn; at any given point, the counting variable `$i` lists the number of words read in the line, and the sum of `$count` and `$i` lists the total number of words read in all input lines.

13

Line 9 adds the value stored in $count to the value stored in $i; if this value, the current word number, is a multiple of 10, lines 10 and 11 call splice and insert the current word number into the list. As a result, every tenth word is followed by its word number.

The scalar variable $added counts the number of elements added to the list; this ensures that the word numbers added by lines 10 and 11 are not included as part of the word count.

After the word numbers have been inserted into the list, line 16 rebuilds the input line by joining the elements of @words; this new input line includes the word numbers. Line 17 then prints the rebuilt line.

Deleting List Elements

You can use splice to delete list elements without replacing them. To do this, call splice and omit the newlist argument. For example:

```
@deleted = splice (@array, 8, 2);
```

This call to splice deletes the ninth and tenth elements of the list stored in @array. If @array contains subsequent elements, these elements are shifted left to fill the gap. The list of deleted elements is returned and stored in @deleted.

Listing 13.15 reads an input file, uses splice to delete all words greater than five characters long, and writes out the result.

TYPE   **Listing 13.15. A program that uses splice to delete words.**

```
1:  # p13_15.pl
2:
3:  while ($line = <STDIN>) {
4:          @words = split(/\s+/, $line);
5:          $i = 0;
6:          while (defined($words[$i])) {
7:                  if (length($words[$i]) > 5) {
8:                          splice(@words, $i, 1);
9:                  } else {
10:                         $i++;
11:                 }
12:         }
13:         $line = join (" ", @words);
14:         print ("$line\n");
15: }
```

OUTPUT
```
C:\> perl p13 15.pl
this is a test of the program which removes long words
^z
this is a test of the which long words
C:\>
```

ANALYSIS This program reads one line of input at a time and breaks each input line into words. Line 7 calls `length` to determine the length of a particular word. If the word is greater than 5 characters in length, line 8 calls `splice` to remove the word from the list.

 NOTE

You also can omit the `length` argument when you call `splice`. If you do, `splice` deletes everything after the element specified by `skipelements`:

```
splice (@array, 7);
```

This deletes the seventh and all subsequent elements of the list stored in `@array`.

To delete the last element of a list, specify `-1` as the `skipelements` argument:

```
splice (@array, -1);
```

In all cases, `splice` returns the list of deleted elements.

The `shift` Function

One list operation that is frequently needed in a program is to remove an element from the front of a list. Because this operation is often performed, Perl provides a special function, `shift`, that handles it.

`shift` removes the first element of the list and moves (or "shifts") every remaining element of the list to the left to cover the gap. `shift` then returns the removed element.

 SYNTAX

The syntax for the `shift` function is

```
element = shift (arrayvar);
```

`shift` is passed one argument: an array variable that contains a list. `element` is the returned element.

 NOTE

`shift` returns the undefined value (equivalent to the null string) if the list is empty.

Here is a simple example using `shift`:

```
@mylist = ("1", "2", "3");
$firstval = shift(@mylist);
```

13

This call to `shift` removes the first element, 1, from the list stored in `@mylist`. This element is assigned to `$firstval`. `@mylist` now contains the list (`"2"`, `"3"`).

If you do not specify an array variable when you call `shift`, the Perl interpreter assumes that `shift` is to remove the first element from the system array variable `@ARGV`. This variable lists the arguments supplied on the command line when the program is started up. For example, if you call a Perl program named `foo` with the following command

```
foo arg1 arg2 arg3
```

`@ARGV` contains the list (`"arg1"`, `"arg2"`, `"arg3"`).

This default feature of `shift` makes it handy for processing command-line arguments. Listing 13.16 is a simple program that prints out its arguments.

TYPE

Listing 13.16. A program that uses `shift` to process the command-line arguments.

```
1:  # p13_16.pl
2:
3:  while (1) {
4:          $currarg = shift;
5:          last if (!defined($currarg));
6:          print ("$currarg\n");
7:  }
```

OUTPUT

```
C:\> perl p13 16.pl arg1 arg2 arg3
arg1
arg2
arg3
C:\>
```

ANALYSIS
When this program is called, the array variable `@ARGV` contains a list of the values supplied as arguments to the program. Line 4 calls `shift` to remove the first argument from the list and assign it to `$currarg`.

If there are no elements (or none remaining), `shift` returns the undefined value, and the call to `defined` in line 5 returns false. This ensures that the loop terminates when there are no more arguments to read.

NOTE

> The `shift` function is equivalent to the following call to `splice`:
>
> ```
> splice (@array, 0, 1);
> ```

13

The `unshift` Function

To undo the effect of a `shift` function, call `unshift`.

SYNTAX

The syntax for the `unshift` function is

```
count = unshift (arrayvar, elements);
```

`arrayvar` is the list (usually stored in an array variable) to add to, and `elements` is the element or list of elements to add. `count` is the number of elements in the resulting list.

The following is an example of a call to `unshift`:

```
unshift (@array, "newitem");
```

This adds the element `newitem` to the front of the list stored in `@array`. The other elements of the list are moved to the right to accommodate the new item.

You can use `unshift` to add more than one element to the front of an array. For example:

```
unshift (@array, @sublist1, "newitem", @sublist2);
```

This statement adds a list consisting of the list stored in `@sublist1`, the element `newitem`, and the list stored in `@sublist2` to the front of the list stored in `@array`.

`unshift` returns the number of elements in the new list, as shown in the following:

```
@array = (1, 2, 3);
$num = unshift (@array, "newitem");
```

This assigns `4` to `$num`.

NOTE

> The `unshift` function is equivalent to calling `splice` with a `skipelements` value of `0` and a `length` value of `0`. For example, the following statements are equivalent:
>
> ```
> unshift (@array, "item1", "item2");
> splice (@array, 0, 0, "item1", "item2");
> ```

13

The `push` Function

As you have seen, the `unshift` function adds an element to the front of a list. To add an element to the end of a list, call the `push` function.

The syntax for the `push` function is

```
push (arrayvar, elements);
```

arrayvar is the list (usually stored in an array variable) to add to, and *elements* is the element or list of elements to add.

The following is an example that uses `push`:

```
push (@array, "newitem");
```

This adds the element `newitem` to the end of the list.

The end of the list is always assumed to be the last defined element. For example, consider the following statements:

```
@array = ("one", "two");
$array[3] = "four";
push (@array, "five");
```

Here, the first statement creates a two-element list and assigns it to `@array`. The second statement assigns `four` to the fourth element of `@array`. Because the fourth element is now the last element of `@array`, the call to `push` creates a fifth element, even though the third element is undefined. `@array` now contains the list

```
("one", "two", "", "four", "five");
```

The undefined third element is, as always, equivalent to the null string.

As with `unshift`, you can use `push` to add multiple elements to the end of a list, as in this example:

```
push (@array, @sublist1, "newitem", @sublist2);
```

Here, the list consisting of the contents of `@sublist1`, the element `newitem`, and the contents of `@sublist2` is added to the end of the list stored in `@array`.

NOTE

> `push` is equivalent to a call to `splice` with the `skiparguments` argument set to the length of the array. This means that the following statements are equivalent:
>
> ```
> push (@array, "newitem");
> splice (@array, @array, 0, "newitem");
> ```

The `pop` Function

The `pop` function undoes the effect of `push`. It removes the last element from the end of a list. The removed element is returned.

The syntax for the pop function is

```
element = pop (arrayvar);
```

arrayvar is the array element from which an element is to be removed. *element* is the returned element.

For example, the following statement removes the last element from the list stored in @array and assigns it to the scalar variable $popped:

```
$popped = pop (@array);
```

If the list passed to pop is empty, pop returns the undefined value.

NOTE

> pop is equivalent to a call to splice with a skipelements value of -1 (indicating the last element of the array). This means that the following statements behave in the same way:
>
> ```
> $popped = pop (@array);
> $popped = splice (@array, -1);
> ```

Creating Stacks and Queues

The functions you have just seen are handy for constructing two commonly used data structures: stacks and queues. The following sections provide examples that use a stack and a queue.

Creating a Stack

A *stack* is a data structure that behaves like a stack of plates in a cupboard: the last item added to the stack is always the first item removed. Data items that are added to the stack are said to be *pushed* onto the stack; items that are removed from the stack are *popped off* the stack.

As you might have guessed, the functions push and pop enable you to create a stack in a Perl program. Listing 13.17 is an example of a program that uses a stack to perform arithmetic operations. It works as follows:

1. Two numbers are pushed onto the stack.
2. The program reads an arithmetic operator, such as + or –. The two numbers are popped off the stack, and the operation is performed.
3. The result of the operation is pushed onto the stack, enabling it to be used in further arithmetic operations.

After all the arithmetic operations have been performed, the stack should consist of a single element, which is the final result.

13

The numbers and operators are read from the standard input file.

Note that Listing 13.17 is the inverse of Listing 9.12. In the latter program, the arithmetic operators appear first, followed by the values.

Listing 13.17. A program that uses a stack to perform arithmetic.

TYPE

```
1:  # p13_17.pl
2:
3:  while (defined ($value = &read_value)) {
4:          if ($value =~ /^\d+$/) {
5:                  push (@stack, $value);
6:          } else {
7:                  $firstpop = pop (@stack);
8:                  $secondpop = pop (@stack);
9:                  push (@stack,
10:                     &do_math ($firstpop, $secondpop, $value));
11:         }
12: }
13: $result = pop (@stack);
14: if (defined ($result)) {
15:         print ("The result is $result.\n");
16: } else {
17:         die ("Stack empty when printing result.\n");
18: }
19:
20: sub read_value {
21:         local ($retval);
22:         $input =~ s/^\s+//;
23:         while ($input eq "") {
24:                 $input = <STDIN>;
25:                 return if ($input eq "");
26:                 $input =~ s/^\s+//;
27:         }
28:         $input =~ s/^\S+//;
29:         $retval = $&;
30: }
31:
32: sub do_math {
33:         local ($val2, $val1, $operator) = @_;
34:         local ($result);
35:
36:         if (!defined($val1) || !defined($val2)) {
37:                 die ("Missing operand");
38:         }
39:         if ($operator =~ m.^[+-/*]$. ) {
40:                 eval ("\$result = \$val2 $operator \$val1");
41:         } else {
42:                 die ("$operator is not an operator");
43:         }
44:         $result;  # ensure the proper return value
45: }
```

13

```
C:\> perl p13 17.pl
11 4 + 26 -
^z
The result is 11.
C:\>
```

Before going into details, let's first take a look at how the program produces the final result, which is 11:

1. The program starts off by reading the numbers 11 and 4 and pushing them onto the stack. If the stack is listed from the top down, it now looks like this:
```
4
11
```

   Another way to look at the stack is this: At present, the list stored in @stack is (11, 4).

2. The program then reads the + operator, pops the 4 and 11 off the stack, and performs the addition, pushing the result onto the stack. The stack now contains a single value:
```
15
```

3. The next value, 26, is pushed onto the stack, which now looks like this:
```
26
15
```

4. The program then reads the – operator, pops 15 and 26 off the stack, and subtracts 15 from 26. The result, 11, is pushed onto the stack.

5. Because there are no more operations to perform, 11 becomes the final result.

This program delegates to the subroutine read_value the task of reading values and operators. This subroutine reads a line of the standard input file and extracts the non-blank items on the line. Each call to read_value extracts one item from an input line; when an input line is exhausted, read_value reads the next one. When the input file is exhausted and there are no more items to return, $input becomes the undefined value, which is equivalent to the null string; the call to defined in line 3 tests for this condition.

If an item returned by read_value is a number, line 5 calls push, which pushes the number onto the stack. If an item is not a number, the program assumes it is an operator. At this point, pop is called twice to remove the last two numbers from the stack, and do_math is called to perform the arithmetic operation.

The do_math subroutine uses a couple of tricks. First, defined is called to see whether there are, in fact, two numbers to add. If one or both of the numbers does not exist, the program terminates.

Next, the subroutine uses the pattern m.^[+-*/]$. to check whether the character string stored in $operator is, in fact, a legal arithmetic operator. (Recall that you can use a pattern

13

delimiter other than / by specifying m followed by the character you want to use as the delimiter. In this case, the period character is the pattern delimiter.)

Finally, the subroutine calls eval to perform the arithmetic operation. eval replaces the name $operator with its current value, and then treats the resulting character string as an executable statement; this performs the arithmetic operation specified by $operator. Using eval here saves space; the only alternative is to use a complicated if-elsif structure.

The result of the operation is returned in $result. Lines 9 and 10 then pass this value to push, which pushes the result onto the stack. This enables you to use the result in subsequent operations.

When the last arithmetic operation has been performed, the final result is stored as the top element of the stack. Line 13 pops this element, and line 15 prints it.

Note that this program always assumes that the last element pushed onto the stack is to be on the left of the arithmetic operation. To reverse this, all you need to do is change the order of $val1 and $val2 in line 33. (Some programs that manipulate stacks also provide an operation that reverses the order of the top two elements of a stack.)

WARNING

The pop function returns the undefined value if the stack is empty. Because the undefined value is equivalent to the null string, and the null string is treated as 0 in arithmetic operations, your program will not complain if you try to pop a number from an empty stack.

To ensure that you get the result you want, always call defined after you call pop, to ensure that a value has actually been popped from the stack.

Creating a Queue

A *queue* is a data structure that processes data in the order in which it is entered; such data structures are known as *first-in, first-out* (or *FIFO*) structures. (A stack, on the other hand, is an example of a *last-in, first-out*, or *LIFO*, structure.)

To create a queue, use the function push to add items to the queue and call shift to remove elements from it. Because push adds to the right of the list and shift removes from the left, elements are processed in the order in which they appear.

Listing 13.18 is an example of a program that uses a queue to add a set of numbers retrieved via a pipe. Each input line can consist of more than one number, and the numbers are added in the order listed.

The Input-Output example shown for this listing assumes that the numbers retrieved via the pipe are 11, 12, and 13.

Listing 13.18. A program that illustrates the use of a queue.

TYPE

```
1:  # p13_18.pl
2:
3:  open (PIPE, "type numbers|") ||
4:          die ("Can't open pipe");
5:  $result = 0;
6:  while (defined ($value = &readnum)) {
7:          $result += $value;
8:  }
9:  print ("The result is $result.\n");
10:
11: sub readnum {
12:         local ($line, @numbers, $retval);
13:         while ($queue[0] eq "") {
14:                 $line = <PIPE>;
15:                 last if ($line eq "");
16:                 $line =~ s/^\s+//;
17:                 @numbers = split (/\s+/, $line);
18:                 push (@queue, @numbers);
19:         }
20:         $retval = shift(@queue);
21: }
```

OUTPUT

```
C:\> perl p13 18.pl
The result is 15.
C:\>
```

ANALYSIS This program assumes that a program named numbers contains the numbers 1, 2, 3, 4, and 5, and that the output of type numbers is a stream of numbers. Multiple numbers can appear on a single line of this output. Lines 3 and 4 associate the file variable PIPE with the output from the numbers command.

Lines 6–8 call the subroutine readnum to obtain a number and then add it to the result stored in $result. This subroutine reads input from the pipe, breaks it into individual numbers, and then calls push to add the numbers to the queue stored in @queue. Line 20 then calls shift to retrieve the first element in the queue, which is returned to the main program.

If an input line is blank, the call to split in line 17 produces the empty list, which means that nothing is added to @queue. This ensures that input is read from the pipe until a non-blank line is read or until the input is exhausted.

13

The `split` Function

The `split` function was first discussed on Day 5, "Lists and Array Variables." It splits a character string into a list of elements.

The usual syntax for the `split` function is

```
list = split (pattern, value);
```

Here, `value` is the character string to be split. `pattern` is a pattern to be searched for. A new element is started every time `pattern` is matched. (`pattern` is not included as part of any element.) The resulting list of elements is returned in `list`.

For example, the following statement breaks the character string stored in `$line` into elements, which are stored in `@list`:

```
@list = split (/:/, $line);
```

A new element is started every time the pattern `/:/` is matched. If `$line` contains `This:is:a:string`, the resulting list is (`"This"`, `"is"`, `"a"`, `"string"`).

If you like, you can specify the maximum number of elements of the list produced by `split` by specifying the maximum as the third argument. For example:

```
$line = "This:is:a:string";
@list = split (/:/, $line, 3);
```

As before, this breaks the string stored in `$line` into elements. After three elements have been created, no more new elements are created. Any subsequent matches of the pattern are ignored. In this case, the list assigned to `@list` is (`"This"`, `"is"`, `"a:string"`).

> **TIP**
>
> If you use `split` with a limit, you can assign to several scalar variables at once:
>
> ```
> $line = "11  12  13  14  15";
> ($var1, $var2, $line) = split (/\s+/, $line, 3);
> ```
>
> This splits `$line` into the list (`"11"`, `"12"`, `"13  14  15"`). `$var1` is assigned 11, `$var2` is assigned 12, and `$line` is assigned `"13  14  15"`. This enables you to assign the leftovers to a single variable, which can then be split again at a later time.

The `sort` and `reverse` Functions

The `sort` function sorts a list in alphabetical order, as follows:

```
@sorted = sort (@list);
```

The sorted list is returned.

The `reverse` function reverses the order of a list:

```
@reversed = reverse (@list);
```

For more information on the `sort` and `reverse` functions, see Day 5. For information on how you can specify the sort order that `sort` is to use, see Day 9, "Using Subroutines."

The `map` Function

The `map` function, defined in Perl 5 for Win32, enables you to use each of the elements of a list, in turn, as an operand in an expression.

The syntax for the `map` function is

```
resultlist = map(expr, list);
```

`list` is the list of elements to be used as operands or arguments; this list is copied by `map`, but is not itself changed. `expr` is the expression to be repeated. The results of the repeated evaluation of the expression are stored in a list, which is returned in `resultlist`.

`expr` assumes that the system variable `$_` contains the element of the list currently being used as an operand. For example:

```
@list = (100, 200, 300);
@results = map($_+1, @list);
```

This evaluates the expression `$_+1` for each of 100, 200, and 300 in turn. The results, 101, 201, and 301, respectively, are formed into the list `(101, 201, 301)`. This list is then assigned to `@results`.

To use `map` with a subroutine, just pass `$_` to the subroutine, as in the following:

```
@results = map(&mysub($_), @list);
```

This calls the subroutine `mysub` once for each element of the list stored in `@list`. The values returned by `mysub` are stored in a list, which is assigned to `@results`.

This also works with built-in functions:

```
@results = map(chr($_), @list);
@results = map(chr, @list);  # same as above,
➥since $_ is the default argument for chr
```

This converts each element of the list in `@list` to its ASCII character equivalent. The resulting list of characters is stored in `@results`.

13

NOTE

For more information on the `$_` system variable, refer to Day 17, "System Variables."

The `wantarray` Function

In Perl, the behavior of some built-in functions depends on whether they are dealing with scalar values or lists. For example, the `chop` function either chops the last character of a single string or chops the last character of every element of a list:

```
chop($scalar);     # chop a single string
chop(@array);      # chop every element of an array
```

Perl 5 for Win32 enables you to define similar two-way behavior for your subroutines using the `wantarray` function. (This function is not defined in Perl 4.)

The syntax for the `wantarray` function is

```
result = wantarray();
```

`result` is a nonzero value if the subroutine is expected to return a list, and is 0 if the subroutine is expected to return a scalar value.

Listing 13.19 illustrates how `wantarray` works.

TYPE   **Listing 13.19. A program that uses the `wantarray` function.**

```
1:  # p13_19.pl
2:
3:  @array = &mysub();
4:  $scalar = &mysub();
5:
6:  sub mysub {
7:          if (wantarray()) {
8:                  print ("true\n");
9:          } else {
10:                 print ("false\n");
11:         }
12: }
```

OUTPUT
```
C:\> perl p13_19.pl
true
false
C:\>
```

ANALYSIS   When `mysub` is first called in line 3, the return value is expected to be a list, which means that `wantarray` returns a nonzero (true) value in line 7. The second call to `mysub` in line 4 expects a scalar return value, which means that `wantarray` returns 0 (false).

Associative-Array Functions

Perl provides a variety of functions that operate on associative arrays. Most of these functions are described in detail on Day 10, "Associative Arrays"; a brief description of each function is presented here.

The `keys` Function

The `keys` function returns a list of the subscripts of the elements of an associative array.

The syntax for `keys` is straightforward:

```
list = keys (assoc_array);
```

`assoc_array` is the associative array from which subscripts are to be extracted, and `list` is the returned list of subscripts.

For example:

```
%array = ("foo", 26, "bar", 17);
@list = keys(%array);
```

This call to `keys` assigns `("foo", "bar")` to `@list`. (The elements of the list might be in a different order. To specify a particular order, sort the list, using the `sort` function.)

`keys` often is used with `foreach`, as in the following example:

```
foreach $subscript (keys (%array)) {
        # stuff goes here
}
```

This loops once for each subscript of the array.

The `values` Function

The `values` function returns a list consisting of all the values in an associative array.

The syntax for the `values` function is

```
list = values (assoc_array);
```

`assoc_array` is the associative array from which values are to be extracted, and `list` is the returned list of values.

13

The following is an example that uses `values`:

```
%array = ("foo", 26, "bar", 17);
@list = values(%array);
```

This assigns the list `(26, 17)` to `@list` (not necessarily in that order).

The `each` **Function**

The `each` function returns an associative-array element as a two-element list. The list consists of the associative array's subscript and its associated value. Successive calls to `each` return another associative-array element.

The syntax for the `each` function is

```
pair = each (assoc_array);
```

`assoc_array` is the associative array from which pairs are to be returned, and `pair` is the subscript-element pair returned.

The following is an example:

```
%array = ("foo", 26, "bar", 17);
@list = each(%array);
```

The first call to `each` assigns either `("foo", 26)` or `("bar", 17)` to `@list`. A subsequent call returns the other element, and a third call returns an empty list. (The order in which the elements are returned depends on how the list is stored; no particular order is guaranteed.)

The `delete` **Function**

The `delete` function deletes an associative-array element.

The syntax for the `delete` function is

```
element = delete (assoc_array_item);
```

`assoc_array_item` is the associative-array element to be deleted, and `element` is the value of the deleted element.

The following is an example:

```
%array = ("foo", 26, "bar", 17);
$retval = delete ($array{"foo"});
```

After `delete` is called, the associative array `%array` contains only one element: the element with the subscript `bar`. `$retval` is assigned the value of the deleted element `foo`, which in this case is 26.

13

The `exists` Function

The `exists` function, defined in Perl 5 for Win32, enables you to determine whether a particular element of an associative array exists.

SYNTAX

The syntax for the `exists` function is

```
result = exists(element);
```

`element` is the element of the associative array that is being tested for existence. `result` is nonzero if the element exists, and `0` if it does not.

The following is an example:

```
$result = exists($myarray{$mykey});
```

`$result` is nonzero if `$myarray{$mykey}` exists.

Summary

Today, you have learned about three types of built-in Perl functions: functions that handle process and program control, functions that manipulate scalar values and convert them from one form to another, and functions that manipulate lists.

With the process- and program-control functions, you can start new processes, stop the current program, or temporarily halt the current program.

The `chop` function removes the last character from a scalar value or from each element of a list.

The `int` function takes a floating-point number and gets rid of everything after the decimal point.

The `defined` function checks whether a scalar variable, array element, or array has been assigned to. The `undef` function enables you to treat a previously defined scalar variable, array element, or array as if it is undefined. `scalar` enables you to treat an array or list as if it is a scalar value.

The other functions described in today's lesson convert values from one form into another. The `hex` and `oct` functions read hexadecimal and octal constants and convert them into decimal form. The `ord` function converts a character into its ASCII decimal equivalent. `pack` and `unpack` convert a scalar value into a format that can be stored in machine memory, and vice versa. `vec` enables you to treat a value as an array of numeric values, each of which is a certain number of bits long.

13

The grep function enables you to extract the elements of a list that match a particular pattern. This function can be used in conjunction with the file-test operators.

The splice function enables you to extract a portion of a list or insert a sublist into a list. The shift and pop functions remove an element from the left and right ends of a list, and the unshift and push functions add one or more elements to the left and right ends of a list. You can use push, pop, and shift to create stacks and queues.

The split function enables you to break a character string into list elements. You can impose an upper limit on the number of list elements to be created.

The sort function sorts a list in a specified order. The reverse function reverses the order of the elements in a list.

The map function copies a list and then performs an operation on every element of the list.

The wantarray function enables you to determine whether the statement that called a subroutine is expecting a scalar return value or a list.

Five functions are defined that manipulate associative arrays:

- [ ] keys, which returns a list of the array subscripts
- [ ] values, which returns a list of the array values
- [ ] each, which returns a two-element list consisting of an array subscript and its value
- [ ] delete, which deletes an element
- [ ] exists, which checks whether a particular element exists

Q&A

Q What programs can be called using system?

A Any program that you can run from your terminal can be run using system.

Q Why is the undefined value equivalent to the null string?

A Basically, to keep Perl programs from blowing up if they try to access a variable that has not yet been assigned to.

Q Why does oct handle hexadecimal constants that start with 0x or 0x?

A There is no particular reason, except that it's a little more convenient. If you find that it bothers you to use oct to convert a hexadecimal constant, get rid of the leading 0x or 0x (using the substitution operator) and call hex instead.

Q Why does int truncate instead of rounding?

A You might find it useful to just retrieve the integer part of a floating-point number. (For example, in earlier chapters, you have seen int used in conjunction with rand to return a random integer.)

13

You can always add 0.5 to your number before calling `int`, which will effectively round it up when necessary.

Q When I pack integers using the s or i pack-format characters, the bits don't appear in the order I was expecting. What's happening?

A Most machines enable you to store integers that are more than one byte long (two- and four-byte integers usually are supported). However, each machine does not store a multibyte integer in the same way. Some machines store the most significant byte of a word at a lower address; these machines are called *big-endian* machines because the big end of a word is first. Other machines, called *little-endian* machines, store the least significant byte of a word at a lower byte address.

If you are not getting the result you expect, you might be expecting big-endian and getting little-endian, or vice versa.

Q Can I use each to work through an associative array in a specified order?

A No. If you need to access the elements of an associative array in a specified order, use `keys` and `sort` to sort the subscripts, and then retrieve the value associated with each element.

Q If I am using values with foreach, can I retrieve the subscript associated with a particular value if I need it?

A No. If you are likely to need the subscripts as well as their values, use `each` or `keys`.

Workshop

The Workshop provides quiz questions to help you solidify your understanding of the material covered and exercises to give you experience in using what you've learned. Try to understand the quiz and exercise answers before you go on to tomorrow's lesson. You can find the answers in Appendix B, "Answers."

Quiz

1. Explain the differences between `system` and `exec`.
2. What format does each of the following pack-format characters specify?

    a. `a`

    b. `A`

    c. `d`

    d. `p`

    e. `@`

13

3. What do these unpack-format specifiers do?

   a. `"a"`

   b. `"@4A10i*"`

   c. `"@*X4C*"`

   d. `"ix4iX8i"`

   e. `"b*X*B*"`

4. What value is stored in `$value` by the following?

   a. The statements

   ```
   $vector = pack ("b*", "10110110");
   $value = vec ($vector, 3, 1);
   ```

   b. The statements

   ```
   $vector = pack ("b*", "10110110");
   $value = vec ($vector, 1, 2);
   ```

5. What's the difference between `defined` and `undef`?

6. Assume `@list` contains (`"1"`, `"2"`, `"3"`, `"4"`, `"5"`). What are the contents of `@list` after the following statement?

   a. `splice (@list, 0, 1, "new");`

   b. `splice (@list, 2, 0, "test1", "test2");`

   c. `splice (@list, -1, 1, "test1", "test2");`

   d. `splice (@list, 2, 1);`

   e. `splice (@list, 3);`

7. What do the following statements return?

   a. `grep (!/^!/, @array);`

   b. `grep (/\b\d+\b/, @array);`

   c. `grep (/./, @array);`

   d. `grep (//, @array);`

8. What is the difference between `shift` and `unshift`?

9. What arguments to `splice` are equivalent to the following function calls?

   a. `shift (@array);`

   b. `pop (@array);`

   c. `push (@array, @sublist);`

   d. `unshift (@array, @sublist);`

10. How can you create a stack using `shift`, `pop`, `push`, or `unshift`?

11. How can you create a queue using `shift`, `pop`, `push`, or `unshift`?

13

Exercises

1. Write a program that reads input from a file named `temp` and writes it to the standard output file. Write another program that reads input from the standard output file, writes it to `temp`, and uses `exec` to call the first program.

2. Write a program that reads two binary strings of *any* length, adds them together, and writes out the binary output. (Hint: This is a really nasty problem. To get this to work, you will need to ensure that your bit strings are multiples of eight bits by adding zeros at the front.)

3. Write a program that reads two hexadecimal strings of any length, adds them together, and writes out the hexadecimal output. (Hint: This is a straightforward modification of Exercise 2.)

4. Write a program that uses `int` to round a value to two decimal places. (Hint: This is trickier than it seems.)

5. Write a program that encrypts a password and then asks the user to guess it. Give the user three chances to get it right.

6. **BUG BUSTER:** What is wrong with the following program?

```
$bitstring = "00000011";
$packed = pack("b*", $bitstring);
$highbit = vec($packed, 0, 1);
print ("The high-order bit is $highbit\n");
```

7. Write a program that uses `splice` to sort a list in numeric order.

8. Write a program that "flips" an associative array; that is, the subscripts of the old array become the values of the new, and vice versa. Print an error message if the old array has two subscripts with identical values.

9. Write a program that reads a file from standard input, breaks each line into words, uses `grep` to get rid of all words longer than five characters, and prints the file.

10. Write a program that reads an input line and uses `split` to read and print one word of the line at a time.

11. **BUG BUSTER:** What is wrong with the following subroutine?

```
sub retrieve_first_element {
        local ($retval);

        $retval = unshift(@array);
}
```

13

Day 14

Packages, Modules, and System Functions

Today's lesson describes the following important features in Perl 5 for Win32:

☐ Packages

☐ Modules

☐ The `require` function, which retrieves code from other files

☐ The `use` function and its difference from the `require` function

☐ System library emulation functions

☐ Socket-manipulation functions

You'll also learn about the miscellaneous features in Perl 5 for Win32:

☐ The `$#array` variables

☐ Alternative methods of string quoting using `q`, `qq`, `qw`, and `<<`

☐ The special internal values `__LINE__`, `__FILE__`, and `__ END__`

☐ Incorporating output from other commands using back quotes

☐ The `??` pattern matching construct and the `reset` function

☐ Using `<>` with indirect file variables and as a filename specifier

☐ Using the `*name` construct globally

What Is a Perl Package?

A Perl program keeps track of the variables and subroutines defined within it by storing their names in a symbol table. In Perl, the collection of names in a symbol table is called a `package`. The following sections describe packages and how to use them.

Perl lets you define more than one package for a program, with each package contained in a separate symbol table. To define a package, use the `package` statement:

```
package mypack;
```

This statement creates a new package named `mypack`. All variable and subroutine names defined from this point on in the program are stored in the symbol table associated with the new package. This process continues until another `package` statement is encountered.

Each symbol table contains its own set of variable and subroutine names, and each set of names is independent. This means that you can use the same variable name in more than one package:

```
$var = 14;
package mypack;
$var = 6;
```

The first statement creates a variable named `$var` and stores it in the main symbol table. The statement following the `package` statement creates another variable named `$var` and stores it in the symbol table for the `mypack` package.

The `main` Package

The default symbol table, in which variable and subroutine names are normally stored, is associated with the package named `main`. If you have defined a package using the `package` statement and you want to switch back to using the normal default symbol table, specify the `main` package as shown here:

```
package main;
```

When this statement is executed, your program resumes behaving as though no `package` statements have ever been seen. Subroutine and variable names are stored as they normally are.

14

The following variables are assumed to be in the main package, even when referenced from inside another package:

- [ ] The file variables STDIN, STDOUT, STDERR, and ARGV
- [ ] The %ENV, %INC, @INC, $ARGV, and @ARGV variables
- [ ] Any system variable with a special character in its name (such as, for example, $_ and $%)

Packages and Subroutines

A package definition affects all the statements in a program, including subroutine definitions. For example:

```
package mypack;
subroutine mysub {
    local ($myvar);
    # stuff goes here
}
```

Here, the names mysub and myvar are both part of the mypack package. To call the subroutine mysub from outside the package mypack, specify &mypack'mysub.

You can change packages in the middle of a subroutine:

```
package pack1;
subroutine mysub {
    $var1 = 1;
    package pack2;
    $var1 = 2;
}
```

This code creates two copies of $var1, one in pack1 and one in pack2.

Using Packages

The following sections introduce more features and applications of packages.

Switching Between Packages

You can switch back and forth between packages at any time. Listing 14.1 shows how you can carry out this action.

14

TYPE **Listing 14.1. A program that switches between packages.**

```
1: # p14_1.pl
2:
3: package pack1;
4: $var = 26;
5: package pack2;
6: $var = 34;
7: package pack1;
8: print ("$var\n");
```

OUTPUT
```
C:\> perl p14_1.pl
26
C:\>
```

ANALYSIS Line 3 defines a package named pack1. Line 4 creates a variable named $var, which is then stored in the symbol table for the pack1 package. Line 5 then defines a new package, pack2. Line 6 creates another variable named $var, which is stored in the symbol table for the pack2 package. Two separate copies of $var now exist, one in each package.

Line 7 specifies the pack1 package again. Because pack1 has already been defined, this statement just sets the current package to be pack1; therefore, all variable and subroutine references and definitions refer to names stored in the symbol table for this package.

As a consequence, when line 8 refers to $var, it refers to the $var stored in the pack1 package. The value stored in this variable, 26, is retrieved and printed.

Specifying No Current Package

Perl 5 enables you to state that there is to be no current package. To do this, specify a package statement without a package name, as in the following:

```
package;
```

The statement tells the Perl interpreter that all variables must have their package names explicitly specified in order for a statement to be valid.

```
$mypack::var = 21;  # OK
$var = 21;          # error - no current package
```

This restriction remains in effect until a current package is explicitly defined by another package statement.

Referring to One Package from Another

To refer to a variable or subroutine defined in one package from inside another package, precede the variable name with the package name followed by a single quotation-mark character. For example:

```
package mypack;
$var = 26;
package main;
print ("$mypack'var\n");
```

Here, $mypack'var refers to the variable named $var located in the package mypack.

WARNING

Do not put any spaces between the quotation-mark character and either the package name or the variable name. The following examples are not correct:

```
$mypack ' var
$mypack' var
$mypack 'var
```

NOTE

In Perl 5, the package name and variable name are separated by a pair of colons instead of a quotation mark:

```
$mypack::var
```

The quotation-mark character is supported for now, but might not be understood in future versions of Perl. Therefore, it is better if you keep using :: instead of the quotation mark '.

Defining Private Data

The most common use of packages is in files containing subroutines and global variables that are used in these subroutines. By defining a package for these subroutines, you can ensure that the global variables used in the subroutines are used nowhere else; such variables are called private data.

Better still, you can ensure that the package name itself is used nowhere else. Listing 14.2 is an example of a file containing a package name and variable names that are used nowhere else.

TYPE **Listing 14.2. A file that contains private data.**

```
1: package privpack;
2: $valtoprint = 46;
3:
4: package main;
5: # This function is the link to the outside world.
```

14

continues

Listing 14.2. continued

```
6: sub printval {
7:      &privpack'printval();
8: }
9:
10: package privpack;
11: sub printval {
12:     print ("$valtoprint\n");
13: }
14:
15: package main;
16: 1;  # return value for require
```

OUTPUT This subroutine, by itself, cannot generate its output until `printval` is called.

ANALYSIS This file can be divided into two parts: the part that communicates with the outside world and the part that does the work. The part that communicates is in the `main` or default package, and the part that does the work is in a special package named `privpack`. This package is defined only in this file.

The subroutine `printval`, defined in lines 6–8, is designed to be called from programs and subroutines defined elsewhere. Its only task is to call the version of `printval` defined in the `privpack` package.

The version of `printval` in the `privpack` package prints the number by retrieving it from the scalar variable `$valtoprint`. This variable is also part of the `privpack` package, and it is defined only inside it.

Lines 15 and 16 ensure that this file behaves properly if it is included in a program by `require`. Line 15 sets the current package to the default package, and line 16 is a nonzero return value to ensure that `require` does not generate an error.

Accessing Symbol Tables

To actually look in a symbol table from within a program, use the associative array `%_package`, in which `package` is the name of the package whose symbol table you want to access. For example, the variable `%_main` contains the default symbol table.

Normally, you will not need to look in the symbol table yourself.

Packages versus Extensions

As you have learned from previous days, Perl has borrowed many features from C programming language. In fact, Perl even allows you to use the extra functions written in C. To do so, Perl implements special packages—extensions. Extensions are enhanced packages that invoke the extra C functions.

More extensions in Perl 5 for Win32 are covered on Day 15, "Perl 5 for Win32 Module Extensions."

Creating a Module

Most large programs are divided into components, each of which performs a specific task or set of tasks. Each component normally contains one or more executable functions, plus the variables needed to make these functions work. The collection of functions and variables in a component is known as a program module. One module can appear in a variety of programs.

Perl 5 for Win32 enables you to use packages to define modules. To define a module, you need to create the package and store it in a file of the same name. For example, a package named Mymodule would be stored in the file Mymodule.pm. (The .pm suffix indicates that the file is a Perl module.)

Listing 14.3 creates a module named Mymodule, containing subroutines myfunc1 and myfunc2 and variables $myvar1 and $myvar2. You would store this code in the file Mymodule.pm.

TYPE **Listing 14.3. Code that creates a Perl module.**

```
1: # p14_3.pl (Mymodule.pm)
2:
3: package Mymodule;
4: require Exporter;
5: @ISA = qw(Exporter);
6: @EXPORT = qw(myfunc1 myfunc2);
7: @EXPORT_OK = qw($myvar1 $myvar2);
8:
9: sub myfunc1 {
10:    $myvar1 += 1;
11: }
12:
13: sub myfunc2 {
14:    $myvar2 += 2;
15: )
16: 1;    # required by caller
```

14

ANALYSIS   Lines 3–7 use the standard Perl module definition conventions. Line 3 defines the
package. Line 4 includes a built-in Perl module, Exporter, which provides information about these definition conventions. Lines 6 and 7 define the subroutines and variables that are to be made available to the outside world.

Line 6 creates a special array named @EXPORT. This array lists the subroutines that can be called by other programs. Here, the subroutines myfunc1 and myfunc2 are accessible. Any subroutine defined inside a module but that is not included in the list assigned to @EXPORT is a private subroutine and can only be called inside the module.

Line 7 creates another special array, called @EXPORT_OK, that lists the variables that can be accessed by other programs. Here, the variables $myvar1 and $myvar2 are accessible from the outside world.

The 1 in line 16 marks the end of the module file, which is required by any other packages that use Mymodule.pm.

More details on modules in Perl are covered on Day 19, "Object-Oriented Programming in Perl".

The use **Function versus the** require **Function**

Generally speaking, you can use both use and require to include Perl modules in your programs. However, use and require are indeed two different Perl functions. The following sections introduce more details about the two functions.

The use **Function**

To import a module into your Perl program, use the use function. For example, the following statement imports the Mymodule module into a program:

```
use Mymodule;
```

The subroutines and variables in Mymodule.pm can now be used in your program.

To undefine a previously imported module, use the no statement. For example, the following statement undefines the Mymodule module:

```
no Mymodule;
```

Listing 14.4 is an example of a program that imports and undefines a module. The integer module referenced here specifies that all arithmetic operations are to be on integers. Floating-point numbers are converted to integers before the arithmetic operations are performed.

TYPE **Listing 14.4. A program that uses the use and no statements.**

```
1: # p14_4.pl
2:
3: use integer;
4: $result = 2.4 + 2.4;
5: print ("$result\n");
6:
7: no integer;
8: $result = 2.4 + 2.4;
9: print ("$result\n");
```

OUTPUT
```
C:\> perl p14_4.pl
4
4.8
C:\>
```

ANALYSIS Line 3 of this program imports the integer module. As a consequence, Line 4 converts 2.4 to 2 before performing the addition, yielding the result 4.

Line 7 undefines the integer module. This tells the Perl interpreter to revert to using floating-point numbers in arithmetic operations.

WARNING

If a use or no statement appears inside a statement block, it remains in effect only for the duration of that block. For example:

```
use integer;
$result1 = 2.4 + 2.4;
if ($result1 == 4) {
    no integer;
    $result2 = 3.4 + 3.4;
}
$result3 = 4.4 + 4.4;
```

Here, the no statement is only in effect inside the if statement. In the statement after the if, the integer module is still in use, which means that 4.4 is converted to 4 before the addition is performed.

The require **Function**

The require function, on the other hand, provides a way to break your program into separate files and create libraries of functions. For example, if you have stored Perl statements in the

14

file `myfile.pl`, you can include them as part of your program by adding the following statement:

```
require ("myfile.pl");
```

When the Perl interpreter sees this `require` statement, it searches the directories specified by the built-in array variable `@INC` for a file named `myfile.pl`. If such a file is found, the statements in the file are executed; if no such file exists, the program terminates and prints the error message

```
Can't find myfile.pl in @INC
```

on your screen (by writing it to the standard error file `STDERR`). (For more details on the `@INC` array, refer to Day 17, "System Variables.")

As in a subroutine call, the last expression evaluated inside a file included by `require` becomes the return value. The `require` function checks whether this value is `0`, and terminates if it is. For example, suppose that the file `myfile.pl` contains the following statements:

```
print ("hello, world!\n");
$var = 14;
```

If the statements in this file are executed by

```
require ("myfile.pl");
```

the return value of `myfile.pl` is the following expression, which has the value `14`:

```
$var = 14
```

Because this value is not zero, the program continues execution with the statement following the `require`.

If `myfile.pl` contains the following statements, the return value of `myfile.pl` is `0`:

```
print ("hello, world!\n");
$var = 0;
```

Because this value is `0`, the Perl interpreter prints the following error message, along with the name and current line number of your program, and then it exits:

```
myfile.pl did not return true value
```

TIP

By convention, files containing Perl statements normally have the suffix `.pl`. This makes it easy to determine which files in a directory contain Perl programs or code included in Perl programs using `require`.

14

You can pass any scalar value to `require`, including those stored in scalar variables or array elements:

```
@reqlist = ("file1.pl", "file2.pl", "file3.pl");
require ($reqlist[$0]);
require ($reqlist[$1]);
require ($reqlist[$2]);
```

Here, the successive calls to `require` include the contents of `file1.pl`, `file2.pl`, and `file3.pl`.

You can also specify no filename, as in the following:

```
require;
```

In this case, the value of the scalar variable `$_` is the filename whose contents are to be executed.

WARNING

One limitation Perl imposes on the `require` statement is that the contents of a particular file can be included only once in a program. To repeat a block of code many times, your only alternative is to put it in a separate program and call it using the `system` function or the `eval` function.

Also, if two directories in `@INC` contain a file named by `require`, only the first one is included.

Also, Perl 5 enables you to use a `require` statement to specify the version of Perl needed to run your program. When Perl sees a `require` statement with a numeric associated value, it runs the program only if the version of Perl is greater than or equal to the number. For example, the following statement indicates that the program is to be run only if the Perl interpreter is version 5.001 or higher:

```
require 5.001;
```

If it is not, the program terminates.

This is useful if your program uses a feature of Perl that you know does not work properly in earlier versions of the language.

Using Predefined Modules

Perl 5 provides a variety of predefined modules that perform useful tasks. Each module can be imported by the `use` statement and removed by the `no` statement.

14

A complete list of the predefined modules included with Perl 5 can be found in your Perl documentation.

System Library Emulation Functions

Several built-in Perl functions enable you to execute various system library calls from within your Perl program. Each one corresponds to a UNIX system library function.

The following sections briefly describe some of the system library functions that are supported by Perl 5 for Win32. For more information on a particular system library function, refer to the online manual page for that function.

Appendix A, "Unsupported Functions in Perl 5 for Win32," lists all functions that are not supported in Perl 5 for Win32.

The gethostbyaddr Function

On Windows NT, the gethostbyaddr function searches the hostname for a given network address.

SYNTAX

The syntax for the gethostbyaddr function is

```
(name, altnames, addrtype, len, addrs) = gethostbyaddr (inaddr, inaddrtype);
```

This function requires two arguments. The first, *inaddr*, is the Internet address to search for, stored in packed four-byte format (identical to that used by getnetbyaddr). The second argument, *inaddrtype*, is the address type; at present, only Internet address types are understood, and *inaddrtype* is normally AF_INET.

gethostbyaddr returns a five-element list. The first element, *name*, is the hostname corresponding to the Internet address specified by *inaddr*. *altnames* is the list of aliases or alternative names that can be used to refer to the host. *addrtype*, like *inaddrtype*, is AF_INET, which is defined as 2.

addrs is a list of addresses (main address and alternatives) corresponding to the host node named *name*. Each address is stored as a four-byte integer. *len* is the length of the *addrs* field; this length is always 4 multiplied by the number of addresses returned in *addrs*.

Listing 14.5 shows how you can use gethostbyaddr to retrieve the Internet address corresponding to a particular machine name.

14

TYPE **Listing 14.5. A program that uses** `gethostbyaddr.`

```
1: # p14_5.pl
2:
3: print ("Enter an Internet address:\n");
4: $machine = <STDIN>;
5: $machine =~ s/^\s+|\s+$//g;
6: @bytes = split (/\./, $machine);
7: $packaddr = pack ("C4", @bytes);
8: if (!(($name, $altnames, $addrtype, $len, @addrlist) =
9:      gethostbyaddr ($packaddr, 2))) {
10:     die ("Address $machine not found.\n");
11: }
12: print ("Principal name: $name\n");
13: if ($altnames ne "") {
14:     print ("Alternative names:\n");
15:     @altlist = split (/\s+/, $altnames);
16:     for ($i = 0; $i < @altlist; $i++) {
17:         print ("\t$altlist[$i]\n");
18:     }
19: }
```

OUTPUT
```
C:\> perl p14_5.pl
Enter an Internet address:
128.174.5.59
Principal name: uxl.cso.uiuc.edu
C:\>
```

ANALYSIS The program starts by prompting you for an Internet address. (In this example, the Internet address specified is `128.174.5.59`, which is the location of a popular public-access Gopher site.) Lines 5–7 then convert the address into a four-byte packed integer, which is stored in `$packaddr`.

Lines 8 and 9 call `gethostbyaddr`. This function looks for an entry matching the specified machine name. If the entry is not found, the conditional expression becomes false, and line 10 calls `die` to terminate the program.

NOTE Line 9 uses the value 2 as the address type to pass to `gethostbyaddr`. If your machine defines a different value of `AF_INET`, replace 2 with that value.

14

If the entry is found, line 12 prints the principal machine name, which was returned by gethostbyaddr and is now stored in the scalar variable $name. Line 13 then checks whether the returned entry lists any alternative machine names corresponding to this Internet address.

If alternative machine names exist, lines 14–18 split the alternative name list into individual names and print each name on a separate line.

WARNING

> gethostbyaddr and the other functions expect the following format for a host entry:
>
> `address mainname altname1 altname2 ...`
>
> Here, *address* is an Internet address; *mainname* is the name associated with the address; and *altname1*, *altname2*, and so on are the (optional) alternative names for the host.

The gethostbyname **Function**

The gethostbyname function is similar to gethostbyaddr, except that it searches for an entry that matches a specified machine name or Internet site name.

SYNTAX

The syntax for the gethostbyname function is

`(name, altnames, addrtype, len, addrs) = gethostbyname (inname);`

Here, *inname* is the machine name or Internet site name to search for. gethostbyname, like gethostbyaddr, returns a five-element list consisting of the machine name, a character string containing a list of alternative names, the address type, the length of the address list, and the address list.

Listing 14.6 is a simple program that searches for an Internet address when given the name of a site.

TYPE   **Listing 14.6. A program that uses** gethostbyname**.**

```
1: # p14_6.pl
2:
3: print ("Enter a machine name or Internet site name:\n");
4: $machine = <STDIN>;
5: $machine =~ s/^\s+|\s+$//g;
6: if (!(($name, $altnames, $addrtype, $len, @addrlist) =
7:     gethostbyname ($machine))) {
8:     die ("Machine name $machine not found.\n");
9: }
```

14

```
10: print ("Equivalent addresses:\n");
11: for ($i = 0; $i < @addrlist; $i++) {
12:     @addrbytes = unpack("C4", $addrlist[$i]);
13:     $realaddr = join (".", @addrbytes);
14:     print ("\t$realaddr\n");
15: }
```

OUTPUT

```
C:\> perl p14_6.pl
Enter a machine name or Internet site name:
ux1.cso.uiuc.edu
Equivalent addresses:
128.174.5.59
C:\>
```

ANALYSIS This program prompts for a machine name and then removes the leading and trailing white space from it. After the machine name has been prepared, lines 6 and 7 call gethostbyname, which searches for the \%SystemRoot%\System32\Drivers\etc\hosts entry matching the specified machine name. If gethostbyname does not find the entry, it returns the null string, the conditional expression becomes false, and line 8 calls die to terminate the program.

If gethostbyname finds the entry, the loop in lines 11–15 examines the list of addresses in @addrlist, assembling and printing one address at a time. Line 12 assembles an address by unpacking one element of @addrlist and storing the individual bytes in @addrbytes. Line 13 joins the bytes into a character string, placing a period between each pair of bytes. The resulting string is a readable Internet address, which line 14 prints.

NOTE The machine name passed to gethostbyname can be either the principal machine name (as specified in the first element of the returned list) or one of the alternative names (aliases).

The getprotobyname **and** getprotobynumber **Functions**

Given a protocol name, the getprotobyname function enables you to search for a particular protocol entry.

The syntax of the getprotobyname function is

```
(name, aliases, number) = getprotobyname (searchname);
```

Here, searchname is the protocol name you are looking for. names, aliases, and number are the same as in getprotoent.

14

Similarly, `getprotobynumber` searches for a protocol entry that matches a particular protocol number.

The syntax of the `getprotobynumber` function is

```
(name, aliases, number) = getprotobynumber (searchnum);
```

`searchnum` is the protocol number to search for. `names`, `aliases`, and `number` are the same as in `getprotoent`.

Both functions return the empty list if no matching protocol database entry is found.

The `getservbyname` and `getservbyport` Functions

The `getservbyname` function provides a way of searching for a particular service name.

The syntax of the `getservbyname` function is

```
(name, aliases, portnum, protoname) = getservbyname (searchname, searchproto);
```

Here, `searchname` and `searchproto` are the service name and service protocol type to be matched. If the name and type are matched, `getservbyname` returns the system service database entry corresponding to this name and type. This entry is the same four-element list as is returned by `getservent`. (The empty list is returned if the name and type are not matched.)

Similarly, the `getservbyport` function searches for a service name that matches a particular service port number.

The syntax of the `getservbyport` function is

```
(name, aliases, portnum, protoname) = getservbyport (searchportnum,
searchproto);
```

`searchportnum` and `searchproto` are the port number and protocol type to search for. `name`, `aliases`, `portnum`, and `protoname` are the same as in `getservbyname` and `getservent`.

Socket-Manipulation Functions

In Berkeley UNIX environments (version 4.3BSD) as well as Windows environments, processes can communicate with one another using a connection device known as a socket. When a socket has been created, one process can write data that can then be read by another process.

Perl 5 for Win32 supports various functions that create sockets and set up connections with them. The following sections describe these functions.

The socket **Function**

To create a socket, call the socket function. This function defines a socket and associates it with a Perl file handle.

SYNTAX

The syntax of the socket function is

socket (*socket, domain, type, format*);

socket is a file variable that is to be associated with the new socket.

domain is the protocol family to use. The legal values for *domain* are listed in the system header file winsock.h from Microsoft; these values are represented by the constants PF_UNIX, PF_INET, PF_IMPLINK, and PF_NS.

type is the type of socket to create. The legal values for *type* are also listed in the file winsock.h. These legal values are represented by the five constants SOCK_STREAM, SOCK_DGRAM, SOCK_RAW, SOCK_SEQPACKET, and SOCK_RDM. (Usually, you can find the winsock.h file in the software package of Microsoft Visual C/C++.)

format is the number of the protocol to be used with the socket. This protocol is normally retrieved by calling getprotobyname.

The socket function returns a nonzero value if the socket has been created and 0 if an error occurs.

The bind **Function**

After you create a socket using socket, the next step is to bind the socket to a particular network address. To do this, use the bind function.

SYNTAX

The syntax of the bind function is

bind (*socket, address*);

Here, *socket* is the file variable corresponding to the socket created by socket.

address is the network address to be associated with the socket. This address consists of the following elements:

- ☐ The address type, which is an unsigned short integer and is always AF_INET
- ☐ The number of the port to use when connecting, which is a short integer in network order
- ☐ The packed four-byte representation of the Internet address of the machine to which the socket is to be bound

14

This function returns a nonzero value if the bind operation succeeds and 0 if an error occurs.

To create an address suitable for passing to bind, call pack:

```
$address = pack ("Sna4x8", 2, $portnum, $intaddress);
```

Here, the pack-format specifier Sna4x8 indicates an unsigned short integer, followed by a short integer in network order (the port number), a four-byte ASCII string (which is the packed address), and eight null bytes. This is the format that bind expects when binding an address to a socket.

The listen **Function**

After an address has been bound to the socket associated with each of the machines that are to communicate, the next step is to define a process that is to be the "listening" process. This process waits for connections to be established with it. (In a client-server architecture, this process corresponds to the server.) To define this listening process, call the listen function.

SYNTAX

The syntax of the listen function is

```
listen (socket, number);
```

socket is the socket created using the socket function. number is the maximum number of processes that can be queued up to connect to this process.

listen returns a nonzero value if it executes successfully, 0 if it does not.

WARNING

The maximum number of processes that can be queued using listen is five. This limitation is imposed by the Berkeley UNIX operating system. Check the latest news for any changes of the limitation.

The accept **Function**

After a process that has been established as the listening process calls listen, the next step is to have this process call the accept function. accept waits until a process wants to connect with it, and then it returns the address of the connecting process.

The syntax of the accept function is

```
accept (procsocket, socket);
```

procsocket is a previously undefined file variable that is to represent the newly created connection. The listening process can then send to or receive from the other process using the file variable specified in *procsocket*. This file variable can be treated like any other file variable: the program can send data through the socket by calling write or print, or it can read data using the <> operator.

socket is the socket created by socket and bound to an address by bind.

Listing 14.7 is an example of a program that uses listen and accept to create a simple server. This server just sends the message Hello, world! to any process that connects to it. (A client program that receives this message is listed in the next section, "The connect Function.")

TYPE   **Listing 14.7. A simple server program.**

```
 1: # p14_7.pl
 2:
 3: $line = "Hello, world!\n";
 4:
 5: $port = 2000;
 6: while (getservbyport ($port, "tcp")) {
 7:     $port++;
 8: }
 9: ($d1, $d2, $prototype) = getprotobyname ("tcp");
10: ($d1, $d2, $d3, $d4, $rawserver) = gethostbyname ("silver");
11: $serveraddr = pack ("Sna4x8", 2, $port, $rawserver);
12: socket (SSOCKET, 2, 1, $prototype) || die ("No socket");
13: bind (SSOCKET, $serveraddr) || die ("Can't bind");
14: listen (SSOCKET, 1) || die ("Can't listen");
15: ($clientaddr = accept (SOCKET, SSOCKET)) ||
16:     die ("Can't accept");
17: select (SOCKET);
18: $| = 1;
19: print SOCKET ("$line\n");
20: close (SOCKET);
21: close (SSOCKET);
```

OUTPUT   This program requires no input and generates no visible output.

ANALYSIS   The first task this server program performs is to search for a port to use when establishing a socket connection. To be on the safe side, the program first checks that the port it is going to use, port 2000, is not reserved for use by another program. If it is reserved, the program checks port 2001, then port 2002, and so on until it finds an unused port.

To do this checking, line 6 calls getservbyport. If getservbyport returns a non-empty list, the port is being used by some other program. In this case, the port number is increased by one, and getservbyport is called again. This process continues until getservbyport returns an empty list, which indicates that the port being checked is unused. When lines 5–8 are no longer executing, the scalar variable $port contains the number of the port to be used.

14

Line 9 calls `getprotobyname` to retrieve the entry associated with the TCP protocol. The protocol number associated with the TCP protocol is retrieved from this entry and is stored in the scalar variable `$prototype`. (The other elements of the list are ignored; the convention used by this program is to store element entries that are not going to be used in variables named `$d1`, `$d2`, and so on; the `d` stands for dummy.)

Line 10 calls `gethostbyname` to retrieve the network address of the machine on which this server is running. This program assumes that the server is running on a local machine named `silver`. To run this program on your own machine, replace `silver` with your machine name.

After `gethostbyname` has been called, the scalar variable `$rawserver` contains the Internet address of your machine. Line 11 calls `pack` to convert the address type, the port number, and this address into the form understood by the operating system. (The address type parameter, `2`, is the local value of `AF_INET`, which is the only address type supported.) This information is stored in the scalar variable `$serveraddr`.

After `pack` is called to build the server address, the program is ready to create a socket. Line 12 does this by calling `socket`. This call to `socket` passes it the file variable `SSOCKET`, the socket domain, the socket type, and the protocol number. After `socket` is called, the file variable `SSOCKET` represents the "master socket" that is to listen for connections. (Note that the values `2` and `1` passed to `socket` are, respectively, the local values of the constants `PF_INET` and `SOCK_STREAM`. `PF_INET` indicates Internet-style protocol, and `SOCK_STREAM` indicates that transmission will be in the form of a stream of bytes. You likely will not need to use any other values for these arguments.)

After the socket has been created, the next step is line 13, which associates the socket with your machine by calling `bind`. This call to `bind` is passed the file variable `SSOCKET` associated with the socket and the server address created by the call to `pack` in line 11.

After the socket is bound to your machine address, you are ready to listen for clients that want to connect to your server. Line 14 does this by calling `listen`. This call to `listen` is passed the file variable `SSOCKET` and the value `1`; the latter indicates that only one client is listened for at any particular time.

Line 15 calls `accept`, which waits until a client process wants to connect to this server. When a connection is established, `accept` creates a new socket associated with this connection and uses the file variable `SOCKET` to represent it. (The address of the client connection is returned in `$clientaddr`; if you want to, you can use `unpack` to obtain the address and then call `gethostbyaddr` to retrieve the name of the machine on which the client process is running.)

When the connection has been established and the file variable `SOCKET` has been associated with it, you can treat `SOCKET` like any other file variable: you can read data from it or write data to it. Lines 17 and 18 turn off buffering for `SOCKET`, which ensures that data sent through the socket is sent right away. (If buffering is left on, the program won't send data until the special internal buffer is full, which means that the client process won't receive the data right away.) After buffering is turned off, line 19 writes the line of data to `SOCKET`, which sends it to the client process.

WARNING

> Although you can both send and receive data through the same socket, doing so is dangerous because you run the risk of deadlock. Deadlock occurs when the client and server processes each think that the other is going to send data. Neither can proceed until the other does.
>
> To avoid a deadlock, make sure that you understand how data flows between the processes you are running.

The connect **Function**

As you have seen, when two processes communicate using a socket, one process is designated as the listening process. This process calls `listen` to indicate that it is the listening process, and then it calls `accept` to wait for a connection from another process. (Listening processes are called `servers`, because they provide service to the processes that connect to them. The processes that connect to servers are called `clients`.)

To connect to a process that has called `accept` and is now waiting for a connection, use the `connect` function.

SYNTAX

The syntax of the `connect` function is

```
connect (socket, address);
```

`socket` is a file variable representing a socket created using `socket` and bound using `bind`. `address` is the internal representation of the Internet address to which you want to connect. In the process to which this process is connecting, this address must have been passed to `bind` to bind it to a socket, and the socket, in turn, must have been specified in calls to `listen` and `accept`.

After `connect` has been called, the program that calls it can send data to or receive data from the other process by means of the file variable specified in `socket`.

Listing 14.8 is an example of a program that uses `connect` to obtain data from another process. (The process that sends the data is displayed back in Listing 14.7.)

14

Listing 14.8. A simple client program.

```
1: # p14_8.pl
2:
3: $port = 2000;
4: while (getservbyport ($port, "tcp")) {
5:     $port++;
6: }
7: ($d1, $d2, $prototype) = getprotobyname ("tcp");
8: ($d1, $d2, $d3, $d4, $rawclient) = gethostbyname ("mercury");
9: ($d1, $d2, $d3, $d4, $rawserver) = gethostbyname ("silver");
10: $clientaddr = pack ("Sna4x8", 2, 0, $rawclient);
11: $serveraddr = pack ("Sna4x8", 2, $port, $rawserver);
12: socket (SOCKET, 2, 1, $prototype) || die ("No socket");
13: bind (SOCKET, $clientaddr) || die ("Can't bind");
14: connect (SOCKET, $serveraddr);
15:
16: $line = <SOCKET>;
17: print ("$line\n");
18: close (SOCKET);
```

OUTPUT
```
C:\> perl p14_8.pl
Hello, world!
C:\>
```

ANALYSIS Lines 3–6 obtain the port to use when receiving data by means of a socket connection. As in Listing 14.7, the port number is compared with the list of ports by calling getservbyport. The first unused port number greater than or equal to 2000 becomes the number of the port to use. (This program and Listing 14.7 assume that the same services file is being examined in both cases. If the services files are different, you will need to choose a port number yourself and specify this port number in both your client program and your server program—in other words, assign a pre-specified value to the variable $port.)

Line 7 calls getprotobyname to retrieve the protocol number associated with the TCP protocol. This protocol number is eventually passed to socket.

Lines 8 and 9 retrieve the Internet addresses of the client (this program) and the server (the process to connect to). $rawclient is assigned the Internet address of the client, and $rawserver is assigned the Internet address of the server; each of these addresses is a four-byte scalar value.

Lines 10 and 11 take the addresses stored in $rawclient and $rawserver and convert them to the form used by the socket-processing functions. In both cases, the 2 passed to pack is the local value for AF_INET. Note that line 10 doesn't bother specifying a port value to pass to pack; this is because the connection uses the port specified in the server address in line 11.

Line 12 now calls socket to create a socket for the current program (the client). As in the call to socket in Listing 14.7, the values 2 and 1 passed to socket are the local values of the

14

constants PF_INIT and SOCK_STREAM; if these values are different on your machine, you need to replace the values shown here with the ones defined for your machine. The call to socket in line 12 associates the file variable SOCKET with the newly created socket.

After the socket has been created, line 13 calls bind to associate the socket with the client program. bind requires two arguments: the file variable associated with the socket that has just been created and the address of the client machine as packed by line 10.

Line 14 now tries to connect to the server process by calling connect and passing it the server address created by line 11. If the connection is successful, you can send and receive data through the socket using the SOCKET file variable.

The SOCKET file handle behaves just like any other file handle. This means that line 16 reads a line of data from the server process. Because the server process is sending the character string Hello, world! (followed by a newline character), this is the string that is assigned to $line. Line 17 then prints $line, which means that the following appears on your screen:

```
Hello, world!
```

After the client process is finished with the socket, line 18 calls close. This call indicates that the program is finished with the socket. (After the socket is closed by both the server and the client programs, the server program can accept a connection from another client process, if desired.)

The shutdown Function

When two processes are communicating using a socket, data can be sent in either direction: The client can receive data from the server, or vice versa. The shutdown function enables you to indicate that traffic in one or both directions is no longer needed.

The syntax for the shutdown function is

```
shutdown (socket, direction);
```

Here, socket is the file variable associated with the socket whose traffic is to be restricted. direction is one of the following values:

- ☐ 0 indicates that the program can send through the socket but can no longer receive data.

- ☐ 1 indicates that the program can receive data from the socket but can no longer send it.

- ☐ 2 indicates that both sending and receiving are disallowed.

14

NOTE

> To terminate communication through a socket, call `close` and pass it the file variable associated with the socket:
>
> `close (SOCKET);`
>
> This line closes the socket represented by `SOCKET`.

The `getsockopt` **and** `setsockopt` **Functions**

The `getsockopt` and `setsockopt` functions enable you to obtain and set socket options.

To obtain the current value of a socket option in your environment, call the `getsockopt` function.

 SYNTAX

The syntax of the `getsockopt` function is

`retval = getsockopt (socket, opttype, optname);`

socket is the file variable associated with the socket whose option you want to retrieve.

opttype is the type of option (or option level). The value of the system constant `SOL_SOCKET` specifies a socket-level option.

optname is the name of the option whose value is to be retrieved; *retval* is the value of this option.

To set a socket option, call `setsockopt`.

 SYNTAX

The syntax of the `setsockopt` function is

`setsockopt (socket, opttype, optname, value);`

Here, *socket*, *opttype*, and *optname* are the same as in `getsockopt`, and *value* is the new value of the *optname* option.

The `getsockname` **and** `getpeername` **Functions**

The `getsockname` and `getpeername` functions enable you to retrieve the addresses of the two ends of a socket connection.

The `getsockname` function returns the address of this end of a socket connection (the end created by the currently running program).

The syntax of the `getsockname` function is

```
retval = getsockname (socket);
```

As in the other socket functions, `socket` is the file variable associated with a particular socket. `retval` is the returned address.

The returned address is in packed format as built by the calls to `pack` in Listing 14.7 and Listing 14.8.

The following code retrieves a socket address and converts it into readable form:

```
$rawaddr = getsockname (SOCKET);
($d1, $d2, @addrbytes) = unpack ("SnC4x8", $rawaddr);
$readable = join (".", @addrbytes);
```

> **NOTE**
>
> Normally, you already have the address returned by `getsockname`, because you need to pass it to `bind` to associate the socket with your machine.

To retrieve the address of the other end of the socket connection, call `getpeername`.

The syntax of the `getpeername` function is

```
retval = getpeername (socket);
```

As in `getsockname`, `socket` is the file variable associated with the socket, and `retval` is the returned address.

> **NOTE**
>
> The address returned by `getpeername` is normally identical to the address returned by `accept`.

Miscellaneous Features of Perl 5 for Win32

The following sections introduce some miscellaneous features ported to Perl 5 for Win32.

14

The `$#array` **Variable**

For each array variable defined in your program, a variable named `$#array`, in which `array` is the name of your array, is also defined. This variable contains the subscript of the last element of the array. Look at this example:

```
@myarray = ("goodbye", "cruel", "world");
$lastsub = $#myarray;
```

Here, there are three elements in `@myarray`, which are referenced by the subscripts 0, 1, and 2. Because the subscript of the last element of the array is 2, `$#myarray` contains the value 2.

NOTE

> Because the value of the maximum subscript is affected by the system variable `$[`, the value of each `$#array` variable is also affected by `$[`. For example:
>
> ```
> $[ = 1;
> @myarray = ("goodbye", "cruel", "world");
> $lastsub = $#myarray;
> ```
>
> Here, the first subscript of the array is 1, because `$[` is set to that value. This means that the maximum subscript is 3 and the value of `$#myarray` is also 3.

Any `$#array` variable that does not correspond to a defined array has the value -1. For example:

```
$sublength = $#notdefined;
```

Here, if the array `@notdefined` does not exist, `$sublength` is assigned -1.

A `$#array` variable is also defined for each built-in array variable. This means, for example, that the `$#ARGV` variable contains the number of elements included on the command line. You can use this variable to check whether files have been specified on the command line:

```
if ($#ARGV == -1) {
    die ("No files specified.\n");
}
```

Controlling Array Length Using `$#array`

You can use `$#array` to control the length of an array variable.

If a `$#array` variable is assigned a value that is larger than the current largest subscript of the corresponding array, the missing elements are created and initialized to the special internal undefined value (equivalent to the null string). For example:

14

```
@myarray = ("hi", "there");
$#myarray = 4;
```

This code sets the maximum subscript of `$#myarray` to 4. Because the subscript of the last defined element is 1, three empty elements are created with subscripts 2, 3, and 4.

You can use this technique to create a large array all at once:

```
$#bigarray = 9999;
```

This statement creates an array large enough to hold 10,000 values (or fails trying). If this statement executes successfully, you know that your machine has enough space to store `@bigarray` before actually assigning to all or part of it.

In Perl 5 for Win32, if the value you assign to a `$#array` variable is less than the current maximum subscript, the leftover array values are destroyed. For example:

```
@myarray = ("hello", "there", "Dave!");
$#myarray = 1;
```

Here, `@myarray` is originally assigned a three-element list, which means that its maximum subscript is 2. Assigning 1 to `$#myarray` sets the maximum subscript to 1, which means that `@myarray` now contains `("hello", "there")`. The third element, `Dave!`, is destroyed.

NOTE

This is one instance in which Perl 5 and Perl 4 behave differently. In Perl 4, array elements are not destroyed when `$#array` is assigned a value less than the current maximum subscript.

In Perl 4, array elements that have been "removed" by assigning to the `$#array` variable can be restored to existence by resetting `$#array` to its original value.

Alternative String Delimiters

As you've seen, Perl for Win32 enables you to enclose character strings in either single quotation marks or double quotation marks. Strings in double quotation marks are searched for variable names, which are replaced with their values when found; strings in single quotation marks are not searched.

Consider the following example:

```
$var = 5;
print ("$var\n");
print ('$var\n');
```

14

The first call to `print` prints 5 followed by a newline character; the second prints the string `$var\n` as is.

Perl for Win32 enables you to use any delimiter you want in place of either single quotation marks or double quotation marks. To specify a string that—like a single-quoted string—is not searched for variable names, use `q` followed by the delimiter you want to use. For example, the following strings are equivalent:

```
q!hello $there!
'hello $there'
```

A useful trick is to use newline characters as delimiters:

```
q
this is my string
```

This example is equivalent to the following because the newline after the `q` indicates the beginning of the string, and the newline after `string` indicates the end of the string:

```
'this is my string'
```

To define a string that is searched for variable names, use `qq`:

```
qq/This string contains $var./
```

The `/` characters delimit the string

```
This string contains $var.
```

which is then searched for variable names. This means that `$var` is replaced by its current value.

NOTE

> If you use a left parenthesis as the opening delimiter for a string defined using `q` or `qq`, the Perl interpreter expects a right parenthesis as the closing delimiter. This method of operation enables you to treat `q` and `qq` as if they were functions:
>
> ```
> q(Here is a single quoted string);
> qq(Here is a double quoted string);
> ```
>
> These are equivalent to both of the following:
>
> ```
> 'Here is a single quoted string'
> "Here is a double quoted string"
> ```
>
> Be careful not to leave a space between the `q` or `qq` and the left parenthesis; if you do, the Perl interpreter will assume that the space character, not the `(`, is the delimiter.

qw, defined in Perl 5 for Win32, provides a convenient way of breaking a string into words. The following statements are equivalent:

```
@words = qw/this is a list of words/;
@words = split(' ', q/this is a list of words/);
```

In each case, @words is assigned the list

```
("this", "is", "a", "list", "of", "words")
```

qw supports any alternative string delimiter supported by q and qq.

Defining Strings Using <<

You can use << (two left angle brackets) to indicate the beginning of a string. This string continues until the next blank line. The following is an example:

```
$longstring = <<
Here is the first part of the string.
Here is the last part of the string.

# here is the next statement
```

This example defines a string consisting of the two input lines

```
Here is the first part of the string.
Here is the last part of the string.
```

and assigns it to $longstring. The newline characters are included as part of the string.

You can specify the characters that indicate "end of string" by including them after the <<. For example:

```
$longstring = <<END
Here is the first part of the string.
Here is the last part of the string.
END
# here is the next statement.
```

Here, END indicates the end of the string.

You can enclose the end-of-string characters in either single or double quotation marks. Single-quoted end-of-string characters behave like normal end-of-string characters:

```
$longstring = <<'END'
Here is the first part of the string.
Here is the last part of the string.
END
# here is the next statement
```

14

Double-quoted end-of-string characters are searched for variable names, which are replaced by their values if found. Take a look at the following:

```
$endchars = "END";
$longstring = <<"$endchars"
Here is the first part of the string.
Here is the last part of the string.
END
# here is the next statement
```

Here, $endchars is replaced by its value, END, which is used to indicate the end of the string.

A string created using << can be used wherever a string is expected. For example, the statement

```
print <<END
Hello there!
This is a test!
END
```

writes the following to the standard output file:

```
Hello there!
This is a test!
```

(This is one place where omitting the parentheses when you pass an argument to a function becomes useful.)

You can use the x operator to write a string more than once:

```
print <<END x 2
Hello there!
END
```

This sends the following to the standard output file:

```
Hello there!
Hello there!
```

You can supply more than one << at a time. If you do, they are processed in the order in which they are received. For example, the statement

```
$longstring = <<END1 . <<END2
This is the first part.
END1
This is the second part.
END2
```

assigns the following (including the trailing newlines) to $longstring:

```
This is the first part.
This is the second part.
```

Do   **Don't**

DON'T leave a space between the << and the end-of-string characters. (If you do, the Perl interpreter will terminate the string when it sees the next blank line.)

DON'T put anything else in the line containing the end-of-string characters.

Special Internal Values

Perl defines three special internal values your program can use: `__LINE__`, `__FILE__`, and `__END__`.

`__LINE__` and `__FILE__` contain, respectively, the current line number and current filename of the program you are running. These are the values that `die` and `warn` use when printing the line number and filename on which an error or a warning occurs.

`__END__` is a special value that indicates "end of file." Everything after `__END__` is treated as data. If the program is contained in a file, you can read the data after `__END__` by reading from the `DATA` file variable:

```
$data - <DATA>;
```

NOTE
> `__LINE__` and `__FILE__` cannot be substituted into double-quoted strings.
>
> You can use the `^D` or `^Z` character (Ctrl+D or Ctrl+Z) in place of `__END__`.

WARNING
> `__END__` does not need to appear on a line by itself as long as some white space separates it from the next item in the file. However, the first line of the file represented by `DATA` is always the line immediately following `__END__`. For example:
> ```
> __END__ Here is some input.
> Here is some more input.
> ```
> In this case, the first line read by `<DATA>` is
> ```
> Here is some more input.
> ```
> The information immediately following `__END__` is lost.

14

Using Back Quotes to Invoke System Commands

Perl provides a way to treat the value printed by a system command as a string. To do this, enclose the system command in back-quote characters (the ` character).

For example:

```
$mytest = `echo A Word`;
print ($mytest);
```

The first statement calls the command echo, which display the string A Word on the screen. This string is passed to $mytest in the second line and printed out by the function print.

The Perl interpreter performs variable substitution on the string enclosed in back quotes before treating it as a system command. Consider this example:

```
$command = "echo A Word";
$mytest = `$command`;
print ($mytest);
```

Here, the value of $command, echo A Word, is substituted into the string enclosed in back quotes, and it becomes the system command that is called.

When a system command is executed, the return code from the command is stored in the system variable $?. To determine whether the system command has executed properly, check this system variable. (Normally, a value of zero indicates successful execution, and any other value indicates an error. The actual error value depends on the command.)

To use a character other than a back quote as a delimiter, use qx:

```
$mytest = qx#echo A Word#;
print ($mytest);
```

As with q and qq, described previously, the first character after qx is treated as the string delimiter. The string continues until another string delimiter—in this case, #—is seen.

NOTE

> If (is used as an opening string delimiter,) becomes the closing string delimiter:
>
> ```
> $myname = qx(whoami);
> ```

Pattern Matching Using `??` and the `reset` Function

The `??` pattern-matching operator is identical to the `//` pattern-matching operator you have been using all along, except that it matches only once, even if it is inside a loop. For example, the following statement loops only once, because the pattern `?abc?` is not matched the second time it is executed:

```
while ($line =~ ?abc?) {
    # stuff goes here
}
```

To make the `??` pattern-matching operator match again, call the `reset` function. This function tells the Perl interpreter that a particular `??` operator can be used to match a pattern again. Listing 14.9 is an example of a program that uses `??` and `reset`.

TYPE Listing 14.9. A demonstration of `??` and the `reset` function.

```
1: # p14_9.pl
2:
3: while ($line = <STDIN>) {
4:     last unless ($line =~ ?\bthe\b?);
5:     print ("$`$'");
6:     reset;
7: }
```

OUTPUT
```
C:\> perl p14_9
this is the first line
this is first line
the next line of input
 next line of input
last line—not matched
C:\>
```

ANALYSIS Line 4 of this program uses the `??` pattern-matching operator to check whether the word `the` appears in the current input line. If it does not, the program terminates. If it does, line 5 uses the `$`` and `$'` variables to print the parts of the line not matched.

Line 6 calls `reset`, which resets the `??` operator in line 4. If `reset` is not called, line 4 will not match even if the new input line contains the word `the`.

14

The `??` operator is deprecated in Perl version 5. This means that the operator is still supported, but is considered obsolete. Future versions of Perl might not support this operator.

Using `reset` with Variables

You also can use the `reset` function to clear all variables whose names begin with a specified character. The following statement assigns the null string to all scalar variables whose names begin with the letter `w` (such as, for instance, `$which`) and assigns the empty list to all array variables whose names begin with that letter:

```
reset ("w");
```

The following statement assigns the null string or the empty list to all variables whose names begin with `a` or `e`:

```
reset ("ae");
```

You can use ranges of letters with `reset`:

```
reset ("a-d");
```

This example resets all variables whose names begin with `a`, `b`, `c`, or `d`.

Be careful with `reset`, because it resets all variables whose names begin with the specified letters, including built-in variables such as `@ARGV`.

Other Features of the `<>` Operator

As you've seen, the `<>` operator reads from the file specified by the enclosed file variable. For example, the following statement reads a line from the file represented by `MYFILE`:

```
$line = <MYFILE>;
```

The following sections describe how to use `<>` with scalar-variable substitution and how to use `<>` to create a list of filenames.

Scalar-Variable Substitution and `<>`

If a scalar variable is contained in the `<>` operator, the value of the variable is assumed to be the name of a file handle. Look at the following example:

```
$filename = "MYFILE";
$line = <$filename>;
```

Here, the value of `$filename`, MYFILE, is assumed to be the file variable associated with the input file to read from. When you change the value of `$filename`, you change the input file.

Creating a List of Filenames

Windows NT commands that manipulate files, such as `copy`, enable you to supply a pattern to generate a list of filenames. Any filename matching this pattern is included as part of the list. For example, the following command copies every file whose name ends in `.pl` to the directory `C:\mydir\srcdir`:

```
C:\> copy *.pl C:\mydir\srcdir
```

In Perl, if the `<>` operator encloses something other than a file variable or a scalar variable containing a file variable, it is assumed to be a pattern that matches a list of files. For example, the following statement assigns a list of the filenames ending in `.pl` to the array variable `@filelist`:

```
@filelist = <*.pl>;
```

You can use filename patterns in loops:

```
while ($line = <*.pl>) {
    print ("$line\n");
}
```

This code prints each filename ending in `.pl` on a separate line.

Global Indirect References and Aliases

On Day 9, "Using Subroutines," you learned that you can pass the name of an array to a subroutine, using an alias. For example:

```
sub my_sub {
    local (*subarray) = @_;
    $arraylength = @subarray;
}
```

14

The `*subarray` definition in `my_sub` tells the Perl interpreter to operate on the actual list instead of making a copy. When this subroutine is called by a statement such as the following, the Perl interpreter realizes that `myarray` and `subarray` refer to the same array variable:

```
&my_sub(*myarray);
```

When a name is given an alias, all variables with that name can be referred to, using the alias. This means, in this example, that the `@subarray` variable and the `@myarray` variable refer to the same array. If the program also defines variables named `$subarray` and `%subarray`, you can use `$myarray` and `%myarray`, respectively, to refer to these variables.

In the earlier example, the following two statements

```
my_sub (*myarray);
local (*subarray) = @_;
```

are equivalent to the assignment

```
local (*subarray) = *myarray;
```

In each case, the name `subarray` is defined to be an alias of the name `myarray`. Because `*subarray` is contained inside a `local` definition in a subroutine, `subarray` and `myarray` are equivalent only while the subroutine is being executed.

If desired, you can define an alias for a name that remains in force throughout your program. For example:

```
*subarray = *myarray;
```

If this statement is part of your main program, `subarray` becomes an alias for `myarray` in all parts of your program, including all subroutines. The values of `$subarray`, `@subarray`, and `%subarray`, if they are defined, are lost.

Listing 14.10 is a simple example of a program that defines and uses a global alias.

TYPE   **Listing 14.10. An example of a global alias.**

```
1:  # p14_10.pl
2:
3:  *name2 = *name1;
4:  $name1 = 14;
5:  print ("$name2\n");
```

OUTPUT
```
C:\> perl p14_10.pl
14
C:\>
```

14

ANALYSIS Line 3 of the program in Listing 14.10 defines `name2` as an alias for `name1`. Every variable that is named `name1` can therefore be referred to using the name `name2`. As a result, `$name1` and `$name2` are really the same scalar variable; this means that line 5 prints the value assigned in line 4.

Translators and Other Supplied Code

The Perl distribution provides programs that translate the following items into Perl:

- [ ] Programs written in the `awk` programming language
- [ ] Scripts written for the `sed` command
- [ ] Commands sent to the `find` command
- [ ] Include files written in the C programming language

For information on these translation programs, refer to the documentation supplied with your Perl distribution.

Summary

Today, you have learned about packages and modules and how to use the Perl functions `use` and `require`. You also learned the Perl functions that emulate system library functions.

Windows NT supports the Berkeley UNIX socket mechanism, which provides interprocess communication using a client-server model.

You have also learned about features of Perl for Win32 that were not discussed on previous days:

- [ ] The `$#array` variable, which returns the largest subscript of an array
- [ ] Alternative methods of enclosing strings using `q`, `qq`, `qw`, `<<`, and `qx`
- [ ] The special internal values `__LINE__`, `__FILE__`, and `__END__`, which retrieve the current filename and line number and which end the program
- [ ] Using back quotes to treat the output from a command as a scalar value
- [ ] Using `??` to match a pattern once, and using `reset` to reset `??` and variables
- [ ] Using `<>` with indirect file variables and file lists
- [ ] Global aliasing using `*`

14

Q&A

Q **Why does a file included by** `require` **need to execute a statement? Why does** `require` **check a return code?**

A Because files included by `require` can contain statements that are immediately executed, checking for a return code enables programs to determine whether code included by `require` generated any errors.

Q **How did sockets get their name?**

A A server process that is listening for clients is like an electrical socket on your wall: any client process with the appropriate protocol can "plug into" it.

Q **Is a** `$#array` **variable defined for system array variables such as** `@ARGV`**?**

A Yes. For example, `$#ARGV` contains the largest subscript of the `@ARGV` array; you can test this to determine whether your program was passed enough arguments.

Q **Are** `$#array` **variables defined for associative arrays?**

A No, because there is no concept of a "largest subscript" in associative arrays.

Q **What happens to system variables when** `reset` **is called? For example, is** `@ARGV` **reset when** `reset` **is passed** `"A"`**?**

A The `reset` function affects all variables, including system variables. For this reason, you should be careful when you use `reset`.

Workshop

The Workshop provides quiz questions to help you solidify your understanding of the material covered and exercises to give you experience in using what you've learned. Try to understand the quiz and exercise answers before you go on to tomorrow's lesson. You can find the answers in Appendix B, "Answers."

Quiz

1. What do these constants contain?

    a. `__LINE__`

    b. `__FILE__`

    c. `__END__`

2. How do you send information using a socket?

3. What is the value of each of the following strings? (Assume that $var has the value hello.)

   a. q(It's time to say $var)

   b. qq "It's time to say $var"; # a comment

   c. qx/echo $var/

4. What is stored in @array after the following statements have been executed?

```
@array = ("one", "two", "three", "four");
$#array = 2;
$array[4] = "five";
```

5. How can you include code from another file in your program?

Exercises

1. Write a program that uses the <> operator to list all the files in a directory in alphabetical order.

2. Write a program that uses a subroutine named sum to add the numbers in a list and return the total. Read the list from standard input (one per line). Assume that the subroutine is contained in the file c:\mydir\perlfiles\sum.pl. Print the total returned by sum.

3. Write a program that creates two packages named pack1 and pack2. For each package, read a line from standard input and assign it to the variable $var. Assume that each $var contains a number, add the two numbers together, and print the total.

4. **BUG BUSTER**: What is wrong with the following statements?

```
print ("Perl files in this directory:\n");
$filepattern = "*.pl";
while ($name = <$filepattern>) {
    print ("$name\n");
}
```

5. **BUG BUSTER**: What is wrong with the following statement?

```
print << EOF
Here is part of my string.
Here is the rest of my string.
EOF
```

14

8

9

10

11

12

13

14

In Review

By now, you know enough about programming in Perl 5 for Win32 to write powerful programs. The program in Listing R2.1 illustrates some of the concepts you've learned during your second week.

It prompts you for a directory name, lists the subdirectories under the specified directory, and stores the names of the subdirectories in an associative array for later usage. It also enables you to move about in the directory hierarchy and print the names of the files in any directory.

Listing R2.1. Browsing directories and printing their contents.

TYPE

```
1:  # pwkr02_1.pl
2:
3:  $dircount = 0;
4:  $curdir = "";
5:  while (1) {
6:      # if we don't have a current directory, get one
7:      if ($curdir eq "") {
8:          print ("Enter directory to list:\n");
9:          $curdir = <STDIN>;
10:         $curdir =~ s/^\s+|\s+$//g;
11:         $curdir = &followlink($curdir);
12:         &readsubdirs($curdir);
13:     }
14:     $curdir = &menudir($curdir);
15: }
16:
17:
18: # find all subdirectories of the given directory,
19: # and store them in an associative array.
20: #
21: # The associative array subscripts ans values are:
22: # <directory name>:      1
23: #       (indicates that directory has been read)
24: # <directory name>.<num> the <num>th subdirectory
25:
26: sub readsubdirs {
27:     local ($dirname) = @_;
28:     local ($dirvar, $subdircount, $name, $index);
29:
30:     # open the current directory;
31:     # $dircount ensures that each file variable is unique
32:     $dirvar = "DIR" . ++$dircount;
33:     if (!opendir ($dirvar, $dirname)) {
34:         warn ("Can't open $dirname.\n");
35:         return;
36:     }
37:
38:     # read all the subdirectories; store in a standard array
39:     chdir ($dirname);
40:     $subdircount = 0;
41:     while ($name = readdir ($dirvar)) {
42:         next if ($name eq ".");
43:         if ($dirname eq "/") {
44:             $name = $dirname . $name;
45:         } else {
46:             $name = $dirname . "/" . $name;
47:         }
48:         if (-d $name) {
49:             $dirarray[$subdircount++] = $name;
50:         }
51:     }
52:     closedir ($dirvar);
53:
```

```
54:     # sort the standard array; assign the sorted array to the
55:     # associative array
56:     @dirarray = sort (@dirarray);
57:     for ($index = 0; $index < $subdircount; $index++) {
58:         $dirarray {$dirname . $index} = $dirarray[$index];
59:     }
60:     undef (@dirarray);
61:     $dirarray{$dirname} = 1;
62: }
63:
64:
65: # display the subdirectories of the current directory and the
66: # available menu options
67:
68: sub menudir {
69:     local ($curdir) = @_;
70:     local ($base) = 0;
71:     local ($command, $count, $subdir);
72:
73:     while (1) {
74:         print ("\nCurrent directory is: $curdir\n");
75:         print ("\nSubdirectories:\n");
76:         if ($base > 0) {
77:             print ("<more up>\n");
78:         }
79:         for ($count = 0; $count < 10; $count++) {
80:             $subdir = $count+$base;
81:             $subdir = $dirarray{$curdir.$subdir};
82:             last if ($subdir eq "");
83:             print ("$count: $subdir\n");
84:         }
85:         if ($dirarray{$curdir.($base+10)} ne "") {
86:             print ("<more down>\n");
87:         }
88:         print ("\nEnter a number to move to the ");
89:         print ("specified directory,\n");
90:         if ($base > 0) {
91:             print ("enter < to move up in the list,\n");
92:         }
93:         if ($dirarray{$curdir.($base+10)} ne "") {
94:             print ("enter > to move down in the list,\n");
95:         }
96:         print ("enter d to display the files, \n");
97:         print ("enter e to specify a new directory, \n");
98:         print ("or enter q to quit entirely. \n");
99:         print ("> ");
100:        $command = <STDIN>;
101:        $command =~ s/^\s+|\s+$//g;
102:        if ($command eq "q") {
103:            exit (0);
104:        } elsif ($command eq ">") {
105:            if ($dirarray{$curdir.($base+10)} ne "") {
106:                $base += 10;
107:            }
108:        } elsif ($command eq "<") {
109:            $base .= 10 if $base > 0;
```

continues

Listing R2.1. continued

```
110:        } elsif ($command eq "d") {
111:            &display ($curdir);
112:        } elsif ($command eq "e") {
113:            # set the current directory to "" to force
114:            # the main program to prompt for a name
115:            return ("");
116:        } elsif ($command =~ /^\d+$/) {
117:            $subdir = $dirarray{$curdir.($command+base)};
118:            # if subdirectory is the parent directory,
119:            # remove .. and the last directory name
120:            # from the path
121:            if ($subdidr =~ /\.\.$/) {
122:                $subdir =~ s#(.*)/.*/..#$1#;
123:            }
124:            # if subdirectory is defined, it becomes
125:            # the new current directory
126:            if ($subdir ne "") {
127:                if ($dirarray{$subdir} != 1) {
128:                    $subdir = &followlink($subdir);
129:                    &readsubdirs($subdir);
130:                }
131:                return ($subdir);
132:            }
133:        }else {
134:            warn ("Invalid command $command\n");
135:        }
136:    }
137:}
138:
139:
140:# Display the files in a directory, three per line.
141:
142:sub display {
143:    local ($dirname) = @_;
144:    local ($file, $filecount, $printfile);
145:    local (@filelist);
146:
147:    if (!opendir(LOCALDIR, "$dirname")) {
148:        warn ("Can't open $dirname\n");
149:        return;
150:    }
151:    chdir ($dirname);
152:    print ("\n\nFiles in directory $dirname:\n");
153:    $filecount = 0;
154:    while ($file = readdir (LOCALDIR)) {
155:        next if (-d $file);
156:        $filelist[$filecount++] = $file;
157:    }
158:    closedir ($dirname);
159:    if ($filecount == 0) {
160:        print ("\tDirectory contains no file.\n");
161:        return;
162:    }
163:    @filelist = sort (@filelist);
```

```
164:    $filecount = 0;
165:    foreach $printfile (@filelist) {
166:        if ($filecount == 30) {
167:            print ("<Press Enter to continue>");
168:            <STDIN>;
169:            $filecount = 0;
170:        }
171:        if ($filecount % 3 == 0) {
172:            print ("\t");
173:        }
174:        printf ("%-20s", $printfile);
175:        $filecount += 1;
176:        if ($filecount % 3 == 0) {
177:            print ("\n");
178:        }
179:    }
180:}
181:
182:
183:# Check whether the directory name is really a symbolic link.
184:# If it is, find the real name and use it.
185:
186:sub followlink {
187:    local ($dirname) = @_;
188:
189:    if (-l $dirname) {
190:        $dirname = readlink ($dirname);
191:    }
192:    $dirname;      # return value
193:}
```

OUTPUT

```
C:\> perl pwk02_1.pl
Enter directory to list:
c:/perl5

Current directory is: c:/perl5

Subdirectories:
0: c:/perl5/..
1: c:/perl5/Lib
2: c:/perl5/Samples
3: c:/perl5/bin
4: c:/perl5/docs
5: c:/perl5/eg
6: c:/perl5/ntt

Enter a number to move to the specified directory,
enter > to move down in the list,
enter d to display the files,
enter e to specify a new directory,
or enter q to quit entirely.
> d
Files in directory c:/perl5:
        INSTALL.BAT     INSTALL.PIF     INSTALL.TXT
        LICENSE.TXT     MANIFEST.TXT    PL2BAT.BAT
```

```
Perl100.dll       README.TXT     STATUS.TXT
UNINSTALL.BAT     WIN95.TXT      install.log
perl.exe          release.txt

Current directoy is: c:/perl5

Subdirectories:
0: c:/perl5/..
1: c:/perl5/Lib
2: c:/perl5/Samples
3: c:/perl5/bin
4: c:/perl5/docs
5: c:/perl5/eg
6: c:/perl5/ntt

Enter a number to move to the specified directory,
enter > to move down in the list,
enter d to display the files,
enter e to specify a new directory,
or enter q to quit entirely.
> 6
Current directory is c:/perl5/ntt

Subdirectories:
0: c:/perl5/ntt/..
1: c:/perl5/ntt/Base
2: c:/perl5/ntt/Cmd
3: c:/perl5/ntt/Comp
4: c:/perl5/ntt/Io
5: c:/perl5/ntt/Lib
6: c:/perl5/ntt/NT
7: c:/perl5/ntt/Op

Enter a number to move to the specified directory,
enter d to display the files,
enter e to specify a new directory,
or enter q to quit entirely.
> q
C:\>
```

ANALYSIS The program in Listing R2.1 consists of five parts:

- [ ] A very simple main program
- [ ] The subroutine &readsudirs, which displays the subdirectories of a directory
- [ ] The subroutine &menudirs, which displays the subdirectories of the current directory, lists the menu options, and processes the menu choices
- [ ] The subroutine &display, which lists the files in the current directory
- [ ] The subroutine &followlink, which checks whether a directory name is really a symbolic link

The main program is quite simple: all it does is prompt for a directory name and call the subroutines &readsudirs and &menudirs. (Many complicated programs are like this: the main portion of the program just calls a few subroutines.)

The subroutine &readsudirs are passed the name of a directory to examine. Line 33 opens the directory using opendir, and lines 38–51 store the subdirectories in a (standard) array named @dirarray. After this, line 56 sorts the array, and lines 57–59 load the sorted elements into an associative array named %directory. (Recall that Perl programs can use the same name for an associated array and for a standard array because the program always can tell them apart.)

The subscripts for the associative array use a simple scheme:

- ☐ When a directory is read, line 61 defines an associative array element whose subscript is the directory name, and sets its value to 1. (For example, if the directory c:/perl5 is being read, the array element $dirarray{"c:/perl5"} is set to 1.) This is the way the program indicates that a particular directory has been read.

- ☐ Line 49 stores the subdirectory names in an associative-array element whose subscripts consist of the name of directory jointed with a unique integer. For example, if the first subdirectory of c:/perl5 is named c:/perl5/Lib, the associative-array element $dirarray{"c:/perl50"} is assigned the value c:/perl5/Lib. Similarly, the second subdirectory of c:/perl5 had its name stored in $dirarray{"c:/perl51"}, and so on.

Line 60 introduces a function you have not yet seen: undef. This function basically just throws away the contents of @dirarray because the program no longer needs them.

The subroutine &menudir uses this associative array to display the subdirectories of the current directory. Line 74 prints the name of the current directory, and lines 79–84 print the names of the subdirectories of the directory. If there are more than 10 subdirectories, &menudir displays only a *window* of 10 subdirectories, and it prints out <more down> or <more up> to show that there are more subdirectories available. Each subdirectory is printed with a corresponding number that you can use to select the subdirectory and set it to be the current directory.

After &menudir prints the subdirectory names, lines 88–99 print a list of the available menu commands. The commands are

- ☐ d, which displays the files stored in the current directory
- ☐ e, which enables you to enter the name of a directory to display
- ☐ q, which enables you to quit the program
- ☐ a number between 0 and 9, which changes the current directory to the specified subdirectory

☐ <, which moves up in the list of subdirectories (if possible)

☐ >, which moves down in the list of subdirectories (again, if possible)

Line 100 reads a command from the standard input file, and line 101 gets rid of any leading or trailing white space. Lines 102–135 determine which command has been entered.

If q has been entered, line 103 calls exit, which terminates the program.

If either < or > has been entered, lines 104–109 move up or down in the directory list. They do this by modifying the value of a variable named $base, which determines how many subdirectory names to skip before lines 79–84 start printing.

If d has been entered, line 111 calls &display, which prints the list of files.

If e has been entered, line 115 exits the subroutine with a return value of the null string. This forces the main program to execute lines 7–13 again, which prompt you for a directory name.

If a number has been entered, line 117 takes the number, joins it to the current directory name, and uses the resulting string as the subscript into the associative array %dirarray. (For example, if the current directory is c:/perl5 and the number 6 has been entered, line 117 accesses the associative-array element %dirarray{"c:/perl56"}). This is one of the array elements that line 49 of &readsubdirs created; its value is the name of a subdirectory.

Line 127 takes the name of this subdirectory and uses it, in turn, as an associative-array subscript. (For example, if the value of %dirarray{"c:/perl56"} is "c:/perl5/ntt", line 127 checks the associative-array element %dirarray{"c:/perl5/ntt"}). If the value of this element is 1, &readsubdirs has already read this directory and stored its subdirectory names in the associative array, so the program does not need to do it again. If this element is not defined, the program calls &readsubdirs, which reads and stores the names of the subdirectories of this directory.

The subroutine &display prints the name of the files stored in a particular directory. To save space, it prints the filenames three per line. &display prints only 10 lines at a time. If there are more than 10 lines (in other words, 30 filenames), line 168 pauses and waits for you to press Enter before continuing to print. This gives you time to read all the currently displayed names.

The final subroutine is &followlink, which is always called immediately before the subroutine &readsubdirs is called. Its job is to check whether a directory name is really a symbolic link. If it is, line 190 calls readlink, which retrieves the real directory name. This directory name is returned to the calling subroutine or main program and then is passed to &readsubdirs.

As you can see, you now know enough about Perl 5 for Win32 to write programs that manipulate the file system and use complex data structures. In Week 3, you'll learn about the remainder of Perl's built-in functions and the rest of the features of Perl 5 for Win32.

WEEK 3

15

16

17

18

19

20

21

At a Glance

You'll know all the features and capabilities of Perl 5 for Win32 by the end of Week 3. More advanced features and applications of Perl, such as references, object-oriented programming, and CGI programming with Perl, are also introduced in Week 3. Take a look at the summary:

Day 15, "Perl 5 for Win32 Module Extensions"
Day 16, "Command-Line Options"
Day 17, "System Variables"
Day 18, "References in Perl 5 for Win32"
Day 19, "Object-Oriented Programming in Perl"
Day 20, "CGI Programming with Perl 5 for Win32"
Day 21, "The Perl Debugger"

Day 15

Perl 5 for Win32 Module Extensions

Today's lesson introduces one of the most important portions of Perl 5 for Win32—Win32 module extensions.

As you already know, Perl 5 for Win32 basically consists of two parts: the directly ported code from the Perl 5 UNIX version and the Windows NT–specific functionality provided via the module extensions.

Those extensions can be classified into four groups:

- [ ] The extensions directly mapped to the Win32 API functions
- [ ] The Win32 extensions
- [ ] The Win32 system modules
- [ ] Other module extensions added by Perl for Win32 users

Today, we'll focus on the first three groups of extensions in Perl 5 for Win32.

What Is Win32?

The term Win32 normally refers to an application programming interface (API) from Microsoft. In the Windows NT system, Win32 is the native and primary subsystem that provides the power, robustness, and speed. You can think of Win32 as a cornerstone for a 32-bit Windows operating system.

Perl for Win32—Perl's NT Version

Perl for Win32 is the name of the Perl language distribution for 32-bit Windows operating systems, such as Windows NT. Because Windows 95 is not a pure 32-bit operating system, some functions in Perl for Win32 cannot be run properly on Windows 95.

Perl 5 for Win32 is the current version of Perl for Win32. The latest build of Perl 5 for Win32, as this book is being written, is build 110 ported from `Perl5.001m`. In fact, the two terms, Perl for Win32 and Perl 5 for Win32, have been used alternately in this book.

As you learned on Day 14, "Packages, Modules, and System Functions," a set of related Perl functions can be put into a place called a *package*. An *extension* is an enhanced package that calls external C code to provide specific functionality. The upcoming sections in today's lesson introduce some useful extensions in Perl 5 for Win32.

NOTE

> I've heard that build 3001 of Perl 5 for Win32 is on the way while I'm writing this book. Because the majority of Perl for Win32 users are still using build 110, I talk about build 110 in this book and use build 110 for reference purposes.
>
> Microsoft owns the copyright for the source code of the Win32-specific portions in Perl for Win32 under the terms of artistic license.

Extensions for Windows NT

The following sections describe some of the Windows NT–specific extensions in Perl for Win32.

15

Extensions Mapped to the Win32 API

Perl 5 for Win32 (build 110) has several built-in extensions directly mapped to Win32 API functions. For example, the following utility functions enable you to find the current user's ID, domain name, node name, and file-system type in your Windows NT system (both workstation and server versions):

NTLoginName	Returns the ID of the user who owns the current process.
NTDomainName	Returns the domain name of the Windows NT on the network.
NTNodeName	Returns the node name of the Windows NT on the network.
NTFsType	Returns the file-system type on the active drive.

Note that there are no arguments required by these functions listed.

Listing 15.1 is an example of verifying the Windows NT system by using these functions.

Listing 15.1. A program that uses NTLoginName, NTDomainName, NTNodeName, **and** NTFsType.

```
1:  # p15_1.pl
2:
3:  $login = &NTLoginName;
4:  $domain = &NTDomainName;
5:  $node = &NTNodeName;
6:  $fstype = &NTFsType;
7:  print ("User ID:         $login\n");
8:  print ("Domain Name:     $domain\n");
9:  print ("Node Name:       $node\n");
10: print ("File System Type: $fstype\n");
```

OUTPUT
```
C:\> perl p15_1.pl
User ID:          TonyZhang
Domain Name:      RNA1996
Node Name:        RNA1996
File System Type:  FAT
C:\>
```

ANALYSIS Lines 3–6 of this program call NTLoginName, NTDomainName, NTNodeName, and NTFsType and then store the returned values from the functions to the variables $login, $domain, $node, and $fstype, respectively.

Lines 7–10 print out the contents of the variables on the screen. (The results shown in the Output section are samples from my computer.)

Event Logging

In addition to the utility functions just introduced, there is a set of functions in Perl for Win32 called the *Event Log extensions* that allows you to query the event log in your Windows NT system.

You can open and close the event log by calling the extensions. Also, you can read from or write to the event log with the help of the corresponding functions in the extensions. Querying the event log is beyond the scope of this book, however. For more details on the event log, refer to the Win32 API programming manuals.

The Windows NT Registry

You may know that on DOS, Windows 3.1, and Windows 95, the system file AUTOEXEC.BAT keeps the initial environment variables. Windows 3.1 and Windows 95 also use several *.INI files to store the initialization parameters. However, the Windows NT system obtains the initial set of environment variables from a database called the Registry.

The Windows NT Registry extensions from Perl for Win32 enable you to connect to the Registry so that you can query, create, or even delete a Registry key. Check the Win32 programming manuals for more details about the API functions for querying and editing the Registry on Windows NT.

The OLE Extensions

OLE stands for *object linking and embedding*. The OLE technology was developed by Microsoft to integrate different software modules. Perl for Win32 has a set of extensions for OLE. Because OLE extensions require more knowledge of Windows programming, though, they are not discussed in this book. *ActiveX Programming Unleashed*, by Sams.net Publishing, provides a very useful discussion of OLE extensions.

Win32 Extensions and Win32 System Modules

Win32 extensions and system modules contain many useful extension routines specified for Windows NT. In Perl for Win32, the Win32 module is a top-level module that consists of extensions and nested modules (or submodules). The extensions within the top-level Win32 module are usually called Win32 extensions.

The nested modules within the Win32 module have their own extensions. Because most of the extensions deal with the Windows NT system, those nested modules are also called the *system module extensions.* The following sections introduce the nested system modules and Win32 extensions.

WARNING

The primary online documentation of Win32 module extensions is located at `http://www.perl.hip.com/man-pages/win32mod.htm`. (Perhaps it will have been moved to ActiveWare's home page when you read this book.)

Please be aware that the current edition of the online document contains some information that causes confusion in real-world applications.

As this book is being written, some of the functions or methods in the current version of Win32 system modules cannot do things that they are supposed to do. I mention some of them in the following sections.

If you figure out ways to get around the errors or bugs found in the Win32 modules, great! Post them to `Perl-Win32-Users@ActiveWare.com` to let other users know about your solutions, if you like. It is also highly recommended that you check the latest news about the Win32 system module extensions from either the home page of Perl for Win32 at `http://www.perl.hip.com`, or `http://www.ActiveWare.com`.

Also, you can search the Perl-Win32 mailing list archive at `http://www.divinf.it/perl-win32`.

The `Win32::Process` Module Extensions

When you first see `Win32::Process`, you may wonder what the double colons (`::`) mean. In Perl 5 for Win32, `::` are used to obtain the reference from a higher-level module. For instance, the `Process` module is one of the nested modules in the `Win32` module. In other words, the `Process` module is a member of the Win32 module. In Perl programs, the string `Win32::Process` is used to mean "the Win32 module's Process module." On Day 19, "Object-Oriented Programming in Perl," you'll learn more about the usage of the double colon.

The `Win32::Process` module extensions consist of one `Create` function and seven methods, which allow you to create various process objects and run applications on Windows NT or Windows 95.

Once you create a process object, you can apply the methods in the `Win32::Process` module to the created object. The seven methods in the module are

☐ Kill	Kills a process object created by the Create function.
☐ Suspend	Suspends an active process.
☐ Resume	Resumes a suspended process.
☐ GetPriorityClass	Obtains the priority of a process.
☐ SetPriorityClass	Sets the priority for a process.
☐ GetExitCode	Finds out how, or if, a process has exited.
☐ Wait	Waits for a process to exit.

The Create function and the seven methods are explained in the following sections.

The Create **Function**

The Create function can start an application and then create a process object that is associated with the launched application.

SYNTAX

The syntax for the Create function is

```
Create ($ProcessObj, $ApplicationName, $CommandLine,
  $InheritHandles, $CreateOptions, $CurrentDir);
```

Here, $ProcessObj is the reference to a created process object. $ApplicationName is the full pathname of the application to run. $CommandLine is the command with necessary arguments to launch the application. $InheritHandles is the flag that is set to 1 if the application does not inherit any open file handles, and is set to 0 otherwise. $CreateOptions is the combination of the following creation-flag values:

CREATE_DEFAULT_ERROR_MODE	Assigns the process object to the default error mode.
CREATE_NEW_CONSOLE	Gives the process object a new console. This flag cannot be used with DETACHED_PROCESS.
CREATE_NEW_PROCESS_GROUP	Sets the created process as the root of a new process group.
CREATE_SEPARATE_WOW_VDM	Runs the new process in its own 16-bit Virtual DOS Machine (VDM).
CREATE_SUSPENDED	Creates the new process in a suspended state.
CREATE_UNICODE_ENVIRONMENT	Uses the Unicode in the new process.
DEBUG_PROCESS	Treats the calling process as a debugger and debugs the new process.
DEBUG_ONLY_THIS_PROCESS	Debugs the calling process only.
DETACHED_PROCESS	Gives the new process no access to the console of the calling process.

And $CurrentDir refers to the location of the working directory for the application.

The `Kill` **Method**

You need to use the `Kill` method to terminate a running process.

The syntax for the `Kill` method is

```
Kill ($ExitCode);
```

Here, `$ExitCode` is the returned value from the process being killed.

The `Suspend` **Method**

The syntax for the `Suspend` method is

```
Suspend ();
```

No argument is needed by the method.

The `Resume` **Method**

The `Resume` method can be used to resume a process that has been suspended either by the `Suspend` method or by the `CREATE_SUSPENDED` flag when the process was created.

The syntax for the `Resume` method is

```
Resume ();
```

No argument is required by the method.

The `GetPriorityClass` **Method**

This method is used to obtain information of the priority level of a process.

The syntax for the `GetPriorityClass` method is

```
GetPriorityClass ($Priority);
```

Here, `$Priority` is the priority level of the process. There are four priority levels:

IDLE_PRIORITY_CLASS	Runs a process only when the system is idle.
NORMAL_PRIORITY_CLASS	Runs a process under the normal process scheduling.
HIGH_PRIORITY_CLASS	Runs a process at above-normal priority level.
REALTIME_PRIORITY_CLASS	Runs a process at the highest priority level. Even preempts the operating-system threads.

The SetPriorityClass **Method**

The SetPriorityClass method enables you to set up the priority level for a process.

The syntax for the SetPriorityClass method is

```
SetPriorityClass ($Priority);
```

Here, $Priority is one of the priority levels of the process listed above, where the syntax of the GetPriorityClass method is introduced.

The GetExitCode **Method**

You apply the GetExitCode method to determine whether a process has exited. You can also find out the way a process exits by applying this method.

The syntax for the GetExitCode method is

```
GetExitCode ($ExitCode);
```

Here, $ExitCode is the exit-code value returned by the method.

The Wait **Method**

The Wait method is used to set up a period of time to wait for a process to exit.

The syntax for the Wait method is

```
Wait ($TimeOut);
```

Here, $TimeOut is the number of milliseconds to wait for a process to end. Use INFINITE if you want to run the process forever.

NOTE

All functions and methods in the system module extensions are supposed to return nonzero (that is, true) on success; zero (that is, false) on failure or unless otherwise noted.

However, there are several exceptions caused by the errors left in some of the functions and methods in the current version of the modules. I'll mention them when we get there in the following sections.

Listing 15.2 is a simple example to create a process object of a Windows application by using the Win32::Process module extensions.

15

TYPE   **Listing 15.2. A program that uses the** `Win32::Process` **module.**

```
 1:  # p15_2.pl
 2:
 3:  use Win32::Process;
 4:
 5:  Win32::Process::Create (
 6:         $ProcessObj,
 7:         "c:\\windows\\calc.exe",
 8:         "",
 9:         0,
10:         DETACHED_PROCESS,
11:         ".") || die "Cannot create the process";
12:
13:  $ProcessObj->SetPriorityClass (NORMAL_PRIORITY_CLASS) ||
14:         die $!;
15:
16:  $ProcessObj->Wait (INFINITE);
17:  print ("Calc program exited. Bye!\n");
```

ANALYSIS   Line 3 includes the `Win32::Process` module in the Perl program. Line 5 calls `Win32::Process::Create`. Here, the `Create` function is a member of the `Process` module, and the `Process` module is a member of the `Win32` module; therefore, the expression `Win32::Process::Create` has been used in the listing.

Line 6 is the reference to the created process object. Line 7 gives the full pathname of the executable `calc.exe`, which is a Windows application program—a working calculator. For Windows NT 4.0, the path shown in line 7 should be `c:\\winnt\\system32\\calc.exe`.

Because no argument is needed to run `calc.exe`, line 8 is left blank for the command line. Line 9 indicates that there is no inheritance to the process. Line 10 tells the Windows NT system that this is a separated process. The `"."` in line 11 means that the current directory is the working directory.

Line 13 sets the priority level for the process by using the method `SetPriorityClass` from the `Win32::Process` module. The `->` statement has been used by `$ProcessObj` in line 13 to refer to the method `SetPriorityClass`. The `->` passes the messages of the process created in lines 5–11 to the `SetPriorityClass` method referred to by `$ProcessObj`. Further details about `->` are introduced on Day 18, "References in Perl 5 for Win32," and Day 19 later in this book.

Line 16 shows that one has to wait for the process until it dies, because the `Wait` method has been passed the argument `INFINITE` for no time-out.

The last line (line 17) in Listing 15.2 just prints out a brief message right after the process is terminated.

A sample calculator on Windows NT, created by running the Perl program in Listing 15.2, is demonstrated in Figure 15.1.

Figure 15.1.

The calculator process created by the Win32::Process *module.*

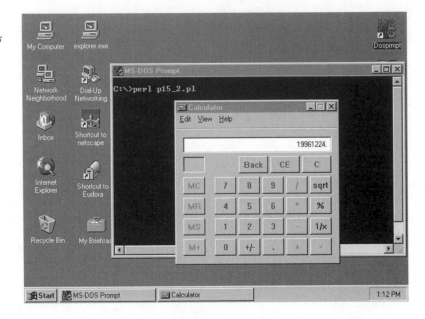

The Win32::Semaphore **Module Extensions**

The *semaphore* is a synchronization facility used for multitasking in many modern operating systems, such as Windows NT and UNIX. The semaphore provides a way to let a specified number of threads of processes run at a given time.

There are two functions, Create and DESTROY, and two methods, Wait and Release, in the Win32::Semaphore module.

NOTE

In the Windows NT system, a *process* refers to an instance of a running program. A process in the Windows NT is inert. A process needs at least one thread to execute the code for an application. A process can own several threads, all of which can execute code simultaneously in the process's address space.

15

The Create **Function**

Call the Create function in the Win32::Semaphore module to create a new semaphore object.

The syntax for the Create function is

```
Create ($SemaphoreObj, $InitialCount, $MaxCount, $SemaphoreName);
```

Here, $SemaphoreObj is the reference to a semaphore object and is returned by the Create function. $InitialCount is used to store the number of the initial counts of the semaphore object. $MaxCount contains the number of maximum counts that have been taken. $SemaphoreName stores the name of the semaphore object.

The DESTROY **Function**

To remove a semaphore object, use the DESTROY function in the semaphore module. The function is automatically called when a semaphore object is out of scope.

The syntax for the DESTROY function is

```
DESTROY ($SemaphoreObj);
```

Here, $Semaphore is the reference to a semaphore object that is about to be removed.

The Wait **and** Release **Methods**

The Wait method tells the calling process to wait on the semaphore.

The syntax for the Wait method is

```
Wait ($TimeOut);
```

Here, $TimeOut is the number of milliseconds to wait on a semaphore. Set $TimeOut to INFINITE for no time-out.

To release a semaphore, you can apply the Release method.

The syntax for the Release method is

```
Release ($ReleaseCount, $LastCount);
```

Here, $ReleaseCount is the count that is incremented when the semaphore is released. $LastCount saves the count of the Semaphore before the release takes place.

A simple example of using the Win32::Semaphore module is demonstrated in Listing 15.3.

TYPE

Listing 15.3. A program that uses the Win32::Semaphore module.

```
1:  # p15_3.pl
2:
3:  use Win32::Semaphore;
4:
5:  Win32::Semaphore::Create ($SemaphoreObj,
6:          1,
7:          0,
8:          "SemaphoreName") || die "Cannot create semaphore";
9:  if ($SemaphoreObj->Wait (INFINITE)){
10:         # Access to the shared resource and do something here
11:         print ("The semaphore has been taken!\n");
12:         $SemaphoreObj->Release (1, $LastCount);
13:         print ("The semaphore has been released.\n");
14: }else{
15:         print ("Cannot access the semaphore\n");
16: }
```

OUTPUT

```
C:\> perl p15_3.pl
The semaphore has been taken!
The semaphore has been released.
C:\>
```

ANALYSIS
Line 3, use Win32::Semaphore, includes the Win32::Semaphore module. Line 5 calls the Create function in the Win32::Semaphore module. Here, the :: is used to remind the Perl interpreter that the Create function is a member of the Semaphore module, and the Semaphore module is a member of the Win32 module.

Line 6 tells the Perl interpreter that there is one initial count of the semaphore; Line 7 sets the maximum count number to 0, which means nobody has taken the initial count. A string of SemahphoreName is given as the name to the semaphore object in line 8.

Lines 9–16 wait for the semaphore in order to access the shared resource. You can do something there after the access. For instance, a brief message is printed in line 11. You should release the semaphore immediately after you get your job done (See line 12.) Line 13 informs you that the semaphore has been released. An error message will be printed out in line 15 if it fails to take the semaphore.

NOTE

Synchronization is needed to control access to the shared resources in a modern operating system. For instance, when two or more processes or threads share a printer, semaphores can be used to ensure that only one process or thread can take the control of the printer at any particular time.

15

> In Windows NT programming, there are four types of process (or
> thread) synchronization facilities: semaphores, mutexes, events, and
> critical sections. For more details on the synchronization facilities,
> check the Windows NT (Win32) programming manuals or references
> from Microsoft.

The `Win32::Mutex` **Module Extensions**

Mutex stands for *mutual exclusion*, which is another synchronization facility used for multitasking in the Windows NT system.

There are three functions, `Create`, `Open`, and `Wait`, and one method, `Release`, in the `Win32::Mutex` module.

The `Create`, `Open`, **and** `Wait` **Functions**

The `Create` function is used to create a mutex object.

The syntax for the `Create` function is

```
Create ($MutexObj, $InitialOwner, $MutexName);
```

Here, *$MutexObj* is the reference to a mutex object. *$MutexObj* is returned by the `Create` function. *$InitialOwner* is a flag that indicates that the process calling the `Create` function has the ownership of the mutex if *$InitialOwner* is not 0. Otherwise, the created mutex is available for everybody. *$MutexName* holds the name of the created mutex that can be referred to by the `Open` function in the `Win32::Mutex` module.

By referring the name of the created mutex ,the `Open` function creates a mutex object for the mutex.

The syntax for the `Open` function is

```
Open ($MutexObj, $MutexName);
```

Here, *$MutexObj* is the reference to a new mutex object to be created. *$MutexName* is the name of an already-created mutex that can be accessed by the `Open` function.

The `Wait` function causes the calling process to wait for the ownership of a created mutex referred to by *$MutexObj*.

The syntax for the Wait function is

```
Wait ($TimeOut);
```

Here, $TimeOut is the number of milliseconds to wait on the mutex. Set $TimeOut to INFINITE for no time-out.

The Release **Method**

The Release method releases the ownership so that anyone waiting on the mutex can take over the ownership.

The syntax for the Release function is

```
Release ();
```

No argument is required by the method.

An example of using the Win32::Mutex module is demonstrated in Listing 15.4. The current version of the module has some problems in doing what has been defined in the Win32mod.htm document. Solutions to those problems are introduced in the example.

 Listing 15.4. A program that uses Win32::Mutex **module.**

```
1:  # p15_4.pl
2:
3:  use Win32::Mutex;
4:
5:  Win32::Mutex::Create($MutObj, 0, "MyMutex") || die $!;
6:
7:  # Note: Use Win32::Mutex::INFINITE, instead of INFINTE
8:  #       Check if Wait returns ZERO, instead of NONZERO
9:  if ( !($MutObj->Wait (Win32::Mutex::INFINITE)) ){
10:     print "The mutex has been accessed to.\n";
11:     $MutObj->Release();
12:     print "The mutex has been released.\n";
13: }else{
14:     print "Cannot access to the mutex.\n";
15: }
```

OUTPUT

```
C:\> perl p15_4.pl
The mutex has been accessed to.
The mutex has been released.
C:\>
```

ANALYSIS
In line 3, use Win32::Mutex includes the Win32::Mutex module in the Perl script. Line 5 calls the Create function in the Win32::Mutex module to create a mutex account. The $InitialOwner argument is set to 0 so that the mutex is available to everybody.

15

As commented in lines 7–8, line 9 calls the Wait function with the time-out set to Win32::Mutex::INFINITE. According to the document of Perl 5 for Win32, one just needs to use INFINITE in the Wait function. But it does not work with the build 110 of Perl 5 for Win32. Also, the Wait function seems to return 0 on success, which is opposite to what the document says.

I believe there are some errors left in the current version of the Wait function. However, if you go about using it in the way shown in line 9, you will be able to get around the errors and access the mutex successfully. (I've already posted the solutions to the Perl-Win32-Users@ActiveWare.com mailing list.)

Line 10 prints out a brief message saying that the mutex has been accessed. Then, line 11 releases the mutex by calling the Release function, making it available to other processes. Line 12 informs us that the mutex has been released.

If somehow you cannot access to the mutex by calling the Wait function, line 14 will let you know about it.

The Win32::ChangeNotification Module Extensions

The Win32::ChangeNotification module is designed to notify a process when a file or directory has been modified in the Windows NT system. This module consists of the FindFirst function and the FindNext, Close, Wait, and DESTROY methods.

The FindFirst Function

The FindFirst function is used to create a notification object with the path to a directory that needs to be monitored.

The syntax for the FindFirst function is

```
FindFirst ($CNObj, $PathName, $WatchSubtree, $Filter);
```

Here, $CNObj is the reference to a notification object. The FindFirst function returns the reference in $CNObj. $PathName contains the full name of the path to the directory that you want to monitor. $WatchSubtree is a flag that can be set to 1 (or any nonzero value) if you want to notify for changes to subtree (or, subdirectory). Otherwise, set $WatchSubtree to 0 if you plan to ignore the subtree.

$Filter specifies the filter conditions that can be a combination of the following options:

FILE_NOTIFY_CHANGE_FILE_NAME	Notifies when a file is created, renamed, or deleted in the monitored directory.
FILE_NOTIFY_CHANGE_DIR_NAME	Notifies when the name of the directory is changed.
FILE_NOTIFY_CHANGE_ATTRIBUTES	Notifies when any attributes are changed.
FILE_NOTIFY_CHANGE_SIZE	Notifies when a file's size is changed and the change is written back to disk.
FILE_NOTIFY_CHANGE_LAST_WRITE	Notifies of any changes to the last write time for a file.
FILE_NOTIFY_CHANGE_SECURITY	Notifies if there are any security-descriptor changes made in the monitored directory.

The FindNext, Close, Wait, and DESTROY Methods

Apply the FindNext method so that the next time the operating system detects any file or directory changes, it will notify the change notification object.

The syntax for the FindNext method is

```
FindNext ();
```

No argument is required by the method.

The Close method shuts down the notification object and stops the monitoring.

The syntax for the Close method is

```
Close ();
```

No argument is needed by the method.

The Wait method asks the calling process to wait for the notification of changes.

The syntax for the Wait method is

```
Wait ($TimeOut);
```

Here, $TimeOut$ is the number of milliseconds to wait on the notification. Set $TimeOut$ to INFINITE if you want to specify no time-out.

The DESTROY method is used to close the notification object if it goes out of scope.

The syntax for the DESTROY method is

```
DESTROY ();
```

No argument is required by the method.

15

15

The current version of Win32::ChangeNotification has similar problems to those found in the Win32::Mutex module. Listing 15.5 is an example of using the Win32::ChangeNotification module, with solutions to these problems.

Listing 15.5. A program that uses the Win32::ChangeNotification module.

TYPE

```
1:  # p15_5.pl
2:
3:  use Win32::ChangeNotification;
4:
5:  Win32::ChangeNotification::FindFirst (
6:          $CNObj,
7:          "C:\\MyDir",
8:          1,
9:          FILE_NOTIFY_CHANGE_FILE_NAME ) || die $!;
10:
11: $CNObj->FindNext();
12:
13: print ("Go ahead to make some changes in the directory...\n");
14:
15: # Note: Use Win32::ChangeNotification::INFINITE, instead of INFINTE
16: #       Check if Wait returns ZERO, instead of NONZERO
17: if (! $CNObj->Wait (Win32::ChangeNotification::INFINITE)) {
18:
19:         # Now, do something with the files in C:\MyDir
20:
21:         print ("Good, the directory has been changed.\n");
22:         $CNObj->Close();
23: }else{
24:         print ("Sorry! Cannot notify the changes.\n");
25: }
```

OUTPUT

```
C:\> perl p15_5.pl
Go ahead to make some changes in the directory...
Good, the directory has been changed.
C:\>
```

ANALYSIS Line 3 includes the Win32::ChangeNotification module into the Perl script. Lines 5–9 call the Create function in the module to create a notification object to any changes, such as renaming, deleting, or creating a file in the monitored directory C:\MyDir. (You can specify other directories in your system.)

If there are any changes made the next time, line 11 asks the operating system to signal the notification object, $CNObj, by applying the FindNext method. Line 13 asks the user to make some changes in the directory to trigger the notification.

Line 17 waits to be notified by the operating system of any changes. If the user just made some changes in the C:\MyDir directory, line 21 prints out a brief message to notify the user that some changes have been made in the monitored directory.

Note that I used `Win32::ChangeNotification::INFINITE`, instead of `INIFINTE`, in line 17. Also, I checked the return value from the `Wait` method to see whether it has been run successfully. Because of the errors in the `Wait` method, the return value is `0` if the method succeeds. The `Win32mod.htm` document says the return value should be nonzero if the `Wait` method runs successfully.

Line 22 closes the notification object by calling the `Close` method. If there are any problems to applying the `Wait` method in line 17, line 24 prints out the warning message.

TIP

Due to the errors in the current version of Win32 modules, it is recommended that you try to include as many of the full pathnames to functions, methods, and even constants as possible, as defined in the Win32 modules. For example, as you've seen, the full pathnames were prefixed to `INFINITE` in `Win32::Mutex::Wait` and `Win32::ChangeNotification::Wait`.

The returned values from some functions or methods are not reliable. Some of the returned values are just the opposite of the expected ones defined by the documentation of Win32 modules.

If you find some functions or methods acting improperly, try the tips mentioned here, or report to the Perl for Win32 user group. Hopefully, those tips will be out of date when the next major release of Perl for Win32 arrives.

The `Win32::IPC` **Module Extensions**

The `Win32::IPC` module is inherited by the `Win32::Process`, `Win32::Semaphore`, `Win32::Mutex`, and `Win32::ChangeNotification` modules. You do not need to implicitly include the `Win32::IPC` module by calling the `use` function.

The `Win32::IPC` module has only one function—`WaitForMultipleObjects`.

The `WaitForMultipleObjects` **Function**

This function can be called to coordinate multiple events in your Perl programs.

The syntax for the `WaitForMultipleObjects` function is

```
WaitForMultipleObjects (@MultiObjs, $WaitAll, $TimeOut);
```

Here, *@MultiObjs* is an array that can hold different types of objects, such as Process, Semaphore, Mutex, or ChangeNotification. The function call waits for all of the objects if *$WaitAll* is set to nonzero; otherwise, the call will return when the first object returns. *$TimeOut* is the number of milliseconds to wait on the events. Set *$TimeOut* to INFINITE if you want to specify no time-out.

WARNING

> In the current build of Perl 5 for Win32, there are some conflicts between the syntax definition of the WaitForMultipleObjects function shown here and the implementation in the Perl interpreter. Check the latest news about this function at http://www.perl.hip.com, or http://www.ActiveWare.com.

The Win32::Eventlog **Module Extensions**

The Win32::Eventlog module is used to track events in the Windows NT system. There are two functions, Open and OpenBackup, to open an event log or a backup event log on a specified computer. There are six methods that can be applied after a log is opened. The following sections introduce these functions and methods.

The Open **and** OpenBackup **Functions**

Let's have a look at the Open function first.

SYNTAX

The syntax for the Open function is

```
Open ($EventObj, $SourceName, [$ServerName]);
```

Here, *$EventObj* is the reference to an event log object. *$SourceName* saves the name of the source for the event. *$ServerName* is optional; this variable can be omitted and the local machine used, if no machine name is assigned to *$ServerName*.

The OpenBackup function opens a backup event log.

SYNTAX

The syntax for the OpenBackup function is

```
OpenBackup ($FileName);
```

Here, *$FileName* contains the name of the file to which the event log is saved.

The `Read` and `Report` **Methods**

The `Read` method is used to read an event log or a backup one.

The syntax for the `Read` method is

```
Read ($ReadFlags, $RecordOffset, %EventInfo);
```

Here, `$ReadFlags` specifies how to read the event log. `$RecordOffset` contains the index number of the first record. `$EventInfo` is the hashed value of the event.

`$ReadFlags` can take a combination of the following options:

EVENTLOG_FORWARDS_READ	Indicates to read an event log in forward chronological order.
EVENTLOG_BACKWARDS_READ	Indicates to read an event log in reverse chronological order.
EVENTLOG_SEEK_READ	Indicates that the read begins at the record specified by `$RecordOffset`. This option has to be used with EVENTLOG_FORWARDS_READ or EVENTLOG_BACKWARDS_READ.
EVENTLOG_SEQUENTIAL_READ	Indicates that the read continues sequentially from the last read call.

The `Report` method is used to report what you have read from an event log.

The syntax for the `Report` method is

```
Report ($Event, %EventInfo);
```

Here, `$Event` specifies the type of the event. `$EventInfo` is the hashed value of the event.

`$Event` has the following options:

EVENTLOG_ERROR_TYPE	Indicates the error event.
EVENTLOG_WARNING_TYPE	Indicates the warning event.
EVENTLOG_INFORMATION_TYPE	Indicates the information event.
EVENTLOG_AUDIT_SUCCESS_TYPE	Indicates the successful audit event.
EVENTLOG_AUDIT_FAILURE_TYPE	Indicates the failed audit event.

`%EventInfo` can be parsed by the following keys:

Category	Contains the integer value for the event category.
EventID	Contains the ID value of the event.
EventRawData	Contains any raw binary data.
Strings	Contains any test strings.
user	Contains the username.

The `Backup`, `GetOldest`, `GetNumber`, `Clear`, and `OpenBackup` **Methods**

The `Backup` method can be applied to save the opened event log to a file.

SYNTAX

The syntax for the `Backup` method is

```
Backup ($FileName);
```

Here, `$FileName` is the name of the file to which the event log is written.

The `GetOldest` method can be used to get the absolute record number of the oldest record in the event log.

SYNTAX

The syntax for the `GetOldest` method is

```
GetOldest ($OldestRecord);
```

Here, `$OldestRecord` saves the absolute record number of the oldest record returned by the method.

Apply the `GetNumber` method to obtain the number of events.

SYNTAX

The syntax for the `GetNumber` method is

```
GetNumber ($EventNumber);
```

Here, `$EventNumber` keeps the number of events returned by the method.

The `Clear` method is called to clear the event log.

SYNTAX

The syntax for the `Clear` method is

```
Clear ([$FileName]);
```

Here, `$FileName` is optional. If `$FileName` is specified, the current event log is written to the file under the `$FileName` name; otherwise, no writing occurs.

The `Win32::Registry` **Module Extensions**

The `Win32::Registry` module is designed to connect and edit the Windows NT Registry. The registry in the Windows NT system provides a way to keep the initial information for the applications. The following sections explain the methods included in the module.

NOTE   In the Windows NT system, a *registry key* is similar to a directory. A *value* is like a file. The top-level keys are more like drivers.

> The Windows NT Registry saves information from device drivers, applications, and users. By using the graphical Registry Editor, the user can also review or update the configuration information saved in the Registry.

The open **and** create **Methods**

The open method is used to open a specified key in the Registry.

 The syntax for the open method is

```
open ($RegistryObj, $Key);
```

Returned by the method, *$RegistryObj* is the reference to the Registry object created by the method. Here, *$Key* specifies the key to access to. In fact, *$Key* can hold any opened key.

There are four predefined Registry objects that are created in the main::namespace when the Win32::Registry module is loaded. The four Registry objects are

- ☐ $HKEY_LOCAL_MACHINE
- ☐ $HKEY_USERS
- ☐ $HKEY_CURRENT_USER
- ☐ $HKEY_CLASSES_ROOT

The create method can be used to create a key if the key does not exist. Otherwise, the create method just opens the existing key. To create a new key, make sure that you have the privilege to write to the Registry file.

The syntax for the create method is

```
create ($RegistryObj, $Key);
```

Returned by the method, *$RegistryObj* is the reference to the Registry object created or opened by the method. *$Key* specifies the key that is accessible to the Registry object.

The SetValue, GetValues, **and** QueryValue **Methods**

The SetValue method assigns the value to a subkey under the current key.

The syntax for the SetValue method is

```
SetValue ($SubKey, $Type, $Value);
```

Here, *$SubKey* holds the subkey name. *$Type* specifies the type of value that has been predefined. *$Value* contains the value to be set.

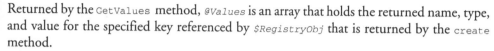

The GetValues method is used to obtain the values of a subkey under the current key.

The syntax for the GetValues method is

```
GetValues (@Values);
```

Returned by the GetValues method, @Values is an array that holds the returned name, type, and value for the specified key referenced by $RegistryObj that is returned by the create method.

The QueryValue method queries the value and type of a specified subkey of the current key.

The syntax for the QueryValue method is

```
QueryValue ($Value, $Type, $Name);
```

Here, $Value keeps the value of $Name. $Type is the type of $Name. $Name contains the name of value to query. $Value and $Type are returned by the method.

The GetKeys and QueryKey Methods

The GetKeys method can be used to obtain a list of subkeys under the current key.

The syntax for the GetKeys method is

```
GetKeys (\@SubKeys);
```

Here, \@SubKeys is a reference to an array that holds a list of names of the subkeys. (Day 18 covers more details about references in Perl.)

The QueryKey method is used to query the class of the key, the number of subkeys, and the number of values in the current key.

The syntax for the QueryKey method is

```
QueryKey ($KeyClass, $NumberOfSubKeys, $NumberOfValues);
```

Here, $KeyClass is a string containing the class of the key. $NumberOfSubKeys is a variable that keeps the number of the subkeys. $NumberOfValues holds the number of values in the current key. The three arguments are returned by the method.

The Save and Load Methods

The Save method saves the current key status to a file.

The syntax for the Save method is

```
Save ($FileName);
```

Here, $FileName holds the name of a file to which the current key status is saved.

The `Load` method helps you load a Registry file.

The syntax for the `Load` method is

```
Load ($SubKey, $FileName);
```

Here, *$SubKey* indicates the name of the subkey to which the Registry file is loaded. *$FileName* holds the Registry file's name.

The `Win32::NetAdmin` **Module Extensions**

The `Win32::NetAdmin` module is useful for systems administrators to maintain the Windows NT system. The following sections introduce the functions included in the module.

> The `Win32::NetAdmin` module works only on Windows NT. Windows 95 cannot run any functions from this module.

The `GetDomainController` **Function**

The `GetDomainController` function returns the name of the domain controller for the network server.

A *domain* is a collection of servers and workstations that share a common-account database and security policy.

The syntax for the `GetDomainController` function is

```
GetDomainController ($ServerName, $DomainName, $ControllerName);
```

Here, *$ServerName* has the name of the server to query. *$DomainName* holds the Windows domain name. *$ControllerName* is the variable that contains the result returned by the function.

The `UserCreate` **and** `UserDelete` **Functions**

You can add or delete a user by calling the `UserCreate` or `UserDelete` functions, respectively, in the `Win32::NetAdmin` module.

The syntax for the `UserCreate` function is

```
UserCreate ($ServerName, $UserName, $Password,
$PasswordAge, $Privilege, $HomeDir, $Comment, $Flags, $ScriptPath);
```

15

Here, *$ServerName* has the name of the server. *$UserName* holds the new username. *$Password* contains the new user's password. *$PasswordAge* specifies the time period before the password expires. *$Privilege* indicates the privilege owned by the new user (see the list of the options for the *$Privilege* below). *$HomeDir* keeps the new user's home-directory name. *$Comment* is a string containing a relevant comment about the new user. *$Flags* is a combination of the options listed below (see the options for the *$Flags*) that control the user creation. *$ScriptPath* holds the pathname of the login script.

The options for the *$Privilege* variable in the function are

- ☐ USER_PRIV_MASK   used for all users
- ☐ USER_PRIV_GUEST   used for all guests
- ☐ USER_PRIV_USER   used for all normal users
- ☐ USER_PRIV_ADMIN   used for the administrative account

The options for the *$Flags* variable in the UserCreate function are

- ☐ UF_TEMP_DUPLICATE_ACCOUNT
- ☐ UF_NORMAL_ACCOUNT
- ☐ UF_INTERDOMAIN_TRUST_ACCOUNT
- ☐ UF_WORKSTATION_TRUST_ACCOUNT
- ☐ UF_SERVER_TRUST_ACCOUNT
- ☐ UF_MACHINE_ACCOUNT_MASK
- ☐ UF_DONT_EXPIRE_PASSWD
- ☐ UF_SETTABLE_BITS
- ☐ UF_SCRIPT
- ☐ UF_ACCOUNTDISABLE
- ☐ UF_HOMEDIR_REQUIRED
- ☐ UF_LOCKOUT
- ☐ UF_PASSWD_NOTREQD
- ☐ UF_PASSWD_CANT_CHANGE

The UserDelete function deletes a user from a specified network server.

SYNTAX

The syntax for the UserDelete function is

```
UserDelete ($ServerName, $UserName);
```

Here, *$ServerName* has the name of the server. *$UserName* holds the username that is about to be deleted by the function.

The `UserGetAttributes` **and** `UserSetAttributes` Functions

The `UserGetAttributes` function is designed to get some useful information, such as password, privilege, home directory, and so on, for a specified user.

The syntax for the `UserGetAttributes` function is

```
UserGetAttributes ($ServerName, $UserName, $Password, $PasswordAge,
$Privilege, $HomeDir, $Comment, $Flags, $ScriptPath)
```

Here, `$ServerName` is a string of the server name. `$UserName` has the name of the user. `$Password` contains the user's password. `$PasswordAge` gives the time before the password expires. `$Privilege` shows the user's privilege. `$HomeDir` indicates the user's home directory. `$Comment` gives the user's comment. `$Flags` is a combination of the flag options listed in the previous section. `$ScriptPath` gives the pathname of the user's login script.

The `UserSetAttributes` function is used to set the password, privilege, home directory, and so on for a specified user.

The syntax for the `UserSetAttributes` function is

```
UserSetAttributes ($ServerName, $UserName, $Password, $PasswordAge,
$Privilege, $HomeDir, $Comment, $Flags, $ScriptPath)
```

Here, the arguments have the same meanings as those in the `UserGetAttributes` function.

Working with a Group

There is a set of functions in the `Win32::NetAdmin` module that has been written to manipulate the groups in the Windows NT system. You can add or delete a group, add or delete a user to a group, or obtain attributes about a group by calling those functions in the module.

To help you understand better about the users and groups in the Windows NT system, Figure 15.2 shows you a sample of the users and groups from the User Manager on my NT machine.

To create a group, you can call either the `LocalGroupCreate` or the `GroupCreate` function.

The syntax for the `LocalGroupCreate` function is

```
LocalGroupCreate ($ServerName, $GroupName, $Comment)
```

The syntax for the `GroupCreate` function is

```
GroupCreate ($ServerName, $GroupName, $Comment)
```

For both functions, `$ServerName` holds the server name. `$GroupName` contains the name of the group to create. `$Comment` is a string of relevant comments for the group.

Figure 15.2.

The users and groups on Tony's Windows NT workstation.

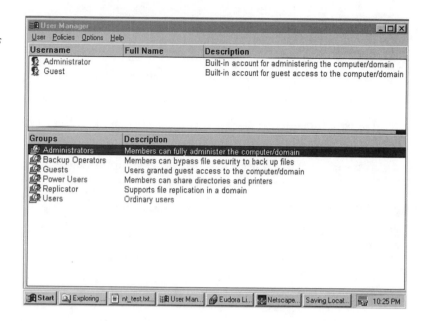

NOTE

A *local group* refers to one or more user accounts logically grouped into a single unit. The single unit is available on the local Windows NT workstation. On the other hand, a *group* (or a *global group*) is available only on a Windows NT domain.

LocalGroupDelete or GroupDelete can be used to delete a group from a network server.

The syntax for the LocalGroupDelete function is

```
LocalGroupDelete ($ServerName, $GroupName)
```

The syntax for the GroupDelete function is

```
GroupDelete ($ServerName, $GroupName)
```

In both instances, *$ServerName* is a string that contains the server name. *$GroupName* has the name of the group to delete.

For a given group in the Windows NT system, LocalGroupGetAttributes or GroupGetAttributes can be used to obtain the group's attributes.

SYNTAX

The syntax for the `LocalGroupGetAttributes` function is

`LocalGroupGetAttributes ($ServerName, $GroupName, $Attributes)`

The syntax for the `GroupGetAttributes` function is

`GroupGetAttributes ($ServerName, $GroupName, $Attributes)`

For both functions, `$ServerName` is a string that holds the server name. `$GroupName` has the name of the group to query. `$Attributes` saves the group attributes returned by the functions.

You can also set the attributes for a given group in the Windows NT system by calling `LocalGroupSetAttributes` or `GroupSetAttributes`.

SYNTAX

The syntax for the `LocalGroupSetAttributes` function is

`LocalGroupSetAttributes ($ServerName, $GroupName, $Attributes)`

The syntax for the `GroupSetAttributes` function is

`GroupSetAttributes ($ServerName, $GroupName, $Attributes)`

In both cases, `$ServerName` is a string that is the network server name. `$GroupName` has the name of the group to work with. `$Attributes` contains the attributes to set for the group specified by `$GroupName`.

To add users to a group, you can call `LocalGroupAddUsers` or `GroupAddUsers`.

SYNTAX

The syntax for the `LocalGroupAddUsers` function is

`LocalGroupAddUsers ($ServerName, $GroupName, @Users)`

The syntax for the `GroupAddUsers` function is

`GroupAddUsers ($ServerName, $GroupName, @Users)`

For each of these functions, `$ServerName` is a string that is the network server name. `$GroupName` has the name of the group to which to add the users. `@Users` contains the names of users to add to the group specified by `$GroupName`.

On the other hand, you can call `LocalGroupDelUsers` or `GroupDelUsers` to delete users from a specified group on a network server.

SYNTAX

The syntax for the `LocalGroupDelUsers` function is

`LocalGroupDelUsers ($ServerName, $GroupName, @Users)`

The syntax for the `GroupDelUsers` function is

`GroupDelUsers ($ServerName, $GroupName, @Users)`

15

For both functions, *$ServerName* is a string that contains the network server name. *$GroupName* has the name of the group. *@Users* contains the names of users to be deleted from the group specified by *$GroupName*.

The `Win32::NetAdmin` module allows you to query a user's membership in a group by providing the `LocalGroupIsMember` and `GroupIsMember` functions.

The syntax for the `LocalGroupIsMember` function is

```
LocalGroupIsMember ($ServerName, $GroupName, $User)
```

The syntax for the `GroupIsMember` function is

```
GroupIsMember ($ServerName, $GroupName, $User)
```

For both functions, *$ServerName* is a string that is the network server name. *$GroupName* has the name of the group. *$User* contains the name of the user whose membership is being queried.

You can also find out all the usernames in a specified group by calling the `LocalGroupGetMembers` or `GroupGetMembers` function, respectively, from the `Win32::NetAdmin` module.

The syntax for the `LocalGroupGetMembers` function is

```
LocalGroupGetMembers ($ServerName, $GroupName, \@Users)
```

The syntax for the `GroupGetMembers` function is

```
GroupGetMembers ($ServerName, $GroupName, \@Users)
```

For these functions, *$ServerName* contains the network server name. *$GroupName* has the name of the group. *\@Users* is a reference to an array of usernames returned by the functions. (References in Perl are explained in detail on Day 18.) *@Users* is returned by both functions.

NOTE

The system symbol `\@` has been used in today's lesson. `\@` is a reference to a regular array. Another system symbol, `\%`, is a reference to a hash array. These two symbols have been introduced in Perl 5. You'll learn more about them on Day 18.

Listing 15.6 is a simple example showing you how to use the `UserGetAttributes` function from the `Win32::NetAdmin` module to get a user's information in the Windows NT system.

TYPE **Listing 15.6. A program that calls** UserGetAttributes **function.**

```
1:  # p15_6.pl
2:
3:  use Win32::NetAdmin;
4:
5:  Win32::NetAdmin::UserGetAttributes (
6:      '',
7:        "Guest",
8:          $Password,
9:            $PasswdAge,
10:             $Privilege,
11:            $HomeDir,
12:          $Comment,
13:        $Flag,
14:     $Script ) || die $!;
15:
16: $result_1 = sprintf (
17:    "Password: %s\n Passwd Age: %x\n Privilege: %s\n",
18:       $Password,
19:         $PasswdAge,
20:           $Privilege );
21:
22: $result_2 = sprintf (
23:    "Home Dirrectory: %s\n Comment: %s\n Flag: %s\n Script: %s\n",
24:       $HomeDir,
25:         $Comment,
26:           $Flag,
27:             $Script );
28:
29: print $result_1 . $result_2;
```

OUTPUT
```
C:\> perl p15_6.pl
Password:
Password Age:    0
Privilege:       0
Home Directory:
Comment:         Built-in account for guest access to the computer/domain
Flag:            66115
Script:
C:\>
```

ANALYSIS Line 3 includes the Win32::NetAdmin module into the Perl script. Lines 5–14 call the UserGetAttributes function to get the password, password age, privilege, home directory, comment, flag, and script for a user called Guest on the local machine. The $ServerName is set to null, that is, '', when the local machine is specified.

Lines 16–20 format a string, $result_1, from the variables $Password, $PasswdAge, and $Privilege, which contain the user information of the password, password age, and privilege, respectively, returned from the UserGetAttributes function.

15

Lines 22–27 format another string, *$result_2*, from the variables *$HomeDir*, *$Comment*, *$Flag*, and *$Script*, which contain the user information about the home directory, comment, flag, and script, respectively, returned also from the UserGetAttributes function.

Line 29 prints out the formatted result of the user attributes on the screen. The Output section here is a sample copied from my machine.

The Win32::File **Module Extensions**

The Win32::File module enables you to get or set attributes for a specified file in the Windows NT (or Windows 95) system. The following section explains the two functions and their usage through an example.

The GetAttributes **and** SetAttributes **Functions**

GetAttributes enables you to obtain the attributes of a file. There are eight attributes defined in Perl 5 for Win32. They are

- [ ] ARCHIVE   It has value of 32.
- [ ] DIRECTORY   It has value of 16.
- [ ] HIDDEN   It has value of 2.
- [ ] NORMAL   It has value of 128.
- [ ] READONLY   It has value of 1.
- [ ] SYSTEM   It has value of 4.
- [ ] TEMPORARYATOMIC_WRITE   It returns the string itself.
- [ ] XACTION_WRITE   It is for future use only.

SYNTAX

The syntax for the GetAttributes function is

```
GetAttributes ($FileName, $Attributes)
```

Here, *$FileName* specifies the name of the file from which you want to obtain the attributes. *$Attributes* contains the returned value of the file attributes listed previously.

To set the attributes for a specified file, call the SetAttributes function.

SYNTAX

The syntax for the SetAttributes function is

```
SetAttributes ($FileName, $Attributes)
```

Here, *$FileName* specifies the name of the file to which you want to set the attributes. *$Attributes* contains the attributes you want to set.

Listing 15.7 gives an example showing you how to use the GetAttributes function from the Win32::File module to obtain a file's attributes.

TYPE **Listing 15.7. A program that uses** GetAttributes **function.**

```
1:  # p15_7.pl
2:
3:  use Win32::File;
4:
5:  print ("Enter a full file name:\n");
6:  my ($filename) = <STDIN>;
7:  chop ($filename);
8:
9:  Win32::File::GetAttributes (
10:     $filename,
11:     $Attributes ) || die $!;
12:
13: if ($Attributes == 32) {
14:     $result = 'archive';
15: } elsif ($Attributes == 16) {
16:     $result = 'directory';
17: } elsif ($Attributes == 2) {
18:     $result = 'hidden';
19: } elsif ($Attributes == 128) {
20:     $result = 'normal';
21: } elsif ($Attributes == 1) {
22:     $result = 'read only';
23: } elsif ($Attributes == 4) {
24:     $result = 'system';
25: } else {
26:     $result = $Attributes;
27: }
28:
29: print ("The $filename is a $result file.\n");
```

OUTPUT
```
C:\> perl p15_7.pl
Enter a full file name:
e:/winnt/notepad.exe
^z
The e:/winnt/notepad.exe is a archive file.
C:\>
```

ANALYSIS   Line 3 includes the Win32::File module into the Perl program. Lines 5–7 ask the user to enter a filename (with a full pathname, if the file is not in the current directory) and assign the chopped filename to the variable $filename. Then the GetAttributes function in line 9 queries the system to get the attributes of the file specified by $filename. If there is an error—for example, the file does not exist—the die function in line 11 will print a brief warning message.

15

Lines 13–27 test the returned value of the attributes to match one of the defined attribute names. Line 29 prints out the final result for the file.

In the Output section, I run the Perl program from Listing 15.7 to get the attribute of a Windows NT application—`notepad.exe`.

The `Win32::Service` **Module Extensions**

The `Win32::Service` module, working only on Windows NT, enables you to start or stop services to which you have the correct privilege. There are six functions in the module; they are introduced in the sections below.

The `StartService` **and** `StopService` **Functions**

The `StartService` function is called to start a service that has been registered with the Service Control Manager in the Windows NT system.

The syntax for the `StartService` function is

```
StartService ($HostName, $ServiceName)
```

Here, `$HostName` specifies the name of the host. Set it to null if the host is the local machine. `$ServiceName` contains the name of the service that you want to start.

If you want to stop a service, call the `StopService` function by passing the service name to the function.

The syntax for the `StopService` function is

```
StopService ($HostName, $ServiceName)
```

Here, `$HostName` specifies the name of the host. Set it to null if the host is the local machine. `$ServiceName` contains the name of the service that you want to stop.

The `PauseService` **and** `ResumeService` **Functions**

Normally, the two functions are used together. If you want to resume a service that has been paused by the `PauseService` function, call the `ResumeService` function by passing the service name to the function.

The syntax for the `PauseService` function is

```
PauseService ($HostName, $ServiceName)
```

Here, `$HostName` specifies the name of the host. Set it to null if the host is the local machine. `$ServiceName` contains the name of the service that you want to pause.

SYNTAX

The syntax for the ResumeService function is

```
ResumeService ($HostName, $ServiceName)
```

Here, $HostName specifies the name of the host. Set it to null if the host is the local machine. $ServiceName contains the name of the service that you want to resume.

The GetStatus **and** EnumServices **Functions**

The GetStatus function is used to return the status of a specified service. The EnumServices function returns a list of available services on a specified host.

The syntax for the GetStatus function is

```
GetStatus ($HostName, $ServiceName, $StatusRef)
```

Here, $HostName specifies the name of the host. Set it to null if the host is the local machine. $ServiceName contains the name of the service whose status you want to know. $StatusRef, returned by the GetStatus function, contains a reference to a hash that can have the following keys:

- ☐ ServiceType
- ☐ CurrentState
- ☐ ControlsAccepted
- ☐ Win32ExitCode
- ☐ ServiceSpecificExitCode
- ☐ CheckPoint
- ☐ WaitHint

The syntax for the EnumServices function is

```
EnumServices ($HostName, \@ServiceList)
```

Here, $HostName specifies the name of the host. Set it to null if the host is the local machine. \@ServiceList is a reference to an array that contains a list of the available services on the host specified by $HostName. \@ServiceList is returned by the function.

The Win32::NetResource **Module Extensions**

The Win32::NetResource module can be used to manipulate the network resources on Windows NT. If you are a systems administrator, you'll find the functions in the module are very useful.

15

Before we go any further, let's take a look at the hash keys in %SHARE_INFO and %NETRESOURCE.

The following keys are available for %SHARE_INFO:

- ☐ netname   Refers to the name of the share.
- ☐ type   Refers to the type of the share.
- ☐ remark   Refers to a string of comment.
- ☐ permissions   Refers to the value of permissions.
- ☐ maxusers   Refers to the maximum number of users.
- ☐ current-users   Refers to the current number of users.
- ☐ path   Refers to the path of the share.
- ☐ passwd   Refers to a password if required.

For %NETRESOURCE, the available keys are

- ☐ Scope   Refers to the scope of an enumeration.
- ☐ Type   Refers to the type of the resource to enumerate.
- ☐ DisplayType   Refers to the way the resource should be displayed.
- ☐ Usage   Refers to the resource usage.
- ☐ LocalName   Refers to the name of the local device.
- ☐ RemoteName   Refers to the network name of the resource.
- ☐ Comment   Refers to a string of comment.
- ☐ Provider   Refers to the provider name of the resource.

The following constants are predefined values for the Scope, Type, DisplayType, and Usage keys.

There are three options for the Scope key:

- ☐ RESOURCE_CONNECTED
- ☐ RESOURCE_REMEMBERED
- ☐ RESOURCE_GLOBALNET

These three options are for the Type key:

- ☐ RESOURCETYPE_ANY
- ☐ RESOURCETYPE_DISK
- ☐ RESOURCETYPE_PRINT

The following three values are used by the `DisplayType` key:

- [ ] RESOURCEDISPLAYTYPE_DOMAIN
- [ ] RESOURCEDISPLAYTYPE_SERVER
- [ ] RESOURCEDISPLAYTYPE_SHARE

The `Usage` key has these two options:

- [ ] RESOURCEUSAGE_CONNECTABLE
- [ ] RESOURCEUSAGE_CONTAINER

The `GetSharedResources` and `GetUNCName` Functions

To obtain a list of all network resources, such as shared printers and disks, call the `GetSharedResources` function in the `Win32::NetResource` module.

SYNTAX

The syntax for the `GetSharedResources` function is

```
GetSharedResources (\@Resources, $Type)
```

Here, `\@Resources` is the reference to the hash array `%NETRESOURCE` (defined in the preceding paragraphs). `$Type` indicates the type of the resource. `\@Resources` is returned by the function.

The `GetUNCName` function in the `Win32::NetResource` module returns the UNC name of the disk share.

UNC is an abbreviation standing for *uniform naming convention*. UNC names are resource names, prefixed with the string `\\`, on the network. (UNC is also known as *universal naming convention*.)

SYNTAX

The syntax for the `GetUNCName` function is

```
GetUNCName ($UNCName, $LocalPath)
```

Here, `$UNCName` contains the UNC name returned by the function. `$LocalPath` indicates the local pathname.

The `AddConnection` and `CancelConnection` Functions

The `AddConnection` function is used to make a connection to a specified network resource. To cancel a connection to a network resource, call the `CancelConnection` function in the `Win32::NetResrouce` module.

15

The syntax for the AddConnection function is

AddConnection (\%NETRESOUCE, $Password, $UserName, $ConnectionOption)

Here, \%NETRESOURCE is a reference to the hash array %NETRESOURCE. The reference is returned by the function. $Password contains the password of the user who makes the connection. $UserName holds the username. $ConnectionOption is set to 1 if the connection should be kept for all logins, and to 0 otherwise.

The CancelConnection function performs the opposite task of the AddConnection function.

The syntax for the CancelConnection function is

CancelConnection ($DeviceName, $ConnectionOption, $ForceOption)

Here, $DeviceName contains the name of the local device to which the resource is connected. $ConnectionOption is set to 1 for persistent connection, and to 0 for non-persistent connection. The connection has to be broken immediately if $ForceOption is set to 1. Otherwise, the connection may remain for a while, if $ForceOption is set to 0.

The GetError and WNetGetLastError Functions

The GetError function returns the last error found from a Win32::NetResource call. If the Win32::GetLastError returns ERROR_EXTENED_ERROR, the WNetGetLastError function can be used to get the extended network error. The Win32::GetLastError extension is introduced in the section titled "The Win32 Miscellaneous Extensions," later in today's lesson.

The syntax for the GetError function is

GetError ($ErrorString)

Here, $ErrorString contains the last error message caused by an improper Win32::NetResource call. $ErrorString is returned by the function.

The syntax for the WNetGetLastError function is

WNetGetLastError ($ErrorString, $ErrorDescription, $ErrorName)

Here, $ErrorString, returned by the function, contains the last error message caused by an improper Win32::NetResource call. $ErrorDescription saves the description of the error. $ErrorName gives the name of the error. $ErrorDescription and $ErrorName are also returned by the function.

The `NetShareAdd`, `NetShareDel`, and `NetShareCheck` Functions

In the `Win32::NetResource` module, there are three functions, `NetShareAdd`, `NetShareDel`, and `NetShareCheck`, that you can use to manipulate the shares on the network.

The syntax for the `NetShareAdd` function is

`NetShareAdd (\%SHARE_INFO, $Error, $ServerName)`

Here, `\%SHARE_INFO` is a reference to the hash array `%SHARE_INFO` defined above. `$Error` returns the value of errors that occurred. `$ServerName` contains the name of the server.

To remove a share from a share list on a computer, call the `NetShareDel` function.

The syntax for the `NetShareDel` function is

`NetShareDel ($ShareName, $ServerName)`

Here, `$ShareName` contains the name of the share to delete. `$ServerName` keeps the name of the server.

The `NetShareCheck` function is used to check whether a share is available for connection for a specified device.

The syntax for the `NetShareCheck` function is

`NetShareCheck ($DeviceName, $ShareType, $ServerName)`

Here, `$DeviceName` holds the name of the device to be checked for shared access. `$ShareType`, returned by the function, gives the type of the share. The value contained in `$ShareType` is not valid unless the function itself returns a nonzero value. `$ServerName` contains the name of the server.

The `NetShareGetInfo` and `NetShareSetInfo` Functions

To get or set information about a specified share, call `NetShareGetInfo` or `NetShareSetInfo`, respectively, from the `Win32::NetResource` module.

The syntax for the `NetShareGetInfo` function is

`NetShareGetInfo ($ShareName, \%SHARE_INFO, $ServerName)`

Here, `$ShareName` specifies the network name of the share. `\%SHARE_INFO`, returned by the function, is a reference to the hash array `%SHARE_INFO`. `$ServerName` gives the name of the server.

15

The NetShareSetInfo function sets the information for a specified share.

15

SYNTAX

The syntax for the NetShareSetInfo function is

NetShareSetInfo ($ShareName, \%SHARE_INFO, $Error, $ServerName)

Here, $ShareName specifies the network name of the share. \%SHARE_INFO is a reference to the %SHARE_INFO hash that describes the share. $Error sets the error status. $ServerName gives the name of the server.

NOTE

Before you finish learning about the Win32 system module extensions, I would like to reiterate that Perl for Win32 is still an ongoing project; many places need to be improved and bugs need to be fixed, especially in some Win32 system module extensions. It is highly recommended that you check the online documents frequently for the latest changes made in Perl for Win32.

The Win32 **Miscellaneous Extensions**

Besides the Win32 nested modules introduced in the preceding sections, the Win32 module itself contains several extensions designed for Win32 programming, especially on Windows NT.

The following extension functions are available in the current version of Perl 5 for Win32:

☐ Win32::GetLastError

If a call to a Win32 API causes an error, use this function to get the error message.

☐ Win32::PerlVersion

Use this function to find the version of Perl for Win32.

☐ Win32::LoginName

Call this function to obtain the name of the user who owns the current Perl process.

☐ Win32::NodeName

Use this function to get the Microsoft Network node-name on the current machine.

☐ Win32::DomainName

Similar to the previous function, except that Win32::DomainName returns the domain name that is logged on by the owner of the current Perl process.

☐ Win32::FsType

Use this function to find the name of the file-system type for the currently active drive.

☐ Win32::GetCwd

Call this function to get the current active drive. (Note: This function does not return a UNC path, so it can't be run on Windows 95.)

☐ Win32::GetOSVersion

This function returns an array of ($string, $major, $minor, $build, $id), where the elements are an arbitrary descriptive string, the major version number of the operating system, the minor version number, the build number, and a digit indicating the actual operating system.

The value of $id is used to determine the operating system name; the value is set to 0 for generic Win32, 1 for Windows 95, and 2 for Windows NT.

☐ Win32::FormatMessage ($ErrorCode)

Call this function to format the Win32 error code, $ErrorCode, returned by function calls (for example, GetLastError) to a descriptive string.

☐ Win32::Spawn ($Command, $Arguments, $ProcessID)

Call this function to spawn a new process using the supplied $Command that contains the full pathname of an application, passing in arguments in the string $Arguments. The new process ID is stored in $ProcessID.

☐ Win32::LookupAccountName ($System, $Account, $Domain, $SID, $SIDType)

This function looks up accounts specified by $Account on the system of $System and returns the domain name $Domain, SID (Security ID) $SID, and SID type $SIDType. For the local machine, $System is set to null.

☐ Win32::LookupAccountSID ($System, $SID, $Account, $Domain, $SIDType)

This function looks up SID on the specified system and returns the account name, domain name, and SID type.

☐ Win32::InitiateSystemShutdown ($Machine, $Message, $Timeout, $ForceClose, $Reboot)

Call this function to shut down the specified machine and notify the user with the supplied $Message, within the interval specified by $Timeout. If the $ForceClose flag is set to true (nonzero), the function forces closing of all documents without prompting the user. If the $Reboot flag is true, the machine will be rebooted after the shutdown.

☐ Win32::AbortSystemShutdown ($Machine)

This function can be called in order to abort a shutdown process on the machine specified by $Machine.

Listing 15.8 demonstrates how to use some of the extensions introduced in this section to obtain a login name, the current version of Perl for Win32, the file-system type, the operating system type, and the version number by querying your machine.

Listing 15.8 also shows you how to call the Win32::Spawn function to launch a Windows application, notepad.exe, and review the saved information in a text file. Finally, Listing 15.8 uses the Win32::GetLastError and Win32::FormatMessage extensions together to check and format the last error caused by a call to Win32 extensions.

TYPE

Listing 15.8. A program that uses the extensions in the Win32 module.

```
 1:  # p15_8.pl
 2:
 3:  use Win32;
 4:
 5:  my ($login_name) = Win32::LoginName;
 6:  &Error;
 7:
 8:  my ($perl_version) = Win32::PerlVersion;
 9:  &Error;
10:
11:  my ($fs_type) = Win32::FsType;
12:  &Error;
13:
14:  my ($string, $major, $minor, $build, $id) = Win32::GetOSVersion;
15:  &Error;
16:
17:  my ($os) = 'unknown';
18:  if ($id == 1) {
19:      $os = 'Windows 95';
20:  } elsif ($id == 2) {
21:      $os = 'Windows NT';
22:  } elsif ($id == 0) {
23:      $os = 'Generic Win32';
24:  }
25:
26:  open MYFILE, "> output15.log";
27:  &Error;
28:
29:  print MYFILE "Login Name:        $login_name\n";
30:  print MYFILE "Perl Version:      $perl_version\n";
31:  print MYFILE "FS Type:           $fs_type\n";
32:  print MYFILE "Operating System:  $os\n";
33:  print MYFILE "OS Version:        $major.$minor\n";
34:  print MYFILE "OS Build:          $build\n";
35:
36:  close (MYFILE);
37:
38:  print ("\nGo ahead to review the ouputs saved in output15.log.\n");
39:  Win32::Spawn ("c:\\windows\\notepad.exe", "notepad output15.log", $pid);
```

continues

Listing 15.8. continued

```
40:  $Error;
41:
42:  sub Error {
43:    print Win32::FormatMessage (Win32::GetLastError());
44:  }
```

OUTPUT
```
C:\> perl p15_8.pl
The operation completed successfully.
The operation completed successfully.
The operation completed successfully.
The operation completed successfully.
The operation completed successfully.

Go ahead to reiew the outputs saved in output15.log.
C:\>
```

ANALYSIS Line 3 includes the Win32 module into the Perl program. Line 5 gets the login name of the user by calling the Win32::LoginName extension. Line 6 checks any errors caused by the call from the Win32::LoginName extension. If there is no error, a brief message, The operation completed successfully., is printed out.

Lines 8–9 query the Perl version and check any errors caused by the Win32::PerlVersion extension. Lines 11–12 find out the file-system type and examine the success of the Win32::FsType extension.

Then, line 14 obtains the major and minor versions of the current operating system. The variable $id in line 14 keeps the value that is tested in lines 17–24 in order to find out the operating system name.

Line 26 opens a file called output15.log, and line 27 reports whether the open function in line 26 runs successfully.

Lines 29–34 dump the information of the login name, the Perl version, the file-system type, and the operating system name and version into the opened file, output15.log. Line 36 closes the handle of the opened file.

Line 38 asks the user to review the outputs saved in output15.log, because the Win32::Spawn in line 39 spawns a Windows application, notepad.exe, to open output15.log, which now contains all the saved information.

The subroutine Error is defined in lines 42–44; it checks and formats the last error by using the Win32::GetLastError and Win32::FormatMessage extensions together.

In the output section for the listing, you see the messages printed by the subroutine Error. Figure 15.3 shows you the saved outputs in the output15.log file.

Figure 15.3.

The sample outputs saved in output15.log, *which is opened by the* Win32::Spawn *extension.*

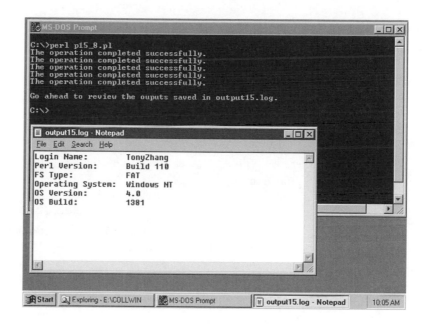

 NOTE

For all modules available in Perl for Win32, check the Web page at http://www.perl.com/perl/CPAN/modules/by-module/Win32/.

Here, CPAN stands for *Comprehensive Perl Archive Network,* which is a Perl archive mirrored around the world.

Writing Module Extensions

The C programming language has a longer history than Perl. C has built up an extremely rich library of functions that can be used to deal with many programming problems. It is very useful to include some of the C functions, in the format of the module extensions, in your Perl programs. To do so, you need to create an interface between Perl and C by using another language—XS.

The key component in XS is the XSUB function, which is used to wrap up a C library function that is needed by Perl. Another major component in XS is xsubpp, which is a compiler used to manipulate Perl data and provide Perl path to access the XSUB.

The basic steps needed to write module extensions are the following:

1. Create an xs file.
2. Compile the xs file with xsubpp, which produces a C++ file.

3. Compile the C++ file into a dynamic linked library (DLL) file. Then, rename the .dll file to a .pll file in order for it to be called by the module interface created in Step 4.

4. Write a Perl interface module that is the link between the .pll file and the Perl interpreter. By default, the module has an extension of .pm.

For more information about writing module extensions for Perl, check the online documentation at http://www.hip.com/man-pages/perlapi.htm.

You can also read http://www.hip.com/man-pages/win32xs.pm for the updated information regarding XS programming.

NOTE

> By the time you read this book, most of the Perl for Win32 documents may have already been moved to ActiveWare's Web site. Keep browsing ActiveWare's home page at http://www.ActiveWare.com/ for the latest news.

Running Perl Programs on Windows 95

As mentioned before, the primary target operating system of Perl for Win32 is Windows NT. Windows 95 is limited when it comes to Perl and does not fully support Perl for Win32, because Windows 95 is not a real 32-bit operating system.

The following summarizes some problems found in running Perl programs on Windows 95:

☐ ^z, the combination keys of Ctrl and Z, does not work properly in the command-line shell on Windows 95.

☐ Exception handling is unreliable.

☐ STDERR redirection is not supported by COMMAND.COM.

☐ Some module extensions introduced in this chapter cannot be run on Windows 95.

Summary

Today's topics make up one of the important portions of Perl for Win32.

You have reviewed the definitions of Win32 and Perl for Win32 and have learned about the directly mapped Perl extensions for Windows NT.

15

The top-level module Win32 consists of many nested modules and extensions. The nested modules in the Win32 modules are sometimes called system module extensions. You learned about the following major system module extensions:

- [ ] `Win32::Process`
- [ ] `Win32::Semaphore`
- [ ] `Win32::Mutex`
- [ ] `Win32::ChangeNotification`
- [ ] `Win32::IPC`
- [ ] `Win32::Eventlog`
- [ ] `Win32::Registry`
- [ ] `Win32::NetAdmin`
- [ ] `Win32::File`
- [ ] `Win32::Service`
- [ ] `Win32::NetResource`

Some extensions within the top-level Win32 module were introduced today, with examples showing how to use the extensions. You also learned about the steps needed to write the module extensions in Perl for Win32, and saw a list of problems found when running Perl programs on Windows 95.

It has been recommended to you to keep checking the online documentation for the latest bug fixes or the next major release of Perl for Win32.

Q&A

Q Why did Microsoft introduce Win32?

A Because of historical reasons, the 16-bit DOS had been the de facto operating system in the PC world. But DOS is neither robust nor user-friendly. DOS cannot run multitasking jobs or access the memory space above the first 1MB unless the user adds some extended features to DOS.

To solve the DOS problems and keep its competitive position in the operating-system market, Microsoft introduced Win32, which became the primary subsystem in Windows NT. As a 32-bit operating system, Windows NT is superior to DOS because it has the power and robustness provided directly by Win32.

Q Why can't some functions of Perl for Win32 run on Windows 95?

A The primary target operating system of Perl for Win32 is 32-bit, such as Windows NT (both the workstation version and the server version). As a transitional operating system, Windows 95 is not really 32-bit. Windows 95 still keeps some 16-bit portions. Therefore, many of the functions designed to run on 32-bit operating systems cannot run on Windows 95.

Q What is a "process" on Windows NT?

A A process on Windows NT is defined as an "instance" of a running program. Each process owns a 4GB address space. Because a process is inert in Windows NT, it needs at least one thread to execute the code for an application. A process can own several threads. All of the threads will execute code simultaneously in the process's address space.

Q What is the purpose of a semaphore?

A A semaphore is a method of ensuring that only one process or thread can run a particular segment of code or access a particular chunk of shared memory storage at any given time.

A full description of how semaphores work is beyond the scope of this book. Many books on operating systems can give you an introduction to the concepts used in semaphores.

Workshop

To help you solidify your understanding of today's lesson, you are encouraged to try to answer the quiz questions and finish the exercises provided in the workshop before you move to next lesson. The answers and hints to the questions and exercises are given in Appendix B, "Answers."

Quiz

1. Define the following terms:
    a. package
    b. module
    c. extension
2. What is the function in the `Win32::Process` module?
3. When do you need to call the `Win32::Mutex::Wait` function if you use a mutex account to synchronize the access to the shared resource?
4. How do you add a user to a group?

Exercises

1. Write a program to extract such information as the node name, domain name, file-system type, and login name from your computer by using the directly mapped extensions in Perl 5 for Win32.

2. Rewrite the program in Exercise 1. This time, you are required to use the extensions in the `Win32` module.

3. Write a program to launch the Windows application Notepad on your computer by calling the extensions in the `Win32::Process` module. (Note: The executable name for Notepad is `notepad.exe`. Be sure that you include the correct pathname for the executable in your Perl script.)

4. Make a subroutine to check and print out the last error caused by a Win32 extension. Then, modify the program in Listing 15.2 to include the subroutine.

5. Write a program that waits for a username entered by the user and then obtains all the attributes, such as password, password age, and privilege, specified by the username.

6. **BUG BUSTER:** What is wrong with the following program?

```
# Exercise 15.6 - bug buster:

Win32::Process::Create (
        $processObj,
        "c:\\windows\\calc.exe",
        "",
        0,
        DETACHED_PROCESS,
        ".") || die "Cannot create the process";
$processObj->SetPriorityClass (NORMAL_PRIORITY_CLASS) ||
        die $!;
$processObj->Wait (INFINITE);
print ("Calc program exited. Bye!\n");
```

Day **16**

Command-Line Options

Today's lesson describes the options you can specify to control how your Perl program operates. These options provide many features, including those that perform the following tasks:

☐ Checking syntax

☐ Printing warnings

☐ Using preprocessor commands

☐ Editing files

☐ Changing the "end of input line" marker

Today's lesson begins with a description of how to supply options to your Perl program.

Specifying Options

There are two ways to supply options to a Perl program:

- ☐ On the command line, when you enter the command that starts your Perl program
- ☐ On the first line of your Perl program

The following sections describe these methods of supplying options.

Specifying Options on the Command Line

One way to specify options for a Perl program is to enter them on the command line when you enter the command that starts your program.

The syntax for specifying options on the command line is

```
perl options program
```

Here, *program* is the name of the Perl program you want to run, and *options* is the list of options you want to supply to the program.

For example, the following command runs the Perl program named `test1.pl` and passes it the options `-s` and `-w` (you'll learn about these, and other options, later today):

```
C:\> perl -s -w test1.pl
```

Some options need to be specified along with a value. For example, the `-0` option requires an integer to be passed with it:

```
C:\> perl -0 26 test1.pl
```

Here, the integer `26` is associated with the option `-0`. (Note that in the option, `0` is the numerical `zero`, not the letter `o`.)

If desired, you can omit the space between the option and its associated value, as in the following:

```
C:\> perl -026 test1.pl
```

As before, this command associates `26` with the `-0` option. In either case, the value associated with an option must always immediately follow the option.

NOTE

> If an option does not require an associated value, you can put another option immediately after it without specifying an additional - character or space. For example, the following commands are equivalent:

```
C:\> perl -s -w test1.pl
C:\> perl -sw test1.pl
```

You can put an option that requires a value as part of a group of options, provided that it is last in the group. For example, the following commands are equivalent:

```
C:\> perl -s -w -0 26 test1.pl
C:\> perl -sw026 test1.pl
```

The -v Option: Printing the Perl for Win32 Version Number

The -v option enables you to find out what version of Perl for Win32 is running on your machine. When the Perl interpreter sees this option, it prints information on itself and then exits without running your program.

This means that if you supply a command such as the following, the file test1.pl is not executed:

```
C:\> perl -v test1.pl
```

Here is sample output from the -v command:

```
This is perl, version 5.001
        Unofficial patch level 1m
Copyright (c) 1987-1994, Larry Wall
Win32 port Copyright © 1995 Microsoft Corporation. All rights reserved.
        Developed by hip communications inc., http://info.hip.com/info/
        Perl for Win32 Build 110
        Built Aug 13 1996@08:18:50
Perl may be copied only under the terms of either the Artistic License
or the GNU General Public License, which may be found in the Perl 5.0
source kit.
```

The only really useful things here, besides the copyright notice, are the version number of the Perl you are running—in this case, 5.001—and the patch level, which indicates how many repairs, or patches, have been made to this version. Here, the patch level is 1m. In Perl 5 for Win32, the build number is used to indicate the release number when the Perl 5 code is ported to the Windows 32-bit operating systems. As you see, the build is 110, which, at this writing, is the latest release of Perl 5 for Win32.

No other options should be specified if you use the -v option, because none of them would do anything in this case anyway.

The -c Option: Checking Your Syntax

You may remember the -c option, because you used it on Day 1, "Getting Started—Perl for Windows NT." The -c option tells the Perl interpreter to check whether your Perl program is correct without actually running it. If it is correct, the Perl interpreter prints the following message (in which *filename* is the name of your program) and then exits without executing your program:

```
filename syntax OK
```

If the Perl interpreter detects errors, it displays them just as it normally does. After printing the error messages, it prints the following message, in which *filename* is the name of your program:

```
filename had compilation errors
```

Again, there is no point in supplying other options if you specify the -c option because the Perl interpreter isn't actually running the program; the only exception is the -w option, which prints warnings. This option is described in the following section.

The -w Option: Printing Warnings

As you have seen on the preceding days, some mistakes are easy to make when you are writing a Perl program, such as accidentally typing the wrong variable name or using == when you really mean to use eq. Because certain mistakes crop up frequently, the Perl interpreter provides an option that checks for them.

This option, the -w option, prints a warning every time the Perl interpreter sees something that might cause a problem. For example, if the interpreter sees the statement

```
$y = $x;
```

and hasn't seen $x before (which means that $x is undefined), it prints a warning message in the following form:

```
Identifier "main::x" used only once: possible typo at filename line linenum.
```

For more information on packages, see Day 14, "Packages, Modules, and Systems Functions."

The following sections provide a partial list of the potential problems detected by the -w option.

16

NOTE

> The -w option can be combined with the -c option to provide a means of checking your syntax for errors and problems before you actually run the program.

Checking for Possible Typos

As you have seen, a statement such as the following one leads to a warning message if $x has not been previously defined:

```
$y = $x;
```

The warning message also appears in the following circumstances, among others:

- ☐ If a variable is assigned to but is never used again
- ☐ If a file variable is referred to without being specified in an open statement

Of course, the warning message might flag lines that don't actually contain typos. Following is one of the most common situations in which a possible typo actually is correct code:

If you call a function that returns a list, and you need only an element of the list, one way to extract that single element is to assign the other elements to dummy variables. For example, if you want to retrieve just the group ID when you call getgrnam, you can do so as shown here:

```
($d1, $d2, $groupid) = getgrnam ($groupname);
```

Here, the scalar variables $d1 and $d2 are dummy variables that hold the elements of the group file entry that you do not need. If (as is likely) $d1 and $d2 are not referred to again, the -w option treats $d1 and $d2 as possible typos.

Checking for Redefined Subroutines

One useful feature of the -w option is that it checks whether two subroutines of the same name have been defined in the program. (Normally, if the Perl interpreter sees two subroutines of the same name, it quietly replaces the first one with the second one and carries on.)

If, for example, two subroutines named x are defined in a program, the -w option prints a message similar to the following one:

```
Subroutine x redefined at file1 line 46.
```

The line number specified is the line that starts the second subroutine.

When the -w option has detected this problem, you can decide which subroutine to rename or throw away.

Checking for Incorrect Comparison Operators

Another really helpful feature of the -w option is that it checks whether you are trying to compare a string using the == operator.

In a statement such as the following

```
if ($x == "humbug") {
       ...
}
```

the conditional expression

```
$x == "humbug"
```

is equivalent to the expression

```
$x == 0
```

because all character strings are converted to 0 when used in a numeric context (a place where a number is expected). This is correct in Perl, but it is not likely to be what you want. Perl 5 for Win32 prints out the following warning:

```
Argument "humbug" isn't numeric for numeric eq at file1 line 26.
```

This warning enables you to detect these incorrect == operators and replace them with eq operators, which compare strings.

WARNING

The -w operator doesn't detect the opposite problem, namely:
```
if ($x eq 46) {
       ...
}
```
In this case, the Perl interpreter converts 46 to the string 46 and performs a string comparison.

Because a number and its string equivalent usually mean the same thing, this normally doesn't cause a problem. Watch out, though, for octal numbers in string comparisons, as in the following example:
```
if ($x eq 046) {
       ...
}
```
Here, the octal value 046 is converted to the number 38 before being converted to a string. If you really want to compare $x to 046, this code will not produce the results you expect.

16

For conditional expressions such as the following

```
if ($x = 0) {
        ...
}
```

Perl 5 flags it with the following message:

```
Found = in conditional, should be == at filename line filenum.
```

16

The -e Option: Executing a Single-Line Program

The -e option enables you to execute a Perl program from your shell command line. For example, the command

```
C:\> perl -e "print ('Hello');"
```

prints the following string on your screen:

```
Hello
```

You can also specify multiple -e options. In this case, the Perl statements are executed left to right. For example, the command

```
C:\> perl -e "print ('Hello');" -e "print (' there');"
```

prints the following string on your screen:

```
Hello there
```

By itself, the -e option is not all that useful. It becomes useful, however, when you use it in conjunction with some of the other options you'll see in today's lesson.

WARNING

You can leave off the closing semicolon in a Perl statement passed via the -e option, if you want to:

```
C:\> perl -e "print ('Hello')"
```

If you are supplying two or more -e options, however, the Perl interpreter strings them together and treats them as though they were a single Perl program. This means that the following command generates an error, because there must be a semicolon after the statement specified with the first -e option:

```
C:\> perl -e "print ('Hello')" -e "print (' there')"
```

The -s Option: Supplying Your Own Command-Line Options

As you can see from this chapter, you can control the behavior of Perl by specifying various command-line options. You can control the behavior of your own Perl programs by specifying command-line options for them, too. To do this, specify the -s option when you call the program.

Here's an example of a command that passes an option to a Perl program:

```
C:\> perl -s testfile.pl -q
```

This command starts the Perl program testfile.pl and passes it the -q option.

WARNING

To be able to pass options to your program, you must specify the Perl -s option. The following command does not pass -q as an option:

```
C:\> perl testfile.pl -q
```

In this case, -q is just an ordinary argument that is passed to your program and stored in the built-in array variable @ARGV.

If an option is specified when you invoke your Perl program, the scalar variable whose name is the same as the option is automatically set to 1 before program execution begins. For example, if a Perl program named testfile.pl is called with the -q option, as in the following, the scalar variable $q is automatically set to 1:

```
C:\> perl -s testfile.pl -q
```

You then can use this variable in a conditional expression to test whether the option has been set.

NOTE

If -q is treated as an option, it does not appear in the system variable @ARGV. A command-line argument either sets an option or is added to @ARGV.

Options can be longer than a single character. For example, the following command sets the value of the scalar variable $potato to 1:

```
C:\> perl -s testfile.pl -potato
```

16

You also can set an option to a value other than 1 by specifying = and the desired value on the command line:

```
C:\> perl -s testfile.pl -potato="hot"
```

This line sets the value of $potato to hot.

Listing 16.1 is a simple example of a program that uses command-line options to control its behavior. This program prints information about the user currently logged in.

Listing 16.1. An example of a program that uses command-line options.

```
1:  # p16_1.pl
2:
3:  # This program prints information as specified by
4:  # the following options:
5:  # -L: print Login Name
6:  # -D: print Domain Name
7:  # -N: print Node Name
8:  # -F: print File System Type
9:  # -all: print everything (overrides other options)
10:
11: $L = $D = $N = $F = 1 if ($all);
12: ($login_name, $domain_name, $node_name, $fs_type) = &GetInfo ($L, $D, $N,
    ➥$F);
13: print "Login Name:        $login_name\n"  if ($L);
14: print "Domain Name:       $domain_name\n" if ($D);
15: print "Node Name:         $node_name\n"   if ($N);
16: print "File System Type:  $fs_type\n"     if ($F);
17:
18: sub GetInfo {
19:    my ($l, $d, $n, $f) = @_;
20:    my @result;
21:    $result[0] = &NTLoginName if $l;
22:    $result[1] = &NTDomainName if $d;
23:    $result[2] = &NTNodeName if $n;
24:    $result[3] = &NTFsType if $f;
25:    return @result;
26: }
```

OUTPUT
```
C:\> perl -s p16_1.pl -L -F
Login Name:        TonyZhang
File System Type:  FAT
C:\>
```

ANALYSIS The comments in lines 3–9 provide information on what options the program supports. This information is useful when someone is reading or modifying the program, because there is no other way to tell which scalar variables are used to test options.

The option -all indicates that the program is to print everything; if this option is specified, the scalar variable $all is set to 1. To cut down on the number of comparisons later, line 11 checks whether $all is 1; if it is, the other scalar variables corresponding to command-line options are set to 1. This technique ensures that the following commands are equivalent:

```
C:\> perl -s p16_1.pl -all
C:\> perl -s p16_1.pl -L -D -N -F
```

The scalar variables listed in line 11 can be assigned to, even though they correspond to possible command-line options, because they behave just like other Perl scalar variables.

Line 12 calls the subroutine, GetInfo, by passing it the values of $L, $D, $N, and $F. The subroutine then returns strings containing the login name, domain name, node name, or file-system type of the current machine depending on whether the value of $L, $D, $N, or $F is set to 1. The subroutine is listed in lines 18–26.

Then, lines 13–16 decide whether to print out the strings by testing $L, $D, $N, and $F.

TIP

Because command-line options can change the initial values of scalar variables, it is a good idea to always assign a value to a scalar variable before you use it. Consider the following example:

```
while ($count < 10) {
        print ("$count\n");
        $count++;
}
```

This program normally prints the numbers from 0 to 9, because $count is assumed to have an initial value of 0. However, if this program is called with the -count option, the initial value of $count becomes something other than 0, and the program behaves differently.

If you add the following statement before the while loop, the program always prints the numbers 0 to 9 regardless of what options are specified on the command line:

```
$count = 0;
```

The -s Option and Other Command-Line Arguments

You can supply both options and command-line arguments to your program (provided that you supply the -s option to Perl). These are the rules that the Perl interpreter follows:

16

☐   Any arguments immediately following the program name that start with a – are assumed to be options.

☐   Any argument that does not start with a – is assumed to be an ordinary argument and not an option.

☐   When the Perl interpreter sees an argument that is not an option, all subsequent arguments are also treated as ordinary arguments, not options, even if they start with a –.

This means, for example, that the following command treats –w as an option to `testfile.pl`, and `foo` and –e as ordinary arguments:

```
C:\> perl -s testfile.pl -w foo -e
```

The special argument – – also indicates end of options. For example, the following command treats –w as an option and –e as an ordinary argument. The – – is thrown away:

```
C:\> perl -s testfile.pl -w - -e
```

The –P Option: Using the C Preprocessor

The C preprocessor is a program that takes code written in the C programming language and searches for special preprocessor statements. In Perl, the –P option enables you to use this preprocessor with your Perl program:

```
C:\> perl -P myprog.pl
```

Here, the Perl program `myprog.pl` is first run through the C preprocessor. The resulting output is then passed to the Perl interpreter for execution.

NOTE

> Perl provides no way to just run the C preprocessor on a Perl program. To do this, you'll need a C compiler that provides an option that specifies "preprocessor only."
>
> Refer to the documentation for your C compiler for details about how to do this.

The -I Option

The -I option is used to add specified directories to the @INC array. In Perl, the @INC keeps the search path for modules that are needed by the require or use functions.

Also, you use the -I option with the -P option. It enables you to specify where to look for include files to be processed by the C preprocessor. For example:

```
perl -P -I /u/dave/myincdir testfile.pl
```

This command tells the Perl interpreter to search the directory /u/dave/myincdir (as well as the default directories) for include files.

To specify multiple directories to search, repeat the -I option:

```
perl -P -I /u/dave/dir1 -I /u/dave/dir2 testfile.pl
```

This command searches in both /u/dave/dir1 and /u/dave/dir2.

The -n Option: Operating on Multiple Files

One of the most common tasks in Perl programs is to read the contents of several input files one line at a time and process each input line as it is read. In these programs and commands, the names of the input files are supplied on the command line.

In Perl, one way to read the contents of several input files, one line at a time, is to enclose the <> operator in a while loop:

```
while ($line = <>) {
        # process $line in here
}
```

Another method is to specify the -n option. This option takes your program and executes it once for each line of input in each of the files specified on the command line.

Listing 16.2 is a simple example of a program that uses the -n option. It puts asterisks around each input line and then prints it.

TYPE **Listing 16.2. A simple program that uses the -n option.**

```
1:  # p16_2.pl
2:
3:  # input line is stored in the system variable $_
4:  $line = $_;
5:  chop ($line);
6:  printf ("* %-52s *\n", $line);
```

OUTPUT

```
C:\> perl -n p16_2.pl
* This test file has only one line in it.                    *
C:\>
```

ANALYSIS The -n option encloses the program shown here in an invisible while loop. Each time the program is executed, the next line of input from one of the input files is read and stored in the system variable $_. Line 4 takes this line and copies it into another scalar variable, $line; line 5 then removes the last character—the trailing newline character—from this line.

Line 6 uses printf to write the input line to the standard output file. Because printf is formatting the input, the asterisks all appear in the same columns (column 1 and column 56) on your screen.

16

NOTE

> The previous program is equivalent to the following Perl program (which does not use the -n option):
>
> ```
> while (<>) {
>         # input line is stored in the system variable $_
>         $line = $_;
>         chop ($line);
>         printf ("* %-72s *\n", $line);
> }
> ```

The -n and -e options work well together. For example,

```
C:\> perl -n -e "print $_;" file1 file2 file3
```

The print $_; argument supplied with the -e option is a one-line Perl program. Because the -n option executes the program once for each input line, and reads each input line into the system variable $_, the statement

```
print $_;
```

prints each input line in turn. (Note that the parentheses that normally enclose the argument passed to print have been omitted in this case.)

The previous command can be made even simpler:

```
C:\> perl -n -e "print" file1 file2 file3
```

By default, if no argument is supplied, print assumes that it is to print the contents of $_. And, if the program consists of a single statement, there is no need to include the closing semicolon.

The pattern-matching and substitution operators also operate on $_ by default. For example, the following statement examines the contents of $_ and searches for a digit:

```
$found = /[0-9]/;
```

This default behavior makes it easy to include a search or a substitution in a single-line command. For example:

```
C:\> perl -n -e "print if /[0-9]/" file1 file2 file3
```

This command reads each line of the files `file1`, `file2`, and `file3`. If an input line contains a digit, it is printed.

> **NOTE**
>
> Several other functions use `$_` as the default scalar variable to operate on, which makes those functions ideal for use with the `-n` and `-e` options. A full list of these functions is provided in the description of the `$_` system variable, which is provided on Day 17, "System Variables".

The `-p` Option: Operating on Files and Printing

The `-p` option is similar to the `-n` option: it reads each line of its input files in turn. However, the `-p` option also prints each line it reads. Look at the following example:

```
C:\> perl -p -e ";" file1 file2 file3
```

Here, the `;` is a Perl program consisting of one statement that does nothing.

The `-p` option is designed for use with the `-i` option, described in the following section.

> **NOTE**
>
> If both the `-p` and the `-n` options are specified, the `-n` option is ignored.

The `-i` Option: Editing Files

As you have seen, the `-n` and `-p` options read lines from the files specified on the command line. The `-i` option, when used with the `-p` option, takes the input lines being read and writes them back out to the files from which they came.

For example, consider the following command:

```
C:\> perl -p -i.bak -e "s/abc/def/g;" file1
```

16

This command contains a one-line Perl program that examines the scalar variable $_ and changes all occurrences of abc into def. (Recall that the substitution operator operates on $_ if the =~ operator is not specified.) The -p option ensures that $_ is assigned each line of each input file in turn and that the program is executed once for each input line. Thus, this command changes all occurrences of abc in the file file1 to def.

Here, the .bak file extension specified with the -i option tells the Perl interpreter to copy file1 to file1.old before editing it.

The file extension specified with the -i option can be any character string. By convention, file extensions usually begin with a period; this convention makes it easier for you to spot them when you list the files in your directory.

WARNING

Do not use the -i option with the -n option unless you know what you're doing. The following command also changes all occurrences of abc to def, but it doesn't write out the input lines after it changes them:

```
C:\> perl -n -i -e "s/abc/def/g;" file1 file2 file3
```

Because the -i option specifies that the input files are to be edited, the result is that the contents of file1, file2, and file3 are completely destroyed.

The -i option also works on programs that do not use the -p option but do contain the <> operator inside a loop. For example, consider the following command:

```
C:\> perl -i file1 file2 file3
```

In this case, the Perl interpreter copies the first file, file1, to a temporary file and opens the temporary file for reading. Then, it opens file1 for writing and sets the default output file (the file used by calls to print, write, and printf) to be file1.

After the program finishes reading the temporary file to which file1 was copied, it then copies file2 to a temporary file, opens it for reading, opens file2 for writing, and sets the default output file to be file2. This process continues until the program runs out of input files.

Listing 16.3 is a simple example of a program that edits using the -i option and the <> operator. This program evaluates any arithmetic expressions (containing integers) it sees on a single line and replaces them with their results.

TYPE   **Listing 16.3. A program that edits files using the** `-i` **option.**

```
1:   # p16_3.pl
2:
3:   while ($line = <>) {
4:         while ($line =~
5:                  s#\d+\s*[*+-/]\s*\d+(\s*[*+-/]\s*\d+)*#<x>#) {
6:                  eval ("\$result = $&;");
7:                  $line =~ s/<x>/$result/;
8:         }
9:         print ($line);
10:  }
```

OUTPUT   This program produces no visible output on the screen because the output is written to the files specified on the command line.

ANALYSIS   The `<>` operator at the beginning of the `while` loop (line 3) reads a line at a time from the input file or files. Each line is searched using the pattern shown in line 5. This pattern matches any substring containing the following elements (in the order given):

☐ One or more digits

☐ Zero or more spaces

☐ An `*`, a `+`, a `-`, or a `/` character

☐ Zero or more spaces

☐ One or more digits

☐ Zero or more of the preceding four subpatterns (which matches the last part of expressions such as `4 + 7 - 3`)

This pattern is replaced by a placeholder substring, `<x>`.

Lines 6 and 7 are executed once for each pattern matched in the input line. The matched pattern, an arithmetic expression, is automatically stored in the system variable `$&`; line 6 substitutes this expression into a character string and passes this character string to the function `eval`. The call to `eval` creates a subprogram that evaluates the expression and returns the result in the scalar variable `$result`. Line 7 replaces the placeholder, `<x>`, with the result returned in `$result`.

When all the arithmetic expressions have been evaluated and substituted for, the inner `while` loop terminates, and line 9 calls `print`. Because the `-i` option has been set, the line is written back to the original input file from which it came.

NOTE

Even though you do not know the name of the file handle that represents the file being edited, you can still set the default output file handle to some other file and change it back later.

To perform this task, recall that the `select` function returns the file variable associated with the current default file:

```
$editfile = select (MYFILE);  # change default file
# do your write operations here
select ($editfile);           # change default file back
```

After the second `select` call has been performed, the default output file is, once again, the file being edited.

The -a **Option: Splitting Lines**

The -a option is used with the -n or -p option. If the -a option is set, each input line that is read is automatically split into a list of "words" (sequences of characters that are not white space); this list of words is stored in a special system variable named @F.

For example, if your input file contains the line

```
This    is    a    test.
```

and if a program that is called with the -a option reads this line, the array @F contains the list

```
("This", "is", "a", "test.")
```

The -a option is useful for extracting information from files. Suppose that your input files contain records of the form

```
company_name      quantity_ordered     total_cost
```

such as, for example,

```
JOHN H. SMITH    10      47.32
```

you can use the -a option to easily produce a program that extracts the quantity and total cost fields from these files. Listing 16.4 shows you how.

Listing 16.4. An example of the -a option.

```
1:  # p16_4.pl
2:
3:  # This program is called with the -a and -n options.
4:  while ($F[0] =~ /[^\d.]/) {
5:          shift (@F);
6:          next if (!defined($F[0]));
7:  }
8:  print ("$F[0] $F[1]\n");
```

OUTPUT
```
C:\> perl -a -n p16_4.pl test.txt
10 47.32
106 11.54
C:\>
```

ANALYSIS Because the program is called with the -a option, the array variable @F contains a list, each element of which is a word from the current input line.

Because the company name in the input file might consist of more than one word (such as JOHN H. SMITH), the while loop in lines 4–7 is needed to get rid of everything that isn't a quantity field or a total-cost field. After these fields have been eliminated, line 8 can print the useful fields.

Note that this program just skips over any nonstandard input lines.

The -F Option: Specifying the Split Pattern

The -F option, defined only in Perl 5, is designed to be used in conjunction with the -a option and specifies the pattern to use when you split input lines into words. For example, suppose Listing 16.4 is called as follows:

```
C:\> perl -a -n -F:: p16_4.pl test.txt
```

In this case, the words in the input file are assumed to be separated by a pair of colons, which means that the program is expecting to read lines such as the following:

```
JOHN H. SMITH::10::47.32
```

NOTE

The -F option ignores opening and closing slashes if they are present, because it interprets them as pattern delimiters. This means that the following program invocations are identical:

```
C:\> perl -a -n -F:: p16_4.pl test.txt
C:\> perl -a -n -F/::/ p16_4.pl test.txt
```

The -0 **Option: Specifying Input End-of-Line**

In all the programs you have seen so far, when the Perl interpreter reads a line from an input file or from the keyboard, it reads until it sees a newline character. You can tell Perl that you want the end-of-line input character to be something other than the newline character by specifying the -0 option. (The 0 here is the digit zero, not the letter O.)

With the -0 option, you specify which character is to be the end-of-line character for your input file by providing its ASCII representation in base 8 (octal). For example, the command

```
C:\> perl -0 040 prog.pl infile
```

calls the Perl program named `prog.pl` and specifies that it is to use the space character (ASCII 32, or 40 octal) as the end-of-line character when it reads the input file `infile` (or any other input file).

This means, for example, that if this program reads an input file containing the following

```
Test input.
Here's another line.
```

it will read a total of four input lines:

- [ ] The first input line consists of the word `Test`.
- [ ] The second input line consists of `input.`, followed by a newline character, followed by `Here's`.
- [ ] The third input line consists of the word `another`.
- [ ] The fourth input line consists of the word `line.`, followed by a newline character.

The -0 option provides a quick way to read an input file one word at a time, assuming that each line ends with at least one blank character. (If it doesn't, you can quickly write a Perl program that uses the -i and -p options to add a space to the end of each line in each file.) Listing 16.5 is an example of a program that uses -0 to read an input file one word at a time.

TYPE   **Listing 16.5. A program that uses the -0 option.**

```
1:  # p16_5.pl
2:
3:  while ($line = <>) {
4:          $line =~ s/\n//g;
5:          next if ($line eq "");
6:          print ("$line\n");
7:  }
```

16

OUTPUT

```
C:\> perl -0040 p16_5.pl file1.txt
This
line
contains
five
words.
C:\>
```

ANALYSIS   The `-0040` option is used to specify that the space character is to become the end-of-line character. (Recall that you do not need a space between an option and the value associated with an option.) This means that line 3 reads from the input file until it sees a blank space.

Not everything read by line 3 is a word, of course. There are two types of lines that are not particularly useful that the program must check for:

- [ ] Empty lines, which are generated when the input file contains two consecutive spaces

- [ ] Lines containing the newline character (remember, the newline character is no longer an end-of-line character, so now it actually appears in input lines)

Line 4 checks whether any newline characters are contained in the current input line. The substitution in this line is a global substitution, because an input line can contain two or more newline characters. (This occurs when an input file contains a blank line.)

After all the newline characters have been eliminated, line 5 checks whether the resulting input line is empty. If it is, the program continues with the next input line. If the resulting input line is not empty, the input line must be a useful word, and line 6 prints it.

 NOTE

> If you specify the value `00` (octal zero) with the `-0` option, the Perl interpreter reads until it sees two newline characters. This enables you to read an entire paragraph at a time.
>
> If you specify no value with the `-0` option, the null character (ASCII 0) is assumed.

The `-l` Option: Specifying Output End-of-Line

The `-l` option enables you to specify an output end-of-line character for use in `print` statements. (Here, l is the lowercase letter l, not the numerical one.)

16

Like the -0 option, the -l option accepts a base-8 (octal) integer that indicates the ASCII representation of the character you want to use.

When the -l option is specified, the Perl interpreter does two things:

☐ If the -n or -p option is specified, each input line read in from the standard input file has its last character (the line terminator) removed. (The Perl interpreter takes this action because it assumes that you want to replace the old end-of-line character with the one specified by the -l option.)

☐ When you call the print function, the output written by print will be immediately followed by the character specified by the -l option.

If you do not specify a value with the -l option, the Perl interpreter uses the character specified by the -0 option, if it is defined. If -0 has not been specified, the end-of-line character is defined to be the newline character.

WARNING

If you are using both the -l and the -0 options and you do not provide a value with the -l option, the order of the options becomes significant, because the options are processed from left to right.

If the -l option appears first, the output end-of-line character is set to the newline character. If the -0 option appears first, the output end-of-line character (set by -l) becomes the same as the input end-of-line character (set by -0).

Listing 16.6 is a simple example of a program that uses -l.

 Listing 16.6. A program that uses the -l option.

```
1:  # p16_6.pl
2:
3:  print ("Hello!");
4:  print ("This is a very simple test program!");
```

OUTPUT
```
C:\> perl -l012 p16_6.pl
Hello!
        This is a very simple test program!
C:\>
```

ANALYSIS The -l012 option in the command line sets the output-line character to the new-line character. This means that every print statement in the program will have a newline character added to it. As a consequence, the output from lines 3 and 4 appear on separate lines.

NOTE You can control the input and output end-of-line characters by using the system variables $/ and $\ as well. For a description of these system variables, refer to Day 17.

The -x Option: Extracting a Program from a Message

The -x option enables you to process a Perl program that appears in the middle of a file (such as a file containing an electronic mail message, which usually contains some mail-routing information). When the -x option is specified, the Perl interpreter ignores every line in the program until it sees a header comment that contains the word perl. A header comment is a comment beginning with the #! characters.

After the Perl interpreter sees the header comment, it then processes the program as usual until one of the following three conditions occurs:

☐ The bottom of the program file is reached.

☐ The program file contains a line consisting of just the Ctrl+D or Ctrl+Z character. (Here, Ctrl+D means the combination of the Ctrl key and D key; Ctrl+Z is the combination of the Ctrl key and Z key.)

☐ The program file contains a line consisting of the following statement (by itself):

_ _END_ _

If the Perl interpreter reads one of the end-of-program lines (the second and third conditions in the preceding list), it ignores everything appearing after that line in the file.

Listing 16.7 is a simple example of a program that works if run with the -x option.

TYPE **Listing 16.7. A Perl program contained in a file.**

```
1: # p16_7.pl
2: Here is a Perl program that appears in the middle
3: of a file.
4: The stuff up here is junk, and the Perl interpreter
5: will ignore it.
6: The next line is the start of the actual program.
7: #!perl
8:
9: print ("Hello, world!\n");
```

16

OUTPUT
```
C:\> perl -x p16_7.pl
Hello, world!
C:\>
```

ANALYSIS If this program is started with the -x option, the Perl interpreter skips over everything until it sees line 7. (Needless to say, if you try to run this program without specifying the -x option, the Perl interpreter will complain.) Line 9 then prints the message Hello, world.

When the Perl interpreter reaches the end of the file, it stops and exits.

Miscellaneous Options

The following sections describe some of the more exotic options you can pass to the Perl interpreter. You are not likely to need any of these options unless you are doing something unusual (and you really know what you are doing).

The -u Option

The -u option, used under UNIX, tells the Perl interpreter to generate a core dump file. This file can then be examined and manipulated. It's not used for Windows NT or Windows 95.

The -U Option

The -U option tells the Perl interpreter to enable you to perform "unsafe" operations in your program. (Basically, you'll know that an operation is considered unsafe when the Perl interpreter doesn't let you perform it without specifying the -U option!)

The -S Option

The -S option tells the Perl interpreter that your program might be contained in any of the directories specified by your PATH environment variable. The Perl interpreter checks each of these directories in turn, in the order in which they are specified, to see whether your program is located there.

NOTE
> You need to use -S only if you are running your Perl program using the perl command, as in
> ```
> C:\> perl -S myprog.pl
> ```

> If you are running the program using a command such as
>
> ```
> C:\> myprog.pl
> ```
>
> your command-line shell (normally) treats it like any other command and searches the directories specified in your PATH environment variable even if you don't specify the -s option.

The -D Option

The -D option sets the Perl interpreter's internal debugging flags. This option is specified with an integer value (for example, -D 256).

Since build 110 of Perl 5 for Win32 is not compiled for debugging, the -D option does nothing.

For details on this option, refer to the online manual page for Perl.

NOTE

> The internal debugging flags specified by -D have nothing to do with the Perl debugger, which is specified by the -d option.
>
> The debugging flags specified by -D provide information on how Perl itself works, not on how your program works.

The -T Option: Writing Secure Programs

The -T option specifies that data obtained from the outside world cannot be used in any command that modifies your file system. This feature enables you to write secure programs for system-administration tasks.

This option is only available in Perl 5 and Perl 5 for Win32.

The -d Option: Using the Perl Debugger

One final option that is quite useful is -d. This option tells the Perl interpreter to run your program using the Perl debugger. For a complete description of the Perl debugger and how to use it, refer to Day 21, "The Perl Debugger."

NOTE

> If you are specifying the -d option, you still can use other options.

16

Summary

Today you have learned how to specify options when you run your Perl programs. An option is a dash followed by a single letter, and optionally followed by a value to be associated with the option. Options lacking associated values can be grouped together.

Available options include those that list the Perl version number, check your syntax, display warnings, allow single-line programs on the command line, invoke the C preprocessor, automatically read from the input files, and edit files in place.

Q&A

Q Why does -v display the Perl version number without running the program?

A This option enables you to check whether the version of Perl you are running is capable of running your program. If an old copy of Perl is running on your machine, your program might not work properly.

Q What options enable me to write a program that edits every line of a file?

A Use the -i (edit in place) and -p (print each line) options. (These options are often used with the -e option to perform an editing command from a command shell.)

Q Why does the -p option override the -n option?

A The -p option tells the Perl interpreter that you want to print each input line that you read, and the -n option tells it that you don't want to do so..

-p overrides -n because -p is safer; -p can do everything that -n does. If you really want -n, you can throw away the output from -p. If you really want -p and get -n, you won't get the output you want.

Workshop

The Workshop provides quiz questions to help you solidify your understanding of the material covered, and exercises to give you experience in using what you've learned. Try to understand the quiz and exercise answers before you go on to tomorrow's lesson. You can find the answers in Appendix B, "Answers."

Quiz

1. What do the following options do?

   a. `-0`

   b. `-s`

   c. `-w`

   d. `-x`

   e. `-n`

2. What happens when `-l` and `-0` are both specified, and

   a. `-l` appears first?

   b. `-0` appears first?

3. Why can the `-i` and `-n` options destroy input files when included together?

4. How does the Perl interpreter distinguish options for the interpreter from options for the program itself?

Exercises

1. Write a program that replaces all the newline characters in the file `testfile` with colons. Use only command-line options to do this.

2. Write a one-line program that prints only the lines containing the word `the`.

3. Write a one-line program that prints the second word of each input line.

4. Write a program that prints `Hello!` if you pass the `-H` switch to it, and that prints `Goodbye!` if you pass the `-G` switch.

5. Write a one-line program that converts all lowercase letters to uppercase.

6. **BUG BUSTER:** What is wrong with this command line?

   ```
   C:\> perl -i -n -e "s/abc/def/g";
   ```

7. **BUG BUSTER:** What is wrong with this command line?

   ```
   C:\> perl -ipe "s/abc/def/g";
   ```

16

Day 17

System Variables

Today's lesson describes the built-in system variables that can be referenced from every Perl program. These system variables are divided into five groups:

- ☐ Global scalar variables
- ☐ Pattern-system variables
- ☐ File-system variables
- ☐ Array-system variables
- ☐ Built-in file variables

The following sections describe these groups of system variables, and also explain how to provide English-language equivalents of their variable names.

Global Scalar Variables

The *global scalar variables* are built-in system variables that behave just like the scalar variables you create in the main body of your program. This means that these variables have the following properties:

☐ Each built-in global scalar variable stores only one scalar value.

☐ Only one copy of a global scalar variable is defined in a program.

Other kinds of built-in scalar variables, which you will see later in this lesson, do not behave in this way.

The following sections describe the global scalar variables your Perl programs can use.

The Default Scalar Variable: $_

The most commonly used global scalar variable is the $_ variable. Many Perl functions and operators modify the contents of $_ if you do not explicitly specify the scalar variable on which they are to operate.

The following functions and operators work with the $_ variable by default:

☐ The pattern-matching operator

☐ The substitution operator

☐ The translation operator

☐ The <> operator, if it appears in a `while` or `for` conditional expression

☐ The `chop` function

☐ The `print` function

☐ The `study` function

The Pattern-Matching Operator and $_

Normally, the pattern-matching operator examines the value stored in the variable specified by a corresponding =~ or !~ operator. For example, the following statement prints `hi` if the string `abc` is contained in the value stored in `$val`:

```
print ("hi") if ($val =~ /abc/);
```

By default, the pattern-matching operator examines the value stored in $_. This means you can leave out the =~ operator if you are searching $_:

```
print ("hi") if ($_ =~ /abc/);
print ("hi") if (/abc/);          # these two are the same
```

NOTE

If you want to use the !~ (true-if-pattern-not-matched) operator, you will always need to specify it explicitly, even if you are examining $_:

```
print ("hi") if ($_ !~ /abc/);
```

If the Perl interpreter sees just a pattern enclosed in / characters, it assumes the existence of an =~ operator.

With $_, you can use pattern-sequence memory to extract subpatterns from a string and assign them to an array variable:

```
$_ = "This string contains the number 25.11.";
@array = /-?(\d+)\.?(\d+)/;
```

In the second statement, each subpattern enclosed in parentheses becomes an element of the list assigned to @array. As a consequence, @array is assigned (25,11).

In Perl 5 for Win32, a statement such as

```
@array = /-?(\d+)\.?(\d+)/;
```

also assigns the extracted subpatterns to the pattern-sequence scalar variables $1, $2, and so on. This means that the statement assigns 25 to $1 and 11 to $2. Perl 4 supports assignment of subpatterns to arrays, but does not assign the subpatterns to the pattern-sequence variables.

The Substitution Operator and $_

The substitution operator, like the pattern-matching operator, normally modifies the contents of the variable specified by the =~ or !~ operator. For example, the following statement searches for abc in the value stored in $val and replaces it with def:

```
$val =~ s/abc/def/;
```

The substitution operator uses the $_ variable if you do not specify a variable using =~. For example, the following statement replaces the first occurrence of abc in $_ with def:

```
s/abc/def/;
```

Similarly, the following statement replaces all white space (spaces, tabs, and newline characters) in $_ with a single space:

```
/\s+/ /g;
```

When you substitute inside $_, the substitution operator returns the number of substitutions performed:

```
$subcount = s/abc/def/g;
```

Here, $subcount contains the number of occurrences of abc that have been replaced by def. If abc is not contained in the value stored in $_, $subcount is assigned 0.

The Translation Operator and $_

The behavior of the translation operator is similar to that of the pattern-matching and substitution operators: it normally operates on the variable specified by =~, and it operates on $_ if no =~ operator is included. For example, the following statement translates all lowercase letters in the value stored in $_ to their uppercase equivalents:

```
tr/a-z/A-Z/;
```

Like the substitution operator, if the translation operator is working with $_, it returns the number of operations performed. For example:

```
$conversions = tr/a-z/A-Z/;
```

Here, $conversions contains the number of lowercase letters converted to uppercase.

You can use this feature of tr to count the number of occurrences of particular characters in a file. Listing 17.1 is an example of a program that performs this operation.

TYPE   **Listing 17.1. A program that counts using tr.**

```
1:  # p17_1.pl
2:
3:  print ("Specify the nonblank characters you want to count:\n");
4:  $countstring = <STDIN>;
5:  chop ($countstring);
6:  @chars = split (/\s*/, $countstring);
7:  while ($input = <>) {
8:          $_ = $input;
9:          foreach $char (@chars) {
10:                 eval ("\$count = tr/$char/$char/;");
11:                 $count{$char} += $count;
12:         }
13: }
14: foreach $char (sort (@chars)) {
15:         print ("$char appears $count{$char} times\n");
16: }
```

OUTPUT
```
C:\> perl p17_1.pl file1
Specify the nonblank characters you want to count:
abc
a appears 8 times
c appears 3 times
b appears 2 times
C:\>
```

17

ANALYSIS This program first asks the user for a line of input containing the characters to be counted. These characters can be separated by spaces or jammed into a single word.

Line 5 takes the line of input containing the characters to be counted and removes the trailing newline character. Line 6 then splits the line of input into separate characters, each of which is stored in an element of the array @chars. The pattern /\s*/ splits on zero or more occurrences of a white-space character; this splits on every nonblank character and skips over the blank characters.

Line 7 reads a line of input from a file whose name is specified on the command line. Line 8 takes this line and stores it in the system variable $_. (In most cases, system variables can be assigned to, just like other variables.)

Lines 9–12 count the number of occurrences of each character in the input string read in line 4. Each character, in turn, is stored in $char, and the value of $char is substituted into the string in line 10. This string is then passed to eval, which executes the translate operation contained in the string.

The translate operation doesn't actually do anything, because it is "translating" a character to itself. However, it returns the number of translations performed, which means that it returns the number of occurrences of the character. This count is assigned to $count.

For example, suppose that the variable $char contains the character e and that $_ contains Hi there!. In this case, the string in line 10 becomes the following because e is substituted for $char in the string:

```
$count = tr/e/e/;
```

The call to eval executes this statement, which counts the number of es in Hi there!. Because there are two es in Hi there!, $count is assigned 2.

An associative array, %count, keeps track of the number of occurrences of each of the characters being counted. Line 11 adds the count returned by line 10 to the associative array element whose subscript is the character currently being counted. For example, if the program is currently counting the number of es, this number is added to the element $count{"e"}.

After all input lines have been read and their characters counted, lines 14–16 print the total number of occurrences of each character by examining the elements of %count.

17

The <> Operator and $_

In Listing 17.1, which you've just seen, the program reads a line of input into a scalar variable named $input and then assigns it to $_. There is a quicker way to carry out this task, however. You can replace

```
while ($input = <>) {
        $_ = $input;
        # more stuff here
}
```

with the following code:

```
while (<>) {
        # more stuff here
}
```

If the <> operator appears in a conditional expression that is part of a loop (an expression that is part of a conditional statement such as while or for) and it is not to the right of an assignment operator, the Perl interpreter automatically assigns the resulting input line to the scalar variable $_.

For example, Listing 17.2 shows a simple way to print the first character of every input line read from the standard input file.

TYPE

Listing 17.2. A simple program that assigns to $_ using <STDIN>.

```
1:  # p17_2.pl
2:
3:  while (<STDIN>) {
4:          ($first) = split (//, $_);
5:          print ("$first\n");
6:  }
```

OUTPUT

```
C:\> perl p17_2.pl
This is a test.
T
Here is another line.
H
^Z
C:\>
```

ANALYSIS   Because <STDIN> is inside a conditional expression and is not assigned to a scalar variable, the Perl interpreter assigns the input line to $_. The program then retrieves the first character by passing $_ to split.

WARNING

The `<>` operator assigns to `$_` only if it is contained in a conditional expression in a loop. The statement

```
<STDIN>;
```

reads a line of input from the standard input file and throws it away without changing the contents of `$_`. Similarly, the following statement does not change the value of `$_`:

```
if (<>) {
        print ("The input files are not all empty.\n");
}
```

The `chop` Function and `$_`

By default, the `chop` function operates on the value stored in the `$_` variable. For example:

```
while (<>) {
      chop;
      # you can do things with $_ here
}
```

Here, the call to `chop` removes the last character from the value stored in `$_`. Because the conditional expression in the `while` statement has just assigned a line of input to `$_`, `chop` gets rid of the newline character that terminates each input line.

The `print` Function and `$_`

The `print` function also operates on `$_` by default. The following statement writes the contents of `$_` to the standard output file:

```
print;
```

Listing 17.3 is an example of a program that simply writes out its input, which it assumes is stored in `$_`.

TYPE **Listing 17.3. An example using `$_`.**

```
1:  # p17_3.pl
2:
3:  print while (<>);
```

 OUTPUT

```
C:\> perl p17_3.pl file1
This is the only line in file "file1".
C:\>
```

17

ANALYSIS   This program uses the <> operator to read one line of input at a time and store it in $_. If the line is non-empty, the print function is called; because no variable is specified with print, it writes out the contents of $_.

WARNING

> You can use this default version of print only if you are writing to the default output file (which is usually STDOUT but can be changed using the select function). If you are specifying a file variable when you call print, you also must specify the value you are printing.
>
> For example, to send the contents of $_ to the output file MYFILE, use the following command:
>
> ```
> print MYFILE ($_);
> ```

The study **Function and** $_

If you do not specify a variable when you call study, this function uses $_ by default:

```
study;
```

The study function increases the efficiency of programs that repeatedly search the same variable. This function is described on Day 12, "File-System, String, and Mathematical Functions."

Benefits of the $_ **Variable**

The default behavior of the functions listed previously is useful to remember when you are writing one-line Perl programs for use with the –e option. For example, the following command is a quick way to display the contents of the files file1, file2, and file3:

```
$ perl -e "print while <>;" file1 file2 file3
```

Similarly, the following command changes all occurrences of abc in file1, file2, and file3 to def:

```
$ perl -ipe "s/abc/def/g" file1 file2 file3
```

 TIP

> Although $_ is useful in cases such as the preceding one, don't overuse it. Many Perl programmers write programs that have references to $_ running like an invisible thread through their programs.
>
> Programs that overuse $_ are hard to read and are easier to break than programs that explicitly reference scalar variables you have named yourself.

17

The Program Name: $0

The $0 variable contains the name of the program you are running. For example, if your program is named perl1, the statement

```
print ("Now executing $0...\n");
```

displays the following on your screen:

```
Now executing perl1...
```

The $0 variable is useful if you are writing programs that call other programs. If an error occurs, you can determine which program detected the error:

```
die ("$0: can't open input file\n");
```

Here, including $0 in the string passed to die enables you to specify the filename in your error message. (Of course, you can always leave off the trailing newline, which tells Perl to print the filename and the line number when printing the error message. However, $0 enables you to print the filename without the line number, if that's what you want.)

NOTE

You can change your program name while it is running by modifying the value stored in $0.

The Version Number: $]

The $] system variable contains the current version number. You can use this variable to ensure that the Perl on which you are running this program is the right version of Perl (or is a version that can run your program).

Normally, $] contains a character string similar to this:

```
$RCSfile: perl.c,v $$Revision: 4.0.1.8 $$Date: 1993/02/05 19:39:30 $
Patch level: 36
```

The useful parts of this string are the revision number and the patch level. The first part of the revision number indicates that this is version 4 of Perl. The version number and the patch level are often combined; in this notation, this is version 4.036 of Perl.

You can use the pattern-matching operator to extract the useful information from $]. Listing 17.4 shows one way to do it.

Listing 17.4. A program that extracts information from the $] variable.

```
1:  # p17_4.pl
2:
3:  $revision = $];
4:  print ("revision $revision\n");
```

OUTPUT
```
C:\> perl p17_4.pl
revision 5.001
C:\>
```

ANALYSIS This program just obtains the revision from $] in line 3. The revision number is printed out in line 4.

WARNING

On some other machines (for example, UNIX machines) the value contained in $] might be completely different from the value used in this example. If you are not sure whether $] has a useful value, write a little program that just prints $]. If this program prints something useful, you'll know that you can run programs that compare $] with an expected value.

The Input Line Separator: $/

When the Perl interpreter is told to read a line of input from a file, it usually reads characters until it reads a newline character. The newline character can be thought of as an input line separator; it indicates the end of a particular line.

The system variable $/ contains the current input line separator. To change the input line separator, change the value of $/. The $/ variable can be more than one character long to handle the case in which lines are separated by more than one character. If you set $/ to the null character, the Perl interpreter assumes that the input line separator is two newline characters.

Listing 17.5 shows how changing $/ can affect your program.

Listing 17.5. A program that changes the value of $/.

```
1:  # p17_5.pl
2:
3:  $/ = ":";
4:  $line = <STDIN>;
5:  print ("$line\n");
```

OUTPUT

```
C:\> perl p17_5.pl
Here is some test input: here is the end.
Here is some test input:
C:\>
```

ANALYSIS Line 3 sets the value of $/ to a colon. This means that when line 4 reads from the standard input file, it reads until it sees a colon. As a consequence, $line contains the following character string:

```
Here is some test input:
```

Note that the colon is included as part of the input line (just as, in the normal case, the trailing newline character is included as part of the line).

WARNING

> The –0 (zero, not the letter O) switch sets the value of $/. If you change the value of $/ in your program, the value specified by –0 will be thrown away.
>
> To temporarily change the value of $/ and then restore it to the value specified by –0, save the current value of $/ in another variable before changing it.
>
> For more information on –0, refer to Day 16, "Command-Line Options."

The Output Line Separator: $\

The system variable $\ contains the current output line separator. This is a character or sequence of characters that is automatically printed after every call to print.

By default, $\ is the null character, which indicates that no output line separator is to be printed. Listing 17.6 shows how you can set an output line separator.

TYPE   **Listing 17.6. A program that uses the** $\backslash$ **variable.**

```
1:  # p17_6.pl
2:
3:  $\ = "\n";
4:  print ("Here is one line.");
5:  print ("Here is another line.");
```

OUTPUT
```
C:\> perl p17_6.pl
Here is one line.
Here is another line.
C:\>
```

ANALYSIS   Line 3 sets the output line separator to the newline character. This means that a list passed to a subsequent print statement will always appear on an output line of its own. Lines 4 and 5 now no longer need to include a newline character as the last character in the line.

WARNING

> The $-l$ option sets the value of $\backslash$. If you change $\backslash$ in your program without saving it first, the value supplied with $-l$ will be lost. Refer to Day 16 for more information on the $-l$ option.

The Output-Field Separator: $,

The $, variable contains the character or sequence of characters to be printed between elements when print is called. For example, in the following statement the Perl interpreter first writes the contents of $a:

```
print ($a, $b);
```

It then writes the contents of $, and then, finally, the contents of $b.

Normally, the $, variable is initialized to the null character, which means that the elements of a print statement are printed next to one another. Listing 17.7 is a program that sets $, before calling print.

TYPE   **Listing 17.7. A program that uses the** $, **variable.**

```
1:  # p17_7.pl
2:
3:  $a = "hello";
4:  $b = "there";
5:  $, = " ";
6:  $\ = "\n";
7:  print ($a, $b);
```

OUTPUT

```
C:\> perl p17_7.pl
hello there
C:\>
```

 ANALYSIS Line 5 sets the value of $, to a space. Consequently, line 7 prints a space after printing $a and before printing $b.

Note that $\, the default output separator, is set to the newline character. This setting ensures that the terminating newline character immediately follows $b. By contrast, the following statement prints a space before printing the trailing newline character:

```
print ($a, $b, "\n");
```

NOTE

> Here's another way to print the newline immediately after the final element that doesn't involve setting $\:
>
> ```
> print ($a, $b . "\n");
> ```
>
> Here, the trailing newline character is part of the second element being printed. Because $b and \n are part of the same element, no space is printed between them.

The Array-Element Separator: $"

Normally, if an array is printed inside a string, the elements of the array are separated by a single space. For example:

```
@array = ("This", "is", "a", "list");
print ("@array\n");
```

Here, the print statement prints

```
This is a list
```

A space is printed between each pair of array elements.

The built-in system variable that controls this situation is the $" variable. By default, $" contains a space. Listing 17.8 shows how you can control your array output by changing the value of $".

TYPE **Listing 17.8. A program that uses the $" variable.**

```
1:  # p17_8.pl
2:
3:  $" = "::";
4:  @array = ("This", "is", "a", "list");
5:  print ("@array\n");
```

`C:\> `**`perl p17_8.pl`**
`This::is::a::list`
`C:\>`

 Line 3 sets the array element separator to `::` (two colons). Array element separators, like other separators you can define, can be more than one character long.

Line 5 prints the contents of `@array`. Each pair of elements is separated by the value stored in `$"`, which is two colons.

> **NOTE**
>
> The `$"` variable affects only entire arrays printed inside strings. If you print two variables together in a string, as in
>
> `print ("$a$b\n");`
>
> the contents of the two variables are printed with nothing separating them regardless of the value of `$"`.
>
> To change how arrays are printed outside strings, use `$\`, described earlier today.

The Number Output Format: `$#`

By default, when the `print` function prints a number, it prints it as a 20-digit floating-point number in compact format. This means that the following statements are identical if the value stored in `$x` is a number:

```
print ($x);
printf ("%.20g", $x);
```

To change the default format that `print` uses to print numbers, change the value of the `$#` variable. For example, to specify only 15 digits of precision, use this statement:

```
$# = "%.15g";
```

This value must be a floating-point field specifier, as used in `printf` and `sprintf`.

> **NOTE**
>
> The `$#` variable does not affect values that are not numbers and has no effect on the `printf`, `write`, and `sprintf` functions.

For more information on the field specifiers you can use as the default value in `$#`, see the section "Formatting Output Using `printf`" of Day 11, "Formatting Your Output."

The $# variable is deprecated in Perl 5. This means that although $# is supported, it is not recommended for use, and might be removed from future versions of Perl.

The `eval` **Error Message:** $@

If a statement executed by the `eval` function contains an error, or an error occurs during the execution of the statement, the error message is stored in the system variable $@. The program that called `eval` can decide either to print the error message or to perform some other action.

For example, the statement

```
eval ("This is not a perl statement");
```

assigns the following string to $@:

```
syntax error in file (eval) at line 1, next 2 tokens "This is"
```

The $@ variable also returns the error generated by a call to `die` inside an `eval`. The following statement assigns this string to $@:

```
eval ("die (\"nothing happened\")");
nothing happened at (eval) line 1.
```

NOTE

The $@ variable also returns error messages generated by the `require` function. See Day 19, "Object-Oriented Programming in Perl," for more information on `require`.

The System Error Code: $?

The $? variable returns the error status generated by calls to the `system` function or by calls to functions enclosed in back quotes, as in the following:

```
$username = 'hostname';
```

The error status stored in $? consists of two parts:

☐ The exit value (return code) of the process called by `system` or specified in back quotes

☐ A status field that indicates how the process was terminated, if it terminated abnormally

The value stored in $?$ is a 16-bit integer. The upper eight bits are the exit value, and the lower eight bits are the status field. To retrieve the exit value, use the $>>$ operator to shift the eight bits to the right:

```
$retcode = $? >> 8;
```

For more information on the status field, refer to the online manual page for the wait function or to the file /usr/include/sys/wait.h. For more information on commands in back quotes, refer to Day 14, "Packages, Modules, and System Functions."

The System Error Message: $!

Some Perl library functions call system library functions. If a system library function generates an error, the error code generated by the function is assigned to the $!$ variable. The Perl library functions that call system library functions vary from machine to machine.

NOTE

The $!$ variable in Perl is equivalent to the errno variable in the C programming language.

The Current Line Number: $.

The $.$ variable contains the line number of the last line read from an input file. If more than one input file is being read, $.$ contains the line number of the last input file read. Listing 17.9 shows how $.$ works.

TYPE **Listing 17.9. A program that uses the $.$ variable.**

```
1:  # p17_9.pl
2:
3:  open (FILE1, "file1") ||
4:          die ("Can't open file1\n");
5:  open (FILE2, "file2") ||
6:          die ("Can't open file2\n");
7:  $input = <FILE1>;
8:  $input = <FILE1>;
9:  print ("line number is $.\n");
10: $input = <FILE2>;
11: print ("line number is $.\n");
12: $input = <FILE1>;
13: print ("line number is $.\n");
```

17

```
C:\> perl p17_9.pl
line number is 2
line number is 1
line number is 3
C:\>
```

 When line 9 is executed, the input file FILE1 has had two lines read from it. This means that $. contains the value 2. Line 10 then reads from FILE2. Because it reads the first line from this file, $. now has the value 1. When line 12 reads a third line from FILE1, $. is set to the value 3. The Perl interpreter remembers that two lines have already been read from FILE1.

NOTE

If the program is reading using <>, which reads from the files listed on the command line, $. treats the input files as if they are one continuous file. The line number is not reset when a new input file is opened.

You can use eof to test whether a particular file has ended, and then reset $. yourself (by assigning zero to it) before reading from the next file.

Multiline Matching: $*

Normally, the operators that match patterns (the pattern-matching operator and the substitution operator) assume that the character string being searched is a single line of text. If the character string being searched consists of more than one line of text (in other words, it contains newline characters), set the system variable $* to 1.

NOTE

By default, $* is set to 0, which indicates that multiline pattern matches are not required.

WARNING

The $* variable is deprecated in Perl 5. If you are running Perl 5, use the m pattern-matching option when matching in a multiple-line string. Refer to Day 7, "Pattern Matching," for more details on this option.

The First Array Subscript: $[

Normally, when a program references the first element of an array, it does so by specifying the subscript 0. For example:

```
@myarray = ("Here", "is", "a", "list");
$here = $myarray[0];
```

The array element `$myarray[0]` contains the string `Here`, which is assigned to `$here`.

If you are not comfortable with using 0 as the subscript for the first element of an array, you can change this setting by changing the value of the `$[` variable. This variable indicates which value is to be used as the subscript for the first array element.

Here is the preceding example, modified to use 1 as the first array element subscript:

```
$[ = 1;
@myarray = ("Here", "is", "a", "list");
$here = $myarray[1];
```

In this case, the subscript 1 now references the first array element. This means that `$here` is assigned `Here`, as before.

 TIP
> Don't change the value of `$[`. It is too easy for a casual reader of your program to forget that the subscript 0 no longer references the first element of the array. Besides, using 0 as the subscript for the first element is standard practice in many programming languages, including C and C++.

 NOTE
> `$[` is deprecated in Perl 5.

Multidimensional Associative Arrays and the $; Variable

So far, all the arrays you've seen have been one-dimensional arrays, which are arrays in which each array element is referenced by only one subscript. For example, the following statement uses the subscript `foo` to access an element of the associative array named `%array`:

```
$myvar = $array{"foo"};
```

(More details on multidimensional associative arrays are covered on Day 18.)

Perl enables you to simulate a multidimensional associative array using the built-in system variable $;.

Here is an example of a statement that accesses a (simulated) multidimensional array:

```
$myvar = $array{"foo","bar"};
```

When the Perl interpreter sees this statement, it converts it to this:

```
$myvar = $array{"foo" . $; . "bar"};
```

The system variable $; serves as a `subscript separator`. It automatically replaces any comma that is separating two array subscripts.

Here is another example of two equivalent statements:

```
$myvar = $array{"s1", 4, "hi there"};
$myvar = $array{"s1".$;.4.$;."hi there"};
```

The second statement shows how the value of the $; variable is inserted into the array subscript.

By default, the value of $; is \034 (the Ctrl+\ character). You can define $; to be any value you want. Listing 17.10 is an example of a program that sets $;.

 Listing 17.10. A program that uses the $; variable.

```
1:  # p17_10.pl
2:
3:  $; = "::";
4:  $array{"hello","there"} = 46;
5:  $test1 = $array{"hello","there"};
6:  $test2 = $array{"hello::there"};
7:  print ("$test1 $test2\n");
```

OUTPUT
```
C:\> perl p17_10.pl
46 46
C:\>
```

ANALYSIS Line 3 sets $; to the string `::`. As a consequence, the subscript `"hello","there"` in lines 4 and 5 is really `hello::there` because the Perl interpreter replaces the comma with the value of $;.

Line 7 shows that both `"hello","there"` and `hello::there` refer to the same element of the associative array.

WARNING

> If you set `$;`, be careful not to set it to a character that you are actually using in a subscript. For example, if you set `$;` to `::`, the following statements reference the same element of the array:
>
> ```
> $array{"a::b", "c"} = 1;
> $array{"a", "b::c"} = 2;
> ```
>
> In each case, the Perl interpreter replaces the comma with `::`, producing the subscript `a::b::c`.

The Word-Break Specifier: `$:`

On Day 11 you learned how to format your output using print formats and the `write` statement. Each print format contains one or more value fields that specify how output is to appear on the page.

If a value field in a print format begins with the `^` character, the Perl interpreter puts a word in the value field only if there is room enough for the entire word. For example, in the following program (a duplicate of Listing 11.9):

```
1:  # p11_9.pl
2:
3:  $string = "Here\nis an unbalanced line of\ntext.\n";
4:  $~ = "OUTLINE";
5:  write;
6:
7:  format OUTLINE =
8:  ^<<<<<<<<<<<<<<<<<<<<<<<<<<
9:  $string
10: .
```

the call to `write` uses the `OUTLINE` print format to write the following to the screen:

```
Here is an unbalanced line
```

Note that the word `of` is not printed because it cannot fit into the `OUTLINE` value field.

To determine whether a word can fit in a value field, the Perl interpreter counts the number of characters between the next character to be formatted and the next word-break character. A *word-break character* is one that denotes either the end of a word or a place where a word can be split into two parts.

By default, the legal word-break characters in Perl are the space character, the newline character, and the – (hyphen) character. The acceptable word-break characters are stored in the system variable `$:`.

17

To change the list of acceptable word-break characters, change the value of `$:`. For example, to ensure that all hyphenated words are in the same line of formatted output, define `$:` as shown here:

```
$: = " \n";
```

Now only the space and newline characters are legal word-break characters.

WARNING

Normally, the tab character is not a word-break character. To allow lines to be broken on tabs, add the tab character to the list specified by the `$:` variable:

```
$: = " \t\n-";
```

The Perl Process ID: `$$`

The `$$` system variable contains the process ID for the Perl interpreter itself. This is also the process ID for your program.

The Current Filename: `$ARGV`

When you use the `<>` operator, the Perl interpreter reads input from each file named on the command line. For example, suppose that you are executing the program `myprog` as shown here:

```
$ myprog test1 test2 test3
```

In `myprog`, the first occurrence of the `<>` operator reads from `test1`. Subsequent occurrences of `<>` continue reading from `test1` until it is exhausted; at this point, `<>` reads from `test2`. This process continues until all the input files have been read.

On Day 6, "Reading from and Writing to Files," you learned that the `@ARGV` array lists the elements of the command line and that the first element of `@ARGV` is removed when the `<>` operator reads a line. (`@ARGV` is discussed in more detail later today.)

When the `<>` operator reads from a file for the first time, it assigns the name of the file to the `$ARGV` system variable. This enables you to keep track of what file is currently being read. Listing 17.11 shows how you can use `$ARGV`.

TYPE **Listing 17.11. A simple file-searching program using** $ARGV.

```
1:  # p17_11.pl
2:
3:  print ("Enter the search pattern:\n");
4:  $string = <STDIN>;
5:  chop ($string);
6:  while ($line = <>) {
7:          if ($line =~ /$string/) {
8:                  print ("$ARGV:$line");
9:          }
10: }
```

OUTPUT
```
C:\> perl p17_11.pl file1 file2 file3
Enter the string to search:
the
file1:This line contains the word "the".
C:\>
```

ANALYSIS This program reads each line of the input files that are supplied on the command line. If a line contains the pattern specified by $string, line 8 prints out the name of the file and then prints the line itself. Note that the pattern in $string can contain special pattern characters.

NOTE

> If <> is reading from the standard input file (which occurs when you have not specified any input files on the command line), $ARGV contains the string - (a single hyphen).

The Write Accumulator: $^A

The $^A variable is used by write to store formatted lines to be printed. The contents of $^A are erased after the line is printed.

This variable is defined only in Perl 5.

The Internal Debugging Value: $^D

The $^D variable displays the current internal debugging value. This variable is defined only when the –D switch has been specified and when your Perl interpreter has been compiled with debugging included.

See your online Perl documentation for more details on debugging Perl. (Unless you are using an experimental version of Perl, you're not likely to need to debug it.)

17

The System File Flag: $^F

The $^F variable controls whether files are to be treated as system files.

Normally, only STDIN, STDOUT, and STDERR are treated as system files, and the value assigned to $^F is 2. Unless you are on a UNIX machine, are familiar with file descriptors, and want to do something exotic with them, you are not likely to need to use the $^F system variable.

Controlling File Editing Using $^I

The $^I variable is set to a nonzero value by the Perl interpreter when you specify the -i option (which edits files as they are read by the <> operator).

The following statement turns off the editing of files being read by <>:

```
undef ($^I);
```

When $^I is undefined, the next input file is opened for reading, and the standard output file is no longer changed.

Do	Don't

DO open the files for input and output yourself if your program wants to edit some of its input files and not others; this process is easier to follow.

DON'T use $^I if you are reading files using the -n or -p option unless you really know what you are doing, because you are not likely to get the behavior you expect. If -i has modified the default output file, undefining $^I does not automatically set the default output file to STDOUT.

The Format Form-Feed Character: $^L

The $^L variable contains the character or characters written out whenever a print format wants to start a new page. The default value is \f, the form-feed character.

Controlling Debugging: $^P

The $^P variable is used by the Perl debugger. When this variable is set to 0, debugging is turned off.

You never want to fiddle with $^P yourself, unless you want to specify that a certain chunk of code does not need to be debugged.

The Program Start Time: $^T

The $^T variable contains the time at which your program began running. This time is in the same format as is returned by the time function: the number of seconds since January 1, 1970.

The time format used by $^T is also the same as that used by the file test operators −A, −C, and −M.

Suppressing Warning Messages: $^W

The $^W system variable controls whether warning messages are to be displayed. Normally, $^W is set to a nonzero value only when the −w option is specified.

You can set $^W to 0 to turn off warnings inside your program. This capability is useful if your program contains statements that generate warnings you want to ignore (because you know that your statements are correct). For example:

```
$^W = 0;    # turn off warning messages
# code that generates warnings goes here
$^W = 1;    # turn warning messages back on
```

WARNING

> Some warnings are printed before program execution starts (for example, warnings of possible typos). You cannot turn off these warnings by setting $^W to 0.

The $^X Variable

The $^X variable displays the first word of the command line you used to start this program. If you started this program by entering its name, the name of the program appears in $^X. If you used the perl command to start this program, $^X contains perl.

The following statement checks to see whether you started this program with the command perl:

```
if ($^X ne "perl") {
        print ("You did not use the 'perl' command ");
        print ("to start this program.\n");
}
```

Pattern-System Variables

The system variables you have seen so far are all defined throughout your program. The following system variables are defined only in the current block of statements you are running. (A block of statements is any group of statements enclosed in the brace characters { and }.) These pattern-system variables are set by the pattern-matching operator and the other operators that use patterns (such as, for example, the substitution operator). Many of these pattern system variables were first introduced on Day 7.

TIP

Even though the pattern-system variables are defined only inside a particular block of statements, your programs should not take advantage of that fact. The safest way to use the pattern-matching variables is to assign any variable that you might need to a scalar variable of your own.

17

Retrieving Matched Subpatterns

When you specify a pattern for the pattern-matching or substitution operator, you can enclose parts of the pattern in parentheses. For example, the following pattern encloses the subpattern \d+ in parentheses (the parentheses themselves are not part of the pattern):

```
/(\d+)\./
```

This subpattern matches one or more digits.

After a pattern has been matched, the system variables $1, $2, and so on match the subpatterns enclosed in parentheses. For example, suppose that the following pattern is successfully matched:

```
/(\d+)([a-z]+)/
```

In this case, the match found must consist of one or more digits followed by one or more lowercase letters. After the match has been found, $1 contains the sequence of one or more digits, and $2 contains the sequence of one or more lowercase letters.

Listing 17.12 is an example of a program that uses $1, $2, and $3 to match subpatterns.

Listing 17.12. A program that uses variables containing matched subpatterns.

TYPE

```
1:  # p17_2.pl
2:  .
3:  while (<>) {
4:        while (/(-?\d+)\.(\d+)([eE][+-]?\d+)?/g) {
5:              print ("integer part $1, decimal part $2");
6:              if ($3 ne "") {
7:                    print (", exponent $3");
8:              }
9:              print ("\n");
10:       }
11: }
```

OUTPUT

```
C:\> perl p17_12.pl file1
integer part 26, decimal part 147, exponent e-02
integer part -8, decimal part 997
C:\>
```

ANALYSIS   This program reads each input line and searches for floating-point numbers. Line 4 matches if a floating-point number is found. (Line 4 is a while statement, not an if, to enable the program to detect lines containing more than one floating-point number. The loop starting in line 4 iterates until no more matches are found on the line.)

When a match is found, the first set of parentheses matches the digits before the decimal point; these digits are copied into $1. The second set of parentheses matches the digits after the decimal point; these matched digits are stored in $2. The third set of parentheses matches an optional exponent; if the exponent exists, it is stored in $3.

Line 5 prints the values of $1 and $2 for each match. If $3 is defined, its value is printed by line 7.

Do	Don't

DO use $1, not $0, to retrieve the first matched subpattern. $0 contains the name of the program you are running.

DON'T confuse $1 with \1. \1, \2, and so on are defined only inside a pattern. See Day 7 for more information on \1.

In patterns, parentheses are counted starting from the left. This rule tells the Perl interpreter how to handle nested parentheses:

```
/(\d+(\.)?\d+)/
```

This pattern matches one or more digits optionally containing a decimal point. When this pattern is matched, the outer set of parentheses is considered to be the first set of parentheses; these parentheses contain the entire matched number, which is stored in $1.

The inner set of parentheses is treated as the second set of parentheses because it includes the second left parenthesis seen by the pattern-matcher. The variable $2, which contains the subpattern matched by the second set of parentheses, contains . (a period) if a decimal point is matched and the empty string if it is not.

Retrieving the Entire Pattern: $&

When a pattern is matched successfully, the matched text string is stored in the system variable $&. This is the only way to retrieve the matched pattern because the pattern-matcher returns a true or false value indicating whether the pattern match is successful. (This is not strictly true, because you could enclose the entire pattern in parentheses and then check the value of $1; however, $& is easier to use in this case.) Listing 17.13 is a program that uses $& to count all the digits in a set of input files.

TYPE **Listing 17.13. A program that uses $&.**

```
1:  # p17_13.pl
2:
3:  while ($line = <>) {
4:          while ($line =~ /\d/g) {
5:                  $digitcount[$&]++;
6:          }
7:  }
8:  print ("Totals for each digit:\n");
9:  for ($i = 0; $i <= 9; $i++) {
10:         print ("$i: $digitcount[$i]\n");
11: }
```

OUTPUT
```
C:\> perl p17_13 file1
Totals for each digit:
0: 11
1: 6
2: 3
3: 1
4: 2
5:
6: 1
7:
8:
9: 1
C:\>
```

This program reads one line at a time from the files specified on the command line. Line 4 matches each digit in the input line in turn; the matched digit is stored in $&.

Line 5 takes the value of $& and uses it as the subscript for the array @digitcount. This array keeps a count of the number of occurrences of each digit.

When the input files have all been read, lines 9–11 print the totals for each digit.

The output is copied from my computer. You may get different outputs depending on the contents of file1.

 NOTE

> If you need the value of $&, be sure to get it before exiting the while loop or other statement block in which the pattern is matched. (A statement block is exited when the Perl interpreter sees a } character.)
>
> For example, the pattern matched in line 4 cannot be accessed outside of lines 4–6 because this copy of $& is defined only in these lines. (This rule also holds true for all the other pattern system variables defined in today's lesson.)
>
> The best rule to follow is to either use or assign a pattern-system variable immediately following the statement that matches the pattern.

Retrieving the Unmatched Text: The $` and $´ Variables

When a pattern is matched, the text of the match is stored in the system variable $&. The rest of the string is stored in two other system variables:

☐ The unmatched text preceding the match is stored in the $` variable.

☐ The unmatched text following the match is stored in the $´ variable.

For example, if the Perl interpreter searches for the /\d+/ pattern in the string qwerty1234uiop, it matches 1234, which is stored in $&. The substring qwerty, which precedes the match, is stored in $`. The rest of the string, uiop, is stored in $´.

If the beginning of a text string is matched, $` is set to the empty string. Similarly, if the last character in the string is part of the match, $´ is set to the empty string.

The $+ Variable

The $+ variable matches the last subpattern enclosed in parentheses. For example, when the following pattern is matched, $+ matches the digits after the decimal point:

```
/(\d+)\.(\d+)/
```

This variable is useful when the last part of a pattern is the only part you really need to look at.

File-System Variables

Several system variables are associated with file variables. One copy of each file-system variable is defined for each file that is referenced in your Perl program. Many of these system variables were first introduced on Day 11. The variables mentioned there are redefined here for your convenience.

The Default Print Format: $~

When the write statement sends formatted output to a file, it uses the value of the $~ system variable for that file to determine the print format to use.

When a program starts running, the default value of $~ for each file is the same as the name of the file variable that represents the file. For example, when you write to the file represented by the file variable MYFILE, the default value of $~ is MYFILE. This means that write normally uses the MYFILE print format. (For the standard output file, this default print format is named STDOUT.)

If you want to specify a different print format, change the value of $~ before calling the write function. For example, to use the print format MYFORMAT when writing to the standard output file, use the following code:

```
select (STDOUT);  # making sure you are writing to STDOUT
$~ = "MYFORMAT";
write;
```

This call to write uses MYFORMAT to format its output.

WARNING

Remember that one copy of $~ is defined for each file variable. Therefore, the following code is incorrect:

```
$~ = "MYFORMAT";
select (MYFILE);
write;
```

In this example, the assignment to $~ changes the default print format for whatever the current output file happens to be. This assignment does not affect the default print format for MYFILE because MYFILE is selected after $~ is assigned. To change the default print format for MYFILE, select it first:

```
select (MYFILE);
$~ = "MYFORMAT";
write;
```

This call to write now uses MYFORMAT to write to MYFILE.

Specifying Page Length: $=

The $= variable defines the page length (number of lines per page) for a particular output file. $= is normally initialized to 60, which is the value that the Perl interpreter assumes is the page length for every output file. This page length includes the lines left for page headers, and it is the length that works for most printers.

If you are directing a particular output file to a printer with a nonstandard page length, change the value of $= for this file before writing to it:

```
select ("WEIRDLENGTH");
$= = 72;
```

This code sets the page length for the WEIRDLENGTH file to 72.

WARNING

$= is set to 60 by default only if a page-header format is defined for the page. If no page header is defined, $= is set to 9999999 because Perl assumes that you want your output to be a continuous stream.

If you want paged output without a page header, define an empty page header for the output file.

Lines Remaining on the Page: $-

The $- variable associated with a particular file variable lists the number of lines left on the current page of that file. Each call to write subtracts the number of lines printed from $-. If write is called when $- is zero, a new page is started. (If $- is greater than zero, but write is printing more lines than the value of $-, write starts a new page in the middle of its printing operation.)

17

When a new page is started, the initial value of $- is the value stored in $=, which is the number of lines on the page.

The program in Listing 17.14 displays the value of $-.

 Listing 17.14. A program that displays $-.

```
1:  # p17_14.pl
2:
3:  open (OUTFILE, ">outfile");
4:  select ("OUTFILE");
5:  write;
6:  print STDOUT ("lines to go before write: $-\n");
7:  write;
8:  print STDOUT ("lines to go after write: $-\n");
9:  format OUTFILE =
10:   This is a test.
11: .
12: format OUTFILE_TOP =
13: This is a test.
14: .
```

```
C:\> perl p17_14.pl
lines to go before write: 58
lines to go after write: 57
C:\>
```

ANALYSIS   Line 3 opens the output file outfile and associates the file variable OUTFILE with this file. Line 4 then calls select, which sets the default output file to OUTFILE.

Line 5 calls write, which starts a new page. Line 6 then sends the value of $- to the standard output file, STDOUT, by specifying STDOUT in the call to print. Note that the copy of $- printed is the copy associated with OUTFILE, not the one associated with STDOUT, because OUTFILE is currently the default output file.

Line 7 calls write, which sends a line of output to OUTFILE and decreases the value of $- by one. Line 8 prints this new value of $-.

NOTE

If you want to force your next output to appear at the beginning of a new page, you can set $- to 0 yourself before calling write.

When a file is opened, the copy of $- for this file is given the initial value of 0. This technique ensures that the first call to write always starts a page (and generates the header for the page).

The Page-Header Print Format: $^

When write starts a new page, you can specify the page header that is to appear on the page. To do this, define a page-header print format for the output file to which the page is to be sent.

The system variable $^ contains the name of the print format to be used for printing page headers. If this format is defined, page headers are printed; if it does not exist, no page headers are printed.

By default, the copy of $^ for a particular file is set equal to the name of the file variable plus the string _TOP. For example, for the file represented by the file variable MYFILE, $^ is given an initial value of MYFILE_TOP.

To change the page header print format for a particular file, set the default output file by calling select, and then set $^ to the print format you want to use. For example:

```
select (MYFILE);
$^ = "MYHEADER";
```

This code changes the default output file to MYFILE and then changes the page-header print format for MYFILE to MYHEADER. As always, you must remember to select the file before changing $^ because each file has its own copy of $^.

Buffering Output: $|

When you send output to a file using print or write, the operating system might not write it right away. Some systems first send the output to a special array known as a buffer; when the buffer becomes full, it is written all at once. This process of output buffering is usually a more efficient way to write data.

In some circumstances, you might want to send output straight to your output file without using an intervening buffer. (For example, two processes might be sending output to the standard output file at the same time.)

The $| system variable indicates whether a particular file is buffered. By default, the Perl interpreter defines a buffer for each output file, and $| is set to 0. To eliminate buffering for a particular file, select the file and then set the $| variable to a nonzero value. For example, the following code eliminates buffering for the MYFILE output file:

```
select ("MYFILE");
$| = 1;
```

These statements set MYFILE as the default output file and then turn on the auto-flush in order to eliminate buffering.

If you want to eliminate buffering for a particular file, you must set $| before writing to the file for the first time because the operating system creates the buffer when it performs the first write operation.

The Current Page Number: $%

Each output file opened by a Perl program has a copy of the $% variable associated with it. This variable stores the current page number. When write starts a new page, it adds 1 to the value of $%. Each copy of $% is initialized to 0, which ensures that $% is set to 1 when the first page is printed. $% often is displayed by page-header print formats.

Array-System Variables

The system variables you've seen so far have all been scalar variables. The following sections describe the array variables that are automatically defined for use in Perl programs. All of these variables, except for the @_ variable, are global variables: their value is the same throughout a program.

The @_ Variable

The @_ variable, which is defined inside each subroutine, is a list of all the arguments passed to the subroutine.

For example, suppose that the subroutine my_sub is called as shown here:

```
&my_sub("hello", 46, $var);
```

The values hello and 46, plus the value stored in $var, are combined into a three-element list. Inside my_sub, this list is stored in @_.

In a subroutine, the @_ array can be referenced or modified, just as with any other array variable. Most subroutines, however, assign @_ to locally defined scalar variables using the local function:

```
sub my_sub {
        local ($arg1, $arg2, $arg3) = @_;
        # more stuff goes here
}
```

Here, the local statement defines three local variables: $arg1, $arg2, and $arg3. $arg1 is assigned the first element of the list stored in @_, $arg2 is assigned the second, and $arg3 is assigned the third.

For more information on subroutines, refer to Day 9, "Using Subroutines."

NOTE

> If the `shift` function is called inside a subroutine with no argument specified, the `@_` variable is assumed, and its first element is removed.

The `@ARGV` **Variable**

When you run a Perl program, you can specify values that are to be passed to the program by including them on the command line. For example, the following command calls the Perl program `myprog` and passes it the values `hello` and `46`:

```
$ myprog "hello" 46
```

Inside the Perl program, these values are stored in a special built-in array named `@ARGV`. In this example, `@ARGV` contains the list `("hello", 46)`.

Here is a simple statement that prints the values passed on the command line:

```
print ("@ARGV\n");
```

The `@ARGV` array also is associated with the `<>` operator. This operator treats the elements in `@ARGV` as filenames; each file named in `@ARGV` is opened and read in turn. Refer to Day 6 for a description of the `<>` operator.

NOTE

> If the `shift` function is called in the main body of a program (outside a subroutine) and no arguments are passed with it, the Perl interpreter assumes that the `@ARGV` array is to have its first element removed.
>
> The following loop assigns each element of `@ARGV`, in turn, to the variable `$var`:
>
> ```
> while ($var = shift) {
>         # stuff
> }
> ```

The `@F` **Variable**

In Perl, if you specify the –n or –p option, you can also supply the -a option. This option tells the Perl interpreter to break each input line into individual words (throwing away all tabs and spaces). These words are stored in the built-in array variable `@F`. After an input line has been (automatically) read, the `@F` array variable behaves like any other array variable.

For more information on the –a, –n, or –p options, refer to Day 16.

NOTE

> When the –a option is specified and an input line is broken into words, the original input line can still be accessed because it is stored in the $_ system variable.

The @INC **Variable**

The @INC array variable contains a list of directories to be searched for files requested by the require and use functions. This list consists of the following items, in order from first to last:

☐ The directories specified by the –I option
☐ The Perl library directory, which is normally c:\perl5\lib
☐ The current working directory (represented by the . character)

Like any array variable, @INC can be added to or modified.

The %INC **Variable**

The built-in associative array %INC lists the files requested by the require function that have already been found.

When require finds a file, the associative-array element $INC{file} is defined, in which file is the name of the file. The value of this associative-array element is the location of the actual file.

When require requests a file, the Perl interpreter first looks to see whether an associative-array element has already been created for this file. This action ensures that the interpreter does not try to include the same code twice.

The %ENV **Variable**

The %ENV associative array lists the environment variables defined for the program and their values. The environment variables are the array subscripts, and the values of the variables are the values of the array elements.

For example, the following statement assigns the value of the environment variable PATH to the scalar variable $path:

```
$path = $ENV{"PATH"};
```

The %SIG **Variable**

In a modern operating-system environment, processes can send signals to other processes. These signals can, for example, interrupt a running program, trigger an alarm in the program, or kill off the program.

You can control how your program responds to signals it receives. To do this, modify the %SIG associative array. This array contains one element for each available signal, with the signal name serving as the subscript for the element. For example, the INT (interrupt) signal is represented by the $SIG{"INT"} element.

The value of a particular element of %SIG is the action that is to be performed when the signal is received. By default, the value of an array element is DEFAULT, which tells the program to do what it normally does when it receives this signal.

You can override the default action for some of the signals in two ways: you can tell the program to ignore the signal or you can define your own signal handler. (Some signals, such as KILL, cannot be overridden.)

To tell the program to ignore a particular type of signal, set the value of the associative-array element for this signal to IGNORE. For example, the following statement indicates that the program is to ignore any INT signals it receives:

```
$SIG{"INT"} = "IGNORE";
```

If you assign any value other than DEFAULT or IGNORE to a signal array element, this value is assumed to be the name of a function that is to be executed when this signal is received. For example, the following statement tells the program to jump to the subroutine named interrupt when it receives an INT signal:

```
$SIG{"INT"} = "interrupt";
```

Subroutines that can be jumped to when a signal is received are called *interrupt handlers*, because signals interrupt normal program execution. Listing 17.15 is an example of a program that defines an interrupt handler.

TYPE **Listing 17.15. A program containing an interrupt handler.**

```
1:  # p17_15.pl
2:
3:  $SIG{"INT"} = "wakeup";
4:  sleep();
5:
6:  sub wakeup {
7:          print ("I have woken up!\n");
8:          exit();
9:  }
```

```
C:\> perl p17_15.pl
^C
I have woken up!
C:\>
```

Line 3 tells the Perl interpreter that the program is to jump to the wakeup subroutine when it receives the INT signal. Line 4 tells the program to go to sleep. Because no argument is passed to sleep, the program will sleep until a signal wakes it up.

To wake up the process, you can send an INT signal to the process using the combination of the keys Ctrl and C—that is, ^C.

When the program receives the INT signal, it executes the wakeup subroutine. This subroutine prints the following message and then exits:

```
I have woken up!
```

If desired, you can use the same subroutine to handle more than one signal. The signal actually sent is passed as an argument to the called subroutine, which ensures that your subroutine can determine which signal triggered it:

```
sub interrupt {
        local ($signal) = @_;

        print ("Interrupted by the $signal signal.\n");
}
```

If a subroutine exits normally, the program returns to where it was executing when it was interrupted. If a subroutine calls exit or die, the program execution is terminated.

> **NOTE**
>
> When a program continues executing after being interrupted, the element of %SIG corresponding to the received signal is reset to DEFAULT. To ensure that repeated signals are trapped by your interrupt handler, redefine the appropriate element of %SIG.

Built-In File Variables

Perl provides several built-in file variables, most of which you have previously seen. The only file variables that have not yet been discussed are DATA and _ (underscore). The others are briefly described here for the sake of completeness.

STDIN, STDOUT, **and** STDERR

The file variable STDIN is, by default, associated with the standard input file. Using STDIN with the <> operator, as in <STDIN>, normally reads data from your keyboard. If your shell has used < or some equivalent redirection operator to specify input from a file, <STDIN> reads from that file.

The file variable STDOUT normally writes to the standard output file, which is usually directed to your screen. If your shell has used > or the equivalent to redirect standard output to a file, writing to STDOUT sends output to that file.

STDERR represents the standard error file, which is almost always directed to your screen. Writing to STDERR ensures that you see error messages even when you have redirected the standard output file.

You can associate STDIN, STDOUT, or STDERR with some other file using open:

```
open (STDIN, "myinputfile");
open (STDOUT, "myoutputfile");
open (STDERR, "myerrorfile");
```

Opening a file and associating it with STDIN overrides the default value of STDIN, which means that you can no longer read from the standard input file. Similarly, opening a file and associating it with STDOUT or STDERR means that writing to that particular file variable no longer sends output to the screen.

To associate a file variable with the standard input file after you have redirected STDIN, specify a filename of –:

```
open (MYSTDIN, "-");
```

To associate a file variable with the standard output file, specify a filename of >–:

```
open (MYSTDOUT, ">-");
```

You can, of course, specify STDIN with – or STDOUT with >– to restore the original values of these file variables.

ARGV

ARGV is a special file variable that is associated with the current input file being read by the <> operator. For example, consider the following statement:

```
$line = <>;
```

This statement reads from the current input file. Because ARGV represents the current input file, the preceding statement is equivalent to this:

```
$line = <ARGV>;
```

You normally will not need to access ARGV yourself except via the <> operator.

DATA

The DATA file variable is used with the __END__ special value, which can be used to indicate the end of a program. Reading from DATA reads the line after __END__, which enables you to include a program and its data in the same file.

Listing 17.16 is an example of a program that reads from DATA.

 Listing 17.16. An example of the DATA file variable.

```
1:  # p17_16.pl
2:
3:  $line = <DATA>;
4:  print ("$line");
5:  __END__
6:  This is my line of data.
```

OUTPUT

```
C:\> perl p17_16.pl
This is my line of data.
C:\>
```

ANALYSIS The __END__ value in line 5 indicates the end of the program. When line 3 reads from the DATA file variable, the first line after __END__ is read in and is assigned to $line. (Subsequent requests for input from DATA read successive lines, if any exist.) Line 6 then prints this input line.

 NOTE

> For more information on __END__ and methods of indicating the end of the program, refer to Day 14.

The Underscore File Variable

The _ (underscore) file variable represents the file specified by the last call to either the stat function or a file-test operator. For example:

```
$readable = -r "C:\mydir\myfile";
$writeable = -w _;
```

Here, the _ file variable used in the second statement refers to C:\mydir\myfile because this is the filename that was passed to −r.

You can use _ anywhere that a file variable can be used, provided that the file has been opened appropriately:

```
if (-T $myoutfile) {
        print _ ("here is my output\n");
}
```

Here, the file whose name is stored in $myoutfile is associated with _ because this name was passed to −T (which tests whether the file is a text file). The call to print writes output to this file.

The main benefit of _ is that it saves time when you are using several file-test operators at once:

```
if (-r "myfile" || -w _ || -x _) {
        print ("I can read, write, or execute myfile.\n");
}
```

Specifying System-Variable Names as Words

As you have seen, the system variables defined by Perl normally consist of a $, @, or % followed by a single, non-alphanumeric character. This ensures that you cannot define a variable whose name is identical to that of a Perl system variable.

If you find Perl system-variable names difficult to remember or type, Perl 5 provides an alternative for most of them. If you add the statement

```
use English;
```

at the top of your program, Perl defines alternative variable names that more closely resemble English words. This makes it easier to understand what your program is doing. Table 17.1 lists these alternative variable names.

Table 17.1. Alternative names for Perl system variables.

Variable	Alternative name(s)
$_	$ARG
$0	$PROGRAM_NAME
$]	$PERL_VERSION
$/	$INPUT_RECORD_SEPARATOR or $RS
$\	$OUTPUT_RECORD_SEPARATOR or $ORS

17

Variable	Alternative name(s)
$,	$OUTPUT_FIELD_SEPARATOR or $OFS
$"	$LIST_SEPARATOR
$#	$OFMT
$@	$EVAL_ERROR
$?	$CHILD_ERROR
$!	$OS_ERROR or $ERRNO
$.	$INPUT_LINE_NUMBER or $NR
$*	$MULTILINE_MATCHING
$[	none (deprecated in Perl 5)
$;	$SUBSCRIPT_SEPARATOR or $SUBSEP
$:	$FORMAT_LINE_BREAK_CHARACTERS
$$	$PROCESS_ID or $PID
$^A	$ACCUMULATOR
$^D	$DEBUGGING
$^F	$SYSTEM_FD_MAX
$^I	$INPLACE_EDIT
$^L	$FORMAT_FORMFEED
$^P	$PERLDB
$^T	$BASETIME
$^W	$WARNING
$^X	$EXECUTABLE_NAME
$&	$MATCH
$'	$PREMATCH
$'	$POSTMATCH
$+	$LAST_PAREN_MATCH
$~	$FORMAT_NAME
$=	$FORMAT_LINES_PER_PAGE
$-	$FORMAT_LINES_LEFT
$^	$FORMAT_TOP_NAME
$|	$OUTPUT_AUTOFLUSH
$%	$FORMAT_PAGE_NUMBER

17

Summary

Today you have learned about the built-in system variables available within every Perl program. These system variables are divided into five groups:

- ☐ Global scalar variables, which are defined everywhere in the program and contain a single scalar value

- ☐ Pattern-system variables, which are defined immediately after a pattern matching or substitution operation has been performed

- ☐ File-system variables, which are defined for each input or output file accessible from the program

- ☐ Array-system variables, each of which contains a list

- ☐ Built-in file variables, which are associated with files that are automatically open or automatically available

You also learned how to specify English-language equivalents for Perl system variables.

Q&A

Q Why do some system variables use special characters rather than letters in their names?

A To distinguish them from variables that you define and to ensure that the `reset` function (described in Chapter 14) cannot affect them.

Q What is the current line number when `$.` is used with the `<>` operator?

A Effectively, the `<>` operator treats its input files as if they are a single file. This means that `$.` contains the total number of lines seen, not the line number of the current input file. (If you want `$.` to contain the line number of the current file, set `$.` to `0` each time `eof` returns true.)

Q Are pattern-system variables local or global?

A Each pattern-system variable is defined only in the current subroutine or block of statements.

Q Why does Perl define both the `$"` and the `$,` system variables?

A Some programs like to treat the following statements differently:
```
print ("@array");
 print (@array);
```

(In fact, by default, the first statement puts a space between each pair of elements in the array, and the second does not.) The `$"` and `$,` variables handle these two separate cases.

17

Workshop

The Workshop provides quiz questions to help you solidify your understanding of the material covered, and exercises to provide you with experience in using what you've learned. Try to understand the answers to the questions before moving to the next chapter. You can find the answers in Appendix B, "Answers."

Quiz

1. List the functions and operators that use `$_` by default.
2. What do the following variables contain?

    a. `$=`

    b. `$/`

    c. `$?`

    d. `$!`

    e. `@_`

3. Explain the differences between ARGV, $ARGV, and @ARGV.
4. Explain the difference between @INC and %INC.
5. Explain the difference between `$0` and `$1`.

Exercises

1. Write a program that reads lines of input, replaces multiple blanks and tabs with a single space, converts all uppercase letters to lowercase, and prints the resulting lines. Use no explicit variable names in this program.
2. Write a program that uses `$'` and `$_` to remove all extra spaces from input lines.
3. Write a program that prints the directories in your PATH environment variable, one per line.
4. Write a program that prints numbers, starting with 1 and continuing until interrupted by an INT signal.
5. Write a program whose data consists of one or more numbers per input line. Put the input lines in the program file itself. Add the numbers and print their total.

Day 18

References in Perl 5 for Win32

The concept of a *reference* is useful in computing languages. References in Perl 5 are introduced in today's lesson, which covers the following topics:

☐ Hard and symbolic references

☐ Creating and de-referencing references

☐ References to arrays, hashes, subroutines, and file handles

☐ References to multidimensional arrays or hashes

Since Perl 5 for Win32 is ported directly from Perl 5, what you'll learn from today's lesson can be applied to Perl 5 for Win32 completely.

Hard and Symbolic References

Like other computing languages, Perl supports references, although it has primarily been developed in favor of flat data structures.

What Is a Reference?

To understand what a reference is, let's first think about an example. I have a mailbox at work. Every day, I check the mailbox to see if any mail has been sent to me. In our department, there are hundreds of engineers and technicians who also have their own mailboxes. So, how can I find mine among the hundreds of mailboxes?

As with others, my mailbox has a unique address (or location). Following the address, I can easily find my mailbox without any confusion. Here, the unique address can be used as a *reference* to my mailbox.

Now, you probably understand what a reference is. When you define a variable in a computing language, you give the variable a name. Sooner or later, the variable is assigned a unique address and given a certain space in the memory. The space is used to contain values passed to the variable. You can think about the variable as a mailbox—the name of the variable is like the label of the mailbox, the address of the variable like the location of the mailbox, and the space of the variable like the mailbox container itself. A *reference variable* is a special one that contains a unique address of another variable. You can think of a reference as just an address to a variable. In other words, a reference points to another variable.

Therefore, by using a reference, you can have access to a variable to which the reference refers. References are useful in creating complex data structures.

Hard References

Introduced in Perl 5, *hard references* are references that always contain the addresses to the contents of variables. In other words, a hard reference points directly to the content of a variable; the content of the variable is the value that you want to manipulate.

In Perl 5, a scalar variable can be used to contain a hard reference.

Symbolic References

A *symbolic reference* points to the name of a variable rather than to the value. Therefore, to obtain the value of the variable, you have to use the symbolic reference to find the address that points to the value of the variable. This is what is called indirectness.

The symbolic references are more complex than the hard references in terms of indirectness. Ironically, the symbolic references were introduced before the hard references in Perl.

To better understand the indirectness, let's take the example of my mailbox again. This time, suppose that I forget the address to my mailbox; I have to go to the secretary for help. The secretary keeps a look-up table of all mailbox addresses for the employees in the department.

Therefore, I give the secretary my name. She helps me to find the address to my mailbox. With the address, I'm able to find my mailbox and check out the mail located there. You see, in this example, I don't have the address to my mailbox at the beginning. In other words, I don't have direct access to my mailbox. I have to go to the secretary to get the address. If the secretary loses the table, then I'll never be able to get access to my mailbox.

In many cases, a hard reference is easier and more straightforward to use than a symbolic reference. The majority of the sections in today's lesson cover hard references. Symbolic references are introduced in the "Symbolic References" section later today.

Creating and De-referencing References

The following four subsections describe how to create references to scalar variables, arrays, and hashes.

In Perl 5, a scalar variable contains one value. Arrays or hashes can be used to contain multiple values. Hashes are also called *associative arrays*. The elements in the one-dimensional arrays or hashes are all simple scalars.

To obtain the values from scalar variables, arrays, or hashes to which a reference points, you have to de-reference the reference. For references on scalar variables or one-dimensional arrays or hashes, you can prefix a $ to the references to de-reference the references.

References to multidimensional arrays or hashes, which contain nested arrays or hashes, are discussed later today.

Creating References with the Backslash Operator (\)

Actually, you saw the usage of the backslash operator in creating references on Day 15, "Perl 5 for Win32 Module Extensions." Basically, you can use the backslash operator to build a reference to any named scalars, arrays, or subroutines.

For instance:

```
$variable = 7;
$hard_ref_to_scalar = \$variable;
```

Here, the scalar variable, $variable, is given the value of 7 in the first statement. Then, in the second statement, the address of the variable is assigned to the hard reference, $hard_ref_to_scalar. The backslash operator in line 2 has the meaning of "the address of." Therefore, \$variable means "the address of $variable."

Similarly, we have the following examples:

```
$hard_ref_to_array = \@Regular_Array;
$hard_ref_to_hash = \%Hash_Array;
$hard_ref_to_subroutine = \&Subroutine;
$hard_ref_to_typeglob = \*FILEHANDLE;
```

Here the four statements assign the addresses of a regular array, an associative array, a subroutine, and the STDOUT to the hard references—$hard_ref_to_array, $hard_ref_to_hash, $hard_ref_to_subroutine, and $hard_ref_to_typeglob, respectively. You will learn about these references later in today's lesson.

NOTE

> If you have done some programming in C, you may find a similarity between the backslash operator (\) in Perl and the ampersand operator (&) in C.

De-referencing References with the $ Operator

To obtain the value of a scalar variable to which a reference points, you can add one dollar sign, $, right before the reference—that is, prefix a $ to the reference—and then assign the de-referenced reference to a new variable. The new variable will contain the value of the referred variable. For instance:

```
$variable = 7;
$hard_ref_to_scalar = \$variable;
$value_of_the_variable = $$hard_ref_to_scalar;
```

Here, line 1 gives the value of 7 to the $variable scalar variable. Line 2 sets up a hard reference to the variable. Then, in line 3, $value_of_the_variable obtains the value of $variable from the hard reference, $hard_ref_to_scalar, by de-referencing the hard reference. The $ sign prefixed to $hard_ref_to_scalar in line 3 does the de-referencing for $value_of_the_variable.

Listing 18.1 gives another example of de-referencing a hard reference.

TYPE **Listing 18.1. Using the backslash operator on arrays.**

```
1  # p18_1.pl
2:
3: $my_mail = "A Greeting Message from a Friend.";
4: $hard_ref = \$my_mail;
5: $a_message = $$hard_ref;
6: print "This is what I found in my mail box:\n";
7: print "  $a_message \n";
```

OUTPUT

```
C:\> perl p18_1.pl
This is what I found in my mail box:
  A Greeting Message from a Friend.
C:\>
```

ANALYSIS   Line 3 in the listing first initializes the `$my_mail` scalar variable with a string of `"A Greeting Message from a Friend."`. Line 4 creates a hard reference to `$my_mail`. Then, line 5 de-references the `$hard_ref` hard reference and assigns the value of `$my_mail` to which `$hard_ref` points to `$a_message`. Here, the value of `$my_mail` is the string initialized in line 3.

Line 7 prints out the value of `$my_mail` now contained in the variable `$a_message`.

References to Arrays

Like the references to scalar variables in Perl, references to arrays can also be created using the backslash operator.

Listing 18.2 demonstrates how to use the backslash operator to create a reference pointing to an array and then de-reference the reference to get the values in the array.

TYPE   **Listing 18.2. Using the backslash operator on an array.**

```
1:  # p18_2.pl
2:
3:  @an_array = ("one", "two", "three", "four", "five");
4:  $hard_ref = \@an_array;
5:  print "The address of the array = $hard_ref\n";
6:  print "The values of the array are:\n";
7:  $i = 0;
8:  foreach (@an_array) {
9:      print "$i : $$hard_ref[$i++]; \n";
10: }
```

OUTPUT

```
C:\> perl p18_2.pl
The address of the array = ARRAY(0x77e8d4)
The values of the array are:
0 : one
1 : two
2 : three
3 : four
4 : five
C:\>
```

ANALYSIS   In Listing 18.2, line 3 initializes an array called `@an_array` with five elements (that is, values). Line 4 creates a hard reference, `$hard_ref`, to the array, `@an_array`. Then `$hard_ref` is used to access the array.

Line 5 prints out the address to the array contained by the hard reference. The address is used by `$hard_ref` to refer to the array. Lines 7–10 obtain and display each individual element (value) in the array with the indexes. Note that in line 9, `$$hard_ref[$i++]` gives the value indexed by `$i` in the array. Here, the first `$` in `$$hard_ref` tells the Perl interpreter to de-reference the `$hard_ref` that points to the array.

Because `$hard_ref` is already created and given the address of `@an_array` in line 4, you can rewrite the statement in line 8 to

```
8:  foreach (@$hard_ref) {
```

Here, `$hard_ref` is used to replace the name of the array, `@an_array`. You should see the same output as in the previous example.

References to Hashes

In this section, you learn to use a reference to refer to a hash (that is, an associative array). Instead of using indexes, you use keys to find the associated values in a hash. The key-value pairs are disordered in a hash, so you can sort out and fetch a value much quicker from a hash than from an array.

Listing 18.3 contains an example showing how to refer to a hash by a reference, as well as to obtain values from the hash by de-referencing the reference.

TYPE   **Listing 18.3. Using the backslash operator on a hash.**

```
1:  # p18_3.pl
2:
3:  %a_hash = ( "01", "one",
4:              "02", "two",
5:              "03", "three",
6:              "04", "four",
7:              "05", "five");
8:  $hard_ref = \%a_hash;
9:  print "The address of the hash = $hard_ref\n";
10: print "The values in the hash are:\n";
11: foreach $key (sort keys %$hard_ref) {
12:     print "$key => $$hard_ref{$key} \n";
13: }
```

OUTPUT
```
C:\> perl p18_3.pl
The address of the hash = HASH(0x77e8e4)
The values in the hash are:
01 => one
02 => two
03 => three
04 => four
05 => five
C:\>
```

Lines 3–7 set up a hash, called `%a_hash`, with five key-value pairs. In other words, The `01`, `02`, `03`, `04`, and `05` keys are associated with values of `one`, `two`, `three`, `four`, and `five` respectively.

Line 8 creates a hard reference and assigns the address of the hash to `$hard_ref`. The address is printed out in line 9.

Lines 11–13 fetch the key-value pairs from the hash by using the hard reference `$hard_ref` and print out the result on your screen. Note that `%$hard_ref` is used, instead of `%a_hash`, in line 11. And in line 12, `$$hard_ref{$key}` fetches the value associated with the key of `$key` in the hash `%a_hash`.

 TIP

If there are many arguments that need to be passed to a subroutine, you can consider putting these arguments into an array or a hash and passing the subroutine a reference that points to the array or hash. For instance, instead of calling

```
&sub_routine( "There", "are", "many", "variables",
"that", "need", "to be", "passed" );,
```

you can pass the subroutine a reference to an array that contains all the arguments:

```
@array = ("There", "are", "many", "variables", "that",
"need", "to be", "passed" );
&sub_routine( \@array );
```

It's more efficient to pass a reference, rather than the multiple arguments, into a subroutine. By passing a reference, the subroutine can manipulate the passed array directly.

Using => in Hashes

As you learned on Day 10, "Associative Arrays," you can use `=>` in your hashes to specify the associative relationship between a key and a value. The `=>` operator has been introduced in Perl 5 and Perl 5 for Win32.

Therefore, you can rewrite the hash in Listing 18.3 as

```
3:  %a_hash = ( "01"=>"one",
4:              "02"=>"two",
5:              "03"=>"three",
6:              "04"=>"four",
7:              "05"=>"five");
```

Listing 18.4 demonstrates how to use `=>` in a hash and refer to the hash by a hard reference.

18

TYPE **Listing 18.4. Using the `=>` and `\` operators on a hash.**

```
1:  # p18_4.pl
2:
3:  %hashed_month = ( "01"=>"January",
4:                    "02"=>"February",
5:                    "03"=>"March",
6:                    "04"=>"April",
7:                    "05"=>"May",
8:                    "06"=>"June",
9:                    "07"=>"July",
10:                   "08"=>"August",
11:                   "09"=>"September",
12:                   "10"=>"October",
13:                   "11"=>"November",
14:                   "12"=>"December");
15: $ref_to_month = \%hashed_month;
16: print "Enter a date in the format of mm-dd-yy\n";
17: print "e.g.,  12-25-96\n\n";
18: $date = <STDIN>;
19: chop ($date);
20: ($month_key, $day, $year) = split ( /-/, $date);
21: $day =~ s/^0//;
22: print "\nThe date you just entered is:\n";
23: print "  $$ref_to_month{$month_key} $day, 19$year \n"
```

OUTPUT

```
C:\> perl p18_4.pl
Enter a date in the format of mm-dd-yy
e.g., 12-25-96

12-09-96

The date you just entered is:
December 9, 1996
C:\>
```

ANALYSIS Lines 3–14 in Listing 18.4 set up a hash, `%hashed_month`, for the names of the months of the year. Here, the `=>` operator is used to associate the strings of the month names with the keys in the hash. Line 15 builds a reference, `$ref_to_month`, that keeps the address to the hash.

Lines 16 and 17 demonstrate the input format required by the program. Lines 18 and 19 get the date entered from the keyboard and chop up any space or return code attached to the date string `$date`.

Line 20 splits the date string into three parts and saves the values in `$month_key`, `$day`, and `$year`, respectively. The value held by `$month_key` is used as the key to fetch the associated month-name string from the hash `%hashed_month`. Line 21 erases the first digit in `$day` if the first digit is zero.

Lines 22 and 23 print out the reformatted date with the help of the reference `$ref_to_month` to extract a month-name string associated with `$month_key` from `%hashed_month`.

18

TIP

The Perl `print` function can be used to print out the content of a reference in order to find out the data type of the variable pointed to by the reference. For instance, if you run the following Perl script

```
$variable = 'Tony';
$ref = \$variable;
print $ref;
```

you get something like `SCALAR(0x77e8d8)`, where `SCALAR` identifies the data type of the variable to which the reference points. `0x77e8d8` is the address in hex format.

Similarly, for a reference to a hash, `$ref` has the word `HASH` followed by an address value, and the word `ARRAY` for an array.

The other built-in types of references are: `REF`, `CODE`, and `GLOB`.

Actually, Perl provides you a function called `ref`, which returns not-zero if the argument passed to `ref` is a reference, or the null string otherwise. The following is an example to use the `ref` function to check the type of reference:

```
$variable = 'Tony';
$ref = \$variable;
if (ref ($ref) eq "SCALAR") {
    print "The reference points to a scalar.\n";
}
elsif (not ref ($ref)) {
    print "\$ref is not a reference.\n";
}
```

On Day 19, "Object-Oriented Programming in Perl," you'll learn more about the `ref` function in retrieving a class name from a reference.

Other Ways to De-reference References

In Perl 5, there are several other ways you can de-reference a reference and obtain the values pointed to by the reference. Today, you're going to learn about two of them.

De-referencing References Using { }

Besides prefixing $ to a reference, you can use the braces {} to wrap up a complex expression as the reference.

The example shown in Listing 18.5 uses {} to de-reference references to subroutines.

Listing 18.5. Using `{}` to de-reference references.

```
 1: # p18_5.pl
 2:
 3: @messages = ( "Execute subroutines that are referred\n",
 4:                 "by an array of references.\n",
 5:                 "This time, use {} to de-reference the references.\n\n");
 6: $ref_to_messages = \@messages;
 7: $ref[0] = \&Sub_1;
 8: $ref[1] = \&Sub_2;
 9: $ref[2] = \&Sub_3;
10:
11: foreach $str (@{$ref_to_messages}) {
12:    print $str;
13: }
14:
15: for ($i=0; $i<3; $i++) {
16:    &{ $ref[$i] } ($i);
17: }
18:
19: sub Sub_1
20: {
21:   my $index = shift (@_);
22:   print "This is Sub_1, referred by \$ref[$index].\n";
23: }
24:
25: sub Sub_2
26: {
27:   my $index = shift (@_);
28:   print "This is Sub_2, referred by \$ref[$index].\n";
29: }
30:
31: sub Sub_3
32: {
33:   my $index = shift (@_);
34:   print "This is Sub_3, referred by \$ref[$index].\n";
35: }
```

```
C:\> perl p18_5.pl
Execute subroutines that are referred
by an array of references
This time, use { } to de-reference the references.

This is Sub_1, referred by $ref[0].
This is Sub_2, referred by $ref[1].
This is Sub_3, referred by $ref[2].
C:\>
```

ANALYSIS Lines 3–5 initialize an array, `@messages`, with the description of the program. Line 6 creates a reference, `$ref_to_messages`, to point to the array.

Lines 7–9 create three references that are the elements in an array called `@ref`. These three references refer to three subroutines in the listing—`Sub_1`, `Sub_2`, and `Sub_3`, respectively.

Lines 11–13 print out the description message saved in @messages. Note that in line 11, the reference $ref_to_messages is wrapped by {} in order to obtain the name of the array.

Then, the three subroutines are executed sequentially in lines 15–17. Note that in line 16, the &{ $ref[$i] } ($i); statement tells the Perl interpreter to invoke the subroutine pointed to by the $ref[$i] with one argument in ($i).

The three subroutines are declared in lines 19–35. They can print out messages to identify themselves when they are executed.

Of course, you do not have to use {} if the references are very straightforward. The only advantage to using {} is that the expression of the reference wrapped by {} can be arbitrary. Usually, the reference inside the {} points to a subroutine that accepts arguments, like the example to execute three subroutines in Listing 18.5.

De-referencing References Using the -> Operator

The -> is another operator you can use to de-reference references in Perl 5, as well as in Perl 5 for Win32. For example, to fetch the first element from the @messages array that is pointed to by the $ref_to_messages reference in Listing 18.5, you can use the -> operator in the following way:

```
$first_element = $ref_to_messages -> [0];
```

which is equivalent to

```
$first_element = $$ref_to_messages[0];
```

Now, let's study an example to learn more about the -> operator. Listing 18.6 gives the example to display the full name of an American state or possession. The -> operator is used to de-reference a reference that points to a hash. The hash contains the full names of all states and possessions associated with the abbreviations as the keys.

TYPE **Listing 18.6. Using -> to de-reference references.**

```
 1:  # p18_6.pl
 2:
 3:  @messages = (
 4:      "This program can print out a full state/possession name, \n",
 5:      "according to the input made by the user.\n",
 6:      "Also, it can display all state/possession names if \n",
 7:      "the input is NULL. \n",
 8:      "\nNow, enter an abbreviation of a state/possession name: \n\n",
 9:  );
10:  %state_poss = (
```

continues

18

Listing 18.6. continued

```
11:       AL => 'ALABAMA',
12:       AK => 'ALASKA',
13:       AS => 'AMERICAN SAMOA',
14:       AZ => 'ARIZONA',
15:       AR => 'ARKANSAS',
16:       CA => 'CALIFORNIA',
17:       CO => 'COLORADO',
18:       CT => 'CONNECTICUT',
19:       DE => 'DELAWARE',
20:       DC => 'DISTRICT OF COLUMBIA',
21:       FM => 'FEDERATED STATES OF MICRONESIA',
22:       FL => 'FLORIDA',
23:       GA => 'GEORGIA',
24:       GU => 'GUAM',
25:       HI => 'HAWAII',
26:       ID => 'IDAHO',
27:       IL => 'ILLINOIS',
28:       IN => 'INDIANA',
29:       IA => 'IOWA',
30:       KS => 'KANSAS',
31:       KY => 'KENTUCKY',
32:       LA => 'LOUISIANA',
33:       ME => 'MAINE',
34:       MH => 'MARSHALL ISLANDS',
35:       MD => 'MARYLAND',
36:       MA => 'MASSACHUSETTS',
37:       MI => 'MICHIGAN',
38:       MN => 'MINNESOTA',
39:       MS => 'MISSISSIPPI',
40:       MO => 'MISSOURI',
41:       MT => 'MONTANA',
42:       NE => 'NEBRASKA',
43:       NV => 'NEVADA',
44:       NH => 'NEW HAMPSHIRE',
45:       NJ => 'NEW JERSEY',
46:       NM => 'NEW MEXICO',
47:       NY => 'NEW YORK',
48:       NC => 'NORTH CAROLINA',
49:       ND => 'NORTH DAKOTA',
50:       MP => 'NORTHERN MARIANA ISLANDS',
51:       OH => 'OHIO',
52:       OK => 'OKLAHOMA',
53:       OR => 'OREGON',
54:       PW => 'PALAU',
55:       PA => 'PENNSYLVANIA',
56:       PR => 'PUERTO RICO',
57:       RI => 'RHODE ISLAND',
58:       SC => 'SOUTH CAROLINA',
59:       SD => 'SOUTH DAKOTA',
60:       TN => 'TENNESSEE',
61:       TX => 'TEXAS',
62:       TT => 'TRUST TERRITORIES',
63:       UT => 'UTAH',
64:       VT => 'VERMONT',
```

```
65:     VI => 'VIRGIN ISLANDS',
66:     VA => 'VIRGINIA',
67:     WA => 'WASHINGTON',
68:     WV => 'WEST VIRGINIA',
69:     WI => 'WISCONSIN',
70:     WY => 'WYOMING',
71: );
72: $ref_to_messages = \@messages;
73: $ref_to_state_poss = \%state_poss;
74:
75: foreach $str (@{$ref_to_messages}) {
76:     print $str;
77: }
78:
79: $input = <STDIN>;
80: chop ($input);
81: $input =~ tr/[a-z]/[A-Z]/;
82:
83: $i=0;
84: if ( $input eq '') {
85:     foreach $key (sort keys %{$ref_to_state_poss}) {
86:         $result .= "$key => $ref_to_state_poss->{$key}, ";
87:         $i++;
88:         $result .= "\n" if !($i % 3);
89:     }
90:     print "$result \n";
91: } else {
92:     if ($value = $ref_to_state_poss->{$input}) {
93:         print "$input => $value \n";
94:     } else {
95:         print "$input is not an American State or Possesion.\n";
96:     }
97: }
```

OUTPUT

```
C:\> perl p18_6.pl
This program can print out a full state/possession name,
according to the input made by the user.
Also, it can display all state/possession names if
the input is NULL.

Now, enter an abbreviation of a state/possession name:

tx
TX => TEXAS
C:\>
```

ANALYSIS Lines 3–9 initialize an array, @messages, with the descriptions about the program. The last element in @messages gives the instruction to the user who wants to obtain the full name of an American state or possession.

Lines 10–71 set up a hash, %state_poss, with the full names of all American states and possessions. The abbreviations of the names are used as keys in the hash.

$ref_to_messages and $ref_to_state_poss are two references that are assigned the addresses of @messages and %state_poss, respectively, in lines 72 and 73.

Lines 75–77 print out the descriptions saved in @messages. As in the previous section, the {} is used to wrap up the $ref_to_messages reference in line 75 to obtain the name of the array.

Lines 79–81 receive the abbreviation (if any) entered by the user, chop off the return character in the input, and convert the rest of the characters in the input to uppercase.

If the user enters nothing but the Enter key, lines 84–90 display the full names of all states and possessions with the corresponding abbreviations. To print three names per row, line 88 adds a newline character to the string whenever the remainder of $i divided by 3 is 0.

If the user types in a correct abbreviation of a state or possession, line 93 prints out the corresponding full name of the state or possession. Otherwise, line 95 tells the user the abbreviation is wrong.

Note that in Listing 18.6, the -> operator is used in lines 86 and 92. In these two places, a value (that is, a full name) of %state_poss is fetched by de-referencing $ref_to_state_poss with the -> operator.

The advantage of using the -> operator will become more obvious when you learn more about multidimensional arrays and hashes in the next section.

Working with Multidimensional Arrays or Hashes

On Day 5, "Lists ands Array Variables," and Day 10, you learned about arrays and hashes (that is, associated arrays). What you've learned about are all one-dimensional—that is, the elements in the arrays or hashes are simply scalar variables. In this section, you're going to learn about multidimensional arrays and hashes and how to de-reference the references that point to those arrays or hashes.

As you know, multiple values can be assigned to the elements inside an array or a hash. If the elements are just scalar variables, the array or hash is one-dimensional. If some of the elements themselves are arrays or hashes nested inside the array or hash, the array or hash is *multidimensional.*

Basically, there are four types of multidimensional arrays and hashes: *arrays of arrays, arrays of hashes, hashes of arrays,* and *hashes of hashes.* The following subsections explain these four types of multidimensional arrays and hashes.

NOTE

Strictly speaking, arrays and hashes in Perl are indeed one-dimensional. Internally, arrays and hashes can only hold scalar values. The phrase "an array of arrays" really means "an array of references to arrays." Similarly, "a hash of hashes" means "a hash of references to hashes."

But it's convenient and descriptive to use the concept of dimensions and phrases like "an array of arrays" in Perl. You just need to remember that the way to create multidimensional arrays or hashes in Perl is by using references to references. You're going to learn more about the references to arrays and hashes in the following sections.

Also, an array or hash may contain both references to hashes and references to arrays.

Arrays of Arrays

For instance, the following is an array, called `@my_family_1`, which contains three elements: `grandparents`, `parents`, and `children`. These three elements are themselves arrays that contain elements called `grandfathers`, `grandmothers`, `father`, `mother`, `brothers`, `sisters`, `me`, and `cat`. Take a look:

```
@my_family_1 = (
    ['grandfathers', 'grandmothers'],
    ['father', 'mother'],
    ['brothers', 'sisters', 'me', 'cat'],
);
```

`@my_family_1` is considered a two-dimensional array, which is also called an *array of arrays*.

Referencing to Arrays of Arrays with [ ]

One way to create a reference to an array of arrays is to use the backslash operator (\). For instance, to `@my_family_1`, you can create a reference like this:

```
$ref = \@my_family_1;
```

Another method to set up a reference to an array of arrays is simply to define the reference in the following way:

```
$ref = [
    ['grandfathers', 'grandmothers'],
    ['father', 'mother'],
    ['brothers', 'sisters', 'me', 'cat'],
];
```

18

Note that the brackets, [], are used to create an anonymous array—an array that only exists as a reference.

To access an element in @my_family_1, you can de-reference a reference that points to the array. For example, you can call

```
print $ref->[0][1];
```

to print out grandmothers on the screen. Here, the -> operator is used to de-reference the reference that has been created to point to the array of arrays.

Arrays of Hashes

If I want to add names to each family member in @my_family_1, I can change the three elements in @my_family_1 to three hashes. Within each hash, the names are assigned to the associated family members. The updated array is called @my_family_2, which is an example of an array of hashes. Take a look:

```
@my_family_2 = (
    {grandfathers => 'Dave & Tom', grandmothers => 'Elise & Mary'},
    {father => 'Steve', mother => 'Nancy'},
    {brothers  => 'Bob & John', sisters => 'Debbie & Linda', me => 'Tony', cat
    ➥ => 'Ellen'},
);
```

Referencing to Arrays of Hashes with [ ]

Similar to the process with arrays of arrays, referencing to an array of hashes can be done by using either the \ or the [] operator. That is, the following two Perl scripts are equivalent:

```
@my_family_2 = (
    {grandfathers => 'Dave & Tom', grandmothers => 'Elise & Mary'},
    {father => 'Steve', mother => 'Nancy'},
    {brothers  => 'Bob & John', sisters => 'Debbie & Linda', me => 'Tony', cat
    ➥ => 'Ellen'},
);
$ref = \@my_family_2;

$ref = [
    {grandfathers => 'Dave & Tom', grandmothers => 'Elise & Mary'},
    {father => 'Steve', mother => 'Nancy'},
    {brothers  => 'Bob & John', sisters => 'Debbie & Linda', me => 'Tony', cat
    ➥ => 'Ellen'},
];
```

Listing 18.7 gives an example of how to create a reference to an array of hashes and then display the content of the array by de-referencing the reference.

TYPE

Listing 18.7. Using [ ] to create a reference to an array of hashes and -> to de-reference the reference.

```
1:  # p18_7.pl
2:
3:  $ref = [   # this is a reference pointing to @my_family_2
4:      {grandfathers => 'Dave & Tom', grandmothers => 'Elise & Mary'},
5:      {father => 'Steve', mother => 'Nancy'},
6:      {brothers  => 'Bob & John', sisters => 'Debbie & Linda', me => 'Tony',
         ↪ cat => 'Ellen'},
7:  ];
8:  $i = 0;
9:  foreach (@{$ref}) {
10:     $ref_tmp = \%{$ref->[$i]};
11:     foreach $key (keys %{$ref_tmp}) {
12:         print "$key => $ref->[$i]{$key} \n";
13:     }
14:     $i++;
15: }
```

OUTPUT

```
C:\> perl p18_7.pl
grandfathers => Dave & Tom
grandmothers => Elise & Mary
father => Steve
mother => Nancy
cat => Ellen
brothers  => Bob & John
me => Tony
sisters => Debbie & Linda
C:\>
```

ANALYSIS
In Listing 18.7, lines 3–7 initialize an array of hashes with the content as shown in @my_family_2 in the previous section and then create a reference, called $ref, to the array. Note that in lines 3 and 7, the brackets ([]) are used in defining the $ref reference.

Line 9 extracts every element from the array pointed to by $ref; line 10 then creates another reference, $ref_tmp, to the hashes inside the array.

Lines 11 and 12 fetch all values in the hashes associated with the keys of $key. In line 12, $ref->[$i]{$key} tells the Perl interpreter to de-reference $ref to the value associated with $key that is the $ith element in the array.

The output shows that the content of the array of hashes has been printed out.

Hashes of Arrays

Now, let's look at another example. This time, I'll classify car manufacturers into two groups, the USA group and the foreign group. The two groups are two elements associated with the keys usa and foreign, respectively, in the %car_makers_1 hash.

Because the two groups themselves are arrays containing the names of some car manufacturers, %car_makers_1 is called a *hash of arrays.*

The following is the example of a hash of arrays:

```
%car_makers_1 = (
    usa => [
        'Chrysler',
        'Ford',
        'GM'
    ],
    foreign => [
        'BMW',
        'Honda',
        'Toyota',
        'Volvo'
    ],
);
```

Referencing to Hashes of Arrays with { }

To create a reference to a hash of arrays, you can use either a backslash or braces ({}). For instance, to build a reference to %car_makers_1, from the previous section, you can write the following statement:

```
$ref = \%car_makers_1;,
```

You could also initialize the reference directly with the help of {}:

```
$ref = {
    usa => [
        'Chrysler',
        'Ford',
        'GM'
    ],
    foreign => [
        'BMW',
        'Honda',
        'Toyota',
        'Volvo'
    ],
};
```

Note that {} is used to pass the address of the hash to $ref.

To access to one of the elements in the hash, you can use -> to de-reference $ref. For example, the following line

```
print STDOUT $ref->{usa}[1];
```

prints out Ford on the screen, because the usa key is used to find the value associated with the key; the value itself is an array, and the index 1 specifies the second element, Ford, in the array.

18

Hashes of Hashes

If I want to associate each car manufacturer listed in `%car_makers_1` with a car name, I can rewrite `%car_makers_1` and assign the car names to their manufacturers. The result is a hash of hashes as shown here in `%car_makers_2`:

```
%car_makers_2 = (
    usa => {
        Chrysler => 'Jeep',
        Ford =>'Mustang' ,
        GM => 'Cadillac'
    },
    foreign => {
        BMW => '728i',
        Honda => 'Accord',
        Toyota =>'Camry',
        Volvo => '960'
    },
);
```

Referencing to Hashes of Arrays with { }

Similarly, both the backslash and braces ({}) can be used to create a reference to a hash of hashes. The following two declarations are equivalent:

```
%car_makers_2 = (
    usa => {
        Chrysler => 'Jeep',
        Ford =>'Mustang' ,
        GM => 'Cadillac'
    },
    foreign => {
        BMW => '728i',
        Honda => 'Accord',
        Toyota =>'Camry',
        Volvo => '960'
    },
);
$ref = \%car_makers_2;

$ref = {
    usa => {
        Chrysler => 'Jeep',
        Ford =>'Mustang' ,
        GM -> 'Cadillac'
    },
    foreign => {
        BMW => '728i',
        Honda => 'Accord',
        Toyota =>'Camry',
        Volvo => '960'
    },
};
```

Here, the braces, {}, are used to create an anonymous hash—a hash that only exists as a reference.

18

Listing 18.8 demonstrates how to create a reference to a hash of hashes and then display the content of the hash by de-referencing the reference.

> **TYPE**
>
> **Listing 18.8. Creating and de-referencing a reference to a hash of hashes.**

```
1:  # p18_8.pl
2:
3:  $ref = {
4:      usa => {
5:          Chrysler => 'Jeep',
6:          Ford =>'Mustang' ,
7:          GM => 'Cadillac'
8:      },
9:      foreign => {
10:         .   BMW => '728i',
11:         Honda => 'Accord',
12:         Toyota =>'Camry',
13:         Volvo => '960'
14:     },
15: };
16: $i = 0;
17: foreach $key_1 (keys %{$ref}) {
18:     $ref_array[$i] = \%{$ref->{$key_1}};
19:     foreach $key_2 (keys %{$ref_array[$i++]}) {
20:         print "$key_1 => $key_2 => $ref->{$key_1}{$key_2} \n";
21:     }
22: }
```

> **OUTPUT**
>
> ```
> C:\> perl p18_8.pl
> usa => Ford => Mustang
> usa => Chrysler => Jeep
> usa => GM => Cadillac
> foreign => Toyota => Camry
> foreign => Volvo => 960
> foreign => BMW => 728i
> foreign => Honda => Accord
> C:\>
> ```

> **ANALYSIS**
>
> In Listing 18.8, lines 3–15 initialize a hash of hashes with the content as shown in %car_makers_2 and then create a reference, called $ref, to the hash. Note that in lines 3 and 15, {} is used in building the reference $ref.

Lines 17 and 19 extract the keys from the hash and the nested hashes, respectively. Line 20 prints out each car name embedded in the hash of hashes by calling $ref->{$key_1}{$key_2}.

The output is a copy from the screen on my computer. Because the elements in hashes are not ordered, the order of the output here is different from the one when the hash is initialized as shown in lines 3–15.

18

NOTE

In today's lesson, the -> operator is used to de-reference references that point to one- or two-dimensional arrays and hashes. You can apply -> to arrays or hashes with more than two dimensions.

For instance, to access the elements of nested arrays, you can use:

$ref->[$index] for a single-dimensional array

$ref->[$index1][$index2] for a two-dimensional array

$ref->[$index1][$index2][$index3] for a three-dimensional array

Similarly, to access the elements of nested hashes, you can use:

$ref->{$key} for a single-dimensional hash

$ref->{$key1}{$key2} for a two-dimensional hash

$ref->{$key1}{$key2}{$key3} for a three-dimensional hash

Using -> in de-referencing references is easier and clearer than using other operators.

References to File Handles

As you learned earlier today, you can create a reference to a file handle. It's handy to use references to pass named file handles to subroutines in Perl programs.

For instance, if you run the following Perl script,

```
Hello (\*STDOUT, 'Hello, world!');
sub Hello {
    my $ref = shift (@_);
    my $str = shift (@_);
    print $ref "$str \n";
}
```

you see the message Hello, world! displayed on the screen because the reference to the standard output handle is passed to the Hello subroutine as the first argument in the first statement.

In Perl, there is an internal data type, called typeglob, which is prefixed with *. File handles can be passed to subroutines in the format of typeglobs (see the first statement in the preceding code).

Take a look at another example, which is shown in Listing 18.9. This example can print out the names of the month and the day in the year 1997 according to the input made by the user. You can run the Perl program in Listing 18.9 with two arguments for input and output file handles.

Listing 18.9. Using references to arrays, hashes, subroutines, and file handles.

TYPE

```
1:  # p18_9.pl
2:
3:  Error( \*STDOUT, "Specify the input and output handles.\n" )
4:      if @ARGV != 2;
5:
6:  my @array_day = (
7:      'Sunday',
8:      'Monday',
9;      'Tuesday',
10:     'Wednesday',
11:     'Thursday',
12:     'Friday',
13:     'Saturday'
14: );
15: my %hashed_month = (
16:     '01'=>'January',
17:     '02'=>'February',
18:     '03'=>'March',
19:     '04'=>'April',
20:     '05'=>'May',
21:     '06'=>'June',
22:     '07'=>'July',
23:     '08'=>'August',
24:     '09'=>'September',
25:     '10'=>'October',
26:     '11'=>'November',
27:     '12'=>'December'
28: );
29: my %Year97 = (
30:     January =>  [ 3, 31 ],
31:     February => [ 6, 28 ],
32:     March => => [ 6, 31 ],
33:     April =>    [ 2, 30 ],
34:     May =>      [ 4, 31 ],
35:     June =>     [ 0, 30 ],
36:     July =>     [ 2, 31 ],
37:     August =>   [ 5, 31 ],
38:     September=> [ 1, 30 ],
39:     October =>  [ 3, 31 ],
40:     November => [ 6, 30 ],
41:     December => [ 1, 31 ]
42: );
43: my $ref_to_day = \@array_day;
44: my $ref_to_month = \%hashed_month;
45: my $ref_to_year = \%Year97;
46: my $ref_to_sub = \&Error;
47: my $ref_to_fh_in = \*{shift(@ARGV)};
48: my $ref_to_fh_out = \*{shift(@ARGV)};
49:
50: #---- print out header ----
51:   Header ($ref_to_fh_out);
52: #---- get input ---
```

18

```
53:    my $date = <$ref_to_fh_in>;
54:    chop ($date);
55:    my ($month_key, $day_key, $year) = split ( /-/, $date);
56: #---- check the year ----
57:    &{$ref_to_sub}($ref_to_fh_out, "The year is not 97! \n" )
58:        if $year ne '97';
59: #---- check the month ----
60:    $month_key = '0' . $month_key if !($month_key =~ /^[0-1][0-9]$/);
61:    my $month_name = $ref_to_month->{$month_key};
62:    &{$ref_to_sub}($ref_to_fh_out, "There is no such month $month_key in a
   year \n" )
63:        if $month_name eq '';
64: #---- check the day ----
65:    $day_key =~ s/^0//;
66:    &{$ref_to_sub}($ref_to_fh_out, "There is no such day $day_key in $month_name
   \n")
67:        if $day_key > $ref_to_year->{$month_name}[1];
68: #---- get the name of the day in a week ----
69:    my $day_index = $ref_to_year->{$month_name}[0] + $day_key - 1;
70:    $day_index %= 7;
71:    my $day_name = $ref_to_day->[$day_index];
72: #---- output the result ----
73:    Result($ref_to_fh_out,
74:        " $ref_to_month->{$month_key} $day_key, 19$year, $day_name \n" );
75:
76: #---- subroutines ----
77: sub Error {
78:    my $ref = shift (@_);
79:    my $str = shift (@_);
80:    print $ref "$str";
81:    print $ref "A nice try :-)\n";
82:    exit;
83: }
84: sub Header {
85:    my $ref = shift (@_);
86:    print $ref "# ---- The 1997 Calendar ---- #\n";
87:    print $ref "Enter a date in the format of mm-dd-97\n";
88:    print $ref "e.g.,  12-25-97\n\n";
89: }
90: sub Result {
91:    my $ref = shift (@_);
92:    my $str = shift (@_);
93:    print $ref "\nThe re-formatted date you just entered is:\n";
94:    print $ref "$str";
95: }
```

OUTPUT

```
C:\> perl p18_9.pl STDIN STDOUT
# ---- The 1997 Calendar ---- #
Enter a date in the format of mm-dd-97
e.g.,  12-25-97


01-25-97


The re-formatted date you just entered is:
January 25, 1997, Saturday
C:\>
```

18

ANALYSIS In Listing 18.9, lines 3 and 4 check the number of the incoming arguments. The user is supposed to enter two arguments: The first one is for the input file handle, and the second one is for the output file handle. Note that in line 3, `\*STDOUT`, the first argument passed to the `Error` subroutine, is the reference to a `typeglob` that holds the `STDOUT` file handle.

Lines 6–14 initialize the `@array_day` array with the names of days in the week. Lines 15–28 set up a hash, called `%hashed_month`, to hold the names of the 12 months of the year. (You may replace the hash with an array. See Exercise 2 at the end of today's lesson.)

`%Year97` is a hash of arrays in which the names of the 12 months are used as the keys that associate with 12 arrays. Each array nested in the hash has two elements; the first one is an index from which you can know the name of the first day in each month. For instance, the first day in January 1997 was on Wednesday, so its index is `3` if Sunday is taken as the beginning of a week and the index starts at `0`.

The second element in each array is the maximum number of days in a month. For instance, the second element in the array associated with the key `January` is `31`, because January has 31 days.

Lines 43–45 create references to `@array_day`, `$hashed_month`, and `%Year97`, respectively. Line 46 builds a reference to the `Error` subroutine. Lines 47 and 48 set references to the two arguments, the first one for the input and the other for the output, both entered by the user. That is, `$ref_to_fh_in` is the reference to the input file handle; `$ref_to_fh_out` is for the output file handle.

The message saved in a header is sent out first to the output file handle in line 51 by calling the `Header` subroutine. The output file handle is referred by `$ref_to_fh_out`. Line 53 waits for the user to enter a date from 1997 in the format of `mm-dd-yy`. Line 54 chops off the return character attached at the end of the input date. Then, line 55 splits the date into three parts that can be used for fetching the names of the day and the month from the array and hashes defined early in the Perl program.

If the user does not enter `97`, line 57 sends the warning message, `"The year is not 97!"`, to the output file handle. To make this message appear, the `Error` subroutine is called by `&{$ref_to_sub}` in line 57. The `$ref_to_sub` reference has the address to the subroutine.

Line 60 adds `0` to `$month_key`—the number in the month part, if `$month_key` is a single digit. Then, `$ref_to_month->{$month_key}` in line 61 finds the month name associated with the value of `$month_key`. If there is not a proper month name associated with `$month_key` that is a portion of the input made by the user, line 62 sends a warning message to the output file handle.

If the value of `$day_key` starts with `0`, line 65 erases the extra `0`. Lines 66 and 67 compare `$day_key` with the maximum number of the days in the month of `$month_name`. The maximum number is fetched by applying `$ref_to_year->{$month_name}[1]` in line 67.

18

Lines 69 and 70 calculate the `$day_index` index that is used in line 71 to extract the name of the day of the week from `@array_day` pointed to by `$ref_to_array`.

Lines 73 and 74 finally send the reformatted date with the names of the month and day in 1997 to the output file handle by calling the `Result` subroutine.

The three subroutines, `Error`, `Header`, and `Result`, are listed in lines 76–95. The first argument passed to these subroutines is the reference to the output file handle to which the messages and results are sent.

The output from the listing is a copy from the screen on my machine. As you see, the standard input and output file handles, `STDIN` and `STDOUT`, are used as the two input arguments.

Symbolic References

So far, you've learned a lot about the hard references in Perl 5. This section introduces how to create and de-reference the symbolic references in Perl.

Remember the mailbox example in which I forget the address to my mailbox and go to the secretary for help? Now I can use Perl language to describe the example.

In the look-up table kept by the secretary, my mailbox address is associated with my first name, which acts as the mailbox label. In Perl language, it can be written something like this:

```
$Tony = 'Row 7, Column 125';.
```

Then, I tell the secretary my name—that is, in Perl language:

```
$Employee_Name = "Tony";
```

The secretary uses the name to extract my mailbox address from the look-up table and print out the address for me, which is equivalent to the following two Perl statements:

```
$Address_of_Mailbox = ${$Employee_Name};
```

```
print $Address_of_Mailbox;.
```

If I run the four preceding Perl statements, I can get the address of my mailbox that is located at row 7 and column 125.

Here, `$Employee_Name` is actually used as a symbolic reference because it contains the mailbox label, rather than the mailbox address. The mailbox label itself is associated with the mailbox address.

`${$Employee_Name}` de-references the symbolic reference that is interpreted as a string. Similar to hard references, you can also de-reference `$Employee_Name` by prefixing a `$` to it—that is, `$$Employee_Name`.

18

Listing 18.10 gives another example of using symbolic references to call subroutines and point to scalar and array variables.

TYPE **Listing 18.10. Using symbolic references to call subroutines and refer to scalars.**

```
1:  # p18_10.pl
2:
3:  @names = (
4:      'sub_or_scalar_1',
5:      'sub_or_scalar_2'
6:  );
7:  local $sub_or_scalar_1 = "Hello, world!";
8:  local $sub_or_scalar_2 = 18;
9:  # create a symbolic reference
10: $sym_ref = "names";
11: foreach $element (@$sym_ref) {
12:     &$element( $$element );
13: }
14:
15: sub sub_or_scalar_1 {
16:     my $str = shift;
17:     print "This is from subroutine sub_or_scalar_1:\n";
18:     print "  $str \n\n";
19: }
20: sub sub_or_scalar_2 {
21:     my $input = shift;
22:     print "This is from subroutine sub_or_scalar_2:\n";
23:     print "  Today is Day $input \n";
24: }
```

OUTPUT
```
C:\> perl p18_10.pl
This is from subroutine sub_or_scalar_1
   Hello, world!
This is from subroutine sub_or_scalar_2
   Today is Day 18
C:\>
```

ANALYSIS In Listing 18.10, lines 3–6 initialize the `@names` array with two strings, `sub_or_scalar_1` and `sub_or_scalar_2`. Lines 7 and 8 declare two scalar variables, called `$sub_or_scalar_1` and `$sub_or_scalar_2`.

Line 10 creates a symbolic reference, `$sym_ref`, to the `@names` array. Then, line 11 fetches all elements in the array. Line 12 uses each of the fetched elements as another symbolic reference to point to the corresponding subroutine and scalar variable. For instance, if `$element` contains `sub_or_scalar_1`, then `&$element($$element)` in line 12 calls a subroutine, called `sub_or_scalar_1`, and passes the value of `$sub_or_scalar_1` to the subroutine. Here, `$element` is another symbolic reference.

Lines 15–24 define the two subroutines, `sub_or_scalar_1` and `sub_or_scalar_2`.

Hard Reference versus Symbolic References

Although a symbolic reference is flexible and powerful, it can cause problems if it is accidentally used in a place where a hard reference is supposed to be used.

To avoid the problems caused by misusing symbolic references in the places of hard references in Perl, you can set a restriction by declaring

```
use strict 'refs';
```

in your Perl program so that only hard references are allowed in the rest of the program after the declaration.

To stop the restriction in your program, just say this:

```
no strict 'refs';
```

NOTE

> If you use a symbolic reference to point to a variable, you cannot declare the variable with `my`, because the variable is not visible to the symbolic reference. Take a look at the following example:
>
> ```
> my $name = 'Tony';
> $ref = 'name';
> print ${$ref};
> ```
>
> The last statement does not print out anything but null, simply because the first statement declares `$name` with `my`, which makes `$name` invisible to `$ref`.
>
> If you replace `my` with `local` in the statement of the example, you can get the desired output, `Tony`, after running the Perl script.

18

Summary

Today, you've learned about the reference—an important concept in Perl. Hard and symbolic references are two types of references in Perl 5, as well as in Perl 5 for Win32.

A hard reference is also called a real reference, because it points to the value of a variable directly. A symbolic reference, on the other hand, refers to the name of a variable instead of to the value. Therefore, a symbolic reference is an indirect reference that can be broken (or lost) more easily.

You've learned how to create a hard or symbolic reference. You now know how to de-reference a reference that points to a scalar, a subroutine, a file handle, an array, or a hash.

You have also learned about multidimensional arrays and hashes, as well as their references, through the examples shown in today's lesson.

References are powerful. You should avoid misusing symbolic references with hard references. The `use strict 'refs';` statement sets a restriction so that only hard references can be used.

Q&A

Q Why are references useful?

A There are many places to use references in Perl. For instance, it's convenient to use references to build complex data structures. Also, it's efficient to pass a reference to an array or a hash to a subroutine instead of passing the array or hash itself so that the subroutine can modify the array or hash directly, instead of modifying their copies.

Q Are there any real multidimensional arrays or hashes in Perl?

A No. Strictly speaking, arrays and hashes in Perl are indeed one-dimensional. Internally, arrays and hashes can only hold scalar values. The phrase of an *array of arrays* really means "an array of references to arrays." Similarly, a *hash of hashes* is only "a hash of references to hashes."

But it's convenient and descriptive to use dimensions and phrases like "an array of arrays" in Perl. You just need to remember that the way to create multidimensional arrays or hashes in Perl is by using references to references.

Q How do I access the innermost elements in a 3-D array or hash?

A Use the `->` operator. For instance, for a 3-D array, you can call `$ref->[$index1][$index2][$index3]` to get an innermost element from the nested arrays.

Similarly, use `$ref_to_hash->{$key1}{$key2}{$key3}` for a 3-D hash.

Q Are `${a_variable}` and `${"a_variable"}` the same?

A No. `${a_variable}` is equivalent to `$a_variable`, which is a scalar variable. But `${"a_variable"}` is interpreted as a symbolic reference in Perl. In this case, `${a_variable}` and `${"a_variable"}` just happen to share the same value.

Workshop

To help you solidify your understanding of today's lesson, you are encouraged to try to answer the quiz questions and finish the exercises provided in the workshop before you move to the next lesson. The answers and hints to the questions and exercises are given in Appendix B, "Answers."

Quiz

1. Besides using the backslash, what is the other way to create a reference to an array?

2. If `$hard_ref` is a hard reference to an array, what's wrong with the following line of code?

   ```
   $element =  $$hard_ref->[$i];
   ```

3. If `$hard_ref` is a hard reference to an array of arrays and I want to obtain the value of the first element in the first array, what's wrong with the following line of code?

   ```
   $element = $hard_ref[0][0];
   ```

4. Are the following two statements equivalent? (Hint: You can write a Perl program to include the two statements, and run the program to see what you can get.)

   ```
   printf "$$ref[$i] \n";

   printf "$ref->[$i] \n";
   ```

Exercises

1. Write a Perl program to print out all elements in an array that contains the names of the 12 months in a year.

2. Rewrite the Perl program in Listing 18.9. This time, replace the `%hashed_month` with an array that contains the names of the 12 months.

3. Explain the differences between

   ```
   &sub_routine( "This", "is a", "subroutine\n");
   ```
   and
   ```
   @array = ( "This", "is a", "subroutine\n");
   ```

4. **BUG BUSTER**: What is wrong with the following Perl program?

   ```
   # Exercise 4: Bug Buster

   @array = ( "Hello, world!\n",
              "This program has a bug.\n"
   );
   $ref = \@array;
   foreach $element (${$ref}) {
       print $element;
   }
   ```

5. **BUG BUSTER**: What is wrong with the following Perl program?

   ```
   # Exercise 5: Bug Buster

   my $string = 'Hello, world!';
   $ref = 'string';
   print ${$ref} . "\n";
   ```

18

Day **19**

Object-Oriented Programming in Perl

Object-oriented programming (OOP) is a new programming methodology that has taken the best ideas of structured programming and combined them with powerful new concepts.

Today's lesson introduces the object-oriented programming in Perl, which applies to Perl 5 for Win32 as well. It covers topics such as construction and destruction of objects, class inheritance, method overriding, and data encapsulation.

An Introduction to Objects, Classes, and Methods

Before going any further, you need to first understand the three important concepts—objects, classes, and methods—involved with object-oriented programming in Perl.

Objects

Generally speaking, an *object* is a concrete entity. In OOP, an object is a logical entity that is made up by a data structure and code that manipulates the data structure.

An object can protect against any unrelated modifications and incorrect use of the private part of the data and code inside the object.

Classes

A class, on the other hand, is abstract. A *class* in OOP is a set of objects that share the same essences, such as a common structure and a common behavior. You cannot group objects into a class if those objects do not share the same structure and behavior.

An object is not a class. Rather, an object demonstrates its behaviors by being an instance of a class.

In Perl 5, a class is a package that contains subroutines to manipulate objects. Refer back to Day 14, "Packages, Modules, and System Functions," when you learned about packages in Perl.

Methods

A method is often referred to as a disciplined process in OOP. In Perl, a *method* is simply a subroutine. Therefore, the two words *method* and *subroutine* are used alternately in today's lesson.

The first argument passed to a method is expected to be an object reference or a class name.

If the first argument is a class name, it is called a *static method*. Otherwise, if a reference to an object is the first argument, the method is a *virtual method*. More details about the two types of methods are explained in the section titled "Methods in Perl" later in this chapter.

Creating a Class

As already defined in this chapter, a class in Perl is simply a package that contains subroutines. The subroutines in the class are called the *methods* of the class.

Now, let's build a very simple class, called My_Class:

```
package My_Class;
sub Hello {
    my @argv = @_;
    print "From My_Class: Hello, world! \n";
}
```

The next section demonstrates how to access to the Hello method inside the My_Class class.

Methods in Perl

As you learned on Day 14, the default package in a Perl program is called main. (You can specify it by declaring package main;.) Now, here is a question: How can you access to the Hello subroutine inside the My_Class class created in the last section?

Listing 19.1 gives an example that tries to access to the Hello subroutine that is inside the My_Class class.

TYPE **Listing 19.1. Trying to call a method inside a class.**

```
1:  # p19_1.pl
2:
3:  package My_Class;
4:  sub Hello {
5:      my @argv = @_;
6:      print "From My_Class: Hello, world! \n";
7:  }
8:  package main;
9:  sub Hello {
10:      my @argv = @_;
11:      print "From main: Hello, world! \n";
12: }
13: Hello ('Testing');
```

OUTPUT
```
C:\> perl p19_1.pl
From main: Hello, world!
C:\>
```

ANALYSIS Whoops! The output result shows that only the Hello subroutine in package main, rather than the Hello method inside the My_Class class, has been accessed and executed.

In Listing 19.1, lines 3–7 create the My_Class class that has a method called Hello. The Hello method can print out a message, From My_Class: Hello, world!, if it is executed.

Line 8 marks the beginning of the default program body, main. Lines 9–12 declare a subroutine, Hello, in main. In Perl, you can assign the same name to subroutines that are in different packages.

But in Listing 19.1, the problem is that the Perl interpreter picks up the Hello subroutine within the main package, not the Hello method within the My_Class class.

In next section, you learn two ways to call a method within a class in Perl.

Accessing Methods

Basically, there are two ways to call a method from a class via the class name. The first one is similar to using the file handles with the Perl `print` or `printf` functions.

Listing 19.2 shows the first way to access a method in a class.

TYPE **Listing 19.2. Accessing a method inside a class.**

```
1:  # p19_2.pl
2:
3:  package My_Class;
4:  sub Hello {
5:      my @argv = @_;
6:      print "From My_Class: Hello, world! \n";
7:  }
8:  package main;
9:  sub Hello {
10:     my @argv = @_;
11:     print "From main: Hello, world! \n";
12: }
13: Hello My_Class 'Testing';
```

OUTPUT
```
C:\> perl p19_2.pl
From My_Class: Hello, world!
C:\>
```

ANALYSIS The Perl code in Listing 19.2 is the same as the one in Listing 19.1, except for line 13. Here, in line 13, the name of the class is used to tell the Perl interpreter to call `Hello` inside the `My_Class` class. The usage of the class name is similar to a file handle used by `print` or `printf`. For example:

```
print My_File_Handle 'Testing';.
```

The output result of the Perl program in Listing 19.2 shows that the `Hello` method (subroutine) inside the `My_Class` class has been accessed and executed correctly.

Now, let's move on to the second way to access a method within a class. This time, the `->` operator is involved in the method access. Listing 19.3 gives an example of accessing a method of a class by using the `->` operator.

TYPE **Listing 19.3. Calling a method from a class by `->`.**

```
1:  # p19_3.pl
2:
3:  package My_Class;
4:  sub Hello {
```

```
5:      my @argv = @_;
6:      print "From My_Class: Hello, world! \n";
7:  }
8:  package main;
9:  sub Hello {
10:      my @argv = @_;
11:      print "From main: Hello, world! \n";
12: }
13: My_Class -> Hello('Testing');
```

OUTPUT

```
C:\> perl p19_3.pl
From My_Class: Hello, world!
C:\>
```

ANALYSIS The only difference between Listing 19.3 and Listing 19.2 is line 13. Here, the `->` operator is used, together with the class name of `My_Class`, to refer to the `Hello` method within the class.

Note that in line 13, the argument, `'Testing'`, is wrapped by the `()` parentheses following the method name `Hello`. The parentheses are required if you use this syntax and pass arguments to a method.

Static Methods

If a method inside a class is accessed via the class name, as shown in the two preceding examples, the method is called *static method*. A static method is also called a *class method*.

You may notice that in Listings 19.2 and 19.3, `Testing` is passed to the `Hello` method, but the method does not do anything with the input arguments.

Now, let's modify the `Hello` method in Listing 19.3 and print out the incoming arguments. The modified Perl program is shown in Listing 19.4.

TYPE **Listing 19.4. Passing the class name to a method.**

```
1:  # p19_4.pl
2:
3:  package My_Class;
4:  sub Hello {
5:      my @argv = @_;
6:      print "From My_Class: Hello, world! \n";
7:      print "The incoming arguments: @argv \n";
8:  }
9:  package main;
10: sub Hello {
11:      my @argv = @_;
12:      print "From main: Hello, world! \n";
13: }
14: My_Class -> Hello('Testing');
```

OUTPUT

```
C:\> perl p19_4.pl
From My_Class: Hello, world!
The incoming arguments:  My_Class  Testing
C:\>
```

ANALYSIS There is nothing special in Listing 19.4, except that the statement `print "The incoming arguments: @argv \n";` (in line 7) is added to the `Hello` method inside the `My_Class` class because we want to see the arguments passed to the method. When the statement in line 14, `My_Class -> Hello('Testing');`, is executed, it displays the output, including the arguments, on the screen.

As you would expect, the first line in the output is the greeting message. Note that in the second line of the output, the class name, `My_Class`, is printed out right before the `Testing` string. But we know the `Testing` string is the only argument passed to the `Hello` method. Where does `My_Class` come from?

When the statement in line 14 is executed, the Perl interpreter knows that `My_Class` is the name of a class from which the `Hello` method is called as a static method, because the statement contains `My_Class->`. Because a static method expects the first argument in `@_` to be the name of a class, the Perl interpreter automatically adds the class name, `My_Class`, into the `@_` array as the first argument. That's why you see the class name in the output.

Virtual Methods and the `bless` Function

As I've mentioned, there is another type of method that expects the first argument in the `@_` array to be a hard reference to an object. This method is called the *virtual method*, or *instance method*. (You should recall that hard references were introduced yesterday.)

To access a method inside a class and treat it as a virtual method, you can use the Perl `bless` function to let the Perl interpreter believe that a referenced object is part of the class. The syntax of using the `bless` function is

```
bless Reference, Class Name;
```

Listing 19.5 shows an example that treats the `Hello` method as a virtual method and passes the blessed reference as the first argument.

TYPE   **Listing 19.5. Accessing a method as a virtual method.**

```
1:  # p19_5.pl
2:
3:  package My_Class;
4:  sub Hello {
5:      my @argv = @_;
6:      print "From My_Class: Hello, world! \n";
7:      print "The incomming arguments:  @argv \n";
```

```
 8:        print "The value of \$x seen from the inside of the class is: $x \n";
 9:    }
10: package main;
11: sub Hello {
12:        my @argv = @_;
13:        print "From main: Hello, world! \n";
14: }
15: $x = 97;
16: $ref = \$x;
17: bless $ref, My_Class;
18: $ref->Hello ( "Testing" );
```

OUTPUT

```
C:\> perl p19_5.pl
From My_Class: Hello, world!
The incoming arguments:  My_Class=SCALAE(0x77ea84) Testing
The value of $x seen from the inside of the class is:
C:\>
```

ANALYSIS

In Listing 19.5, lines 3–9 declare the My_Class class that contains a subroutine called Hello. Line 10 indicates the beginning of the main package. Lines 11–14 define a subroutine, also called Hello, inside the main package.

Line 15 declares a scalar variable, $x, and initializes it with the value of 97. Then, a hard reference, $ref, is created and assigned the address of $x in line 16.

Line 17 uses the bless function to make the Perl interpreter think that $x referred by $ref is part of the My_Class class. After the blessing, $ref can be used to refer to the Hello method inside the My_Class class. (See line 18.) In this way, the Hello method is treated as a virtual method. You can check the output to find the evidence.

The first line in the output shows that the Hello method inside the My_Class class has been executed. The second line displays the contents in @_ that have been passed to the method:

```
My_Class=SCALAR(0x77ea84) Testing.
```

Here, you see that the address kept by $ref is assigned to the name of the class. The Perl interpreter truly believes that $x is part of the My_Class class because of the blessing in line 17 of Listing 19.5.

It should be pointed out that the $x, being considered as part of My_Class, is *not* part of My_Class in reality. That's why in the third line of the output, the value of $x, 97, is not printed out.

Line 18 can be rewritten as

```
Hello $ref "Testing";,
```

where the relationship between $ref and Hello is similar to the one between a file handle and the print function in Perl.

19

> **NOTE**
>
> For either a static method or a virtual method, you can assign the method name to a variable and then access the method by pointing to the variable with the class name or reference name. For instance, in Listing 19.5, you can use
>
> ```
> $method_name = 'Hello';
> $ref->$method_name ( "Testing" );
> ```
>
> to replace
>
> ```
> $ref->Hello ( "Testing" );.
> ```

Classes and Objects in Perl

If an object is defined as a concrete entity, the $x scalar variable you saw in Listing 19.5 can be considered an object. In line 17 of that listing, $x is incarnated and assigned the behaviors by being an instance of the My_Class class. This is why a virtual method is also called an instance method.

However, $x in Listing 19.5 is defined outside the My_Class class. Can $x be created within the My_Class class and called from the code outside the class? Let's go to the next section for the answer.

Object Constructors

The Perl code in Listing 19.5 can be modified; lines 15–17 can be moved into the My_Class class. As shown in Listing 19.6, a method, called new, is added into My_Class. The new method contains the code shown in lines 15–17 of Listing 19.5.

TYPE   **Listing 19.6. Defining an object constructor.**

```
 1:  # p19_6.pl
 2:
 3:  package My_Class;
 4:  sub new {
 5:      my $x = 97;
 6:      my $ref = \$x;
 7:      bless $ref, My_Class;
 8:      return $ref;
 9:  }
10:  sub Hello {
11:      my @argv = @_;
12:      print "From My_Class: Hello, world! \n";
13:      print "The incomming arguments:  @argv \n";
```

```
14: }
15: package main;
16: sub Hello {
17:     my @argv = @_;
18:     print "From main: Hello, world! \n";
19: }
20: $new_ref = new My_Class;
21: $new_ref->Hello ( "Testing ", $$new_ref );
```

OUTPUT

```
C:\> perl p19_6.pl
From My_Class: Hello, world!
The incoming arguments:  My_Class=SCALAR(0x77e928) Testing 97
C:\>
```

ANALYSIS In Listing 19.6, lines 4–9 declare a method (subroutine), called new, within the My_Class class. Line 5 initializes the $x scalar variable with 97. Line 6 creates a reference, $ref, which refers to $x. The bless function is used in line 7 to connect the name of the class, My_Class, to the $ref reference. Line 8 returns the $ref reference to the caller.

Lines 10–14 define the Hello method within the My_Class class. Then, lines 16–19 declare another Hello subroutine in main, beginning at line 15.

Line 20 creates a new object by calling the statement new My_Class;. $new_ref is a reference returned by the new method within the My_Class class. In line 21, $new_ref is used to call another method, Hello, within My_Class. The two arguments, "Testing " and $$new_ref, are passed to Hello in line 21. According to what you learned on Day 18, "References in Perl 5 for Win32," $$new_ref contains the value of a variable to which $new_ref points.

The output from the Perl program in Listing 19.6 indicates that the Hello method within My_Class has been executed and the two arguments passed to Hello are printed out along with the address of $x defined within My_Class and referred by $ref.

In Listing 19.6, the new method within the My_Class class is a special method that acts as an object constructor. You can create objects with an object constructor in your Perl program.

19

NOTE

You may use any name for a method that constructs objects. So far, new has been commonly used in Perl.

You can also rewrite line 20 in Listing 19.6 to

```
$new_ref = My_Class -> new;
```

which is equivalent to

```
$new_ref = new My_Class;.
```

One more thing you need to notice is that the syntax of using the bless function is

```
bless Reference, Class-Name; ,
```

where `Class-Name` is optional. The default class name is the current class (that is, package) name.

If a referenced object has been blessed into a class, you can use the Perl `ref` function to retrieve the class name from the reference that points to the object. (The `ref` function was introduced on Day 18.) The following example demonstrates how to use `ref` to retrieve the name of a class:

```
package My_Class;
sub new {
    my $x = 97;
    my $ref = \$x;
    bless $ref, My_Class;
    return $ref;
}
package main;
$new_ref = new My_Class;
my $retrieved_name = ref ($new_ref);
print "The class name is: $retrieved_name.\n";
```

If you run the above Perl scripts, you'll see the retrieved class name displayed on the screen.

Data Encapsulation Within an Object

On Day 18, you learned to create a reference to an anonymous array or hash by using `[]` or `{}`, respectively.

You can use an anonymous array or hash inside an object to encapsulate data. The data within an object cannot be manipulated from the outside of the object unless the reference, returned by the object constructor, is used.

Listing 19.7 shows how to create a reference to an anonymous array in an object constructor and manipulate the encapsulated data within a class. Note that an object constructor can take a class name by parsing the incoming first argument.

Listing 19.7. Creating a reference to an anonymous array in an object constructor.

| TYPE |

```
1:  # p19_7.pl
2:
3:  package My_Class;
4:  sub new {
5:      my ($class, @rest) = @_;
```

19

```
 6:      my $ref = [];
 7:      @$ref = @rest;
 8:      bless $ref, $class;
 9:      return $ref;
10: }
11: sub ArrayUpdate {
12:      my ($ref_to_array, @data) = @_;
13:      @$ref_to_array = @data;
14: }
15: sub ArrayPrint {
16:      my $ref_to_array = shift @_;
17:      my $str;
18:      my $i = 0;
19:      print "The elements in an array from My_Class: \n";
20:      foreach $str (@$ref_to_array) {
21:          print "$ref_to_array [$i]: $str \n";
22:          $i++;
23:      }
24: }
25: package main;
26: $new_ref = new My_Class '1', '2', '3';
27: $new_ref->ArrayPrint( );
28: print "\nNow, update the array in My_Class ... \n\n";
29: $new_ref->ArrayUpdate( '100', '200', '300');
30: $new_ref->ArrayPrint( );
```

OUTPUT

```
C:\> perl p19_7.pl
The elements in an array from My_Class:
My_Class=ARRAY(0x77ec34) [0]: 1
My_Class=ARRAY(0x77ec34) [1]: 2
My_Class=ARRAY(0x77ec34) [2]: 3

Now, update the array in My_Class ...

The elements in an array from My_Class:
My_Class=ARRAY(0x77ec34) [0]: 100
My_Class=ARRAY(0x77ec34) [1]: 200
My_Class=ARRAY(0x77ec34) [2]: 300
C:\>
```

ANALYSIS   Line 3 in Listing 19.7 marks the beginning of the My_Class class. Lines 4–10 declare an object constructor called new.

Note that line 6 creates a reference to an anonymous array, and line 7 initializes the array with the incoming elements if there are any.

Lines 11–14 declare a method (subroutine) called ArrayUpdate that takes the incoming reference to an array and then sets up the values of the elements in the array with the incoming values. Lines 15–24 define another method (subroutine), ArrayPrint, to print out the values of an array pointed to by the reference passed to the method (subroutine).

Line 25 marks the beginning of the main package. Then, line 26 creates an object by calling new My_Class '1', '2', '3';, where the arguments of 1, 2, and 3 are passed to the object to initialize the array within the object. In line 26, $new_ref, returned by the new object constructor, is a reference to the array. Line 27 prints out the values of the array pointed to by $new_ref.

If you want to update the array inside the object, you cannot access the elements of the array from the outside of the object without the help of the $new_ref reference. Line 29 shows how to call the built-in method (subroutine), ArrayUpdate, to manipulate the values of the array pointed to by $new_ref. Here, ArrayUpdate is applied as a virtual method. Values of 100, 200, and 300 are used to replace the initial ones, 1, 2, and 3. Line 30 prints out the updated values of the array.

The output results show that the values of the array have been updated successfully.

Similarly, you can create a reference to an anonymous hash within an object constructor. (See Listing 19.8.)

TYPE

Listing 19.8. Creating a reference to an anonymous hash in an object constructor.

```
1:  # p19_8.pl
2:
3:  package My_Class;
4:  sub new {
5:      my ($class, @rest) = @_;
6:      my $ref = {};
7:      %$ref = (%$ref, @rest);
8:      bless $ref, $class;
9:      return $ref;
10: }
11: sub HashUpdate {
12:     my ($ref_to_hash, @data) = @_;
13:     %$ref_to_hash = (%$ref_to_hash, @data);
14: }
15: sub HashPrint {
16:     my $ref_to_hash = shift @_;
17:     my $key;
18:     print "The elements in a hash from My_Class: \n";
19:     foreach $key (sort keys %$ref_to_hash) {
20:         print "$ref_to_hash {$key}: $ref_to_hash->{$key} \n";
21:     }
22: }
23: package main;
24: $new_ref = new My_Class key1, 1, key2, 2, key3, 3;
25: $new_ref->HashPrint ( );
26: print "\nNow, update the hash in My_Class ... \n\n";
27: $new_ref->HashUpdate ( key1, 100, key2, 200, key3, 300);
28: $new_ref->HashPrint ( );
```

19

OUTPUT

```
C:\> perl p19_8.pl
The elements in a hash from My_Class:
My_Class=HASH(0x77d184) {key1}: 1
My_Class=HASH(0x77d184) {key2}: 2
My_Class=HASH(0x77d184) {key3}: 3

Now, update the hash in My_Class ...

The elements in a hash from My_Class:
My_Class=HASH(0x77d184) {key1}: 100
My_Class=HASH(0x77d184) {key2}: 200
My_Class=HASH(0x77d184) {key3}: 300
C:\>
```

ANALYSIS The Perl program shown in Listing 19.8 is similar to the one in Listing 19.7, except the former creates a reference, called $ref, that points to an anonymous hash in line 6. Line 7 in Listing 19.8 initializes the hash with the incoming elements, if any. In line 8, the $ref reference is blessed with the class name that is the first incoming argument to the new object constructor.

Similarly, lines 11–14 in Listing 19.8 declare a method (subroutine) called HashUpdate, and lines 15–22 define another method, HashPrint, to print out the values of a hash pointed to by the reference passed to the method.

In the main package that starts in line 23, the values of the hash inside an object are printed out before and after the values are updated. The hash referred by the $new_ref reference has the initial key-value pairs of key1=>1, key2=>2, and key3=>3. Line 27 updates them with the key-value pairs of key1=>100, key2=>200, and key3=>300 by applying the virtual method, HashUpdate, to which the $new_ref reference points.

The output from the Perl program in Listing 19.8 proves that the values of the hash referred to by $new_ref have been manipulated correctly.

Let's have a look at one more example that manipulates a scalar variable within an object. Take a look at Listing 19.9.

19

TYPE
Listing 19.9. Creating a reference to a scalar variable in an object constructor.

```
1:  # p19_9.pl
2:
3:  package My_Class;
4:  local $my_scalar;
5:  sub new {
6:      my ($class, $rest) = @_;
7:      my $ref = \$my_scalar;
8:      $$ref = $rest;
9:      bless $ref, $class;
10:     return $ref;
```

continues

Listing 19.9. continued

```
11: }
12: sub ScalarUpdate {
13:     my ($ref_to_scalar, $data) = @_;
14:     $$ref_to_scalar = $data;
15: }
16: sub ScalarPrint {
17:     my $ref_to_scalar = shift @_;
18:     print "The scalar in My_Class: \n";
19:     print "$$ref_to_scalar \n";
20: }
21: package main;
22: $new_ref = new My_Class 1;
23: $new_ref->ScalarPrint( );
24: print "\nNow, update the scalar in My_Class ... \n\n";
25: $new_ref->ScalarUpdate(100);
26: $new_ref->ScalarPrint( );
```

OUTPUT

```
C:\> perl p19_9.pl
The scalar in My_Class:
1

Now, update the scalar in My_Class ...

The scalar in My_Class:
100
C:\>
```

ANALYSIS   Similar to Listings 19.7 and 19.8, Listing 19.9 demonstrates how to manipulate scalar variables that are located inside an object. This time, a hard reference to a scalar variable is created in line 7.

When an object that is an instance of the My_Class class is created in line 22, the object constructor returns a reference to $new_ref. The reference points to a scalar variable that is initialized with 1 in line 22. The initial value of the scalar variable is printed out in line 23.

Line 25 changes the value of the scalar to 100 by applying the virtual method of ScalarUpdate, referred to by $new_ref. Line 26 displays the updated value on the screen. (See the results in the Output section.)

So far, you've learned about data encapsulation in an object and how to manipulate the data with the help of a reference that points to a scalar, an array, or a hash. The next section introduces inheritance, another important feature of OOP.

Inheritance

In object-oriented programming, you can create a new class by defining a new one or by inheriting properties from an existing class. The class from which a new one is derived is called the *base class.* In Perl, a class can be derived from more than one base class.

To create a new class that inherits the characteristics of its parent (that is, base) classes, an @ISA array is added to the derived class to contain the names of those parent classes. The Perl interpreter will automatically search the @ISA array for the names of the classes that may contain a method that is not declared as part of the derived class.

A very simple example of deriving a class from a base class is shown in Listing 19.10. An @ISA array is used in the derived class.

TYPE **Listing 19.10. Using @ISA to inherit a base class.**

```
1:  # p19_10.pl
2:
3:  package Parent_Class;
4:  local $my_scalar;
5:  sub new {
6:      my ($class, $rest) = @_;
7:      my $ref = \$my_scalar;
8:      $$ref = $rest;
9:      bless $ref, $class;
10:     return $ref;
11: }
12: sub ScalarUpdate {
13:     my ($ref_to_scalar, $data) = @_;
14:     $$ref_to_scalar = $data;
15: }
16: sub ScalarPrint {
17:     my $ref_to_scalar = shift @_;
18:     print "The scalar referred to by $ref_to_scalar: \n";
19:     print "$$ref_to_scalar \n";
20: }
21:
22: package Child_Class;
23: @ISA = ('Parent_Class');
24:
25: package main;
26: $parent = new Parent_Class 1;
27: $parent->ScalarPrint();
28: $child = new Child_Class 2;
29: $child->ScalarPrint();
30: $child->ScalarUpdate(3);
31: $child->ScalarPrint();
```

OUTPUT
```
C:\> perl p19_10.pl
The scalar referred to by Parent_Class=SCALAR(0x770b20):
1
The scalar referred to by Child_Class=SCALAR(0x770b20):
2
The scalar referred to by Child_Class=SCALAR(0x770b20):
3
C:\>
```

19

ANALYSIS Line 3 in Listing 19.10 marks the beginning of the `Parent_Class` class. Lines 4–11 declare the `new` object constructor. The `ScalarUpdate` method (subroutine) is defined in lines 12–15. Lines 16–20 define another method, `ScalarPrint`, inside the `Parent_Class` class.

Line 22 starts a new class, called `Child_Class`, that has only a single (but very important) statement, `@ISA = ('Parent_Class');`, shown in line 23. It is the `@ISA` array that keeps the base class name, `Parent_Class`, and tells the Perl interpreter that the `Child_Class` class is derived from `Parent_Class`. How can we prove it? Well, let's keep going by looking at what lines 26–31 do in the `main` package.

Line 26 creates an object that is an instance of the base class, `Parent_Class`. Also, the `$my_scalar` variable inside the object is initialized with 1. Line 27 calls the `ScalarPrint` method to display the initialized value of `$my_scalar`. So far, nothing is new.

But in line 28, another object is created by calling the statement `new Child_Class;`. As you know, there is no subroutine or method called `new` declared in the `Child_Class` class. Actually, the class contains nothing but an `@ISA` array.

Well, that's good enough for the Perl interpreter. When the interpreter does not find the `new` method (as an object constructor) inside the `Child_Class` class, it automatically searches the `@ISA` array for the name of the base class from which `Child_Class` is derived. Then, the Perl interpreter invokes the `new` object constructor found in the base class `Parent_Class` to create an object as an instance of the derived class, `Child_Class`. In other words, `Child_Class` inherits the `new` object constructor from its base class.

Based on the inheritance, lines 29–31 print out the value of `$my_scalar` that has been manipulated by calling the inherited methods of `ScalarUpdate` and `ScalarPrint` through the `$child` reference. `$child` is the reference returned by the object of `Child_Class`. Note that `$child` has the same address, `SCALAR(0x770b20)`, as `$parent` does. (See the output.)

The output shows that the derived class `Child_Class` in Listing 19.10 has completely inherited the characteristics of the `Parent_Class` base class.

TIP

On Day 14, you learned about `qw`, which is defined in Perl 5 as well as in Perl 5 for Win32. `qw` provides a convenient way to break a string into words. For instance, instead of using

```
@array = ('element1', 'element2', 'element3');
```

you can employ

```
@array = qw(element1  element2  element3);
```

19

Therefore, the statement

```
@ISA = ('Parent_Class');
```

in Listing 19.10 can be replaced by

```
@ISA = qw(Parent_Class);
```

Now, let's modify the Perl code in Listing 19.10 and add some guts to the Child_Class class. This time, we allow Child_Class to have its own object constructor and scalar variable. The modified Perl code is shown in Listing 19.11.

TYPE | **Listing 19.11. Calling the inherited methods.**

```
1:  # p19_11.pl
2:
3:  package Parent_Class;
4:  local $my_scalar;
5:  sub new {
6:      my ($class, $rest) = @_;
7:      my $ref = \$my_scalar;
8:      $$ref = $rest;
9:      bless $ref, $class;
10:     return $ref;
11: }
12: sub ScalarUpdate {
13:     my ($ref_to_scalar, $data) = @_;
14:     $$ref_to_scalar = $data;
15: }
16: sub ScalarPrint {
17:     my $ref_to_scalar = shift;
18:     print "The scalar referred to by $ref_to_scalar: \n";
19:     print "$$ref_to_scalar \n";
20: }
21:
22: package Child_Class;
23: @ISA = qw(Parent_Class);
24: local $child_scalar;
25: sub new {
26:     my ($class, $rest) = @_;
27:     my $ref = \$child_scalar;
28:     $$ref = $rest;
29:     bless $ref, $class;
30:     return $ref;
31: }
32:
33: package main;
34: $parent = new Parent_Class 1;
35: $parent->ScalarPrint();
36: $child = new Child_Class 2;
37: $child->ScalarPrint();
38: $child->ScalarUpdate(3);
39: $child->ScalarPrint();
```

19

```
C:\> perl p19_11.pl
The scalar referred to by Parent_Class=SCALAR(0x770b20):
1
The scalar referred to by Child_Class=SCALAR(0x77e8b0):
2
The scalar referred to by Child_Class=SCALAR(0x77e8b0):
3
C:\>
```

The behavior of the Perl program shown in Listing 19.11 is similar to that of the program in Listing 19.10, except the derived class Child_Class in Listing 19.11 has its own object constructor and scalar variable.

Because Child_Class has its own object constructor, the $child reference returned by the object of Child_Class in line 36 has a different address than what $parent has. The $parent reference is set up in line 34 when the object of Parent_Class is created.

The output results show that $child contains the address of SCALAR(0x77e8b0), while $parent has SCALAR(0x770b20). (Remember in Listing 19.10, both $child and $parent have the same address, SCALAR(0x770b20).)

Inheriting from More than One Base Class

Like in some other computing languages, a class in Perl can be derived from more than one base class. In other words, the derived class can inherit characteristics from several base classes.

An example of deriving a class from two base classes is shown in Listing 19.12.

TYPE **Listing 19.12. Deriving a class from two base classes.**

```
1:  # p19_12.pl
2:
3:  package Mother_Class;
4:  sub HashUpdate {
5:      my ($ref_to_hash, @data) = @_;
6:      %$ref_to_hash = (%$ref_to_hash, @data);
7:  }
8:
9:  package Father_Class;
10: sub HashPrint {
11:     my $ref_to_hash = shift @_;
12:     my $key;
13:     foreach $key (keys %$ref_to_hash) {
14:         print "$ref_to_hash {$key} => $ref_to_hash->{$key} \n";
15:     }
16: }
17:
18: package Child_Class;
19: @ISA = qw(Mother_Class  Father_Class);
20: sub new {
```

```
21:     my ($class, @rest) = @_;
22:     my $ref = {};
23:     %$ref = (%$ref, @rest);
24:     bless $ref, $class;
25:     return $ref;
26: }
27:
28: package main;
29: print "Create an object by new Child_Class: \n";
30: $child = new Child_Class ('key1', '100', 'key2', '200', 'key3', '300');
31: $child->HashPrint();
32: print "\nUpdate the object: \n";
33: $child->HashUpdate('key1', 'One Hundred', 'key2', 'Two Hundred', 'key3',
➥'Three Hundred');
34: $child->HashPrint();
```

OUTPUT

```
C:\> perl p19_12.pl
Create an object by new Child_Class:
Child_Class=HASH(0x780fa0) {key1} => 100
Child_Class=HASH(0x780fa0) {key2} => 200
Child_Class=HASH(0x780fa0) {key3} => 300

Update the object:
Child_Class=HASH(0x780fa0) {key1} => One Hundred
Child_Class=HASH(0x780fa0) {key2} => Two Hundred
Child_Class=HASH(0x780fa0) {key3} => Three Hundred
C:\>
```

ANALYSIS Lines 3–7 in Listing 19.12 declare a base class called Mother_Class. In the class, there is a method, HashUpdate, that can be applied to update an anonymous hash referred to by $ref_to_hash.

Lines 9–16 declare another base class, Father_Class, that contains the HashPrint method. Lines 13 and 14 demonstrate that HashPrint can print out the values of an anonymous hash pointed to by the incoming reference, $ref_to_hash.

The derived class, Child_Class, defined in lines 18–26, has its own object constructor. Note that in line 19, the @ISA array is assigned the names of the two base classes, Mother_Class and Father_Class, from which Child_Class is derived.

Line 30 creates an object of Child_Class with the initial key-value pairs of key1=>100, key2=>200, and key3=>300. An anonymous hash is initialized by the key-value pairs while the object of Child_Class is being created.

Line 31 displays the initialized key-value pairs in the hash by calling the inherited method, HashPrint, from one of the base classes.

Line 33 then calls another inherited method, HashUpdate, to change the values associated with the keys key1, key2, and key3 in the anonymous hash within the object of Child_Class. The

19

updated hash now contains the key-value pairs of key1=>'One Hundred', key2=>'Two Hundred', and key3=>'Three Hundred', which are printed out in line 34 by the inherited HashPrint method.

The output results prove that the Child_Class has inherited the methods from its parent classes—the two base classes, Mother_Class and Father_Class.

The has-a Relationship

Besides the inheritance relationship, which is also called an is-a relationship, there are several other relationships that classes may have. One of them is the has-a relationship.

In object-oriented programming, the has-a relationship means that a class contains instances of other classes. In other words, the has-a relationship is a whole-versus-part relationship. (Sometimes the word *aggregation* is used to refer to the has-a relationship.)

Listing 19.13 gives an example demonstrating a has-a relationship between two classes.

TYPE   **Listing 19.13. A has-a relationship between two classes.**

```
1:  # p19_13.pl
2:
3:  package Texas_Class;
4:  sub new {
5:      my $class = shift;
6:      my $ref = {};
7:      $ref->{Texas} = 'The second largest state in USA.';
8:      bless $ref, $class;
9:      return $ref;
10: }
11: package USA_Class;
12: sub new {
13:     my $class = shift;
14:     my $ref = {};
15:     $ref->{Texas_Class} = new Texas_Class;
16:     $ref->{USA} = 'Has total 50 states.';
17:     bless $ref, $class;
18:     return $ref;
19: }
20: package main;
21: $usa = new USA_Class;
22: print "From object of USA_Class: \n";
23: foreach $key (keys(%$usa)) {
24:     print "$key => $usa->{$key} \n";
25: }
26: print "\nFrom object of $usa->{Texas_Class}: \n";
27: foreach $key (keys(%{$usa->{Texas_Class}})) {
28:     print "$key => $usa->{Texas_Class}->{$key} \n";
29: }
```

19

```
C:\> perl p19_13.pl
From object of USA_Class:
USA => Has total 50 states.
Texas_Class => Texas_Class=HASH(0x77e8bc)

From object of Texas_Class=HASH(0x77e8bc):
Texas => The second largest state in USA.
C:\>
```

ANALYSIS Lines 3–10 in Listing 19.13 declare a class called `Texas_Class`. Lines 6 and 7 create an anonymous hash and initialize the hash with a key-value pair, `Texas => 'The second largest state in USA.'`. Then, the `$ref` reference to the hash is blessed into the class in line 8.

Lines 11–19 declare another, bigger class, called `USA_Class`. Line 14 creates a reference, `$ref`, that points to an anonymous hash. Line 15 then builds a new object as an instance of the `Texas_Class` class. The reference returned by the object is kept in the anonymous hash associated with the key of `Texas_Class`. In this way, a `has-a` relationship is set up between the `USA_Class` class and the `Texas_Class` class. In other words, `USA_Class` contains `Texas_Class` (just like the country itself contains a state called Texas).

Line 16 adds another key-value pair, `USA => 'Has total 50 states.'`, into the hash. Lines 17 and 18, blessing the reference to the anonymous hash and returning it to the caller, complete the object constructor, `new`, in the `USA_Class` class.

Then, in the `main` package starting in line 20, a new object of `USA_Class` is created in line 21. Lines 23–25 print out what is contained in the anonymous hash initialized within `USA_Class`. From the output, you can see that the address to the hash created within `Texas_Class` has been saved by the hash in `USA_Class` (again, because `USA_Class` contains `Texas_Class`).

By using the address, lines 26–29 can find the hash within `Texas_Class` and print out the values of the hash. (See the second portion of the output section.)

Object Destructors

In Perl, a reference count is used to keep track of references to an object. When the count reaches 0, as there are no references to the object, the Perl interpreter automatically destroys the object to which the reference points. The memory associated with an object is released after the object is destroyed.

You can add a method (subroutine) named `DESTROY` to a class. The method is called whenever the object of the class is about to be destroyed. The method is called an `object destructor`.

Listing 19.14 contains the Perl program shown in Listing 19.11 with an object destructor added.

19

TYPE   **Listing 19.14. Calling DESTROY—an object destructor.**

```
 1: # p19_14.pl
 2:
 3: package Parent_Class;
 4: local $my_scalar;
 5: sub new {
 6:     my ($class, $rest) = @_;
 7:     my $ref = \$my_scalar;
 8:     $$ref = $rest;
 9:     bless $ref, $class;
10:     return $ref;
11: }
12: sub ScalarUpdate {
13:     my ($ref_to_scalar, $data) = @_;
14:     $$ref_to_scalar = $data;
15: }
16: sub ScalarPrint {
17:     my $ref_to_scalar = shift;
18:     print "The scalar referred to by $ref_to_scalar: \n";
19:     print "$$ref_to_scalar \n";
20: }
21: sub DESTROY {
22:     print "Destroy the object at @_ .\n";
23: }
24: package Child_Class;
25: @ISA = qw(Parent_Class);
26: local $child_scalar;
27: sub new {
28:     my ($class, $rest) = @_;
29:     my $ref = \$child_scalar;
30:     $$ref = $rest;
31:     bless $ref, $class;
32:     return $ref;
33: }
34:
35: package main;
36: $parent = new Parent_Class 1;
37: $parent->ScalarPrint();
38: $child = new Child_Class 2;
39: $child->ScalarPrint();
40: $child->ScalarUpdate(3);
41: $child->ScalarPrint();
```

OUTPUT
```
C:\> perl p19_14.pl
The scalar referred to by Parent_Class=SCALAR(0x770b20):
1
The scalar referred to by Child_Class=SCALAR(0x77e904):
2
The scalar referred to by Child_Class=SCALAR(0x77e904):
3
Destroy the object at Parent_Class=SCALAR(0x770b20).
Destroy the object at Child_Class=SCALAR(0x77e904).
C:\>
```

19

ANALYSIS Lines 21–23 set up an object destructor by adding the DESTROY method (subroutine) to the Parent_Class class.

The output of the Perl program in Listing 19.14 is the same as the one from Listing 19.11, except that the former has the additional messages sent from the object destructor, DESTROY, showing that Parent_Class and Child_Class are consequently destroyed.

> **NOTE**
>
> The has-a relationship (aggregation) among classes is more appropriate than the is-a relationship (inheritance) in many cases. One of reasons is that the Perl interpreter can automatically destroy an object contained within another object. (That is, there is a has-a relationship between the two objects.) But in the case of the is-a relationship, the nested object re-blessed by a base class may not be destroyed automatically unless the object destructor, DESTROY, is called.

More About Methods

Before the end of today's lesson, it's worth it to introduce several other features of methods in OOP. One of them is overriding methods within a base class.

Overriding Methods

In object-oriented programming, it is possible for a derived class to have some methods that share the same names with the methods within a base class. If you call such inherited methods from a derived class, you can prefix the name of the base class to the method name so that the Perl interpreter knows which method you want to call.

Listing 19.15 shows an example of overriding methods of a base class.

TYPE **Listing 19.15. Overriding methods of a base class.**

```
1:  # p19_15.pl
2:
3:  package Dad;
4:  sub FirstName {
5:      print 'John ';
6:  }
7:  sub MiddleName {
8:      print 'K. ';
9:  }
```

continues

Listing 19.15. continued

```
10: sub LastName {
11:     print 'Smith ';
12: }
13: package Son;
14: @ISA = qw(Dad);
15: sub new {
16:     my $class = shift;
17:     my $ref = [];
18:     bless $ref, $class;
19:     return $ref;
20: }
21: sub FirstName {
22:     my $ref = shift;
23:     $ref->Dad::FirstName();
24: }
25: sub MiddleName {
26:     my $ref = shift;
27:     $ref->Dad::MiddleName();
28: }
29: sub LastName {
30:     my $ref = shift;
31:     $ref->Dad::LastName();
32:     print "Jr. \n";
33: }
34: package main;
35: $son_name = new Son;
36: print "The name of Smith's son is: \n";
37: $son_name->FirstName;
38: $son_name->MiddleName;
39: $son_name->LastName;
```

OUTPUT

```
C:\> perl p19_15.pl
The name of Smith's son is:
John K. Smith Jr.
C:\>
```

ANALYSIS In Listing 19.15, there are two classes, Dad and Son, declared in lines 3–12 and lines 13–33, respectively. The Son class is derived from the Dad class. Both classes have three methods. The methods inside Son have the same names as the methods in Dad: FirstName, MiddleName, and LastName.

When the methods within the Dad class are called from the Son class, the name of the base class, Dad, is prefixed to the names of the inherited methods. (See lines 23, 27, and 31 for the usage of the base class name in distinguishing the inherited methods, FirstName, MiddleName, and LastName, from the ones within the derived Son class.)

Then, lines 37–39 print out the name of the son, John K. Smith Jr., by directly calling the three methods, FirstName, MiddleName, and LastName, within the Son class. These three methods invoke the corresponding inherited methods within the Dad class to get the job done.

NOTE

Starting with Perl version 5.2, you can use the name of a pseudoclass called SUPER to refer to a base class in which methods are overridden if you don't know the exact name of the base class.

When you get this book, build 300 of Perl 5 for Win32 will probably be ready. Build 300 supports SUPER, too.

Exporting Methods

In the previous sections, classes (including base and derived ones) in every example were all put into the same file, because it's easy and convenient for a simple application. However, for a large and complex application, you may want to group relative classes and save them into modules.

As you learned on Day 14, in Perl, a module is a reusable package that is saved in the format of a library file. The name of a module file has the .pm extension. For instance, you can save a group of classes into a module file called MyModule.pm.

In order to export the methods of the classes saved in the MyModule.pm module file, you can include the Perl library module Exporter.pm into MyModule.pm by calling the statement require Exporter;. Then you need to add the library module name, Exporter, into the @ISA array. The names of the methods inside the classes have to be listed in an array called @EXPORT. The names of the methods, treated as symbols, are exported later by the Exporter module into the symbol table of any other package that requires MyModule.pm.

A sample module file is demonstrated in Listing 19.16.

TYPE **Listing 19.16. An example to build a module file that uses the exportation semantics provided by the Exporter module.**

```
1:  package Parent_Class;
2:  require Exporter;
3:  @ISA = qw(Exporter);
4:  @EXPORT = qw( HashUpdate  HashPrint);
5:  sub new {
6:      my ($class, @rest) = @_;
7:      my $ref = {};
8:      %$ref = (%$ref, @rest);
9:      bless $ref, $class;
10:     return $ref;
11: }
12: sub HashUpdate {
13:     my ($ref_to_hash, @data) = @_;
```

continues

Listing 19.16. continued

```
14:     %$ref_to_hash = (%$ref_to_hash, @data);
15: }
16: sub HashPrint {
17:     my $ref_to_hash = shift @_;
18:     my $key;
19:     foreach $key (sort keys %$ref_to_hash) {
20:         print "$ref_to_hash {$key}: $ref_to_hash->{$key} \n";
21:     }
22: }
23: 1;
```

OUTPUT No visible output from the example.

In this listing, line 1 marks the beginning of the class called `Parent_Class`. Line 2 asks the Perl interpreter to include the `Exporter.pm` module file. The name of the `Exporter` module is saved into the `@ISA` array in line 3. Line 4 then adds the names of the methods `HashUdpate` and `HashPrint` in the module into the `@EXPORT` array. Later, the two names `HashUdpate` and `HashPrint`, treated as symbols, are exported into the symbol table of any other package that calls the module file shown in Listing 19.16.

You don't need to add `new`, the name of the object constructor, into the `@EXPORT` array. The Perl interpreter can find it when you create an object with the constructor.

Last but not least, put `1;` in the last line, line 23 in this case, to mark the end of the module file.

Do	Don't

DO initialize variables in modules with the object constructor.

DO use `my` to set the scope of variables in a method.

DON'T use global variables in modules.

DON'T use `local` to variables in a method unless you really do want the variables to be passed down to other subroutines.

Autoloading Methods

The first step the Perl interpreter takes when looking for a method is to check the current package. If the method is not defined in the package, the interpreter goes to the `@ISA` array and tries to find the method in one of the classes whose names are listed in the @ISA array. If it still does not find the method, the Perl interpreter looks for an AUTOLOAD subroutine. The AUTOLOAD subroutine tries to find and load the method from the installed Perl libraries. Finally, the Perl interpreter tries to find the method within the UNIVERSAL class. If it still fails, the Perl interpreter produces an error message about the unresolved method.

The AUTOLOAD subroutine is defined in Autoload.pm module file. Put the statement use Autoload; into the current package when you attempt to use the AUTOLOAD subroutine.

One way to learn more about Autoload.pm and AUTOLOAD subroutine is to study the Autoload.pm module file itself. By default, the module file is saved in the Lib subdirectory of your Perl5 directory.

Summary

Today's lesson provides a brief introduction to object-oriented programming (OOP) in Perl. You can apply what you've learned to the applications developed with Perl 5 for Win32.

A class in Perl is a package that contains methods to manipulate objects. An object, created by a constructor, is an instance of a class. In Perl, a method is simply a subroutine.

There are two types of methods: static and virtual.

bless is an important Perl built-in library function that can connect a reference to an object with the name of a class. The default class name is the name of the current class (package). The bless function is normally used in an object constructor. An object constructor in Perl is commonly called new.

With inheritance, a base class is the class from which a new class can be derived. An object constructor can be inherited from a base class. Also, multiple inheritance is allowed in Perl, which means a class can be derived from more than one base class.

Besides the inheritance that is called an is-a relationship, there is another relationship that classes can have—a has-a relationship. In many cases, the has-a relationship is clearer and cleaner than the is-a one.

In today's lesson, you have learned about data encapsulation with scalars, arrays, or hashes within a class. You have also learned how to apply the methods to manipulate the data structures within a class. You can override the methods defined in base classes in Perl. For more complex applications, classes can be grouped and saved into Perl library files in the form of modules.

19

NOTE

> If you are interested in learning more about object-oriented programming, I'd like to recommend an excellent book, *Object-oriented Analysis and Design with Applications*, written by Grady Booch (published by The Benjamin/Cummings Publishing Company, Inc.)

Q&A

Q What's the difference between a class and an object?

A A class is abstract, whereas an object is a concrete entity. In object-oriented programming, an object is an instance of a class.

Q What are static and virtual methods?

A A static method, also called a class method, is a method that expects a class name as the first argument. A virtual method expects a reference to an object as the first argument. A virtual method is also known as an instance method.

Q What does the Perl `bless` function do?

A The `bless` function connects a reference to an object with the name of a class. The first argument to the `bless` function is a reference to an object. The second argument specifies the name of a class. The default class name is the name of the current class (package).

Q How do I export methods saved in a module file?

A Use the `require Exporter;` statement, put the name of `Exporter` into the `@ISA` array, and list the names of the methods (subroutines) in the `@EXPORTER` array. Make sure to put `1;` at the end of the module file.

Workshop

To help you solidify your understanding of today's lesson, you are encouraged to try to answer the quiz questions and finish the exercises provided in the workshop before you move to next lesson. The answers and hints to the questions and exercises are given in Appendix B, "Answers."

Quiz

1. Are these two statements equivalent?

   ```
   new A_Class;
   ```

   and

   ```
   A_Class->new;
   ```

2. Given that the `a_method` method (subroutine) is defined in the `A_Class` class and `$ref = new A_Class;`, does the statement

   ```
   $ref->a_method;
   ```

   treat the `a_method` method as a static method in the class?

3. How do you build an object constructor that can initialize a hash within a class?

4. Given that there is a method within a derived class and the method shares the same name with a method in a base class, how do you call the method of the base class from the derived class?

Exercises

1. Given the `My_Class` class below, access the `Hello` method from the `main` package in two ways.

   ```
   package My_Class;
   sub Hello {
       my @argv = @_;
       print "From My_Class: Hello, world! \n";
   }
   ```

2. Add a statement `print "@argv \n";` to the `Hello` method in the `My_Class` class from Exercise 1. Now, what do you get when you call `Hello` in each of the two different ways?

3. Build an object constructor called `new` into the `My_Class` class from Exercise 1 and create an object of `My_Class`. Then use the reference returned from `new` to access the `Hello` method. Put all of them together to make a Perl program. What do you get after running the Perl program?

4. **BUG BUSTER**: Assume that the `Child_Class` class is derived from the `Parent_Class` class. What is wrong with the following code?

   ```
   # Exercise 4: Bug Buster

   package Parent_Class;
   sub new {
       my ($class, $rest) = @_;
       my $my_scalar;
       my $ref = \$my_scalar;
       $$ref = $rest;
       bless $ref, $class;
   ```

```
        return $ref;
}
sub ScalarPrint {
    my $ref_to_scalar = shift;
    print "The scalar referred by $ref_to_scalar: \n";
    print "$$ref_to_scalar \n";
}
package Child_Class;
sub new {
    my ($class, $rest) = @_;
    my $child_scalar;
    my $ref = \$child_scalar;
    $$ref = $rest;
    bless $ref, $class;
    return $ref;
}
package main;
$ref = new Child_Class 1;
$ref->ScalarPrint;
```

5. **BUG BUSTER:** What is wrong with the following code?

```
# Exercise 5: Bug Buster

package Parent_Class;
sub new {
    my ($class, $rest) = @_;
    my $my_scalar;
    my $ref = \$my_scalar;
    $$ref = $rest;
    bless $ref;
    return $ref;
}
package Child_Class;
@ISA = qw(Parent_Class);
sub ScalarPrint {
    my $ref_to_scalar = shift;
    print "The scalar referred by $ref_to_scalar: \n";
    print "$$ref_to_scalar \n";
}
package main;
$ref = new Child_Class 1;
$ref->ScalarPrint;
```

Week 3

Day 20

CGI Programming with Perl 5 for Win32

Common Gateway Interface (CGI) programming—one of the most exciting and important applications of Perl—is today's main topic. You'll also gain some knowledge about the following:

☐ TCP/IP and the Internet

☐ The client/server architecture

☐ HTML, HTTP, CGI, and Web-page design

☐ HTML forms and CGI programming

☐ Microsoft's IIS and Windows NT Server

☐ The CGI.pm module

☐ CGI versus ISAPI

Of course, a comprehensive discussion on these topics alone requires a thick book. Today's lesson is an introduction simply to help you to start with CGI programming. You will need to read more books or online documents that explain the details of CGI programming.

The Internet Basics

Currently, the *Internet* refers to an independent and vast system that loosely connects millions of people, computers, databases, and other information repositories all over the world. You can think of the Internet as the network of networks.

The Internet, as a mass of computerized communication networks, has been exploding in popularity and affecting the ways people work and live.

What Is TCP/IP?

TCP stands for Transmission Control Protocol, and *IP* stands for Internet Protocol. TCP and IP need to work together to provide connections among computers across the Internet. That's the reason you hear people use TCP/IP as one word to refer to the connection. TCP/IP was actually developed back in the 1970s to support an experimental network sponsored by the U.S. government.

TCP/IP is within the transport stack. You can think of TCP as a higher-level layer on top of the IP layer. The TCP layer is used to handle huge amounts of data and ensure data integrity. The IP layer's responsibility is to deliver packets of data among computers networked with TCP/IP protocols.

NOTE

> Based on the Internet concepts, the recently coined word *intranet* refers to private networks having specific owners. Information on an intranet is shared internally.

What Can the Internet Do?

Among the many services offered by the Internet are World Wide Web (WWW) publishing, electronic mailing (e-mail), online chatting, and using FTP for file transfers, all provided by the servers globally connected on the Internet.

Actually, when you download Perl 5 for Win32, you're most likely using the FTP service to transfer the software package from a remote location to your computer. You can also download Perl packages using the HTTP protocol (WWW documents) or SMTP (mail).

You can use the e-mail service on the Internet, if, for instance, you want to discuss problems found in Perl for Win32 with your friends. Figure 20.1 is an example of an e-mail message that I plan to send to the Perl for Win32 user mailing list. (Of course, you always have to make sure that it's proper and necessary to send out your messages to the hundreds of users on the mailing list.)

Figure 20.1.

A sample e-mail message I want to post to the Perl for Win32 user mailing list.

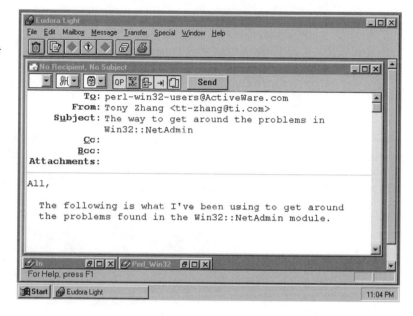

To send out your e-mail, you have to know the receiver's e-mail address. For instance, the address to the Perl for Win32 user mailing list is `perl-win32-users@ActiveWare.com`, which I've used in the sample e-mail message in the figure.

You've probably seen many different Web pages on the Internet—the interactive World Wide Web (WWW, or just Web) publishing displayed using your favorite Internet browser—including the one shown in Figure 20.2. Web publishing is the most popular service provided by the Internet; companies use it to provide product catalogs, online shopping, technical support, and more. By using the WWW, you can obtain or provide information and interact with millions of Internet users worldwide.

NOTE

The WWW was first created and used by Tim Berners-Lee at the European Laboratory for Particle Physics. Now, the WWW is a vast collection of interconnected information resources from which you can fetch an interesting document or find a piece of news almost instantly.

A *browser*, as it is usually called, is the application program you need to access a WWW site (or Web site). With the help of communication protocols, a browser can "talk" with the server at the Web site, receive documents from the server or other resources, and display the results on your screen.

20

Currently, you can get a browser that can access Web sites and obtain documents via communication protocols such as HTTP, FTP, and Gopher. (The HTTP protocol is explained later today.) Some browsers can even send and receive electronic mail, known as e-mail.

Figure 20.2.

A sample Web page: Netscape's home page on the Internet.

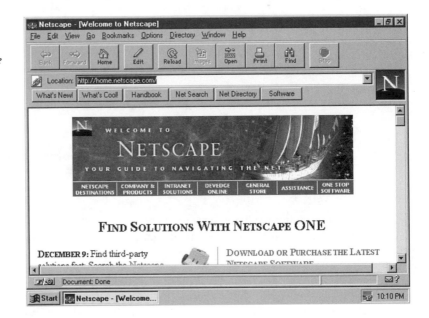

What Is a URL?

URL stands for Uniform Resource Locator. You can think of a URL as an address for a Web site. A URL consists of three fields: protocol, hostname, and required file. The format of a URL is

```
[protocol]://[host name]:[port number]/[required file]
```

The Protocol Field and HTTP

The protocol field specifies the service protocol (or agreement) used to transfer data (information) between the user's Web browser and one of the Web servers connected to the Internet.

There are many protocols in the service-specific section, such as HTTP, FTP, WAIS, Gopher, and Telnet, from which you can choose to fill in the protocol field. Among them,

20

HTTP is probably the most frequently used. (The service-specific section is above the transport stack layer in which TCP/IP resides.)

HTTP stands for Hypertext Transfer Protocol. It's a very popular transport mechanism used in WWW publishing. You'll learn more about HTTP in the following sections. You also can check the Web site at

```
http://www.w3.org/pub/WWW/Protocols/
```

for the official specification for the HTTP standard.

The Hostname Field and Port Number

The hostname field specifies the hostname of a Web server on the Internet. For instance, as you may know, the URL of Netscape Communications Corporation's home Web site is

```
http://home.netscape.com/
```

Here, `home.netscape.com` is the hostname of the Web server at Netscape Communications Corporation.

Specifying the port number is optional. For the HTTP protocol, 80 is the default port number.

The Required-File Field

The required-file field indicates the name of the file in which you are interested.

For example, you can check a list of the unsupported functions in Perl for Win32 at

```
URL: http://www.perl.hip.com/man-pages/status.htm
```

Here again, `http` is the protocol. `www.perl.hip.com` is the hostname of the Web server. `man-pages` is the pathname (similar to a directory name) that leads to the file, `status.htm`. The `status.htm` file contains the information about the unsupported functions in Perl for Win32.

If you type in this URL correctly and the Web server is running, your Web browser should be able to receive information from the `status.htm` file and display the contents of the file on your screen.

Some examples of the URLs that you may have used are

```
http://www.ActiveWare.com/default.htm
```

and

```
ftp://ftp.linux.activeware.com/pub/PerlWin32/perl5.001m/CurreBuild/110i86.zip
```

20

IIS and Windows NT Server

IIS refers to the Internet Information Server—one of the latest products from Microsoft. IIS provides services, such as document publishing, file transmission, and information searching and indexing, for hosting an Internet or intranet information repository on a Windows NT system.

IIS offers many services by manipulating the WWW server, FTP server, and Gopher server running on Windows NT Server. TCP/IP is the network protocol used during the data transmission.

Like Windows NT Workstation, Windows NT Server is built on the Win32 core technologies. Besides IIS, a Windows NT Server offers additional features, such as the increased capacity for servicing more simultaneous connections, enhanced TCP/IP services, network client administration, and more.

You can use IIS to build a WWW or FTP site for your organization or even for yourself. IIS can also be used to create an intranet Web site for a company's internal use.

The Client/Server Architecture

You may have already heard about client/server. Primarily, in the computer world, the word *server* stands for a process that provides services. *Client*, on the other hand, usually refers to a process that consumes services. The client/server architecture defines a relationship between processes normally running on separate computers.

The WWW is a typical example of a client/server relationship. As mentioned in the last section, when you want to find out about the unsupported functions in Perl for Win32, you start up a Web browser and type in the URL:

```
http://www.perl.hip.com/man-pages/status.htm
```

At this moment, you, as a client, are asking for a service that allows you to review the file called `status.htm` for the information about the unsupported functions.

When the Web server under the hostname `www.perl.hip.com` receives your request, it will provide the service by finding the file under the pathname `man-pages` and sending your Web browser the data from the file over the Internet. Your browser then displays the data on your screen. Figure 20.3 illustrates the relationship between you and the Web server.

Figure 20.3.

An example of client/ server: Checking the status.htm *file over the Internet.*

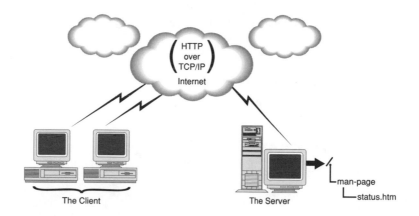

How a Web Page Works

Let's first look at an example. The user sends a request to a Web server by clicking a button on the Web page shown by a Web browser on the client side. The request asks for a stock price. When the Web server on the server side receives the request, it goes to a database to fetch the information about the stock price and send the information back to the Web browser on the client side. The browser then displays the stock price on the Web page so that the user can read it from the screen.

Usually, a Web page uses the HTML form to collect input data from the users on the Internet. The next section gives the definitions of HTML and HTML tags. HTML forms are explained later today, in the CGI programming sections.

What Is HTML?

HTML stands for Hypertext Markup Language. HTML provides an efficient way to build graphical user interfaces on the client machines. With HTML, you use tags to describe important parts of the text, such as titles, lists, and citations, and to tell your computer what size and color the text should be and where to put the text on the screen.

Tags

In HTML, the format of a tag is `<tag name>`. There are two types of tags that are paired and used together: the beginning tag and the ending tag. The format of the beginning tag is `<tag name>`. The ending tag has the format of `</tag name>`.

For example, to start your HTML file, you use this HTML tag:

```
<HTML>
```

20

Then you put your HTML content after the tag. When you want to indicate the end of your content, you use the tag:

```
</HTML>
```

Here, the `<HTML>` tag indicates that your HTML file starts immediately. The `</HTML>` tag closes the HTML file.

The Structure of HTML

An HTML file usually consists of a head and a body. Listing 20.1 is a very simple HTML file.

TYPE   **Listing 20.1. An HTML file that prints out** `Hello, world!`.

```
1:   <HTML>
2:   <HEAD>
3:   <TITLE>An Example of an HTML File Structure</TITLE>
4:   </HEAD>
5:
6:   <BODY BGCOLOR='white'>
7:   Hello, world!
8:   </BODY>
9:   </HTML>
```

ANALYSIS   Line 1 indicates the beginning of the HTML file by using the beginning tag `<HTML>`. In line 2, `<HEAD>` is the beginning tag for the head. Then, line 3 inserts the title of the HTML file, `An Example of an HTML File Structure`, within a pair of title tags, `<TITLE>` and `</TITLE>`. The title of the HTML file will be displayed on the title bar of a browser window.

Line 4 tells the Web browser to end the head portion. The body portion of the HTML file starts at line 6 with the beginning tag of `<BODY>`. Line 6 also tells the Web browser to set the background color to white with the statement `BGCOLOR='white'`.

The content of the body in this HTML file is only one sentence, `Hello, World!`, shown in line 7.

The ending tags in lines 8 and 9 close the body and the entire file, respectively.

If you save the content in Listing 20.1 under a filename with the extension `.htm`, you should be able to execute the file directly from the desktop Explorer on Windows NT or Windows 95.

You can also run the HTML file through your favorite Internet browser, such as Netscape Navigator or Microsoft Internet Explorer. In our case, the HTML file is saved in a file called `20L01.htm`. I'm using Netscape Navigator as my Web browser. Figure 20.4 is what I get by running the file `20101.htm` through the browser.

Figure 20.4.

The HTML file from Listing 20.1, as displayed in my Web browser.

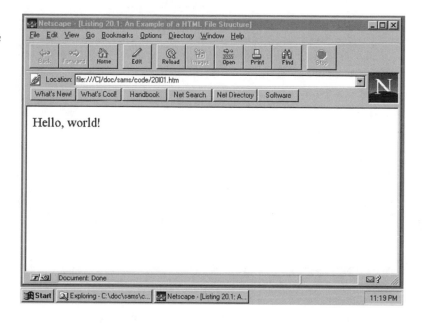

NOTE

> For more information about HTML, check out the Sams book *Teach Yourself HTML in 14 Days*, written by Laura Lemay, which gives a complete description of HTML syntax.

Making Your Web Site Interactive

You've seen a simple HTML file displayed by a Web browser. Although you may change the text attributes in an HTML file and add many fancy features such as fonts, tables, graphics, and more, a plain-text HTML file is displayed statically in a Web browser. This means that the content of a plain-text HTML file never changes unless you open the HTML file itself and make the changes manually.

The WWW would not be very attractive if Web pages contained only static text or pictures that could not be updated dynamically according to the user's requests.

One of the important reasons that the WWW is so successful today is that CGI programming makes it possible to create interactive Web pages. (Later in this chapter, you'll learn that ISAPI is another way to do so.)

For example, say that a vendor sells music CDs over the Internet by interacting with the customers and taking the online orders sent from the customers' Web browsers. To assist this process, a CGI program can be designed to fetch the data from the incoming orders and save the data in the CD vendor's database. Then, the CGI program returns a message to inform the customers that their orders have been taken successfully and that the ordered CDs will be delivered within a certain number of days.

To make a Web page interactive, HTML, HTTP, and CGI programs have to work closely. Here, HTML is responsible for collecting, formatting, and sending data to CGI programs. The primary way to do so in HTML is to use the HTML forms. The HTTP headers pave the way for communications between a Web browser and a Web server. A CGI program's job is to interact with the users who are browsing the Web page provided by the Web server.

The basics of CGI programming are introduced in the next section. An example of an interactive Web page based on the HTML form and CGI programming is shown in the section titled "CGI Programming and HTML Forms."

Introduction to CGI Programming

As mentioned in the previous sections, CGI is designed to run programs on Web servers for clients across the Internet. Perl is one of the most popular languages used to create CGI applications.

For Web servers like IIS, running on a Windows NT Server, Perl 5 for Win32 is one of the best choices for CGI programming.

 NOTE

> CGI itself is not a language. Rather, it is just an interface between a client and a server across the Internet. The CGI script refers to a program that supports CGI and is written in a computing language, such as Perl, C/C++, or Visual Basic.
>
> With the help of CGI programming, you can create a Web page on-the-fly in order to interact and communicate with the Web user.

CGI Scripts in Perl

To start learning CGI programming in Perl, let's rewrite the HTML file in Listing 20.1 and create a CGI script in Perl for Win32. Listing 20.2 is the CGI script.

TYPE **Listing 20.2. A CGI program written in Perl.**

```
1:  # p20_02.pl
2:
3:  print "Content-type: text/html\n\n";
4:
5:  print "<HTML>\n";
6:  print "<HEAD>\n";
7:  print "<TITLE>An Example of a CGI script in Perl</TITLE>\n";
8:  print "</HEAD>\n";
9:
10: print "<BODY BGCOLOR='white'>\n";
11: print "Hello, world!\n";
12: print "</BODY>\n";
13: print "</HTML>\n";
```

ANALYSIS Line 3 in Listing 20.2 generates a string to be used in an HTTP header by specifying the content type. In this example, the content type is text/html, which means a plain-text HTML file. Note the characters \n\n in line 3, which are always used for adding two new lines.

Lines 5–8 indicate the head portion with the title, An Example of a CGI script in Perl.

Line 10 starts the body of the HTML file with the white background color. Line 11 prints out the body of the HTML file, that is, Hello, world!. Finally, lines 12 and 13 close the body and the entire HTML file, respectively.

Listing 20.2 is almost identical to Listing 20.1, except that the Perl function print is used in Listing 20.2 to send the HTML file to the standard output.

When you ask a Web server on Windows NT to run the CGI script in Listing 20.2, the Perl interpreter, perl.exe, from Perl 5 for Win32 is needed to interpret the CGI script. In this case, the Perl function print is executed; the output from the function is sent to you (that is, the client). The output is actually an HTML file. Your Web browser then displays the output and shows you a screen similar to the one in Figure 20.4.

Of course, the CGI script shown in Listing 20.2 can be treated as a regular Perl program; you can run the CGI script from a command-line shell and thoroughly test the Perl portion in the CGI script before you load it onto your Web server.

20

HTTP Headers and Content Type

In the example shown in Listing 20.2, there are actually two parts generated when the CGI program is executed. The first part is called the HTTP header; the second one is the body of an HTML file.

You are already familiar with the structure of an HTML file. Here, let's focus on the HTTP header.

A CGI program has to generate an HTTP header first to tell the Web server the content type of the data stream made by the CGI program. An HTTP header is terminated by two new (blank) lines.

The content type can be one of the following:

- [ ] text/html
- [ ] image/gif
- [ ] www/source

Besides the HTTP header for content type, there are several other HTTP headers, such as the one for location and the one for status. Again, check the Web site at

```
http://www.w3.org/pub/WWW/Protocols/
```

for the official specification for the HTTP standard and a complete list of HTTP headers.

Using the `CGI.pm` Module

Introduced in Perl 5, the `CGI.pm` module is an object that provides a simplified method for parsing and interpreting query strings passed to CGI scripts from the clients. (Recall that you learned about object-oriented programming on Day 19, "Object-Oriented Programming in Perl.")

On Windows NT, the `CGI.pm` module can be used in CGI programming to work with Microsoft's IIS.

When you use the `CGI.pm` module on Windows NT, make sure to update the variable `$OS` in `CGI.pm` and assign `NT` to it:

```
$OS = 'NT';
```

Assign `'Windows'` to `$OS`—that is, `$OS = 'WINDOWS'`—if you are running Windows 95. You can do it simply by commenting out the previous setting for `$OS` and un-commenting out an available `$OS` with the proper operating-system name in the `CGI.pm` file.

Where Do I Get `CGI.pm`?

Read the online document `cgi_docs.html` at the Web site:

```
http://www.genome.wi.mit.edu/ftp/pub/software/WWW/cgi_docs.html
```

Then, go to the Downloading & Installation section within the document to download a compressed (or uncompressed, if you'd rather) CGI.pm module. After you uncompress the CGI.pm file, make sure you read the readme file first, and then follow the instructions to install the CGI.pm module properly on your machine.

Where Do I Put CGI.pm?

You must put the CGI.pm module in the perl5 library directory and put all CGI scripts that use CGI.pm in another specified directory. For instance, I put the CGI.pm module into the directory C:\perl5\lib on my machine.

Also, you need to either associate the .pl suffix with the Perl interpreter (perl.exe) or install the Perl DLL library so that a CGI script written in Perl can be executed as a regular executable file by the operating system on your machine.

An Example of Using CGI.pm in CGI Scripts

You can call functions (written in Perl) provided by the CGI.pm module, instead of just printing HTML tags, to build a Web page. More importantly, by using the CGI.pm module, the state of the form is preserved from one request to another because the form is initialized by the previous query value.

Listing 20.3 demonstrates how to use the CGI.pm module in a CGI script. CGI.pm provides many useful library functions (also known as methods) that you can use to make your program clearer and cleaner.

TYPE   **Listing 20.3. A CGI program using the CGI.pm module.**

```
1:  # p20_3.pl
2:
3:  use CGI;
4:
5:  $wp = new CGI;
6:
7:  print $wp->header;
8:
9:  print $wp->start_html (
10:    -title=>'Using CGI.pm in a CGI script',
11:    -BGCOLOR=>'white');
12:
13: print "<BODY>\n";
14: print "Hello, world!\n";
15: print "</BODY>\n";
16:
17: print $wp->end_html;
```

20

Line 3 calls the CGI.pm module. Line 5 creates a new CGI object, $wp, by using the new method. (More details about object creation have been introduced on Day 19.)

Line 7 generates the HTTP header that indicates the content type of the output data stream from the CGI script.

By calling the start_html method from CGI.pm, lines 9–11 output the beginning tags of the HTML file for the Web page, along with the title, Using CGI.pm in a CGI script, and the white background color. Note that -title=> is used to set the title for the Web page. Similarly, the white is passed to BGCOLOR by using -BGCOLOR=> to set the background color to white.

Lines 13–15 output the body portion of the Web page, which is the string Hello, world!. Line 17 then closes the HTML file for the Web page by calling $wp->end_html. Here, end_html, as a method in CGI.pm, returns the HTML tags </BODY> and </HTML> to end the HTML file.

Testing CGI Scripts

As mentioned earlier, you can test CGI scripts from a command-line shell, such as the DOS command-line shell, on a Windows NT or Windows 95 system. In this way, you can fix any errors found in the Perl portion of the CGI script before you start the online test for the script.

The following is the output of the CGI script testing:

```
C:\> perl p20_3.pl
(offline mode: enter name=value pairs on standard input)
^z
Content-type: text/html


<HTML><HEAD><TITLE>Using CGI.pm in a CGI script</TITLE>
</HEAD><BODY BGCOLOR="white"><BODY>
Hello, world!
</BODY>
</BODY></HTML>
C:\>
```

The CGI script is switched to the offline mode when it is run from the command-line shell. You can pass the names and values of input fields, if any, or you can simply press the Ctrl+Z (^z) key combination to continue running the CGI script.

In the offline-mode test shown in the preceding output section, the content type is displayed first and is always followed by two new lines. Then the beginning tags <HTML> and <HEAD> are printed out, followed by the title string, Using CGI.pm in a CGI script, paired with the <TITLE> and </TITLE> tags

After the ending </HEAD> tag, the beginning <BODY> tag starts with the white background color. The content of the body, Hello, world!, is printed out before the ending </BODY> and </HTML> tags.

20

After the offline test, it's confirmed that the CGI script using `CGI.pm` in Listing 20.3 can produce the exact format of the HTML file shown in Listing 20.1. By using `CGI.pm`, people like you who are familiar with Perl programming can easily build a Web page on a Windows Web server.

CGI Programming and HTML Forms

As mentioned in the previous sections, the HTML form is the most-frequently used format in a Web page for collecting data and interacting with the user. This section demonstrates how to create a simple HTML form to obtain the username and execute a CGI script that prints out a greeting message with that username.

The <FORM> Tag

The `<FORM>` tag is used to start an HTML form and to specify the URL location of the CGI script that you want to run. For the latter task, you assign the URL to the `ACTION` attribute within the `<FORM>` tag.

To end a form, simply put the ending tag `</FORM>` in your HTML code.

For instance, you can start an HTML form by setting the `<FORM>` tag in this way:

```
<FORM ACTION="http://MyWebServerDomainName/cgi-bin/MyCGI.pl" METHOD="POST">
```

Here, the `ACTION` attribute is given the URL of your CGI script called `MyCGI.pl`. There is another attribute in the `<FORM>` tag—the `METHOD` attribute. The `METHOD` attribute contains the name of a method that can be used to send data to the CGI scripts.

The POST and GET Methods

`POST` and `GET` are two methods used to send data collected from an HTML form to the CGI scripts running on the Web server.

The way to send data by the `POST` method is different from how you send data using the `GET` method. Simply put, the `POST` method uses the standard input to send data to your CGI script. The `GET` method sends it by using the environment variables.

The environment variables are used by the Web server to communicate with the CGI script. (*TY CGI Programming with Perl 5, Second Edition* by Eric Herrmann provides a useful discussion about environment variables.)

20

A Data-Entry HTML Form

Listing 20.4 contains the code for building a very simple HTML form to obtain the user's name.

TYPE   **Listing 20.4. An HTML form to obtain the user's name.**

```
1:  <HTML>
2:  <HEAD>
3:  <TITLE>An HTML Form</TITLE>
4:  </HEAD>
5:
6:  <BODY>
7:  <FORM ACTION="http://MyWebServerDomainName/PerlCode/CGI/p20_4.pl"
    ➥ METHOD="POST">
8:  This Web Page is designed to obtain the user's name
9:  <P>
10: Please enter your name: <INPUT TYPE="text" NAME="user" SIZE=40>
11: <P>
12: <INPUT TYPE="submit" VALUE="Click this button to send your name to the Web
    ➥ server">
13: </FORM>
14: </BODY>
15: </HTML>
```

Figure 20.5 illustrates the HTML form created in Listing 20.4. In the figure, the HTML form is displayed with Netscape Navigator.

Figure 20.5.

The HTML form in Listing 20.4, as displayed in my Web browser.

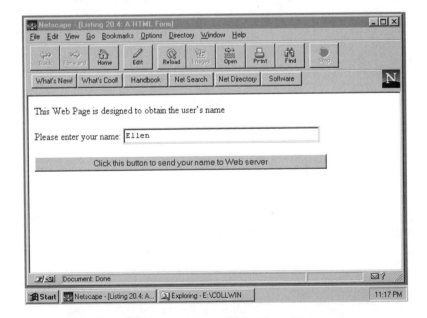

ANALYSIS As you may already have figured out, lines 1–4 start the HTML file and set the title name as An HTML Form. Line 6 indicates the beginning of the body of the HTML file.

Line 7 is the beginning form tag that assigns the URL of your CGI script to the ACTION attribute and specifies the METHOD with POST.

Line 8 displays a message to describe the Web page. Line 9 sets up a paragraph break with the <P> tag. You can use <P> to separate different contents on your Web page.

Line 10 contains a new HTML tag, <INPUT>, which specifies a data-entry field. The type of the data field is defined as a text type. The field is named user. The total length of the field is set to 40 characters long. The <P> tag in line 11 sets up another paragraph break.

Line 12 is another example of using the <INPUT> tag. This time, the <INPUT> tag is used to build a pushbutton by assigning submit to TYPE. The VALUE in line 12 contains the name string that is displayed on the button. After the user clicks the button, the user's name will be sent to the Web server and the CGI script specified in line 7 will be triggered to process the information from the HTML form.

Lines 13–15 close the HTML form, body, and the file itself by calling the ending tags </FORM>, </BODY>, and </HTML>, respectively.

A CGI Script for Interacting with the User

Listing 20.5 shows the CGI script p20_5.pl, which is referred to by the HTML form discussed in the previous section.

The CGI script can retrieve the username and then send the user a greeting message embedded with his or her name. This is an example of making a Web page interactive.

TYPE

Listing 20.5. A CGI script that sends the user a greeting message.

```
1:  # p20_5.pl
2:
3:  use CGI;
4:  $wp = new CGI;
5:  # Fetch the user name entered in HTML form
6:  $user_name = $wp->param ('user');
7:  print $wp->header;
8:  print $wp->start_html (
9:     -title=>'A CGI script to Interact with the User',
10:    -BGCOLOR=>'white');
11: # Send a greeting message back to the user
12: print "<BODY>\n";
```

continues

20

Listing 20.5. continued

```
13: print "Hello, $user_name,\n";
14: print "Welcome to my Web page!\n";
15: print "This message is sent to $user_name by the Web server.\n";
16: print "</BODY>\n";
17:
18: print $wp->end_html;
```

 Lines 3 and 4 call the CGI.pm module and create a new CGI object, $wp, by using the new method.

Line 6 extracts the username entered in the HTML form by calling the param subroutine in the CGI.pm module. The argument in the param subroutine must contain the same name, user, as the name entered in the data-entry field in the HTML code shown in Listing 20.4.

Line 7 makes an HTTP header specifying the content type. Lines 8–10 set up the title for the CGI script.

Lines 16 and 18 close the HTML body and file, respectively.

Then, lines 13 and 15 send the user a greeting message with the user's name embedded in the $user_name variable.

If everything is set up correctly, the user will see the greeting message, complete with her name, displayed in the Web browser after she enters her name in the data-entry field and clicks the button on the HTML form shown in Figure 20.5.

In obtaining the user's name and sending the user a greeting message, the CGI script and the HTML form work together to make the user feel like she is interacting with the Web page.

Figure 20.6 illustrates the greeting message to the user, Ellen, after she enters her name and clicks the enter button.

Figure 20.6.

The output of the CGI script in Listing 20.5, as displayed in my Web browser.

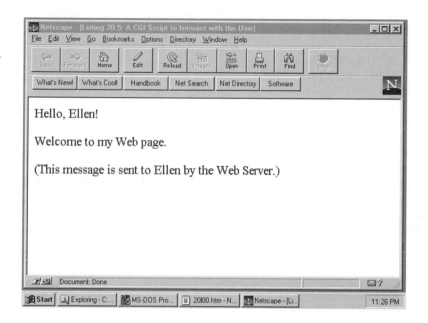

CGI Programming in Other Languages

Besides Perl 5 for Win32, you can use other computing languages, such as C/C++, Visual Basic, FORTRAN, and Pascal, to create CGI programs for Windows NT or Windows 95. CGI programming with those languages is beyond the scope of this book, however.

Security Issues

You have to pay much attention to CGI scripts that take input from the users on the Internet and pass the input as command-line arguments. If you are not careful, a malicious client may take advantage of the CGI scripts, and steal or even destroy the private or confidential data on your Web server (or in your database).

For the same reason, you should not put the Perl interpreter, `perl.exe`, in any directories that are accessible to the clients. Rather, place `perl.exe` into a directory that is hidden from outsiders. You need to configure the script mapping for `perl.exe` with the Registry editor so that only your CGI scripts written in Perl can access the Perl interpreter.

Check your Web server or CGI programming documents for more information on security issues.

20

CGI versus ISAPI

ISAPI (Internet Server Application Programming Interface) is an alternative interface that provides functionality similar to CGI programs. It is created by Microsoft's IIS SDK (Internet Information Server Software Developer's Kit).

Because an ISAPI application is indeed a Windows dynamic link library (DLL), it is different from a CGI application in the following ways:

☐ An ISAPI application is executed as an internal part of the Web server; a CGI application, in contrast, is considered an external program.

☐ Because an ISAPI application is a multithreaded DLL file, only one copy is kept in the memory to support multiple clients simultaneously. However, multiple copies (that is, processes) of a CGI application must be executed in order to support more than one client at the same time.

☐ Also, as one of the DLL's features, the functionality provided by an ISAPI application can be loaded into or unloaded from the memory dynamically according to the client's requests.

Therefore, you can expect that the performance of your Web server can be improved by using ISAPI applications.

To take full advantage of the DLL feature in ISAPI, `PerlIS.dll` has been introduced in Perl 5 for Win32. You can use `PerlIS.dll` to run your Perl scripts on IIS or other Web servers that support ISAPI.

ISAPI is a relatively new technology that is still under development. CGI and ISAPI are expected to coexist for a while in the world of the Internet.

NOTE

> As in the Win32 modules, things are still being updated in the `CGI.pm` module, CGI programming with Perl for Win32, ISAPI programming with `PerlIS.dll`, and HTML. Also, new features are being added to Web browsers.
>
> You are encouraged to keep checking the online documents or the latest news about `CGI.pm`, CGI programming, and ISAPI programming.

Summary

In today's lesson, you learned about the basics of CGI programming with Perl 5 for Win32 and other relevant topics.

TCP/IP is the communication protocol employed by the Internet to manipulate and deliver huge amounts of data among the computers connected to the Internet. The client/server architecture is a popular model to define the relationship between two processes or systems. The WWW is an example of the client/server model.

HTML, HTTP, and CGI have to work together closely to make a Web page interactive. The HTML form is the primary way to collect data entered by the Web user. POST and GET are two methods used in HTML forms to send the collected data to the Web server. The CGI scripts, running on the Web server on the Internet, can extract the input data and send back the processed data to the user. With CGI programming, you can build a Web page on-the-fly.

The CGI.pm module is a new module added in Perl 5 that provides an easy way to write CGI scripts in Perl. You can use the CGI.pm module with Perl 5 for Win32 to write CGI scripts for Web servers on Windows NT systems.

Besides Perl 5 for Win32, a CGI script can be written in another computing language available for Windows NT, such as C/C++, Visual Basic, FORTRAN, and so on.

Microsoft IIS is a popular Web server that can be run on a Windows NT system. There are two versions of Windows NT—Windows NT Workstation and Windows NT Server. Both versions were developed based on the Win32 API.

Remember that security is always a key issue you have to deal with when you plan to build a Web server connected to the Internet.

The introduction and sample programs presented in today's lesson have given you the basic knowledge you need for your continuous study of Web-page design and CGI programming with Perl 5 for Win32.

Q&A

Q Why is CGI programming so important?

A Because a static Web page is neither attractive nor useful, an interactive Web page is the right choice in the WWW publishing business. CGI programming is one of the important technologies that enables people to create interactive Web pages to display across the Internet.

Q What is client/server, anyway?

A The client/server architecture defines a relationship between two entities (or processes). For example, when you order a pizza over the phone, you are a client who requires and consumes the service. The pizza parlor is the server because it provides the service you just requested.

20

A few minutes later, a delivery person delivers the pizza to your home. You can think of him as a transport mechanism, and the phone is a network layer.

In the computer world, the client/server architecture provides an efficient way to define a relationship between two processes in a complex system.

Q What is the structure of TCP/IP?

A Within TCP/IP, there are four portions. From top to bottom, they are the application portion, the transport portion, the Internet portion, and the physical portion. Here, a portion is also called as a layer.

Q What is the relationship between HTTP and TCP/IP?

A TCP/IP belongs to the transport stack layer that is underneath the network operating-system (for example, Windows NT) layer. HTTP, on the other hand, is in the service-specific layer. The service-specific layer is on the top of the network operating-system layer. Therefore, the communication between HTTP and TCP/IP must be interpreted by the network operating system.

Workshop

To help you solidify your understanding of today's lesson, you are encouraged to try to answer the quiz questions and finish the exercises provided in the workshop before you move on to the next lesson. The answers to the questions and exercises are given in Appendix B, "Answers."

Quiz

1. What do these HTML tags do?

    a. `<HTML>`

    b. `</HTML>`

    c. `<BODY>`

    d. `</BODY>`

    e. `<TITLE>`

    f. `</TITLE>`

    g. `<FORM>`

    h. `</FORM>`

2. How do you create a new CGI object in a CGI script?

3. What is the HTML equivalent for the following CGI script?

```
print $wp->start_html (
  -title=>'Using CGI.pm in a CGI script',
  -BGCOLOR=>'white');
print $wp->end_html;
```

4. What are the differences between a CGI application and an ISAPI application?

5. How do you build a data-entry field and an enter button by using the `<INPUT>` tag?

6. How do you fetch the data sent from an HTML form in a CGI script by using the `CGI.pm` module?

Exercises

1. Write an HTML file that can display the message `This is my first HTML file` with a title string of `Exercise 1, Day 20`. Set the background color to blue. Run the HTML file from your favorite Web browser.

2. Write a CGI script with the same message and title name from Exercise 1. Set the background color to yellow and test the script as a regular Perl script.

3. Rewrite the CGI script in Exercise 2 to use the `CGI.pm` module. This time, set the background color to red. Test the script in offline mode.

4. **BUG BUSTER**: What is wrong with the following CGI script?

```
use CGI;

print $wp->header;
print $wp->start_html (
   -title=>'Using CGI.pm in a CGI script',
   -BGCOLOR=>'white');
print "<BODY>\n";
print "Hello, world!\n";
print "</BODY>\n";
print $wp->end_html;
```

5. **BUG BUSTER**: What is wrong with the following CGI script?

```
use CGI;
$wp = new CGI;
print $wp->header;
print $wp->start_html (
   -title=>'Using CGI.pm in a CGI script',
   -BGCOLOR=>'white');
print "<BODY>\n";
print "Hello, world!\n";
print "</BODY>\n";
```

20

Day 21

The Perl Debugger

Today's lesson describes the Perl debugging facility. You'll learn the following:

- ☐ How to enter and exit the Perl debugger
- ☐ How to list parts of your program
- ☐ How to execute one statement at a time
- ☐ How to set breakpoints and trace program execution
- ☐ How to perform line actions
- ☐ About other useful debugging commands

The following two sections describe how to start the Perl debugger and how to exit it.

Entering the Debugger

To debug a Perl program, specify the `-d` option when you run the program. For example, to debug a program named `debugtest`, specify the following command:

```
C:\> perl -d debugtest.pl
```

You can supply other options along with -d if you want to.

When the Perl interpreter sees the -d option, it starts the Perl debugger. The debugger begins by displaying a message similar to the following one on your screen:

```
Loading DB routines from $RCSfile: perl5db.pl,v  $$Revision: 4.0.1
$$Date: 92/08/07 18:24:07 $
Emacs support available.

Enter h for help.

main::(debugtest:3):          $dircount = 0;
  DB<1>
```

The first few lines display the date on which this version of the debugger was created. The only lines of interest are the last two.

The second-to-last line in this display lists the line that the debugger is about to execute. When the debugger starts, the first executable line of the program is displayed.

When the debugger displays a line that it is about to execute, it also provides the following information about the line:

- ☐ The package in which the line is contained (in this case, the default package, which is main).
- ☐ The name of the file containing the line (here, the file is named debugtest).
- ☐ The current line number (which, in this example, is 3).

The last line of the display prompts you for a debugging command. The number enclosed in angle brackets indicates the command number; in this case, the number is 1 because you are about to specify the first debugging command.

Later today you will learn how to use the debugging command number to re-enter debugging commands you have previously executed.

NOTE

To enter the debugger without supplying a program, supply the -e option with the -d option:

```
C:\> perl -d -e "1;"
```

This line starts the debugger with a program—if you can call it that—consisting of a single statement:

```
1;
```

(which is an expression that doesn't do anything meaningful).

Starting the debugger without a program enables you to examine the predefined system variables or supply statements to be executed. You will learn how to perform both of these tasks later in today's lesson.

21

Exiting the Debugger

To exit the debugger, enter the debugging command q:

```
DB<1> q
```

This command halts program execution immediately and returns you to the command shell.

Listing Your Program

You can list any part of your program from within the debugger. The following sections describe debugging commands that perform the display operations.

The 1 Command

The simplest way to list part of your program is with the 1 command, which lists the next few statements in your program:

```
  DB<1> 1
3:        $dircount = 0;
4:        $curdir = "";
5:        while (1) {
6:              # if we don't have a current directory, get one
7:              if ($curdir eq "") {
8:                    print ("Enter directory to list:\n");
9:                    $curdir = <STDIN>;
10:                   $curdir =~ s/^\s+|\s+$//g;
11:                   $curdir = &followlink($curdir);
12:                   &readsubdirs($curdir);
```

The 1 command lists a *window* of executable statements, which is a group of statements small enough to be easily displayed on your screen. A window usually consists of about 10 statements. The line number of each statement is displayed at the beginning of its line.

NOTE | The statements displayed in today's lesson are taken from the program presented in "Week 2 in Review."

Entering the 1 command again displays the window of statements immediately following the last displayed line, which in this example is line 12:

```
  DB<1> 1
13:             }
14:             $curdir = &menudir($curdir);
15:       }
16:
```

21

```
17:
18:     # Find all subdirectories of the given directory,
19:     # and store them in an associative array.
20:     #
21:     # The associative array subscripts and values are:
22:     # <directory name>:        1
```

You can specify the lines displayed by the l command. If you specify a single line number with the l command, it displays that line:

```
DB<1> l 10
10:                              $curdir =~ s/^\s+|\s+$//g;
```

To display a range of lines, specify the first and last line number and separate them with a hyphen:

```
DB<1> l 10-15
10:                              $curdir =~ s/^\s+|\s+$//g;
11:                              $curdir = &followlink($curdir);
12:                              &readsubdirs($curdir);
13:             }
14:             $curdir = &menudir($curdir);
15:     }
```

To display a specified number of lines starting at a certain point, supply the starting line number, a + character, and a number of additional lines to display:

```
DB<1> l 10+5
10:                              $curdir =~ s/^\s+|\s+$//g;
11:                              $curdir = &followlink($curdir);
12:                              &readsubdirs($curdir);
13:             }
14:             $curdir = &menudir($curdir);
15:     }
```

You also can use the l command to specify a subroutine to display. To do this, provide the name of the subroutine to display:

```
DB<1> l readsubdirs
26:     sub readsubdirs {
27:             local ($dirname) = @_;
28:             local ($dirvar, $subdircount, $name, $index);
29:
30:             # open the current directory;
31:             # $dircount ensures that each file variable is unique
32:             $dirvar = "DIR" . ++$dircount;
33:             if (!opendir ($dirvar, $dirname)) {
34:                     warn ("Can't open $dirname\n");
35:                     return;
```

This command lists the statements in the subroutine. If the subroutine is too large to fit in a single window, only the first few statements are listed; you can list subsequent statements by entering l with no arguments.

The - Command

You can display the lines immediately preceding the last displayed line by entering the –
command. For example, the following – command lists the window of lines immediately
preceding the subroutine `readsubdirs`:

```
  DB<1> -
16:
17:
18:      # Find all subdirectories of the given directory,
19:      # and store them in an associative array.
20:      #
21:      # The associative array subscripts and values are:
22:      # <directory name>:        1
23:      #      (indicates that directory has been read)
24:      # <directory name>.<num>  the <num>th subdirectory
25:
```

Subsequent – commands go back farther in the file.

The w Command

To list a window of lines containing a specified line, use the w command and specify the
number of the line to be included:

```
  DB<1> w 7
4:      $curdir = "";
5:      while (1) {
6:              # if we don't have a current directory, get one
7:              if ($curdir eq "") {
8:                      print ("Enter directory to list:\n");
9:                      $curdir = <STDIN>;
10:                     $curdir =~ s/^\s+|\s+$//g;
11:                     $curdir = &followlink($curdir);
12:                     &readsubdirs($curdir);
13:              }
```

The w command displays the three lines before the specified line and fills the window with
the lines following it.

The // and ?? Commands

You can search for a line containing a particular pattern by enclosing the pattern in slashes:

```
  DB<1> /Find/
18:     # Find all subdirectories of the given directory,
```

The debugger searches forward from the last displayed line for a line matching the specified
pattern. If it finds such a line, the line is displayed.

21

To search backward for a particular pattern, enclose the pattern in question marks:

```
  DB<1> ?readsubdirs?
12:                          &readsubdirs($curdir);
```

This command starts with the last displayed line and searches backward until it finds a line matching the specified pattern.

NOTE

Patterns specified by // and ?? can contain any special character understood by the Perl interpreter.

You have the option to omit the final / or ? character when you match a pattern.

The s Command

The s command lists all the subroutines in the current file, one subroutine per line:

```
  DB<> S
main::display
main::followlink
main::menudir
main::readsubdirs
```

Each subroutine name is preceded by the package name and double colons.

Stepping Through Programs

One of the most useful features of the Perl debugger is the capability to execute a program one statement at a time. The following sections describe the statements that carry out this action.

The s Command

To execute a single statement of your program, use the s command:

```
  DB<2> s
main::(debugtest:4):         $curdir = "";
```

This command executes one statement of your program and then displays the next statement to be executed. If the statement executed needs to read from the standard input file, the debugger waits until the input is provided before displaying the next line to execute.

21

TIP

If you have forgotten which line is the next line to execute (because, for example, you have displayed lines using the l command), you can list the next line to execute using the L command:

```
  DB<2> L
3:        $dircount = 0;
```

The L command lists the last lines executed by the program. It also lists any breakpoints and line actions that have been defined for particular lines. Breakpoints, line actions, and the L command are discussed later today.

If the statement executed by the s command calls a subroutine, the Perl debugger enters the subroutine but does not execute any statements in it. Instead, it stops at the first executable statement in the subroutine and displays it. For example, if the following is the current line,

```
main::(debugtest:12):                    &readsubdirs($curdir);
```

specifying the s command tells the Perl debugger to enter readsubdirs and display the following, which is the first executable line of readsubdirs:

```
main::readsubdirs(debugtest:27):    local ($dirname) = @_;
```

The s command assumes that you want to debug the subroutine you have entered. If you know that a particular subroutine works properly and you don't want to step through it one statement at a time, use the n command, described in the following section.

The n Command

The n command, like the s command, executes one line of your program and displays the next line to be executed:

```
  DB<2> n
main::(debugtest:5):        while (1) {
```

The n statement, however, does not enter any subroutines. If the statement executed by n contains a subroutine call, the subroutine is executed in its entirety. After the subroutine is executed, the debugger displays the line immediately following the call.

For example, if the current line is

```
main::(debugtest:12):                    &readsubdirs($curdir);
```

the n command tells the debugger to execute readsubdirs and then display the next line in the program, which is

```
main::(debugtest:13:):             }
```

21

Combining the use of s and n ensures that the debugger examines only the subroutines you want to see.

NOTE The Perl debugger does not enable you to enter any built-in library functions. You can enter only subroutines that you have created yourself or that have been created previously and added to a subroutine library.

The f command

The f command is used to switch to a different file:

```
DB<2> f filename
```

Here, *filename* is the name of a different file you want to view.

The Carriage-Return Command

If you are stepping through a program using s or n, you can save yourself some typing by just pressing the Enter key when you want to execute another statement. When you press Enter, the debugger repeats the last s or n command executed.

For example, to step from line 5 to line 7, you can use the s command as usual:

```
  DB<3> s
main::(debugtest:7):                    if ($curdir eq "") {
```

(Line 6 is skipped because it contains no executable statements.) To execute line 7, you can now just press Enter:

```
  DB<2>
main::(debugtest:8):                    print ("Enter directory to list:\n");
```

NOTE Pressing the Enter key has no effect if you have not specified any s or n commands.

21

The r Command

If you are inside a subroutine and decide that you no longer need to step through it, you can tell the Perl debugger to finish executing the subroutine and return to the statement after the subroutine call. To do this, use the r command:

```
  DB<4> r
main::(debugtest:13:):                         }
```

The statement displayed by the debugger is the first statement following the call to the subroutine.

Displaying Variable Values

Another powerful feature of the Perl debugger is the capability to display the value of any variable at any time. The following sections describe the commands that perform this action.

The x Command

The x command displays variables in the current package (which is main if no other package has been specified). If the x command is specified by itself, it lists all the variables in the current package, including the system-defined variables and the variables used by the Perl interpreter itself. Usually, you won't want to use the x command by itself because there are a lot of system-defined and internal variables known to the Perl interpreter.

To print the value of a particular variable or variables, specify the variable name or names with the x command:

```
  DB<5> X dircount
$dircount = '0'
```

This capability often is useful when you are checking for errors in your program.

WARNING

> You must not supply the $ character with the variable name when you use the x command. If you supply the $ character (or the @ or % characters for arrays), the debugger displays nothing.

21

You can use x to display the values of array variables and associative array variables:

```
  DB<6> X regarray
@regarray = (
  0      14
  1      'hello'
  2      36
)
  DB<7> X assocarray
%assoc_array = (
  'hi'   1
  'there' 2
)
```

Each command prints the subscripts of the array and their values. Regular arrays are printed in order of subscript; associative arrays are printed in no particular order.

NOTE

> If you have an array variable and a scalar variable with the same name, the x command prints both variables:
>
> ```
>   DB<8> X var
> $var = '0'
> @var = (
>   0      'test1'
>   1      'test2'
> )
> ```
>
> There is no way to use x to display one variable but not the other.

The v Command

The v command is identical to the x command except that it prints the values of variables in any package. If you specify just a package name, as in the following, this command displays the values of all variables in the package (including system-defined and internal variables):

```
DB<9> V mypack
```

If you specify a package name and one or more variable names, as in the following, the debugger prints the values of the variables (if they are defined in that package):

```
  DB<10> V main dircount
$dircount = '0'
```

Breakpoints

As you have seen, you can tell the Perl debugger to execute one statement at a time. Another way of controlling program execution is to tell the debugger to execute up to a certain specified point in the program, called a *breakpoint*.

The following sections describe the commands that create breakpoints and the command that executes until a breakpoint is detected.

The b Command

To set a breakpoint in your program, use the b command. This command tells the debugger to halt program execution whenever it is about to execute the specified line. For example, the following command tells the debugger to halt when it is about to execute line 10:

```
DB<11> b 10
```

(If the line is not breakable, the debugger will return Line 10 is not breakable.)

NOTE

> You can have as many breakpoints in your program as you want. The debugger will halt program execution if it is about to execute any of the statements at which a breakpoint has been defined.

The b command also accepts subroutine names:

```
DB<12> b menudir
```

This sets a breakpoint at the first executable statement of the subroutine menudir.

You can use the b command to tell the program to halt only when a specified condition is true. For example, the following command tells the debugger to halt if it is about to execute line 10 and the variable $curdir is equal to the null string:

```
DB<12> b 10 ($curdir eq "")
```

The condition specified with the b statement can be any legal Perl conditional expression.

WARNING

> If a statement is longer than a single line, you can set a breakpoint only at the first line of the statement:
> ```
> 71:     print ("Test",
> 72:      " here is more output");
> ```
> Here, you can set a breakpoint at line 71, but not at line 72.

21

The c **Command**

After you have set a breakpoint, you can tell the debugger to execute until it reaches either the breakpoint or the end of the program. To do this, use the c command:

```
DB<13> c
main::(debugtest:10):                          $curdir =~ s/^\s+|\s+$//g;
DB<14>
```

When the debugger detects that it is about to execute line 10—the line at which the breakpoint was set—it halts and displays the line. (Recall that the debugger always displays the line it is about to execute.)

The debugger now prompts you for another debugging command. This action enables you to start executing one statement at a time using n or s, continue execution using c, set more breakpoints using b, or perform any other debugging operation.

You can specify a temporary (one-time-only) breakpoint with the c command by supplying a line number:

```
DB<15> c 12
main::(debugtest:12):                          &readsubdirs($curdir);
```

The argument 12 supplied with the c command tells the debugger to define a temporary breakpoint at line 12 and then resume execution. When the debugger reaches line 12, it halts execution, displays the line, and deletes the breakpoint. (The line itself still exists, of course.)

Using c to define a temporary breakpoint is useful if you want to skip a few lines without wasting your time executing the program one statement at a time. Using c also means that you don't have to bother defining a breakpoint using b and deleting it using d (described in the following section).

TIP

> If you intend to define breakpoints using c or b, it is a good idea to ensure that each line of your program contains at most one statement. If you are in the habit of writing lines that contain more than one statement, such as
>
> $x++; $y++;
>
> you won't get as much use out of the debugger, because it can't stop in the middle of a line.

The L Command and Breakpoints

To list all your breakpoints, use the L command. This command lists the last few lines executed, the current line, the breakpoints you have defined, and the conditions under which the breakpoints go into effect:

```
  DB<16> L
3:        $dircount = 0;
4:        $curdir = "";
5:        while (1) {
7:                if ($curdir eq "") {
10:                      $curdir =~ s/^\s+|\s+$//g;
  break if (1)
```

Here, the program has executed lines 3–7, and a breakpoint is defined for line 10. (Line 6 is not listed because it is a comment.) You can distinguish breakpoints from executed lines by looking for the *breakpoint conditional expression*, which immediately follows the breakpoint. Here, the conditional expression is (1), which indicates that the breakpoint is always in effect.

The d and D Commands

When you are finished with a breakpoint, you can delete it using the d command:

```
DB<16> d 10
```

This command tells the debugger to delete the breakpoint in line 10. The line itself remains in the program.

If you do not specify a breakpoint to delete, the debugger assumes that a breakpoint is defined for the next line to be executed and deletes that breakpoint.

```
main::(debugtest:12):                          &readsubdirs($curdir);
  DB<17> d
```

Here, line 12 is the next line to be executed, so the debugger deletes the breakpoint in line 12.

To delete all your breakpoints, use the D command:

```
DB<18> D
```

This command deletes all the breakpoints you have defined with the b command.

Tracing Program Execution

When you run a program using the Perl debugger, you can tell it to display each line as it is executed. When the debugger is doing this, it is said to be in *trace mode*.

21

To turn on trace mode, use the `t` command:

```
  DB<18> t
Trace = on
```

When a statement is executed in trace mode, the statement is displayed. For example, if the current line is line 5 and the command `c 10` (which executes up to line 10) is entered, the following is displayed:

```
  DB<18> c 10
main::(debugtest:5):        while (1) {
main::(debugtest:7):                if ($curdir eq "") {
main::(debugtest:10):                    $curdir =~ s/^\s+|\s+$//g;
  DB<19>
```

The debugger prints and executes line 5 and line 7, and then displays line 10 and waits for further instructions.

To turn off trace mode, specify the `t` command again:

```
  DB<19> t
Trace = off
```

At this point, trace mode is turned off until another `t` command is entered.

Line Actions

The Perl debugger allows you to specify one or more statements to be executed whenever the program reaches a specified line. Such statements are known as *line actions*. The most common line actions are printing the value of a variable and resetting a variable containing an erroneous value to the value you want.

The following sections describe the debugging commands that define line actions.

The a Command

To specify a line action for a particular line, use the `a` command:

```
DB<19> a 10 print ("curdir is $curdir\n");
```

This command tells the debugger to execute the statement

```
print ("curdir is $curdir\n");
```

whenever it is about to execute line 10 of the program. The debugger performs the action just after it displays the current line and before it asks for the next debugging command.

To create a line action containing more than one statement, just string the statements together. If you need more than one line for the statements, put a backslash at the end of the first line:

```
 DB<20> a 10 print ("curdir is $curdir\n"); print \
("this is a long line action\n");
```

In this case, when the debugger reaches line 10, it executes the following statements:

```
print ("curdir is $curdir\n");
print ("this is a long line action\n");
```

The A Command

To delete the line actions defined using the a command, use the A command:

```
DB<21> A
```

This command deletes all line actions currently defined.

NOTE

> The A command does not affect the < and > commands, which are described in the following section.

The < and > Commands

To define a line action that is to be executed before the debugger executes any further statements, use the > command:

```
DB<21> > print ("curdir before execution is $curdir\n");
```

This command tells the debugger to print the value of $curdir before continuing.

Similarly, the < command defines a line action that is to be performed after the debugger has finished executing statements and before it asks for another debugging command. This command tells the debugger to print the value of $curdir before halting execution again:

```
DB<22> < print ("curdir after execution is $curdir\n");
```

The < and > commands are useful when you know that one of your variables has the wrong value, but you don't know which statement assigned the wrong value to the variable. By single-stepping through the program using s or n and printing the variable either before or after executing each statement, you can determine where the variable was given its incorrect value.

21

NOTE

To delete a line action defined by the < command, enter another < command with no line action defined:

```
DB<23> <
```

Similarly, the following command undoes the effects of a > command:

```
DB<24> >
```

Displaying Line Actions Using the L Command

The L command prints any line actions you have defined using the a command (as well as breakpoints and executed lines). For example, suppose that you have defined a line action using the following command:

```
DB<25> a 10 print ("curdir is $curdir\n");
```

The L command then displays this line action:

```
main::(debugtest:10):                        $curdir =~ s/^\s+|\s+$//g;
  action:  print ("curdir is $curdir\n");
```

The line action is always displayed immediately after the line for which it is defined. This method of display enables you to distinguish lines containing line actions from other lines displayed by the L command.

Other Debugging Commands

The following sections describe the debugging commands that don't fall into the preceding categories.

Executing Other Perl Statements

In the debugger, anything that is not a debugging command is assumed to be a Perl statement and is performed right away. Take a look at the following example:

```
DB<4> @array = (1, 2, 3);
```

You can use statements such as this to alter values in your program as it is being executed. This capability is useful when you are testing your code.

NOTE

If you want to, you can omit the semicolon at the end of the statement.

The R Command

The R command is used to restart the Perl debugger. You have to re-initialize the internal settings and re-enter command line options because they may be lost in the new session of the debugger.

The H Command: Listing Preceding Commands

The H (for *history*) command lists the last few commands you have entered:

```
DB<4> H -number
```

Here, the *number* specifies how many commands need to be listed. Note that *number* is optional. If *number* is omitted, all preceding commands that are longer than one character are listed.

The commands are listed in reverse order, with the most recently executed command listed first. Each command is preceded by its command number, which is used by the ! command (described in the following section).

The ! Command: Executing Previous Commands

Each command that is saved by the debugger and can be listed by the H command has a *command number*. You can use this command number to repeat a previously executed command. For example, to repeat command number 5, make the following entry:

```
  DB <11> !5
b 8
  DB <12>
```

The debugger displays command number 5—in this case, the command b 8— and then executes it.

If you omit the number, the debugger repeats the last command executed:

```
  DB <12> $foo += $bar + 1
  DB <13> !
$foo += $bar + 1
  DB <14>
```

If you specify a negative number with !, the debugger skips back that many commands:

```
  DB <14> $foo += $bar + 1
  DB <15> $foo *= 2
  DB <16> ! -2
$foo += $bar + 1
  DB <17>
```

Here, the ! -2 command refers to the command $foo += $bar + 1.

21

The T Command: Stack Tracing

The T command enables you to display a *stack trace*, which is a collection of all the subroutines that are in progress, listed in reverse order. Here is an example:

```
DB <16> T
$ = &main::sub2('hi') from file debug1 line 7
$ = &main::sub1('hi') from file debug1 line 3
```

Here, the T command indicates that the program is currently inside subroutine sub2, which was called from line 7 of your program; this subroutine is part of the main package. The call to sub2 was passed the argument 'hi'.

The $ = preceding the subroutine name indicates that the subroutine call is expecting a scalar return value. If the call is expecting a list to be returned, the characters @ = appear in front of the subroutine name.

The next line of the displayed output tells you that sub2 was called by another subroutine, sub1. This subroutine was also passed the argument 'hi', and it was called by line 3 of the program. Because the stack trace lists no more subroutines, line 3 is part of your main program.

NOTE

The list of arguments passed to a subroutine that is displayed by the stack trace is the list of actual values after variable substitution and expression evaluation are performed. This procedure enables you to use the stack trace to check whether your subroutines are being passed the values you expect.

The p Command: Printing an Expression

An easy way to print the value of an expression from inside the debugger is to use the p command:

```
DB <17> p $curdir + 1
1
```

21

The p command evaluates the expression and displays the result.

NOTE

The `p` command writes to the screen even when the program has redirected `STDOUT` to a file.

The = Command: Defining Aliases

If you find yourself repeatedly entering a long debugging command and you want to save yourself some typing, you can define an alias for the long command by using the `=` command. For example:

```
  DB <15> = pc print ("curdir is $curdir\n");
= pc print ("curdir is $curdir\n");
```

The `=` command prints the alias you have just defined and then stores it in the associative array `%DB::alias` (package `DB`, array name `alias`) for future reference. From here on, the command

```
DB <16> pc
```

is equivalent to the command

```
DB <16> print ("curdir is $curdir\n");
```

To list the aliases you have defined so far, enter the `=` command by itself:

```
  DB <17> =
pc =  print ("curdir is $curdir\n")
```

This command displays your defined aliases and their equivalent values.

Predefining Aliases

You can define aliases that are to be created every time you enter the Perl debugger.

When the debugger starts, it first searches for a file named `perldb.ini` in the current directory. If the debugger finds this file, it executes the statements contained there.

To create an alias, add it to the `.perldb` file. For example, to add the alias

```
= pc print ("curdir is $curdir\n");
```

add the following statement to your `.perldb` file:

```
$DB'alias{"pc"} = 's/^pc/print ("curdir is $curdir\n");/';
```

Here's how this works: when the Perl debugger creates an alias, it adds an element to the `$DB'alias` associative array. The subscript for this element is the alias you are defining, and the value is a substitution command that replaces the alias with the actual command you want

21

to use. In the preceding example, the substitution takes any command starting with `pc` and replaces it with

```
print ("curdir is $curdir\n");
```

WARNING

Be careful when you define aliases this way. For example, your substitution should match only the beginning of a command, as in `/^pc/`. Otherwise, the alias will replace any occurrence of the letters `pc` with your print command, which is not what you want.

The h Command: Debugger Help

The `h` (for *help*) command provides a list of each of the debugger commands you've seen in today's lesson, along with a one-line explanation of each. This is handy if you are in the middle of debugging a program and forget the syntax of a particular command.

Summary

Today, you have learned about the Perl debugger. This debugger enables you to perform the following tasks, among others:

- ☐ List any part of your source file
- ☐ Step through your program one statement at a time
- ☐ Display any variables you have defined
- ☐ Set breakpoints, which tell the debugger when to stop and request further commands
- ☐ Set line actions, which are statements to be executed when the program reaches a particular line
- ☐ Trace program execution as it happens
- ☐ Print a stack trace, which lists the current subroutine you are in and the subroutines that called it

Q&A

Q **Is it possible to enter more than one debugging command at a time?**

A No; however, there's no real need to do so. If you want to perform several single steps at once, use the c command to skip ahead to a specified point. If you want to both step ahead and print the value of a variable, use the < or > command.

Q **Is it possible to examine variables in one package while inside another?**

A Yes. Use the v command or the standard Perl package/variable syntax.

Q **If I discover that my program works and I want to turn off debugging, what do I do?**

A You cannot exit the debugger in the middle of a program. However, if you delete all breakpoints and line actions and then enter the c command, the program begins executing normally and is no longer under control of the debugger.

Q **How can I convert to a reusable breakpoint a one-time breakpoint created using c?**

A By default, the b command sets a breakpoint at the line that is about to be executed. This is the line at which c has set its one-time breakpoint.

Q **How can I execute DOS commands from inside the debugger?**

A Enter a statement containing a call to the Perl system function. For example, to display the contents of the current directory, enter the following command:

```
DB <11> system ("dir");
```

Q **What special built-in variables can be accessed from inside the debugger?**

A All of them.

Workshop

The Workshop provides quiz questions to help you solidify your understanding of the material covered. Try to understand the answers before moving on to the next lesson. You can find the answers in Appendix B, "Answers."

Quiz

1. Define the following terms:
    a. trace mode
    b. stack trace
    c. breakpoint
    d. line action

21

2. Explain the differences between the x and v commands.

3. Explain the differences between the // and ?? commands.

4. Explain the differences between the < and > commands.

5. Explain the differences between the s and n commands.

6. What do the following commands do?

    a. 1

    b. 1 26

    c. 1 5-7

    d. 1 5+7

    e. w

 WEEK **3**

 15

16

17

18

19

20

21

In Review

Congratulations! You've spent 21 days studying the 21 lessons in this book.

In the final week of teaching yourself how to use Perl 5 for Win32, you've learned about the extensive Perl function library and Win32 extensions and modules, as well as some other important features and applications of Perl. The pair of programs in Listings R3.1 and R3.2 illustrates some of the concepts you've learned during your second week.

You've probably sent and received e-mails at work or home by using some commercial or shareware (free) software; the programs in Listings R3.1 and R3.2 provide a simple service that can send out your e-mails.

Now let's take a look at Listing R3.1, which contains a Perl program that launches a Windows application, `notepad.exe`, and calls the `SendMail` subroutine from the `pwkr03_2.pl` file to send out e-mails.

Listing R3.1. The main console that launches a Windows application and calls a module to send e-mails.

`TYPE`

```perl
1:  # pwkr03_1.pl
2:  #**********************************************************
3:  # maincnsl.pl (saved under the name of pwkr03_1.pl):
4:  #     This is a main console that you can use to
5:  #     issue commands saved in the command array
6:  #     %Commands
7:  #
8:  # author:   Tony Zhang,  December 29, 1996
9:  # version:  1.0
10: #**********************************************************
11:
12: require 'pwkr03_2.pl';
13:
14: %Errors = {
15:         '-1' => 'mail host unknown',
16:         '-2' => 'socket() failed',
17:         '-3' => 'connect() failed',
18:         '-4' => 'service not available',
19:         '-5' => 'unspecified communication error',
20:         '-6' => 'local user $to unknown on host $smpt',
21:         '-7' => 'transmission of message failed'
22: };
23: #------------------------------------------------------
24: # Define the user-level commands.
25: #------------------------------------------------------
26: &Help('<QUIT>     Terminate the Perl program');
27: sub mainQUIT {
28:   $Echo = 0;
29:   &Output('Bye!');
30:   close (MF) if MF;
31:   exit 0;
32: }
33: $Commands{'<QUIT>'} = 'mainQUIT';
34:
35: &Help('<SADDR    Set address of receiver');
36: sub mainSEND_ADDR {
37:   $Send_Addr = shift (@Inputs);
38:   &Output($Send_Addr);
39: }
40: $Commands{'<SADDR>'} = 'mainSEND_ADDR';
41:
42: &Help('<RADDR    Set address for replying mails');
43: sub mainREPLY_ADDR {
44:   $Reply_Addr = shift (@Inputs);
45:   &Output($Reply_Addr);
46: }
47: $Commands{'<RADDR>'} = 'mainREPLY_ADDR';
48:
49: &Help('<FADDR    Set address of sender');
50: sub mainFROM_ADDR {
51:   $From_Addr = shift (@Inputs);
52:   &Output($From_Addr);
```

```
53:   }
54:   $Commands{'<FADDR>'} = 'mainFROM_ADDR';
55:
56:   &Help('<SUBJ>    Set the subject');
57:   sub mainSUBJECT {
58:     my (@tmp) = @Inputs;
59:     $Subject = join (' ', @tmp);
60:   }
61:   $Commands{'<SUBJ>'} = 'mainSUBJECT';
62:
63:   &Help('<MSG>      The message body');
64:   sub mainMSG {
65:     my (@tmp) = @Inputs;
66:     my ($str) = join (' ', @tmp);
67:     push (@Msg, $str);
68:   }
69:   $Commands{'<MSG>'} = 'mainMSG';
70:
71:   &Help('<MSG_BGN> The beginning of the e-mail body');
72:   sub mainMSGBGN {
73:     $Is_Msg = 1;
74:   }
75:   $Commands{'<MSG_BGN>'} = 'mainMSGBGN';
76:
77:   &Help('<MSG_END> The end of the e-mail');
78:   sub mainMSGEND {
79:     $Is_Msg = 0;
80:     shift (@Msg);
81:     $msg = join ("\n", @Msg);
82:     &Output($msg);
83:     &Output(' ');
84:     &Output('If you want to send the message, enter <mail> now.');
85:   }
86:   $Commands{'<MSG_END>'} = 'mainMSGEND';
87:
88:   &Help('<MAIL>     Start to mail the e-mail');
89:   sub mainMAIL {
90:     my ($return) = &SendMail ($From_Addr,
91:                               $Reply_Addr,
92:                               $Send_Addr,
93:                               'mail_server_name',  # make sure to update
                                 ➥the mail server name
94:                               $Subject, $msg);
95:     if ($return == 1) {
96:       &Output("The mail has been sent out successfull.");
97:     } else {
98:       &Output("Have problem(s):  %Errors{$return} ");
99:       &Output('Nice try!  :-) ');
100:   }
101: }
102: $Commands{'<MAIL>'} = 'mainMAIL';
103:
104: &Help('<?>       On-line help');
105: &Help('<HELP>    On-line help');
106: sub mainHELP {
107:   foreach $ele (sort @Help) {
```

continues

Listing R3.1. continued

```
108:      &Output($ele);
109:    }
110:    &Output(' ');   # add a new line
111: }
112: $Commands{'<?>'} = 'mainHELP';
113: $Commands{'<HELP>'} = 'mainHELP';
114: #--------------------------------------------------------
115: # Invoke the Windows application, notepad.exe, which
116: # can be used in editing the e-mail.
117: #--------------------------------------------------------
118: use Win32::Process;
119:
120: &Help('<EDIT>     Edit your e-mail in notepad');
121: sub mainEDIT {
122:    Win32::Process::Create (
123:             $processObj,
124:             "c:\\windows\\notepad.exe",   # make sure to update the path
125:             "notepad tmp_mail.txt",
126:             0,
127:             DETACHED_PROCESS,
128:             ".") or die "Cannot create the process object.";
129:
130:    $processObj->SetPriorityClass (NORMAL_PRIORITY_CLASS) or
131:             die $!;
132:    $processObj->Wait (INFINITE);
133:    Output ("The notepad.exe program exited.");
134:    open (MF, "tmp_mail.txt");
135: }
136: $Commands{'<EDIT>'} = 'mainEDIT';
137: #--------------------------------------------------------
138: # other subroutines
139: #--------------------------------------------------------
140: sub Help {
141:    push(@Help, @_);
142: }
143: sub Output {
144:    my (@output) = @_;
145:    print STDOUT "@output\n" if @output > 0;
146: }
147: sub MakeCall {
148:    local($sub, @args) = split(/\s+/, join(' ', @_));
149:    if (defined(&$sub)) {
150:      &$sub(@args);
151:    } else {
152:      &Output("Undefined subroutine: $sub @args");
153:      die('');
154:    }
155: }
156: sub ProcessCommands {
157:    for (;;)
158:    {
159:      $cmd = ($cmd_1=<MF>) ? $cmd_1:($cmd_2=<STDIN>);
160:      if ($cmd) {
```

```
161:        chop ($cmd);
162:        ($_, @Inputs) = split (/\s+/, $cmd);
163:        $_ =~ tr/a-z/A-Z/;
164:        if ($v = $Commands{$_}){
165:          &MakeCall ($v);
166:        }
167:        if ($Is_Msg) {
168:          push (@Msg, $cmd);
169:        }
170:        $cmd = '';
171:     }
172:   }
173: }
174: #--------------------------------------------------------
175: # the main loop
176: #--------------------------------------------------------
177: &Output('The following is a list of commands:');
178: &MakeCall ($v) if ($v = $Commands{'<?>'});
179: &Output('Enter <EDIT> to start edit your e-mail');
180: &Output('or, <QUIT> to quit.');
181: for (;;) {
182:   eval { &ProcessCommands };
183: }
184: #------ the end of pwkr03_1.pl ---------#
```

OUTPUT

```
C:\> perl pwkr03_1.pl
The following is a list of the commands:
<?>        On-line help
<EDIT>     Edit your e-mail in notepad
<FADDR>    Set address of sender
<HELP>     On-line help
<MAIL>     Start to mail the e-mail
<MSG>      The message body
<MSG_BGN>  The beginning of the e-mail body
<MSG_END>  The end of the e-mail
<QUIT>     Terminate the Perl program
<RADDR>    Set address for replying mails
<SADDR>    Set address of receiver
<SUBJ>     Set the subject

Enter <EDIT> to start editing your e-mail
or, <QUIT> to quit:
<quit>
Bye!
C:\>
```

ANALYSIS There are three parts in Listing R3.1. Lines 23–136 declare the user-level commands. Lines 137–173 give the subroutines called by the other subroutines in the pwkr03_1.pl file. Lines 174–184 show the main loop that is used to process the commands entered by the user.

Line 12 asks the Perl interpreter to include the pwkr03_2.pl file that contains the SendMail subroutine. Lines 14–22 define the %Errors hash (associative array). %Errors contains the error messages associated with the keys that are the values of the error code returned by the SendMail subroutine.

The Help subroutine is called in several lines, such as 25, 26, and 42, to save the description of the commands into the @Help array. Note that in line 141, the online help information is pushed into @Help by applying the Perl function push.

The syntax of a user-level command is <Command Name>. The commands supplied in pwkr03_1.pl are

```
<?>        On-line help
<EDIT>     Edit your e-mail in notepad
<FADDR>    Set address of sender
<HELP>     On-line help
<MAIL>     Start to mail the e-mail
<MSG>      The message body
<MSG_BGN>  The beginning of the e-mail body
<MSG_END>  The end of the e-mail
<QUIT>     Terminate the Perl program
<RADDR>    Set address for replying mails
<SADDR>    Set address of receiver
<SUBJ>     Set the subject.
```

These commands are shown in the output section after pwkr03_1.pl is executed. Among them, <?> and <HELP> are the commands displaying all commands on the screen. Normally, the user enters the <EDIT> command to launch a Windows application, notepad.exe, in order to edit an e-mail. Note in line 118, that the Win32::Process module is included, so that the Create function can be called to create a new process that starts the notepad.exe program in lines 122–128.

Figure R3.1 shows an example that a notepad is created and used in editing my e-mail after the <EDIT> command is entered. As you can see, the foreground window in Figure R3.1 is the Notepad window that contains an e-mail I've written. The background is the DOS window, in which you can see a portion of the list of commands and the <edit> command I just entered. When the ProcessCommands subroutine, declared in lines 156–163, gets the command I entered, it translates the edit to EDIT automatically (see line 163).

When the user finishes the editing and closes the Notepad window, he is asked to enter the <MAIL> command to send out the e-mail if he wants to. When <MAIL> is entered, the SendMail subroutine is called to establish a connection and send out the e-mail. Note that in line 93, I use mail_server_name as the mail server name. You have to replace this with your mail server's name before you run the Perl program.

The pwkr03_2.pl file, shown in Listing R3.2, contains the SendMail subroutine, as well as another one, called Error. pwkr03_2.pl is required by the Perl program of the main console saved in the pwkr03_1.pl file.

Figure R3.1.

A sample e-mail message that I edited in Notepad launched by entering the <EDIT> command.

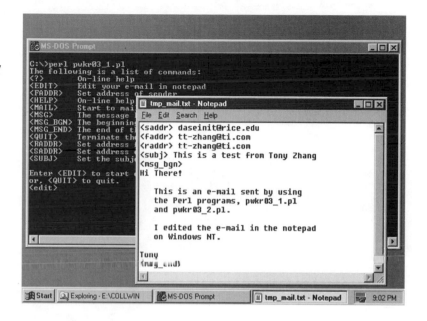

Listing R3.2. The package file required by the Perl program of the main console.

```
1:   # pwkr03_2.pl
2:
3:   #-----------------------------------------------------------------------
4:   # pwkr03_2.pl: Contains two subroutines, Error and SendMail,
5:   #              which are required by pwkr03_1.pl.
6:   # Error: Displays errors during a mail sending.
7:   # SendMail: Establishes connection and sends out e-mails.
8:   # (Do NOT give me credit. SendMail is a freely-shared program I downloaded
9:   #  from the user group of Perl 5 for Win32. I don't know who is
10:  #  the original author.Also, I've modified it.)
11:  #
12:  # syntax:
13:  #    Error( $error_string );
14:  #    SendMail( $from,
15:  #              $reply,
16:  #              $to,
17:  #              $smtpserver, $subject, $message );
18:  #-----------------------------------------------------------------------
19:
20:  sub Error {
21:    my ($str) = @_;
22:    my ($error_flag) = 0;
23:    if ($str =~/^[45]/) {
24:      $error_flag = 1;
25:      print STDOUT "$str \n";
26:    }
```

continues

Listing R3.2. continued

```
27:    return $error_flag;
28:  }
29:  sub SendMail {
30:      my ($from, $reply, $to, $smtp, $subject, $message) = @_;
31:      my ($proto, $port, $smptaddr);
32:      my ($ret);
33:      my ($AF_INET)    = 2;
34:      my ($SOCK_STREAM) = 1;
35:
36:      $smptaddr = ($smtp =~ /^(\d{1,3})\.(\d{1,3})\.(\d{1,3})\.(\d{1,3})$/)
37:                  ? pack('C4',$1,$2,$3,$4)
38:                  : (gethostbyname($smtp))[4];
39:      $proto = (getprotobyname('tcp'))[2];
40:      $port  = 25;
41:      if (!defined($smptaddr)) {
42:          return -1;
43:      }
44:      if (!socket(S, $AF_INET, $SOCK_STREAM, $proto)) {
45:          return -2;
46:      }
47:      if (!connect(S, pack('Sna4x8', $AF_INET, $port, $smptaddr))) {
48:          return -3;
49:      }
50:      my($oldfh) = select(S); $| = 1; select($oldfh);
51:      if (Error ($ret=<S>)) {
52:          close S;
53:          return -4;
54:      }
55:      print S "mail from: $from\n";
56:      if (Error ($ret=<S>)) {
57:          close S;
58:          return -5;
59:      }
60:      print S "rcpt to: $to\n";    # "rcpt to: $to\n"
61:      if (Error ($ret=<S>)) {
62:          close S;
63:          return -6;
64:      }
65:      print S "data\n";
66:      if (Error ($ret=<S>)) {
67:          close S;
68:          return -5;
69:      }
70:      print S "Reply-to: $reply\nSubject: $subject\n$message\n.\n";
71:      if (Error ($ret=<S>)) {
72:          close S;
73:          return -7;
74:      }
75:      print S "quit\n";
76:      close S;
77:      return 1;
78:  }
79:  1;  # required by the caller.
```

In Listing R3.2, lines 20–28 declare the `Error` subroutine that is called by the `SendMail` subroutine, declared in lines 29–78, to determine whether the string returned by the socket is an error message.

The `Error` subroutine detects errors by checking the incoming string. If the first character in the string is 4 or 5, it means the string contains an error message. Lines 23–26 show the `if` block that prints out the incoming error string and sets up the error flag to inform the caller that something went wrong during the e-mail sending.

Lines 36–38 obtain the mail-host address. To do so, the Perl `gethostbyname` function is employed as one of the methods in line 38. Line 39 gets the communication protocol by calling another Perl `getprotobyname` function. Line 40 sets the port number with 25. Line 44 creates a socket and associates the file handle `s` with the socket. (On Day 14, "Packages, Modules, and System Functions," you learned about the Perl `socket` functions and other socket-manipulation functions supported in Perl 5 for Win32.)

Then, another Perl `connect` function is called to connect the `s` file handle, representing the socket created in line 44, with the internal value of the Internet address created by `pack('Sna4x8', $AF_INET, $port, $smptaddr)` in line 47.

Line 50 eliminates buffering for the file to which `s` is the file handle. Lines 51–75 send out the communication-level commands combined with the address of the receiver, the address of the sender, and the e-mail message itself to the output file pointed by the `s` file handle. The returned strings from the socket are checked for errors by applying the `Error` subroutine.

If everything is correct and the e-mail is sent out successfully, line 76 closes the `s` file handle, and line 77 returns 1. The last line in Listing R3.2, line 79, marks the end of the `pwkr03_2.pl` file.

Before you close this book, I'd like to remind you that all examples shown in this book are not necessarily the best. As is sometimes said, in Perl there's more than one way to do it. Now it's your turn to apply what you've learned from this book and do it your way.

Good luck!

Unsupported Functions in Perl 5 for Win32

As you have learned in the past three weeks, Perl 5 for Win32 does not support all the built-in functions found in Perl 5 (the UNIX version). The main reason is that, on the Windows NT system, it's difficult to find the equivalents for some of the UNIX-version Perl functions. The situation is even worse for the Windows 95 system.

The following list gives the unsupported functions in Perl 5 for Win32. In many cases, the Perl 5 for Win32 interpreter will give you a warning message or simply quit if you try to use one of the unsupported functions in your Perl programs.

However, there are several unsupported functions that the Perl interpreter won't complain about when you use them in your Perl programs, which means you will not get any warning messages when calling those unsupported functions. These functions are marked with an * in the following table.

Please note that the list of unsupported functions in Table A.1 is a copy from the original on-line document saved at

`http://www.perl.hip.com`

We do recommend you check the latest news regarding the unsupported functions at

`http://www.perl.hip.com` **or,**
`http://www.ActiveWare.com`

Table A.1. Unsupported functions in Perl 5 for Win32 (Build 110).

alarm	getpgrp	setgrent
chmod *	getppid	sethostent
chroot	getpriority	setnetent
crypt	getprotoent	setpgrp
dbmclose *	getpwent	setpriority
dbmopen *	getpwnam	setprotoent
dump *	getpwuid	setpwent
endgrent	getservent	setservent
endhostent	ioctl *	shmctl
endnetent	kill	shmget
endprotoent	link	shmread
endpwent	lstat *	shmwrite
fcntl *	msgget	symlink
flock	msgrcv	syscall
fork	msgsnd	sysread *

getgrent	pipe	syswrite *
getgrgid	readlink *	times
getgrnam	select *	umask *
getlogin *	semctl	utime *
getnetbyaddr	semget	wait
getnetbyname	semop	waitpid
getnetent		

NOTE

The single-argument version of the select function has been implemented in Perl 5 for Win32. For instance, to select a socket and make it the new current socket, you can use the select function by passing the socket's file handle to it:

```
select (A_Socket_File_Handle)
```

in your programs written in Perl 5 for Win32.

APPENDIX

B

Answers

This appendix contains the answers for the Quiz sections and possible solutions for the Exercise sections you've seen throughout the book.

Answers for Day 1, "Getting Started—Perl for Windows NT"

Quiz

1. You can get Perl 5 for Win32 at the FTP site, `ftp.perl.hip.com`, or you can visit the Perl for Win32 home page at `http://www.perl.hip.com` or `http://www.ActiveWare.com`.

2. The Perl interpreter executes your Perl program (starting from the beginning and continuing one statement at a time).

3. The answers are as follows:

   a. A statement is one particular task or instruction (usually corresponding to a line of code). A statement is terminated by a semicolon (`;`).

   b. A token is the smallest unit of information understood by the Perl interpreter. A statement consists of several tokens.

   c. An argument is an item passed to a library function (such as `$mystring` to `print`).

   d. The standard input file is the file that stores the characters you enter at the keyboard.

   e. The standard output file is the file that stores the characters you want to display the screen.

4. A comment is any text that is preceded by a `#`. A comment can appear anywhere in your program. Everything after the `#` character is assumed to be part of the comment.

5. Perl 5 for Win32 is ported directly from Perl 5, a UNIX version of Perl.

6. A library function is defined as part of the Perl interpreter and performs a specific task.

7. There are basically three methods to run a Perl program on Windows NT:

   Method One: Run a Perl program from a command prompt by typing `perl Perl-Program-Name`. Make sure the Perl program is accessible to the Perl interpreter.

Method Two: Convert a Perl program to a batch file and then run it in the way you would run the other batch files.

Method Three: Configure the File Manager on Windows NT and make a Perl program recognized by the Perl interpreter automatically.

Exercises

1. The following is one possible solution:

```
# 01a01.pl
$mystring = <STDIN>;
print ($mystring, $mystring);
```

2. The following is one possible solution:

```
# 01a02.pl
$mystring = <STDIN>;
print ($mystring);
$mystring = <STDIN>;
print ($mystring);
```

3. The following is one possible solution:

```
# 01a03.pl
$mystring = <STDIN>;
$mystring = <STDIN>;     # this throws away the previous input line
print ($mystring);
```

4. The second line of the program is missing a semicolon at the end of the statement. It should look like this:

```
# Exercise 4 - bug buster
$mystring = <STDIN>;
print ($mystring);
```

5. The `print ($mystring)` line is ignored because the entire third line is being treated as a comment. You want the following instead:

```
# The correct one:
$mystring = <STDIN>;
print ($mystring);   # print my line!
```

6. This program reads two lines of input and prints them in reverse order (second line first).

Answers for Day 2, "Basic Operators and Control Flow"

Quiz

1. The answers are as follows:

   a. An expression is a collection of operators and the values on which they operate.

   b. An operand is a value associated with an operator.

   c. A conditional statement is a statement that is executed only when its conditional expression is true.

   d. A statement block is a collection of statements contained inside the braces of a conditional statement. The statement block is executed only when the conditional expression associated with its conditional statement is true.

   e. An infinite loop is a conditional statement whose conditional expression is always true.

2. A `while` statement stops looping when its conditional expression is false.

3. An `until` statement stops looping when its conditional expression is true.

4. The `==` operator compares its two operands. If they are numerically equal, the `==` operator yields a result of true; otherwise, it yields false.

5. 27.

6. The legal ones are a, c, and f.

Exercises

1. Here is one possible solution:

```
print ("Enter a number to be multiplied by 2:\n");
$number = <STDIN>;
chop ($number);
$number = $number * 2;
print ("The result is ", $number, "\n");
```

2. Here is one possible solution:

```
print ("Enter the dividend (number to divide):\n");
$dividend = <STDIN>;
```

```
chop ($dividend);
print ("Enter the divisor (number to divide by):\n");
$divisor = <STDIN>;
chop ($divisor);
if ($divisor == 0) {
        print ("Error: can't divide by zero!\n");
} elsif ($dividend == 0) {
        $result = $dividend;
} elsif ($divisor == 1) {
        $result = $dividend;
} else {
        $result = $divisor / $dividend;
}
if ($divisor == 0) {
        # skip the print, since we detected an error
} else {
        print ("The result is ", $result, "\n");
}
```

3. Here is one possible solution:

```
$count = 1;
$done = 0;
while ($done == 0) {
        print ($count, "\n");
        if ($count == 10) {
                $done = 1;
        }
        $count = $count + 1;
}
```

4. Here is one possible solution:

```
$count = 10;
until ($count == 0) {
        print ($count, "\n");
        $count = $count - 1;
}
```

5. There are, in fact, three separate bugs in this program:

   a. You must call `chop` to get rid of the trailing newline character in `$value` before comparing it to 17.

   b. The conditional expression should read `$value == 17`, **not** `$value = 17`.

   c. There should be a closing brace `(}` before the `else`.

6. This program contains an infinite loop. To fix it, add the following statement just before the closing brace `(})`:

```
$input = $input + 1;
```

   Also, the statement

```
$input = $terminate + 5;
```

   should read

```
$terminate = $input + 5;
```

Answers for Day 3, "Understanding Scalar Values"

Quiz

1. The answers are as follows:

   a. A round-off error is the difference between the floating-point number that appears in a program and the number as it is represented in the machine.

   b. Octal notation is another way of referring to base-8 notation: Each digit can be a number from 0 to 7 and is multiplied by 8 to the exponent n, where n is the number of digits to skip.

   c. The precision of a floating-point representation on a machine is the number of significant digits it can hold.

   d. Scientific notation is a way of writing floating-point numbers. It consists of one digit before the decimal point, as many digits as required after the decimal point, and an exponent.

2. The answers are as follows:

   a. 255 (the ASCII end-of-file character)

   b. 6

   c. 601

3. The answers are as follows:

   a. 255

   b. 17

   c. 48,813

4. This line prints `I am bored`, and then backspaces over `bored` and replaces it with `happy!`. (I don't know a lot of practical uses for the `\b` escape character, but it's fun to watch.)

5. The answers are as follows:

   a. `This string contains 21.`

   b. `\21 is my favorite number.`

   c. `Assign \$num to this string.`

6. The answers are as follows:

   a. `4.371e01`

   b. `6.0e-08` (the `.0` is optional)

   c. `3.0e+00` (actually, `3` by itself is acceptable)

   d. `-1.04e+00`

Exercises

1. Here is one possible solution:

```
$count = 1;
$number = 0.1;
until ($count == 10) {
        print ("$number\n");
        $number = $number + 0.1;
        $count = $count + 1;
}
```

2. Here is one possible solution:

```
$inputline = <STDIN>;
chop ($inputline);
if ($inputline == 0) {
        print ("0\n");
} else {
        print ("1\n");
}
```

3. Here is one possible solution:

```
print ("Enter a number:\n");
$number = <STDIN>;
chop ($number);
until ($number == 47) {
        print ("Wrong! Try again!\n");
        $number = <STDIN>;
        chop ($number);
}
print ("\aCorrect!\n");
```

4. The first string in the `print` statement is not terminated properly, because there is a backslash `(\)` before the final `'`. To fix this, add another quote:

   ```
   print ('here is the value of \$inputline\'', ": $inputline");
   ```

5. This code fragment does not produce the expected result because of a round-off error. Try subtracting `$num3` from `$num1` before adding `$num2` and `$num4`.

6. `"0xce"` converts to `0`, not to the hexadecimal constant `0xce`. To fix this, leave the quotes off.

Answers for Day 4, "More Operators"

Quiz

1. The answers are as follows:

    a. An operator is a character or string of characters that represents a particular Perl operation.

    b. An operand is a value used by an operator. In Perl, operators require one, two, or three operands.

    c. An expression is a collection of operators and operands, yielding a final result.

    d. Operator precedence is the order in which different types of operations are performed.

    e. Operator associativity is the order in which operations of the same precedence are performed.

2. The answers are as follows:

    a. Logical AND

    b. Bitwise AND

    c. Bitwise XOR

    d. String inequality

    e. String concatenation

3. The answers are as follows:

    a. `eq`

    b. `%`

    c. `x`

    d. `|`

    e. `>=`

4. The answers are as follows:

    a. `0000000010101011`

    b. `0000010001010001`

    c. `0` (or `00000000`)

5. The answers are as follows:

    a. `100`

    b. `15`

    c. `65`

6. The answers are as follows:

    a. 4

    b. 0 (I hope you didn't calculate all of the expression! Once you see the first 0, you should know that the result is 0.)

    c. 1819

    d. "abcdede"

Exercises

1. The following is just one of many possible answers:

```
$value = 1;
$counter = 0;
while ($counter < 16) {
        print ("2 to the power $counter is $value\n");
        $value = $value << 1;
        $counter++;
}
```

2. The answer is as follows:

```
$result = $var1 == 5 || $var2 == 7 ?
        $var1 * $var2 + 16.5 :
        (print("condition is false\n"), 0);
```

3. The answer is as follows:

```
if ($var1 <= 26) {
        $result = ++$var2;
} else {
        $result = 0;
}
```

4. The following is just one of many possible answers:

```
print("Enter the integer to be divided:\n");
$dividend = <STDIN>;
print("Enter the integer to divide by:\n");
$divisor = <STDIN>;
# check for division by zero
if ($divisor == 0) {
        print("error: can't divide by zero\n");
} else {
        $quotient = $dividend / $divisor;
        $remainder = $dividend % $divisor;
        print("The result is $quotient\n");
        print("The remainder is $remainder\n");
}
```

5. Adding 100005.2 and then subtracting it causes round-off errors, which means that the final value isn't exactly the same as 5.1.

6. `($result = ((($var1 * 2) << (5 + 3)) || ($var2 ** 3))), $var3;`

7. `81`

8. Here is the corrected program, with the fixed errors listed:

```
$num = <STDIN>;
chop ($num);
$x = "";
$x .= "hello";      # += is for integers
if ($x ne "goodbye" || $x eq "farewell") {
        # the previous line had two problems:
        #    the operators were numeric, not string;
        #    the or operator was bitwise, not logical.
        $result = $num == 0 ? 43 : 0;
        # the : and third operand were missing in the previous
        # line; eq replaced by ==
} else {
        $result = ++$num;   # can't have ++ on both sides
}
print("the result is $result\n");
```

Answers for Day 5, "Lists and Array Variables"

Quiz

1. The answers are as follows:

   a. A list is an ordered collection of scalar values.

   b. An empty list is a list with zero elements in it.

   c. An array variable is a variable that can store a list.

   d. A subscript is a scalar value that refers to an element of a list. The subscript 0 refers to the first element, the subscript 1 refers to the second, and so on.

   e. An array slice is a list consisting of some elements of an array variable. (Notice that the elements do not have to be in order.)

2. The answers are as follows:

   a. `(1, 2, 3)`

   b. `(3, 2)`

   c. `("hello", 2, 2)`

   d. `("", 3, 2, 2)`

   e. The contents of the standard input file, one line per list element.

3. The answers are as follows:

    a. `2`

    b. `4`

    c. `"one"`

    d. `2`

    e. `"three"`

    f. `""` (Only three elements in the list are stored in `@list2`.)

4. A list is a collection of scalar values. An array variable is a place where you can store a list.

5. The brackets (`[]`) enclosing the subscript distinguish an array element from a scalar variable.

6. You can do this in many ways. The two easiest are

    ☐ Use single-quoted strings, which do not allow substitutions.

    ☐ Put a backslash (`\`) before the character that you want left as is.

7. You can obtain the length of a list stored in an array variable by assigning the array variable to a scalar variable.

8. All undefined array elements are assumed to contain the null string `""`.

9. When you assign to an array element that is larger than the current length of the array, the array grows to include the new element.

Exercises

1. Here is one possible solution:

```
$thecount = 0;
$line = <STDIN>;
while ($line ne "") {
        chop ($line);
        @words = split(/ /, $line);
        $wordindex = 1;
        while ($wordindex <= @words) {
                if ($words[$wordindex-1] eq "the") {
                        $thecount += 1;
                }
                $wordindex++;
        }
        $line = <STDIN>;
}
print ("Total occurrences of \"the\": $thecount\n");
```

2. Here is one possible solution:

```
$grandtotal = 0;
$line = <STDIN>;
```

```
while ($line ne "") {
        $linetotal = 0;
        @numbers = split(/ /, $line);
        $numbercount = 1;
        while ($numbercount <= @numbers) {
                $linetotal += $numbers[$numbercount-1];
                $numbercount++;
        }
        print("line total: $linetotal\n");
        $grandtotal += $linetotal;
        $line = <STDIN>;
}
print("grand total: $grandtotal\n");
```

3. Here is one possible solution:

```
@lines = <STDIN>;
chop (@lines);
$longlongline = join(" ", @lines);
@words = split(/ /, $longlongline);
@words = reverse sort (@words);
$index = 0;
print("Words sorted in reverse order:\n");
while ($index < @words) {
        # note that the first time through, the following
        # comparison references $words[-1]. This is all
        # right, as $words[-1] is replaced by the null
        # string, and we want the first word to be printed
        if ($words[$index] ne $words[$index-1]) {
                print ("$words[$index]\n");
        }
        $index++;
}
```

4. The array element reference should be `$array[4]`, not `@array[4]`.

5. There are four separate bugs in this program:

    a. You must call `chop` to remove the newline characters from the input lines stored in `@input`. Otherwise, they make your output unreadable.

    b. Similarly, you have to append a newline when calling `join`:

    ```
    $input[$currline] = join(" ", @words, "\n");
    ```

    c. The conditional expression should read

    ```
    $currline <= @input
    ```

    instead of

    ```
    $currline < @input
    ```

    to make sure that the last line of the input file is read.

    d. Your subscripts should read `[$currline-1]`, not `[$currline]`. (This bug will keep coming up in your programs because it's easy to forget that subscripts start with zero.)

Answers for Day 6, "Reading from and Writing to Files"

Quiz

1. The answers are as follows:

    a. A file variable is a name that represents an open file.

    b. A reserved word is a word that can't be used as a variable name because it has a special meaning in Perl (such as `if`).

    c. The file mode specifies how you want to access a file when you open it (read, write, or append).

    d. Append mode indicates that you want to open the file for writing and append anything you write to the existing contents of the file.

    e. A pipe is a connection between output from one program and input to another.

2. The `<>` operator reads its data from the files specified on the command line.

3. The answers are as follows:

    a. `-e` tests whether a file exists.

    b. `-r` tests whether you have permission to read a file.

    c. `-w` tests whether you have permission to write to a file.

4. `@ARGV` contains the following list:

    ```
    ("file1", "file2", "file3")
    ```

5. The answers are as follows:

    a. To open a file in write mode, put a `>` character in front of the filename.

    b. To open a file in append mode, put two `>` characters (`>>`) in front of the filename.

    c. To open a file in read mode, just specify the filename. By default, files are opened in read mode.

    d. To open a pipe, put a `|` character in front of the command to be piped to.

6. The `<>` operator reads data from the files whose names are stored in the array variable `@ARGV`. When the `<>` operator runs out of data in one file, it opens the file named in `$ARGV[0]` and then calls `shift` to move the elements of `@ARGV` over.

Exercises

1. Here is one possible solution:

```
$total = 0;
$count = 1;
while ($count <= @ARGV) {
        $total += $ARGV[$count-1];
        $count++;
}
print ("The total is $total.\n");
```

2. Here is one possible solution:

```
$count = 1;
while ($count <= @ARGV) {
        if (-e $ARGV[$count-1] && -s $ARGV[$count-1] > 10000) {
                print ("File $ARGV[$count-1] is a big file!\n");
        }
        $count++;
}
```

3. Here is one possible solution:

```
open (INFILE, "file1") ||
        die ("Can't open file1 for reading\n");
open (OUTFILE, ">file2") ||
        die ("Can't open file2 for writing\n");
# the following only works if file1 isn't too big
@contents = <INFILE>;
print OUTFILE (@contents);
# we don't really need the call to close, but they
# make things a little clearer
close (OUTFILE);
open (OUTFILE, ">>file2") ||
        die ("Can't append to file2\n");
print OUTFILE (@contents);
```

4. Here is one possible solution:

```
$count = 1;
while ($count <= @ARGV) {
        print ("File $ARGV[$count-1]:");
        if (!(-e $ARGV[$count-1])) {
                print (" does not exist\n");
        } else {
                if (-r $ARGV[$count-1]) {
                        print (" read");
                }
                if (-w $ARGV[$count-1]) {
                        print (" write");
                }
                if (-x $ARGV[$count-1]) {
                        print (" execute");
                }
                print ("\n");
        }
        $count++;
}
```

5. This program is opening `outfile` in read mode, not write mode. To open in write mode, change the call to `open` to

```
open (OUTFILE, ">outfile");
```

Answers for Day 7, "Pattern Matching"

Quiz

1. The answers are as follows:

    a. Either the letter `a` or `b`, followed by zero or more occurrences of `c`.

    b. One, two, or three digits.

    c. The words `cat`, `cot`, and `cut`. (This pattern does not match these letters if they are in the middle of a word.)

    d. The first part of this pattern matches a subpattern consisting of `x`, one or more of `y`, and `z`. The rest of the pattern then matches a period, followed by the subpattern first matched.

    e. This matches an empty line (the null string).

2. The answers are as follows:

    a. `/[a-z]{5,}/`

    b. `/1|one/`

    c. `/\d+\.?\d+/`

    d. `/([A-Za-z])[aeiou]\1/`

    e. `/\++/`

3. Items a, b, c, and f are true; d and e are false.

4. The answers are as follows:

    a. `"def123abc"`

    b. `"X123X"`

    c. `"aWc123abc"`

    d. `"abd"`

    e. `"abc246abc"`

5. The answers are as follows:

    a. `"ABC123ABC"`

    b. `"abc456abc"`

c. "abc456abc"

d. "abc abc"

e. "123"

Exercises

1. Here is one possible solution:

```
while ($line = <STDIN>) {
        $line =~ tr/aeiou/AEIOU/;
        print ($line);
}
```

2. Here is one possible solution:

```
while ($inputline = <STDIN>) {
        $inputline =~ tr/0-9/ /c;
        $inputline =~ s/ +//g;
        @digits = split(//, $inputline);
        $total += @digits;
        $count = 1;
        while ($count <= @digits) {
                $dtotal[$digits[$count-1]] += 1;
                $count++;
        }
}
print ("Total number of digits found: $total\n");
print ("Breakdown:\n");
$count = 0;
while ($count <= 9) {
        if ($dtotal[$count] > 0) {
                print ("\tdigit $count: $dtotal[$count]\n");
        }
        $count++;
}
```

3. Here is one possible solution:

```
while ($line = <STDIN>) {
        $line =~ s/(\w+)(\s+)(\w+)(\s+)(\w+)/$5$2$3$4$1/;
        print ($line);
}
```

4. Here is one possible solution:

```
while ($line = <STDIN>) {
        $line =~ s/\d+/$&+1/eg;
        print ($line);
}
```

5. There are two problems. The first is that the pattern matches the entire line, including the closing newline. You do not want to put a quotation mark after the closing newline of each line.

The first problem is that the program has omitted the s operator, which specifies substitution.

The second problem is that the replacement string should contain $1, not \1. \1 is defined only inside the search pattern.

6. The pattern uses the * special character, which matches zero or more occurrences of any digit. This means the pattern always matches.

The pattern should use the + special character, which matches one or more occurrences of any digit.

Answers for Day 8, "More Control Structures"

Quiz

1. 7
2. 11
3. 5
4. 6
5. `last if ($x eq "done");`
6. `redo if ($list[0] == 26);`
7. `next LABEL if ($scalar eq "#");`
8. `print ("$count\n") while ($count++ < 10);`
9. The `continue` statement defines a block of code to be executed each time a `while` or an `until` statement loops.

Exercises

1. Here is one possible solution:
```
$count = 1;
do {
        print ("$count\n");
        $count++;
} while ($count <= 10);
```

2. Here is one possible solution:
```
for ($count = 1; $count <= 10; $count++) {
        print ("$count\n");
}
```

3. Here is one possible solution:

```
for ($count = 1; $count <= 5; $count++) {
        $line = <STDIN>;
        last if ($line eq "");
        print ($line);
}
```

4. Here is one possible solution:

```
for ($count = 1; $count <= 20; $count++) {
        next if ($count % 2 == 1);
        print ("$count\n");
}
```

5. Here is one possible solution:

```
$linenum = 0;
while ($line = <STDIN>) {
        $linenum += 1;
        $occurs = 0;
        $line =~ tr/A-Z/a-z/;
        @words = split(/\s+/, $line);
        foreach $word (@words) {
                $occurs += 1 if ($word eq "the");
        }
        if ($occurs > 0) {
                print ("line $linenum: $occurs occurrences\n");
        }
}
```

6. Here is one possible solution:

```
$count = 10;
while ($count >= 1) {
        print ("$count\n");
}
continue {
        $count-;
}
```

7. You can't use the `last` statement inside a `do` statement. To get around this problem, use another loop construct such as `while` or `for`, or put the conditional expression in the `while` statement at the bottom.

Answers for Day 9, "Using Subroutines"

Quiz

1. The answers are as follows:

   a. A subroutine is a separate body of code designed to perform a particular task.

B

b. An invocation is a statement that tells the Perl interpreter to execute a particular subroutine.

c. An argument is a value that is passed to a subroutine when it is invoked.

2. The answers are as follows:

   a. 0

   b. (4, 5, 6)

   c. (4, 5, 6)

3. False (or zero), because the conditional expression $count <= 10 is the last expression evaluated in the subroutine.

4. (1, 5, 3)

Exercises

1. Here is one possible solution:

```
sub add_two {
        local ($arg1, $arg2) = @_;

        $result = $arg1 + $arg2;
}
```

2. Here is one possible solution:

```
sub count_t {
        local ($string) = @_;

        # There are a couple of tricks you can use to do this.
        # This one splits the string into words using "t" as
        # the split pattern. The number of occurrences of "t"
        # is one less than the number of words resulting from
        # the split.
        @dummy = split(/t/, $string);
        $retval = @dummy - 1;
}
```

3. Here is one possible solution:

```
sub diff {
        local ($file1, $file2) = @_;

        # return false if we can't open a file
        return (0) unless open (FILE1, "$file1");
        return (0) unless open (FILE2, "$file2");
        while (1) {
                $line1 = <FILE1>;
                $line2 = <FILE2>;
                if ($line1 eq "") {
                        $retval = ($line2 eq "");
                        last;
```

```
                }
                if ($line2 eq "" || $line1 ne $line2) {
                        $retval = 0;
                        last;
                }
        }
        # you should use close here, as this subroutine may
        # be called many times
        close (FILE1);
        close (FILE2);
        # ensure that the return value is the last evaluated
        # expression
        $retval;
}
```

4. Here is one possible solution:

```
sub dieroll {
        $retval = int (rand(6)) + 1;
}
```

5. Here is one possible solution:

```
# assume that the first call to printlist passes the argument
# 0 as the value for $index
sub printlist {
        local ($index, @list) = @_;

        if ($index + 1 < @list) {
                &printlist ($index+1, @list);
        }
        # the conditional handles the case of an empty list
        print ("$list[$index]\n") if (@list > 0);
}
```

6. The subroutine print_ten overwrites the value stored in the global variable $count. To fix this problem, define $count as a local variable. (You also should define $printval as a local variable, in case someone adds this variable to the main program at a later time.)

7. The local statement in the subroutine assigns both the list and the search word to @searchlist, which means that $searchword is assigned the empty string. To fix this problem, switch the order of the arguments, putting the search word first.

8. If split produces a nonempty list, the last expression evaluated in the subroutine is the conditional expression, which has the value 0 (false):

```
@words == 0
```

Therefore, the return value of this subroutine is 0, not the list of words.

To get around this problem, put the following statement after the if statement:

```
@words;
```

This ensures that the list of words is always the return value.

Answers for Day 10, "Associative Arrays"

Quiz

1. The answers are as follows:

   a. An associative array is an array whose subscripts can be any scalar value.

   b. A pointer is an associative-array element whose value is the subscript of another associative-array element.

   c. A linked list is an associative array in which each element of the array points to the next.

   d. A binary tree is a data structure in which each element points to (at most) two other elements.

   e. A node is an element of a binary tree.

   f. A child is an element of a binary tree that is pointed to by another element.

2. This statement creates an associative array containing three elements:

   ☐ An element with subscript `17.2` whose value is `hello`

   ☐ An element with subscript `there` whose value is `46`

   ☐ An element with subscript `e+6` whose value is `88`

3. When you assign an associative array to an ordinary array variable, the value of the array variable becomes a list consisting of all of the subscript/value pairs of the associative array (in the order in which they were stored in the associative array, which is random).

4. Define a scalar variable containing the value of the list's first element. Then, use the value of one associative-array element as the subscript for the next.

5. This is a trick question: Because the associative array `%list` stores its elements in random order, it is not clear how many times the `foreach` loop iterates. It could be one, two, or three.

Exercises

1. Here is one possible solution:
```
while ($line = <STDIN>) {
        $line =~ s/^\s+|\s+$//g;
        ($subscript, $value) = split(/\s+/, $line);
        $array{$subscript} = $value;
}
```

2. Here is one possible solution:

```perl
$linenum = 0;
while ($line = <STDIN>) {
        $linenum += 1;
        $line =~ s/^\s+|\s+$//g;
        @words = split(/\s+/, $line);
        if ($words[0] eq "index" &&
                $index{$words[1]} eq "") {
                $index{$words[1]} = $linenum;
        }
}
foreach $item (sort keys (%index)) {
        print ("$item: $index{$item}\n");
}
```

3. Here is one possible solution:

```perl
$linenum = 0;
while ($line = <STDIN>) {
        $linenum += 1;
        $line =~ s/^\s+|\s+$//g;
        @words = split(/\s+/, $line);
        # This program uses a trick: for each word, the array
        # item $index{"word"} stores the number of occurrences
        # of that word. Each occurrence is stored in the
        # element $index{"word#n"}, where[]is a
        # positive integer.
        if ($words[0] eq "index") {
                if ($index{$words[1]} eq "") {
                        $index{$words[1]} = 1;
                        $occurrence = 1;
                } else {
                        $index{$words[1]} += 1;
                        $occurrence = $index{$words[1]};
                }
                $index{$words[1]."#".$occurrence} = $linenum;
        }
}

# The loop that prints the index takes advantage of the fact
# that, when the list is sorted, the elements that count
# occurrences are always processed just before the
# corresponding elements that store occurrences. For example:
# $index{word}
# $index{word#1}
# $index{word#2}
foreach $item (sort keys (%index)) {
        if ($item =~ /#/) {
                print ("\n$item:");
        } else {
                print (" $index{$item}");
        }
}
print ("\n");
```

4. Here is one possible solution:

```
$student = 0;
@subjects = ("English", "history", "mathematics",
             "science", "geography");
while ($line = <STDIN>) {
        $line =~ s/^\s+|\s+$//g;
        @words = split (/\s+/, $line);
        @students[$student++] = $words[0];
    for ($count = 1; $count <= 5; $count++) {
            $marks{$words[0].$subjects[$count-1]} =
                    $words[$count];
        }
}

# now print the failing grades, one student per line
foreach $student (sort (@students)) {
    $has_failed = 0;
    foreach $subject (sort (@subjects)) {
            if ($marks{$student.$subject} < 50) {
                    if ($has_failed == 0) {
                            $has_failed - 1;
                            print ("$student failed:");
                    }
                    print (" $subject");
            }
    }
    if ($has_failed == 1) {
            print ("\n");
    }
}
```

5. There is one problem and one unwanted feature in this program.

The problem: Adding a new element to %list in the middle of a foreach loop that uses the function keys yields unpredictable results.

The unwanted feature: The foreach loop doubles the size of the associative array because the original elements Fred, John, Jack, and Mary are not deleted.

Answers for Day 11, "Formatting Your Output"

Quiz

1. The answers are as follows:

   a. @<<<<<<<<<

   b. @>>>>

   c. @|

    d. `@####.###`

    e. `~~ ^<<<<<<<<<<<<<<<<<<<<<<<<<<<<<<<`

2. The answers are as follows:

    a. Five left-justified characters.

    b. Seven centered characters.

    c. One character.

    d. Multiple (unformatted) lines of text.

    e. Ten right-justified characters, with the line being printed only if the line is not blank.

3. The answers are as follows:

    a. An integer (base 10) in a field of at least five digits.

    b. A floating-point number with a total field width of 11 characters, four of which are to the right of the decimal point.

    c. A base-10 integer in a field of at least 10 digits. Empty characters in the field are filled with zeroes.

    d. A character string of at least 12 characters, left-justified.

    e. An integer in hexadecimal (base-16) form.

4. Numbers with rounding problems are numbers that normally round up but cannot be exactly stored on the machine. The closest equivalent that can be stored rounds down.

5. To create a page header for an output file, define a print format named `filename_TOP`, where `filename` is the file variable associated with the file. (You could also create a print format of any name and assign the name to the system variable `$^`.)

Exercises

1. Here is one possible solution:

```
for ($count = 1; $count <= 9; $count += 3) {
        $num1 = 2 ** $count;
        $num2 = 2 ** ($count + 1);
        $num3 = 2 ** ($count + 2);
        write;
}
$num1 = 2 ** 10;
$num2 = $num3 = "";
write;
```

```
format STDOUT =
^>>> ^>>> ^>>>
$num1 $num2 $num3
.
```

2. Here is one possible solution:

```
for ($count = 1; $count <= 10; $count++) {
        printf ("%4d", 2 ** $count);
        if ($count % 3 == 0) {
                print ("\n");
        } else {
                print (" ");
        }
}
print ("\n");
```

3. Here is one possible solution:

```
@text = <STDIN>;
$line = join("", @text);
write;
format STDOUT =
*****************************************
~~^<<<<<<<<<<<<<<<<<<<<<<<<<<<<<<<<<<<<<<<
$line
*****************************************
.
```

4. Here is one possible solution:

```
$total1 = $total2 = 0;
while (1) {
        $num1 = <STDIN>;
        last if ($num1 eq "");
        chop ($num1);
        $num2 = <STDIN>;
        last if ($num2 eq "");
        chop ($num2);
        $~ = "LINE";
        write;
        $total1 += $num1;
        $total2 += $num2;
}
$~ = "TOTAL";
write;
$~ = "GRAND_TOTAL";
write;

format LINE =
                   @####.##   @####.##
                   $num1      $num2
.
format TOTAL =
   column totals:  @#####.##  @#####.##
                   $total1    $total2
.
format GRAND_TOTAL =
grand total:                  @#####.##
                   $total1 + $total2
.
```

5. When `print` writes a line to the page, the `$-` variable is not automatically updated. This means that the line count is off. To fix this, subtract one from the `$-` variable yourself.

Also, you must specify what is to be printed by the STDOUT print format:

```
format STDOUT =
@*
$line
.
```

Answers for Day 12, "File-System, String, and Mathematical Functions"

Quiz

1. The answers are as follows:
   a. `file1` is open for reading only.
   b. `file2` is actually a pipe that is sending the output from a command to this program (where it is treated as input).
   c. `file3` is open for reading and writing. (`+<file3` is equivalent.)
   d. MYFILE is being treated as identical to STDOUT (the two file variables now refer to the same file).

2. The answers are as follows:
   a. `%x`
   b. `%o`
   c. `%e`
   d. `%f`

3. The answers are as follows:
   a. `"abc"`
   b. `"efgh"`
   c. `"gh"`
   d. The null string (a length of 0 is being specified)

4. The answers are as follows:
   a. `4`
   b. `9`

Exercises

1. Here is one possible solution:

```
opendir(HOMEDIR, "c:/perl5") ||
        die ("Unable to open directory");
$i = 0;
while ($filename = readdir(HOMEDIR)) {
        $array[$i++] = $filename;
}
closedir(HOMEDIR);
foreach $filename (sort @array) {
        print ("$filename\n");
}
```

2. Here is one possible solution:

```
for ($val = 1; $val <= 100; $val++) {
        print ("log of $val is ", log($val), "\n");
}
```

3. Here is one possible solution:

```
for ($i = 1; $i <= 6; $i++) {
        &sum(10 ** $i);
}
sub sum {
        local($limit) = @_;
        local(@startval, @stopval);
        local($i, $count);
        $count = 0;
        @startval = times();
        for ($i = 1; $i <= $limit; $i++) {
                $count += $i;
        }
        @stopval = times();
        print ("sum $limit: ", $stopval[0]-$startval[0], "\n");
}
```

4. Here is one possible solution:

```
$degrees = <STDIN>;
chop ($degrees);
$radians = $degrees * atan2(1,1) / 45;
$sin = sin ($radians);
$cos = cos ($radians);
print ("sin of $degrees is ", $sin, "\n");
print ("cos of $degrees is ", $cos, "\n");
print ("tan of $degrees is ", $sin/$cos, "\n");
```

5. Here is one possible solution:

```
$_ = <STDIN>;   # reads to $_ by default
print ("number of a's found: ", tr/a/a/, "\n");
print ("number of e's found: ", tr/e/e/, "\n");
print ("number of i's found: ", tr/i/i/, "\n");
print ("number of o's found: ", tr/o/o/, "\n");
print ("number of u's found: ", tr/u/u/, "\n");
```

B

6. This program is trying to use `eof()` to test for the end of a particular input file. In Perl, `eof()` tests for the end of the entire set of input files, and `eof` (with no parentheses) tests for the end of a particular input file.

Answers for Day 13, "Process, Scalar-Conversion, and List-Manipulation Functions"

Quiz

1. `system` starts a completely different program that runs concurrently (at the same time as the current program). `exec` terminates the current program and starts a new one.

2. The answers are as follows:

   a. A character string, padded with null characters if necessary.

   b. A character string, padded with blanks if necessary.

   c. A floating-point number (double-precision).

   d. A pointer to a string (as in the C programming language).

   e. Skip to the position specified.

3. The answers are as follows:

   a. Unpack a character string (unstripped).

   b. Skip four bytes, unpack a 10-character string (stripping null characters and blanks), then treat the rest of the packed string as integers.

   c. Skip to the end of the packed string, back up four bytes, and unpack four unsigned characters.

   d. Unpack the first integer, skip four bytes, unpack an integer, skip back eight bytes, and unpack another integer. (This, effectively, unpacks the first, third, and second integers in that order.)

   e. Unpack a string of bits in low-to-high order, back up to the beginning, and unpack the same string of bits in high-to-low order.

4. The answers are as follows:

   a. `1`

   b. `3`

5. `defined` tests whether a particular value is equivalent to the special "undefined" value. `undef` sets a scalar variable, array element, or array variable to be equal to the special undefined value.

6. The answers are as follows:

   a. `("new", "2", "3", "4", "5")`

   b. `("1", "2", "test1", "test2", "3", "4", "5")`

   c. `("1", "2", "3", "4", "test1", "test2")`

   d. `("1", "2", "4", "5")`

   e. `("1", "2", "3")`

7. The answers are as follows:

   a. This returns every list element that does not start with an exclamation mark.

   b. This returns every list element that contains a word that consists entirely of digits.

   c. This returns every nonempty list element.

   d. This returns every list element.

8. `unshift` adds one or more elements to the left end of a list. `shift` removes an element from the left end of a list.

9. The answers are as follows:

   a. `splice (@array, 0, 1);`

   b. `splice (@array, @array-1, 1);`

   c. `splice (@array, scalar(@array), 0, @sublist);`

   d. `splice (@array, 0, 0, @sublist);`

10. You can create a stack using `push` to add elements, and `pop` to remove them (or by using `shift` and `unshift` in the same way).

11. You can create a queue using `push` to add elements, and `shift` to remove them (or by using `unshift` and `pop` in the same way).

Exercises

1. Here is a program that reads from `temp`:

```
open (INFILE, "temp") || die ("Can't open input");
while ($line = <INFILE>) {
        print ($line);
}
close (INFILE);
```

Here is a program that writes to `temp` and calls the first program (which is assumed to be named `13a01.pl`):

```
open (OUTFILE, ">temp") || die ("Can't open output");
while ($line = <STDIN>) {
        print OUTFILE ($line);
}
close (OUTFILE);
exec ("13a01.pl");
```

2. Here is one possible solution:

```
$string1 = <STDIN>;
chop ($string1);
$len1 = length ($string1);
$string2 = <STDIN>;
chop ($string2);
$len2 = length ($string2);
if ($len1 % 8 != 0) {
        $string1 = "0" x (8 - $len1 % 8) . $string1;
        $len1 += 8 - $len1 % 8;
}
if ($len2 % 8 != 0) {
        $string2 = "0" x (8 - $len2 % 8) . $string2;
        $len2 += 8 - $len2 % 8;
}
if ($len1 > $len2) {
        $string2 = "0" x ($len1 - $len2) . $string2;
} else {
        $string1 = "0" x ($len2 - $len1) . $string1;
        $len1 += ($len2 - $len1);
}
$bytes1 = pack ("b*", $string1);
$bytes2 = pack ("b*", $string2);
$carry = 0;
$count = $len1 - 1;
while ($count >= 0) {
        $bit1 = vec ($bytes1, $count, 1);
        $bit2 = vec ($bytes2, $count, 1);
        $result = ($bit1 + $bit2 + $carry) & 1;
        $carry = ($bit1 + $bit2 + $carry) >> 1;
        vec ($bytes1, $count, 1) = $result;
        $count-;
}
$resultstring = unpack ("b*", $bytes1);
$resultstring = $carry . $resultstring if ($carry > 0);
print ("$resultstring\n");
```

3. Here is one possible solution:

```
$string1 = <STDIN>;
chop ($string1);
$len1 = length ($string1);
$string2 = <STDIN>;
chop ($string2);
$len2 = length ($string2);
if ($len1 % 8 != 0) {
        $string1 = "0" x (8 - $len1 % 8) . $string1;
        $len1 += 8 - $len1 % 8;
}
```

```
        if ($len2 % 8 != 0) {
                $string2 = "0" x (8 - $len2 % 8) . $string2;
                $len2 += 8 - $len2 % 8;
        }
        if ($len1 > $len2) {
                $string2 = "0" x ($len1 - $len2) . $string2;
        } else {
                $string1 = "0" x ($len2 - $len1) . $string1;
                $len1 += ($len2 - $len1);
        }
        $bytes1 = pack ("h*", $string1);
        $bytes2 = pack ("h*", $string2);
        $carry = 0;
        $count = $len1 - 1;
        while ($count >= 0) {
                $nybble1 = vec ($bytes1, $count, 4);
                $nybble2 = vec ($bytes2, $count, 4);
                $result = ($nybble1 + $nybble2 + $carry) & 15;
                $carry = ($nybble1 + $nybble2 + $carry) >> 4;
                vec ($bytes1, $count, 4) = $result;
                $count--;
        }
        $resultstring = unpack ("h*", $bytes1);
        $resultstring = $carry . $resultstring if ($carry > 0);
        print ("$resultstring\n");
```

4. Here is one possible solution:

```
        $value = <STDIN>;
        $value *= 100;
        $value = int ($value + 0.5);
        $value = sprintf ("%.2f", $value / 100);
        print ("$value\n");
```

5. This program is actually reading the low-order bit of the bit vector. To read the high-order bit, use `vec ($packed, 7, 1)`.

6. Here is one possible solution:

```
        # This program uses a very dumb sorting algorithm.
        @list = (41, 26, 11, 9, 8);     # sample list to sort
        for ($outer = 0; $outer < @list; $outer++) {
                for ($inner = 0; $inner < @list; $inner++) {
                        if ($list[$inner] > $list[$inner+1]) {
                                $x = splice (@list, $inner, 1);
                                splice (@list, $inner+1, 0, $x);
                        }
                }
        }
```

7. Here is one possible solution:

```
        # assume %oldarray is assigned here
        while (($subscript, $value) = each (%oldarray)) {
                if (defined ($newarray{$value})) {
                        print STDERR ("$value already defined\n");
                } else {
                        $newarray{$value} = $subscript;
                }
        }
```

8. Here is one possible solution:

```
while ($line = <STDIN>) {
        @words = split (/\s+/, $line);
        @shortwords = grep (/^.{1,5}$/, @words);
        print ("@shortwords\n");
}
```

9. Here is one possible solution:

```
$line = <STDIN>;
$line =~ s/^\s+//;
while (1) {
        last if ($line eq "");
        ($word, $line) = split (/\s+/, $line, 2);
        print ("$word\n");
}
```

10. This subroutine is trying to remove an element from a list using `unshift`. The subroutine should use `shift`, not `unshift`.

Answers for Day 14, "Packages, Modules, and System Functions"

Quiz

1. The answers are as follows:

   a. `__LINE__` contains the current line number of the executing program or subroutine.

   b. `__FILE__` contains the current file being executed.

   c. `__END__` indicates the end of the Perl program.

2. To send information using a socket, use an output function such as `print` or `printf`, and specify the file variable associated with the socket.

3. The answers are as follows:

   a. `It's time to say $var`

   b. `"It's time to say hello";` (including the quotes and the semicolon)

   c. `hello`

4. `("one", "two", "three", "", "five")`

5. There are two ways:

   ☐ With the `#include` preprocessor command.

   ☐ Adding the file's directory to `@INC` and then passing the filename to `require`.

Exercises

1. Here is one possible solution:

```
@filelist = <*>;
foreach $file (sort (@filelist)) {
        print ("$file\n");
}
```

2. Here is one possible solution:

```
unshift (@INC, "/user/perlcode");
require ("sum.pl");
@numlist = <STDIN>;
chop (@numlist);
$total = &sum (@numlist);
print ("The total is $total.\n");
```

3. Here is one possible solution:

```
package pack1;
$var = <STDIN>;
chop ($var);
package pack2;
$var = <STDIN>;
chop ($var);
package main;
$total = $pack1'var + $pack2'var;
print ("The total is $total.\n");
```

4. In this case, `<$filepattern>` is treated as a scalar variable containing the name of a file variable, not as a scalar variable containing a file list pattern. (To obtain the latter, use `<${filepattern}>`.)

5. There should be no space between the `<<` and the EOF. The space after the `<<` means that the end-of-string character string is assumed to be null; therefore, `print` prints only the first of the two lines in the string.

Answers for Day 15, "Perl 5 for Win32 Module Extensions"

Quiz

1. The answers are as follows:

   a. A package in Perl is a block of programs that contains a set of related Perl variables and subroutines. The names of the variables and subroutines are saved in a symbolic table for the Perl program to keep track of these variables and subroutines.

b. A module is a package that is saved in the format of a library file.

c. An extension is an enhanced package that calls external C code to provide specific functionality.

2. The `Create` function is the only function in the `Win32::Process` module.

3. The `Win32::Mutex::Wait` function is used when a process has to wait for the ownership of a created mutex in order to access to the shared resource.

4. To add users to a group, you can call `LocalGroupAddUsers` or `GroupAddUsers` from the `Win32::NetAdmin` module.

Exercises

1. Here is one possible solution:

```
my ($node_name) = &NTNodeName;
my ($domain_name) = &NTDomainName;
my ($fs_type) = &NTFsType;
my ($login_name) = &NTLoginName;

print STDOUT "Node Name:        $node_name\n";
print STDOUT "Domain Name:      $domain_name\n";
print STDOUT "FS Type:          $fs_type\n";
print STDOUT "Login Name:       $login_name\n";
```

2. Here is one possible solution:

```
use Win32;

my ($node_name) = Win32::NodeName;
my ($domain_name) = Win32::DomainName;
my ($fs_type) = Win32::FsType;
my ($login_name) = Win32::LoginName;

print STDOUT "Node Name:        $node_name\n";
print STDOUT "Domain Name:      $domain_name\n";
print STDOUT "FS Type:          $fs_type\n";
print STDOUT "Login Name:       $login_name\n";
```

3. Here is one possible solution:

```
use Win32::Process;

Win32::Process::Create (
      $ProcessObj,
      "c:\\windows\\notepad.exe",
      "",
      0,
      DETACHED_PROCESS,
      ".") || die "Cannot create the process";

$ProcessObj->SetPriorityClass (NORMAL_PRIORITY_CLASS) ||
      die $!;

$ProcessObj->Wait (INFINITE);
print ("The notepad.exe program exited. Bye!\n");
```

4. Here is one possible solution:

```
use Win32::Process;
use Win32;

Win32::Process::Create (
        $ProcessObj,
        "c:\\windows\\calc.exe",
        "",
        0,
        DETACHED_PROCESS,
        ".") || die "Cannot create the process";
&Error;
$ProcessObj->SetPriorityClass (NORMAL_PRIORITY_CLASS) ||
        die $!;
&Error;
$ProcessObj->Wait (INFINITE);
print ("The calc.exe program exited. Bye!\n");
&Error;

sub Error {
    print Win32::FormatMessage (Win32::GetLastError());
}
```

5. Here is one possible solution:

```
use Win32::NetAdmin;
use Win32;
$user_name = <STDIN>;
chop ($user_name);

Win32::NetAdmin::UserGetAttributes (
        '',
        $user_name,
        $Password,
        $PasswdAge,
        $Privilege,
        $HomeDir,
        $Comment,
        $Flag,
        $Script ) || die $!;
&Error;
$result_1 = sprintf (
        "Password: %s\n Passwd Age: %x\n Privilege: %s\n",
        $Password,
        $PasswdAge,
        $Privilege );
$result_2 = sprintf (
        "Home Directory: %s\n Comment: %s\n Flag: %s\n Script: %s\n",
        $HomeDir,
        $Comment,
        $Flag,
        $Script );

print $result_1 . $result_2;

sub Error {
    print Win32::FormatMessage (Win32::GetLastError());
}
```

6. The `Win32::Process` module is not included in the Perl program. Use the following statement to include the `Win32::Process` module:

```
use Win32::Process;
```

Answers for Day 16, "Command-Line Options"

Quiz

1. The answers are as follows:

   a. The `-0` option specifies the end-of-file character for the input line.

   b. The `-s` option enables you to specify options for your program.

   c. The `-w` option tells the Perl interpreter to warn you if it sees something it thinks is erroneous.

   d. The `-x` option tells the Perl interpreter that your program is to be extracted from a file.

   e. The `-n` option indicates that each line of the files specified on the command line is to be read.

2. The answers are as follows:

   a. The input end-of-line character becomes either a newline or the character specified by `-l`. The output end-of-line character becomes either null or the character specified by `-0`.

   b. The input end-of-line character becomes either the character specified by `-l` or the character specified by `-0`; if neither option has a value supplied with it, the input line character becomes null. The output end-of-line character becomes either null or the character specified by `-0`.

3. The `-n` option tells the Perl interpreter to read each line of the input file, but does not explicitly tell it to write out its input. The `-i` option copies the input file to a temporary file and then opens the input file for writing. If you do not explicitly write to the file yourself, nothing gets written to it.

4. The options for the interpreter appear before the Perl program name in the command line, or in the header comment for the program. The options for the program appear after the program name.

Exercises

1. Here is one possible solution:

```
C:\> perl -i -p -l072 -e ";" testfile
```

Note that `-e ";"` indicates an empty program. (Otherwise, the Perl interpreter would assume that `testfile` was the program, not the input file.)

2. Here is one possible solution:

```
C:\> perl -ne "print if (/\bthe\b/);" file1 file2 ...
```

3. Here is one possible solution:

```
C:\> perl -nae 'print ("$F[1]\n");' file1 file2 ...
```

4. Here is one possible solution:

```
print ("Hello\n") if ($H == 1);
print ("Goodbye\n") if ($G == 1);
```

(When you run these Perl scripts, use the `-s` option.)

5. Here is one possible solution:

```
C:\> perl -i -pe "tr/a-z/A-Z/;" file1 file2 ...
```

6. This command line wipes out all your input files. Use the `-p` option instead of the `-n` option.

7. The `-i` option can be specified with a value (for creating a backup version of the file). The Perl interpreter thinks that `pe` is the suffix to append to the filename, and does not realize that these are supposed to be options. (I get tripped up by this problem all the time.)

Answers for Day 17, "System Variables"

Quiz

1. The pattern-matching operator, the substitution operator, the translation operator, the `<>` operator (if it appears in a `while` or `for` conditional expression), the `chop` function, the `print` function, and the `study` function.

2. The answers are as follows:

   a. The `$=` variable contains the page length of a particular output file.

   b. The `$/` variable contains the input end-of-line character.

    c. The `$?` variable contains the return code returned by a command called by
the `system` function or enclosed in back quotes.

    d. The `$!` variable contains the error code generated by a system library routine.

    e. The `@_` variable contains the list of arguments passed to a subroutine by the
calling program or calling subroutine.

3. `ARGV` is the file variable used by the `<>` operator to read from the list of input files
specified on the command line. `$ARGV` is the name of the current file being read by
the `<>` operator. `@ARGV` is the list of arguments (or files) specified on the command
line.

4. `@INC` contains the directories to search when looking for files to be included. `%INC`
lists the files requested by the `require` function that have already been found.

5. `$0` is the name of the program you are running. `$1` is defined when a pattern is
matched, and is the first subpattern enclosed in parentheses in the matched pattern.

Exercises

1. Here is one possible solution:

```
while (<>) {
        s/[ \t]+/ /g;
        tr/A-Z/a-z/;
        print;
}
```

All these statements use the system variable `$_` by default. Use the `-i` option when
you run the Perl script.

2. Here is one possible solution:

```
while ($line = <>) {
        while ($line =~ /  +/g) {
                $line = $` . " " . $';
        }
        print ($line);
}
```

Use the `-i` option when you run the Perl script.

3. Here is one possible solution:

```
@dirlist = split (/:/, $ENV{"PATH"});
foreach $dir (@dirlist) {
        print ("$dir\n");
}
```

Note that if your machine uses a character other than `:` to separate entries in the
value of your PATH environment variable, you should use this character instead.

4. Here is one possible solution:

```
$SIG{"INT"} = stopnum;
$num = 1;
while (1) {
        print ("$num\n");
        $num++;
}

sub stopnum {
        print ("\nInterrupted.\n");
        exit (0);
}
```

5. Here is one possible solution:

```
$total = 0;
while ($line = <DATA>) {
        @nums = split (/\s+/, $line);
        foreach $num (@nums) {
                $total += $num;
        }
}
print ("The total is $total.\n");
__ __END__ __
4 17   26
11
9     5
```

Answers for Day 18, "References in Perl 5 for Win32"

Quiz

1. The second way to create a reference to an array is to declare the reference directly with the elements of the array wrapped by []. For example:

   ```
   $ref = ['This', 'is', 'an', 'array'];
   ```

2. To get the value of an element inside an array, you can call the statement

   ```
   $element = $hard_ref->[$i];
   ```

   or

   ```
   $element = $$hard_ref[$i];
   ```

   but not

   ```
   $element = $$hard_ref >[$i];
   ```

3. The correct answer is `$element = $hard_ref->[0][0];`.

4. Yes.

Exercises

1. Here is one possible solution:

```
$ref_to_month = [
  'January',
  'February',
  'March',
  'April',
  'May',
  'June',
  'July',
  'August',
  'September',
  'October',
  'November',
  'December'
];
foreach $ele (@{$ref_to_month}) {
    print "$ele \n";
}
```

2. Here is one possible solution:

```
Error( \*STDOUT, "Specify the input and output handles.\n" )
      if @ARGV != 2;

my @array_day = (
    'Sunday',
    'Monday',
    'Tuesday',
    'Wednesday',
    'Thursday',
    'Friday',
    'Saturday'
);
my @array_month = (
    'January',
    'February',
    'March',
    'April',
    'May',
    'June',
    'July',
    'August',
    'September',
    'October',
    'November',
    'December'
);
my %Year97 = (
    January =>  [ 3, 31 ],
    February => [ 6, 28 ],
    March => => [ 6, 31 ],
    April =>    [ 2, 30 ],
    May =>      [ 4, 31 ],
    June =>     [ 0, 30 ],
```

```perl
        July =>     [ 2, 31 ],
        August =>   [ 5, 31 ],
        September=> [ 1, 30 ],
        October =>  [ 3, 31 ],
        November => [ 6, 30 ],
        December => [ 1, 31 ]
);
my $ref_to_day = \@array_day;
my $ref_to_month = \@array_month;
my $ref_to_year = \%Year97;
my $ref_to_sub = \&Error;
my $ref_to_fh1 = \*{shift(@ARGV)};
my $ref_to_fh2 = \*{shift(@ARGV)};


#---- print out header ----
   Header ($ref_to_fh2);
#---- get input ----
   my $date = <$ref_to_fh1>;
   chop ($date);
   my ($month_key, $day_key, $year) = split ( /-/, $date);
#---- check the year ----
   &{$ref_to_sub}($ref_to_fh2, "The year is not 97! \n" )
       if $year ne '97';
#---- check the month ----
   $month_key =~ s/^0//;
   $month_key --;
   my $month_name = $ref_to_month->[$month_key];
   &{$ref_to_sub}($ref_to_fh2, "There is no such month in a year \n" )
       if $month_name eq '';
#---- check the day ----
   $day_key =~ s/^0//;
   &{$ref_to_sub}($ref_to_fh2, "There no such day $day_key in $month_name
➥\n")
       if $day_key > $ref_to_year->{$month_name}[1];
#---- get the name of the day in a week ----
   my $day_index = $ref_to_year->{$month_name}[0] + $day_key - 1;
   $day_index %= 7;
   my $day_name = $ref_to_day->[$day_index];
#---- output the result ----
   Result($ref_to_fh2,
       " $ref_to_month->[$month_key] $day_key, 19$year, $day_name \n" );


#---- subroutines ----
sub Error {
   my $ref = shift (@_);
   my $str = shift (@_);
   print $ref "$str";
   print $ref "A nice try :-)\n";
   exit;
}
sub Header {
   my $ref = shift (@_);
   print $ref "# ---- The 1997 Calendar ---- #\n";
   print $ref "Enter a date in the format of mm-dd-97\n";
   print $ref "e.g.,  12-25-97\n\n";
}
```

```
sub Result {
  my $ref = shift (@_);
  my $str = shift (@_);
  print $ref "\nThe re-formatted date you just entered is:\n";
  print $ref "$str";
}
```

3. In &sub_routine("This", "is a", "subroutine\n");, there are three arguments
    that need to be passed to the subroutine, but there is only one argument passed to
    the subroutine in &sub_routine(\@array);.

4. @{$ref}, instead of ${$ref}, should be used for the foreach loop.

5. The $string scalar declared with my is not visible to the symbolic reference $ref,
    unless you declare the scalar variable with local.

Answers for Day 19, "Object-Oriented Programming in Perl"

Quiz

1. Yes.

2. No. The statement $ref->a_method; treats the a_method method as a virtual
    method.

3. Here is one possible solution:

```
sub new {
    my ($class, @rest) = @_;
    my $ref = {};
    %$ref = (%$ref, @rest);
    bless $ref, $class;
    return $ref;
}
```

4. By prefixing the name of the base class, with ::, to the method; for example,
    Base_Class_Name::Method.

Exercises

1. The two ways are

    ```
    Hello My_Class;
    ```
    and
    ```
    My_Class -> Hello;
    ```

2. `print "@argv \n";` displays `My_Class` in the two ways.

3. Here is what I get from my machine:
```
From My_Class: Hello, world!
My_Class=SCALAR(0x77ea04)
```

4. `@ISA = qw(Parent_Class);` is missed inside the derived class.

5. The `bless` function in the base class uses only the base class name as the default name, while the derived class attempts to inherit the object constructor from the base class. One solution to correct the error is to modify the statement, `bless $ref;`, in the base class to `bless $ref, $class;`.

B

Answers for Day 20, "CGI Programming with Perl 5 for Win32"

Quiz

1. The answers are as follows:
   a. `<HTML>` marks the beginning of an HTML file.
   b. `</HTML>` marks the end of an HTML file.
   c. `<BODY>` marks the beginning of the body of an HTML file.
   d. `</BODY>` marks the end of the body of an HTML file.
   e. `<TITLE>` marks the beginning of the title of an HTML file.
   f. `</TITLE>` marks the end of the title of an HTML file.
   g. `<FORM>` marks the beginning of the form of an HTML file.
   h. `</FORM>` marks the end of the form of an HTML file.

2. You have to include the `CGI.pm` in your Perl program, and then call the object constructor, `new`, to create a CGI object, for example,
```
use CGI;
$wp = new CGI;
```

3. Here is one possible solution:
```
<HTML>
<HEAD>
<TITLE>Using CDI.pm in a CGI script</TITLE>
</HEAD>
<BODY BGCOLOR='white'>
</BODY>
</HTML>
```

4. The main differences are

☐ An ISAPI application is executed as an internal part of the Web server, not like a CGI application that is considered as an external program.

☐ Because an ISAPI application is a multithreaded DLL file, only one copy is kept in the memory to support multiple clients simultaneously. However, multiple copies (that is, processes) of a CGI application must be executed in order to support more than one client at the same time.

☐ Also, as one of the DLL's features, the functionality provided by an ISAPI application can be loaded into or unloaded from the memory dynamically according to the client's requests.

5. Here is one possible solution:

```
<INPUT TYPE="text" NAME="user" SIZE=20>
```

This specifies a data-entry field. The type of the data field is defined as a text type. The field is named as user. The total length of the field is set to 20 characters long.

6. By calling the param method in the library CGI.pm module file. For instance, to get the username sent from an HTML form, one possible solution is

```
use CGI;
$wp = new CGI;
# Fetch the user name enter in HTML form
$user_name = $wp->param ('user');
```

Exercises

1. Here is one possible solution:

```
<HTML>
<HEAD>
<TITLE>Exercise 1, Day 20</TITLE>
</HEAD>
<BODY BGCOLOR='blue'>
This is my first HTML file.
</BODY>
</HTML>
```

2. Here is one possible solution:

```
print "Content-type: text/html\n\n";
print "<HTML>\n";
print "<HEAD>\n";
print "<TITLE>Exercise 1, Day 20</TITLE>\n";
print "</HEAD>\n";
print "<BODY BGCOLOR='yellow'>\n";
print "This is my first HTML file.\n";
print "</BODY>\n";
print "</HTML>\n";
```

3. Here is one possible solution:

```
use CGI;
$wp = new CGI;
    print $wp->header;
        print $wp->start_html (
            -title=>'Exercise 1, Day 20',
            -BGCOLOR=>'red');
        print "<BODY>\n";
    print "This is my first time HTML file.\n";
  print "</BODY>\n";
print $wp->end_html;
```

4. The CGI script is missing the `$wp = new CGI;` statement, so no CGI object is created.

5. The CGI script is missing the following statement:

```
print $wp->end html;
```

Answers for Day 21, "The Perl Debugger"

Quiz

1. The answers are as follows:

   a. Trace mode controls whether lines are displayed as they are executed. If trace mode is on, lines are displayed; if it is off, they are not.

   b. A stack trace is a display of the current subroutine being executed, plus a listing of the subroutine that called this one, and so on back to the original main program.

   c. A breakpoint is a line in the program before which execution is halted and further debugging commands are requested.

   d. A line action is a statement that is executed whenever a particular line of the program is reached.

2. The x command displays only variables in the current package. The v command can display variables in any package.

3. The // command searches forward in the file for a line matching the specified pattern; the ?? command searches backward.

4. The > command defines a line action that is to be executed before the debugger executes any further statements. The < command defines a line action that is to be performed after the debugger has finished executing the next statement or group of statements.

5. The s command steps into a subroutine when it encounters one; the n command executes the subroutine without stepping into it, stopping at the statement following the subroutine.

6. The answers are as follows:

    a. This displays the next window of statements, continuing where the last l command left off.

    b. This displays just line 26.

    c. This displays lines 5–7.

    d. This displays lines 5–12.

    e. This displays the window of statements surrounding the current line.

ASCII Character Set

The original ASCII character set only includes characters with decimal values of 0 through 127. The following character set is actually an IBM-PC character set which covers characters 0 through 255.

Dec X_{10}	Hex X_{16}	ASCII Character
000	00	null
001	01	☺
002	02	☻
003	03	♥
004	04	♦
005	05	♣
006	06	♠
007	07	•
008	08	◘
009	09	○
010	0A	◙
011	0B	♂
012	0C	♀
013	0D	♪
014	0E	♫
015	0F	☼
016	10	►
017	11	◄
018	12	↕
019	13	‼
020	14	¶
021	15	§
022	16	▬
023	17	↨
024	18	↑
025	19	↓
026	1A	→
027	1B	←
028	1C	∟
029	1D	↔
030	1E	▲
031	1F	▼

Dec X_{10}	Hex X_{16}	ASCII Character
032	20	space
033	21	!
034	22	"
035	23	#
036	24	$
037	25	%
038	26	&
039	27	'
040	28	(
041	29	)
042	2A	*
043	2B	+
044	2C	,
045	2D	-
046	2E	.
047	2F	/
048	30	0
049	31	1
050	32	2
051	33	3
052	34	4
053	35	5
054	36	6
055	37	7
056	38	8
057	39	9
058	3A	:
059	3B	;
060	3C	<
061	3D	=
062	3E	>
063	3F	?

C

continues

Dec X_{10}	Hex X_{16}	ASCII Character
064	40	@
065	41	A
066	42	B
067	43	C
068	44	D
069	45	E
070	46	F
071	47	G
072	48	H
073	49	I
074	4A	J
075	4B	K
076	4C	L
077	4D	M
078	4E	N
079	4F	O
080	50	P
081	51	Q
082	52	R
083	53	S
084	54	T
085	55	U
086	56	V
087	57	W
088	58	X
089	59	Y
090	5A	Z
091	5B	[
092	5C	\
093	5D	]
094	5E	^
095	5F	–

Dec X_{10}	Hex X_{16}	ASCII Character
096	60	`
097	61	a
098	62	b
099	63	c
100	64	d
101	65	e
102	66	f
103	67	g
104	68	h
105	69	i
106	6A	j
107	6B	k
108	6C	l
109	6D	m
110	6E	n
111	6F	o
112	70	p
113	71	q
114	72	r
115	73	s
116	74	t
117	75	u
118	76	v
119	77	w
120	78	x
121	79	y
122	7A	z
123	7B	{
124	7C	¦
125	7D	}
126	7E	~
127	7F	Δ

C

continues

Dec X_{10}	Hex X_{16}	ASCII Character
128	80	Ç
129	81	ü
130	82	é
131	83	â
132	84	ä
133	85	à
134	86	å
135	87	ç
136	88	ê
137	89	ë
138	8A	è
139	8B	ï
140	8C	î
141	8D	ì
142	8E	Ä
143	8F	Å
144	90	É
145	91	æ
146	92	Æ
147	93	ô
148	94	ö
149	95	ò
150	96	û
151	97	ù
152	98	ÿ
153	99	Ö
154	9A	Ü
155	9B	¢
156	9C	£
157	9D	¥
158	9E	₧
159	9F	ƒ

Dec X_{10}	Hex X_{16}	ASCII Character
160	A0	á
161	A1	í
162	A2	ó
163	A3	ú
164	A4	ñ
165	A5	Ñ
166	A6	ª
167	A7	º
168	A8	º
169	A9	¿
170	AA	⌐
171	AB	¬
172	AC	½
173	AD	¼
174	AE	¡
175	AF	«
176	B0	»
177	B1	░
178	B2	▒
179	B3	│
180	B4	┤
181	B5	╡
182	B6	╢
183	B7	╖
184	B8	╕
185	B9	╣
186	BA	║
187	BB	╗
188	BC	╝
189	BD	╜
190	BE	╛
191	BF	┐

continues

Dec X_{10}	Hex X_{16}	ASCII Character
192	C0	┐
193	C1	└
194	C2	┴
195	C3	┬
196	C4	├
197	C5	─
198	C6	+
199	C7	╟
200	C8	╢
201	C9	╚
202	CA	╔
203	CB	╩
204	CC	╦
205	CD	╠
206	CE	=
207	CF	╬
208	D0	╧
209	D1	╨
210	D2	╤
211	D3	╥
212	D4	╙
213	D5	╘
214	D6	╒
215	D7	╓
216	D8	╫
217	D9	╪
218	DA	┘
219	DB	┌
220	DC	■
221	DD	■
222	DE	▌
223	DF	▐

Dec X_{10}	Hex X_{16}	ASCII Character
224	E0	■
225	E1	α
226	E2	β
227	E3	Γ
228	E4	π
229	E5	Σ
230	E6	σ
231	E7	μ
232	E8	γ
233	E9	Φ
234	EA	θ
235	EB	Ω
236	EC	δ
237	ED	∞
238	EE	$\emptyset$
239	EF	$\in$
240	F0	$\cap$
241	F1	$\equiv$
242	F2	$\pm$
243	F3	$\geq$
244	F4	$\leq$
245	F5	$\lceil$
246	F6	$\rfloor$
247	F7	$\div$
248	F8	$\approx$
249	F9	$\circ$
250	FA	$\bullet$
251	FB	$\cdot$
252	FC	$\sqrt{}$
253	FD	^{n}
254	FE	^{2}
255	FF	■

C

INDEX

Symbols

MACMILLAN COMPUTER PUBLISHING USA
A VIACOM COMPANY

Technical ---- Support:

If you need assistance with the information in this book or with a CD/Disk
accompanying the book, please access the Knowledge Base on our Web
site at **http://www.superlibrary.com/general/support**. Our most
Frequently Asked Questions are answered there. If you do not find the
answer to your questions on our Web site, you may contact Macmillan
Technical Support **(317) 581-3833** or e-mail us at **support@mcp.com**.

Microsoft BackOffice 2.0 Administrator's Survival Guide, Second Edition

Arthur Knowles

This all-in-one reference describes how to make the components of BackOffice version 2.0 work best together and with other networks. BackOffice is Microsoft's complete reference for networking, database, and system-management products. This book covers the fundamental concepts required for daily maintenance, troubleshooting, and problem solving. The CD-ROM that accompanies the book includes product demos, commercial and shareware utilities, and technical notes from Microsoft technical support personnel.

Price: $59.99 USA/$84.95 CDN *User Level: Accomplished*
ISBN: 0-672-30977-7 *1,200 pages*

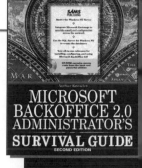

Microsoft BackOffice 2 Unleashed

Joe Greene, et al.

Microsoft BackOffice 2 Unleashed is an instrumental tool for anyone in charge of developing or managing BackOffice. This book covers the individual pieces of BackOffice, as well as key phases in the development, integration, and administration of the BackOffice environment. It covers using BackOffice as the infrastructure of an intranet or for the Internet, and instructs readers on integrating individual BackOffice products. The CD-ROM that accompanies the book includes source code, third-party products, and utilities.

Price: $59.99 USA/$84.95 CDN *User Level: Accomplished–Expert*
ISBN: 0-672-30816-9 *1,200 pages*

Designing and Implementing Microsoft Internet Information Server 2

Arthur Knowles & Sanjaya Hettihewa

This book details the specific tasks of setting up and running a Microsoft Internet Information Server. Readers will learn troubleshooting, network design, security, and cross-platform integration procedures. This book covers security issues, and discusses ways to maintain an efficient, secure network. Readers learn everything from planning to implementation.

Price: $39.99 USA/$56.95 CDN *User Level: Casual–Expert*
ISBN: 1-57521-168-8 *336 pages*

Microsoft Internet Information Server 2 Unleashed

Arthur Knowles, et al.

The power of the Microsoft Internet Information Server 2 is meticulously detailed in this 800 page volume. Readers will learn how to create and maintain a Web server, integrate IIS with BackOffice, and create interactive databases that can be used on the Internet or on a corporate intranet. This book also teaches advanced security techniques, as well as how to configure the server. The CD-ROM that accompanies this book includes source code from the book and powerful utilities.

Price: $49.99 USA/$70.95 CDN *User Level: Accomplished–Expert*
ISBN: 1-57521-109-2 *800 pages*

Microsoft Exchange Server Survival Guide

Greg Todd, et al.

Readers will learn the difference between Exchange and other groupware, such as Lotus Notes, as well as everything about the Exchange Server, including troubleshooting, development, and how to interact with other BackOffice components. This book covers everything operators need to run an Exchange server, and teaches readers how to prepare, plan, and install the Exchange server. This book also explores ways to migrate from other mail applications, such as Microsoft Mail and cc:Mail.

Price: $49.99 USA/$70.95 CDN   *User Level: Advanced–Expert*
ISBN: 0-672-30890-8   *800 pages*

Intranets Unleashed

Sams.net Development Group

Intranets, internal Web sites that can be accessed within a company's firewalls, are quickly becoming the status quo in business. This book shows IS managers and personnel how to effectively set up and run large or small intranets. Everything from design to security is discussed. The CD-ROM that accompanies this book contains source code and valuable utilities.

Price: $59.99 USA/$84.95 CDN   *User Level: Accomplished–Expert*
ISBN: 1-57521-115-7   *900 pages*

Microsoft SQL Server 6.5 Unleashed, Second Edition

David Solomon & Daniel Woodbeck, et al.

This comprehensive reference details the steps needed to plan, design, install, administer, and tune large and small databases. This book covers programming topics, including SQL, data structures, programming constructs, stored procedures, referential integrity, large table strategies, and more. It also includes updates to cover all new features of SQL Server 6.5, including the new transaction processing monitor and Internet/database connectivity through SQL Server's new Web wizard. The CD-ROM that accompanies this book includes source code, libraries, and administration tools.

Price: $59.99 USA/$84.95 CDN   *User Level: Accomplished–Expert*
ISBN: 0-672-30956-4   *1,100 pages*

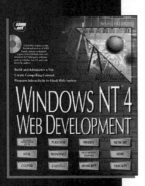

Windows NT 4 Web Development

Sanjaya Hettihewa

Windows NT and Microsoft's newly developed Internet Information Server are making it easier and more cost-effective to set up, manage, and administer a good Web site. Because the Windows NT environment is relatively new, few books on the market adequately discuss its full potential. *Windows NT Web Development* addresses that potential by providing information on all key aspects of server setup, maintenance, design, and implementation. The CD-ROM that accompanies this book contains valuable source code and powerful utilities.

Price: $59.99 USA/$84.95 CDN   *User Level: Accomplished–Expert*
ISBN: 1-57521-089-4   *744 pages*

Add to Your Sams Library Today with the Best Books for Programming, Operating Systems, and New Technologies

The easiest way to order is to pick up the phone and call
1-800-428-5331
between 9:00 a.m. and 5:00 p.m. EST.
For faster service please have your credit card available.

ISBN	Quantity	Description of Item	Unit Cost	Total Cost
0-672-30977-7		Microsoft BackOffice 2.0 Administrator's Survival Guide, Second Edition (Book/CD-ROM)	$59.99	
0-672-30816-9		Microsoft BackOffice 2 Unleashed (Book/CD-ROM)	$59.99	
1-57521-168-8		Designing & Implementing Microsoft Internet Information Server 2	$39.99	
1-57521-109-2		Microsoft Internet Information Server 2 Unleashed (Book/CD-ROM)	$49.99	
0-672-30890-8		Microsoft Exchange Server Survival Guide (Book/CD-ROM)	$49.99	
1-57521-115-7		Intranets Unleashed (Book/CD-ROM)	$59.99	
0-672-30956-4		Microsoft SQL Server 6.5 Unleashed, Second Edition (Book/CD-ROM)	$59.99	
1-57521-089-4		Windows NT 4 Web Development (Book/CD-ROM)	$59.99	
❑ 3 ½" Disk		Shipping and Handling: See information below.		
❑ 5 ¼" Disk		TOTAL		

Shipping and Handling: $4.00 for the first book, and $1.75 for each additional book. Floppy disk: add $1.75 for shipping and handling. If you need to have it NOW, we can ship the product to you in 24 hours for an additional charge of approximately $18.00, and you will receive your item overnight or in two days. Overseas shipping and handling adds $2.00 per book and $8.00 for up to three disks. Prices are subject to change. Call for availability and pricing information on latest editions.

201 W. 103rd Street, Indianapolis, Indiana 46290

1-800-428-5331 — Orders   1-800-835-3202 — FAX   1-800-858-7674 — Customer Service

Book ISBN 0-672-31047-3